THE HANDBOOK OF STUDENT AFFAIRS ADMINISTRATION

THE HANDBOOK OF STUDENT AFFAIRS ADMINISTRATION

THIRD EDITION

George S. McClellan,
Jeremy Stringer,
and Associates

JOSSEY-BASS
A Wiley Imprint
www.josseybass.com

Published by Jossey-Bass
A Wiley Imprint
989 Market Street, San Francisco, CA 94103-1741—www.josseybass.com

Readers should be aware that Internet Web sites offered as citations and/or sources for further
information may have changed or disappeared between the time this was written and when it is read.

Limit of Liability/Disclaimer of Warranty: While the publisher and author have used their best
efforts in preparing this book, they make no representations or warranties with respect to the accuracy
or completeness of the contents of this book and specifically disclaim any implied warranties of
merchantability or fitness for a particular purpose. No warranty may be created or extended by sales
representatives or written sales materials. The advice and strategies contained herein may not be suitable
for your situation. You should consult with a professional where appropriate. Neither the publisher nor
author shall be liable for any loss of profit or any other commercial damages, including but not limited to
special, incidental, consequential, or other damages.

Jossey-Bass books and products are available through most bookstores. To contact Jossey-Bass directly
call our Customer Care Department within the U.S. at 800-956-7739, outside the U.S. at 317-572-3986,
or fax 317-572-4002.

Jossey-Bass also publishes its books in a variety of electronic formats. Some content that appears in print
may not be available in electronic books.

Library of Congress Cataloging-in-Publication Data
McClellan, George S.
    The handbook of student affairs administration / George S. McClellan, Jeremy Stringer, and
associates. — 3rd ed.
        p.   cm.
    Prev. eds. entered under: Barr, Margaret J.
    ISBN 978-0-7879-9733-5 (alk. paper)
        1. Student affairs services—United States—Handbooks, manuals, etc.   2. Student activities—
United States—Management—Handbooks, manuals, etc.   I. Stringer, Jeremy.   II. Barr, Margaret J.
Handbook of student affairs administration.   III. Title.
    LB2342.92.B37   2008
    378.1'940973—dc22
                                                                                            2008047328

Printed in the United States of America
THIRD EDITION

HB Printing   10 9 8 7 6 5 4

CONTENTS

Figures and Tables   xvii

National Association of Student Personnel Administrators   xix

Preface   xxi

Acknowledgments   xxiii

The Authors   xxv

PART ONE: CONTEXTS OF PROFESSIONAL PRACTICE   1

1   From the People Up: A Brief History of Student Affairs
Administration   3

James J. Rhatigan

Beginnings   3

The Deans and the Personnel Workers   4

The Student Personnel Point of View   10

The Modern Era   11

Conclusion   14

References   16

2 The Importance of Institutional Mission   19

Joan B. Hirt

Institutional Classification Systems   20

Institutional Mission Statements   22

How Mission Informs Student Affairs Professional Practice   29

Student Affairs Professional Mobility: Individual and Institutional
Perspectives   36

Conclusion   38

References   38

3 Institutional Governance and the Interests of Students   41

John S. Levin

Narratives of Governance   42

Multiple Ways of Viewing Governance   47

Governance as Institutional Identity   52

The Governance Connection for Student Affairs   53

Governance: How Can Student Affairs Practitioners Respond?   55

References   56

4 Understanding Campus Environments   59

George D. Kuh

Institutional Context and Student Success   60

A Framework for Assessing the Influence of Contextual
Conditions on Student Learning   61

Key Issues in Assessing Environmental Influences on Learning   72

Conclusion   76

References   77

5 Fiscal Pressures on Higher Education and Student Affairs   81

John H. Schuh

Demographic and Social Trends   82

Federal Higher Education Initiatives   85

Selected Factors Influencing the Financial Health of Institutions   92

Fund Raising   99

Conclusion   101

References   101

6 Accountability   105

Sherry L. Mallory and Linda M. Clement

Accountability Defined   106

Why All the Fuss About Accountability?   107

Who Are the Stakeholders in Institutional Accountability?   109

For What Is Student Affairs Accountable?   110

The Role of the Accreditation Process   111

Council for the Advancement of Standards and Accountability   112

Accreditation by Student Affairs Professional Organizations   112

Best Practices in Accountability in Student Affairs   113

Additional Resources   114

Conclusion   115

References   116

7 Internationalization in Higher Education and
Student Affairs   120

Kenneth J. Osfield and Patricia Smith Terrell

Internationalization Defined   121

History of Internationalization in U.S. Higher Education   121

Benefits of Internationalization in Higher Education   121

Leading the Way Toward Internationalization   122

Opportunities for International Education   127

Supporting Study Abroad   136

International Opportunities for Student Affairs Professionals   137

Student Affairs Graduate Preparation Programs   137

Staff and Faculty Opportunities for Study Abroad   138

Opportunities for Research and International Education   139

Conclusion   139

References   140

PART TWO: FRAMEWORKS FOR PROFESSIONAL PRACTICE   145

8   Using Reflection to Reframe Theory-to-Practice in
    Student Affairs   147

Lori D. Patton and Shaun R. Harper

Explaining Theoretical Resistance: Five Assumptions to Consider   148

An Overview of Theories That Inform Student Affairs Practice   150

Environmental Theories   155

Other Bodies of Theory Relevant to Student Affairs   157

Applying Theory to Practice: A Cross-Case Example   157

Conclusion   160

References   161

9   Maintaining and Modeling Everyday
    Ethics in Student Affairs   166

Jon C. Dalton, Pamela C. Crosby, Aurelio Valente, and
David Eberhardt

What Is Ethics?   167

Ethics as the Art of Making Wise and Responsible Decisions   168

Why Be Concerned About Ethics?   169

Five Domains of Ethical Responsibility   169

Ethics in the Student Affairs Profession   173

A Multi-Lens Perspective on Managing and
Modeling Everyday Ethics   179

The Moral Landscape of Student Affairs Work   180

Deciding and Acting in Ethical Conflict Situations   183

Using a Moral Compass in Everyday Ethics   184

Conclusion   185

References   186

10 Applying Professional Standards   187

Jan Arminio

Standards in Education   188

Standards in Higher Education   189

Standards in Student Affairs   190

Case Illustrations   200

Conclusion   202

References   203

11 Professional Associations in Student Affairs   206

Nancy J. Evans and Jessica J. Ranero

The Functions of Professional Associations   206

The History of Student Affairs Professional Associations   207

Specialty Associations   212

The Structure of Professional Associations   216

Benefits of Membership in Professional Associations   216

Involvement and Leadership Opportunities   217

Conclusion   219

References   219

PART THREE: STUDENTS: THE REASON FOR OUR PROFESSIONAL PRACTICE   223

12 The Changing Student Population   225

George S. McClellan and Jim Larimore

Diversity as a Global Issue in Higher Education   226

Defining Diversity   227

Yesterday, Today, and Tomorrow   228

Benefits of Diversity   234

Challenges to Diversity   235

Recommendations   236

Conclusion   237

References   238

13 Continuing the Journey Toward Multicultural
    Campus Communities   242

Jason A. Laker and Tracy L. Davis

Identity: A Critical Individual-Institutional Nexus   243

Pedagogical Issues at the Individual Level   245

The Conversation Must Become More Uncomfortable   249

Language Matters   250

Looking Inward: Student Affairs and Identity Politics   252

Epistemological Privilege   254

To Whom Much Is Given   255

Promoting Structural Transformation   256

Conclusion   261

References   262

14 Helping Students with Health and Wellness Issues   265

John H. Dunkle and Cheryl A. Presley

Historical Context   266

Student Physical and Mental Health Issues   267

Major Administrative Issues   275

Conclusion   282

References   284

15 Supporting Online Students   288

Anita Crawley and Christine LeGore

The Explosive Growth of Online Learning   288

Changing Enrollment Trends   289

A Closer Look at the Online Learner   291

Online Students: Whose Responsibility?   295

Best Practices in Online Student Services   298

Conclusion   304

References   306

PART FOUR: HUMAN RESOURCES IN PROFESSIONAL PRACTICE 311

16 The Dynamics of Organizational Models Within Student Affairs 313

Linda Kuk

Organizational Design Issues in Student Affairs 314

Common Student Affairs Organizational Models 318

Theory and Research Related to Organizational Design 321

New Approaches to Organizational Design and Structure 326

A Systematic Approach to Organization Structural Design 328

Conclusion 331

References 332

17 Effective Management of Human Capital in Student Affairs 333

Michael L. Jackson, Larry Moneta, and Kelly Anne Nelson

Recruitment 334

Selection 337

Supervision 340

Staff Awards and Recognition 341

Helping Staff Manage Their Time 342

Meetings 343

Staff and Professional Development 344

Staff Retention 352

Conclusion 353

References 353

Recommended Reading 354

18 Middle Managers: Roles and Responsibilities Spanning
the Student Affairs Career 355

Donald B. Mills

Management in Student Affairs 356

Role Issues for Management 359

The Generational Challenge 362

Managing Up (and Down) the Organization 365

Mobility   366

Conclusion   368

References   369

19 Professional Development as Lifelong Learning   371

    Susan R. Komives and Stan Carpenter

    Lifelong Professional Learning   372

    Professional Competencies   372

    Defining Professional Development   374

    A Model of Professional Development   377

    Exemplary Practices   383

    Conclusion   385

    References   386

20 Doctoral Education and Beyond   388

    Mary F. Howard-Hamilton and Randy E. Hyman

    Why a Doctorate?   389

    Where to Go?   390

    Ed.D. or Ph.D.?   393

    Area of Program Emphasis   394

    The Doctoral Study Journey   394

    Career Paths After the Doctorate   396

    Implications for Best Practice in Doctoral Education   399

    References   400

**PART FIVE: INTERPERSONAL DYNAMICS IN
PROFESSIONAL PRACTICE   403**

21 Supporting and Enhancing Student Learning
    Through Partnerships with Academic Colleagues   405

    Adrianna Kezar

    Reflection 1: Remember History   407

    Reflection 2: Logic Overcomes Barriers   408

Reflection 3: Fortuitous Timing   411

Reflection 4: Collaboration Is Deepening   411

Action Step 1: Start with a Problem and Success Area   414

Action Step 2: Leadership for Success   416

Action Step 3: Attend to Culture, People, and Planning   418

Action Step 4: Sustaining Partnerships   420

Conclusion   421

References   422

22 The Political Environment of the Student Affairs Administrator   425

Jeremy Stringer

The University as a Political System   426

Political Behavior as a Concern for Student Affairs   430

Traditional Political Concepts   434

Emergent Political Concepts and Values   440

Limitations of the Political Metaphor   444

References   445

23 Developing Effective Relationships on Campus and
in the Community   447

Shannon Ellis

The Importance of Relationships   448

Types of Relationships   448

Relationships with Individuals and Constituencies   452

How Relationships Are Formed   455

Relationships in Conflict   458

Conclusion   459

References   459

24 Understanding and Managing Conflict   463

Dale Nienow and Jeremy Stringer

Understanding Our Differing Approaches to Conflict   464

Types of Conflict Interventions   466

Internal and External Responses to Conflict   469

Conflict Resolution Scenario   471

Moving Beyond Conflict Management   473

Gracious Space   474

Conclusion   477

References   478

PART SIX: SKILLS AND COMPETENCIES OF PROFESSIONAL PRACTICE   479

25 Budgeting and Fiscal Management for Student Affairs   481
    Margaret J. Barr
    The General Fiscal Environment for Student Affairs   482

    Sources of Funds   483

    Public Versus Private Financial Issues   491

    The Purposes of a Budget   493

    Types of Budgets   496

    Budget Models   497

    The Budget Cycle   499

    Dealing with Budget Cuts   502

    Conclusion   503

    References   504

26 Legal Issues in Student Affairs   505
    Beverly E. Ledbetter
    The University's Contractual Responsibilities to Students   506

    The University's Noncontractual Obligations to Students   507

    Higher Education and the Constitution   515

    Federal and State Statutes and Regulations   518

    Conclusion   524

    References   524

    Cases Cited   524

Federal Laws and Regulations Cited   525

27 Implementing Assessment to Improve Student Learning and Development   526

Marilee J. Bresciani

Historical Overview   527

Evaluating Contributions to Student Learning and Development   528

Assessment Approaches   530

Implementing Assessment   536

References   543

28 Program Planning and Implementation   545

Michael J. Cuyjet and Sue Weitz

The Model   546

Planning and Implementing Major Initiatives   546

Case Example: Changing the Culture in a Residence Hall   550

Planning and Implementing Specific Activities   552

Case Example: Providing a Nonalcoholic Activity Night   560

Recommendations for Practice   562

References   563

29 Facilities Planning and Development   565

Jerry Price

Developing a Strategic Plan   566

Developing an Operational Plan   569

Facility Development   577

Conclusion   583

References   584

30 Technology: Innovations and Implications   586

Kevin Kruger

Students and Technology   587

Beyond the Administrative Core   592

Electronic Portfolios   595

Technology Challenges   596

Conclusion   598

References   598

31 Responding to Campus Crisis   602
    Keith M. Miser and Cynthia Cherrey

Crisis Defined   603

Management of Crisis Work   604

Transitions After a Catastrophic Event   613

Lessons Learned   616

Conclusion   620

References   621

Other Resources   622

Epilogue: Continuing the Conversation   623
    George S. McClellan and Jeremy Stringer

Change as Metatheme   623

Timeless Values Frame Our Practice   624

Ethical Principles Inform Our Actions   625

The Importance of Context   626

Investing in Higher Expectations   627

Fostering Learning   629

Developing Whole Students and Whole Communities   629

Eroding Boundaries   631

Strengthening Networks and Relationships   632

Keeping Our Profession Vital   632

References   634

Name Index   637

Subject Index   649

FIGURES, TABLES, AND EXHIBITS

Figures

7.1   Financial Support to Students for Study Abroad (by Country)   124
7.2   Anticipated Freshman Study Abroad Participation Rate   129
7.3   Study Abroad Versus Higher Education Enrollment (by Ethnicity)   130
9.1   Domains of Ethical Responsibility   170
15.1   Student Services for Online Learners   299
18.1   Sample Student Affairs Organization   357
22.1   Political Map for a Senior Student Affairs Officer   432
28.1   Typical Process of Program Planning and Implementation   547

Tables

3.1   Characteristics of Public Research Extensive Universities and Community Colleges   50
9.1   Components of Ethical Deliberation and Action   184
15.1   Strengths of Online Learning   294
16.1   Traditional Models of Student Affairs Practice   324
16.2   Innovative Models of Student Affairs Practice   325
18.1   Generational Workplace Characteristics   363

19.1 The CAS Curriculum 373
19.2 The Nature of Professional Development 375
19.3 Sample Professional Development Activities and
      the PREPARE Model 381
19.4 Examples of Continuing Professional Development by Primary Sources
      of Delivery 382

Exhibits

11.1 A Sample Listing of Professional Associations 213

NASPA–STUDENT AFFAIRS ADMINISTRATORS IN HIGHER EDUCATION

NASPA–Student Affairs Administrators in Higher Education is the leading voice for student affairs administration, policy, and practice and affirms the commitment of the student affairs profession to educating the whole student and integrating student life and learning. With more than 11,000 members at 1,400 campuses, and representing 29 countries, NASPA is the foremost professional association for student affairs administrators, faculty, and graduate and undergraduate students. NASPA members are committed to serving college students by embracing the core values of diversity, learning, integrity, collaboration, access, service, fellowship, and the spirit of inquiry.

NASPA members serve a variety of functions and roles, including the vice president and dean for student life, as well as professionals working within housing and residence life, student unions, student activities, counseling, career development, orientation, enrollment management, racial and ethnic minority support services, and retention and assessment.

For more information about NASPA publications and professional development programs, contact:

NASPA–Student Affairs Administrators in Higher Education

1875 Connecticut Ave, NW, Suite 418

Washington, DC 20009–5728

202–265–7500

office@naspa.org

www.naspa.org

PREFACE

The third edition of the *Handbook of Student Affairs Administration (HSAA3)* is intended to serve as a practical and informative resource for those interested in the student affairs profession. This edition of the handbook is organized into seven broad constructs. They include:

1. Contexts of professional practice,
2. Frameworks of professional practice,
3. Students: the reason for our professional practice,
4. Human resources in professional practice,
5. Interpersonal dynamics in professional practice,
6. Skills and competencies of professional practice, and
7. Epilogue: continuing the conversation.

The third edition of *HSAA* honors and builds on the success of the preceding editions. It continues the emphasis on practical and timely information for student affairs and includes revised and updated iterations of key chapters from previous editions that continue to have relevance today and in the future. Chapters focus on day-to-day professional practice in student affairs, reference both classic and recent literature, and feature case studies and examples from a multitude of functional areas and a host of institutional settings.

HSAA3 features several new chapters. Among these are the chapters on accountability (Chapter Six), serving online students (Chapter Fifteen), and internationalization in higher education (Chapter Seven). A fourth chapter, the one on student health and wellness issues (Chapter Fourteen), returns to the handbook, having appeared in the first edition but having been absent from the second. Size constraints dictated that two chapters that appeared in second edition had to be cut from this edition. While the chapters on identifying and working with key constituent groups and the chapter on measuring student satisfaction and needs do not appear here, key information from those chapters has been included in other places in this edition of the handbook.

The authors contributing to *HSAA3* include the profession's most prominent scholar practitioners as well as some of the notable rising scholar practitioners. They are as diverse as our field itself. The authors reflect an array of experiences at a variety of institutional types and sizes. Their personal backgrounds reflect the diversity within our profession, as do the theoretical frameworks with which they approach their work.

Audience

HSAA3 is written to meet the needs of entry-, mid-, and senior-level student affairs practitioners for a ready reference guide for professional practice. It should be helpful to those entering the profession through nontraditional pathways (for example, from the faculty or through administrative realignment) as well as to those who came into the profession through graduate preparation programs in higher education or student affairs. The third edition also serves as resource for graduate faculty in professional preparation programs and as a text for students in those programs.

ACKNOWLEDGMENTS

There are no words sufficient to express our thanks to the authors who agreed to participate in this handbook. Their diligent and thoughtful efforts are the source of its strength.

Thanks as well to Peggy Barr for serving as the primary editor for the first two editions of the handbook. Her example informed our work, and we appreciate the wise counsel she shared with us. Thanks also to Mary Desler for her contribution to the second edition.

We wish to acknowledge the support we received from NASPA and the NASPA staff, particularly Gwen Dungy and Kevin Kruger, in initiating the third edition of this handbook. We are also honored to have David Brightman and Erin Null, both with Jossey-Bass, as colleagues and partners throughout the development of this edition.

George McClellan is thankful to and for his colleagues at both Dickinson State University and Indiana University Purdue University Fort Wayne, particularly President Lee Vickers and Chancellor Mike Wartell. Bertie Kudrna provided invaluable service and an unflagging positive spirit that made it possible to keep going even on the tough days. Jay Anstett helped clean up the myriad of "just one more things" as we wrapped up this project. Jeremy Stringer particularly appreciates the support and encouragement of Dean Sue Schmitt at Seattle University. Sarah Postel provided awesome assistance with proofing and references, and Eunice MacGill was also helpful with aspects of this project.

Jeremy Stringer is especially thankful for the love and support of his wife, Susan, and his three precious daughters: Shannon, Kelly, and Courtney. He is grateful for the many invaluable professional and personal lessons he has learned from current and former colleagues. He is forever aware that most of his closest personal friends have been student affairs professionals. He is ever mindful of the importance of his mentors in the field, especially the late Bill Swift, who gave him his first job, Jim Appleton, Fr. William Sullivan, S.J., and Phil Beal, who started as a professional mentor and became his life coach. George McClellan is thankful to his parents, teachers, faculty members, colleagues (particularly Jason Laker and Shelly Lowe), and mentors who have offered challenge and support. Special thanks to Koko and Pops Taylor, Willie Dixon, and Peggy Barr for some of life's richest lessons.

Finally, we wish to thank the many students who have allowed us in one way or another to be a part of their lives. They are the reason for our work and the work of all of our fellow student affairs professionals, and it is our most sincere hope that this handbook will serve them through serving our profession.

George S. McClellan
Jeremy Stringer

THE AUTHORS

Jan Arminio is currently professor and chair of the Department of Counseling and College Student Personnel at Shippensburg University. She also served as president of the Council for the Advancement of Standards in Higher Education (CAS) from 2004 to 2008 and represented the National Association for Campus Activities (NACA) to CAS from 1987 to 2008. She coauthored *Negotiating the Complexities of Qualitative Research* (2006), is a Senior Scholar for the American College Personnel Association, and received the 2007 Thomas M. Magoon Distinguished Alumni award from the University of Maryland, College Park.

Margaret J. Barr is professor emeritus in the School of Education and Social Policy at Northwestern University and is retired vice president for student affairs at that same institution. She previously served in a variety of administrative positions, including vice president for student affairs at Northern Illinois University and vice chancellor for student affairs at Texas Christian University. Her recent work includes the *Academic Administrator's Guide to Budgets and Financial Management* (2002), and with Arthur Sandeen she wrote *Critical Issues for Student Affairs* (2006).

Marilee J. Bresciani is associate professor of postsecondary education at San Diego State University and faculty coordinator of the master's and doctorate in postsecondary educational leadership. Bresciani previously served as the assistant vice president for institutional assessment at Texas A&M University and director of assessment at North Carolina State University. Her areas of research focus on organizational evaluation of student learning and development. Bresciani has authored four books, along with multiple chapters, refereed journal articles, and other publications. In addition, she is a frequent facilitator of workshops and conversations about evaluating student learning centeredness across the globe.

Stan Carpenter is professor and chair of the Educational Administration and Psychological Services Department at Texas State University-San Marcos. He has served as the executive director of the Association for the Study of Higher Education (ASHE) and as editor/chair of the ACPA Media Board, as well as on the NASPA Board of Directors. He has published more than seventy-five articles, chapters, and other works, most recently on professional development in student affairs and on scholarship as an ethos for student affairs. He has received awards for teaching (Texas A&M College of Education), scholarship (Senior Scholar of ACPA, 2000; Southern Association for College Student Affairs Melvene Hardee Award), and service (Distinguished Service Award from ASHE; Esther Lloyd Jones Award from ACPA in 2004).

Cynthia Cherrey is the vice president for student affairs and dean of students at Tulane University and clinical professor in the A. B. Freeman School of Business. Prior to coming to Tulane University, Cherrey served as the associate vice president for student affairs at the University of Southern California. She is a Senior Fellow at the James McGregor Burns Academy of Leadership, a Fellow at the World Business Academy and a J. W. Fulbright Scholar. In her thirty years in student affairs work, she has been involved in crisis management, from student tragedies and protests to earthquakes and the 1992 Los Angeles riots, and the worst national natural disaster of Hurricane Katrina in 2005.

Linda M. Clement is vice president for student affairs and an affiliate associate professor in the college student personnel program at the University of Maryland. She currently serves as a member of the NASPA Faculty Fellows, and recently completed a ten-year term as a trustee for the College Board.

Anita Crawley is the interim director of distance learning at Montgomery College, Maryland. She has served as student development faculty/counselor at two community colleges: Montgomery and Harper Colleges. In addition, she has been an online instructor since 1999 teaching student development courses for both community colleges as well as teaching online learning, faculty development, counseling, and online student services courses for University of California, Los Angeles Extension, Illinois Online Network, Student Affairs.com, and NASPA/ACPA. She is actively involved with Western Cooperative for

Educational Telecommunications serving as a consultant and a member of the planning committee for the national conference.

Pamela C. Crosby is coeditor of the *Journal of College and Character* and a doctoral student in history and philosophy of education at Florida State University. Her research interests include philosophy of higher education, the pragmatic philosophy of William James, and the influence of nineteenth-century German philosophy of education on U.S. higher education.

Michael J. Cuyjet is an associate professor in the Department of Educational and Counseling Psychology, College Student Personnel Program in the College of Education and Human Development at the University of Louisville, where he has also served as associate graduate dean and acting associate provost for student life. Prior to joining the faculty in 1993, he served more than twenty years as a student affairs practitioner at Northern Illinois University and the University of Maryland, College Park. He has been involved in professional organizations for more than thirty-five years, having served in numerous leadership roles including memberships on the boards of directors of NACA, ACPA, and NASPA and the editorial boards of the *NASAP Journal* and the *Journal of College and Character*. In 2006, he was named a Diamond Honoree by the ACPA Educational Leadership Foundation.

Jon C. Dalton is associate professor of higher education and director of the Hardee Center for Leadership and Ethics at Florida State University. He serves as coeditor of the *Journal of College and Character*. He is a former president of NASPA, a Senior Scholar of ACPA, and vice president for student affairs at Florida State University and Northern Illinois University. He is coauthor of *Encouraging Authenticity and Spirituality in Higher Education* (2006).

Tracy L. Davis currently serves as professor and college student personnel coordinator in the Department of Educational and Interdisciplinary Studies at Western Illinois University. He has also served as an instructor for the Iowa Governor's Institute and the National Scholars Academy with the Connie Belin and Jacqueline N. Blank International Center for Gifted Education and Talent Development, and was an assistant director for the Office of Student Life at the University of Iowa. Davis is a frequent consultant and presenter and has numerous publications in the areas of issues of social justice, identity development, and gender. He has served on several dissertation committees and is currently an editorial board member for the *Journal of College Student Development*.

John H. Dunkle is the executive director of Counseling and Psychological Services at Northwestern University. He is a licensed psychologist in Illinois and New York and is credentialed by the National Register of Health Service Providers in Psychology. He is a member of NASPA, the Association for University and College Counseling Center Directors, and the American Psychological Association. He is also on the board of advisors for the Center for the Study of College Student Mental Health.

David Eberhardt is the dean of students at Birmingham Southern College. He was a research associate in the Hardee Center for Leadership and Ethics while completing doctoral studies in higher education at Florida State University. His professional interests include college student ethical and spiritual development and ethical issues for professionals who work with college students.

Shannon Ellis serves as vice president for student services and a member of the faculty at the University of Nevada, Reno. She has worked in the field of higher education for nearly thirty years as a faculty member and administrator at the University of Massachusetts, Amherst, University of Southern California, Seattle University, and Evergreen State College. She has served as president of NASPA and is active on several editorial and foundation boards. In addition to presenting hundreds of keynotes and workshops, Ellis has published numerous articles and chapters in professional journals and books, including authoring *Dreams, Nightmares and Pursuing the Passion: Personal Perspectives on College and University Leadership.*

Nancy J. Evans is a professor of higher education in the Department of Educational Leadership and Policy Studies at Iowa State University and coordinator of the master's program in student affairs. She received her doctorate in counseling psychology from the University of Missouri in 1978. She served as president of the American College Personnel Association in 2001–02, received the Contribution to Knowledge Award from ACPA in 1998, and was named an ACPA Senior Scholar in 1999. She has published seven books, including *Student Development in College, Foundations of Student Affairs Practice,* and most recently *Developing Social Justice Allies,* along with numerous book chapters and journal articles. Her research and scholarship focuses on social justice in higher education and the impact of the college environment on student development, particularly with regard to the experiences of nondominant populations, including lesbian, gay, and bisexual students and students with disabilities.

Shaun R. Harper is an assistant professor of higher education management at the University of Pennsylvania and director of research on the NASPA Board of Directors. He maintains an active research agenda that examines race and gender in higher education; Black male college achievement; the effects of college environments on student behaviors and outcomes; student affairs at historically Black colleges and universities; and gains associated with educationally purposeful student engagement. Harper has published four books and monographs and more than forty articles and book chapters. Additionally, he has presented more than one hundred research papers and workshops at national higher education and student affairs conferences. Harper received the 2004 NASPA Melvene D. Hardee Dissertation of the Year Award and the 2006 ACPA Annuit Coeptis Award. His Ph.D. in higher education administration is from Indiana University.

Joan B. Hirt is associate professor of higher education in the Department of Educational Leadership and Policy Studies at Virginia Tech. She spent fifteen years as a student affairs professional, working in residence life, housing and dining services, and a dean of students office before becoming a faculty member in 1994. Hirt has authored or coauthored more than thirty refereed articles, book chapters, and monograph chapters. While her secondary research endeavors have focused on issues of diversity in higher education, her abiding interest centers on professionalization in student affairs. Her book, *Where You Work Matters: Student Affairs Administration at Different Types of Institutions* (2005), examines that topic more closely.

Mary F. Howard-Hamilton is a professor of higher education in the Department of Educational Leadership, Administration, and Foundations at Indiana State University. She has published more than eighty articles and is the coauthor of *Unleashing Suppressed Voices on College Campuses: Diversity Issues in Higher Education.* She received the Robert S. Shaffer Award for Academic Excellence as a Graduate Faculty Member from NASPA and the Standing Committee for Women Wise Woman Award from ACPA in 2007. The University of Iowa Albert Hood Distinguished Alumni Award was presented to her in 2002. She is a member of the NASPA Faculty Fellows and cofacilitated the NASPA doctoral colloquium in 2006 and 2007.

Randy E. Hyman is vice chancellor for academic support and student life and associate professor of higher education at the University of Minnesota, Duluth. He has published articles and reviews in the *NASPA Journal*, the *Journal of College Student Development*, and the *College and University Journal*. He received the Melvene Hardee Dissertation of the Year Award from NASPA in 1985. He has served NASPA on the board of directors as director of the research division, the *NASPA Journal* editorial board, and as a NASPA Faculty Fellow, cofacilitating the annual doctoral colloquium in 2006 and 2007. He also serves as associate editor for the *College Student Affairs Journal* and is a consultant evaluator for the Higher Learning Commission of the North Central Association of Colleges and Schools.

Michael L. Jackson is vice president for student affairs at the University of Southern California. His is also professor of higher education in the Rossier School of Education at the University of Southern California. A former NASPA president, he served on the NASPA Foundation Board and received the NASPA Scott Goodnight Award in 2008. He also served as dean of students at Stanford University.

Adrianna Kezar is associate professor of higher education at the University of Southern California. She studies higher education collaboration, change, and leadership. She has several articles and books focused on the topic of academic and student affairs collaboration, including *Understanding the Role of Academic and Student Affairs Collaboration in Creating a Successful Learning Environment* (a monograph in the New Directions in Student Affairs series) and a forthcoming book, *Reorganizing for Collaboration in Higher Education.* She served on the boards of the American Association for Higher Education and the Association of American Colleges and Universities.

Susan R. Komives is professor in college student personnel at the University of Maryland. A former president of ACPA: College Student Educators International and former vice president for student affairs at Stephens College and the University of Tampa, she is currently president of the Council for the Advancement of Standards in Higher Education (CAS). Coeditor of two editions of *Student Services* and coauthor of two editions of *Exploring Leadership,* she is also research director of the National Clearinghouse for Leadership Programs and Senior Scholar with the James MacGregor Burns Academy of Leadership. Komives is the spring 2006 recipient of both the NASPA Contribution of Scholarship and Literature Award and the ACPA Contribution to Knowledge Award and is the 2004 recipient of the NASPA Robert H. Shaffer Award for Academic Excellence as a Graduate Faculty Member.

Kevin Kruger is currently the associate executive director of the National Association of Student Personnel Administrators (NASPA). He previously was associate vice president for Student Affairs at the University of Maryland, Baltimore County. He has edited two books on technology in student affairs and has authored numerous book chapters and journal articles on a wide range of higher education topics.

George D. Kuh is Chancellor's Professor of Higher Education and director of the Center for Postsecondary Research at Indiana University Bloomington. A past president of the Association for the Study of Higher Education (ASHE), he has published widely and received awards from several national organizations for his academic leadership and contributions to the literature. His two most recent books are *Piecing Together the Student Success Puzzle* (2007) and *Student Success in College: Creating Conditions That Matter* (2005).

Linda Kuk is associate professor of education at Colorado State University, where she also serves as chair of the Student Affairs in Higher Education graduate program. She previously served for twenty-two years as vice president of student Affairs at Colorado State University, the Rochester Institute of Technology, and State University of New York, Cortland. She has served on both the NASPA and ACPA boards of directors and *the NASPA Journal* board. She was NASPA region II vice president and is currently a NASPA Faculty Fellow. She also serves as an organizational consultant for higher education and nonprofit organizations.

Jason Laker was born and educated in the United States and moved to Canada in 2006 to serve as associate vice principal and dean of student affairs at Queen's University in Kingston, Ontario. He also teaches in the Women's Studies Department there. Previously, he was the dean of campus life at Saint John's University in Collegeville, Minnesota. He also served as an adjunct instructor at Saint Cloud State University, where he taught undergraduate general and honors courses about community engagement, gender, race, and ethnicity and graduate-level courses in student development, and where he was awarded Honors Teacher of the Year by vote of students. He has also worked at the University of Arizona, in student affairs and in continuing education; University of Delaware, and Fort Lewis College in Colorado.

Jim Larimore is the dean of students at Swarthmore College, outside of Philadelphia, Pennsylvania. He has previously served as dean of the college at Dartmouth College and in a variety of roles at Stanford University, including assistant dean and director of the American Indian Program, acting dean of students, and assistant to the provost.

Beverly E. Ledbetter is vice president and general counsel for Brown University. Prior to Brown University, she was legal counsel for the University of Oklahoma and adjunct professor at the University of Oklahoma College of Law and at the Center for Higher Education, College of Education. She is on the faculty of the Management Development Program at Harvard University and has been an adjunct professor at Harvard. She lectures frequently on higher education issues including employment, civil rights, sexual and racial harassment, and federal regulatory compliance and is regarded as an expert in the field of higher education law. A past president of the National Association of College & University Attorneys, and a former member of the NCAA Infractions Committee, she is a member of the International Advisory Board of the Center for Excellence in Higher

Education Law and Policy of Stetson University College Law, and is a faculty member of the Higher Education Resource Services Programs at Wellesley and Bryn Mawr, the Western Association of College and University Business Officers Business Management Institute at the University of California, Santa Barbara, and the College of Business Management Institute at the University of Kentucky.

Christine LeGore is the director of distance education for the University of Maine system, where she oversees central support services for students and faculty participating in distance courses and programs offered by the system's seven universities. Ten university system off-campus centers, known as "University College," are also under her leadership. She holds the rank of associate professor of mathematics at the University of Maine at Augusta, where she continues to teach part time. She is an active participant in WCET, having coordinated the student services workshop strand for the 2007 annual conference, and she co-led the first-ever online conference for student services professionals for the Sloan Consortium in 2006.

John S. Levin is the Bank of America Professor of Education Leadership and the director and principal investigator of the California Community College Collaborative (C4). His books in this decade include *Globalizing the Community College* (2001), *Community College Faculty: At Work in the New Economy* (2006), with Susan Kater and Richard Wagoner, and *Non-Traditional Students and Community Colleges: The Conflict of Justice and Neo-Liberalism* (2007).

Sherry L. Mallory is special assistant to the vice president for student affairs at Western Washington University, where she also teaches in the student affairs graduate program. She served on the NASPA board as public policy division chair and has served on the editorial board for both the *NASPA Journal* and the *College Student Affairs Journal*.

George S. McClellan is the vice chancellor for student affairs at Indiana University Purdue University Fort Wayne (IPFW). Before coming to IPFW, he was vice president for student development at Dickinson State University and served students in a variety of roles at the University of Arizona and Northwestern University. He is a member of the NASPA Foundation Board and was a founding member of NASPA's Administrators in Graduate and Professional Student Services and Indigenous Peoples knowledge communities, among other leadership roles in that association. He serves as a member of the editorial boards of the *Journal of College Student Development* and the *Journal of College and Character*, was coeditor of New Directions in Student Services monographs on college gambling and serving Native American students, and has authored or coauthored a variety of other articles, papers, and chapters.

Donald B. Mills is the vice chancellor for student affairs at Texas Christian University. His special interests include the effect of environment on student learning, generational influences on values and behavior, and organizational challenges for student affairs. He has been honored as a Pillar of the Profession by the NASPA Foundation and with the Silver Medal by the National Interfraternity Council.

Keith M. Miser is special assistant to the chancellor for international programs at the University of Hawai`i at Hilo. He began his career in 1971 at the University of Vermont, where he served as director of residential life, dean of students, and associate vice president for administration. He then served as vice president for student affairs at Colorado State University. and as vice chancellor for student affairs at the University of Hawai`i at Hilo. He has been involved directly in managing the response to many crisis situations in thirty-five years of administration, from student protests and arrests to a catastrophic flood at Colorado State University, to the tragic death of Matthew Shephard, and to preparing for hurricanes and tsunamis in Hawai`i.

Larry Moneta serves as the vice president for student affairs at Duke University. He joined the Duke community in 2001 after nearly ten years at the University of Pennsylvania, most recently as associate vice president for campus services. Moneta holds adjunct faculty appointments at Duke in the Hart Leadership Program at the Sanford Institute of Public Policy, and at the Graduate School of Education at the University of Pennsylvania, where he teaches in the Higher Education Executive Doctorate Program. He has written numerous publications, presents frequently at professional meetings, and serves on a number of corporate boards.

Kelly Anne Nelson is a doctoral student in educational leadership at the University of Southern California (USC). Prior to her enrollment at USC, she worked in various residence life positions at the University of Southern California, the University of Miami, Southern Methodist University, and the University of Tampa.

Dale Nienow is executive director of the Center for Ethical Leadership, a nonprofit that builds leadership to advance the common good. He consults with organizations across sectors and leads the national Kellogg Leadership for Community Change program on behalf of the W. K. Kellogg Foundation. In addition, he serves on the Seattle University Student Development Administration Master's Degree Program Advisory Board and as senior adjunct instructor.

Kenneth J. Osfield currently serves as the Americans with Disabilities compliance officer and an instructor at the College of Education in the Department of

Education Administration and Policy at the University of Florida, where he has worked since 1989 when he was hired as an assistant dean of students/director of disability resources. Active within NASPA since 1989, he is past NASPA International Education Knowledge Community Chair (2004–06) and past director of the NASPA International Symposium (2002–04). He is the founding network chair of NASPA Disability Concerns Network (1992–94) (now the Disability Concerns Knowledge Community). He is the recipient of the NASPA Region III James E. Scott Mid-Level Student Affairs Professional Award (2003) and the Region III William Leftwich New Professional Award (1991).

Lori D. Patton is an assistant professor of higher education in the Department of Educational Leadership and Policy Studies at Iowa State University. She has administrative experiences in a wide range of student affairs functional areas, including student activities, Greek life, admissions, and residence life. Patton's research spans broadly across social justice issues in higher education including race, gender, and sexual identities. She has studied the effects of Hurricane Katrina, lesbian/gay/bisexual/transgender populations at historically Black colleges and universities, and spiritual dimensions of student development. Most notably, her research has highlighted the relevance of Black culture centers in higher education. Patton serves on the ACPA Governing Board as the director of equity and inclusion. In 2004 she was recognized as an ACPA Emerging Scholar and was an ACPA Annuit Coeptis Award recipient. She has published, edited, and contributed to numerous books, articles, and book chapters. Patton regularly presents educational sessions at ACPA, NASPA, Association for the Study of Higher Education, and American Educational Research Association annual conferences.

Cheryl A. Presley is the director of the Student Health Center at Southern Illinois University in Carbondale, Illinois. She is the director of the Core Institute for Alcohol and Other Drug Studies at Southern Illinois University and is on the Directorate for Alcohol and Other Drugs for ACPA. She is a member of American College Health Association, where she is a past member of the board of directors. She currently is the chair of the board of directors for Prevention First in the state of Illinois.

Jerry Price is vice chancellor for student affairs and dean of students at Chapman University. He previously served as associate vice president and dean of students at the University of Texas Pan American and as dean of students at Drake University. He also taught graduate classes on student affairs organization and administration at Iowa State University.

Jessica J. Ranero is a doctoral student in the Educational Leadership and Policy Studies program at Iowa State University. Her research interests include social justice, college access, the role of multicultural affairs on college campuses, and critical race theory. Before returning to school full time, she worked in the area of multicultural affairs for seven years.

James J. Rhatigan served Wichita State University (WSU) as vice president for student affairs and dean of students from 1965 to 1996, and as senior vice president from 1996 to 2002. Currently he is a consultant for the WSU Foundation. He was the NASPA historian from 1978 to 1996 and was president of NASPA in 1975–76. He has written extensively in student affairs journals and in other publications and has been a speaker and consultant throughout his career.

John H. Schuh is distinguished professor of educational leadership and policy studies at Iowa State University. Previously he held administrative and faculty appointments at Arizona State University, Indiana University (Bloomington), and Wichita State University. He is particularly interested in the experiences of college students, assessment in student affairs, and higher education finance. Schuh is editor of the New Directions for Student Services sourcebook series and book review editor for the *Review of Higher Education*. He served as associate editor of the *Journal of College Student Development* for fourteen years.

Jeremy Stringer is founder and director of the master's program in Student Development Administration at Seattle University. He has served as a vice president for student development, associate provost, chief housing officer, and department chair for several academic programs. He received the Distinguished Service to the Profession Award from NASPA Region V. A member of the inaugural class of the NASPA Faculty Fellows, he served as chair of the group for two years.

Patricia Smith Terrell is the former vice president for student affairs at the University of Kentucky. She earned her B.S.Ed. and M.S. degrees from the University of Louisville and her Ed.D. in higher education administration from the University of Kentucky. She currently serves on the NASPA Foundation board of directors and previously served NASPA as the Region III vice president and the international exchange coordinator. She is board member emeritus for the Golden Key International Honour Society, where she assisted in chartering the first international chapters of the Society in Australia. She was previously the vice president for student services at Utah State University; associate vice president for student affairs and dean of students at Southern Methodist University, and assistant vice president for student affairs at the University of Louisville.

Aurelio Valente is assistant dean of student development at Philadelphia University. He is a doctoral student in higher education at Florida State University, where he recently served as associate director of the Hardee Center for Leadership and Ethics in Higher Education. His research interests include programs and services that foster student development and academic success in the first year of college.

Sue Weitz is the vice president for student life at Gonzaga University. She has been active in NASPA leadership positions for many years and is a former member of the NASPA Foundation board of directors. In 2000 she received the Ignatian Medal for Outstanding Achievement in Jesuit Institutions, and in 2004 she was honored by NASPA as a Pillar of the Profession. She has also received the Fred Turner Award for Outstanding Service to NASPA. She has participated in the Semester at Sea program as director of student life in 1996 and executive dean in 2004.

THE HANDBOOK OF STUDENT AFFAIRS ADMINISTRATION

PART ONE

CONTEXTS OF PROFESSIONAL PRACTICE

Our work as student affairs professionals takes places in a variety of economic, historic, political, and social contexts. Those contexts shape and are in turn shaped by our efforts. We begin our conversation of student affairs by discussing several of those contextual dimensions of professional practice. In Chapter One, Jim Rhatigan presents a brief history of our field, focusing on the early practitioners, positions, and perspectives. Joan Hirt delineates the importance of institutional mission in shaping the work of student affairs staff in Chapter Two. Institutional governance, a critically important but often misunderstood or overlooked construct in higher education, is addressed by John Levin in Chapter Three, with particular attention given to the ways in which students are affected by and involved (or not) in governance structures and processes. George Kuh discusses the context of campus environment in Chapter Four. He recounts the influence of environment on student success and identifies issues to be addressed in assessing campus environment. In Chapter Five, John Schuh describes the fiscal context for higher education within which we in student affairs conduct our work. Given the relationship between fiscal pressures and calls for accountability, it is no accident that Sherry Mallory and Linda Clement present a portrait of the accountability landscape of contemporary professional practice in Chapter Six. Kenneth Osfield and Pat Terrell discuss the implications for student affairs of the growing internationalization in higher education in Chapter Seven, the final chapter in the first part of the handbook.

CHAPTER ONE

FROM THE PEOPLE UP

A Brief History of Student Affairs Administration

James J. Rhatigan

The intent of student affairs has always been to connect people who need with people who care (Chambers, 1987). The many ways this happens provides the story of student affairs. This story is framed by the individual efforts of men and women who built our profession from the ground up. This chapter attempts to tell that story by first focusing on the pioneering men and women in our field and their involvement with the profound changes that shaped our field. A primary focus will be on the roles and philosophies of the deans—both deans of men and women—and the personnel workers. A discussion of the influence of the *Student Personnel Point of View* (National Association of Student Personnel Administrators [NASPA], 1989) and subsequent documents in stating and affirming the core values of our profession is also presented. A brief discussion of the modern era in student affairs professional practice follows. The chapter concludes with a view of our professional future as it is shaped by these historical perspectives.

Beginnings

Some writers have pointed to antecedents of student affairs in Athenian education (Bathurst, 1938), others to universities in the Middle Ages (Cowley, 1940; Haskins, 1940; Kibre, 1948; Leonard, 1956; Rait, 1912; and Rashdall, 1895).

However, student affairs is largely an American higher education invention. It had a small but important beginning in the nineteenth century, but for the most part is a twentieth-century phenomenon.

Several factors influenced the early evolution of our field, including the development of land-grant institutions and the rise of public colleges and universities; expanding enrollments and the accompanying increase in the heterogeneity of student populations; social, political, and intellectual ferment in the United States; the rise of coeducation and the increase in numbers of women entering educational institutions; the introduction of the elective system in higher education; and an emphasis on vocationalism as a competitor to the traditional liberal arts. In addition, the impact of science and the scientific method; impersonalism on the part of faculty educated in German institutions; expanding industrialization and urbanization and the closing of the American frontier; the view of higher education as a social status phenomenon, with less student motivation for academic subjects; the establishment of a true university system; massive European immigration; and the changing roles of students in higher education influenced the development of student affairs. Undeniably other factors exist, but certainly all of those mentioned are related to the formation and development of what we know today as the student affairs profession.

The Deans and the Personnel Workers

Factors contributing to the emergence of the field surfaced in different ways and places, and for different reasons. Three distinct groups were involved in addressing the implications of these factors on the lives of college students: the deans of men, the deans of women, and the personnel workers.

Over time each of these groups formed its own professional associations. Those early associations were the genesis of today's largest student affairs professional associations (see Chapter Eleven for further discussion of student affairs professional associations).

A review of the proceedings of the early deans of men and deans of women reveals a collection of diverse people with high ideals, warmth, optimism, and genuineness. Students writing later about these deans emphasized their affection, compassion, and concern for students. The deans also evidenced strong qualities of leadership, and many of them were deeply religious. Most of them came from teaching roles in the liberal arts. The profession's kinship with liberal arts is a facet of our history that warrants further attention (Kuh, Shedd, and Whitt, 1997).

Deans of Men

Cowley (1937) identified the first of student personnel deans as LeBaron Russell Briggs of Harvard, who assumed his position in 1890. Thomas Arkle Clark of Illinois claimed to be the first administrator to carry the title "Dean of Men," beginning in 1909, although he assumed the responsibilities earlier.

The roles and activities of the early deans emerged as they worked. Dean Stanley Coulter of Purdue observed, "When the Board of Trustees elected me Dean of Men, I wrote them very respectfully and asked them to give me the duties of the Dean of Men. They wrote back that they did not know but when I found out to let them know." Thomas Arkle Clark noted, "I had no specific duties, no specific authority, no precedents either to guide me or to handicap me. It was an untried sea upon which I was about to set sail. My only chart was the action of the Board of Trustees when they said I was to interest myself in the individual student" (Secretarial Notes, 1924, p. 9). While the early deans of men might not have had a particularly well-articulated set of expectations from their institutions, Fley (1977), writing on the life of Dean Briggs, offers an insight from Briggs's biographer, Rollo Brown, of the ways in which at least one of these early deans was making an impact on the lives of students: "Of President Eliot I saw very little. . . . But about Dean Briggs there could be no doubt. He was human: he was intimate, personal, vastly gentle and kind. To me and to my brethren he meant Harvard, and Harvard meant nothing less than Dean Briggs" (p. 24).

Slowly, definitions began to take shape. A typical definition of the dean of men was "that officer in the administration who undertakes to assist the men students [to] achieve the utmost of which they are individually capable, through personal effort on their behalf, and through mobilizing in their behalf all the forces within the University which can be made to serve this end" (Secretarial Notes, 1928, p. 37). President Cloyd Heck Marvin of George Washington observed, "The Dean of Men is most free to interpret his position in terms of modern university life because he is handling problems dealing with the adaptation of student life to the constantly changing social surroundings. . . . You are dealing in men, helping the student to get hold of life, to find the right environment in which he can develop himself to his fullest capacity" (Secretarial Notes, 1929, p. 23).

An emphasis on the welfare of the whole student, responsibility for student discipline, and genuine care for offering students advice and support were hallmarks of the work of many of the early deans of men. These early student affairs administrators moved without the benefit of prior history or professional preparation as we know it today. They lacked both budget and clearly outlined duties. There was little communication across campuses, no agreed-upon agendas, and no tools of any kind save their own education, values, personal skills, and leadership ability. Nevertheless, they began the process of preparing a foundation upon which a field of work could later be built (Schwartz, 2002).

Deans of Women

Blackburn (1969) reports the existence of women deans by a variety of names, but believes the title was first used at the University of Chicago in 1892, with Alice Freeman Palmer and Marion Talbot as central figures. Tuttle (1996) believes that Adelia Johnston was first, serving from 1869 at Oberlin as lady principal and designated as dean of women in 1894.

Issues facing the early deans of women overlapped with those of their male counterparts but had understandably unique features. Many educators were unenthusiastic about the increasing enrollment of women students, feeling they were physically and emotionally ill equipped to cope with the rigors of higher education. As early as the mid-1800s, Horace Mann commented on women's enrollment to the Regents of the University of Michigan, who were considering coeducation. "The advantages of a joint education are great. The dangers of it are terrible" (Fley, 1966, p. 108). He argued that either the moral dangers facing women had to be dealt with or he would prefer that the "young women of that age" not have the advantages of an education. Deans of women were expected to deal with these issues. While the deans may have privately despaired of their situation, they embraced the opportunity to participate. Many of them reported to the president and were given campuswide visibility and opportunities to serve in policy-making settings. Being in these circles did not exempt them from the skepticism, but it was a matter of importance.

Most of the early deans of women were nonconformists. They were a first-of-a-kind in institutions that were first-of-a-kind (coeducational). The frustrations they encountered were enormous, a function of working in an alien environment dominated by men. Nonetheless, the inroads they made were permanent. Their ambitions for women were not always respected, but through nuance, poise, and skill they worked to expand opportunities for women students (Nidifer, 2000).

In 1903, Martha Foote Crow, the dean of women at Northwestern, and her colleague, Marion Talbot at the University of Chicago, founded a group that later would become the American Association of University Women (AAUW). This was a vigorous voice for women in the years that followed, yet the historical role of deans of women in AAUW is not well remembered (Truex, 1971).

Student discipline was thrust upon them. Many faculty saw this as a central role for the deans of women, whose annoyance was circumspect and often translated into language and behavior that could serve women. Matthews (1915) set the pattern for women writers who acknowledged the obligations they had to endure but who then set out to broaden perspectives, inspire, and subtly advocate change. She identified academic, administrative, and social roles for the deans and argued that the dean of women was to be a specialist in women's education. One could imagine this kind of language had special meaning to her informed colleagues.

As was the case with their male counterparts, the position of dean of women varied greatly from campus to campus. In an early history, Holmes (1939) observed that the position was not standardized and, given the uniqueness of each campus, probably should not be. Hopkins (1926) and Cowley (1937) would make the same observations about deans of men. Holmes identified diverse obstacles, opportunities, and quality programs in her study of various campuses. She belied the stereotype of these women as gray-haired ladies looking after routine chores, reporting that 60 percent had faculty rank and taught regularly. The early deans saw this recognition not only as earned but as essential to their credibility as deans. Nidifer (2000) and Fley (1963) have observed of these women that a remarkable breadth of interest, keen insight, and scholarship were evident from the beginning. When William Rainey Harper created the University of Chicago, for example, he chose Alice Freeman Palmer as the first dean of women. She had been the longtime president of Wellesley and was one of the most prominent women in America in the closing years of the nineteenth century (Palmer, 1908).

Personnel Workers

The third group comprising the field was the personnel worker. It appears none of the early deans of men or deans of women thought of themselves as personnel workers, as one seldom finds the word *personnel* used by them.

In 1911, Walter Dill Scott, a psychologist at Northwestern University, published the first book known to apply principles of psychology to employees in industry. As World War I approached, Scott was asked to offer assistance to the U.S. Army to develop a classification system for the Army. In 1917, a Committee on Classification of Personnel was formed that, in retrospect, included a "Who's Who" in the emerging field of psychology, measurement, and educational psychology. Among them were E. K. Strong Jr., E. L. Thorndike, W. V. Bingham, John B. Watson, Lewis M. Terman, Robert M. Yerkes, and J. K. Angell.

When Scott accepted the presidency of Northwestern in 1919, he did so with the understanding that he could develop a personnel program for the institution. In a meeting with the Northwestern Board of Trustees, Scott described his concept of personnel work: "It is my belief that the emphasis would be on the individuality of the student and his present needs and interests. The student should be looked upon as more than a candidate for a degree, he is an individuality that must be developed and must be trained for a life of service. . . . Inadequate attention has been given to the fundamental problem of personnel. The great problem in our nation today is the problem of people" (Blackburn, 1969).

The focus Scott chose was to guide students intelligently into the proper field of work. Vocational guidance was to be performed by the personnel administrator. The work was a natural extension of Parsons' pioneering effort, offering psychological measurement as an indispensable tool in vocational guidance. Both the number of personnel workers and the variety of services they offered multiplied rapidly, but the emphasis on vocational guidance became such a dominant theme that, in time, for many the terms *guidance* and *student personnel* were seen as nearly synonymous (Cowley, 1937).

A number of other events, involving the scholars engaged in the activities of the Army Classification System, coincided with the work of Scott. Psychological measurement gained considerable momentum both from the Army classification test and from seminal work in the field of intelligence. Although Cattell has been credited with instituting the first American testing and data collection (at Columbia University), the work of Alfred Binet was of major influence. His tests were translated into English and produced in several versions, the most important of which was the Stanford-Binet, first produced by Lewis Terman in 1916. A discussion of these issues would require an outline of the history of psychology in the United States. This discussion is available elsewhere (Hunt, 1993), but the impact of these influences on the field of student personnel administration must be acknowledged.

The status of psychology in the United States was altered by John B. Watson. The introspective psychology that Wundt had formulated proved frustrating because it was found lacking in objectivity. Predictability was difficult and replication was nearly impossible. Lowe (1969) argues that disillusionment with introspection led to behaviorism—the application of the objective methods of animal psychologists to human beings. This opened a field of study that has remained popular since. It is clear that the field of student personnel owes a debt to behaviorism, but as is characteristic of much of our dilemma, the weighting of that debt could be enhanced by historical analysis.

A final personnel element emerged from the field of mental health. "It came to be recognized that mental health really depended on the way people got along with each other on the college campus. Increasingly, it was seen that it was closely tied up with the morale of the college, with the presence or absence of conflicts in the environment or within personality" (Brubacher and Rudy, 1976, p. 342). (An examination of the college environment would develop later.) The American public had a growing interest in mental health, stimulated by Clifford Beers' *A Mind That Found Itself,* published in 1909. Mental health came to be considered as one aspect of the whole student. Its roots are found in the medical profession, but Blackburn (1969) believes the "medical model" and its focus on "adjustment" has been a mixed blessing for student affairs.

Other issues in the rapidly changing United States affected the development of student affairs, and certainly those touched upon above were complex and interacted in ways that we do not fully understand. Still, they do explain the separate emergence of the personnel professional. From the beginning, these persons sought to use the tools of science and humanistic learning to the extent those tools were available, adapting them to the needs of the student.

Deans of Students

The introduction of the Servicemen's Readjustment Act in 1944 (also known as the G.I. Bill) spurred huge increases in college enrollments across the United States, and the students who came to campus were different in many important ways from those who had come before them. These changes spurred growth in the number of higher education institutions, their size, and complexity. Student affairs units too grew larger and more complex, and one result was the emergence of the role of dean of students.

The early deans of men focused to large extent on the affective dimensions of the student experience and relied largely on their experience and intuition in performing their duties. The deans of women emphasized a more scholarly approach and held out the need for graduate preparation for professional practice (Schwartz, 2002). The personnel workers focused on measurement and counseling. Which of these three perspectives emerged as the preferred model in the profession as it sought to address the changes on campus? The answer is that a bit of each of them informed postwar student affairs practice.

The personnel workers' perspective, articulated in the *Student Personnel Point of View* (NASPA, 1989), discussed in greater detail later in this chapter, became the predominant perspective within student affairs. The increasing specialization and complexity of professional practice necessitated greater academic preparation for those entering into or advancing in a career in student affairs. The deans of students, purportedly selected for administrative abilities, tended to be the former deans of men.

The Student Personnel Point of View

It can be argued that the foundational document for our work is *The Student Personnel Point of View*, 1937 (NASPA, 1989). In 1937, the American Council on Education (ACE) called together an influential group of educators interested in examining the status of growing out-of-class programs and activities loosely called personnel services. Hardee (1987) provides useful information on the background of these participants. From the discussions held by the group, two members took the responsibility for preparing a summary document. They were W. H. Cowley, professor and director of the personnel bureau at Ohio State University, and Esther Lloyd-Jones, chair of guidance and student personnel, Teachers College, Columbia University. The document was entitled *The Student Personnel Point of View*.

When Walter Dill Scott established the Personnel Office, as he had promised the trustees at Northwestern, he selected L. B. Hopkins to direct the office. Esther Lloyd-Jones was an outstanding undergraduate student who worked with Hopkins but felt his program was geared mostly to men. She conducted a study of women undergraduates and their needs that so impressed Scott that he sponsored her master's program at Teachers College, Columbia, and established an associate director of personnel position for her when she returned. She returned to Teachers College in 1926, beginning a forty-year career there. She would become one of the most influential figures in our professional history.

As Lloyd-Jones began her career at Teachers College, only a few blocks away John Dewey was concluding his long tenure at Columbia University. The humanist influence in the United States—referred to varyingly as experimentalism, instrumentalism, or pragmatism—was reformulated in Dewey's work. We see his influence in the present day.

Dewey believed in the humanist propositions of human growth and development and gave to the schools an important role in encouraging these outcomes. Central to his work was an analysis of the psychology of learning, his belief in the wholeness of students, and his advocacy for student-centered learning. He did not abandon the centrality of intellectual development but argued that it would prosper if it was accompanied by experience. He saw both the successes and the abuses of the Industrial Revolution and believed the tools of science could be used in service to the nation (Dewey, [1916] 1952).

At the time of the 1937 ACE meeting, Cowley had developed an interest in the growing field of student personnel. He wrote during that period about the variety of functions performed and argued for closer cooperation among the various campus programs and national organizations, a point of view that found its way into the document.

The perspective articulated in the *Student Personnel Point of View* went largely unchallenged for thirty years and has not been superseded even now. The core philosophy is contained within two concise paragraphs that reflect a humanist perspective:

> One of the basic purposes of higher education is the preservation, transmission, and enrichment of the important elements of culture: the product of scholarship, research, creative imagination, and human experience. It is the task of colleges and universities to utilize this and other educational purposes as to assist the student in developing to the limits of his potential and in making his contribution to the betterment of society.
>
> This philosophy imposes upon educational institutions the obligation to consider the student as a whole—his intellectual capacity and achievement, his emotional make-up, his physical condition, his social relationships, his vocational aptitudes and skills, his moral and religious values, his economic resources, and his aesthetic appreciation. It puts emphasis, in brief, upon the development of the student as a person rather than upon his intellectual training alone [NASPA, 1989].

The document was redrafted by American Council on Education in 1949 to reflect the major changes in American life and on the campus following World War II. Only Cowley and Lloyd-Jones were left from the original committee. E. G. Williamson (University of Minnesota) chaired the new effort, and three new goals were offered:

1. Education for a fuller realization of democracy in every phase of living
2. Education directly and explicitly for understanding and cooperation, and
3. Education for the application of creative imagination and trained intelligence to the solution of social problems and to the administration of public affairs (NASPA, 1989)

The "preservation, transmission, and enrichment of the culture" changed from one of higher education's basic purposes (1937) to the basic purpose (1949). This may reflect Williamson's concern that student personnel administration was seen as soft intellectually. This caused him to comment on one occasion that the field needed to consider the whole student, "intellect and all" (Williamson, 1961, p. 429).

The Modern Era

In one sense, the end of World War II transformed student personnel administration. The enterprise grew phenomenally, both in the introduction of new programs and services and the expansion of old ones. Philosophical issues in student affairs were secondary to the requirements of time and energy needed to serve the returning veteran. The role of women in the war effort, whether in the military or in industry, led them to college in greater numbers. Racial minorities, while small as a percentage, grew substantially in absolute numbers from the prewar years.

Blaesser (1945) and his colleagues were concerned about a number of these issues. Rules and regulations, they correctly predicted, "are probably in for a bad time." They believed that mental health would be an issue, particularly for veterans with combat experience. What would racial attitudes be like, they pondered. Would religious counseling need to be expanded?

Of course, most worrisome of all, what would be the needs of a postwar America, and how should a college education be altered to meet those needs? The G.I. Bill of Rights introduced students to the campus who were the first in their families to attend college. Hundreds of thousands of students would flock to newly developed public two-year colleges across the United States. Married students would be coming to campus in huge numbers. Where would they live? What would be their requirements?'

The 1960s and 1970s

A number of issues coalesced in the 1960s to make the decade violent on and off the campus. The assassination of three national leaders, John F. Kennedy, Robert F. Kennedy, and Martin Luther King Jr. demonstrated the fragile nature of human progress. The undeclared war in Vietnam hardened hearts and minds, dividing the nation. A counterculture emerged with drugs as a sacrament. Efforts to increase rights along racial lines intensified. A revolution in communication and information introduced messages into one's living room nearly simultaneous to their occurrence across the globe.

College students were not isolated from these events. In fact, in some instances students led the dissent. Many were disturbed by the collaboration between war industries and higher education institutions. Eisenhower (1961) warned the country about "the military-industrial complex," and his admonition was taken seriously on the campus. College students' ideals led them to politics, but what they found there was not appealing. Campus dissent became violent in a number of instances and occasionally was met by repressive responses that worsened matters.

Serious as these issues were, the decade of the 1960s produced successful legislation that would transform civil rights. The Civil Rights Act of 1965 contained a number of separate titles that over the years would be pervasive influences. The Higher Education Acts of 1965 (amended in 1972) improved the lives of students in a number of ways, not the least of which was financial support unparalleled in the nation's history. Wolf-Wendel (2004) and a number of her colleagues have written about the role of student affairs in this volatile time.

Much of what we know as the contemporary practice of student affairs evolved during the 1970s as a direct result of the social upheaval of the preceding decade. Not the least of these developments was the emerging prominence of a new position: the vice president for student affairs. The change resulted from a growing acceptance of student affairs as a major division of the institution. The title proliferated during the period of student unrest in the 1960s. For a period of time, the title "vice president for student affairs and dean of students" reflected both a reluctance of senior student affairs officers to move further from the lives of students and the beckoning of the executive role many would find more useful in their campus efforts.

The long history of women in student affairs resurfaced in the 1980s with the vice president's position. On most campuses, no women were employed at a vice presidential level in the university administration. Student affairs became a natural area of entry. Today a substantial number of vice presidents of student affairs are women, perhaps a final vindication of the dean of women.

When the "student development" movement emerged in the late 1960s, writers differentiated the "service" function attributed to the early deans from their own conceptions about students (Brown, 1972; Crookston, 1972). These later writers took the view that service was an insufficient basis upon which the profession could develop a future. Regardless of the merit of their position, it is regrettable that they used a superficial definition of service and applied it to the work of the early deans. A more accurate picture is provided by Cowley, in 1983: "Personnel work constitutes all activities undertaken or sponsored by an educational institution, aside from curricular instruction, in which the student's personal development is the primary concern" (p. 65).

The 1980s and 1990s

The last quarter of the twentieth century was an energizing time for student affairs. Existing professional associations grew substantially in size, quality, and diversity. A sense of greater inclusiveness was evident. Minority and women professionals became involved in larger numbers and in leadership roles. Interagency cooperation gave attention to standards (through the Council for the Advancement of Standards), alcohol abuse (Boosting Alcohol Consciousness Concerning the Health of University Students [BACCHUS]), and the mental health of students. Assessment of programs became more formal, to better understand the impact of our work, but in reality they were mandated from outside sources (governing boards and legislative bodies) wondering about the effectiveness of their support of higher education.

On individual campuses, new organizations were added to the structure of student affairs, and smaller ones blossomed. They were called to service on behalf of students with specific needs and issues not well enough addressed before. Students with physical disabilities, minority students, first-generation students, students with differing sexual orientations, students bringing a large number of mental health issues to their campus experience, students asking for more opportunities to express faith and values issues on secular campuses are examples of needs that saw a response in organizational and financial support. These new or expanded programs demonstrate how the adaptability of senior student affairs officers and their staffs created the conditions for change that remained consistent with the history and philosophy of student affairs.

New campus responsibilities came to student affairs in the last quarter of the century. Senior officers on various campuses assumed responsibilities for intercollegiate athletic programs, campus human relations programs, public (external) relations, cooperative education efforts, and developing their own fund raising programs. Today they run golf courses, swimming pools, office complexes, and a number of other activities idiosyncratic to the skills and personalities of student affairs personnel on any one campus.

Research on the campus has expanded to address theories of developmental change, psychosocial behavior, organizational change, typology, community, and the effects of college on students. The work of these outstanding scholars has been summarized by Sandeen and Barr (2006). It also seems significant that other scholars, having looked at the field, see the enduring values and beliefs that have underpinned student affairs from the beginning (Woodard, Love, and Komives, 2000). This was the conclusion of a group of student affairs leaders who studied *The Student Personnel Point of View* on the fiftieth year anniversary of its publication (NASPA, 1989).

Conclusion

How will our profession transform itself to better serve the students of the future? How will our practice change to respond to new environmental imperatives? How will we change as teachers and learners as the boundaries of cognition and communication form and reform rapidly as a result of technological innovation? How will we help assure access, affordability, and accountability within the constructs of constrained resources and in light of heightened expectations? How will the decisions of our past shape the direction of our future?

History unfolding need not be a spectator sport. We all need to think, write, and participate in our time about matters of importance if we hope to influence the future. Writing about current issues in student affairs and beyond should be considered a matter of stewardship. We owe our present circumstances to the earlier deans who made it possible. We repay this debt not to them, but to those who follow us. This responsibility cannot be met solely through segmented, restrictive articles in research journals. Scholars will need to introduce broader ideas for discussion among practitioners. There is evidence of progress we should find encouraging (Kuh, Kinzie, Schuh, and Whitt, 2005; Pascarella and Terenzini, 2005; Sandeen and Barr, 2006; Schuh and Whitt, 1999; and Woodard, Love, and Komives, 2000).

There are other reasons to be encouraged. A handful of dissertations in recent years have uncovered primary documents on individual campuses (Bashaw, 1992; Gilroy, 1987; and Tuttle, 1996). Sheeley (1991) found sufficient archival material to profile all of the past presidents of American College Personnel Association (ACPA), and Sandeen (2001) profiled a number of successful leaders in NASPA. Murphy (1988) demonstrated that a writer without formal training in history can present material effectively as he summarized the first hundred years of student affairs history at Oklahoma State University. Herdlein (2005) provides another illustration in his student affairs history of the University of Pittsburgh. Burlingame (2007) encourages the writing of local campus history and suggests strategies for accomplishing it. He sees the importance of establishing information from the campus up, as a way of developing a full understanding of our work. More of these efforts undoubtedly exist and a comprehensive effort to find them is underway (Coomes, 2007). A number of professional associations are now depositing their papers on a regular basis in the impressive student affairs archival collection housed at Bowling Green State University. NASPA has established a History Advisory Committee in its formal bylaws. History articles offering new perspectives are appearing more frequently in our professional journals (Blimling and Alschuler, 1996; Caple, 1996; Coomes, Whitt, and Kuh, 1987; Cross, 1998; Roberts, 1998; and Ruekel and Harris, 1986). Indications are that one day, sufficient sources will be developed to enable one among us to write the definitive history our predecessors deserve and our successors can use.

In an effort to encourage active participation in the large events that await us, the ordinary, pressing issues of the day cannot be neglected. This is a problem for dedicated student affairs professionals who must choose how to spend their energy. Reading and writing may not be their first choice (Rhatigan and Crawford, 1978). We do not need to write for publication to be effective. In campus committees, memoranda, classes, newspapers, seminars, presentations, and conversations, we can use the tools of history to achieve goals seen as important.

Campus practitioners will need to find a way to retreat from their labors to be active learners. A major limitation in work is lacking the ability to see possibilities, failing to employ imagination, wasting time on undeserving tasks, or doing things others have identified as important. Yet, the professional literature must take practitioners into account in far more effective ways than seem to exist at the time of this writing.

Practitioners do not enjoy the luxury of certainty. It is profoundly true that student affairs administrators must often proceed without knowing exactly what they are doing. We either act or step aside. This requires judgment and faith, the willingness to be vulnerable and to take risks. There is much to celebrate in these ordinary days of our lives, part of the fellowship we share with those who came before. We must work hard to allow colleagues years from now to glimpse this evidence of goodness.

References

Bashaw, C. T. "We Who Live off on the Edges: Deans of Women at Southern Coeducational Institutions and Access to the Community of Higher Education, 1907–1960." Unpublished doctoral dissertation, University of Georgia, 1992.

Bathurst, J. E. "What Is Student Personnel Work?" *Educational Record,* 1938, 19, 502–515.

Blackburn, J. L. "Perceived Purposes of Student Personnel Programs by Chief Student Personnel Officers as a Function of Academic Preparation and Experience." Unpublished doctoral dissertation, Florida State University, 1969.

Blaesser, W. W., and others. *Student Personnel Work in the Postwar College.* Washington, D.C.: American Council on Education, 1945.

Blimling, G. S., and Alschuler, A. S. "Creating a Home for the Spirit of Learning: Contributions of Student Development Directors." *Journal of College Student Development,* 1996, 37(2), 203–223.

Brown, R. D. *Student Development in Tomorrow's Higher Education: A Return to the Academy.* Monograph 16, Association of College Personnel Administrators, 1972.

Brubacher, J., and Rudy, W. R. *Higher Education in Transition* (3rd ed.). New York: Harper Collins, 1976.

Burlingame, P. J. "Writing Local Student Affairs History." Unpublished manuscript, 2007.

Caple, R. B. "The Learning Debate: A Historical Perspective." *Journal of College Student Development,* 1996, 37(2), 203–223.

Chambers, J. Untitled Remarks, Opening Session. Presented at ACPA/NASPA Joint Conference, Chicago, March 1987. Audiotape.

Coomes, M. D., Whitt, E. J., and Kuh, G. D. "Woman for a Changing World." *Journal of Counseling and Development*, 1987, 65, 407–414.

Coomes, M. D. "A Bibliographic Guide for Student Affairs Historians." Unpublished manuscript, 2007.

Cowley, W. H. "The Disappearing Dean of Men." *Proceedings of the Nineteenth Annual Conference of Deans and Advisors to Men*. Austin: University of Texas, 1937, 85–99. Mimeograph.

Cowley, W. H. "The History and Philosophy of Student Personnel Work." *Journal of the National Association of Deans of Women*, 1940, 3, 153–162.

Cowley, W. H. "The Nature of Student Personnel Work." In G. L. Saddlemire and A. L. Rentz (Eds.), *Student Affairs: A Profession's Heritage*. Carbondale: Southern Illinois Press, 1983, 47–73.

Crookston, B. B. "An Organizational Model for Student Development." *Journal of the National Association of Student Personnel Administrators*, 1972, 10(1), 3–13.

Cross, K. P. "Why Learning Communities? Why Now?" *About Campus*, 1998, 3(3), 4–11.

Dewey, J. *Democracy and Education*. New York: Macmillan Company, 1952. (Originally published 1916).

Eisenhower, D. D. "A Farewell Address." Delivered on radio and television, January 17, 1961.

Fley, J. "Discipline in Student Personnel Work: The Changing Views of Deans and Personnel Workers." Unpublished doctoral dissertation, University of Illinois, 1963.

Fley, J. "An Honorable Tradition." *Journal of the National Association of Women Deans and Counselors*, 1966, 29(3), 106–110.

Fley, J. "LeBaron Russell Briggs: He Meant Harvard." *Journal of the National Association of Women Deans, Advisors and Counselors*, 1977, 40(Fall), 21–24.

Gilroy, M. "The Contributions of Selected Teachers College Women to the Field of Student Personnel." Unpublished doctoral dissertation, Teachers College, Columbia University, 1987.

Hardee, M. D. Untitled Keynote Address. Presented at ACPA/NASPA Joint Conference, Chicago, March 15, 1987.

Haskins, C. H. *The Rise of Universities*. New York: Peter Smith, 1940.

Herdlein, R. J. *A History of Innovation at the University of Pittsburg*. Lewiston: The Edwin Mellen Press, 2005.

Holmes, L. *A History of the Position of Dean of Women in a Selected Group of Co-educational Colleges and Universities in the United States*. New York: Teachers College, Columbia, University, 1939.

Hopkins, L. B. "Personnel Procedure in Education," *The Educational Record*, 1926, 3, 3–96.

Hunt, M. *The Story of Psychology*. New York: Doubleday, 1993.

Kibre, P. *The Nations in the Medieval Universities*. Cambridge: Medieval Academy of America, 1948.

Kuh, G. D., Kinzie, J., Schuh, J. H., and Whitt, E. J., and Associates. *Student Success in College: Creating Conditions That Matter*. San Francisco: Jossey-Bass, 2005.

Kuh, G. D., Schuh, J. H., and Whitt, E. J. *Involving Colleges: Successful Approaches to Fostering Student Learning and Development Outside the Classroom*. San Francisco: Jossey-Bass, 1991.

Kuh, G. D., Shedd, J. D., and Whitt, E. J. "Student Affairs and Liberal Education: Unrecognized (and Unappreciated) Common Law Partners." In E. J. Whitt (Ed.), *College Student Affairs Administration*. ASHE Reader Series. Needham Heights, Mass.: Simon & Schuster, 1997, 60–69.

Leonard, E. A. *Origins of Personnel Services in American Higher Education*. Minneapolis: University of Minnesota Press, 1956.

Lowe, C. M. *Value Orientations in Counseling and Psychotherapy*. San Francisco: Chandler Company, 1969.

Matthews, L. K. *The Dean of Women*. Boston: Houghton Mifflin, 1915.

Murphy, P. M. *Student Life and Services*. Stillwater: Oklahoma State University Centennial Series, 1988.

National Association of Student Personnel Administrators. *Points of View*. Washington, D.C.: National Association of Student Personnel Administrators, 1989.

Nidifer, J. *Pioneering Deans of Women: More Than Wise and Pious Matrons*. New York: Teachers College Press, 2000.

Palmer, G. H. *The Life of Alice Freeman Palmer*. New York: Houghton-Mifflin, 1908.

Pascarella E. T., and Terenzini, P. T. *How College Affects Students*, vol. 2: *A Third Decade of Research*. San Francisco: Jossey-Bass, 2005.

Rait, R. S. *Life in the Medieval University*. Cambridge, Mass.: Harvard University Press, 1912.

Rashdall, H. *The Universities of Europe in the Middle Ages*. 3 vols. New York: Oxford University Press, 1895.

Rhatigan, J. J., and Crawford, A. E. III. "Professional Development Preferences of Student Affairs Administrators." *National Association of Student Personnel Administrators Journal*, 1978, 15(3), 45–52.

Roberts, D. C. "Student Learning Was Always Supposed to Be the Core of Our Work." *About Campus*, 1998, 3(3), 18–22.

Ruekel, P., and Harris, A. R. (Eds.). "NAWDAC Celebrates Seventy Years." *Journal of the National Association for Women Deans, Administrators and Counselors*, 1986, 49(2).

Sandeen, A. *Making a Difference: Profiles of Successful Student Affairs Leaders*. Washington, D.C.: National Association of Student Personnel Administrators, 2001.

Sandeen, A., and Barr, M. J. *Critical Issues for Student Affairs*. San Francisco: Jossey-Bass, 2006.

Schuh, J. H., and Whitt, E. J. *Creating Successful Partnerships Between Academic and Student Affairs*. New Directions for Student Services Sourcebook, no. 87. San Francisco: Jossey-Bass, 1999.

Schwartz, R. A. "The Rise and Demise of Deans of Men." *The Review of Higher Education*. 2002, 26(2), 217–239.

Secretarial Notes on the Sixth Annual Conference of Deans and Advisers of Men held at the University of Michigan, April 24–26, 1924, p. 9.

Secretarial Notes on Tenth Annual Conference of Deans and Advisers of Men held at University of Colorado, May 10–12, 1928, p. 37.

Secretarial Notes on Eleventh Annual Conference of Deans and Advisers of Men held at Washington, D.C., April 11–13, 1929, p. 23.

Servicemen's Readjustment Act of 1944, PL346, 58 *Statutes at Large* 284.

Sheeley, V. L. *Fulfilling Visions: Emerging Leaders of ACPA*. Alexandria, VA: American College Personnel Association, 1991.

Truex, D. "Education of Women, the Student Personnel Profession, and the New Feminism." *Journal of the National Association of Women Deans and Counselors*, 1971, 34, 13–20.

Tuttle, K. N. "What Became of the Dean of Women? Changing Roles for Women Administrators in American Higher Education, 1940–1980." Unpublished doctoral dissertation, University of Kansas, 1996.

Williamson, E. G. *Student Personnel Services in Colleges and Universities*. New York: McGraw Hill, 1961.

Wolf-Wendel, L., and Associates. *Reflecting Back, Looking Forward: Civil Rights and Student Affairs*. Washington, D.C.: National Association of Student Personnel Administrators, 2004.

Woodard, D. B. Jr., Love, P. G., and Komives, S. R. *Leadership and Management Skills for the New Century*. New Directions for Student Services, no. 92. San Francisco: Jossey Bass, 2000.

CHAPTER TWO

THE IMPORTANCE OF INSTITUTIONAL MISSION

Joan B. Hirt

The American system of higher education is the envy of the world, largely because of its rich array of institutional types (Carnegie Foundation for the Advancement of Teaching, 2000). Many colleges and universities focus on teaching arts and sciences. Some offer vocational training and workforce development opportunities, while others conduct groundbreaking research or engage in outreach activities to benefit citizens at the local, national, or international level. An assortment of variables differentiate institutions, including the number of students they enroll, their type of control (public versus independent campus), and the number and type of certificates and degrees they offer, to name but a few. Indeed, the breadth and scope of the higher education enterprise is so complex it can seem indecipherable, at times. Yet there is a mechanism that can assist in decoding that complexity: the institutional mission statement.

The mission statement of a college or university serves several purposes. First and foremost, it captures the essence and distinctive character of the organization. A mission statement describes why a college or university was founded, who it serves, and what it strives to accomplish. In short, the statement reveals where the institution came from, where it is heading, and how it plans to get there (Barr, 2000; and Martin, 1982). It communicates elemental information about the institution to key external and internal constituents.

To those outside the organization, the mission expresses the goals of the institution. It defines intentions so that external audiences can understand the span of activities and academic offerings of the college or university as well as the types of students it serves (Barr, 2000). Such public proclamations of purpose and intent convey important information to critical external groups. Prospective students may evaluate the mission to see if an institution would enable them to achieve their educational aspirations. Potential faculty members look to the mission to gain a sense of institutional purpose and relevance of that purpose to their areas of expertise. Public officials may rely on the mission when identifying criteria by which to assess the organization's effectiveness.

For external groups, the mission statement serves to *inform,* but for those inside the institution the mission statement serves to *conform.* It identifies the role that the college or university plays in the higher education enterprise. That helps academic leaders determine what falls within the scope of the organization and where to allocate resources. The mission statement guides decision makers when they consider adopting, expanding, revising, or eliminating programs and services. In an era of declining resources and increasing demands, the mission of an institution can serve as a beacon to guide institutional managers.

Understanding institutional mission is particularly important for student affairs leaders. As Barr (2000) notes, "Failure to understand, appreciate, and translate the mission of the institution into programs and services can rank among the biggest mistakes a student affairs administrator can make" (p. 25). While other chapters in this volume offer insights into models of professional practice and the competencies considered fundamental to successful practice, this one focuses on the milieus in which that practice is enacted. The chapter opens by describing different frameworks for classifying colleges and universities. Next, the social, economic, and political trends that influenced the emergence and mission of different institutional types are described. This is followed by a discussion on how mission influences the work of student affairs administrators at different types of institutions. Finally, the relationship between institutional mission and professional mobility is explored.

Institutional Classification Systems

Unlike other countries of the world, the United States does not have a centrally coordinated national system of postsecondary education. Instead, higher education has always fallen under the domain of the states. As a result, there are literally fifty systems of higher education, not including those in the District of Columbia, Puerto Rico, and other affiliated territories. While there are some common organizing patterns, the structure of higher education in each state has its own unique qualities and quirks. This renders comparisons across state systems somewhat challenging. To address that challenge, experts have developed a number of frameworks to sort colleges and universities into comprehensive (and comprehensible) categories. For example, Barr (2000) identified factors that influence mission, including institutional affiliation, history, and governance system. Nexus of control (public, private, tribal), purpose of charter (not-for-profit, proprietary), size, and athletic league are other ways of categorizing colleges and universities. This chapter is organized around one of the most well-known and frequently used frameworks: the Carnegie Classification of Institutions of Higher Education.

The Carnegie framework identifies categories of like colleges and universities. Originally published in 1973, the system was refined, revised, and reissued in 1976, 1987, 1994, 2000 (Carnegie Foundation, 2000), and 2005. The first five iterations of the classification system grouped colleges and universities according to their mission. Categories included doctoral and research universities, master's colleges and universities, baccalaureate colleges, associate's colleges, specialized institutions (for example, seminaries, schools of art), and tribal colleges and universities.

Over the years, scholars and administrators have used the system to conduct research and assessment projects. The framework has also been used in unintended ways, however: as an institutional ranking system or a mechanism for allocating funds, for example. These more pernicious uses of the classification system prompted leaders at the Carnegie Foundation for the Advancement of Teaching to reconceptualize it. In addition to grouping institutions by mission (albeit with some new subcategories), the framework that debuted in 2005 also classifies institutions by the nature of their undergraduate instructional program, graduate instructional program, enrollment profile, undergraduate profile, size and setting, and level of community engagement. These new categories are intended to paint a richer picture of the higher education landscape (Carnegie Classification of Institutions of Higher Education, 2005).

The 2005 Carnegie framework categorizes a total of 4,392 institutions. Most (3,483) are two- or four-year not-for-profit colleges and universities. The rest (909) are for-profit (proprietary) institutions. The remainder of this chapter employs a modified version of the 2005 Carnegie Classification model. Missions for baccalaureate colleges (both secular and sectarian), master's colleges and universities, research and doctoral granting universities, and associate's colleges are described. Added to these are discussions of tribally controlled colleges, historically Black colleges and universities, Hispanic-serving institutions, and for-profit organizations.

Institutional Mission Statements

In order to fully appreciate the profound and pervasive influence that mission statements have on institutions, it is imperative to understand the historical contexts in which different types of colleges and universities emerged. Scholars have produced works on the history of education in America (for example, see Brubacher and Rudy, 1997, or Rudolph, 1962) that are far richer than what is offered here. Rather, this chapter simply touches upon the conditions under which certain types of colleges and universities developed in the United States so that the discussion of mission statements is placed in some pertinent historical context.

Baccalaureate Colleges

The first type of institution established in America was the baccalaureate college. Baccalaureate colleges were modeled after Cambridge and Oxford universities in England (Brubacher and Rudy, 1997; Rudolph, 1962; and Urban and Wagoner, 2000). Colonial leaders founded these early institutions in order to educate those who would serve the religious and political interests of the colony (O'Grady, 1969). The number of colleges swelled as the country expanded, and over time baccalaureate institutions took one of two paths. Some moved away from their religious roots and evolved into secular colleges. Others retained their religious affiliations.

The 2005 Carnegie Classification system assigns 3,483 not-for-profit institutions to various categories. Of those, 693 (19.9 percent) are classified as baccalaureate colleges, and 314 (9 percent) are labeled Special Faith Focused Institutions. The latter group includes some baccalaureate colleges as well as seminaries, bible colleges, and other faith-based institutions. This makes it difficult to clearly delineate sectarian from secular colleges. However, the difference between these two forms of baccalaureate colleges is evident in their mission statements.

Liberal Arts Colleges. To distinguish between the two types of baccalaureate colleges, secular institutions hereafter are referred to as "liberal arts colleges." These colleges tend to be independent (as opposed to public), residential campuses that typically serve eighteen- to twenty-four-year-old undergraduates. They are small, on average enrolling between 1,600 and 1,800 students, and offer traditional curricula: a broad array of general education classes and majors in the arts and sciences.

The mission statements for liberal arts colleges reflect their character. They tend to be brief—only a paragraph or two—and often highlight the campus's historical roots. The statements address a holistic approach to education, referring to the outcomes that these colleges endeavor to achieve for their students: intellectual sophistication, the ability to think clearly and communicate effectively, a future as socially aware citizens of the world. In general, students are at the center of the mission for liberal arts colleges.

Religiously Affiliated Colleges. Those baccalaureate colleges that retained their sectarian ties are hereafter referred to as "religiously affiliated colleges." These institutions tend to be independent, small, and enroll primarily traditional-aged students. Their mission statements talk about a liberal education that is grounded in the arts and sciences. What sets religiously affiliated colleges apart from secular liberal arts institutions is the clear enunciation of religious ties in their mission statements. Denominational campuses spotlight spiritual development and talk about the role of the institution in glorifying a higher power, serving the relevant church, or encouraging the evangelical spirit. The mission statements of these colleges openly and proudly proclaim their sectarian nature.

Master's Colleges and Universities

While baccalaureate colleges and universities dominated the landscape through the first 250 years of American higher education, other institutional forms did eventually emerge. Master's colleges and universities are one such form. Most of the 621 not-for-profit institutions assigned to this classification in the 2005 Carnegie framework arrived at their current status in one of two ways. Some started out as baccalaureate colleges and thrived through the middle of the twentieth century until the Baby Boomers completed their undergraduate educations. At that time, enrollments threatened to drop precipitously, and some of these tuition-dependent campuses elected to introduce professional (for example, business, teacher education) and graduate programs to their curricula to survive (Breneman, 1990, 1994). This led to their reassignment in the Carnegie system from baccalaureate to master's colleges and universities.

The bulk of institutions in this category, however, followed a historical path that was closely linked to the development of K–12 education. It may seem surprising, but the current tiered system of elementary, middle, and secondary education was not fully developed in the United States until the 1940s. As these lower forms of education became institutionalized, the need for teachers grew. Teacher training programs, or "normal schools," developed to meet this demand. As industrialization gripped the country in the early twentieth century, many normal schools expanded their curricula and morphed from normal schools to state colleges, then to state universities, and many ultimately became part of a state university system. During the latter part of the twentieth century, most of these campuses increased their span of influence regionally and added graduate education through the master's degree, and in some instances a limited number of doctoral programs, to their curricula (Cohen, 1998; Lucas, 1994; and Urban and Wagoner, 2000).

Most master's institutions are midsized, enrolling 4,000–8,000 students. About half are public, and the rest are independent (many of those former baccalaureate campuses). A review of their mission statements reveals the many transformations their development has taken. They typically educate students from their regions, often serving as pathways to upward mobility for students who might not otherwise have access to higher education. Their graduate programs serve working adults who seek professional advancement. The mission statements of these institutions characteristically are lengthy and talk about the various roles the institutions fulfill, from offering liberal arts degrees to undergraduates and professional programs to graduate students to serving as cultural hubs for their regions.

Research and Doctoral Granting Universities

Research and doctoral granting universities are another form of higher education that emerged in the post–Civil War era. A confluence of factors in the latter half of the nineteenth century catalyzed the development of this sector. First, the Enlightenment produced rapid advancements in science and technology, leading to new curricular offerings. Second, higher education started enrolling students from a broader socioeconomic spectrum in an effort to provide trained workers for emerging industries. Additionally, states striving to recover from the Civil War and capitalize on postwar industrialization sought to expand higher education. Indeed, the federal government endorsed this expansion through the Morrill Acts (1862 and 1890), which encouraged states to establish public universities. Finally, the introduction of graduate education in the United States occurred in the last quarter of the nineteenth century (Fincher, 1989). Collectively, these factors spawned the growth of research and doctoral granting universities (Cohen, 1998; Lucas, 1994; and Urban and Wagoner, 2000).

As of 2005, 274 of the 3,483 institutions in the Carnegie framework were classified as research or doctoral granting. While their numbers reflect just 7.9 percent of all not-for-profit institutions, they serve 27.9 percent of the 17.5 million students enrolled in higher education; most are large campuses with average enrollments over 20,000. The majority (66 percent) are public institutions. Their size is often reflective of their complexity. All offer undergraduate, graduate, and professional programs, and most are home to research institutes and crossdisciplinary endeavors that add a further layer of density to the organization (Anderson, 2001; Etzkowitz, Webster, and Healey, 1998; and Slaughter and Leslie, 1997).

Mission statements of research and doctoral institutions reflect both this density and a sense of elitism. Nearly all discuss their tripartite mission of teaching, research, and service, but research is clearly the crown jewel. References to research as the bedrock for the university, enabling it to attract high-quality students, top-notch scholars, and international recognition are rampant. These mission statements also proclaim their elite status. Phrases like "world class" and "cutting edge" are sprinkled throughout research university mission statements. In fact, the term *statement* does not really capture the nature of these documents; most are several pages long and might better be termed reports.

Associate's Colleges

Associate's colleges, also referred to as "community colleges," were the sixth type of postsecondary organization to evolve in the postbellum era and represent 34.7 percent of all not-for-profit institutions (Carnegie Classification, 2005). They offer multiple types of programs and have distinct service (geographic) areas that tie them to their communities. These ties are linked to the historical era in which they materialized. At the start of the twentieth century, there was an emergent educational ladder (elementary, middle, secondary, college levels). Curricular development, however, was not as clear. Colleges sought students who had studied math, science, and languages, among other subjects. Secondary schools, on the other hand, were designed to offer terminal education. A debate ensued, and associate's colleges initially served two purposes: vocational training for those who completed high school and did not aspire to a college degree, and transfer education for high school graduates who were ill prepared for the academic rigors of college. Over the course of the twentieth century, they added two more functions to their rosters: remedial education, particularly for the growing numbers of immigrants in America, and continuing education opportunities for people in their service areas (Cohen, 1998; Cohen and Brawer, 2003; and Urban and Wagoner, 2000).

The 1,212 community colleges educate 38.6 percent of students, suggesting that most are relatively small in terms of enrollment. Perhaps most notable about associate's colleges, however, is their variety. In fact, the Carnegie system identifies fourteen different forms of community colleges: small rural, single campus suburban, and urban multicampus, among others. This represents a significant departure from the 2000 classification, where all such campuses were grouped in a single category.

Despite their differences, the mission statements of associate's colleges share some commonalties. They tend to be very straightforward: many statements consist of enumerated lists of the programs the institution offers. Almost without exception, however, these public pronouncements identify the four traditional missions of associate's colleges: vocational development, transfer education, remedial or developmental education, and continuing education. Most also acknowledge their role as a community resource and their commitment to serving the interests of their local districts.

Tribally Controlled Colleges

Scholars (Carney, 1999; and McClellan, Tippeconnic Fox, and Lowe, 2005) have written about the history of Native American higher education far more fully than can be captured here. The first tribally controlled community college was established in 1968, and since then thirty-three other institutions have opened (McClellan and others, 2005). Nearly all of these offer associate's degrees, and a handful offer bachelor's or master's degrees (Carney, 1999). Most of these campuses are small, enrolling fewer than 1,000 students. Those enrollees tend to be older women who often have children, typically come from low-income backgrounds, and are first-generation students (Belgarde, 1996) who see higher education as a means to improve their lives.

The mission statements for tribally controlled colleges reflect their students' aspirations. Most are short, typically a single paragraph. Without exception these statements talk about serving Natives in general and members of the specific tribe in particular. Nearly all see their mission as providing vocational training and educational opportunities that will better individuals, families, and tribal communities. Indeed, the focus on the welfare of the community is a distinguishing characteristic of tribally controlled institutions. They play a key role in tribal economic development and preservation of language and culture. Since tribes, not state governments, control them, these colleges are powerful symbols of tribal sovereignty.

Historically Black Colleges and Universities

"Historically Black Colleges and Universities" (HBCUs) is not a Carnegie Classification, per se. Some HBCUs are baccalaureate colleges, while others are master's or doctoral granting universities (Coaxum, 2001). They constitute a unique type of institution, however, because many were founded to educate a certain segment of the population: the sons and daughters of slaves. Allen and Jewell (2002) and Brown and Davis (2001) are excellent sources of history on these colleges and universities. For purposes of this discussion, some basic statistics serve to illustrate the need for HBCUs. On the eve of the Civil War, there were 4 million people in the United States, but only twenty-nine Blacks earned a bachelor's degree between 1619 and 1850 (Humphries, 1995). The emancipation of slaves after the Civil War created an urgent need for educational services. A number of religious and secular groups stepped up to fill this gap, but most HBCUs started out offering elementary education to illiterate slaves and gradually increased their curricular offerings to include secondary, postsecondary, and graduate education.

The numbers of HBCUs have varied over time. The general consensus is that there are currently 103 such institutions in the United States (Brown, Donahoo, and Bertrand, 2001), representing 2.9 percent of the not-for-profit campuses included in the 2005 Carnegie Classification system. Collectively, they enroll 300,000 students, meaning that most HBCUs are relatively small (3,000 or fewer students) (Brown and Davis, 2001). Despite their relatively limited numbers, these colleges and universities confer 28 percent of all bachelor's, 15 percent of all master's, and 10 percent of all doctoral degrees earned by Blacks in the United States.

The mission statements of most HBCUs are hybridized. On one hand, they typically discuss functions reflective of their Carnegie type. Those that are baccalaureate colleges refer to liberal education, while those that are master's institutions talk about serving their regions and offering graduate education. On the other hand, nearly all make mention of their commitment to educating Blacks, and many mention their role in educating offspring of former slaves. This is an overriding theme in the mission statements of HBCUs: they are public declarations about the preservation of Blacks and Black culture in America.

Hispanic-Serving Institutions

"Hispanic-Serving Institutions" (HSIs) is not a category of colleges and universities in the Carnegie Classification system either. Although definitions about what constitutes an HSI vary, the U.S. Department of Education defines a Hispanic-Serving Institution as "a non-profit institution that has at least 25% Hispanic full-time equivalent (FTE) enrollment" (U.S. Department of Education, 2008). They may be baccalaureate, master's, research, or associate's colleges in terms of their mission. Like their HBCU and tribal counterparts, it is the students served by HSIs that distinguish them from other colleges and universities. Demographic shifts over the past thirty years have spawned these institutions (Benitez, 1998). Their numbers in the United States have quadrupled since 1960, since Hispanics now comprise 13 percent of the population, a proportion expected to climb to 22 percent by the year 2015 (U.S. Census Bureau, 2002). Federal initiatives in the 1990s coupled with efforts of Hispanic leaders led to the recognition of postsecondary institutions that served large numbers of Hispanic students. Inclusion of HSI status in both Title III of the 1992 Higher Education Reauthorization Act and Title V of the same act in 1998 made these institutions eligible for extra funding, further cementing their presence in the higher education hierarchy.

Estimates about the number of HSIs vary from 131 to 738, depending on what threshold of Hispanic enrollment must be met to qualify for HSI status. Puerto Rico accounts for the largest number of HSIs (Laden, 2001). The rest are primarily located in states like California, New York, and Arizona, where large numbers of Hispanics reside. While exact numbers are elusive, educated guesses suggest that enrollments at HSIs have increased by 14 percent during the past decade (U.S. Department of Education, 2002). There is little doubt that HSIs are major providers of higher education to Hispanics and will play an increasingly critical role as the Hispanic population in this county proliferates (Gregory, 2003).

Mission statements for HSIs typically parallel those of other institutions in their Carnegie group. HSIs that are associate's colleges talk about the four traditional missions of community colleges, while statements from HSIs that are baccalaureate colleges focus on a liberal education. In this sense, HSIs are unlike their HBCU counterparts. Service to Hispanic students is not usually mentioned in HSI missions. The ways in which Hispanic students are served at these campuses is evident in what they do rather than in the ways they talk about themselves in mission statements.

Proprietary Colleges and Universities

Proprietary schools are perhaps the least understood sector of the higher education system in America. Kinser (2006) identifies some common misperceptions about these institutions. First, they are not recent additions to the postsecondary landscape. For-profit education has existed since the early nineteenth century, and many of these colleges have served students for more than 100 years (Kinser, 2005). Second, proprietary campuses are not typically distance education providers; most are brick-and-mortar operations. Nor are most for-profit colleges and universities publicly traded corporations; the majority of such institutions are privately owned. Finally, while national attention has focused on mega-organizations like the University of Phoenix or Devry University, multicampus institutions, enrolling tens of thousands of students, are not representative of this sector (Davidson, 2008; Kinser, 2006).

Since the 1980s for-profit education has experienced unprecedented expansion. The number of institutions has grown by 29 percent, and enrollment has increased by an astonishing 125 percent (Davidson, 2008; National Center for Educational Statistics, 2006), resulting in a spate of research about this sector of higher education (Breneman, 2005; Kelly, 2001; Kinser, 2005, 2006). The Carnegie classification system identifies 909 for-profit colleges and universities that span the institutional spectrum, from associate's colleges to doctoral-granting universities. These campuses enroll 899,972 students, but most are relatively small; average enrollment is 990 students. Two recent taxonomies offer other ways to conceptualize these colleges and universities. The first identifies three types of proprietary institutions: small single-campus organizations, distance education providers, and large multicampus operations (Kelly, 2001). The other (Kinser, 2006) suggests assorting proprietary campuses by their geographic span, level of degree offerings, and type of ownership.

Regardless of which classification system is used, proprietary institutions are just like not-for-profit campuses in many ways. They offer certificates, associate's, bachelor's, master's, doctoral, and professional degrees to students from all types of backgrounds. The proprietary sector differs in one important way, however: it is revenue driven. Kinser (2007) offers a glimpse at the complexity of this difference in his discussion of publicly owned education corporations. In the final analysis, missions for proprietary schools are influenced by a profit motive that distinguishes them from the not-for-profit segment of postsecondary education.

How Mission Informs Student Affairs Professional Practice

The discussion, thus far, has focused on the variety of institutional types in the American schema of higher education. Institutions within these categories, to a large extent, have similar missions. These missions, in turn, have a direct influence on the work of administrators, the relationships they form with students and others in their campus environments, and the rewards they reap from their jobs. A number of studies (Hirt, 2006; Hirt, Amelink, and Schneiter, 2004; Hirt and Collins, 2005; and Hirt, Strayhorn, Amelink, and Bennett, 2006; Kinser, 2006) have examined the nature of professional life for student affairs administrators at different types of colleges and universities and inform this discussion.

Liberal Arts Colleges

Most liberal arts colleges are small, and this impacts professional life in a number of ways. First, there are limited numbers of staff, so many student affairs administrators have both primary and ancillary job responsibilities (for example, residence hall director and assistant director of student activities). Because staff numbers are small, practitioners at these colleges tend to work very collaboratively—they need to rely on one another if large-scale programs are to succeed. As a result, they operate much like a family and know one another both personally and professionally. Those with spouses, partners, or children find it easy to incorporate their family life into campus life. For those without families, opportunities to meet others outside of work may be limited, particularly at the many liberal arts colleges located in small towns. Finally, the family-like atmosphere fosters institutional loyalty. Professionals find a niche, and it is not at all unusual for people to work twenty or more years at the same campus. So job advancement occurs either very slowly or by moving to a new college.

The signature element of working at these institutions is the close, enduring ties that professionals and students sustain. Student affairs administrators at liberal arts colleges know about their students' academic, social, personal, and emotional lives. They frequently deal with the parents and families, furthering their insights into their students. In describing their work, those at liberal arts colleges often refer to seeing students develop over their undergraduate years, and their work with students nourishes them.

The mission of liberal arts colleges influences the functions that professionals serve. These campuses are, at their core, teaching institutions that are student centered. Hence, the faculty exerts a great deal of influence, and professionals would be well served to understand and appreciate the role the faculty plays on these campuses. Engaging faculty in the design of programs and services is important to professional success. The student-centered nature of the campus translates to a need for professionals who are well versed in communication and counseling skills. These skills enable them to engage deeply with students over time to maximize the educational experience for those students.

Religiously Affiliated Colleges

Professional life at religiously affiliated colleges is similar to that at liberal arts colleges. Staff members often have ancillary responsibilities, their numbers are limited so they work closely together, and they can incorporate their families into the life of the college. There are two distinctive aspects to working at a sectarian college, however. First, there is an additional layer to campus life at religiously affiliated colleges: denominational issues. At sectarian institutions, the politics of the church are strongly present and must be addressed in professional life. Student affairs administrators at these institutions must be politically savvy to succeed. They often find themselves interpreting denominational issues to students and student issues to both denominational and campus leaders.

The second distinction has to do with matters of personal faith. Student affairs administrators at religiously affiliated institutions know the academic, social, emotional, and personal lives of their students, but they also get involved in students' spiritual lives. In doing so, they are able to incorporate their own faith into their work. In fact, they often refer to their work as a calling or a mission, and it is the allure of incorporating their religious beliefs into their professional work that draws them to these campuses in this first place and sustains them once they are there.

Student affairs functions at religiously affiliated campuses can be closely linked to the sectarian mission. For instance, while many liberal arts colleges have a chapel on campus (often an artifact of their sectarian roots), most religiously affiliated campuses have large and active campus ministry offices. Religious services are commonplace, as are programs with a denominational focus. Service is also fundamental, and service-learning centers are often very active on campus.

Master's Colleges and Universities

Professional life at master's colleges and universities is unique in several ways. First, although student affairs administrators at these campuses tend to have a single job assignment, they have many opportunities to work with professionals in other functional areas. Serving on campuswide committees is a hallmark of work at master's colleges and universities. Second, because many campuses are members of a statewide system, professionals at these institutions are adept at cross-institutional work, in particular strategic planning on a systemwide basis. Many policies and procedures at such campuses are enacted systemwide in order to routinize work.

Their exposure to a broad spectrum of functional areas mirrors their exposure to a broad array of students. Master's colleges and universities offer both undergraduate and graduate education and primarily serve students from the region in which they are located. Their undergraduate students are often those who might not otherwise have access to higher education. Graduate students tend to be working adults who seek professional training to advance in their careers. Student affairs professionals at these campuses value the opportunity to work with both populations of students and are deeply committed to providing opportunities to students whose circumstances might otherwise prevent them from seeking higher education.

Mission influences functions for student affairs professionals at master's colleges and universities. These institutions typically serve underrepresented and/or adult students who live within commuting distance of the campus. Consequently, they may have smaller residence hall systems but offer more programs to assist students in their transition to college and emphasize tutoring and career services. Because they offer graduate education, services for graduate students are also evident at these campuses. Finally, many of their students are working adults, so special services, like child care, are often provided, and hours of operation for programs and services frequently extend to evening and weekends.

Research and Doctoral Granting Universities

Unlike baccalaureate and master's campuses, many research and doctoral granting universities are mammoth, often enrolling tens of thousands of students. Student affairs administrators at these institutions usually operate in a single functional area (for example, career services, judicial affairs) and become specialists in that area. They work quite closely with other professionals within their functional area, and usually with colleagues in one or two other departments on campus, but typically do not know most other student affairs staff members on campus. These universities strive for excellence, creating a politically charged and often competitive environment for professionals. Administrators need to understand and appreciate campus politics. One advantage to working in this large, complex environment is advancement opportunity. Those at research and doctoral granting universities can move up to higher levels of responsibility at the same institution, unlike their counterparts at baccalaureate campuses, who may need to relocate to another college to assume higher-level positions.

The nature of relationships between administrators and students is also markedly different. Those at liberal arts and religiously affiliated colleges get to know many of their students personally and talk about seeing their students develop over time. At research and doctoral universities, professionals know most students only in the context of their functional area. For example, fraternity and sorority life professionals deal with students about issues associated with Greek life but not necessarily with personal or emotional issues. Instead of *seeing* students develop, those at doctoral and research campuses *believe* that what they do makes a difference in the lives of students.

The mission of these universities influences the breadth and scope of services for students. At many, for example, auxiliary programs like housing, the student newspaper, or campus radio station operate almost as independent enterprises. Some activities, like career advising, may take place within academic colleges rather than through a central office. Perhaps the most distinctive difference in functional areas relates to graduate students. In addition to services for master's and doctoral students in the arts and sciences, programs for those in law, medicine, nursing, pharmacy, architecture, veterinary science, and business, to name but a few, require student affairs professionals with a unique knowledge base and skills set.

Associate's Colleges

Professional life at associate's colleges offers a different set of challenges and rewards. To start, most community colleges are relatively small. That means that student affairs professionals often work quite closely with their students and get to know them personally. They frequently talk about the changes they see in their students between matriculation and graduation. Since community colleges serve a localized population, professionals frequently have contact with family members, adding another dimension to their relationships with students.

The nature of work for those at associate's colleges is very fast paced. Staffs tend to be small, and they get to know one another quite well. Turnover is usually low, so they may work together for many years. Their work is highly bureaucratized and routinized, so professionals have to be able to produce at a high level of quality as well as a high level of productivity on a daily basis. This entails a fair amount of strategic planning on the part of administrators. To offset that pressure to produce, community college professionals work evenings and weekends very infrequently. Hence, they are able to balance their work and personal lives in fairly predictable ways.

The mission of community colleges also has a direct impact on the types of services they offer. Given their local service districts, for example, very few offer residence halls. Most, however, require students to complete academic skill assessments prior to enrolling, so testing services is often a major component of a student affairs division. On a related note, most community colleges offer the first two years of baccalaureate education and prepare students to transfer to other four-year institutions. Consequently, experts in articulation agreements (policies governing what classes transfer to which four-year institution) are standard at community colleges.

Tribally Controlled Colleges

Information about the nature of work for student affairs professionals at tribally controlled institutions is sparse, perhaps because a different tribe (hence tribal history and traditions) controls each college. Nevertheless, Cajete (2005) characterizes tribal college education as "learning about life through participation and relationship to community, including not only people, but plants, animals, and the whole of nature" (p. 70). Students learn through experience and explore that learning through storytelling, ritual and ceremony, dreaming, apprenticeship, and artistic creation.

The work of student affairs professionals needs to be understood in light of tribal epistemologies. Nearly all tribes believe they exist at the center of seven directions: East, West, North, South, Zenith, Nadir, and the Center (Cajete, 2005, p. 73). Learning and development are guided by seven foundations, including the environmental, the mythic, the visionary, the artistic, the affective, the communal, and the spiritual (Cajete, 2005, pp. 74–76). In the broadest sense, there seem to be parallels between student affairs work at tribally controlled colleges and the holistic approach to education that characterizes work at liberal arts, religiously affiliated, and community colleges. Far more information about professional life at tribal institutions is needed, however, to confirm any such assumption.

The mission of tribal colleges suggests some specific functions and skills not found at liberal arts, master's, or research and doctoral granting institutions. For example, knowledge of tribal history and customs is essential, and programming to tribal interests is common. Likewise, given the role of tribal colleges in economic development, close ties with the tribal community are necessary. Finally, the student population at tribal colleges suggests that certain services, like child care and financial aid, are more important than at some other types of campuses.

Historically Black Colleges and Universities

HBCUs reflect a variety of institutional types, from community colleges to liberal arts colleges, master's, and research universities. Yet there are common threads in professional life at many of these campuses. Many student affairs professionals are themselves graduates of HBCUs. Often they are alumni of the campus for which they work. Administrators view themselves as surrogate family members for students and often talk about themselves as students' mother, father, sibling, or grandparent. This approach to education, referred to as "othermothering," is an artifact of the damage done to Black families during slavery (see Guiffrida, 2005, for a detailed discussion of this phenomenon). HBCU professionals are irrevocably committed to providing educational opportunities for their students and believe that serving as family surrogates helps students achieve their potential.

Notions of family and commitment to racial uplift translate to other professional arenas of work life. To start, staff turnover at most HBCUs is limited.

People tend to stay in the employ of the institution for many years, so staff become like family to one another. Additionally, resources at HBCUs, most of which are independent campuses, are incredibly limited. Yet despite the deprivations imposed by limited resources, professionals at HBCUs are profoundly committed not only to their own campuses, but also to HBCUs in general. They see themselves as guardians of a species of higher education institutions that is threatened with extinction, and they are determined to protect the educational opportunities for Blacks that HBCUs offer.

HBCUs' missions can influence the breadth and scope of student affairs functions. Their dedication to racial uplift often extends to the local community, and community service offices are common on these campuses. Likewise, events celebrating Black history and culture dominate the work of those in student activities. In fact, some organizations, like fraternities and sororities, operate very differently than their counterparts at predominately White institutions, and experts who understand and appreciate those differences are indispensable.

Hispanic-Serving Institutions

Like their HBCU counterparts, HSIs include the full range of institutional types: community colleges, master's, and doctoral granting universities, among others. Yet certain aspects of work life for student affairs professionals transcend those institutional differences. To start, their work with students is grounded in the notion of respect. HSI professionals often talk about the respect they have for their students and the families of students. Administrators are open about the fact that dealing with a student often means dealing with the student's family.

Some of this respect also translates to how HSI professionals view their work. They acknowledge that they serve students who might not otherwise participate in higher education and genuinely marvel at their students. For many, serving students from underrepresented groups is what motivates and sustains them. Their dedication is admirable, particularly since many HSIs face severe resource deficits despite enrollments that continue to mushroom. As the Hispanic population in the United States continues to expand, those at HSIs will play an increasingly important role in higher education.

Because the missions of HSIs cross many institutional types, it is more difficult to discern how mission influences the scope of student affairs work at these campuses. Certain offices and functions, however, stand out at HSI campuses. Programs and services for parents and families are particularly evident, because of the significance of family in many cultures associated with Hispanics. Likewise, an ability to speak Spanish and an understanding of the many and varied Spanish-speaking cultures are much needed skills for professionals at these institutions.

Proprietary Colleges and Universities

The for-profit sector runs the gamut of institutional types, from associate's colleges to doctoral granting universities. Yet the work of student services professionals is narrower and more focused at these campuses. Only a limited number of proprietary colleges offer traditional student services like housing, student activities, or athletics. Nearly, all, however, offer programs and services associated with access (admission, financial aid), retention (academic advising, learning assistance), and vocational planning (career services, internships) (Davidson, 2008). Professional work on these campuses consists of getting students in, getting them through, and finding them work.

In large part, students drive the nature of work at for-profit institutions. These campuses serve disproportionately high numbers of racial and ethnic minorities, part-time students, and adult learners. Many of their students are employed and have families, hence are juggling multiple roles in their lives (Kinser, 2006). Proprietary colleges and universities appeal to these students because they operate on a corporate model. Instruction is offered during evening and weekend hours, typically on a year-round basis, for the convenience of learners. Student services are available when courses are offered so students can get seek assistance when they are on site for classes. These institutions strive to deliver education in an effective and efficient manner.

This focus is consistent with the mission of proprietary institutions. They are profit-driven organizations that identify an educational market niche and develop their business model to serve that niche. Institutional goals typically reflect student demands, and student affairs professionals align their work to achieve institutional goals. This often requires administrators to partner with faculty so that curricular and co-curricular demands are addressed concurrently. In fact, Kinser (2006) argues that managers at not-for-profit colleges and universities might learn something about academic-student affairs partnerships from their for-profit colleagues. Student affairs professionals who seek to work closely with faculty, and who respect and appreciate issues like cost containment and efficiency, might appreciate professional life at these institutions.

Student Affairs Professional Mobility: Individual and Institutional Perspectives

It seems clear that institutional mission shapes professional practice in student affairs. Less clear, however, is whether mission also shapes professional mobility. Any student affairs administrator who has conducted a job search in recent years has probably fallen victim to the myopia that institutional mission can create. Most job announcements include language that refers to mission. Baccalaureate colleges seek individuals who understand and appreciate the value of a liberal education. Associate's colleges often require candidates to have prior experience in a community college setting. Once professionals are inculcated into the environment of a particular type of institution, they may assume that only others who have experience at a like campus will be able to successfully transition to that institution. This is an increasing concern among student affairs professionals. Indeed, some young professionals are convinced that the first position they assume will dictate the institutional sector in which they will spend their entire careers.

Yet the preceding discussion about professional life at different types of campuses suggests that there are certain elements of professional life that might translate across institutional types. For instance, student affairs administrators at both liberal arts colleges and community colleges develop relationships with students that are sufficiently close that they can see development in those they serve. Professionals at both these types of campuses, along with their counterparts at sectarian colleges and HSIs, deal extensively with families of students. Political savvy is a particularly important skill at both religiously affiliated colleges and doctoral granting universities. Work for professionals at master's campuses is often highly bureaucratized, requiring strategic planning skills, which is also descriptive of work at community colleges. It would seem counterproductive to limit applicant pools to those who have worked in certain settings without examining the skills they might have garnered in those settings. Both employers and candidates need to ensure that individual talents, as opposed to experience at select institutional types, drive professional mobility.

Employers can start by determining whether experience at a particular type of institution is really a necessary prerequisite for a job at their campus. Instead of focusing on where a candidate has worked, they might identify the skill sets and talents they seek in applicants. Writing job announcements and descriptions accordingly would be a first step in broadening the applicant pool. They might also shape interview processes around those skill sets. Professional development programs can offer candidates with requisite skills insights into the peculiarities of the institutional type.

Student affairs professionals also need to be proactive. If a job announcement calls for experience at a certain type of campus, some applicants may self-select out of the process without further consideration. Instead, professionals would be well served to appreciate particular talents that would transfer readily from one institutional setting to another. They then need to highlight those talents during the job search process. Addressing the commonalities in the nature of work between the two institutional types is likely to go a long way in convincing employers that a candidate has an understanding of the new work environment.

Conclusion

The diversity of institutional types in the American higher education enterprise is one of its greatest strengths. The variety of missions these institutions serve is impressive, even daunting. There is little doubt that institutional mission shapes professional practice for student affairs professionals. Yet recognizing and appreciating differences in mission provides an avenue of professional mobility within the student affairs profession.

References

Allen, W. R., and Jewell, J. O. "A Backward Glance Forward: Past, Present, and Future Perspectives on Historically Black Colleges and Universities." *Review of Higher Education,* 2002, 25(3), 241–261.

Anderson, M. S. "The Complex Relations Between the Academy and Industry: Views from the Literature." *The Journal of Higher Education,* 2001, 72, 226–246.

Barr, M. J. "The Importance of the Institutional Mission." In M. J. Barr, M. K. Desler, and Associates (Eds.), *The Handbook of Student Affairs Administration* (2nd ed.). San Francisco: Jossey-Bass, 2000.

Belgarde, W. L. "History of American Indian Community Colleges." In C. Turner, M. Garcia, A. Nora, and L. I. Rendon (Eds.), *Racial and Ethnic Diversity in Higher Education.* ASHE Reader Series. Boston: Pearson, 1996.

Benitez, M. "Hispanic Serving Institutions: Challenges and Opportunities." In J. P. Merisotis and C. T. O'Brien (Eds.), *Minority-Serving Institutions: Distinct Purposes, Common Goals.* San Francisco: Jossey-Bass, 1998.

Breneman, D. W. "Are We Losing Our Liberal Arts Colleges?" *College Board Review,* 1990, 156, 16–21, 29.

Breneman, D. W. *Liberal Arts Colleges: Thriving, Surviving, or Endangered?* Washington, D.C.: Brookings Institution, 1994.

Breneman, D. "Entrepreneurship in Higher Education." In B. Pusser (Ed.), *Arenas of Entrepreneurship: Where Nonprofit and For-Profit Institutions Compete.* New Directions for Higher Education, no. 129. San Francisco: Jossey-Bass, 2005.

Brown, M. C., and Davis, J. E. "The Historically Black College as Social Contract, Social Capital, and Social Equalizer." *Peabody Journal of Education,* 2001, 76(1), 31–49.

Brown, M. C., Donahoo, S., and Bertrand, R. D. "The Black College and the Quest for Educational Opportunity." *Urban Education,* 2001, 36(5), 553–571.

Brubacher, J. S., and Rudy, W. *Higher Education in Transition: A History of Colleges and Universities* (4th ed). New Brunswick, N.J.: Transaction, 1997.

Cajete, G. A. "American Indian Epistemologies." In M. J. Tippeconnic Fox, S. C. Lowe, and G. S. McClellan (Eds.), *Serving Native American Students*. New Directions for Student Services, no. 109. San Francisco: Jossey-Bass, 2005.

Carnegie Foundation for the Advancement of Teaching. *A Classification of Institutions of Higher Education*. Princeton, N.J.: Carnegie Council for the Advancement of Teaching, 2000.

Carnegie Classification of Institutions of Higher Education. [http://www.carnegiefoundation.org/about/sub.asp?key=18&subkey=405]. 2005.

Carney, C. M. *Native American Higher Education in the United States*. New Brunswick, N.J.: Transaction, 1999.

Coaxum, J. "The Misalignment Between the Carnegie Classifications and Black Colleges." *Urban Education*, 2001, 36(5), 572–584.

Cohen, A. M. *The Shaping of American Higher Education*. San Francisco: Jossey-Bass, 1998.

Cohen, A. M., and Brawer, F. B. *The American Community College* (4th ed.). San Francisco: Jossey-Bass, 2003.

Davidson, D. L. "Including all Institutional Types: Student Services at For-Profit Institutions." Paper presented at the annual conference of the American College Personnel Association, Atlanta, April 2008.

Etzkowitz, H., Webster, A., and Healey, P. (Eds.). *Capitalizing Knowledge: New Intersections of Industry and Academia*. Albany: State University of New York Press, 1998.

Fincher, C. "The Influence of British and German Universities on the Historical Development of American Universities." Paper presented at the Annual Forum of the European Association for Institutional Research, Trier, Germany, August 1989. ERIC Document Reproduction Service No. ED443301.

Gregory, S. T. "Planning for the Increasing Number of Latino Students." *Planning for Higher Education*, 2003, 31(4), 13–19.

Guiffrida, D. "Othermothering as a Framework for Understanding African American Students' Definitions of Student-Centered Faculty." *The Journal of Higher Education*, 2005, 76(6), 701–723.

Hirt, J. B. *Where You Work Matters: Student Affairs Administration at Different Types of Institutions*. Washington, D.C.: American College Personnel Association, 2006.

Hirt, J. B., Amelink, C., and Schneiter, S. "The Nature of Professional Life at Liberal Arts Colleges." *NASPA Journal*, 2004, 42, 94–110.

Hirt, J. B., and Collins, D. "Work, Relationships, and Rewards in Student Affairs: Differences by Institutional Type." *College Student Affairs Journal*, 2005, 24(1), 4–19.

Hirt, J. B., Strayhorn, T. L., Amelink, C. T., and Bennett, B. R. "The Nature of Student Affairs Work at Historically Black Colleges and Universities." *Journal of College Student Development*, 2006, 47, 661–676.

Humphries, F. S. "A Short History of Blacks in Higher Education." *The Journal of Blacks in Higher Education*. 1995, 6, 57.

Kelly, K. F. *Meeting the Needs and Making Profits: The Rise of the For-Profit Degree Granting Institutions*. Denver: Education Commission of the States, 2001.

Kinser, K. "A Profile of Regionally Accredited For-Profit Institutions of Higher Education." In B. Pusser (Ed.), *Arenas of Entrepreneurship: Where Nonprofit and For-Profit Institutions Compete*. New Directions for Higher Education, no. 129. San Francisco: Jossey-Bass, 2005.

Kinser, K. "Principles of Student Affairs in For-Profit Higher Education." *NASPA Journal*, 2006, 43, 264–279.

Kinser, K. "Dimensions of Corporate Ownership in For-Profit Education." *Review of Higher Education*, 2007, 30, 217–245.

Laden, B. V. "Hispanic-Serving Institutions: Myths and Realities." *Peabody Journal of Education,* 2001, 76, 73–92.

Lucas, C. J. *American Higher Education.* New York: St. Martin's Griffin, 1994.

Martin, W. B. *A College of Character.* San Francisco: Jossey-Bass, 1982.

McClellan, G. S., Tippeconnic Fox, M. J., and Lowe, S. C. "Where We Have Been: A History of Native American Higher Education." In M. J. Tippeconnic Fox, S. C. Lowe, and G. S. McClellan (Eds.), *Serving Native American Students.* New Directions for Student Services, no. 109. San Francisco: Jossey-Bass, 2005.

National Center for Education Statistics. *Digest of Education Statistics: 2005.* [http://nces. ed.gov/programs/digest/d05/tables/dt05_170.asp]. 2006.

O'Grady, J. P. "Control of Church-Related Institutions of Higher Learning." *Journal of Higher Education,* 1969, 40, 108–121.

Rudolph, F. *The American College and University: A History.* New York: Knopf, 1962.

Slaughter, S., and Leslie, L. L. *Academic Capitalism: Politics, Policies and the Entrepreneurial University.* Baltimore: Johns Hopkins University Press, 1997.

Urban, W., and Wagoner, J. *American Education: A History* (2nd ed.). Boston: McGraw-Hill, 2000.

U.S. Census Bureau. *Resident Population Estimates of the United States by Sex, Race and Hispanic Origin: April 1 to July 1, 1999, with Short-Term Projection to June 1, 2001.* Washington, D.C.: U.S. Census Bureau, 2002.

U.S. Department of Education. "Definition of Hispanic-Serving Institutions." [http://www. ed.gov/programs/idueshsi/definition.html]. 2008.

U.S. Department of Education, National Center for Education Statistics. *Hispanic Serving Institutions: Statistical Trends from 1990 to 1999* (NCES 2002–051, by Christina Stearns and Satoshi Watanbe. Project Officer: Thomas D. Snyder). Washington, D.C.: U.S. Department of Education, 2002.

CHAPTER THREE

INSTITUTIONAL GOVERNANCE AND THE INTERESTS OF STUDENTS

John S. Levin

Governance in colleges and universities is customarily viewed as the domain of executive officers, boards of trustees, and faculty senates. In the literature student affairs divisions are not characteristically connected to governance; yet these divisions are part of colleges and universities; student affairs divisions are both participants in the organization and management of these institutions and subject to governance processes and outcomes. This chapter provides scholarly perspectives on governance, one of which is not at all a traditional one, and also centers governance on the interests of students.

This chapter begins with two narratives that offer examples of governance in action. These narratives, both dramatic but salutary examples, suggest that governance can reflect the patterned behaviors and cultural values found within higher education institutions. As well, they show that in the highest levels of institutional decision making, students and student interests are not necessarily the central concerns—a matter of some concern to student affairs practitioners.

The author of this chapter was an observer of the two events described in this section. Some of the behaviors are slightly modified so as to avoid exact reproduction and therefore ethical infringement, as release forms from the parties were not obtained. Nonetheless, both events were public, with the press in attendance.

Narratives of Governance

Narrative One: The Senate

The chairperson of the university senate at a large research university calls the meeting to order. Eighty faculty members representing university units, a dozen or so administrative personnel (deans, directors, provost, university president), and four students diminish their social exchanges, take their seats, and look at a long agenda that will wend its way from 4 P.M. to 6 P.M. on a Monday, when the business of the senate concludes. After an hour of reporting, which includes the university president's state of the university address—where all is upbeat except for the reference to "conservative forces" in the state legislature whose disrespect for education is displayed by paltry allocations to the university, "this year just 20 percent of our total budget," and the provost's descriptions about "centers of excellence" and reallocation of resources—the business of the senate is underway. The audience's attention is focused on three eagerly awaited agenda items: the disciplining of a faculty member for unethical behavior, the university's impending contract with an athletic apparel company for outfitting athletic teams, and the merit review of faculty. The real business is at hand.

On the first item, the chair of the senate subcommittee reports on the findings of the subcommittee and its recommendations. While the findings suggest gross negligence on the part of a biochemist on her management of her laboratory and treatment of student research assistants, they are inconclusive about her fabrication of evidence to bolster the results of her nationally funded investigation on chemical interventions for blood cancers. The committee's recommendations are, on the one hand, for the establishment of a national panel of experts to determine the extent of evidence fabrication and its consequences, and, on the other hand, to turn the laboratory mismanagement actions over to a university committee on faculty misconduct and discipline. Numerous faculty senators rise to give both pro and con views on the faculty member in question, on the subcommittee's handling of the case, and on the recommendations. The university president rises to inform the senate that he, recently, personally met with the biochemist and finds her explanations to be both "unconvincing and insincere." He has thus taken his administrative prerogative and suspended her without pay pending an investigation by the university legal counsel. At this announcement a handful of faculty begin to protest. To which the president responds, "I am accountable to the board of regents and as chief executive officer of this university I must protect not only the university but also the students who are potentially in harm's way." The exchanges continue for forty minutes, with the secretary of the faculty informing the faculty chair that the time period for the senate meeting has almost concluded, leaving one senate member calling for tabling the subcommittee's report until next month and another member making a motion to call for an extraordinary meeting the next week for the senate to censure the university president for his unilateral action of suspension. The parliamentarian of the senate adds a few remarks about the rules of senate proceedings. A faculty senator who is in the law school rises on a point of privilege to ask the university president why he did not seek out senate advice before acting to suspend the faculty member. The university president responded that his action was a legal matter and that the senate is not a legal agent of the university. "I needed to act immediately for the sake of the reputation of the university and for the safety of the students. I did chat briefly with a few faculty in the biochemistry department who viewed the situation as serious, with the treatment of graduate students as egregious behavior. There was no time to consult with the senate even if I had wanted to do that." At that point, the secretary of the faculty notes that it is 6 P.M. and the appointed time for adjournment. One senator makes a motion to adjourn; another makes a motion to postpone the other two main agenda items to the next meeting; and the parliamentarian notes that there were already two motions on the floor. Each motion is brought forward consecutively: first, the motion for an extraordinary meeting, which is defeated without discussion; second, the motion to censure the president, which is withdrawn; third, the motion to postpone the other agenda items, which is passed without discussion; and finally, the motion to adjourn, which is seconded, and the meeting ends.

As the faculty senate members file out of the meeting room, several groups form, some of which argue about the president's actions; and others simply discuss personal issues. They are off to their homes for dinner, back to their offices, or off to classes to teach a night course. The administrative senate members walk together back to their offices, engaging in little except for some social conversation. The student senators disperse individually, finding their way home.

The Scholarly View. Robert Birnbaum once described both the senate and its activities as symbolic (Birnbaum, 1989), suggesting that it has importance to university life but largely as a cultural artifact. His description indicates that the senate does little of substance in the actions of the institution. Yet, the senate has value because it gives meaning to institutional members and to the actions of those members. For some, the senate is emblematic of faculty authority within a university or college. The faculty as a whole can be seen as significant players in the life of the university; the administration sits down in a formal venue with the faculty to discuss important matters; students have a prominent role in the senate and thus have equality with faculty members who sit on the senate; and the president and provost are answerable to the senate, even if they act first and then explain later.

The senate as a structure that represents college and university decision making and serves as a vehicle for decisions sits within a complex context. Faced with forces and pressures to act, both internally and externally, higher education institutions can hardly depend upon the senate for more than a narrow range of decisions, mostly pertinent to academic matters. Senates have a difficult task with such specific matters as university contracts with apparel companies or with more general behaviors of academic capitalism and entrepreneurialism (Clark, 1998; Marginson and Considine, 2000; Slaughter and Leslie, 1997). Decisions about those matters reside with senior administrators and governing boards.

Narrative Two: The Board of Trustees

The monthly meeting of the board of trustees at this community college is open to the public and involves the participation of numerous officials and groups. First, the college chancellor of this two-college district is an ex officio member of the board, and both college presidents as well as the district executive administrators are expected to attend the board meeting. Second, the student association presidents of both colleges and the faculty senate presidents of both colleges attend. Moreover, the presidents of the faculty union and the staff union for the community college district attend. All of these representatives are invited and are expected to give reports or address the board at this meeting. The meeting is thus a forum for formal and public accountability.

The formal monthly board meeting provides the board with an opportunity to hear from various constituencies and to vote on actions that the colleges will take on matters ranging from tuition and fee setting to faculty and staff salaries. While a number of issues have already been reviewed and deliberated upon by board members prior to the formal meeting, it is here that board members must make their views and decisions public.

This board, not necessarily identical to those in other states, is made up of five publicly elected members and two nonvoting student elected by the student body. Together they are a "corporate body," legally responsible for the operations of a two college district, which has an annual budget of approximately $200 million. They are guided by the district chancellor, but it is their legislated mandate to make institutional decisions, including the appointment of the chancellor.

There are about forty visitors at the board meeting, mostly faculty and administrators of the two colleges. They are here today in the main because the board will be considering a non-confidence vote taken and passed on the district chancellor by the two colleges' faculty, a vote administered by the faculty union. While there is a hefty agenda of business items today, including the expansion of a student center and the renovation of one college's swimming pool, the large turnout is a consequence of the non-confidence vote and the board's reaction to that vote.

After two hours of reports and board members' questioning of those reporting, the business of the board meeting turns to the anticipated issue, which is introduced by the president of the faculty union. With the look and sound of an early twentieth-century orator, the union president—a man in his late fifties or early sixties, a man who has been at his college for more than twenty years as a full-time instructor, and a man who is well known statewide as a union activist—begins speaking slowly and deliberately. "For almost ten years, the administration and the faculty of our two colleges have worked together harmoniously, with respect for each others' expertise and responsibilities, and in concert, to maintain our nationally prominent reputation. However, this collegiality has abruptly ended." He stops, then raises his voice as he points to the community college district chancellor. "You, sir, have eroded the cooperative working partnership between faculty and administration; you have betrayed our trust in the administrators of our colleges. You have treated us badly and have made our colleges suffer. You have made decisions without consultation; you have ignored standing committees and even the spirit of our collective bargaining agreement." He continues along these lines, informing both the board of trustees as well as the audience that the chancellor reneged on various promises and committed several other unpalatable actions. He stops, takes a deep breath, and begins again, this time in a loud voice. "But these actions do not approach the egregious behavior of invading our privacy, of spying on faculty by you and your minions. You, sir, have treated all of us as if we were criminals, not professionals." He then explains that the chancellor authorized administrators to review all electronic mail messages sent by faculty and required these administrators to conduct periodic surveillance of two specific faculty members. The justification for this action was that the two faculty members allegedly were using electronic mail to communicate their dissatisfaction with one college's administration to faculty at other state colleges. The chancellor viewed this action as potentially damaging to the institution and as insubordination under labor law. The union president then concludes his speech by calling for the board to fire the chancellor.

The chair of the board first thanks the union president for coming forward with his concerns and the information on the vote by the faculty union. The board chair then reminds the union president that the board does not conduct personnel matters in public, but that she would ensure that the board in a closed session would discuss the matter. At that point, she turns to the chancellor and asks if he has any remarks he wants to make. The chancellor nods and begins to talk about the good of the colleges, his vision for the institution, and that the union president has falsely characterized his actions. "Of course," he notes, "we are in the middle of bargaining a new collective agreement and our union wants to get as much press on their plight as possible so that they can achieve a stronger bargaining position. They are not making much headway at the bargaining table so they have created a scenario where they can discredit me. They are used to getting their own way and they do not like someone who stands up to them and says 'no.'" Looking very pleased with himself, the chancellor glares at the union president, then at the vice chancellor of human resources, who nods and smiles at the chancellor.

The two student board members want to speak, but the board chair says that their remarks must be left for a closed session. One student ignores this command and begins to give her view. "As students on the board, we are not permitted to vote on any matters and in fact we are excluded from most personnel discussion. So I suspect we will not be included in the closed session. I just want to say in public that the morale of the college I attend is very low and faculty are upset. I have heard that the administration is reading faculty e-mail, and I think that is illegal. If the board does not stop this practice, I will no longer serve on the board as I cannot support the reading of faculty e-mail." The board chair thanks the student.

Some members of the audience begin to ask questions of the board; others make statements. The board chair reiterates that this is a personnel matter and that the board cannot discuss this publicly. A group of faculty in the audience begins to grumble. Several begin to raise their voices loudly. A heated verbal exchange erupts between the chancellor and three faculty members in the audience. The board chair then claims that the board meeting is adjourned. Several media reporters, one from the local newspaper and another from the local television station, shout out questions to the board chair. The board members depart, and all the administrators depart, leaving the faculty members and the three local community members who attended the meeting talking with each other and with the media reporters. The union president thanks the faculty present for their support and promises that this matter will not go away.

The Scholarly View. Scholars of governance in higher education usually offer one of two judgments on the behaviors of those involved in the process. One reflects a rather rational, well-ordered system in which there are rules, guidelines, and behavioral precedents established so that civilized exchanges occur among equals (Baldridge, Curtis, Ecker, and Riley, 1977; Hines, 2000). The other reflects a political process where power stands at the center and conflict and contest are normal behaviors (Pusser, 2003). From this later perspective, concepts of governance are aligned with power, what Mintzberg (1983) and others refer to as the ability to realize intentions by influencing or convincing others to act. In organizations, various players form alliances in order to attain desired results. In the previous example, the union is one alliance formed to "negotiate" and lobby collectively for the interests of faculty in the face of the governing board, the legal authority for the higher education institution, and its agents the administrators, headed by the chancellor. While the union holds no legal or formal authority on board matters such as the setting of tuition fees, the establishment of programs, or the hiring and the firing of personnel, including the chancellor, they do have potential influence because of their collective accumulation of expertise and criticality. The union membership—the faculty—are the core operators of the institution, and without them the institution cannot fulfill its public expectations and legal mandate. Thus, as a collective or alliance, faculty can and do influence the management and governance of the institution, including the actions of the board.

Multiple Ways of Viewing Governance

To state that governance of higher education institutions—either the understanding of the concept of governance or the practice of governing—is straightforward and without considerable complexity is to ignore the multiple strands of discourse and the experiences of practitioners during the past several decades. Institutional governance is on the one hand what shapes institutional behaviors and on the other hand what defines the character of the institution. Governance of higher education institutions both structures the actions of the institution and its members and gives meaning to organizational action. That is, governance is both a verbal construct and a noun: it connotes action as well as a condition. Practitioners who work in unionized environments can readily acknowledge the ways that union-management contracts guide and regulate not only individual behaviors but also interaction between parties. Practitioners who work in overly hierarchical systems or under autocratic leadership recognize that their individuality and personal freedom are limited and their organizational identities diminutive. Governance includes both how institutional behaviors and actions are carried out—the methods—and what actions are taken—the goals realized.

The Traditional Perspective

The scholarly discourse on governance during the past four decades has included multiple frameworks for explaining, analyzing, and indeed prescribing governance. One of the more common frameworks has been that which addresses the roles and goals of the players in governance (Hines, 2000; Miller, 2000). This framework describes governance as a formal structure held together by actors, such as trustees, presidents, administrators, and faculty, who fulfill or are expected to fulfill specific roles with attached goals. This is the more traditional view that asserts that governance is a system of decision making comprised of processes and structures. It assumes that the institution is a rational system, functioning as a modern organization to realize specific predetermined outcomes. It assumes as well an ordered and hierarchical system, with an institutional structure organized around functions, such as executive action, management and administration, core operations (for example, teaching), administrative support, and services (for example, advising). This traditional view in the main excludes both external actors and students, although advanced modifications to this traditional view suggest a role for students (Hines, 2000).

One of the more prominent of these traditional perspectives was articulated by Baldridge, Curtis, Ecker, and Riley in 1977 (Pusser, 2003): an understanding of higher education institutions as homogeneous, decidedly influenced by higher education discourse involving research universities and ignoring the diversity of institutional types. They suggested models of governance—bureaucracy, collegium, political arena, and organized anarchy; and these models have shaped understandings of higher education governance and management for three decades. Baldridge and others' parsimonious categorization fit the developing scholarship on both organizations generally and higher education specifically. The metaphors of organization were aligned with the times: machine, culture, political system, and loosely coupled—some might say chaotic—system. These metaphors were easily connected to practice, from hierarchical and rigid management of the organization (machine), to ideological grounding for action (culture), to collective bargaining (political system), and to ambiguity in all facets of the organization, including mission, technology, and authority (loosely coupled system).

These models and the underlying assumptions about higher education governance reflect a second characteristic of traditional perspectives of governance: the tendency to conceive of governance as situated within an institution that either is or aspires to be autonomous—separate from externalities such as governments, corporations, the public, the media, and the like. Indeed, Corson (1960) views institutional autonomy as the cornerstone of higher education institutions' unique character. Higher education institutions, asserts this perspective, have sovereignty over student admissions, teaching assignments, compensation, promotion and tenure of faculty, course content, curricula, educational standards, the awarding of degrees, the relative emphasis upon teaching, research, and service, and finally the allocation of resources (Carnegie Commission on Higher Education, 1973; Corson, 1960).

Challenges to the Traditional Perspective

By the end of the 1990s, there was considerable acknowledgment that forces and parties external to higher education institutions played a prominent role in governance, thus challenging the central place of institutional autonomy in understanding colleges and universities (Hines, 2000; Slaughter and Leslie, 1997). Indeed, Collis (2004) argues that the core of the university began to decline in influence as external players such as private sector businesses grew in their connectivity through partnerships, corporate training, and sponsored research, and as outsourcing became a way of institutional economic survival. That is, full-time faculty and the traditional symbols of the university—liberal arts and scientific education as well as developmental aspects of student services—lost their primacy in influence. Instead, the economic marketplace and the externally legitimating activities of the university, such as funded research and revenue generation through ancillary services such as housing and sales, became ascendant (Slaughter and Rhoades, 2004).

This shift in view from institutional autonomy to the college and university as instrument is furthered by both Marginson (2004) and Levin (J. Levin, 2001). While Marginson adds the global dimension to the governance of universities—that universities are globally engaged—Levin addresses community colleges, which are hardly the institutions that scholars of higher education have addressed in their examination of governance. The neglect of the external, indeed global, environment in the traditional views of governance is to ignore the webs and networks of influence that impinge upon college and university behaviors. To neglect community colleges and other non-elite institutions is to ignore the variety of college and university contexts.

Institutional Type as a Perspective

The omission of institutional types in the examination of governance is serious because of the wide range of higher education institutions and the preponderance of those institutions that are not research universities. Of the 4,387 public and private universities and colleges in the United States in 2005, research universities total 199, arts and sciences colleges 274, and public community colleges—the most numerous institutional type—total 1,057 (Carnegie Foundation, 2007). Institutional type may constitute one of the most influential variables in how colleges and universities operate, in their purposes, their student body, and their outcomes (Clark, 1987). Governance, too, is affected by institutional type.

The Community College as a Case. The community college provides an illustrative case. Indeed, institutional characteristics of community colleges compared to the prototypical institution of scholarship and prescriptive guides for practitioners are telling. The community college as an institutional type is distinctly different from other types, such as the public research extensive university. This suggests not only that organizational behaviors are distinctive but also that governance is contingent upon institutional context.

As Table 3.1 indicates, community colleges are significantly different from public research extensive universities—those most commonly discussed in traditional views of governance—even on the most overt characteristics. Students are predominantly nontraditional: more likely to be over twenty-four years of age, more likely to be in the lower economic strata of postsecondary students, more

TABLE 3.1 CHARACTERISTICS OF PUBLIC RESEARCH EXTENSIVE UNIVERSITIES AND COMMUNITY COLLEGES

Characteristics	Prototypical Public Research Extensive University	Prototypical Public Community College
Students	Traditional: Full-time, 18–21 years of age, middle and upper income, European descent, undergraduate and graduate	Nontraditional: Part time, 27 years of age, lower income, close to 50% non-European origin, pre-college, college entry, and two-year college
Admissions	Selective/competitive	Open access, except for specialized programs
Faculty	Doctoral degree, research focus, mobile, tenure track	Master's degree, teaching focus, local, part time
Curriculum	Undergraduate and graduate disciplinary and professional programs	Pre-college and first two levels of college academic and occupational programs
Legal authority for decision making	Bicameral: Governing board and administration for financial and administrative matters; faculty-dominated senate for educational matters	Unicameral: Governing board and president (delegated) for all matters, superseded by state officials on specific issues such as facilities, tuition setting

likely to possess academic disadvantages such as lack of high school credential or in need of remedial coursework in college, and more likely to be first in their family to attend college. As well, there is close to a 50 percent chance that a community college student is classified as an underrepresented minority (J. S. Levin, 2007b). The community college is customarily characterized as an open access institution, which means that adults do not need to possess particular academic qualifications to attend the institution. The open access mission of the community college has led to various outcomes for students, from social mobility to social reproduction (Brint, 2003; Brint and Karabel, 1989; Cohen and Brawer, 2003; J. Levin, 2001).

Faculty are hired to teach, and they develop a particular culture around this activity, referred to by McGrath and Spear (1991) as a "practitioner's culture"— one that reflects shared experience, not analytical or disciplinary discourse, as a base and is distinct from university faculty who engage in critical analysis and debate. Faculty have been roundly criticized for both their practices and their culture (Grubb, 1999; Richardson, Fisk, and Okun, 1983; Seidman, 1985), but a major component of their condition as workers—part time, overly managed, peripheral to major institutional decisions—is overlooked by these critics (J. Levin, Kater, and Wagoner, 2006). Indeed, the condition of community college faculty, with 67 percent of them classified as part time, has considerable implications for governance and both differentiates the community college from other higher education institutions and suggests that there are dramatic differences in the governance of institution by type.

Indeed, in research universities, governance from the traditional perspective of numerous scholars from Corson to Baldridge and others to Mortimer and McConnell to Schuster and others and to Tierney is centered on the role and primacy of faculty rights, including academic freedom, tenure, and professional autonomy (Mortimer and McConnell, 1978; Schuster, Smith, Corak, and Yamada, 1994; Tierney, 2004). These attributes are largely absent in community colleges, and governance involving faculty is primarily advisory, with boards, presidents, and state governments the legal authority (Kater and Levin, 2005).

Clearly, institutional type has salience not only in organizational functioning but also in governance, where public institutions are more closely tied to state policy of economic and social development and private institutions are wedded to alumni, philanthropic, and private sector interests, including religious denominations for religiously affiliated institutions. A similar observation on the salience of institutional type is presented by Joan Hirt in her examination of student affairs practitioners, indicating that the practice of student affairs is contingent upon institutional type (Hirt, 2006).

Governance as Institutional Identity

Customarily, governance in colleges and universities is viewed in line with what James March and Johan Olsen refer to as the "exchange perspective" (March and Olsen, 1995). According to the exchange perspective, collective behaviors and actions are based upon exchanges among individuals, and individuals are motivated largely by self-interest. Individuals do band together for common interests, forming coalitions, and forms of bargaining and negotiation ensue. In the context of higher education institutions, this perspective rationalizes union-management relationships; faculty and administration-board relationships; relationships within colleges among faculty, among administrators, and among staff. Thus, governance is viewed as a political activity that endeavors to mediate interests based upon exchanges of resources (for example, work for pay). This perspective views institutional actions as a consequence of structures and the dynamics of these structures. For example, the determination of institutional policy is the end result of the negotiation between and among parties. Such an approach is largely a political one, where those in positions of strength or formal authority reign. Underlying this condition of institutional power is its source, and, as some of the literature suggests, that source is largely external to the institution, found in legislatures, corporate boardrooms, and in resource rich sectors. The implications for students are profound.

In contrast, college and university governance from an "institutional perspective" acknowledges collective actions that are based upon understandings among institutional participants or affiliated parties of an existing or developing common identity, a common situation, or common behaviors. From this perspective, individuals work together or interact in order to develop identities, establish rules, regulations, and duties. In this perspective, the ongoing molding of institutional life (some would say "culture") is intended to meet the ends of all. Thus, consent is achieved if the institution is viewed as the product of all participating parties. The development of community is a continuing goal, and trust between and among groups is both an ideal sentiment and a necessity for productive relationships. The implications for students in this perspective, too, are considerable and different from those found in the exchange perspective. The exchange perspective has long dominated governance in higher education, and an individual's sense of belonging is more to a special interest than to a community.

Lack of Engagement in Governance

The lack of engagement of college members and units in the governing of the institution is in part a consequence of several factors: new models and approaches of management; changing priorities of higher education; and pressures from external forces and stakeholders, which include government and business (Aronowitz and Di Fazio, 1994; Bok, 2003; Labaree, 1997; Marginson and Considine, 2000; Readings, 1997; Slaughter and Leslie, 1997; Tierney, 2004). This lack of engagement both signals and reinforces the undoing of community on campuses, relinquishing not only responsibility for but also influence over student learning and student development. Furthermore, this behavior fashions institutional identity as colleges and universities become more marketplaces and virtual worlds than socially democratic and personally enriching spaces. The exchange is that for money, and traditional four-year college students gain a time-out on the road to their adult development with 50 percent attaining a credential. These conditions are likely what Readings (1997) meant with the term "the university in ruins"—that the institution as a community of trust is in disarray. The building of communities does not happen when the institution's participants are disengaged and detached from decision making at all levels.

On their participation in institutional decision making, students are relatively muted, particularly on larger educational issues. Students' views are most evident during periods of social concern. Student activism both in the present and historically might constitute students' major vehicle for their participation in governance (Olausen, 2007). Through activism, students effect change not only on campuses but also nationally. However, such efforts are limited to a handful of colleges and universities, with examples ranging from unionization of graduate teaching assistants and pay raises for custodial staff to university partnerships with an athletic apparel company and its practices of using "sweatshop" labor. These examples certainly constitute student participation, even illegitimate participation, in institutional governance. In lesser nationally prominent institutions, student activism can affect local issues, such as immigration policy. Outside of activism, generally, students' roles in institutional governance are relatively limited.

The Governance Connection for Student Affairs

The link of student affairs to institutional governance should not be a mystery. Yet, the connection is not always apparent. The saliency of student and student affairs involvement in institutional governance is a viewpoint customarily absent in both the discussions of student affairs and in the graduate programs that prepare practitioners (Laker, 2007). This oversight needs to be corrected. The discussion that follows identifies norms that are asserted about the practice of student affairs and then places these norms and their assumptions within a context of new economy values that prize the private good; valorize individual achievement; and diminish the worth of the public good. The operative term for this context is neoliberal, and universities and colleges increasingly reflect this context (J. S. Levin, 2007a; Slaughter and Rhoades, 2000). This neoliberal context is likely at-odds with the traditional principles of student affairs practice.

Seven of these principles identified by Whitt and Blimling (2000) include engaging students in active learning, helping students build coherent values and ethical standards, setting and communicating high expectations for student learning, using systematic inquiry to improve student and institutional performance, using resources effectively to help achieve institutional mission and goals, forging educational partnerships that advance student learning, building supportive and inclusive communities. The bulk of these suggest that student learning is an end, and institutional actions—governance and management, for example—are a means. They include, certainly, more than student affairs professionals: they suggest the involvement of faculty as the educators of students, the administration as institutional managers, and staff as technical supporters; they also suggest that the flow of institutional operations and decisions move in the direction to favor student development and outcomes. The principles, in short, are not only institutionally based—for example, "the institution shall help the students"—but also institutionally contingent—for example, "these principles depend upon the institution." These principles do not exist within a vacuum, but instead are enmeshed with institutional governance. The connection between major actions and behaviors in higher education institutions and those principles mentioned for student affairs administration is that these principles in practice are mediated by institutional governance behaviors and patterns.

Within the new economy or neoliberal context, these connections can appear to be tenuous. Colleges and universities are engaged in commercial activities that are reportedly unprecedented (Bok, 2003), including athletic competition (Sperber, 2000) as well as government training grants for business and industry, where revenue generation is the prime motive. Beyond providing more funds for institutions, how are these endeavors serving students' interests? Pressures from numerous sectors for an increase in the use of their products, from food products to clothing to electronic gadgets, are endemic on campuses throughout the United States. How are students' interests served in this rhetorical free market environment (Slaughter and Rhoades, 2004)? The efforts of colleges to economize—conserve institutional resources—coupled with declining state revenues lead to decision making about the allocation of resources. These allocations are documented as serving ventures and programs that have economic utility to the institution (J. Levin, 2001; Slaughter, 1998), with student interests underserved (Slaughter and Rhoades, 2004).

A number of institutional behaviors reflect gaps in aligning higher education with the needs of students. This may be a consequence of the low profile of institutional governance in the student affairs' divisions in universities and colleges. At a time in higher education when numerous constituents are clambering to have their needs met, student developmental interests are often neglected. Private sector business and industry are clearly making their way to the forefront of recipients of higher education institutions (Slaughter and Rhoades, 2004) as colleges and universities both train students for the labor force and either conduct research or provide services that are aimed at the private sector. How are students' interests served in these endeavors?

The exchange perspective of governance has dominated practitioners' and scholars' understandings of actions and behaviors at colleges and universities. The institutional perspective of governance has been overshadowed by the exchange perspective, in a sense implying that politics and economics are more salient on college and university campuses than culture. While it is difficult and perhaps unreasonable to expect that in a postindustrial, economically globalized environment institutions can maintain community and commonality, they might be able to rebalance the scales so that higher education institutions can move student interests, such as personal development, to the center of institutional actions. This is unlikely without the participation and engagement of both student affairs practitioners and students (National Survey of Student Engagement, 2006).

Governance: How Can Student Affairs Practitioners Respond?

The current trajectory of institutional actions is arguably directed and influenced by external forces, including state governments, accreditation agencies, private sector interests, the federal government, and multinational corporations (Slaughter and Leslie, 1997). Institutional actions have a tendency to become isomorphic as colleges and universities faced with similar external pressures imitate each other in how they respond to these. As such pressures as competition for external sources of revenues increase, higher education institutions will look outward to the marketplace in order to survive. As mandates from government to demonstrate outcomes such as graduation rates and job placement are maintained and even tied to funding, higher education institutions may operate more and more like private sector businesses. As student demands for personal benefits, such as more convenient access to courses and better services on campus, escalate, higher education institutions may look more like service sector enterprises that cater to consumption. Student services and student affairs in numerous colleges and universities are increasingly business functions, ensuring that students find their way to particular programs and are maintained as satisfied customers (Slaughter and Rhoades, 2004). From some perspectives, decision making is less and less about the development of students and more and more about selling goods and services to students who have become redefined as customers (Slaughter and Rhoades, 2004). All in all, the trajectory for colleges and universities (à la for-profit institutions) approaches a credentialing factory for students and a labor market for business and industry. Such dire conditions are connected to governance—how the institution is led, managed, and experienced. These tendencies of leadership, management, and participant understandings characterize the culture of colleges and universities.

Governance is becoming detached from educational processes and behaviors, and this gap may be greater given the ascendancy of commercialization (Bok, 2003), entrepreneurialism (Marginson and Considine, 2000), academic capitalism (Slaughter and Rhoades, 2000), globalization (J. Levin, 2001), and the reliance upon education mediated by technology (Aronowitz and Di Fazio, 1994; Noble, 1998). The reformation of governance so that it is about community building and not about economic exchange might alter this trajectory. A first step is to replace the current exchange perspective and replace it with an institutional perspective. Without the connection of governance to students' education and development—which necessitates the participation of the various constituents of institutions in governance, including students and their champions—universities and colleges may fail to live up to their potential as higher educational institutions.

References

Aronowitz, S., and Di Fazio, W. *The Jobless Future: Sci-tech and the Dogma of Work.* Minneapolis: University of Minnesota Press, 1994.
Baldridge, J. V., Curtis, D. V., Ecker, G. P., and Riley, G. L. "Alternative Models of Governance in Higher Education." In J. V. Baldridge (Ed.), *Governing Academic Organizations: New Problems New Perspectives.* Berkeley: McCutchan, 1977.
Birnbaum, R. "The Latent Organizational Functions of the Academic Senate: Why Senates Do Not Work But Will Not Go Away." *The Journal of Higher Education*, 1989, 6(4), 424–443.
Bok, D. *Universities in the Marketplace: The Commercialization of Higher Education.* Princeton: Princeton University Press, 2003.
Brint, S. "Few Remaining Dreams: Community Colleges Since 1985." *The Annals of the American Academy of Political and Social Sciences*, 2003 (March), 16–37.
Brint, S., and Karabel, J. *The Diverted Dream: Community Colleges and the Promise of Educational Opportunity in America, 1900–1985.* New York: Oxford University Press, 1989.

Carnegie Commission on Higher Education. *Governance of Higher Education.* New York: McGraw Hill, 1973.

Carnegie Foundation. (2007). *Carnegie Foundation for the Advancement of Teaching.* Retrieved November 2007, from www.carnegiefoundation.org

Clark, B. *The Academic Life: Small Worlds, Different Worlds.* Princeton, N.J.: Carnegie Foundation for the Advancement of Teaching, 1987.

Clark, B. *Creating Entrepreneurial Universities: Organizational Pathways of Transformation.* Oxford, U.K.: Pergamon, 1998.

Cohen, A., and Brawer, F. *The American Community College.* San Francisco: Jossey-Bass, 2003.

Collis, D. J. "The Paradox of Scope: A Challenge to the Governance of Higher Education." In W. G. Tierney (Ed.), *Competing Conceptions of Academic Governance: Negotiating the Perfect Storm.* Baltimore, MD: Johns Hopkins University Press, 2004.

Corson, J. *Governance of Colleges and Universities.* New York: McGraw Hill, 1960.

Grubb, W. N. *Honored but Invisible: An Inside Look at Teaching in Community Colleges.* New York: Routledge, 1999.

Hines, E. "The Governance of Higher Education." In J. Smart and W. Tierney (Eds.), *Higher Education: Handbook of Theory and Research, XV.* New York: Agathon, 2000.

Hirt, J. *Where You Work Matters: Student Affairs Administration at Different Types of Institutions.* Lanham, Md.: University Press of America, 2006.

Kater, S., and Levin, J. "Shared Governance in Community Colleges in the Global Economy." *Community College Journal of Research and Practice,* 2005, 29(1), 1–24.

Labaree, D. "Public Goods, Private Goods: The American Struggle Over Educational Goals." *American Educational Research Journal,* 1997, 34(1), 39–81.

Laker, J. "Book Review." Unpublished manuscript, Kingston, Ontario, 2007.

Levin, J. *Globalizing the Community College: Strategies for Change in the Twenty-First Century.* New York: Palgrave, 2001.

Levin, J., Kater, S., and Wagoner, R. *Community College Faculty: At Work in the New Economy.* New York: Palgrave MacMillan, 2006.

Levin, J. S. "Globalizing Higher Education: Neo-Liberal Policies and Faculty Work." In J. Smart and W. Tierney (Eds.), *Handbook of Higher Education,* vol. 22. Norwell, Mass.: Kluwer Academic, 2007a.

Levin, J. S. *Non-Traditional Students and Community Colleges: The Conflict of Justice and Neo-Liberalism.* New York: Palgrave Macmillan, 2007b.

March, J. G., and Olsen, J. P. *Democratic Governance.* New York: Free Press, 1995.

Marginson, S. (2004, November 3). Response to Burton Clark. Paper presented at the annual meeting of the Association for the Study of Higher Education, Kansas City, MO.

Marginson, S., and Considine, M. *The Enterprise University: Power, Governance and Reinvention in Australia.* New York: Cambridge University Press, 2000.

McGrath, D., and Spear, M. *The Academic Crisis of the Community College.* Albany: State University of New York Press, 1991.

Miller, T. E. "Institutional Governance and the Role of Student Affairs." In M. J. Barr, M. K. Desler, and Associates (Eds.), *The Handbook of Student Affairs Administration* (2nd ed.). San Francisco: Jossey-Bass, 2000.

Mintzberg, H. *Power In and Around Organizations.* Englewood Cliffs, N.J.: Prentice Hall, 1983.

Mortimer, K., and McConnell, T. R. *Sharing Authority Effectively* (1st ed.). San Francisco: Jossey Bass, 1978.

National Survey of Student Engagement. *Engaged Learning: Fostering Success for All Students* (Annual report). Bloomington, Ind.: National Survey of Student Engagement, 2006.

Noble, D. *Digital Diploma Mills: The Automation of Higher Education.* [http://www.firstmonday.dk/issues/issue3_1/noble/]. 1998.

Olausen, K. R. "Protests Without Tear Gas: Portrayals of Campus Activism in the Print Media 1996–2004." Unpublished doctoral dissertation, North Carolina State University, Raleigh, 2007.

Pusser, B. (2003). "Beyond Baldridge: Extending the Political Model of Higher Education Organization and Governance." *Educational Policy*, 2003, 17(1), 121–140.

Readings, B. *The University in Ruins.* Cambridge, Mass.: Harvard University Press, 1997.

Richardson, R., Fisk, E., and Okun, M. *Literacy in the Open-Access College.* San Francisco: Jossey-Bass, 1983.

Schuster, J., Smith, D., Corak, K., and Yamada, M. *Strategic Governance: How to Make Big Decision Better.* Phoenix, Ariz.: American Council on Education and Oryx Press, 1994.

Seidman, E. *In the Words of the Faculty.* San Francisco: Jossey-Bass, 1985.

Slaughter, S. "Federal Policy and Supply-Side Institutional Resource Allocation at Public Research Universities." *The Review of Higher Education*, 1998, 21(3), 209–244.

Slaughter, S., and Leslie, L. *Academic Capitalism, Politics, Policies, and the Entrepreneurial University.* Baltimore: Johns Hopkins University Press, 1997.

Slaughter, S., and Rhoades, G. *Academic Capitalism and the New Economy: Markets, State, and Higher Education.* Baltimore, Md.: Johns Hopkins University Press, 2004.

Slaughter, S., and Rhoades, G. "The Neo-Liberal University." *New Labor Forum*, 2000, Spring/Summer, 73–79.

Sperber, M. *Beer and Circus: How Big-Time Sports Is Crippling Undergraduate Education.* New York: Holt, 2000.

Tierney, W. (Ed.). *Competing Conceptions of Academic Governance: Negotiating the Perfect Storm.* Baltimore, Md.: Johns Hopkins University Press, 2004.

Whitt, E. J., and Blimling, G. S., "Applying Professional Standards and Principles of Good Practice in Student Affairs." In M. J. Barr, M. K. Desler, and Associates (Eds.), *The Handbook of Student Affairs Administration* (2nd ed). San Francisco: Jossey-Bass, 2000.

CHAPTER FOUR

UNDERSTANDING CAMPUS ENVIRONMENTS

George D. Kuh

Colleges and universities have many things in common. Most institutions offer training in a variety of major fields. Academic years are usually divided into semesters or quarters. Classrooms, laboratories, and studios provide structured settings for regular interactions between teachers and students. Through out-of-class learning experiences, students acquire practical competence in such areas as making decisions and working with people who are different from themselves. Even though asynchronous, "virtual" learning opportunities such as distance education are increasing exponentially, patterns and rhythms continue to characterize the undergraduate experience, especially for full-time students and those taking classes at brick-and-mortar campuses.

At the same time, institutions of higher education differ in many respects, such as size, control (public or private), curricular emphasis (for example, liberal arts, science and technology), and the amount and type of external funding. Prospective students often consider these factors in choosing a college, even though variables such as institutional size, prestige, and affluence generally are unrelated to student learning and personal development (Kuh and Pascarella, 2004; and Pascarella and Terenzini, 2005). All things considered, what and how much a student learns is more a function of what the student *does* in college than of institutional characteristics such as size and affluence. In addition, as Pascarella and Terenzini (2005) concluded, an institution's contextual conditions are more important in encouraging student engagement in learning opportunities than organizational or programmatic variables. Equally important, the amount of effort students devote to learning is, in part, a function of the degree to which their institution provides opportunities for, supports, and rewards student learning (Kuh, Kinzie, Schuh, and Whitt, 2005a).

The accountability movement demands that colleges and universities become more transparent in terms of what students gain from college as well as the steps the institution is taking to improve teaching and learning (Kuh, 2007b). As experts on students and learning environments (National Association of Student Personnel Administrators, 1987), student affairs professionals must help their institutions make the case for why college matters and implement policies and practices that create and sustain developmentally powerful learning environments, inside and outside the classroom.

This chapter provides an overview of some of the more important "contextual conditions" that foster student learning and personal development and outlines a process for assessing these conditions. Key concepts are discussed that can help student affairs professionals understand and positively shape learning environments. First, the relationship between the institutional context and student learning and personal development is briefly summarized. Then, a framework is presented for identifying and understanding how contextual conditions work together to influence student success in college. The chapter closes with a discussion of key issues that need to be addressed when assessing environmental influences on student learning and success.

Institutional Context and Student Success

In their most recent synthesis of the student development research, Pascarella and Terenzini (2005) confirmed that

> what happens to students after they enroll at a college or university is more important than the structural characteristics of the institution they attend. What matters is the nature of the experiences students have after matriculation: the courses they take, the instructional methods their teachers use, the interactions they have with their peers and faculty members outside the classroom, the variety of people and ideas they encounter, and the extent of their active involvement in the academic and social systems of their institutions. (p. 642)

In addition, student development is a holistic, not segmented, process and is influenced by a variety of experiences across different venues, on and off the campus. That is, "students' in- and out-of-class experiences are interconnected components of complex processes shaping student change and development [associated with] classroom experiences and pedagogies, coursework, institutional environments and cultures, and an array of out-of-class activities" (Pascarella and Terenzini, 2005, p. 629).

When students' expectations match their experiences in college, students are more likely to be satisfied and persist to graduation. The area where the greatest gap exists between what students expect college to be like and what they experience is the nature of the college environment (Braxton, Vesper, and Hossler, 1995; and Kuh, Gonyea, and Williams, 2005).

Finally, students who feel they belong and are valued as individuals are more likely to take advantage of the resources the institution provides for their learning. When ethics of membership and care characterize a college, students are more likely to perceive that the institution is concerned about their welfare and committed to their success (Kuh, Schuh, Whitt, and Associates, 1991; and Kuh, Kinzie, Schuh, Whitt, and Associates, 2005b).

Taken together, these empirically based conclusions about student development and institutional performance demand that student affairs professionals know how the various aspects of their campus environments influence student behavior (American College Personnel Association, 1994; and Keeling, 2006). To acquire this knowledge, student affairs staff must discover how such institutional properties as location, physical, social, and psychological environments and faculty and student cultures work together to promote or inhibit students' engagement with learning and personal development opportunities.

A Framework for Assessing the Influence of Contextual Conditions on Student Learning

A complex web of factors and conditions interact in a myriad of ways to create an institution's context for learning (Banning, 1978; Barker, 1968; Western Interstate Commission for Higher Education, 1973). Student affairs professionals must know how their college's environment affects students and be able to the extent possible to modify these contextual conditions in ways that induce students to engage more frequently in educationally productive activities. Toward these ends, two frameworks are useful in identifying and examining an institution's environment for learning. The first, the *substantive frame*, identifies the various physical and psychological properties that influence student development, such as the size and shape of built structures, the use of campus green space, and students' perceptions of what the institution emphasizes and quality of relations among faculty, students, and administrators. The second lens is the *interpretive framework* that student affairs professionals can use to analyze and understand how the institution's contextual conditions influence student behavior. Aspects of the institution's environment are rarely neutral; most positively or negatively influence the nature and quality of the interactions students have with their peers and faculty members as well as the effects of these interactions on student effort and success.

As with any theoretical or conceptual framework, what one attends to is in large part a function of the perspective used. For example, just as some student development theories account for certain aspects of growth and behavior but not others, so it is with interpretive views of the effects of interactions between students and their college environments.

Substantive Frames

In this section, three sets of institutional properties and conditions are discussed that can substantially influence student success: (1) institutional mission and philosophy; (2) student engagement in educationally purposeful activities; and (3) and campus cultures.

Institutional Mission and Philosophy. Colleges and universities that align their mission with their educational policies and programs are generally more effective in fostering student success (Kuh and others, 1991; and Kuh and others, 2005b). As Chickering and Reisser (1993) put it:

> Clear and consistent objectives, stated in terms of desired outcomes for learning and personal development, are critically important in creating an educationally powerful institution. These should not have to be deduced from course descriptions. They should be explicit and compelling. They should be defined by the members of the college community, taken to heart by campus leaders, and invoked as guides to decision making. (p. 287)

Clarifying the mission seems to be a fairly straightforward task. But while every college has a mission, that mission may or may not be congruent with how the college describes itself in its publications, such as the statement of educational purposes in the catalog or other documents. In addition, institutional missions may change, intentionally or in response to the external environment, such as what occurred at many single-sex colleges when the vast majority of students began opting for coeducational learning experiences. For these reasons, a necessary step is discovering the institution's enacted mission by talking with students, faculty, administrators, graduates, and others in order to learn what the college is at present and what it aspires to be (Kuh and others, 2005a).

One indication that an institution's mission is clear and coherent is that members of various groups consistently use similar terms to describe what their college is trying to do with its resources. In some instances, particularly small colleges and universities, the institutional mission may be salient, meaning that even people who are not "insiders" (people who live and work in close proximity to the institution and call it their own), or are not members of one of the college's major constituent groups, have a fairly clear understanding of what the institution stands for and is trying to accomplish (Clark, 1970; Kuh and others, 1991; Kuh and others, 2005b; and Townsend, Newell, and Wiese, 1992). For example, institutions such as Alverno College, Berea College, California State University Monterey Bay, Earlham College, Luther College, Mount Holyoke College, University of Michigan Ann Arbor, Wabash College, and Wheaton College (Massachusetts) attract students and faculty with aspirations consistent with those the institution values. For example, when Wheaton College decided to admit men, it focused on developing a curriculum that was gender balanced to incorporate both female and male perspectives. This allowed the institution to honor its past as a women's college while at the same time realigning its curriculum and learning environment with its new academic mission as a coeducational institution (Kuh and others, 2005b).

A salient mission also clarifies expectations for behavior. Too often, however, institutions are unclear about what they are trying to accomplish or communicate their aims in confused or convoluted ways. As a result, they send mixed messages about their purposes and values. When institutional leaders assert that both research and teaching are important, but tenure decisions depend primarily on research contributions, faculty can become confused or jaded about what their institution values.

Just as every college has a mission, each has a philosophy (Kuh and others, 1991). Although rarely stated in writing, an institution's philosophy can be discerned from how it distributes its resources, the decisions it makes, and its standard operating procedures (Kuh, 1993a). As colleges grow larger, their philosophies and core values tend to erode; curricular and co-curricular experiences also become less coherent and, in some instances, inconsistent with the educational aims of the institution. When students are told at orientation that the faculty have high expectations for student achievement but then encounter a steady diet of multiple choice tests and little or no feedback on written work other than a letter grade, students understandably may become confused. Students may respond in similar fashion if they are exhorted to manage their own affairs but are continually monitored by the student affairs staff. Enacting a clear, coherent institutional mission and educational philosophy is essential to provide direction to students and others and to create an environment conducive to student success.

Effective Educational Practices. Since the appearance of the *Seven Principles of Good Practice in Undergraduate Education* (Chickering and Gamson, 1987), considerable attention has focused on promoting more effective teaching and learning approaches. The Association of American Colleges and Universities (2007) identified ten potentially high-impact practices based on the student development research:

1. First-year seminars and experiences
2. Common intellectual experiences
3. Learning communities
4. Writing-intensive courses
5. Collaborative assignments and projects
6. Undergraduate research experiences
7. Diversity and global learning experiences
8. Service learning and community-based learning
9. Internships
10. Capstone courses and projects

The widely used National Survey of Student Engagement features five clusters made up of many of the student behaviors and institutional conditions identified by Chickering and Gamson and Association of American Colleges and Universities (AAC&U) (Kuh, 2001, 2003). The clusters are

1. Level of academic challenge
2. Active and collaborative learning
3. Student-faculty interaction
4. Enriching educational experiences
5. Supportive campus environment

The Community College Survey of Student Engagement (CCSSE) measures similar desirable aspects of the learning environment.

To illustrate, academic challenge represents the amount of time and effort students devote to (1) studying and other academic work, (2) preparing for class, (3) reading assigned and other books, and (4) writing reports and papers. Academic challenge also addresses whether instructors set high expectations for student performance and the extent to which students engage in activities that require analyzing, synthesizing, applying theories, and making judgments, as well as the extent to which instructors set standards that compel students to work harder than they thought possible. Taken together, engaging in these kinds of activities sets a tone for campus life that emphasizes serious academic work. Ursinus College requires a Common Intellectual Experience (CIE) of all first-year students to cultivate a climate of rigorous intellectual discourse. Interdisciplinary in orientation, CIE exposes students to a wide range of challenging readings on complex philosophical topics from original texts and writing assignments that address such daunting questions as "What does it mean to be human?" Ursinus also reassigned student residences so that all first-year students now live in close proximity, which makes it easier to organize enriching programs outside the classroom that complement CIE course content, thus adding an additional measure of intellectual vitality to campus life (Kuh and others, 2005b).

Creating and maintaining supportive campus environments is important because students perform better and are more satisfied at colleges where positive working and social relations exist among different groups on campus. Salient characteristics of a supportive campus environment include (1) providing support to help students succeed academically and socially; (2) supporting students in meeting their nonacademic responsibilities; and (3) fostering high-quality student relationships with other students, faculty, and the institution's administrative personnel. Educationally effective institutions provide programs and practices to create supportive environments through transition programs, advising networks, peer support, safety nets, special student support initiatives, learning communities, and living environments organized around educational themes. At Fayetteville State University, for example, an ethos of concern, nurturance, and support for student success permeates all facets of institutional life. Faculty and staff members routinely follow up on students who miss classes, experience academic difficulty, or seem to be struggling to succeed. The cultural messages to students and everyone else is clear: students matter and the institution is committed to helping them succeed (Kuh and others, 2005b).

By using effective educational practices inside and outside the classroom, institutions create learning environments that essentially guarantee that students will:

- Invest time and effort in activities associated with desired learning outcomes,
- Interact with faculty and peers about substantive matters,
- Experience diversity,
- Get frequent feedback in formal and informal ways, and
- Discover relevance of their learning through real-world applications.

Campus Cultures. Student learning is in large part a function of academic effort and the frequency and quality of interactions between students and important agents of socialization: faculty, student affairs professionals, peers (Pascarella and Terenzini, 2005). Therefore, it is important to determine whether faculty and student cultures encourage or discourage student engagement in educationally purposeful activities.

The amount of time faculty devote to students is influenced to a degree by the type of institution in which they work and the expectations that institutional leaders and others have for faculty and student performance. Teachers at many institutions spend less time with undergraduates outside the classroom than their counterparts of several decades ago. Of course, there always have been and will continue to be exceptions, institutions where the quality of interaction between students and faculty are unusually rich and rewarding (Kuh and others, 1991). Moreover, there is perceptible shift in the role of the faculty member from dispensing information to arranging activities that promote student learning (Barr and Tagg, 1995; and Tagg, 2003) and in the amount of attention being given to undergraduate education, even at research universities (Diamond and Adam, 1997).

Even so, this shift toward a student- or learner-centered philosophy is a long way from being fully realized in most colleges and universities. For example, in state-assisted colleges, where the heavy emphasis on undergraduate instruction is often coupled with aspirations to move up in the prestige pecking order, teaching loads remain heavy even as expectations for scholarly productivity increase. In addition, many faculty members often feel conflicted between devoting time to research (to which many were socialized to value over teaching in graduate school) and the daily demands of teaching and student advising. At some types of institutions, such as community colleges, faculty members have heavy teaching loads and many students in their classes who require compensatory assistance to succeed academically.

Understanding what students expect of and from their college experience is crucial for fashioning policies and practices that effectively address students' learning needs (Kuh, Gonyea, and Williams, 2005), but what students expect and what faculty expect can differ substantially (Schilling and Schilling, 1999). Many traditional-age students start college with a cumulative deficit in terms of attitudes, study habits, and academic skills. For example, in the mid-1990s, high school seniors reported studying only about six hours per week on average, well below the amount traditionally assumed necessary to do well in college. More recent studies (McCarthy and Kuh, 2006) show similar findings. Compared with their counterparts of a decade earlier, high school seniors were more frequently bored in class and missed more classes as a result of oversleeping or other obligations (Sax and others, 2003). Even so, record numbers reported B+ or better high school grades and expected to earn at least a B average in college. Because behavioral patterns established in elementary and secondary school tend to persist through the college years, we should not be surprised that the majority of first-year students—about 70 percent—report working just hard enough to get by (Kuh, 2007a).

Assuming many students matriculate with an entitlement mentality, what they expect to do in college and what faculty members and postsecondary institutions provide portends a potentially debilitating condition (Moneta and Kuh, 2005). For example, if a student does not expect to do research with a faculty member, take part in cultural events, or study abroad, chances are that opportunities to pursue these activities will be overlooked or dismissed out of hand.

The combination of demands on faculty to improve their instructional approaches, incorporate technology in their work, and engage in scholarly inquiry and the entitlement expectation students bring with them to college has given rise to a tacit agreement between students and faculty—a disengagement compact—that essentially says, "You leave me alone and I will leave you alone" (Kuh, Schuh, and Whitt, 1991). That is, faculty members do not require much from students who in turn demand relatively little from faculty in terms of making appointments to talk or challenging a grade. The trade-off is that students expect a reasonably good grade, at least a B.

Taken together, student cultures and peers exert a nontrivial influence on student learning because they determine the kinds of people with whom a student spends time and, therefore, the values and attitudes to which a student is exposed. It seems that no matter what institutional agents say or do, within four to six weeks following the start of an academic term new students learn from their peers what classes and instructors are to be taken seriously, and where, how much, and what to study (Holland and Eisenhart, 1990; and Moffatt, 1989).

Complicating attempts to understand the influence of the institution's cultures on student behavior is that different student affinity groups develop and perpetuate their own distinctive interaction patterns and norms that influence how their members behave and relate to others. These groups include but are not limited to Greek organizations, students who live together on or off campus, honors students, athletes, and members of minority racial and ethnic groups, including international students. For example, such student groups as fraternities organize around social themes while athletes are focused on competition; both value orientations may conflict with those of the faculty.

One unfortunate irony of college life is that most colleges and universities ignore what student subcultures teach their student members. Only by becoming more knowledgeable about the various student cultures on our campuses will we have a good chance of effecting positive change with those groups that are antithetical to the institution's educational aims (Kuh, 1994). There is always more to learn about the influence of student cultures on student learning, as the characteristics, aspirations, and attitudes of students change from one cohort to the next. Of course, to do this task well some resources must be committed to it.

Interpretive Frames

In this section, three perspectives are discussed that can be used to understand how a college's contextual conditions influence student learning: (1) ecology; (2) climates; and (3) cultures. The terms *ecology, climate,* and *culture* often are used interchangeably, but they emphasize different aspects of an institution's environment that influence student learning and personal development. Ecology is the broadest of these concepts, encompassing both climate and culture. The plural forms of *climate* and *culture* suggest that multiple subenvironments exist on a campus; they can be identified by examining climates and cultures at different levels: the institution, academic department or major field, living unit, and affinity group(s). Institutional environments also have variable influences on student behavior. This explains why campus climates and cultures have competing, sometimes contradictory effects on the behavior of students, faculty, and student affairs professionals.

Ecology. Student learning and personal development are products of transactional interactions between individuals or groups of students, faculty and administrators, and the physical, perceived, and enacted environments of the college (Banning, 1978; Barker, 1968; Western Interstate Commission on Higher Education, 1973). That is, behavior is a function of students interacting with the college environment broadly defined to include physical spaces, policies, people, and other physical, biological, chemical, and cultural stimuli (Strange and Banning, 2001). Said another way, students shape their environment and are shaped by it (Outcalt and Skewes-Cox, 2002).

The physical or built environments affect—for better or worse—students' behavioral patterns and social choices. For example, the amount, locations, and arrangement of physical spaces shape behavior by facilitating or discouraging social interaction. The proximity of academic buildings to student residences can promote or inhibit interactions between students from different majors, facilitating or discouraging learning and development (Strange and Banning, 2001).

Collegiate environments tend to encourage students to behave in similar ways. Some environments are more congruent with certain students' needs than others. For example, "if a student reported a high need for achievement and the campus environment was consensually identified as exerting a press for achievement, a congruent situation would exist, leading to satisfaction and good functioning" (Huebner, 1989, p. 169). Similarly, if a student is surrounded by people with compatible personality characteristics, the environmental setting can be said to be congruent (Holland, 1973; and Strange and Banning, 2001). Substantial mismatches between environmental demands and student needs create dissonance, which in turn can lead to dissatisfaction, poor academic performance, and even premature departure from the institution (Braxton, Hirshy, and McClendon, 2004; and Tinto, 1993).

The ecology frame (institutional size, location, facilities, open spaces, and other permanent attributes) can also help interpret the influence of campus physical properties on behavior. The amount, locations, and arrangement of physical spaces facilitate or inhibit social interaction and the development of group cohesiveness (Myrick and Marx, 1968). In general, the less crowded and more organized and neat the physical environment, the lower the stress level (Ahrentzen and others, 1982). In densely populated areas, such as high-rise residences, indicators of social pathology such as deviant behavior and frustration tend to be higher (Moos, 1979). The proximity of academic buildings to accessible socially catalytic spaces can promote or discourage interaction between students from different majors. When the engineering building is in a far corner of the campus some distance from the student union, the amount of interaction engineering students will have with students in other fields will likely be low. Locating enrollment-related offices such as registrar, financial aid, admissions, and bursar in different parts of the campus affects student satisfaction. The physical design of counseling centers (Iwai and others, 1983), the dean of students office (Hurst and Ragle, 1979), college unions (Banning and Cunard, 1986), commencement programs (Banning, 1983), and campus markings (Banning, 1992) can also affect student perceptions and performance.

Territoriality also warrants attention. When arriving in a new environment, it is not uncommon for people from similar backgrounds or who knew one another prior to coming to the university to congregate in a specific public area at certain times of the day. At one urban university, African American students were comfortable in socializing in only a few places on campus, one of which was around a red couch in the middle of the ground floor of the student union. Whether this and other similar behaviors expands or places limits on their network of social relations is not known. However, when student affinity groups are highly segmented by ethnic background, academic interest, or other characteristics, learning and personal development may be unnecessarily blunted. This is especially problematic if students perceive that the university environment discourages interacting with students from other groups.

Climate. Climate refers to how students, faculty, student affairs staff, and other institutional agents *perceive and experience* their institution (Baird, 1988; and Peterson and Spencer, 1990). For example, institutions differ in the degree to which students believe faculty and administrators are supportive of their learning and personal development goals (Kuh, Vesper, Connolly, and Pace, 1997). If students view the campus as "chilly" or "inhospitable," it can negatively affect their academic performance (Lyons, 1990; Torres, 2003). Indeed, students' perceptions of their institution almost always have a nontrivial, indirect influence on learning and personal development (Pike and Kuh, 2006; and Pascarella and Terenzini, 2005). Most climate measures focus on (1) perceptions of organizational functioning, such as goal setting, decision making, and resource allocation; and/or (2) affective responses to experiences with the institution, such as feelings of loyalty and commitment, morale and satisfaction, and a general sense of belonging (Baird, 1988).

Such instruments as the College and University Environment Scales (CUES) assess institutional attributes that encourage students to behave in certain ways, such as a high need for achievement or the quality of relations between faculty and students. The College Student Experience Questionnaire (CSEQ) measures that amount of effort students devote to various learning activities and also includes ten scales that represent students' perceptions of other aspects of the institution. Seven of the scales depict the degree to which students feel that their college emphasizes scholarship, estheticism, critical thinking, diversity, information literacy, vocational competence, and the practical relevance of courses. The remaining three CSEQ environment scales refer to the quality of relations among students, faculty, and administrators. The National Survey of Student Engagement (NSSE) and the Community College Survey of Student Engagement (CCSSE) include the same three CSEQ quality of relations scales along with other measures such as the Supportive Campus Environment item cluster mentioned earlier.

The University Residence Environments Scale (URES) provides information about the climates of residential subenvironments, such as whether residents are more interested in social activities or academic pursuits, and whether these same students view their living environments as structured and competitive, or interpersonally supportive and achievement oriented. Student affairs professionals can use these data to intentionally modify, through indirect or direct means, the climate of residences by grouping students with certain characteristics in order to create the desired climate.

Results from the CUES, CSEQ, NSSE, CCSSE, URES, and similar instruments, such as the College Student Questionnaire and Institutional Functioning Inventory (Baird, 1988), can be disaggregated by students' sex, year in school, major field, and race and ethnicity to discover the perceptions of different groups of students. By administering climate measures periodically, student affairs staff can monitor progress toward making living unit environments, attitudes of subgroups of students, such as fraternities, and the general campus climate more congruent with the institution's educational purposes.

Culture. Whereas measures of climate reflect individual or group perceptions of certain aspects of the institution, campus culture encompasses both the espoused and enacted character of an institution (Kuh, 1993a). Institutional culture is the collective, mutually shaping patterns of institutional history, mission, physical settings, norms, traditions, values, practices, beliefs, and assumptions that guide the behavior of individuals and groups in college or university (Kuh and Whitt, 1988). The espoused character of an institution's culture is that which people on and off the campus wish the institution to be, its best public image congruent with its announced educational values and programs. The enacted character of the institution's culture is the myriad elements and interactions that make up institutional life on a daily basis and may or may not be consistent with espoused values and commitments. For example, at some colleges, the dominant student culture values activities that complement the institution's educational purposes, while at other institutions students routinely engage in activities that are antithetical to their college's mission (Kuh, 1990). Viewing institutional life through a cultural lens provides a frame of reference with which to interpret the meaning of events and actions on and off campus (Kuh and Whitt, 1988).

Specifying a college's culture is a challenging task. This is because collegiate cultures are made up of holistic, complex webs of physical and verbal artifacts, enduring behavioral patterns, embedded values and beliefs, and ideologies and assumptions that represent learned products of group experience (Kuh and Whitt, 1988). Cultural values and beliefs are perpetuated through traditions (graduation ceremonies, induction experiences for new students and faculty), major campus events, heroic individuals, and language (Kuh, 1998; London, 1989; and Magolda, 2000). The meanings that various members of the campus community attach to these cultural elements, however, are not always easy to deduce nor can they be easily derived by people unfamiliar with the institution. As increasing numbers of students start at two-year colleges or commute to four-year institutions, the classroom becomes even more important as a cultural venue, as it is the only point of regular contact students have with the institution (Kuh, 2007c).

Institutional cultures tend to be relatively stable, but they are not stagnant. Cultures change over time through a dynamic interplay between the institution's structural and cultural elements, forces in the external environment (shifting demographics), cataclysmic events (destruction of facilities or accidents that take the lives of senior administrators or athletic teams) (Peterson and others, 1986), and the presence of individuals—such as women and members of historically underrepresented ethnic and racial groups—with beliefs and assumptions that differ somewhat from those held by the majority.

Cultures also change as a result of the mutual shaping of cultural properties. That is, the physical attributes of a campus, established practices, celebratory events, symbols and symbolic actions, and subcultures influence each other while simultaneously shaping the behavior of students, faculty, and staff. Similarly, the arrival of newcomers whose backgrounds are different than those of previous cohorts of students and faculty members also can affect cultural properties. In this sense, culture is both product and process (Peterson and others, 1986), influencing such behavioral outcomes as student performance and satisfaction as well as being shaped by the characteristics, attitudes, and behavior of faculty, staff, and students and the external environment.

Earlier an example was given of African American students congregating around a red couch in the student union where they enjoy the only meaningful social interaction they have on campus. The cultural lens is useful here, as the red couch is not only an important gathering place for African American students; it is to them their most visible symbol of a Black presence on campus.

Key Issues in Assessing Environmental Influences on Learning

To discover how the contextual conditions of a campus influence student learning and success, a comprehensive, in-depth study of an institution's culture and its policies and practices is needed. This section discusses some key issues related to conducting an audit of how a college's contextual conditions influence student learning. Although the presentation assumes a comprehensive campuswide audit, the same issues pertain if the focus of the project is circumscribed, such as assessing the impact of the residence halls or the campus union on student performance.

As will become evident, institutional audits are labor intensive. However, they provide high-quality, policy-relevant information that cannot be obtained any other way. The following suggestions are informed by Austin (1990), Fetterman (1990), Kuh (1993a), Kuh and others, (1991), Schein (1985), Whitt

(1993), and Whitt and Kuh (1991). Especially relevant for those seeking a step-by-step approach is the *Inventory for Student Engagement and Success,* which provides a detailed template for guiding investigations of the influence of campus cultures on student performance (Kuh and others, 2005a).

Determine the Commitment of Key Campus Personnel to the Project

Clarifying the purpose of an audit is critical. No matter what the study team has been asked to focus on, support from the highest administrative levels, including the governing board, is essential for a successful campus audit. Ideally, the audit itself should be commissioned by the president or provost and cosponsored by academic and student affairs as a collaborative endeavor. Also, it is essential to publicize the project in a variety of venues, such as the student newspaper, faculty newsletters, alumni publications, e-mail, and local as well as campus radio and television. Finally, institutional leaders must be willing to confront what Collins (2001, p. 71) calls "the brutal facts of reality"—what actually is going on as contrasted with what people would like to think is happening.

Assemble a Credible, Qualified Study Team

Assuming that campus decision makers are committed to a comprehensive study of the student experience, the next step is to create a partnership of people familiar with the institution (insiders) and consultants (outsiders) knowledgeable about conditions that foster student learning. Outsiders are needed to help insiders "make the familiar strange" (Whitt, 1993, p. 82). That is, most faculty, student affairs staff, and students are so familiar with the institution that they are unable to discern the effects of taken-for-granted aspects of campus life such as traditions and ritualistic practices on the experiences of members of different groups, such as women, minorities, and older students. The team must be perceived as credible, fair, tactful, discrete, truthful, and trustworthy by the various stakeholders likely to be affected by the findings or charged with implementing recommendations from the study. Sensitivity to and appreciation for the institution's mission and educational purposes are essential. While many student affairs professionals embody these characteristics, it also will be important that faculty members and academic administrators be represented on the study team. Faculty members are more likely to talk freely with another faculty member or with a respected outsider; therefore, a study team that includes several faculty members will likely obtain higher-quality data. The team should reflect an appropriate gender and racial and ethnic balance to the extent possible.

Obtain as Much Relevant Information as Possible from Different Sources

It is essential to obtain high-quality information from a variety of sources including faculty, current, former and prospective students, graduates, student affairs staff, and governing board members using multiple data collection methods such as interviews, observations, survey data, and document analysis. To yield the most useful results, audits should incorporate some combination of interviews, observations, and self-report pencil-and-paper instruments completed by students and perhaps others such as faculty and student affairs professionals (Austin, 1990; Kuh, 1990).

One approach is to use open-ended interviews with students, faculty, and others to identify critical issues that deserve immediate attention. Based on this information, an appropriate instrument, such as the CSEQ, NSSE, or CCSSE, could be used to collect additional information from a larger number of students. In certain instances, the best approach may be to construct a survey designed to obtain the needed information. Following the collection of survey data, additional interviews with individual and groups of students, faculty members, and student affairs staff will provide more detailed insights into how the institutional context affects student learning and personal development.

To determine if the espoused values and aspirations of the institution are congruent with the enacted policies and practices that shape daily interactions, the audit team must examine the written and oral statements of institutional leaders and important institutional documents, such as the mission statement, past and current catalogs, and statements of student rights, responsibilities and ethics. Such documents and pronouncements often contain tacit assumptions about what is valued or preferred that often go unchallenged and unrecognized, which makes their influence on student learning and success difficult to ascertain and address.

Seek Different Points of View

Obtain as much relevant information as possible by seeking out contradictions and differences of opinion. Avoid simplifying complicated issues and prematurely drawing conclusions. Particular attention should be given to what the institution *espouses* (says about itself in publications and public statements but may or may not actually do) with regard to the philosophy, values, policies, and practices and what seems to be *enacted* (what people put into practice). Espoused values may take the form of institutional aspirations, such as an announced commitment to health-enhancing behavior or to increasing the number of students and faculty from historically underserved groups. If these goals are not realized, however, the gap between espoused and enacted values can create considerable confusion in students and others. Insiders, institutional agents with the best intentions and skilled in audit methods, simply cannot get their colleagues to talk about these issues in ways that outsiders can.

Test Impressions Early and Often

Feedback from insiders about emerging interpretations is critical to obtaining high-quality data. That is, as mentioned previously, the audit team must have their emerging understandings and impressions validated and corrected by those whose experiences are being described. Participating in the study should be educative; that is, through the data collection and reporting processes the team and various groups should learn a good deal about themselves and student learning before any "final report" is circulated. Indeed, perhaps the most important outcome of the audit process is getting people together to talk about or discover matters of mutual interest and importance to institutional vitality and student learning.

Whitt's (1993) cautions warrant emphasis here. Those cautions included (1) obtain the permission of participants; (2) be clear about the audit purposes and the ways information obtained from participants will be used; (3) do not report preliminary findings except to check evolving impressions, explanations, and interpretations; (4) be explicit about how the results of the campus audit can and cannot be used.

Treat Every Participant and Every Piece of Information as Important

Attention must be given to the routine as well as the more unusual, celebratory aspects of campus life. By focusing on events that are the most obvious or most colorful, such as new student orientation, induction ceremonies, honors programs, scholarship banquets, and commencement, the audit team may overlook the mundane routines by which institutional values are expressed and reinforced for most students and that shape faculty and student aspirations and behavior on an ongoing basis (Kuh, 1998).

Significant Improvements in Institutional Conditions for Learning Take Time

Audits often shed light on the "shadow side" of campus culture, aspects of faculty and student cultures about which just enough is known so that people know they are not to discuss such matters (Kuh, 1993b, p. 117). Therefore, it probably will be useful to have people from different groups of faculty, students, and administrators participate in some aspects of the investigation. Expect the audit results to confirm as well as challenge one or more taken-for-granted assumptions about student life. Certain physical attributes of a campus are not always viewed as welcoming or hospitable by people who have been historically underrepresented and may belie espoused institutional aspirations to be open to members of these groups. For example, artwork and portraits featured in public places often reflect the institution's history and preferences of administrators. As a result, artifacts manifest mostly white, mostly male views. While it seems a simple matter to add some artifacts that reflect the experiences of different groups of people, a college usually cannot exchange one set paintings for another. Some will object to what appears to be revisionist history or "politically correct" behavior. Moreover, a college must determine whether its enacted values are consistent with its educational purposes.

No institution is perfect, so it is easy to criticize the current state of affairs anywhere. At the same time, the most important goal of an audit is to help faculty, student affairs professionals, and students become aware of the rich harvest of learning opportunities inherent in collegiate environments and how their institution can encourage more students to greater advantage of these opportunities. This means that, among other things, faculty and staff must have current relevant information about the characteristics of their students in order to understand and interpret the findings from a campus audit and use the information to improve the learning climate.

Conclusion

An institution of higher education is more than a collection of students and faculty, buildings, and green spaces. Greater than the sum of its many parts, a college or university is at once a behavior setting that regulates the behavior of its members, a theater-in-the-round where the scripts of the past get played out in the process of seeking solutions to contemporary ills, a highly leveraged subsidiary that annually consumes an increasing amount of its parent company's resources, a social club with numerous cliques of faculty, students, and administrators, a cultural and recreational oasis where the number and variety of events and activities outstrip any one individual's capacity to partake of them all, a game of chance in which members of various groups are assigned to physical spaces not always compatible with their personal or academic preferences and aspirations, and an intellectual theme park where the only limits to what one can discover are imposed by the learner.

All of the actions and events described, and more, occur simultaneously. At some colleges, this maelstrom of activity is more coherent and consistent with the institution's educational purposes than at others. This is because the various properties of a college work together in complicated, almost mysterious ways to promote or discourage student learning and success. While the way these properties work together may seem mysterious, the properties themselves are not.

Student affairs staff can use the substantive and interpretive frames described in this chapter to identify and better understand the influence of their institution on the learning and personal development of students. Such knowledge, coupled with intentional use of demonstrably effective educational practices and a firm belief in what their college stands for, will enable student affairs professionals to make even more valuable contributions to their institutions and students.

References

Ahrentzen, S., Jue, B. M., Skorpanish, M. A., and Evans, G. W. "School Environment and Stress." In G. Evans (Ed.), *Environmental Stress*. Cambridge, Mass.: MIT Press, 1982.

American College Personnel Association. *The Student Learning Imperative*. Washington, D.C.: American College Personnel Association, 1994.

Association of American Colleges and Universities. *College Learning for the New Global Century*. Washington, D.C.: Association of American Colleges and Universities, 2007.

Austin, A. E. "Faculty Cultures, Faculty Values." In W. G. Tierney (Ed.), *Assessing Academic Climates and Cultures*. New Directions for Institutional Research, no. 68. San Francisco: Jossey-Bass, 1990.

Baird, L. L. "The College Environment Revisited: A Review of Research and Theory." In J. C. Smart (Ed.), *Higher Education: Handbook of Theory and Research*, Vol. 4. New York: Agathon, 1988.

Banning, J. H. *Campus Ecology: A Perspective for Student Affairs*. Cincinnati, Ohio: NASPA, 1978.

Banning, J. H. "The Built Environment: Do Ivy Walls Have Memories?" *Campus Ecologist*, 1983, 1(2), 1–3.

Banning, J. H. "Visual Anthropology: Viewing the Campus Ecology for Messages of Sexism." *The Campus Ecologist*, 1992, 10(1), 1–4.

Banning, J. H., and Cunard, M. "Environment Supports Student Development." *ACU-I Bulletin*, 1986, 54(1), 8–10.

Barker, R. *Ecological Psychology*. Palo Alto, Calif.: Stanford University Press, 1968.

Barr, R. B., and Tagg, J. "From Teaching to Learning: A New Paradigm for Undergraduate Education." *Change*, 1995, 27(6), 12–25.

Braxton, J. M., Hirschy, A. S., and McClendon, S. A. *Understanding and Reducing College Student Departure*. ASHE-ERIC Higher Education Report, Vol. 30, no. 3. Washington, D.C.: George Washington University, School of Education and Human Development, 2004.

Braxton, J. M., Vesper, N., and Hossler, D. "Expectations for College and Student Persistence." *Research in Higher Education*, 1995, 36(5), 595–612.

Chickering, A. W., and Gamson, Z. F. (Eds.). "Seven Principles for Good Practice in Undergraduate Education." *AAHE Bulletin*, 1987, March, 3–7.

Chickering, A. W., and Reisser, L. *Education and Identity* (2nd ed.). San Francisco: Jossey-Bass, 1993.

Clark, B. R. *The Distinctive College: Antioch, Reed and Swarthmore.* Chicago: Aldine, 1970.

Collins, J. C. *Good to Great: Why Some Companies Make the Leap—and Others Don't.* New York: Harper Business, 2001.

Diamond, R. M., and Adam, B. E. *Changing Priorities at Research Universities: 1991–1996.* Syracuse, N.Y.: Syracuse University Center for Instructional Development, 1997.

Fetterman, D. *"Ethnographic Auditing: A New Approach to Evaluating Management."* In W. G. Tierney (Ed.), *Assessing Academic Climates and Cultures.* New Directions for Institutional Research, no. 68. San Francisco: Jossey-Bass, 1990.

Holland, J. L. *Making Vocational Choices: A Theory of Careers.* Englewood Cliffs, N.J.: Prentice-Hall, 1973.

Holland, D. C., and Eisenhart, M. A. *Educated in Romance: Women, Achievement, and College Culture.* Chicago: University of Chicago Press, 1990.

Huebner, L. A. *"Interaction of Student and Campus."* In U. Delworth and G. Hanson (Eds.), *Student Services: A Handbook for the Profession* (2nd ed.). San Francisco: Jossey-Bass, 1989.

Hurst, J. C., and Ragle, J. D. *"Application of the Ecosystem Perspective to a Dean of Students' Office."* In L. Huebner (Ed.), *Redesigning Campus Environments.* New Directions for Student Services, no. 8. San Francisco: Jossey-Bass, 1979.

Iwai, S., Churchill, W., and Cummings, L. "The Physical Characteristics of College and University Counseling Services." *Journal of College Student Personnel,* 1983, 24, 55–60.

Keeling, R. (Ed.). *Learning Reconsidered 2: Implementing a Campus-Wide Focus on the Student Experience.* Various: American College Personnel Association, Association of College and University Housing Officers-International, Association of College Unions-International, National Academic Advising Association, National Association for Campus Activities, National Association of Student Personnel Administrators, National Intramural-Recreational Sports Association, 2006.

Kuh, G. D. "Assessing Student Culture." In W. G. Tierney (Ed.), *Assessing Academic Climates and Cultures.* New Directions for Institutional Research, no. 68. San Francisco: Jossey-Bass, 1990.

Kuh, G. D. "Appraising the Character of a College." *Journal of Counseling and Development,* 1993a, 71, 661–668.

Kuh, G. D. "Some Implications of Cultural Perspectives for Student Affairs." In G. D. Kuh (Ed.), *Using Cultural Perspectives in Student Affairs Work.* Alexandria, Va.: ACPA Media, 1993b.

Kuh, G. D. *"Creating Campus Climates That Foster Student Learning."* In C. Schroeder and P. Mable (Eds.), *Realizing the Educational Potential of Residence Halls.* San Francisco: Jossey-Bass, 1994.

Kuh, G. D. "Strengthening the Ties That Bind: Cultural Events, Traditions, and Rituals." In J. N. Gardner and G. Van der Veer (Eds.), *The Senior Year Experience: Facilitating Integration, Reflection, Closure, and Transition.* San Francisco: Jossey-Bass, 1998.

Kuh, G. D. "Assessing What Really Matters to Student Learning: Inside the National Survey of Student Engagement. "*Change,* 2001, 33(3), 10–17, 66.

Kuh, G. D. "What We're Learning About Student Engagement from NSSE." *Change,* 2003, 35(2), 24–32.

Kuh, G. D. "What Student Engagement Data Tell Us About College Readiness." *Peer Review,* 2007a, 9(1), 4–8.

Kuh, G. D. "The Common Reporting Template: Promises, Pitfalls, and Pathways to Responsible Use." *Change,* 2007b.

Kuh, G. D. "Promoting Student Success: What Institutions Can Do." In P. Lingenfelter (ed.), *More Student Success*. Boulder, Colo.: State Higher Education Executive Officers, 2007c.

Kuh, G. D., Gonyea, R. M., and Williams, J. M. "What Students Expect from College and What They Get." In T. Miller, B. Bender, J. Schuh, and Associates (Eds.), *Promoting Reasonable Expectations: Aligning Student and Institutional Thinking About the College Experience*. San Francisco: Jossey-Bass/National Association of Student Personnel Administrators, 2005.

Kuh, G. D., Kinzie, J., Schuh, J. H., and Whitt, E. J. *Assessing Conditions to Enhance Educational Effectiveness: The Inventory for Student Engagement and Success*. San Francisco: Jossey-Bass, 2005a.

Kuh, G. D., Kinzie, J., Schuh, J. H., Whitt, E. J., and Associates. *Student Success in College: Creating Conditions That Matter*. San Francisco: Jossey-Bass, 2005b.

Kuh, G. D., and Pascarella, E. T. What Does Institutional Selectivity Tell Us About Educational Quality? *Change*, 2004, 36(5), 52–58.

Kuh, G. D., Schuh, J. H., and Whitt, E. J. (1991). "Some Good News About Campus Life: How 'Involving Colleges' Promote Learning Outside the Classroom." *Change*, 1991, 23(5), 48–55.

Kuh, G. D., Schuh, J. H., Whitt, E. J., Andreas, R. E., Lyons, J. W., Strange, C. C., Krehbiel, L. E., and MacKay, K. A. *Involving Colleges: Successful Approaches to Fostering Student Learning and Development Outside the Classroom*. San Francisco: Jossey-Bass, 1991.

Kuh, G. D., Vesper, N., Connolly, M. R., and Pace, C. R. *College Student Experiences Questionnaire: Revised Norms for the Third Edition*. Bloomington, Ind.: Center for Postsecondary Research and Planning, Indiana University, 1997.

Kuh, G. D., and Whitt, E. J. *The Invisible Tapestry: Culture in American Colleges and Universities*. ASHE-ERIC Higher Education Report, No. 1. Washington, D.C.: Association for the Study of Higher Education, 1988.

London, H. B. "Breaking Away: A Study of First-Generation College Students and Their Families." *American Journal of Education*, 1989, 97(1), 144–170.

Lyons, J. W. "Examining the Validity of Basic Assumptions and Beliefs." In M. J. Barr, M. L. Upcraft, and Associates (Eds.), *New Futures for Student Affairs*. San Francisco: Jossey-Bass, 1990.

McCarthy, M. M., and Kuh, G. D. "Are Students Ready for College? What Student Engagement Data Say." *Phi Delta Kappan*, 2006, 87, 664–669.

Magolda, P. M. "The Campus Tour ritual: Exploring Community Discourses in Higher Education." *Anthropology and Education Quarterly*, 2000, 31(1), 24–36.

Moffatt, M. *Coming of Age in New Jersey: College and American Culture*. New Brunswick, N.J.: Rutgers University Press, 1989.

Moneta, L., and Kuh, G. D. "When Expectations and Realities Collide: Environmental Influences on Student Expectations and Student Experiences." In T. Miller, B. Bender, J. Schuh, and Associates (Eds.), *Promoting Reasonable Expectations: Aligning Student and Institutional Thinking About the College Experience*. San Francisco: Jossey-Bass/National Association of Student Personnel Administrators, 2005.

Moos, R. *Evaluating Educational Environments*. San Francisco: Jossey-Bass, 1979.

Myrick, R., and Marx, B. S. *An Exploratory Study of the Relationship Between High School Building Design and Student Learning*. Washington, D.C: U. S. Department of Health, Education and Welfare, Bureau of Research, Office of Education 1968.

National Association of Student Personnel Administrators. *A Perspective on Student Affairs*. Iowa City, Iowa: American College Testing Program, 1987.

Outcalt, C. L., and Skewes-Cox, T. E. "Involvement, Interaction, and Satisfaction: The Human Environment at HBCUs." *The Review of Higher Education*, 2002, 25(3), 331–347.

Pascarella, E .T., and Terenzini, P. T. *How College Affects Students: A Third Decade of Research.* San Francisco: Jossey-Bass, 2005.

Peterson, M. W., and Spencer, M. G. *"Understanding Academic Climate and Culture."* In W. G. Tierney (Ed.), *Assessing Academic Climates and Cultures.* New Directions for Institutional Research, no. 68. San Francisco: Jossey-Bass, 1990.

Peterson, M. W., Cameron, K. S., Mets, L. A., Jones, P., and Ettington, D. *The Organizational Context for Teaching and Learning: A Review of the Research Literature.* Ann Arbor: National Center for Research to Improve Postsecondary Teaching and Learning, 1986.

Pike, G. R., and Kuh, G. D. "Relationships Among Structural Diversity, Informal Peer Interactions and Perceptions of the Campus Environment." *Review of Higher Education*, 2006, 29, 425–450.

Sax, L. J., and Others. *The American Freshman: National Norms for Fall 2003.* Los Angeles: University of California, Los Angeles, Higher Education Research Institute, 2003.

Schein, E. H. *Organizational Culture and Leadership.* San Francisco: Jossey-Bass, 1985.

Schilling, K. M., and Schilling, K. L. "Increasing Expectations for Student Effort." *About Campus*, 1999, 4(2), 4–10.

Strange, C., and Banning, J. *Educating by Design: Creating Campus Learning Environments That Work.* San Francisco: Jossey-Bass, 2001.

Tagg, J. *The Learning Paradigm College.* Bolton, Mass.: Anker, 2003.

Tinto, V. *Leaving College.* Chicago: University of Chicago Press, 1993.

Torres, V. "Mi Casa: Is Not Exactly Like Your House." *About Campus: Enriching the Student Learning Experience*, 2003, May-June, 2–7.

Townsend, B. K., Newell, L. J., and Wiese, M. D. *Creating Distinctiveness: Lessons from Uncommon Colleges and Universities.* ASHE-ERIC Higher Education Report, no. 6. Washington, D.C.: George Washington University, School of Education and Human Development, 1992.

Western Interstate Commission for Higher Education. *The Ecosystem Model: Designing Campus Environments.* Boulder, Colo.: Western Interstate Commission for Higher Education, 1973.

Whitt, E. J. "Making the Familiar Strange: Discovering Culture." In G. D. Kuh (Ed.), *Using Cultural Perspectives in Student Affairs Work.* Alexandria, Va.: ACPA Media, 1993.

Whitt, E. J., and Kuh, G. D. (1991). "Qualitative Research in Higher Education: A Team Approach to Multiple Site Investigation." *Review of Higher Education*, 1991, 14, 317–337.

CHAPTER FIVE

FISCAL PRESSURES ON HIGHER EDUCATION AND STUDENT AFFAIRS

John H. Schuh

These are challenging economic times for higher education. Raines (2000) has described the fiscal environment of higher education in dismal terms: "The effect of financial constraints on higher education from the 1980s to the present has been extensive. University administrators have had to modify their institutions' academic programs, administrative services and student affairs operations to contain costs and increase revenue" (p. 71). Sandeen and Barr (2006, p. 106) concluded, "If student affairs leaders are to achieve their goals on their campus, it is essential that they become expert fiscal managers, articulate advocates for their programs, creative resource procurers, and knowledgeable contributors to their institution's overall budget process."

As this chapter describes, many students are coming to our institutions from economic and social backgrounds that place them at risk; the federal government's agenda for higher education has resulted in increased costs for colleges and universities; and the overall costs of obtaining a higher education continue to escalate faster than the cost of living. In addition, institutions of higher education face increased costs for services, and deteriorating physical plants (nationally deferred maintenance is estimated to be $26 billion according to one study [National Commission on the Cost of Higher Education, 1998]) place further financial burdens on both public and private institutions. Perhaps most important, as Balderston (1995, p. xi) asserts, "In the past these institutions were capable of growing in many directions without having to assess mission or scope and without being specifically accountable, financially or otherwise, to funding agencies, the taxpaying public, faculty or students. That period is over, and universities are now asked to justify themselves."

Fiscal policies, economic constraints, and social conditions have a profound effect on the programs, services, learning opportunities, and activities developed by and offered in the student affairs division. This chapter examines a variety of factors that influence the fiscal environment in which the student affairs division operates. First, the economic implications of selected demographic and social trends are examined. Second, several federal initiatives are identified in the context of their economic impact on institutions of higher education. Third, trends related to state support of higher education will be provided. Finally, the cost to students of attending institutions of higher education and financial aid are discussed. Brief implications for student affairs are presented in each section.

Demographic and Social Trends

This section discusses selected demographic and social trends in the context of their financial implications for higher education. In 1990, Kuh observed that student affairs officers would have to deal with social issues that will affect the practice of student affairs in the future. Fifteen years later, Reason and Davis (2005) reported, "To maximize student learning both in and out of the classroom, we must improve intergroup relations on campus and create an environment that nurtures all students equitably" (p. 5). For reasons that will be examined later, many college students of the future may be at risk and may need additional support to be successful. This assistance will take the form of tutorial help, counseling, financial aid, and other assistance specific to individual campuses. Consider the following information about the students who are coming to college in the twenty-first century.

The Family

The number of two-parent households with children under eighteen has declined in the United States from 1990 to 2004 by 3.3 percent while single parent households with at last one natural child has increased (Snyder, Tan, and Hoffman, 2006, Table 18). From 1990 to 2005, the percentage of children under eighteen years old living in a family with both parents declined from 72.5 percent to 67.4 percent, according to the U.S. Census Bureau (2007). Those living in a family with just the mother present increased from 21.6 percent in

1990 to 23.4 percent in 2005. Using an international lens, compared with ten economically developed countries, the United States had the largest percentage of single-parent households in 2005. The United States also heads a list of twelve developed countries in divorce rates (U.S. Census Bureau, 2007).

Income distribution over the most recently reported ten- and twenty-year periods of time (1985 to 2005 and 1995 to 2005) has resulted in a greater concentration of income in the highest 20 percent of families (U.S. Census Bureau, 2008). From 1985 to 2005, the share of household income received by the lowest, second, third, and fourth quintile declined to the point where 80 percent of all families received less than 50 percent of all income. The share of income received by the highest quintile families increased from 46.1 percent in 1985 to 50.4 percent in 2005. The concentration of wealth in the highest quintile will make it difficult for institutions of higher education to make higher education available to students from families other than those that have the most robust economic circumstances.

Many traditional-age college students will continue to come from homes where divorce has occurred. As a result, many of these students may need help from their institution of higher education in the form of support groups, individual counseling, or other assistance in order to cope with a changed family structure. Expansion of or introduction of such services very well may result in additional fiscal pressures on student affairs divisions. These statistics lead to the second demographic trend that will affect students of the future: economic deprivation.

Poverty

Absence of a parent often means limited financial support, lack of nurturing, and negative psychological and social effects on children (Bianchi, 1990). The economic consequences of growing up in single-parent households are of particular concern. The U.S. Census Bureau (2007) estimates that the median family income for two-parent families was $62,281 in 2003, compared with $26,550 for families with only the female parent present.

The U.S. Census Bureau (2007) reported that 17.3 percent of all children lived in poverty in 2004, a decline from 17.9 percent in 1990 but an increase from 15.6 percent in 2000. Families headed by females only were far more likely to live in poverty (28.4 percent) than families headed by married couples (5.5 percent). In 2005 more than two thirds of all African American (70 percent), Hispanic (73 percent), and American Indian (65 percent) fourth graders were eligible for free or reduced-price lunch programs (U.S. Department of Education, 2006b, p. 33).

Many traditional-age students of the future will come from one-parent families in which the only provider is the mother. As we have seen, the data reveal that the income of these families often falls below the poverty line. Students from these families potentially will require substantial amounts of financial aid in order to enroll in college. Additionally, the students may require special efforts on the part of colleges and universities to attract them to college in the first place, because many of them may come from families in which the remaining parent has not graduated from college or even thought about attending an institution of higher education. This situation, in turn, will make it more costly to recruit these students. It is incumbent on institutions to provide more programming for parents that describes the benefits of college attendance, because individuals unfamiliar with institutions of higher education may find the language, traditions, and culture of colleges complex and difficult to understand (Kuh and Whitt, 1988).

School Enrollment

The percentage of young people of color enrolled in elementary and secondary schools has grown dramatically over the past two decades and should be an indication of this century's college population. Unfortunately, young people from underrepresented minority groups do not enroll in institutions of higher education to the extent that they attend elementary and secondary schools, according to federal reports. Whites comprised 78 percent of the enrollment in elementary and secondary schools in 1972 and were 57 percent of the enrollment in 2004 (Snyder and others, 2006, p. 342). African Americans have increased their numbers from 15 percent of children attending elementary and secondary schools in 1972 to 16 percent of those enrolled in 2004 (U.S. Department of Education, 2006b, p. 32). But they constituted only 9.4 percent of all students attending college in 1976 and 12.5 percent in 2004 (Snyder and others, 2006, p. 342), although that percentage of such students had increased from 4.8 percent in 1965 (U.S. Department of Education, 1997, p. 221).

Similarly, the representation of Latino/a youth has increased in elementary and secondary schools, but they are not enrolled proportionately in institutions of postsecondary education. The percentage of Latino/a children enrolled in elementary and secondary schools grew from 6 percent of all those enrolled in 1976 to 19 percent in 2006 (U.S. Department of Education, 2006b, p. 32). These students, however, made up only 3.5 percent of college students in 1976 and 10.5 percent in 2004 (Snyder and others, 2006, p. 342).

Another dimension of the students of the future is worthy of note: the percentage of students ages five to seventeen who come from homes where a language other than English is spoken at home is increasing. As a percentage of the total population, these students have grown from 8.5 percent in 1979 to 18.8 percent in 2004. While the percentage of those who spoke a language other than English at home has grown, the percentage that spoke English with difficulty has declined, however, from 34.2 percent in 1979 to 27.9 percent in 2004 (U.S. Department of Education, 2006b).

It is clear that student bodies of the future will contain an increasingly larger percentage of students of color and students from families where English has not been spoken as the primary language. Additional financial investments may be required to provide staff time, perhaps staff members, and targeted programs, as has been recommended many times in the student affairs literature (for example, Cuyjet, 1998; Tippeconnic Fox, Lowe, and McClellan, 2005; Howard-Hamilton, 2003; and Ortiz, 2004). Brown, Hinton, and Howard-Hamilton (2007) conclude that "without appropriate amount of assets (academic preparation, financial aid, social capital, mentoring, faculty of color) they (students from under represented populations) continue to struggle in these often indifferent and unwelcoming institutions" (p. 3).

Federal Higher Education Initiatives

This section reviews selected federal legislative and regulatory developments of recent years. Specific attention is given to the fiscal implications of these initiatives.

Access for Those with Disabilities

One category of federal regulation in higher education is access for those with disabilities. With the passage of Section 504 of the Rehabilitation Act of 1973 (reauthorized in 1992) and the Americans with Disabilities Act (1990), colleges and universities incurred additional costs in the course of serving students who heretofore had not participated in campus life and who are entitled to reasonable accommodations in pursing their educational aspirations. A particular area of growth and expense has been the enrollment of and corresponding services for students with learning disabilities.

Among the implications of these initiatives for student affairs officers are that reserves may be tapped for residence hall, student union, or other facility modifications; staff must be identified and programs developed to assist those with disabilities; accessible Web sites, documents, brochures, and other printed material may have to be provided in formats to meet the needs of the visually impaired; interpreters will be needed for public events; assistive technology will need to be provided; and that those with disabilities will expect student affairs officers to serve as their advocates, even though the potential costs associated with the changes they desire may be substantial.

Regulatory Compliance

Another category of federal initiatives deals with regulatory compliance. The burdens of some of these regulations are relatively light because all that is required is a certain degree of documentation. In other cases, a substantial amount of legislation has been passed that in turn requires institutions to engage in compliance activities that can be changed quite frequently, thereby incurring additional costs. For example, the Family Educational Rights and Privacy Act has been changed nine times according to Jackson, Terrell, and Heard (2007), and in each case institutions have had to adjust their practices to stay in compliance with the federal legislation. Hunter and Gehring (2005) estimated that at one institution the cost of compliance with federal legislation was 11.7 cents out of every tuition dollar received. In cases such as campus safety, draft registration, or other similar activities, there is no funding to help institutions stay in compliance.

Consumer Protection

A third category on the federal agenda, which might be termed "consumer protection legislation," has placed additional financial burdens on colleges and universities for the foreseeable future. Federal law has stipulated that institutions of higher education notify faculty and students on a regular basis about the institution's substance abuse policy, laws related to the use of alcohol and other drugs, and programs available to provide assistance to those who seek help (Drug-Free Schools and Communities Act Amendments of 1989, Public Law 101–226). Starting with the 1992–93 academic year, institutions have been required to provide each current student and employee with information related to graduation rates, campus safety, and criminal activity (Student Right-to-Know and Campus Security Act, Public Law 101–542, more recently amended and known as the Jeanne Clery Act) (U. S. Department of Education, 2005). Failure to comply with Department of Education regulations can result in financial penalties for institutions. Lowery (2007) cites one instance where an institution paid a fine of $200,000 for failure to comply with certain elements of the Clery Act. Some institutions have published such reports and provided printed copies to members of the campus community. Lowery (2007) has indicated, "Using the

Internet to distribute the Annual Security Reports is a far more cost-effective method of sharing this information" (p. 210).

The implications of consumer legislation include costs related to preparation and distribution of materials. For example, the law requires that every student receive certain information about campus crime each year. At a college where each student has a campus mailbox this has minimal implications, but the costs associated with a commuter student body may be considerably greater. As crimes are detected and members of the campus advised of criminal activity, including providing timely warnings about criminal activity (Lowery, 2007), additional costs will be incurred in the notification process.

The agenda of the federal government is captured in the report from the Spellings Commission (U.S. Department of Education, 2006a). The report indicated that greater accountability, among other things, is being sought from institutions of higher education. Concern about the cost of higher education was expressed in the report, particularly as it affects access to institutions of higher education. These dimensions of the report have implications for the financial framework of our institutions, ranging from having to justify increases in the cost of attendance to providing more information to stakeholders about how institutional resources are deployed.

Issues Related to State Finance

Before reviewing specific factors and trends influencing the financing of higher education, it is useful to take a moment to describe some of the financial issues faced by the states. State governments have had to contend with a fundamental shift in their relationship with the federal government that has had dramatic implications for their budgets. Consider several issues, listed here in cursory form, that have both short- and long-term implications for higher education.

A number of the programs that have been transferred to the states have become competitors with higher education for state funding. Included in this group are hazardous waste control, transportation, and welfare. In addition, there are the costs of operating prisons for an ever-growing population, health care and housing, rising costs of PK–12 education, and a continuous pressure to reduce taxes. Just one example illustrates the situation. As a percentage of the population, adults who are on probation, in jail or prison, or on parole has grown from 1.7 percent to 3.2 percent from 1985 to 2004 according to the U.S. Census Bureau (2007). All of these people need to be provided with supervision that comes with a cost that must be funded. The competition higher education faces for state support has become keen, indeed. When one examines sources of current fund revenue for public institutions of higher education, state appropriations as percentage of revenue received by public institutions of higher education have declined from 1980–81 to 2000–01. In 1980–81, state appropriations comprised 45.6 percentage of all current fund revenue. In 2000–01, this funding had declined to 35.6 percent (Snyder and others, 2006, p. 533). Much of the decline has been made up by tuition increases. Over this same period of time, tuition income at public degree-granting institutions as a percentage of income increased from 12.9 percent to 18.1 percent (Snyder and others).

Institutions should not look to their states for relief from regulation. State governmental regulation has also placed additional burdens on colleges and universities. State involvement has taken on many forms (budgeting, program assessment, and political intrusion) and exists for many purposes (improving academic quality, economic competitiveness, access, and degree attainment [Fenske and Johnson, 1990]).

The pressures on state budgets continue to be manifested in declining support for higher education as measured by the percentage of revenue received by public degree-granting institutions. Consequently, it is also clear that many public institutions of higher education will not be able to turn to their legislatures for substantial increases in funding. In the best scenario, public institutions may be able to receive adjustments in their budgets that correspond to the cost of inflation. In the worst scenario, institutions may experience continued disappointment, as was reported recently in Oregon, where "six of the Oregon University system's seven campuses—all but the University of Oregon—had their budgets reduced during the last two-year budget period" (Fischer, 2007, p. A16). It is unlikely that a majority of public colleges and universities will be successful in their attempts to receive substantially greater support from their state governments in the future.

Private institutions have experienced similar economic pressures. At private not-for-profit institutions, tuition income as percentage of total revenues has increased from 27 percent in 1996–97 to 34 percent in 2002–03 (Snyder and others, 2006, p. 541). Aggressive fund raising and gift and endowment income at these institutions cannot meet all the perceived needs of these institutions. Indeed, as a percentage of general fund revenue, private gifts and grants have increased only slightly from 1980–81 (12.31 percent) to 2002–03 (13.6 percent) at private institutions (Snyder and others, 2006, p. 541), which helped compensate for tuition shortfalls.

As institutions of higher education are adversely affected by state budget problems, student affairs units have been fortunate to maintain the status quo that has existed over the past two decades. Student affairs expenditures at all public universities were 4.6 percent of all educational and general expenditures in 1980–81 and were 4.9 percent in 2000–01 (Snyder and others, 2006,

p. 553). Those student affairs units funded by general revenues (state support and tuition) will be in fierce competition with academic units for resources. Those funded by user fees and fees for service (such as student housing or student unions) can expect to contribute more money to their institutions through overhead charges for human resources, accounting and purchasing services, security, and the like. Plus, those units funded by student fees will be subject to the vagaries of enrollment. If enrollment declines, so will revenue on a per student basis. Regardless of the funding source, student affairs units will be challenged to maintain an adequate funding base for the foreseeable future.

Factors Affecting State Finance of Higher Education

When one examines the relationship of higher education to the states, it is important to remember that the United States does not have a national system of higher education. "State governments, more than any other single element in American society, have assumed the responsibility of financing public higher education" (Alexander, 2003, p. 15). As a consequence, a study of state financing of higher education is really a study of fifty different entities rather than just one. Moreover, Alexander asserts, "The apparent result of the overall federal policy is to reward richer states for the lack of tax effort for public higher education" (2003, p. 14).

Review of Expenditures. Increasingly, governing boards, legislatures, coordinating councils, students, parents, and virtually anyone else who has a perceived interest in this area are scrutinizing expenditures of higher education institutions. As mentioned earlier, state funding is being squeezed, and the result is that careful attention is being paid to how financial resources are being spent.

Lowry (2003) studied the effects of governance structures on public university prices and spending. What he found was that "public universities in institutional settings that enhance political oversight tend to charge lower prices than public universities that have more autonomy" (p. 51). He adds, however, that "I cannot say what students in high-tuition systems get for their money, but increased spending on activities such as instruction, student services and academic support may lead to benefits for many students" (p. 51).

Student affairs officers can expect that expenditures will continue to receive careful scrutiny. This is not to suggest that care has not been exercised in the past. It has. But as resources become increasingly restricted, institutions likely will examine their funding for student affairs and other nonacademic units with a more powerful microscope and perhaps with an eye to finding resources that could be diverted to support other institutional activities.

Disenchanted Taxpayers. As witnessed by the tax revolt in California (Proposition 13) more than a quarter of a century ago, taxpayers across the country are demanding and winning cuts in property taxes (Yinger, 1990). "Many state governments, in response to their own fiscal and deficit problems, have reduced subsidies for state institutions of higher education and scholarship programs for private institutions" (Lennington, 1996, p. ix). States vary dramatically in the amount of effort they exert in providing funding for public university and community colleges and private, not for private institutions (Alexander, 2003). As noted previously, higher education has become a competitor with other activities for state funds: "Citizen movements like California's Proposition 13 can have an impact on higher education, as a decline in local tax revenues places greater burdens on the state to provide services previously assumed by the localities" (Hauptman, 1990, p. 16).

Productivity. As part of the call for increased accountability, institutions have been asked to develop measures of productivity. Benchmarking has become a common form of measuring how well institutions do relative to each other (Bender and Schuh, 2002), and strategic indicators have been developed help institutions as they engage in self-evaluations (Taylor and Massy, 1996).

Faculty and academic administrators represent the largest concentration of expenditures in higher education (Lennington, 1996, p. 116) and will be called upon to demonstrate increasingly greater levels of productivity because they represent the largest proportions of institutional expenditures. Similar demonstrations of effectiveness will be required of student affairs practitioners. Sandeen and Barr (2006) assert that assessment is now "at the center stage of colleges and universities and it may be the dominant issued in American higher education now, as the forces driving assessment have in effect moved many of the critical decisions institutions make increasingly to external bodies, such as state legislatures and accrediting associations" (p. 136). Schuh and Upcraft (2001) assert that student affairs needs to respond to global pressures of accountability as well as to internal pressure to justify the allocation of resources to programs and services that appear to be nonacademic and, therefore, less essential. Woodard, Love, and Komives (2000, p. 77) add, "Assessment and evaluation processes should be in place such that we are able to demonstrate, with empirical evidence, the importance of our work and the student outcomes that result from our programs and services."

Student affairs units are seen by some (for example, Lennington, 1996) as adding to the cost of higher education. Balderston (1995) recommends that (student) service units should be self-financing and "charge each user a price that will ostensibly at least, cover the cost" (pp. 128–129). Charging user fees, however, is merely a means of shifting the costs from tuition charges to other sources and has little or no benefit to the student, who pays for the service either as part of a tuition bill or a fee bill. Still another option is to charge specific users for services. Schuh (2003) provides more detailed information about student fees.

In the future, staff can expect to work more efficiently, harder, and perhaps longer, but technology will not necessarily make jobs easier or help staff be more productive. In fact, as Moneta (2005) points out, while technology has provided improved information for administrators, it has come with a cost. "Administrators naively predicted great cost savings while anticipating the achievement of widespread access to better and more reliable data. Generally the latter objective was achieved, but seldom with significant cost savings" (2005, p. 8).

One approach to limiting costs related to technology has been an increasing reliance on partnerships and outsourcing. Such units as bookstores and food services have been outsourced on some campuses, meaning that contractual arrangements have been established with an outside vendor to provide goods, services, or both. Askew (2001) adds, "As colleges and universities recognize the necessity of diversifying their sources of revenue for operating the institution, senior officers in student affairs must develop a new mind-set and find new ways to enlarge the resource base for departments within their purview" (p. 81).

The Public-Private Dilemma

An especially vexing issue confronting the financing of higher education by state governments is the extent to which government ought to support private institutions. Though private colleges and universities constitute over half of the country's institutions of higher education ("Almanac," 2006, p. 8), their total enrollment is less than a quarter of all individuals attending institutions of higher education ("Almanac," 2006, p. 16). The average in-state resident charges for tuition, fees, room and board at a four-year public institution in 2006–07 totaled $12,796, whereas similar charges at a residential four-year private institution averaged $30,367 (College Board, 2006a, p. 5). Direct aid from states to private not-for-profit institutions has remained less than 1.5 percent from 1996–97 through 2002–03 (Snyder and others, 2006, p. 541).

Tax strategies vary dramatically from state to state and region to region. Alexander (2003) observed, "Many wealthy states located primarily in the Northeast advance fiscal strategies of high tuition and high aid for their public campuses while investing comparatively little public resources directly to their public colleges and universities. New York, Maine, New Hampshire, Vermont, and Massachusetts spend comparatively little resources on students attending public campuses, but these same states are among the leaders in allocating public resources to private college and university students and institutions" (pp. 22–23).

Although public institutions rely on state support to a much greater degree than private institutions, virtually every college or university in the country is affected to some degree by the amount of financing that the states can provide, whether through direct support to institutions or financial aid programs to students. There is little doubt that the competition between public and private institutions for state dollars—often revolving around whether states ought to provide direct support to students (through financial aid programs, thereby favoring private colleges) or direct support to institutions (thereby favoring public colleges)—has the potential to become more heated. Regardless of the direction of the debate, Lennington (1996) asserts, "Many state governments, in response to their own fiscal and deficit problems, have reduced subsidies for state institutions of higher education and scholarship programs for private institutions" (p. ix).

Selected Factors Influencing the Financial Health of Institutions

A variety of factors influence the fiscal health of colleges and universities. Several are discussed in detail in this section.

Revenues

Revenues have a dramatic and important effect on the financial status of colleges and universities. "Institutions generally rely on six main sources for revenues: students or parents, federal government, state government, private gifts, endowments, and auxiliary enterprises" (Toutkoushian, 2003, p. 27). Students and their families pay tuition, fees, room-and-board expenses and buy books and supplies. State governments, as mentioned earlier, provide direct aid to public institutions and financial aid to students who attend private institutions. The federal government sponsors financial aid programs and supports research and creative activities. Individuals, foundations, and corporations furnish gifts and grants to colleges and universities; and financial markets provide income for these institutions through revenue generated from investments of endowments and operating funds. In general, the mix of revenues has changed from 1980–81 to 2000–01. Income from tuition and fees, private gifts and contracts, and sales and services has grown over this period of time, whereas federal support and state appropriations declined as revenue sources (Snyder and others, 2006, p. 533).

Tuition. Tuition is the most important source of income for many not-for-profit degree-granting private institutions of higher education. In 1996–97, tuition represented 27.79 percent of total revenue, whereas by 2002–03, this percentage had increased to 34.09 percent (Snyder and others, 2006, p. 541). Taylor and Massy (1996) concluded as a result of a study of nearly 1,000 institutions that almost all private institutions are tuition driven, and, of course, tuition and fee income is also significant for public institutions.

Fund Raising. Private colleges depend more on private, foundation, and corporate contributions than do public institutions, but the latter have also begun to rely more on donations—a situation that puts them squarely in competition for these funds with the private sector. During the 2004–05 fiscal year, seven of the ten institutions that were the "top fund raisers" were private ("Almanac," 2006, p. 30). Revenues from investments reflect the fruits of gifts and donations. In some years the returns are relatively robust, but in other years, reflecting a difficult investment environment, returns may be disappointing. The implications of poor investment returns are obvious: less money may be available from one year to the next and hence other sources of funding to support the activity, project, scholarship, and so on would be available. Other sources may not be easy to come by, and the activity may have to be limited or cut.

Student Costs

This section uses the term, "costs," in the sense that students and their families typically use it: cost to them. The cost of attending college continues to rise at a rate much higher than the commonly accepted measure of inflation, the Consumer Price Index. To illustrate the growth in student costs, the average in-state cost of attending a four-year public institution in 1986–87 was $2,628 for tuition and fees. By 2006–07, the cost had risen to $5,836. Similarly, the cost of private higher education had risen dramatically. In 1986–87, the average cost of tuition and fees at a private institution was $12,375. By 2006–07, the cost of tuition and fees for a year at a private college had grown to $22,218, according to the College Board (2006a, p. 7). These costs were reported in constant 2006 dollars. At public two-year colleges, the cost of tuition and fees increased from $1,227 to $2,272 from 1986–87 to 2006–07.

Cost of attendance varies widely along a number of dimensions: geographical location, state policy, type of control (public versus private), type of institution (such as regional baccalaureate granting versus doctoral granting with an international profile), and perceived prestige of the institution, among others. A student attending a private institution in one state very well could face a lower cost of attendance than a student attending a public four-year institution in another. To be sure, however, no claims are made to equate cost with quality. More data on this subject are available from Snyder and others (2006).

Financial Aid Trends

Clearly, one of the responses to the growth in the cost of attendance has been the widespread development of financial aid programs. Sixty percent of all full-time undergraduate students who attended college in 1989–90 received some form of financial aid, but participation in financial aid programs increased to 74 percent in 1999–2000 (Wei, Li, and Berkner, 2004, p. 14). Students attending private not-for-profit institutions were more likely to participate in financial aid programs in 2003–04 (88.6 percent) than those attending public institutions (71.1 percent) (Snyder and others, 2006, Table 320). This difference, in part, can be attributed to participation in institutional aid programs. More than half of the students who attended private colleges and universities (64.9 percent) participated in institutional aid programs, compared with 23.6 percent of students who attended public institutions. These data reflect full-time enrollment (Snyder and others, 2006, Table 319).

From 1991–92 through 2005–06, the emphasis of financial aid to undergraduates has shifted from grants to loans. In 1991–92, just over 40 percent of all aid to undergraduates took the form of loans, but by 2005–06, 52 percent of all aid was loans. Aid in the form of grants has declined from just under 60 percent in 1991–92 to 42 percent in 2005–06 (College Board, 2006b, p. 15). The purchasing power of Pell grants has gained modestly over the past decade. In 1995–96, the average Pell grant was worth $1,946. By 2002–03, it was worth $2,648, but by 2005–06 it was worth $2,354 in constant 2005 dollars (College Board, 2006b, Table 3).

Loan Programs. Loans have become the most common form of federal aid during the time period from 1992–93 to 2003–04. Thirty-one percent of all undergraduates received federal loans in 1992–93, but by 2003–04, 48 percent of all undergraduates received federal loans. Students receiving federal grants increased from 30 percent in 1992–93 to 34 percent in 2003–04. Low-income dependent undergraduates with federal loans decreased from 48 percent in 1992–93 to 47 percent in 2003–04 (U.S. Department of Education, 2006b, p. 100).

The percentage increase in participation in loan programs is about equal whether the student attended a public or private four-year institution. The growth was from 25.5 percent in 1992–93 to 42.6 percent participation in loan programs at public institutions in 2003–04, and from 45.4 percent to 66 percent at private not-for-profit colleges and universities in 2003–04. Students who attended two-year public colleges borrowed less than their counterparts who enrolled at four-year institutions. For two-year college students the increase was from 12.1 percent in 1992–93 to 26.4 percent (Snyder and others, 2006, Table 320).

In the 2003–04 academic year, full-time undergraduates who borrowed at community colleges borrowed, on average, $4,100. At public four-year institutions, full-time undergraduate students borrowed, on average, $5,800. Full-time undergraduate students who attended private not-for-profit four-year institutions borrowed on average $7,200, and 80 percent of all full-time undergraduate students who attended private for-profit institutions borrowed, averaging $7,800 per student (Berkner and Wei, 2006).

Students attending graduate or professional school have to deal with even greater financial challenges. The data indicate that a substantial majority of students seeking a first professional degree borrow. According to Snyder and others (2006, Table 325) 67.8 percent of first professional students received loans, compared with 25.8 percent of doctor's degree students and 32.1 percent of master's degree students in 1992–93. By 2003–04, the percentage of full-time professional degree-seeking students who borrowed increased to 84.7 percent, compared with 58.4 percent of master's degree-seeking students and 38.4 percent of doctor's degree-seeking students. The difference between these cohorts of students presumably lies in the greater availability of graduate assistantships for master's and doctoral students. Such support typically is not as readily available for students seeking professional degrees.

Clearly, loans have emerged as the most common form of federal student financial aid. More than half of all financial aid consists of federal loans ($68.6 billion) according to the College Board (2006b). Subsidized and unsubsidized Stafford loans account for 68 percent of all student loans (College Board, 2006b). Federal loans are especially common for students at private, not-for-profit four-year colleges and universities, where 64.4 percent of all undergraduates participated in some form of federal loan program (Snyder and others, 2006, Table 320).

Tuition Discounting. Another strategy is the development of tuition discounting, which is an increasingly common strategy at private institutions. "Under tuition discounting plans, colleges use their institutional grants to reduce the tuition and fee charges students would otherwise be unable or unwilling to pay to attend particular higher education institutions. The discounts may be funded by tuition and fee revenue (the collective amounts of tuition and fees students and their families pay to attend postsecondary education institutions), donations from alumni or other private sources, and earnings from endowments" (Redd, 2000, p. 5).

Discounting, however, does not always work to the financial advantage of the institution. "Unfortunately, at least one quarter of the private colleges and universities paid a steep price for this achievement. The rapid use of tuition discounting led to large losses in net tuition revenue and have resulted in decreased spending on instruction and other services to students" (Redd, 2000, p. 3). Davis (2003) reached the same conclusion from another study of institutions that had discounted their tuition: "Another unexpected consequence of tuition discounting is that it does not always increase an institution's net revenue" (p. 24). The consequence of a circumstance such as this for student affairs is obvious: less institutional income means that potential budget reductions are a very real possibility, meaning that student affairs units will have fewer resources to support the delivery of their programs and services to students.

In the twenty-first century, those from families with modest financial resources who are considering becoming college students are likely to be forced to work more hours to finance their education, to take on greater debt burden, or both. In a study of the working poor, McSwain and Davis (2007) concluded that youth from working poor backgrounds "often find themselves in a precarious position—reaching for the education that many of their parents have not attained, yet lacking the financial and auxiliary support to help them achieve their goal" (p. 6). Institutions seeking to attract students from families with modest financial resources will be confronted with the expenses related to offering additional financial aid, additional campus employment, and additional support services.

As an economic policy issue, the matter of students increasingly turning to loans to finance their college education does not augur well for the future financial health of the United States, where consumer spending represents a significant proportion of all economic activity. Students who are strapped with heavy college loan debts will be less able to buy appliances, cars, homes, or other items that require long-term financing.

College Attendance and Low Income

One of the objectives of federal policy, almost regardless of administration, has been to provide greater access to postsecondary education for students from modest economic backgrounds. In some respects, financial aid programs have been developed to increase access to students, but in actual practice institutional aid has been awarded to students from middle- to high-income families in amounts that suggest using aid to attract able students is as important to institutions of higher education as opening doors to students from the modest economic circumstances.

Federal Aid. The demographic trends in the first section of this chapter indicate that an increasing proportion of college students will be from low-income backgrounds, so this objective is consistent with the population trends of the country. Using a definition of low income as "the bottom 20 percent of all family incomes" (U.S. Department of Education, 2006, p. 225), a substantial proportion of low-income students participated in financial aid programs. More than 85.5 percent received grants, whereas 49 percent received loans in 2003–04. Nearly half (47.5 percent) participated in federal loan programs (U.S. Department of Education, 2006, p. 211). Students from middle-income families were slightly more likely to borrow (49.5 percent) but were less likely to receive grants (58 percent).

Institutional Aid. Institutional aid to low-income students has increased from 1992–93 to 1999–2000 (U.S. Department of Education, 2006, p. 211). The percentage of students from low-income families receiving institutional aid has increased from 52.8 percent in 1992–93 to 55 percent in 1999–2000, and the amount of institutional aid received by students, in constant 1999 dollars, has increased on average from $5,500 in 1992–93 to $6,200 in 1999–2000. The amount of aid low-income students received ($6,200 per student), however, is less than the institutional aid received by students from middle-income families, who, on average, received $7,500 in institutional aid in 2003–04. In addition, while the percentage of students from high-income families who received institutional aid is less than those from low-income families (51.2 percent compared with 55.7 percent), on average students from high-income received more aid ($6,800 per student compared with $6,200 per student) (U.S. Department of Education, 2004, p. 182). What these data demonstrate is that institutions use available financial aid not only to widen access to students from modest economic backgrounds but also to attract students from middle- and high-income families.

Work as a Financing Option

One other option for students who attend institutions of higher education is to work while they are enrolled. This is an option that a large proportion of undergraduates use to finance college attendance, at least in part. For example, in 1999–2000, 80.1 percent of undergraduates reported working. Full-time students worked 25.5 hours per week on average (U.S. Department of Education, 2006, Table 37–1). Including students who can be defined as employees who study (U.S. Department of Education, 2004, p. 82), students who attended community colleges worked the most hours, 36.0 hours week, followed by those who attended public colleges and universities (27.3 hours per week) and private not-for-profit colleges and universities (26.5 hours per week) (U.S. Department of Education, 2004, p. 198).

Students who worked more hours reported that work had some negative effects on their college experiences. For example, fewer than 20 percent of students who worked 1–15 hours per week reported that work had a negative effect on their experiences. Students who indicated that they worked 16–20 hours per week reported that work had a negative effect on their grades (30.2 percent), whereas 39.9 percent of those who reported working 21–34 hours per week indicated that working had a negative effect on their grades. Of those who reported working 35 or more hours per week, 47.9 percent reported that work had a negative effect on their grades, 63.3 percent that working limited the number of classes they could take, 70.0 percent that working limited their class schedules, and 47.9 percent that it limited their access to the library. More than half (53 percent) indicated that working 35 or more hours reduced their choice of classes. According to another study, "Among students who worked to pay school expenses, the more hours they worked, the more likely they were to report that their work schedule limited their class schedule, reduced the number of classes they could take and reduced their class choices" (U.S. Department of Education, 1998, p. 122). Students who worked more hours, however, were less likely to borrow to pay for their education. Those who worked 1 to 15 hours per week participated in loan programs at a 49 percent rate, compared with 32 percent of those who worked 35 or more hours per week (U.S. Department of Education, 2002, p. 101).

Still, not all students who work are affected adversely from the experience. Pascarella, Edison, Nora, Hagedorn, and Terenzini (1998) found in a study of 3,840 students enrolled at twenty-three institutions that "for the most part, work during college that does not exceed 15–20 hours per week does not seriously inhibit students' intellectual growth." They added in a summary of empirical research, "The research on the effects of employment on persistence and degree completion consistently indicates that the more hours students work, the more likely they are to shift from full-time to part-time enrollment and the less likely they are to persist from one year to the next or to complete a bachelor's degree program" (Pascarella and Terenzini, 2005, p. 415).

Managing Debt

With an increase in the number of students who are borrowing and the amount of money that students borrow increasing, a logical concern centers on the long-term effect of borrowing the lives of the borrowers. Just under half the graduates who received their degrees in 1992–93 borrowed, on average, $12,100 (in 1999 constant dollars). A larger percentage of 1999–2000 students borrowed (65.4 percent), and they borrowed a larger amount ($19,300). Students from families from the lower-income quartile were more likely to borrow in 1999–2000 (72.1 percent), but they borrowed a lesser amount ($17,800) than their colleagues from wealthier families (U.S. Department of Education, 2004, p. 183).

To date, college graduates have been able to manage their debt. The average amount that college graduates who completed their degrees in 1992–93 paid each month to service their debt was $150, with the median amount being $130 (Choy and Li, 2006, p. 29). Nearly three quarters (74 percent) of those who had not enrolled in an additional degree program had paid off their student loans (Choy and Li, 2006). Just under 10 percent had defaulted, but 44.5 percent of those who had defaulted reentered repayment (Choy and Li, 2006, p. 43). Since more students are borrowing, and they are borrowing in ever-increasing amounts, it is difficult to predict if current borrowers will be as successful in repaying their loans as their predecessors have been.

It is difficult to predict the future of higher education, but the financial aid trends identified may have a serious impact on higher education delivery systems of the future. The longitudinal data suggest the following:

- More students are participating in financial aid programs.
- More students are participating in institutional financial aid programs and are receiving institutional grants, particularly at private, not-for-profit institutions.
- More students are working, and they are working long hours to pay for their educations.
- More students are borrowing money to pay for their educations, and those who borrow are borrowing more money than in the past.

Fund Raising

One option that student affairs practitioners can employ to increase their resource base is to engage in fund raising. Fund raising can be conducted to create endowments for specific projects, such as securing support for an annual event such as a dinner for student leaders, or for an ongoing project, such as scholarships for students who meet certain criteria—participation in community service or being a single parent. Fund raising also can be targeted toward capital projects such as building new facilities, renovating buildings, purchasing equipment, and so on.

Jackson (2000) provides an excellent primer on the basic elements of fund raising. Without question, he is correct in urging student affairs officers to engage in fund-raising activities at their institutions. It is important to note that developing relationships with prospective donors can take a substantial amount of time. In many respects, fund raising is a process by which the interests of potential benefactors have to be matched with institutional needs. That does not occur overnight; rather it is the result of a process that can take an extended period of time.

Not all potential donors will decide to support a project. Thus, the results of fund-raising efforts can be disappointing when substantial time in invested in a potential donor who chooses to contribute to other projects on campus or chooses not to support any project at all.

Development work does not occur in an institutional vacuum. That is, fund raising requires developing partnerships with the institution's development office. In many respects, development offices are charged with making sure that institutional priorities are addressed through coordinated efforts. The point of such coordination is to ensure that a single prospect is not asked repeatedly for small gifts—for example, for student leaders to attend a regional conference—when a large gift for a building may be the institution's highest priority.

It is also important to note that funds raised for endowments such as a fund developed to support a leadership dinner form a corpus from which only a portion of the income can be spent. The amount of spendable income can increase or decline depending on investment results. While different formulas are applied to spending from endowments, one approach is to use an average of the return on the endowment for the three previous years. So, if the endowment returned 4 percent in Year 1, 5 percent in Year 2, and 6 percent in Year 3, in Year 4 the average of the previous three years would be 5 percent, and that amount could be spent in line with the purpose of the endowment. The amount of money that institutions spend on their endowment has been a subject of concern in recent months (Wolverton, 2008) and has resulted in different formulas being devised by some institutions to govern spending practices (Fain, 2008).

Institutions with foundations or development offices, or both, will have guidelines that govern development activities. These must be adhered to in the fund-raising process. A student body president from twenty years ago might be a logical prospect for the student affairs division, but this person might already be "spoken for" by the dean of the academic college from which the person received a degree. So, constituencies need to be developed much as is the case with campus libraries and museums. Several natural constituency groups can be developed while students are still undergraduates, and they can become prospects as they develop the financial wherewithal to make gifts to their alma mater. Among these are student government officers, resident assistants, union board members, student leaders in recreational sports, and so on. They will have a good understanding of the contributions various student affairs units have made to their education, and they very well may be supportive of fund-raising efforts in student affairs long after they have graduated. Developing resources through fund raising should be crafted carefully as part of a long-range resource enhancement plan for student affairs, but this process will start with the development of good relationships with student constituencies while they are undergraduates.

Conclusion

This chapter has been developed during a period of relatively poor economic times. Unemployment rates are increasing and state revenues have declined from the stronger economic years of the middle part of this decade. Typically, in times of economic hardship, enrollments increase but state support declines. That would provide a set of challenges for institutions of higher education to resolve, although the typical approach has been to increase the cost of attendance at an accelerated rate, resulting in higher costs for students. The economic challenges that higher education has faced in periods of relative economic health have been difficult to manage. No doubt the fiscal challenges to higher education will prove even more difficult in tough economic times. Perhaps one can take comfort in higher education's resiliency and ability to manage such challenges in the past. The economic experiences of the 1930s and 1970s are examples of time periods when higher education leaders faced enormous problems and managed to address them satisfactorily in the face of increasing enrollments and demands by various stakeholders. On that point of optimism, one can hope that the past is prologue.

References

Alexander, F. K. "Comparative Study of State Tax Effort and the Role of Federal Government Policy in Shaping Revenue Reliance Patterns." In F. K. Alexander and R. C. Ehrenberg (Eds.), *Maximizing Revenue in Higher Education*. New Directions for Institutional Research, no. 119. San Francisco: Jossey-Bass, 2003.

"Almanac." *Chronicle of Higher Education.* August 25, 2006, pp. 3–42.

Americans with Disabilities Act of 1990. Public Law 101–336, 42 U.S.C. 12101–12132.

Askew, P. E. "The University as a Source for Community and Academic Partnerships." In L. H. Dietz and E. J. Enchelmayer (Eds.), *Developing External Partnerships for Cost-Effective, Enhanced Service.* New Directions for Student Services, no. 96. San Francisco: Jossey-Bass, 2001.

Balderston, F. E. *Managing Today's University* (2nd ed.) San Francisco: Jossey-Bass, 1995.

Bender, B. E., and Schuh, J. H. (Eds.). *Using Benchmarking to Inform Practice in Higher Education.* New Directions for Higher Education, no. 118. San Francisco: Jossey-Bass, 2002.

Berkner, L., and Wei, C. C. *Student Financing of Undergraduate Education: 2003–04.* (NCES 2006–186). U.S. Department of Education. Washington, D.C.: National Center for Education Statistics, 2006.

Bianchi, S. M. "America's Children: Mixed Results." *Population Bulletin,* 1990, 45(4), 3–41.

Brown, O. G., Hinton, K. G., and Howard-Hamilton, M. "Unleashing Suppressed Voices at Colleges and Universities: The Role of Case Studies in Understanding Diversity in Higher Education." In *Unleashing Suppressed Voices on College Campuses.* New York: Lang, 2007.

Choy, S. P., and Li, X. *Dealing with Debt: 1992–1993 Bachelor's Degree Recipients 10 Years Later* (NCES 2006–156). Washington, D.C.: National Center for Education Statistics, 2006.

The College Board. *Trends in College Pricing.* Washington, D.C.: Author, 2006a.

The College Board. *Trends in Student Aid.* Washington, D.C.: Author, 2006b.

Cuyjet, M. J. (Ed.). *Helping African American Men Succeed in College.* New Directions for Student Services, no. 80. San Francisco: Jossey-Bass, 1998.

Davis, J. S. *Unintended Consequences of Tuition Discounting.* Indianapolis, Ind.: Lumina Foundation, 2003.

Drug-Free Schools and Communities Act, Public Law 101–226, 1989.

Fain, P. "Yale Commits to Spend More from Its Endowment." *Chronicle of Higher Education,* January 18, 2008, A10.

Fenske, R. H., and Johnson, E. A. "Changing Regulatory and Legal Environments." In M. J. Barr, M. L. Upcraft, and Associates (Eds.), *New Futures for Student Affairs: Building a Vision for Professional Leadership and Practice.* San Francisco: Jossey-Bass, 1990.

Fischer, K. "In Oregon, Regional Colleges Struggle to Overcome Shortfalls." *Chronicle of Higher Education,* May 18, 2007, A16–17.

Hauptman, A. M. "Helping Colleges Survive Bad Times." *State Government News,* 1990, 33(9), 16–17.

Howard-Hamilton, M. F. (Ed.). *Meeting the Needs of African American Women.* New Directions for Student Services, no. 104. San Francisco: Jossey-Bass, 2003.

Hunter, B., and Gehring, D. D. "The Cost of Federal Legislation on Higher Education: The Hidden Tax on Tuition." *NASPA Journal,* 2005, 42(4), 478–497.

Jackson, J. F. L., Terrell, M. C., and Heard, R. L. "The Complexities of Maintaining a Safe Campus in Higher Education." In J. F. L. Jackson and M. C. Terrell (Eds.), *Creating and Maintaining Safe College Campuses.* Sterling, Va.: Stylus, 2007.

Jackson, M. L. "Fund Raising and Development." In M. L. Barr, M. K. Desler, and Associates (Eds.), *The Handbook of Student Affairs Administration* (2nd ed.). San Francisco: Jossey-Bass, 2000.

Kuh, G. D. "The Demographic Juggernaut." In M. J. Barr, M. L. Upcraft, and Associates, *New Futures for Student Affairs: Building a Vision for Professional Leadership and Practice.* San Francisco: Jossey-Bass, 1990.

Kuh, G. D., and Whitt, E. J. *The Invisible Tapestry: Culture in American Colleges and Universities,* ASHE-ERIC Higher Education Report, no. 1. Washington, D.C.: Association for the Study of Higher Education, 1988.

Lennington, R. L. *Managing Higher Education as a Business*. Phoenix, Ariz: Oryx, 1996.

Lowery, J. W. "The Legal Implications of Campus Crime for Student Affairs Professionals." In J. F. L. Jackson and M. C. Terrell (Eds.), *Creating and Maintaining Safe College Campuses*. Sterling, Va.: Stylus, 2007.

Lowry, R. C. "Effects of State Postsecondary Education Structures on Public University Prices and Spending." In F. K. Alexander and R. C. Ehrenberg (Eds.), *Maximizing Revenue in Higher Education*. New Directions for Institutional Research, no. 119. San Francisco: Jossey-Bass, 2003.

McSwain, C., and Davis, R. *College Access for the Working Poor*. Washington, D.C.: Institute for Higher Education Policy, 2007.

Moneta, L. "Technology and Student Services: Redux." In K. Kruger (Ed.), *Technology in Student Affairs: Supporting Student Learning and Services*. New Directions for Student Services, no. 112. San Francisco: Jossey-Bass, 2005.

National Commission on the Cost of Higher Education. *Straight Talk About College Costs and Prices*. Washington, D.C.: American Council on Education, 1998.

Ortiz, A. M. (Ed.). *Addressing the Unique Needs of Latino American Students*. New Directions for Student Services, no. 105. San Francisco: Jossey-Bass, 2004.

Pascarella, E. T., Edison, M. I., Nora, A., Hagedorn, L. S., and Terenzini, P. T. "Does Work Inhibit Cognitive Development During College?" *Educational Research and Policy Analysis*, 1998, 20, 75–93.

Pascarella, E. T., and Terenzini, P. T. *How College Affects Students*, vol. 2. San Francisco: Jossey-Bass, 2005.

Raines, M. P. "Effect of Fiscal Constraints on Student Affairs Services." *NASPA Journal*, 2000, 38(1), 70–81.

Reason, R. D., and Davis, T. J. "Antecedents, Precursors, and Concurrent Concepts in the Development of Social Justice Attitudes and Actions." In R D. Reason, E. M. Broido, T. J. Davis, and N. J. Evans, (Eds.), *Developing Social Justice Allies*. New Directions for Student Services, no. 110. San Francisco: Jossey-Bass, 2005.

Redd, K. E. *Discounting Toward Disaster: Tuition Discounting, College Finances, and Enrollments of Low-Income Undergraduates*. Indianapolis, Ind.: Lumina Foundation, 2000.

Sandeen, A., and Barr, M. J. *Critical Issues for Student Affairs: Challenges and Opportunities*. San Francisco: Jossey-Bass, 2006.

Schuh, J. H. (Ed.). *Contemporary Financial Issues in Student Affairs*. New Directions for Student Services, no. 103. San Francisco: Jossey-Bass, 2003.

Schuh, J. H., and Upcraft, M. L. *Assessment Practice in Student Affairs*. San Francisco: Jossey-Bass, 2001.

Snyder, T. D. Tan, A. G., and Hoffman, C. M. *Digest of Education Statistics 2005* (NCES 2006–030). U.S. Department of Education, National Center for Education Statistics. Washington, D.C.: U.S. Government Printing Office, 2006.

Taylor, B. E., and Massy, W. F. *Strategic Indicators for Higher Education*. Princeton, N.J.: Peterson's, 1996.

Tippeconnic Fox, M. J., Lowe, S. C., and McClellan, G. S. (Eds.). *Serving Native American Students*. New Directions for Student Services, no. 109. San Francisco: Jossey-Bass, 2005.

Toutkoushian, R. K. "Weathering the Storm: Generating Revenues for Higher Education During a Recession." In F. K. Alexander and R. C. Ehrenberg (Eds.), *Maximizing Revenue in Higher Education*. New Directions for Institutional Research, no. 119. San Francisco: Jossey-Bass, 2003.

U.S. Census Bureau. *Income*. [http://www.census.gov/hhes/www/income/histinc/ineqtoc.html]. 2008

U.S. Census Bureau. *The 2007 Statistical Abstract. The National Data Book.* [http://www.census.gov/compendia/statab/]. 2007

U.S. Department of Education. *The Handbook for Campus Crime Reporting.* Washington, D.C.: U.S. Department of Education, Office of Postsecondary Education, 2005.

U.S. Department of Education. *A Test of Leadership: Charting the Future of U.S. Higher Education.* Washington, D.C.: U.S. Department of Education, 2006a.

U.S. Department of Education, National Center for Education Statistics. *The Condition of Education 1998.* Washington, D.C.: U.S. Department of Education, 1998.

U.S. Department of Education, National Center for Education Statistics. *The Condition of Education 2002* (NCES 2002–025). Washington, D.C.: U.S. Government Printing Office, 2002.

U.S. Department of Education, National Center for Education Statistics. *Digest of Education Statistics 1997.* Washington, D.C.: U.S. Department of Education, 1997.

U.S. Department of Education, National Center for Education Statistics. *The Condition of Education 2004* (NCES 2004–077). Washington, D.C.: U.S. Government Printing Office, 2004.

U.S. Department of Education, National Center for Education Statistics. *The Condition of Education 2006* (NCES 2006–071). Washington, D.C.: U.S. Government Printing Office, 2006b.

Wei, C. C., Li, X., and Berkner, L. *A Decade of Undergraduate Student Aid: 1989–90 to 1999–2000* (NCES 2004–158). U.S. Department of Education, National Center for Education Statistics. Washington, D.C.: U.S. Government Printing Office, 2004.

Wolverton, B. Senators' letter grills 136 wealthy colleges about endowment-spending and financial-aid policies. *Chronicle of Higher Education.* [http://chronicle.com/daily/2008/01/1377n.htm]. January 25, 2008.

Woodard, D. B. Jr., Love, P., and Komives, S. R. *Leadership and Management Issues for a New Century.* New Directions for Student Services, no. 92. San Francisco: Jossey-Bass, 2000.

Yinger, J. "States to the Rescue? Aid to Central Cities Under the New Federalism." *Public Budgeting and Finance,* 1990, 10(2), 27–44.

CHAPTER SIX

ACCOUNTABILITY

Sherry L. Mallory and Linda M. Clement

Accountability is certainly not a new issue in higher education or student affairs. As noted by Wellman (2006), "Access, quality, and accountability have been framing the context for. . .higher education in the United States since the 1950s" (p. 113). It is, however, an issue that has gained considerable attention in recent decades. From campuses to state houses, in news stories and in Congress, accountability is being discussed and the general consensus seems clear: greater accountability is needed in higher education.

Two key catalysts have served to "raise the stakes" in this discussion. In January 2002, President George Bush signed the No Child Left Behind Act into law, "ushering in an era of unprecedented federal control" over education (Carey, 2007, p. 27). The higher education community responded, Carey asserts, by launching "a new round of efforts to get the accountability equation right" (p. 27).

Then, in October 2005, U.S. Secretary of Education Margaret Spellings appointed a task force to lead a national conversation on issues of quality, access, affordability, and accountability in higher education. While the group stopped short of calling for mandatory testing for college students—a hallmark of No Child Left Behind—it did urge the creation of "a robust culture of accountability and transparency throughout higher education" (National Commission on the Future of Higher Education, 2006, p. 21).

Student affairs professionals must pay attention as this discussion continues to unfold. As Blimling and Whitt (1999) assert, while "student affairs organizations are not at the center of controversy over accountability in higher education . . . [we] are part of a much larger agenda of reform that has caused scrutiny of virtually every element of higher education" (p. 8).

This chapter presents an overview of the growing accountability movement in higher education, with specific emphasis on the implications of this movement for student affairs. Three primary questions will be considered: (1) To whom are we accountable? (2) For what are we accountable? and (3) More broadly, what constitutes accountability? To address these issues, we first define accountability, then discuss the reasons why accountability in higher education has become such a salient issue. We then review who the stakeholders are in institutional accountability, and the areas for which student affairs is accountable. The chapter delves briefly into the accreditation movement and its role in accountability and concludes with a summary of strategies, best practices, and resources.

Accountability Defined

Accountability, in the context of higher education and student affairs, is difficult to define. It is not a monolithic concept; multiple definitions exist (Neave, 1980). Moreover, perspectives on higher education accountability have changed over time (Eaton, 2007; McLendon, Hearn, and Deaton, 2006).

In the 1970s and 1980s, when higher education first began to face increased public scrutiny, a primary focus of accountability was the responsible stewardship of resources. As Harpel (1976) noted, "Being accountable means being a good steward. We have been entrusted with physical and financial resources. . . . It is not unreasonable that we should be called upon periodically to account for our stewardship" (p. ii). During this period, accountability was primarily decentralized and institution based.

In the 1990s, as competition for public resources increased and criticism of higher education began to grow, accountability focused more on institutional productivity and student performance. State governments took an active role in this process, defining performance indicators and requiring annual accountability reports. With an emphasis on such issues as student access, retention and graduation rates, and institutional efficiency (McClendon and others, 2006), accountability moved from being decentralized and institution based, to being coordinated at the state level.

In recent years, accountability has shifted again, to what many have dubbed the "new accountability" (Burke and Minassians, 2002; McLendon and others, 2006; Welsh and Metcalf, 2003). A key characteristic of this approach is its focus on institutions from the outside in, rather than the inside out. Public accountability for the public agenda, as Wellman (2006) refers to it, is less about the institution as a unit of performance and more about the role it plays in meeting "general social, cultural, and economic needs" (p. 113).

Accountability, in this context, has become a public-oriented process, designed to "assure public constituents of the value, effectiveness, and quality of higher education" (Leveille, 2005, p. 3). It requires greater attention to "cross-sector measures of student academic preparation . . . student flow across institutions, and measures of student learning outcomes" (Wellman, 2006, p. 115). According to Reville (2006), a key question of the movement is, "What specifically should students know and be able to do as a result of their education?" (p. 19).

It is no longer enough for institutions to measure the effectiveness of what they do, including the outcomes their students achieve. They must now be purposeful, aligning departmental goals with institutional goals, and institutional goals with state and federal goals. They must also share the information they've collected with a range of constituents, presenting it in ways that are both easy to understand and readily accessible. Put simply, accountability in higher education and student affairs has become about "publicly acceptable performance and results" (Ewell, 2004, p. 3).

Why All the Fuss About Accountability?

Upcraft and Schuh (1996) put it best when they posed the question, "Why all the fuss about accountability?" After all, "For about 350 years, our citizenry accepted as a matter of faith that . . . higher education was doing its job, and doing it well" (p. 5).

A critical turning point for higher education came in the mid-1980s, with the publication of *A Nation at Risk* (National Commission on Excellence in Education, 1983), a scathing report on the state of education in the United States. Although the report focused primarily on K–12 education, the resulting cries for reform in public schools began to echo "in calls for change on college campuses" (Burke and Minassians, 2002, p. 6).

Not long after, U.S. Secretary of Energy James Watkins charged Sandia National Laboratories with examining the state of public education. The *Sandia Report* shared a more positive view than *A Nation at Risk*, citing steady or slight improvement on a number of indicators of educational progress. Yet, it still called for "upgrading the quality of educational data" and making "major improvements . . . in the data used to analyze U.S. education" (Sandia National Laboratories, 1993, pp. 309–310).

In the early 1990s, the nation experienced a major recession. For the first time in decades, higher education faced a decline in state support. In 1993, the Wingspread Group on Higher Education released *An American Imperative: Higher*

Expectations for Higher Education. The report charged higher education with failing to meet society's needs for a better educated, more skilled and more adaptable citizenry, and urged society to hold colleges and universities to higher standards. Calls for change began to intensify.

In recent years—spurred, at least in part, by rising college costs, graduation rates that have not significantly increased over time, and employer concerns that graduates do not have the skills necessary to succeed in the workplace—accountability in higher education has become an issue of national importance (Miller, 2003). Calls for change are clearly here to stay.

A number of recent events illustrate this. In April 2004, the Business-Higher Education Forum issued the report, *Public Accountability for Student Learning in Higher Education.* It called on colleges and universities to conduct rigorous learning outcomes assessments and publicly report their results. Less than a year later, in March 2005, the National Commission on Accountability in Higher Education issued the report, *Accountability for Better Results: A National Imperative for Higher Education.* It called for a new approach to accountability, grounded in public responsibility, and urged policymakers and educators to work together to create a system that emphasizes student learning.

The National Commission on the Future of Higher Education issued their final report in September 2006. In the report, they cited "inadequate . . . accountability for measuring institutional performance" (p. 13) and called on higher education to embrace and implement "serious accountability measures" (p. 20). This was followed, more recently, by the Educational Testing Services' three-part *Culture of Evidence* series—*Postsecondary Assessment and Learning Outcomes* (2006); *Critical Features of Assessments for Postsecondary Student Learning* (2007); and *An Evidence-Centered Approach to Accountability for Student Learning Outcomes* (2008)—which asserted the need for "a systemic, data-driven . . . approach to understanding the quality of . . . postsecondary education" (Educational Testing Service, 2006, p. 1).

So, why all the fuss about accountability? First, higher education represents a significant public investment. Each year, the United States spends roughly $330 billion on higher education. Of that, a little more than half comes from private support (including tuition payments, gifts, auxiliary revenue); the rest comes from state and federal governments (Duderstadt, 2005).

Second, the stakes are high. Shulock (2006) notes, "Problems of low college-going rates, low graduation rates, inadequate preparation among college graduates . . . and persistent gaps in educational attainment across income and racial lines bode poorly for the future social and economic health of the nation" (pp. 1–2). The United States once ranked first in the world in both the proportion of its population that graduated from high school and the proportion that enrolled in postsecondary education; it now ranks seventh and ninth, respectively (Kirwan, 2007).

Third, despite the large amounts of data provided by colleges and universities to regional accrediting bodies, state governing boards, and the federal government in the name of accountability each year, significant change has yet to occur. Until higher education is able to get in front of the calls for performance and outcomes, transparency and accountability in ways that have meaning and motivate substantive change, accountability will likely continue to cause a fuss (McCormick, 2007; McPherson and Shulenberger, 2006; Shulock, 2006).

There are many involved in higher education and student affairs that are skeptical of the movement toward greater accountability. Reactions to a national push, as noted by Campbell (2007), range from "cynical hostility to blithe acquiescence" (p. 99). Critics fear that institutions will be measured against a single template—a "one-size-fits-all" approach—that doesn't respect the diversity of our missions and goals, or the students we serve (Warren, 2004).

As noted by McCormick (2007), a well-designed accountability system can motivate substantive change. However, a system that requires institutions to use common assessments to measure common outcomes could "undermine useful diagnostic tools" and "seriously hamper efforts to improve college quality." Notwithstanding critics, the drive for greater accountability in higher education remains a resounding imperative that will continue to be a focus for our institutions and the profession.

Who Are the Stakeholders in Institutional Accountability?

There are three primary types of stakeholders in higher education: those who provide funding and support, those who ensure that institutions fulfill their various fiduciary and educational responsibilities, and those who are consumers of higher education.

The federal government provides funding for student aid as well as for research and development. State policymakers provide funding for operating and capital expenditures, for public and—in some cases—private institutions, and for need- and merit-based aid. Corporations and the greater public provide support through gifts and service. These stakeholders believe their investment should result in the development of "human capital" for the workforce and view education as the key to competitiveness in today's global society (Zumeta, 2001).

State higher education coordinating agencies and institutional governing boards also have a stake. There is a fiduciary responsibility inherent in their roles, as well as a responsibility to make sure that institutions are achieving their mission. In doing so, these stakeholders perform a service for the public and society as a whole. They play a clear role in ensuring that institutions are responsive to current realities (Zumeta, 2001).

Last, students and their families are stakeholders. With the costs of higher education rising, those who invest their personal resources expect outcomes: well-educated individuals who can achieve their full potential to lead productive lives. Given studies showing that the average American worker changes jobs ten times in his or her lifetime, the learning, understandings, and skills acquired in college are critical (Association of American Colleges and Universities, 2007).

For What Is Student Affairs Accountable?

Priorities and expectations have changed over time as student affairs has evolved. The *Student Personnel Point of View* (American Council on Education, [1937] 1949), a seminal document of the profession, urged the development of services; it also called for intentional assessment in order to improve services. The profession looked to measures of efficiency, like usage data and satisfaction, to assess success.

In the decades that followed, talented professionals developed theories about how students mature in such areas as cognitive development (Gilligan, 1982; Perry, 1968), identity development (Chickering, 1969), and moral reasoning (Kohlberg, 1976). These theories were operationalized, as were the means for measuring them, and a body of literature around student development emerged. In 1972, Robert Brown published *Tomorrow's Higher Education: A Return to the Academy;* in it, he advised student affairs professionals to fully embrace student development as their leading priority and integrate it into their daily practice.

More recently, in 1994, the *Student Learning Imperative* encouraged practitioners to be intentional about creating conditions that enhance student learning (American College Personnel Association, 1994). Blimling and Whitt (1999) expanded on this concept, focusing on how to integrate learning into our work. This was followed, in 2004, by the publication of *Learning Reconsidered: A Campus-Wide Focus on the Student Experience* (Keeling, 2004); in 2006, by the publication of *Learning Reconsidered 2: A Practical Guide to Implementing a Campus-Wide Focus on the Student Experience* (Keeling, 2006); and, in 2008, by the publication of *Assessment Reconsidered: Institutional Effectiveness for Student Success* (Keeling, Wall, Underhile, and Dungy, 2008). All emphasized the role student affairs plays as a partner in the broader campus curriculum and the resulting positive impact on student learning and development.

It is clear that student affairs practitioners need to accomplish all three ends—to provide high-quality services delivered in an efficient manner, to facilitate students' development, and to contribute to student learning (Barham and Scott, 2006). Chapter Twenty-Seven discusses different approaches to assessment and offers practical suggestions for student affairs leaders who want to develop and implement a comprehensive assessment plan.

The Role of the Accreditation Process

The accreditation process has long been viewed as the primary mechanism for institutional accountability (Merisotis, 2006). Originally conceived by college presidents, the process has widespread buy-in among institutions of higher education because it involves peer reviewers, can be applied to all institutions of higher education, utilizes standards approved by the institutions themselves, and is focused on development and improvement (Wolff, 2005).

Three approved types of institutional accreditation typically occur: regional, national, and specialized. Regional accrediting agencies operate within geographical parameters—for example, Middle States or Southern—and are viewed as a stable and revered mechanism for accreditation. National accrediting agencies focus on specific types of institutions, for example, distance education or religious education. Specialized accrediting agencies focus on specific disciplines, for example, business, teacher education, or engineering.

Accreditation processes typically involve a complex and intensive self-study as well as a site visit by a team composed primarily of faculty but increasingly inclusive of others, including student affairs administrators. The costs for these processes are borne by the institution in the form of annual dues and site visit expenses. Institutional responsibility for meeting accrediting standards has largely fallen to the academic sector of higher education institutions.

In the past, as noted by Wolff (2005), accreditation tended to focus on inputs such as faculty characteristics, resources (for example, library books), and processes (for example, course approval). Increasingly, accreditation now focuses on results, often in the form of learning outcomes. Defined by the Council for Higher Education Accreditation (2003) as "the knowledge, skills, and abilities that a student has attained at the end (or as a result) of his or her . . . higher education experiences" (p. 5), these outcomes may include critical reasoning, written and oral communications, quantitative reasoning, information literary, or technology fluency.

As the emphasis on learning outcomes continues to grow, student affairs has a key role to play in the accreditation process. Accordingly, useful tools have been developed through the Council for the Advancement of Standards in Higher Education and other professional organizations.

Council for the Advancement of Standards and Accountability

The Council for the Advancement of Standards in Higher Education (CAS), discussed in greater detail in Chapter Ten, has responded to calls for increasing accountability in higher education by developing a series of self-assessment guides and frameworks for assessing student learning and development (Dean, 2006; Strayhorn, 2006). Together with the CAS Standards, these guides and frameworks represent a key force in promoting standards within student affairs. Examples of how CAS and other professional standards can be used as tools for promoting accountability are available in Dean (2006), Strayhorn (2006), and Whitt and Blimling (2000).

Accreditation by Student Affairs Professional Organizations

Currently, there are no general national accreditation mechanisms within the student affairs profession. However, in an effort to be accountable, three health- and wellness-related organizations—to which many student affairs professionals belong—have fashioned processes that are similar in nature to those of regional, national, and specialized accrediting bodies. These include the International Association of Counseling Services (IACS); the American Psychological Association (APA); and the American College Health Association.

The International Association of Counseling Services has established a comprehensive set of standards that address such areas as the relationship of the center to the campus, ethical standards, roles and functions, and personnel (Kiracofe and others, 1994). To maintain accreditation, centers must complete a written self-study that is reviewed by the accreditation board—made up of IACS members—every five years. Every seven years, they must undergo a site visit by a team of peers (International Association of Counseling Services, 2000).

The American Psychological Association has developed a voluntary accreditation process for internship training programs that are executed by university counseling centers. The APA Committee on Accreditation publishes annual guidelines and procedures as well as a list of accredited programs. Having an accredited training program facilitates the licensing process for those trained and assures public accountability for institutions and counseling centers. To maintain accreditation, programs must submit an annual report; periodic self-study reports and site visits are also required (American Psychological Association, 2007).

The American College Health Association provides a consultation service to help institutions navigate the accreditation process for ambulatory health care. This volunteer process assists health centers in assessing the quality of services provided relative to a set of nationally recognized standards, including administration, quality of care provided, clinical records and health information, and facilities (Accreditation Association for Ambulatory Health Care, 2007). To maintain accreditation, health centers must conduct a full survey every three years. As with other accreditation processes, this involves extensive self-study and peer site visits.

Best Practices in Accountability in Student Affairs

Many institutions are still working to develop and implement accountability measures in the form of clearly defined outcomes for student learning. However, an informal survey of peers identified three institutions that are considered to be "ahead of the curve": Alverno College, North Carolina State University, and California State University Channel Islands.

At Alverno College, a small Catholic women's college in Wisconsin, student learning and development are integrated into the curriculum and co-curriculum. Faculty and staff have identified eight abilities that all graduates should possess: aesthetic engagement, analysis, communication, a global perspective, effective citizenship, problem solving, social interaction, and valuing in decision making. Students are evaluated through course-based and integrative assessments, or "real-life" situations in which trained assessors judge a student's performance based on explicit criteria. Students also take part in a continuous loop of self-assessment, evaluating their own performances on the basis of criteria provided by the college.

Alverno's Office of Educational Research and Evaluation takes the evaluation of student learning a step further by tracking cohorts of students from entry to graduation and up to five years after college. The findings are used to enhance student learning and development, as well as for continuous improvement (Alverno College, 2008).

North Carolina State University, a large public land-grant university, relies on outcomes-based planning and assessment to inform decision making and to provide evidence about the quality of teaching, learning, and engagement that occurs at the university. All curricular and co-curricular departments, including those in student affairs, engage in ongoing outcomes-based assessment and evaluation; they also take part in more extensive reviews and compact planning. Through compact planning, departments focus on specific initiatives—aligned with the university's mission and goals—that they plan to achieve (North Carolina State University, 2008).

California State University Channel Islands is a relatively new campus in the California State University (CSU) System; it opened to students in fall 2002. As such, it has built an outcomes-focused approach into its mission. Mission-based outcomes at CSU Channel Islands include being able to identify and describe the modern world and issues facing societies from multiple perspectives; to analyze issues; and to develop and convey to others solutions to problems using the methodologies, tools, and techniques of an academic discipline.

A cross-divisional council at CSU Channel Islands provides support for continuous outcome-focused assessment and evaluation. A set of "dashboard indicators," or key performance indicators, focuses on six areas: students, faculty instruction, program quality, infrastructure, finance, and funding. A Center for Integrative and Interdisciplinary Studies was also established to support the institution's integrated approach to learning—both inside and outside of the classroom (California State University Channel Islands, 2008).

Additional Resources

Since the release of the Spellings Commission report in 2006, a number of key higher education associations have weighed in, creating resources and issuing subsequent reports. Several of those resources are discussed in this section.

International Center for Student Success and Institutional Accountability

In February 2007, the National Association of Student Personnel Administrators (NASPA) and Keeling and Associates joined together to create the International Center for Student Success and Institutional Accountability (ICSSIA). The center—which seeks to help institutions improve student success and learning through professional development, applied research, and the creation and sharing of resources—also offers discussion forums and communities of practice (International Center for Student Success and Accountability, 2008).

University and College Accountability Network

In September 2007, the National Association of Independent Colleges and Universities launched the University and College Accountability Network

(U-CAN). The Web site, designed to give prospective students and their families concise, consumer-friendly information on private colleges and universities, includes information on admissions criteria, student demographics, graduation rates, faculty information, tuition and fee trends, and campus safety (National Association of Independent Colleges and Universities, 2008).

Voluntary System of Accountability

In November 2007, the American Association of State Colleges and Universities and the National Association of State Universities and Land Grant Colleges unveiled a Voluntary System of Accountability, designed to improve public understanding of how public colleges and universities operate. Through a Web reporting template—*College Portrait*—the system seeks to provide "consistent, comparable, and transparent information . . . to key higher education stakeholders, including prospective students and their families" on a range of measures including retention and graduation rates, financial aid, student engagement with the learning process, and outcomes (American Association of State Colleges and Universities and National Association of State Universities and Land Grant Colleges, 2007, p. 2).

Conclusion

It has become clear in recent years that accountability in higher education and student affairs is here to stay. As noted by Mundhenk (2006), "higher education is being asked by many groups, both within and outside higher education, to be publicly accountable and demonstrate its worth to stakeholders" (p. 44). For student affairs professionals, this means not only providing high-quality services delivered in an efficient manner, facilitating students' development, and contributing to student learning (Barham and Scott, 2006), but also finding ways to measure the effectiveness of these activities and share the results with a variety of stakeholders—including students, parents, state and federal government, higher education coordinating agencies, and governing boards—in ways that are both easy to understand and readily accessible.

Increasingly, student affairs professional organizations are beginning to weigh in on accountability. While only a few currently have accreditation processes and/or measures in place, there are other initiatives, including the development of the CAS Frameworks for Assessing Learning and Development Outcomes and the launch of the International Center for Student Success and Institutional Accountability. Several national organizations—including the National Association of State Universities and Land Grant Colleges and the National Association of Independent Colleges and Universities—have developed voluntary accountability systems.

Lee Shulman (2007) has likened the growing volume of calls for accountability to a powerful current over which we, in higher education, believe we can exert little influence. As noted by Shulman, we have three options for responding: we can "paddle upstream, resisting all the way"; we can "go with the flow, adopting a stance of minimal compliance"; or we can take the approach that a skilled whitewater rafter or canoeist would—negotiating the rapids by paddling faster than the current (p. 25).

It is time, Shulman asserts, for higher education to take control. Accordingly, we must "summon the creative energy and ambition to take advantage of the momentum (and resources) unleashed by [this movement] . . . and exploit them to initiate the long-overdue progress in assessment needed to improve the quality of learning in higher education" (p. 25).

References

Alverno College. "Educational Research and Evaluation at Alverno College." [http://depts. alverno.edu/ere/index.html]. May 2008.

American Association of State Colleges and Universities and National Association of State Universities and Land Grant Colleges. "The Voluntary System of Accountability: Summary and Background Materials." [http://www.nasulgc.org]. October 2007.

Accreditation Association for Ambulatory Health Care. "Survey Eligibility Criteria." [http://www.aaahc.org/]. May 2007.

American College Personnel Association. *The Student Learning Imperative: Implications for Student Affairs.* Alexandria, Va.: Author, 1994.

American Council on Education. *The Student Personnel Point of View.* Washington, D.C.: Author, 1949. (Originally published 1937).

American Psychological Association. *Guidelines and Principles for Accreditation of Programs in Professional Psychology.* Washington, D.C.: Author, 2007.

Association of American Colleges and Universities. *College Learning for the New Global Century.* Washington, D.C.: Author, 2007.

Barham, J. D., and Scott, J. H. "Increasing Accountability in Student Affairs Through a New Comprehensive Assessment Model." *College Student Affairs Journal*, 2006, 25(2), 209–219.

Blimling, G. S., and Whitt, E. J. "Identifying the Principles That Guide Student Affairs Practice." In G. S. Blimling and E. J. Whitt (Eds.), *Good Practice in Student Affairs: Principles to Foster Student Learning.* San Francisco: Jossey-Bass, 1999.

Brown, R. D. *Student Development in Tomorrow's Higher Education: A Return to the Academy.* Student Personnel Series, no. 16. Washington, D.C.: American Personnel and Guidance Association, 1972.

Burke, J. C., and Minassians, H. P. "The New Accountability: From Regulations to Results." In J. C. Burke and H. P. Minassians (Eds.), *Reporting Higher Education Results: Missing Links in the Performance Chain.* New Directions for Institutional Research, no. 116. San Francisco: Jossey-Bass, 2002.

Business-Higher Education Forum. *Public Accountability for Student Learning in Higher Education: Issues and Options.* Washington, D.C.: American Council on Education, 2004.

California State University Channel Islands. "Institutional Research Office." [http://www.csuci.edu/about/ir/]. May 2008.

Campbell, K. J. "Assessment Advice for Beginners." *PS: Political Science and Politics,* 2007, 40(1), 99.

Carey, K. "Truth Without Action: The Myth of Higher-Education Accountability." *Change,* 2007, 39(5), 24–29.

Chickering, A. *Education and Identity.* San Francisco: Jossey-Bass, 1969.

Council for Higher Education Accreditation. *Statement of Mutual Responsibilities for Student Learning Outcomes: Accreditation, Institutions, and Programs.* Washington, D.C.: Author, 2003.

Dean, L. A. (Ed.). *CAS Professional Standards for Higher Education* (6th ed). Washington, D.C.: Council for the Advancement of Standards in Higher Education, 2006.

Duderstadt, J. J. *The Crisis in Financing Public Higher Education.* Ann Arbor: University of Michigan, 2005.

Eaton, J. S. "Nationalization and Transparency: On Our Own Terms." *Inside Accreditation with the President of CHEA,* 2007, 3(1).

Educational Testing Service. *A Culture of Evidence: Postsecondary Assessment and Learning Outcomes.* Princeton, N.J.: Educational Testing Service, 2006.

Educational Testing Service. *A Culture of Evidence: Critical Features of Assessments for Postsecondary Student Learning.* Princeton, N.J.: Educational Testing Service, 2007.

Educational Testing Service. *A Culture of Evidence: An Evidence-Centered Approach to Accountability for Student Learning Outcomes.* Princeton, N.J.: Educational Testing Service, 2008.

Ewell, P. T. "The Changing Nature of Accountability in Higher Education." Paper prepared for the Western Association of Schools and Colleges (WASC) Senior Commission, November 2004.

Gilligan, C. *In a Different Voice.* Cambridge, Mass.: Harvard University Press, 1982.

Harpel, R. L. "Planning, Budgeting, and Evaluation in Student Affairs Programs: A Manual for Administrators." *NASPA Journal,* 1976, 14(1), i–xx.

International Association of Counseling Services. *Accreditation Standards for University and College Counseling Centers.* Alexandria, Va.: International Association of Counseling Services, 2000.

International Center for Student Success and Institutional Accountability. "About Us." [http://www.icssia.org/about/index.cfm]. May 2008.

Keeling, R. (Ed.). *Learning Reconsidered 2: Implementing a Campus-Wide Focus on the Student Experience.* Various: American College Personnel Association, Association of College and University Housing Officers-International, Association of College Unions-International, National Academic Advising Association, National Association for Campus Activities, National Association of Student Personnel Administrators, National Intramural-Recreational Sports Association, 2004.

Keeling, R. P. (Ed.). *Learning Reconsidered 2: A Practical Guide to Implementing a Campus-Wide Focus on the Student Experience.* Washington, D.C.: American College Personnel Association, and Others, 2006.

Keeling, R. P., Wall, A. F., Underhile, R., and Dungy, G. J. *Assessment Reconsidered: Institutional Effectiveness for Student Success.* Washington, D.C.: International Center for Student Success and Institutional Accountability, 2008.

Kiracofe, N., and Others. "Accreditation Standards for University and College Counseling Centers." *Journal of Counseling and Development*, 1994, 73(1), 38–43.

Kirwan, W. E. "Higher Education's 'Accountability' Imperative: How the University System of Maryland Responded." *Change: The Magazine of Higher Learning*, 2007, 39(2), 21–25.

Kohlberg, L. "Moral Stages and Moralization: The Cognitive-Developmental Approach." In T. Lickona (Ed.), *Moral Development and Behavior: Theory, Research, and Social Issues*. New York: Holt, Rinehart and Winston, 1976.

Leveille, D. E. *An Emerging View on Accountability in American Higher Education*. CSHE Research and Occasional Paper Series: CSHE.8.05. Berkeley: University of California, 2005.

McCormick, A. C. "First, Do No Harm." *Carnegie Perspectives*. [http://www.carnegiefoundation.org]. April 2007.

McLendon, M. K., Hearn, J. C., and Deaton, R. "Called to Account: Analyzing the Origins and Spread of State Performance-Accountability Policies for Higher Education." *Educational Evaluation and Policy Analysis*, 2006, 28(1), 1–24.

McPherson, P., and Shulenberger, D. *Improving Student Learning in Higher Education Through Better Accountability and Assessment: A Discussion Paper*. Washington, D.C.: National Association of State Land Grant Colleges and Universities, 2006.

Merisotis, J. P. "Accountability and Leadership for Learning." Paper presented at the Council of Independent Colleges 34th Annual Institute for Chief Academic Officers and Student Affairs Officers, St. Petersburg, FL, November 2006.

Miller, C. O. "Is There a Need for a New Approach to Higher Education Accountability?" Testimony Provided to the U.S. Committee on Education and the Workforce, May 13, 2003.

Mundhenk, R. T. "Embracing Accountability." *American Academic*, 2006, 2(1), 39–53.

National Association of Independent Colleges and Universities. "University and College Accountability Network." [http://www.ucan-network.org/about]. May 2008.

National Association of State Universities and Land Grant Colleges. *The Voluntary System of Accountability: Summary and Background Materials*. Washington, D.C.: National Association of State Universities and Land Grant Colleges, 2007.

National Commission on Accountability in Higher Education. *Accountability for Better Results: A National Imperative for Higher Education*. Denver, Colo.: State Higher Education Executive Officers, 2005.

National Commission on Excellence in Education. *A Nation at Risk: The Imperative for Educational Reform*. Washington, D.C.: U.S. Government Printing Office, 1983.

National Commission on the Future of Higher Education. *A Test of Leadership: Charting the Future of U. S. Higher Education*. Washington, D.C.: U.S. Department of Education, 2006.

Neave, G. "Accountability and Control." *European Journal of Education*, 1980, 15(1), 49–60.

North Carolina State University. "University Planning and Analysis." [http://www2.acs.ncsu.edu/UPA/index.html]. May 2008.

Perry, W. G. Jr. *Forms of Intellectual and Ethical Development in the College Years: A Scheme*. New York: Holt, Rinehart, and Winston, 1968.

Reville, S. P. "Coming Soon to a College Near You: Accountability." *Connection, New England's Journal of Higher Education*, 2006, 20(5), 19.

Sandia National Laboratories. "Summary of Issues." *Journal of Educational Research*, 1993, 86(5), 309–310.

Shulman, L. S. "Counting and Recounting: Assessment and the Quest for Quality Improvement." *Change: The Magazine of Higher Learning*, 2007, 39(1), 20–25.

Shulock, N. B. "Editor's Notes." In N. B. Shulock (Ed.), *Practitioners on Making Accountability Work for the Public*. New Directions for Higher Education, no. 135. San Francisco: Jossey-Bass, 2006.

Strayhorn, T. L. *Frameworks for Assessing Learning and Development Outcomes*. Washington, D.C.: Council for the Advancement of Standards in Higher Education, 2006.

Upcraft, M. L., and Schuh, J. H. *Assessment in Student Affairs: A Guide for Practitioners*. San Francisco: Jossey-Bass, 1996.

Warren, D. "Appropriate Accountability." Testimony before the National Commission on Accountability in Higher Education, April 8, 2004.

Wellman, J. V. "Accountability for the Public Trust." In N. B. Shulock (Ed.), *Practitioners on Making Accountability Work for the Public*. New Directions for Higher Education, no. 135. San Francisco: Jossey-Bass, 2006.

Welsh, J. F., and Metcalf, J. "Administrative Support for Institutional Effectiveness Activities: Responses to the New Accountability." *Journal of Higher Education Policy and Management*, 2003, 25(2), 183–193.

Whitt, E. J., and Blimling, G. S. "Applying Professional Standards and Principles of Good Practice in Student Affairs." In M. J. Barr and M. K. Desler (Eds.), *The Handbook of Student Affairs Administration* (2nd ed.). San Francisco: Jossey-Bass, 2000.

Wingspread Group on Higher Education. *An American Imperative: Higher Expectations for Higher Education*. Racine, Wisc.: Johnson Foundation, 1993.

Wolff, R. A. "Accountability and Accreditation: Can Reforms Match Increasing Demands?" In J. C. Burke (Ed.), *Achieving Accountability in Higher Education: Balancing Public, Academic and Market Demands*. San Francisco: Jossey-Bass, 2005.

Zumeta, W. "Accountability Challenges for Higher Education." *The NEA 2000 Almanac of Higher Education*. Washington, D.C.: National Education Association, 2001.

CHAPTER SEVEN

INTERNATIONALIZATION IN HIGHER EDUCATION AND STUDENT AFFAIRS

Kenneth J. Osfield and Patricia Smith Terrell

Higher education is becoming increasingly international in practice. As modern nations are making increasing use of international education as a means to advance policy goals, economic interests require the development of a workforce prepared to compete in the global economy (Bartell, 2003; and Haigh, 2002), and students continue to be interested and see study abroad as a worthwhile part of their education (Sax, Hurtado, Lindholm, Astin, Korn, and Mahoney, 2004). Higher education in the United States is no exception, and student affairs plays an important role in the extent to which efforts to internationalize campuses and the student experience are successful (Schulz, Lee, Cantwell, McClellan, and Woodard, 2007).

This chapter presents a discussion of the internationalization of higher education and the role of student affairs in that process in the United States. The discussion opens with a definition of the term *internationalization* as used in the chapter followed by a brief history of the internationalization of higher education in this country. Next, the importance of internationalization as a goal is addressed. The chapter then presents an overview of efforts among governments, universities, and professional associations to further advance internationalization in U.S. higher education. The discussion then turns to curricular and co-curricular programs which enhance internationalization and to the planning of those programs. The role of student affairs in developing and supporting such programs is a specific focus of this section. Next, suggestions are shared for ways in which student affairs professionals can better prepare themselves to fulfill their professional role in the internationalization of campuses. Finally, the chapter concludes with summary comments and recommendations.

Internationalization Defined

"Internationalization," "globalization," and "intercultural" are often confusing terms offering different definitions to different people (Olson, Green, and Hill, 2006). For purposes of this chapter, the authors have chosen to use the term "internationalization" and define it as follows: *Internationalization* refers to the process of fostering intentional, multidimensional, and interdisciplinary leadership-driven activities that expand global learning, for example, knowledge, skills, and attitudes (Olson Green, and Hill, 2006; Ellingboe, 1998).

History of Internationalization in U.S. Higher Education

There have been two periods of marked activity in internationalization in the history of the United States. With the advent of the Cold War following World War II, the United States entered an era in which fostering knowledge of other cultures and languages became an important strategy in competing with other emerging national powers (De Wit, 2000; and Engberg and Green, 2002). More recently, the increasingly global marketplace and international tensions of the past twenty years have sparked renewed attention to and investment in programs in U.S. higher education designed to promote internationalization (Knight, 2004). There has also been a marked increase during this time in international mobility among students, staff, and faculty in higher education worldwide (Organisation for Economic Co-operation and Development, 2005).

Benefits of Internationalization in Higher Education

There are a number of potential benefits for any country seeking to internationalize its higher education system. One potential benefit is heightened national and global security. People who understand and appreciate different cultures, religions, histories, and governments are less likely to engage in conflict and more likely to develop a greater understanding of each other (Rice, 2006). Encouraging students to study abroad and welcoming international students to study on campus are both important means of advancing intercultural understanding and appreciation.

Economic gain is another potential benefit from internationalizing higher education. Bain and Cummings (2005) report that "national governments are increasingly concerned about their competitive share in the internationally mobile student market" (p. 20). Between 2003 and 2006, international students on the average contributed approximately $13 billion annually to the U.S. economy, according to the National Association of Foreign Student Advisors (NAFSA) (National Association of Foreign Student Advisors [NAFSA], n.d.c).

A third potential benefit is enhanced foreign policy. World governments are important stakeholders in the move to internationalize higher education. In Europe, the Bologna Declaration is a prime example of a foreign policy change aimed specifically at enhancing mobility for international study for people living within the European Union (EU). For example, one of the important features of the Bologna Declaration is the development of articulation agreements among European countries that will permit students to attend or transfer to a university in another country and earn credit toward a degree (Bell and Watkins, 2006).

Finally, international education provides significant learning outcomes that are essential to living in this age. There are numerous potential learning outcomes associated with internationalized higher education experiences. Among these are developing a better understanding of self; identifying different models of successful leadership; learning about and appreciating differences; developing multiple perspectives on international issues and being less ethnocentric; and developing interpersonal networks across the globe and social responsibility. One of the essential learning outcomes that students must have for success in the twenty-first century is "intercultural knowledge and competence" (American Association of Colleges and Universities, 2007).

Leading the Way Toward Internationalization

Leadership on several fronts is critical if we are to realize the educational potential of internationalization. World leaders must be joined by those at the national level and those in higher education communities to bring about the necessary transformation. Examples of such leadership are discussed in this section of the chapter.

World Leadership

The European Union has sought to provide one common educational system for all its member countries. By the year 2010, the world will see a unified European educational system that will exemplify the spirit of internationalism (Bell and Watkins, 2006).

National Leadership

Several countries provide programmatic support, research, and/or the distribution of financial support in order to improve international education. Departments and ministries in individual countries include the U.S. Departments of State, Education (ED), and Defense; the Ministry of Public Education, Higher Education and Research, the Ministry of National Education, and the Ministry of Foreign Services in France; the Deutsches Studentenwerk and the Federal Ministry of Education and Research in Germany; the Higher Education Authority and the Department of Education and Science in Ireland; the Ministry of Education and Science in Spain; the Department of Education and Skills in the United Kingdom; and the European Commission in the European Union. These are just a few of the governmental agencies in various countries that are involved in attempting to improve international education.

Since 1945, the U.S. Department of State has been providing Fulbright Awards to students and scholars in an effort to encourage international exchanges between the United States and other countries (Commission on Abraham Lincoln Study Abroad Fellowship Program [CALSAFP], 2005; and Osfield and Associates, in press). The Department of State also offers the Benjamin A. Gilman International Scholarship for low-income students to study abroad (CALSAFP). The U.S. Department of Education provides many funding opportunities for students interested in expanding their international education, such as the Fulbright-Hays Program, which encourages teachers (new and current) to study abroad and undergraduate students to enrich their understanding of careers in government and international development. ED, under Title VI of the Higher Education Act (HEA), also funds the Foreign Languages and International Education programs. In addition, under Title IV of the HEA, ED provides student financial assistance which can be used for study abroad. Two other long-standing programs within the ED, the Fund for the Improvement of Postsecondary Education (FIPSE) and the TRIO programs, also provide international funding opportunities for international exchanges and study abroad (CALSAFP, 2005).

In Europe, financial support to students for study abroad varies from country to country within the European Union (see Figure 7.1). The proportion of students receiving state assistance is highest in the United Kingdom, with 85 percent of students receiving some form of state assistance. Finland and the Netherlands are right behind, with 71 percent and 62 percent, respectively. In France, the state assistance rate is 53 percent, which is above the European average. The percentage of students receiving state support in Ireland is approximately 31 percent and in Austria, Germany, Spain, and Portugal, 1 in 4 students receives state support (Eurostudent Report, 2005, p. 99).

FIGURE 7.1 FINANCIAL SUPPORT TO STUDENTS FOR STUDY ABROAD (BY COUNTRY)

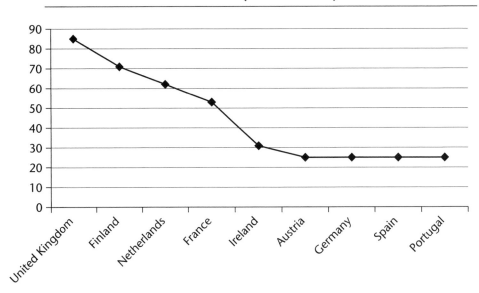

Source: Eurostudent Report (2005).

Organization Leadership

One of the foremost leaders of internationalization in higher education is the American Council on Education (ACE). Their publication, *A Handbook for Advancing Comprehensive Internationalization: What Institutions Can Do and What Students Should Learn* (2006), provides information for each campus on forming an internationalization project team: identifying and assessing global learning outcomes, conducting an internationalization review, and developing an internationalization plan. In addition, the ACE Center for International Initiatives offers programs and services that enhance and support campus internationalization, engagement, advocacy, and resources.

The Institute of International Education (IIE) is an independent organization that seeks to promote higher education internationalization around the world through a variety of services and programs (IIE, 2006a). One of IIE's programs is *Open Doors*, a series of reports on the number of international students studying in the United States, as well as the number of Americans studying abroad (IIE, 2004).

Student Affairs Professional Associations. Within the student services profession, associations in the United States such as NASPA, ACPA (American College Personnel Association), ACUHO-I (Association of College and University Housing Officers International), and ACUI (Association of College Unions International) have focused on expanding their missions and services to include an international perspective. Internationally, associations such as the European Council of Student Affairs (ECStA), as well as country-specific associations in the United Kingdom, France, Canada, Australia, South Africa, China, Spain, Germany, Mexico, Ireland, and Hong Kong, have all initiated new programs aimed at encouraging international exchanges and understanding. Some have set as a primary focus of their missions to internationalize the profession, and some have changed their name to reflect an international commitment. Others have even joined resources and have initiated a joint international exchange program for their members, such as the agreement between NASPA and ten international professional associations. This collaboration is a very important innovation in internationalization of student affairs and student services.

These associations are just a few of the groups working on the issue of internationalization in student services. In addition, NAFSA is a truly world association and one of the leading voices in promoting internationalization. NAFSA's primary mission is to promote international education and provide professional opportunities to its members. The association provides student services assistance to its members around the world, and has been involved in international education and exchange since 1948 (NAFSA, n.d.a).

College and University Leadership

While the number of students taking part in international education (study abroad) continues to rise each year, only 108 institutions out of 4,200 American colleges and universities account for 50 percent of the total number of students studying abroad (CALSAFP, 2005, p. 15). Several seem to stand out among their peers.

Of the 108 institutions heavily involved in promoting international and global education, institutions like the University of Minnesota, Harvard University, San Francisco State University, and Goucher College are exceptional. The University of Minnesota has established a goal that 50 percent of its undergraduates will participate in study abroad, and San Francisco State University has set in motion plans to double the number of students studying abroad by 2010. Harvard University has announced that it "plans to make study abroad a degree requirement," following in the footsteps of Goucher College, which in 1996 opted to make study abroad a degree requirement (CALSAFP, 2005).

Other institutions have also been successful in increasing the number of students who study abroad. In the 2003–04 academic year, the University of North Carolina at Chapel Hill and the University of Virginia already had more than a third of their undergraduates participating in study abroad. The University of California-Los Angeles, the University of Wisconsin, Michigan State University, and the University of Georgia also had at least a fourth of their undergraduates participating in study abroad (CALSAFP, 2005). Many institutions have or are in the process of establishing a campus abroad. Students are often attracted to these campuses since they are viewed as an extension of their current campus and more likely to provide essential academic, personal, social, and cultural support commensurate with their home institution.

Collaborative Leadership

In order for internationalization to succeed, efforts must include citizens, government, and educational systems from around the world. The American Council on Education suggests that successful internationalization efforts on our campuses will include bringing together several individuals and groups: senior faculty with international expertise or interest, committed faculty, academic deans, at least one administrator specializing in assessment, faculty serving on key governance committees, and senior administrators (ACE, 2006). Student affairs representation on such a group is essential.

Student affairs professionals can play multiple partnership roles in the effort to internationalize higher education. First, they can assist in identifying and assessing learning outcomes related to internationalization. California State University at Stanislaus has identified four internationalization learning outcomes. They are multiple perspectives, interdependence, social justice, and sustainability. They have hierarchical levels ranging from level 1, where a student is able to define or give an example of the goal, to level 4, where the student can analyze and argue more than one point of view (ACE, 2006). Second, student affairs professionals can ensure that all international education programs are open to all students, that safety and security issues are addressed, and that appropriate policies and procedures are in place for any scenario that may arise on and off campus. Third, student affairs professionals can plan, identify, and facilitate programs, services, and activities that provide students an opportunity to learn and apply internationalization skills.

In Ireland, the Irish Universities Quality Board (2006) has produced a publication that outlines the national guidelines for how student support services and student affairs should interact with the various constituencies on campus (stakeholders, senior management, each other, students, academics, external agencies). This publication was developed in an effort "by the seven Irish universities to increase the level of inter-university co-operation in developing their quality assurance procedures and processes, in line with best international systems and to represent the Irish university quality assurance system nationally and internationally" (Irish Universities Quality Board [IUQB], 2006).

In South Africa the Centre for Higher Education Transformation (CHET) developed "A Guide to Student Services" for South African student services professionals. The publication is "essentially a critical reflection on, and a re-envisioning of the role of, student services in the context of the transformation of the higher education system" (Mandew, 2003, p. x).

On January 5–6, 2006, U.S. Secretary of State Condoleezza Rice and Secretary of Education Margaret Spellings co-hosted a Summit in Washington, D.C., of more than 120 U.S. university presidents to discuss the need to strengthen international education and emphasize its importance to the national interest. The goal of the summit was to identify how the federal government and the higher education sector could forge an alliance to enhance connections between the United States and the world (Rice, 2006).

Opportunities for International Education

Opportunities for enhanced international education abound on most college campuses. Students have a variety of choices, including, but not limited to, curricular and co-curricular offerings, academic study abroad, living learning communities, and co-curricular study abroad. We briefly discuss each of these opportunities.

Curricular Offerings

In addition to the usual plethora of courses and disciplines that focus on attaining international knowledge and perspectives, many campuses have sought to imbed international education perspectives throughout the curriculum. The University of Minnesota and Michigan State University have begun to use the term "curriculum integration" (University of Minnesota, 2006, and Michigan State University, n.d.), when addressing the internationalization of their curriculum. The Michigan State program states that the "study abroad curriculum integration project seeks to closely integrate study abroad options into the undergraduate experiences and curricula for all students in all majors" (Michigan State University, n.d.). Institutions focused on "seamless learning" realize that integration of international education and issues throughout a student's undergraduate, and in some cases, graduate years, are essential to the development of a well-rounded liberal education.

Academic Study Abroad

When addressing the impact of internationalization on higher education and student affairs, we need to look at the impact of academic study abroad. An academic study abroad program is one that is usually sponsored by an academic department, offered and taught by the faculty and bearing academic credit. Study abroad has been on the rise for the past twenty years and is no longer considered a "junior year abroad" experience (Institute of International Education, 2006b).

While some universities participate in academic consortia, others run a significant number of their own international study programs. The University of Wisconsin-Madison "offers more than 100 different study abroad programs around the world. More than 80 of these programs are offered by International Academic Programs (IAP) to UW-Madison students across campus" (University of Wisconsin-Madison, n.d.).

For several years, the University of Florida International Center, in an effort to meet the university's strategic goal of internationalizing the campus and curriculum, has made grants available for faculty to incorporate international components into existing or new courses with substantial international content (University of Florida, 2007). During 2007, the University of Florida offered sixteen awards of $3,000 each. In addition, the University of Florida Center for European Studies has also offered European travel grants of up to $1,000 and course enhancement grants up to $3,000 (University of Florida, n.d.).

The benefits and the reasons for international study vary from person to person. Some of the most frequently cited reasons include (1) to accumulate enough credits to graduate; (2) to fulfill a degree requirement; (3) to fulfill a desire to travel and experience another part of the world; (4) to learn a new language or improve existing language skills; (5) to meet and experience firsthand the people and the culture of the country that is the focus of their study; (6) to take specific course work or study academic disciplines that may not be offered in their native country; and (7) to study in their ancestral home country and learn about their genealogy. The study abroad and exchange components of any campus are crucial to an effort to internationalize an institution.

More students are coming to college interested in an international experience. According to the fall 2004 Annual Freshman Survey, 27.1 percent of all first-year university students said their chances were "very good" that they would participate in study abroad, and 45.5 percent said that "improving their understanding of other countries and cultures was "essential" or "very important" (Sax and others, 2004). These expectations appear to be increasing sharply. In the fall 2006 Annual Freshman Survey, 31.8 percent said that their chances were "very good" that they would participate in a study abroad, program and 53 percent said that improving their understanding of other countries and cultures was "essential" or "very important" (Pryor, Hurtado, Saenz, Korn, Santos, and Korn, 2006). Clearly, students' interest in study abroad continues to increase (see Figure 7.2).

In the past decade alone, the number of U.S. students studying abroad has increased 144 percent, increasing from 84,403 students in 1994–95 to 205,983 in 2004–05 (IIE, 2006c; IIE, 2006d). In addition, the number of international students studying in the United States has risen from 48,486 students in 1959–60 to 564,766 in 2005–06 (IIE, 2006b). Although the number of international students increased significantly from 1959 to 2006, there was a three-year decline from 2003–06 in the total number of international students enrolled. In contrast, the number of U.S. students taking part in study abroad has risen continuously since 1985 with steady growth during the past three years, increasing from approximately 175,000 in 2002–03 to 205,983 students in 2004–05 (IIE, 2006e).

FIGURE 7.2 ANTICIPATED FRESHMAN STUDY ABROAD PARTICIPATION RATE

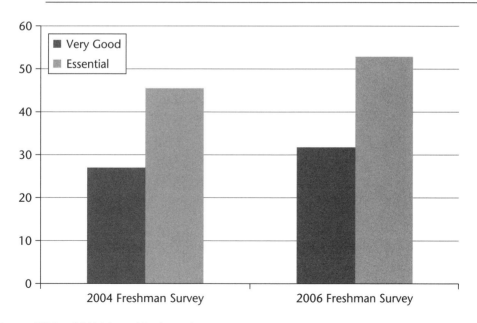

Source: 2004 and 2006 Annual Freshman Survey.

During the 2003–04 academic year, approximately 191,321 students studied abroad. The demographic makeup of students going abroad, based on race and ethnicity, has continued to be disproportionate, with 83.7 percent Caucasian students, 3.4 percent African Americans, 6.1 percent Asian Americans, and 5.0 percent Hispanic/Latino Americans participating (NAFSA, n.d.c). This contrasts sharply with U.S. postsecondary enrollment for the same year. During 2003–04 Caucasian students made up a total of 66.7 percent of the overall group of students enrolled in higher education. University enrollment for African Americans and Hispanic/Latino Americans was significantly higher than the study abroad cohorts for these groups. African Americans accounted for 12.2 percent, while Hispanic/Latino Americans accounted for 10.2 percent of the total higher education enrollment. The Asian American numbers only varied by .3 percent (NAFSA, n.d.b) (see Figure 7.3).

In spite of their stated interest and the increases in the number of U.S. students studying abroad, higher education institutions, as a group, fall far short

FIGURE 7.3 STUDY ABROAD VERSUS HIGHER EDUCATION ENROLLMENT (BY ETHNICITY)

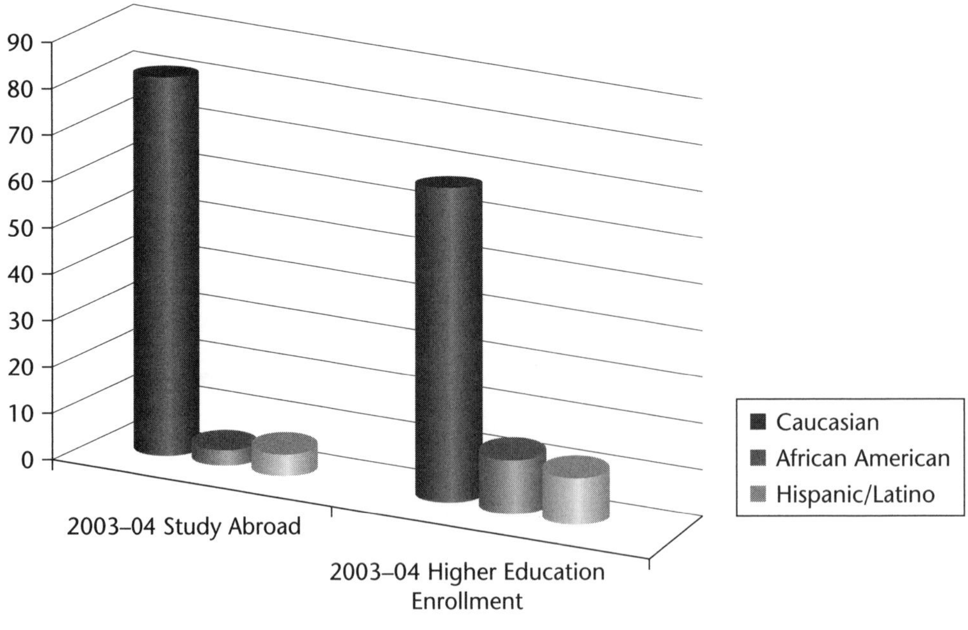

Source: National Association of Foreign Student Advisors.

of institutional and the Lincoln Commission goal of increasing the number of students studying abroad. On the other hand, when looking at the international student market share, the United States leads the way when it comes to hosting international students, with 28 percent of the world market share, followed by the United Kingdom (14 percent), Germany (12 percent), France (8 percent), and Australia (7 percent) (Bain and Cummings, 2005).

Students Studying Around the World

According to the Institute of International Education's annual Open Doors report (2006c), approximately 45 percent of U.S. students taking part in study abroad selected locations in Western Europe as their destination of choice, with the United Kingdom first, followed by Italy, Spain, and France. Of the top twenty study abroad locations around the world, only five are primarily English-speaking countries (United Kingdom, Australia, Ireland, New Zealand, and South Africa).

In Germany, nearly two thirds of students studying abroad pick Europe as their exchange destination, while only 16 percent travel to North America (Schnitzer, Isserstedt, Müßig-Trapp, and Schreiber, 1999). In the German *16th Social Survey* (Schnitzer, Isserstedt, and Middendorff, 2002), it was reported that the percentage studying aboard increased from 27 to 29 percent from the previous *15th Social Survey*, published three years earlier. In France, the Centre National des Œuvres Universitaires et Scolaires (CNOUS) reported in their 2005–06 "Key Figures" brochure that 10 percent of students registered in French higher education are international students. In France, from 1999 to 2004 the number of international students rose from 158,000 to 245,000 (CNOUS, 2005–06). In Ireland, from 2001 to 2002, 9 percent of students in Irish universities came from outside the country, with 41 percent of them from the European Union (IUQB, 2006). In Mexico, the Technologico de Monterrey system "works constantly to increase its academic exchange programs," and, at the time the publication, *Committed to Development*, was printed, it had more than 320 international collaboration agreements (*Committed to Development*, n.d.).

Regrettably, one of the immediate outcomes of the September 11, 2001, tragedy was a reduction in the number of international students studying in the United States. However, the negative impact of 9/11 on international student enrollment may not have been as bad as some may have feared. In *Opendoors 2006 Fast Facts* (IIE, 2006b), the reduction in the number of international students coming to the United States began to drop off from 2001–02 to 2002–03. During that period, enrollment growth declined from a 6.4 percent (2001–02) to 0.6 percent in 2002–03. The drop in actual enrollment started in 2003–04 when there was a 2.4 percent drop and was followed in 2004–05 with a

1.3 percent decrease and in 2005–06 with a 0.05 percent drop. During the three-year period from 2002–03 to 2005–06, the number of international students declined from 586,323 to 564,766.

In the Fall 2006 International Student Enrollment Survey, the Institute of International Education (2006c) reported numerous reasons for declines in international student enrollment in the United States. Twenty percent of institutions experiencing declines in international enrollment stated that the visa application process was the major reason for decline, followed by 16 percent of institutions reporting that high tuition and fees at U.S. institutions was the determining factor. The previous year, 35 percent of institutions reported that visa issues were the major reason for decline (IIE, 2006d). In spite of this three-year decline, the number of international students studying in the United States seems once again on the rise.

Both academic and student affairs must play a crucial role in ensuring that all students have opportunities to study abroad, especially first-generation, low-income, and ethnic minority students. Student participation may be improved by:

- Continuing to internationalize the curriculum,
- Developing grant and scholarship programs to fund experiences,
- Developing special outreach programs for underserved groups,
- Highlighting programs offered by the federal government, and
- Educating parents on the benefits of studying abroad.

Co-Curricular International Education

Student affairs can enhance students' understanding of and interest in international education through co-curricular programming on campus. For example, student affairs can:

- Develop language or cultural interest floors in residence halls,
- Develop international residential living areas that invite native and international students to live together and share culture, language, and friendship,
- Promote cross-cultural programming within student government, residential life, student activities, international student clubs and organizations, and orientation activities on campus,
- Create international cultural centers where students can meet and share ideas, friendships, language, and culture,
- Encourage participation by international students and native students in regular day-to-day programming as well as initiatives by various cultural groups on campus,

- Schedule international speakers, and
- Include international perspectives in leadership development programs.

Seamless support services to international and native students are essential. No professional cadre is better able to anticipate, plan, organize and implement these programs for native and international students than student affairs professionals.

Co-Curricular Study Abroad Opportunities

There is a significant increase in the number of students who want to participate in international service learning and experiential education. According to the Fall 2006 Freshman Survey, 53.1 percent of first-year public and 57.4 percent of first-year private university students said that their high school required community service (Pryor and others, 2006). About 25.7 percent of public and 41.4 percent of private university first-year students said their chances were "very good" that they would participate in community service in college (Pryor and others, 2006.)

Many universities sponsor service projects all over the world, with and without academic credit, during spring break and/or the summer. During the 2005 spring break, members of the University of Louisville dental school faculty and students provided dental care for indigents in Belize. In the spring of 2007, thirteen students in the Physician Assistant (PA) program at the University of Kentucky, without academic credit, along with a professor, spent a week in Mexico, where they provided basic medical care and vaccines to families who otherwise were unable to get care.

Duke University has established a $30 million-dollar program, called DukeEngage, to support students who participate in community service projects around the world. The fund's interest earnings will provide financial support for travel expenses as well as a stipend to cover either a summer- or semester-long project. Both faculty and staff who mentor the student participants will also be paid for their participation (Duke Magazine, 2007; University Business, n.d.).

Student affairs divisions can also provide opportunities for undergraduate and graduate students enrolled in student affairs programs to take part in international study abroad and study tours sponsored or cosponsored by student affairs divisions or by a student affairs preparation program. Examples of such programs are the University of Kentucky student leader study abroad program for undergraduates and the University of Florida program for master's degree students in the College Student Personnel Program.

There is heightened interest in initiating new co-curricular study abroad programs sponsored by student affairs. In order to be effective, these programs should consider the following issues for a successful program: student interest, intended learning outcomes, linking outcomes with program sessions/topics, location(s), schedule, cost, policies, orientation, knowledge about participants, and assessment.

Student Interest. Student affairs professionals interested in this area should collate a list of current opportunities for curricular and co-curricular study abroad and identify gaps. Surveys of students are helpful for identifying countries and cultures of interest. For example, universities may not offer service learning or study abroad programs in many third world countries.

Learning Outcomes. For an excellent list of possible learning outcomes, review Appendix E: "International/Intercultural Competencies" (p. 88) in the ACE's publication on Advancing Comprehensive Internationalization (Olson and others, 2006).

Linking Outcomes with Program Sessions/Topics. If one of the learning outcomes is recognizing individual and cultural differences, the program planner will want to ensure that there are multiple opportunities for participants to interact with diverse members of the population of the host country. Students can be encouraged to learn about the heritage and history of the country, visit culturally important sites, and discuss the country's values and perspectives.

Location. Cost may be a major determinant of the location. Other factors are logistics (a major airport), the availability of in-country travel by train or bus; and low-cost lodging, including the availability of residence halls.

Schedule. The schedule must reflect adequate time for adapting to the local time zone; a balance of formal in-class versus informal interaction; sufficient travel time from one site to another; and sightseeing. Sometimes opportunities occur that were not anticipated that add value to the program. Allow for a flexible schedule to accommodate those opportunities.

Cost. The projected cost per participant should include honoraria for presenters, in-country travel and lodging, admission to sightseeing locales, tips for guides and drivers, publications and handouts, audio-visual equipment, commemorative gifts and certificates for participants, and health insurance for presenters and participants. Also, bring a receipt book for reimbursement of any out-of-pocket expenses and cash tips.

Policies. U.S. laws differ from those of other countries. The program should specifically state whether the participants are expected to follow U.S. and/or campus policies or the laws of the host country. If students can legally drink at eighteen years of age in the host country and the program follows the host country's laws, then clear expectations about attendance and attentiveness, especially in the early morning hours, are essential. Consequences if a student violates a policy, is disruptive, leaves the program, arrives late every day, or does not actively participate should also be clear. Students should be asked for permission for the program director to contact their family in the event that any student leaves the program for any reason.

Orientation. Orientation should include information on security and crime in the host country; monetary exchange; the importance of keeping valuables (such as a passport) safe; cultural differences and establishing respect for local customs; appropriate clothing; weather extremes; and materials to bring.

In addition, the name of the on-site coordinator who should be contacted in the event of a home emergency requiring contact with the student should be provided to students and parents before departure. Likewise, the on-site coordinator should have the name and phone number of an emergency contact for each student.

Knowledge About Participants. Planning and preparation include knowing as much as possible about the student participants. It's important to know if students have any special accommodation, dietary needs, or medical issues. What are their expectations for the program? Have they traveled abroad previously? What questions or concerns do they have?

Assessment. Assess learning outcomes as well as logistics at the end of each day as well as during the last session. Recognize and reward participants (students and faculty) and send notes to the students' parents about their involvement. Follow-up six months later with the participants to see if their learning outcomes have changed. Using the assessment feedback, revise the succeeding year's program.

Miscellaneous. The on-site coordinator should know the location of the nearest medical facilities (ambulatory and emergency care), pharmacy (which may be called something else in an international country), and grocery store, and how to obtain a passport if one is stolen or lost.

Barriers to Curricular and Co-Curricular Study Abroad

Some students may be reluctant to study abroad due to their perceptions of security issues. Front-page articles about missing young people and crimes in other countries may give the misperception that crime is rampant and the country is not safe. Others may have difficulty juggling a study abroad experience within the curricular requirements of their academic programs, especially if required courses are offered only once each academic year. Extending a student's college career to spend a semester or quarter abroad can affect a student's finances. In addition, study abroad can be an extra expense, even if the student is paying the same tuition, fees, and room and board. Students studying abroad may be required to purchase extra health insurance as well as pay for flights to and from their international city of study. In some cases, parents of students resist study abroad initiatives because of safety and financial concerns.

Universities are still struggling with how to address these issues. Many universities discuss the importance of study abroad at their orientation programs or classes in hopes of encouraging more student participation. These universities encourage first-year students to work closely with their academic advisors to incorporate a study abroad experience. Successful study abroad programs are those that offer academic credit and are integrated into the students' program of study as seamlessly as possible. Some institutions provide travel scholarships through the establishment of special student fees that are awarded based on financial need.

Supporting Study Abroad

There is usually one central department designated to conduct outreach, recruitment, and support to students interested in curricular study abroad. If this department is not in student affairs and student affairs staff are not primarily responsible, it is highly recommended that the staff partner and become familiar with who is responsible and what programs are offered where and when. Planning for co-curricular study abroad may be more decentralized, but the expectations of support from student affairs are commensurate with curricular study abroad. By the nature of student affairs' campus responsibilities, it is likely that at some point they will be asked to collaborate or offer advice on some aspect of study abroad. Disability resource staff may be consulted when students with disabilities want to study abroad and need accommodations. Judicial services staff may be consulted to handle off-campus infractions of the campus judicial code and to interpret conduct policies' application outside the United States. In addition, some of the most important professionals within student affairs who need to be active players in study abroad are the members of the multicultural or intercultural staff. They can mentor students on campus and assist in recruitment of students to study abroad programs.

International Opportunities for Student Affairs Professionals

Though the movement to internationalize higher education focuses mainly on undergraduate students, more professional staff are interested in participating in exchanges, either to support their own students or for their own learning enhancement and professional development. Some professional staff seek opportunities to expand their international awareness through government programs such as the Fulbright, while others look to their professional associations and on-campus programs for opportunities.

Student Affairs Graduate Preparation Programs

Until recently, the profession has been bereft of research and scholarship on the importance of internationalizing student affairs graduate preparation programs. Schulz and others (2007) believe internationalization is paramount in order to (1) prepare U.S. students to live and work in a global society and economy, especially as student affairs practitioners and faculty; (2) learn about new best practices that exist in higher education around the world; (3) decrease ethnocentrism within the profession and expand concepts of multiculturalism and pluralism; (4) better understand and serve the needs of international students on our campuses; and (5) return the United States to its pre-9/11 condition as an appealing site for higher education study among international students (Schulz and others).

Unfortunately, student affairs professional preparation does not appear to be keeping pace with the global movement toward internationalization. Schultz and others conducted a study of student affairs graduate professional programs and learned that 73 percent of the programs that responded had internationalized in some way, but only 20 percent had an "international cognate and a mere 11% would qualify as being internationalized" (p. 3).

Though universities have been providing study abroad services to international students and native students for decades, only recently have students in and alumni of student affairs preparation programs begun to consider and seek international employment opportunities. The University of Arizona Center for the Study of Higher Education's Web site lists several student affairs preparation programs that provide coursework and other opportunities to learn about international student affairs work (University of Arizona, n.d.). Each of the programs listed offers a varied amount of course work and practical experience.

Owen (in press) reports that student affairs professionals "must become cultural educators" and "in order to facilitate the development of a globally competent individual it is paramount that student services professionals recognize the importance of international education" (p. 133). Coursework, internships, and practica in international student affairs should be a required component of any student affairs graduate preparation program. International student affairs is a wonderful place to learn about student development theory, intercultural issues, student behavior, cross-cultural issues, and refine and improve counseling and helping skills.

Staff and Faculty Opportunities for Study Abroad

Many student services professional associations offer opportunities for participation in short-term international exchanges. NASPA, for instance, developed an International Exchange Program in 1995 when the first U.S. delegation was invited to France to meet with CNOUS. That same year NASPA also started the annual NASPA International Symposium (Ludeman, Osfield, and Sullivan, 2005). Since then NASPA has signed reciprocal international exchange agreements with student affairs professional associations in ten other countries (Australia/New Zealand, China, Germany, Ireland, Mexico, South Africa, Spain, United Arab Emirates, and United Kingdom) (Terrell and Osfield, 2006). Some professional associations have partnered in order to share staff, skills, and resources. A prime example is the initiative offered during the summers of 2006 and 2007 by ASPA, ACPA, ACUI, and ACUHO-I to offer an opportunity to its members for an International Student Services Study Tour (ACUI, n.d.), which has taken student affairs professionals and graduate students to visit institutions on the continents of Australia and Africa.

International opportunities for student affairs staff are still in their infancy. The Florida and Kentucky programs are a good example of how student affairs professionals are developing new opportunities to ensure that more students can learn and travel abroad. The authors of this chapter had an opportunity to take part in a NASPA exchange to Ireland, and this trip inspired the development of the Florida and Kentucky programs. With the increased emphasis on internationalizing the campus and curriculum, student affairs professionals have opportunities to become leaders in the promotion of internationalism.

One of the premier opportunities for student services staff and faculty to become involved with international student services and higher education is through the Fulbright International Exchange Program, especially the Education Administrators Program for staff. One past participant in the Fulbright program has stated that "my exchange experiences through NASPA prior to the Fulbright . . . coupled with the IEKC (International Education Knowledge Community) were the 'springboards' leading me to think globally. Fulbright was only the 'icing on the cake,' in terms of deepening my appreciation" (H. Holmes, personal communication, February 1, 2007).

Participation in international exchange and study abroad programs provides numerous benefits to student affairs staff. Among these are (1) visiting other countries and meeting students and learning about their goals, needs and issues, their interest in exchange opportunities, and learning about higher education systems outside the United States; (2) sharing ideas and best practices; (3) developing and nurturing networks and relationships with colleagues around the world; and (4) exploring avenues for collaborative and cooperative agreements that benefit all parties. These same benefits can also accrue to the staff members' institutions.

Opportunities for Research and International Education

Opportunities in the area of international student affairs are plentiful, especially in comparative research. Research that examines differences and similarities in alcohol education and abuse, sexual assault, disability accommodations and legislation, auxiliary service operations, and finance and budget among institutions, just to name a few, are areas for inquiry.

There are also opportunities for student affairs staff to consult with international colleges and universities on various student services topics. Student affairs professionals from the United States are also being called upon to lead newly created colleges, universities, and student affairs divisions around the world. For example, one colleague, formerly the senior student affairs officer at a midwestern university, now holds a commensurate position in the United Arab Emirates. In addition, student affairs professionals are frequently asked to be speakers at international student services conferences.

Conclusion

The demands and sustainability of democracy around the globe require an informed citizenry that can understand and articulate the commonalities and differences found among the histories, cultures, politics, religions, and economies of other regions as well as how these forces impact our global community. From such an understanding comes an appreciation of, respect for, and an acknowledgment that each unique culture has certain rights and privileges that are neither better nor less than others. We are no longer citizens of just one country, but citizens of the world.

The American Association of Colleges and Universities (AAC&U) in 2007 noted that "this is a pivotal moment for higher education, a time when we must work together for the kind of learning [that] graduates need for an interdependent and volatile world. And it is also a precarious moment when short-sighted educational choices may prove permanently limiting to America's prospects" (p. 7). This publication noted that, according to the Academic Profile from the Educational Testing Service (2003–04), today's college students' global knowledge and skills indicate that less than 13 percent of them achieve basic competence in a language other than English. Less than 34 percent earn credit for an international studies class and of those who do, only 13 percent enroll in more than four classes. Less than 10 percent study abroad (AAC&U, 2007).

We should also know how to collaborate with our academic partners and our external communities to imbed learning outcomes that complement what students are learning in the classroom. Student services professionals who want to advance in higher education will take note of the opportunities mentioned herein and strengthen these skills in their portfolio. The resulting benefits accrue to all.

There will be increasingly more opportunities for students, faculty, and staff, especially student affairs professionals, to engage with others in international study and exchange, both on and off campus. Student affairs professionals must make the same commitment that we ask our students to make, to become internationally and culturally knowledgeable and competent. We must be willing to step outside our own comfort zones and explore our interconnections. Serving as an advisor and/or accompanying students or other professionals on international study abroad programs provides an experience rich with insights into our own and others' beliefs and attitudes and challenges us to develop a world perspective rather than ethno- or nation-centric ones. Student affairs professionals frequently have the requisite skills to lead, plan, implement, and assess such experiences.

References

American Association of Colleges and Universities. *Liberal Education & America's Promise.* Washington, D.C.: American Association of Colleges and Universities, 2007.

American Council on Education. *A Handbook for Advancing Comprehensive Internationalization: What Institutions Can Do and What Students Should Learn.* Washington, D.C.: American Council on Education, 2006.

Association of College Unions International. "International Study Tour: South Africa." [http://www.acui.org/programs/professional/program.aspx?id=596&xsl=con]. n.d.

Bain, O., and Cummings, W. K. "Where Have the International Students Gone?" *International Educator*, 2005, March/April, 18–26.

Bartell, M. "Internationalization of Universities: A University Culture-Based Framework." *Higher Education*, 2003, 45, 43–70.

Bell, J. E., and Watkins, R. A. "Strategies in Dealing with the Bologna Process." *International Educator*, 2006, September/October, 70–75.

Centre National des Œuvres Universitaires et Scolaires. *Key numbers.* Paris: Centre National des Œuvres Universitaires et Scolaires, 2005/2006.

Commission on the Abraham Lincoln Study Abroad Fellowship Program. *Global Competence and National Needs: One Million Americans Studying Abroad.* Washington, D.C.: Commission on the Abraham Lincoln Study Abroad Fellowship Program, November 2005.

"Committed to Development." Monterrey, Mexico: Technologico de Monterrey, n.d.

De Wit, H. "Changing Rationales for the Internationalization of Higher Education." In L. C. Barrows (Ed.), *Internationalization of Higher Education: An Institutional Perspective. Papers on Higher Education.* Bucharest, Romania: Administrative Officer (CEPES/UNESCO), 2000.

Duke Magazine. "Engaging Students." [http://www.dukemagazine.duke.edu/dukemag/cgibin/printout.pl?date=030407&article=depgaz]. March/April 2007.

Ellingboe, B. J. "Divisional Strategies to Internationalize a Campus Portrait: Results, Resistance, and Recommendations from a Case Study at a U.S. University." In A. J. Mestenhauser and B. J. Ellingboe (Eds.), *Reforming the Higher Education Curriculum: Internationalizing the Campus.* Phoenix, Ariz.: American Council on Education and Oryx Press, 1998.

Engberg, D., and Green, M. F. *Promising Practices: Spotlighting Excellence in Comprehensive Internationalization.* Washington, D.C.: American Council on Education, 2002.

Eurostudent Report. *Social and Economic Conditions of Student Life in Europe 2005.* Hannover, Germany: HIS Hochschul-Information-System, 2005.

Haigh, M. J. "Internationalization of the Curriculum: Designing Inclusive Education for a Small World." *Journal of Geography in Higher Education*, 2002, 26(1), 49–66.

Institute of International Education. "About IIE." [http://www.iie.org//Content/NavigationMenu/About_IIE1/Mission_and_Profile/MissionandProfile.htm]. 2006a.

Institute of International Education. "U.S. Students Abroad Top 200,000, Increase By 8 Percent." [http://opendoors.iienetwork.org/?p=89252]. 2006b.

Institute of International Education. "Open Doors Online: Open Doors Report 2006—Open Doors 2006 Fast Facts." [http://opendoors.iienetwork.org]. 2006c.

Institute of International Education. "Fall 2006 International Student Enrollment Survey." [http://opendoors.iienetwork.org/?p=Fall2006Survey]. 2006d.

Institute of International Education. "Open Doors Online: Press Releases—Fall 2006 Enrollment Survey." [http://opendoors.iienetwork.org]. 2006e.

Institute of International Education. "Open Doors Press Room." [http://opendoors.iienetwork.org/?p=28645]. 2004.

Irish Universities Quality Board. *Good Practice: In the Organization of Student Services in Irish Universities.* Dublin, Ireland: Higher Education Authority, 2006.

Knight, J. "Internationalization Remodeled: Definition, Approaches, and Rationales." *Journal of Studies in International Education*, 2004, 8, 5–31.

Ludeman, R. B., Osfield, K. J., and Sullivan, M. "The NASPA International Symposium: A Decade of Global Dialogue." *Leadership Exchange*, 2005, 3(1), 25.

Mandew, M. (Ed.) *A Guide to Student Services in South Africa*. South Africa: Centre for Higher Education Transformation (CHET), 2003.

Michigan State University. "MSU Study Abroad Curriculum Integration Project." [http://studyabroad.msu.edu/currintegration/project.html]. n.d.

National Association of Foreign Student Advisors. "About NAFSA: Frequently Asked Questions." [http://www.nafsa.org/about.sec/faqs.pg]. n.d.a.

National Association of Foreign Student Advisors. "Demographics of student abroad." [http://www.nafsa.org/public_policy.sec/study_abroad_2/demographics_of_study]. n.d.b.

National Association of Foreign Student Advisors. "Public Policy: International Students Contribute over $13 Billion to the U.S. Economy." [http://www.nafsa.org/public_policy. sec/international_education_1/the_economic_benefits]. n.d.c.

Olson, C. L., Green, M. F., and Hill, B. A. *A Handbook for Advancing Comprehensive Internationalization: What Institutions Can Do and What Students Should Learn*. Washington, D.C.: American Council on Education, 2006.

Organisation for Economic Co-operation and Development. *Guidelines for Quality Provision in Cross-Border Higher Education*. Paris: Organisation for Economic Co-operation and Development, 2005.

Osfield, K. J., and Associates (in press). *The Internationalization of Student Affairs and Services in Higher Education: An Emerging Global Perspective*. Washington, D.C.: National Association of Student Personnel Administrators.

Owen, L. A. (in press). *"Serving International Students."* In K. J. Osfield and Associates, *The Internationalization of Student Affairs and Services in Higher Education: An Emerging Global Perspective*. Washington, D.C.: National Association of Student Personnel Administrators.

Pryor, J. H., Hurtado, S., Saenz, V. B., Korn, J. S., Santos, J. L., and Korn, W. S. *The American Freshman: National Norms for Fall 2006*. Los Angeles: University of California, Higher Education Research Institute, 2006.

Rice, C. "Speech Delivered During the U.S. Summit on International Education, Washington, D.C." [http:www.state.gov/secretary/rm/2006/58750.htm]. 2006.

Sax, L. J., Hurtado, S., Lindholm, J. A., Astin, A. W., Korn, W. S., and Mahoney, K. M. *The American Freshman: National Norms for Fall 2004*. Los Angeles: UCLA, Higher Education Research Institute, 2004.

Schnitzer, K, Isserstedt, W., and Middendorff, E. *Student Life in Germany: The Socio-Economic Picture. Summary of the 16th Social Survey*. Bonn, Germany: HIS Federal Ministry of Education and Research, 2002.

Schnitzer, K, Isserstedt, W., Müßig-Trapp, P., and Schreiber, J. *Student Life in Germany; The Socio-Economic Picture. Summary of the 15th Social Survey*. Bonn, Germany: Federal Ministry of Education and Research, 1999.

Schulz, S. A., Lee, J. J., Cantwell, B., McClellan, G., and Woodard, D. B. "Moving Toward a Global Community: An Analysis of the Internationalization of Student Affairs Graduate Preparation Programs." *NASPA Journal*, 44(3). [http://publications.naspa.org/naspajournal/vol44/iss3/art12/]. 2007.

Terrell, P. S., and Osfield, K. J. "Reap the Benefits of an International Exchange." *Leadership Exchange*, 2006, 4(1), 30–31.

University of Arizona. "Directory of College Student Personnel Preparation Programs with International Emphasis." [http://www.ed.arizona.edu/csppp/index2.asp]. n.d.

University Business "Duke to Spend $30 Million on Student Service Initiative." [www2.universitybusiness.com/newssummary.aspx?news_date=2007–02–14&news_id=13762]. n.d.

University of Florida . "The Center for European Studies at UF." [http://grove.ufl.edu/~ces]. n.d.

University of Florida. "Internationalizing the Curriculum Awards 2007." [http://www.ufic.ufl.edu/ica.htm]. 2007.

University of Minnesota "What Is Curriculum Integration?" [http://www.umabroad.umn.edu/ci/whatisCI/index.html]. 2006.

University of Wisconsin-Madison. "Study Abroad Web Site." [http://www.studyabroad.wisc.edu]. n.d.

PART TWO

FRAMEWORKS FOR PROFESSIONAL PRACTICE

Just as our professional practice takes place in a variety of contexts, so too is it conducted within a variety of frameworks. Theory is the first of those frameworks discussed in this part of the handbook. Lori Patton and Shaun Harper use Chapter Eight to briefly describe a variety of theories important to student affairs and then encourage colleagues to be active, intentional, and reflective in bringing theory to practice. John Dalton, Pam Crosby, Aurelio Valente, and David Eberhart tackle the thorny subject of ethics in Chapter Nine, suggesting that everyday ethics are essential as a framework for those working in student affairs. Professionals standards, addressed in Chapter Ten by Jan Arminio, are another valuable resource to assure the quality of student affairs professional practice. Not surprisingly, she presents a thorough discussion of the standards promulgated by the Council for the Advancement of Standards in Higher Education and also outlines professional standards for student affairs from a variety of other sources. Associations serve as a structural framework for professions, and student affairs professional associations play an important role within our field. Nancy Evans and Jessica Ranero share a description of a variety of generalist and specialist student affairs professional associations and articulate ways in which individual professionals can benefit from and be engaged in association activities.

CHAPTER EIGHT

USING REFLECTION TO REFRAME THEORY-TO-PRACTICE IN STUDENT AFFAIRS

Lori D. Patton and Shaun R. Harper

A group comprised primarily of senior student affairs administrators was recently engaged in a discussion about the role of scholarship in the profession. The dean of students from a large research university shared his belief that one of the major journals in student affairs had become "too theoretical" in recent years. In fact, he claimed to have found hardly any useful articles to guide his administrative work. One of the few faculty members participating in the conversation argued the exact opposite: she felt the journal focused too heavily on practice. Tension regarding the best direction in which to take the publication remained unresolved, as group members could not agree. Perhaps this dilemma could have been mediated via a "both-and" perspective. That is, the disagreement centered mostly on whether to focus more on theory *or* practice. The group instead might have asked themselves, "Why not both?" This example is in many ways reflective of the compartmentalization of theory and practice in student affairs administration.

In this chapter, we explore the undercurrents of the compartmentalization of theory and practice. We also provide a broad overview of theories commonly used in the profession and focus on using theory reflectively in practice. We conclude with a cross-case example of how theory and reflection can be introspectively used to inform and enhance sense making and action among student affairs administrators.

Explaining Theoretical Resistance: Five Assumptions to Consider

In their 1998 book, *Student Development in College: Theory, Research, and Practice,* Nancy J. Evans, Deanna S. Forney, and Florence Guido-DiBrito made a compelling case for the use of theory in student affairs. They provided a comprehensive overview of theories that help explain student development in cognitive, affective, and behavioral domains. Other scholars have also highlighted the benefits associated with incorporating theory into work with students in general (Brown, 1972; Knefelkamp, Widick, and Parker, 1978; McEwen, 2003; Miller and Prince, 1976; Rodgers, 1990; and Strange, 1994) and diverse populations in particular (Harper and Quaye, 2008; Howard-Hamilton, 1997, 2003; Patton, McEwen, Rendón, and Howard-Hamilton, 2007; and Torres, Howard-Hamilton, and Cooper, 2003). As such, McEwen and Talbot (1998) noted, "the concept of student development and the related student development theories represent one of the hallmarks of the student affairs profession" (p. 133). Most student affairs graduate programs, particularly those that are in compliance with the Council for the Advancement of Standards in Higher Education (CAS), offer at least one course on student development theory.

Despite its well-noted importance in the student affairs profession, theory is often misunderstood in ways that limit its use in practice. While there are a variety of reasons why educators and administrators decide against incorporating theory into their work on college and university campuses, we find the following five misconceptions particularly noteworthy and problematic:

1. *"Theory" was a course taught in graduate school.* As mentioned earlier, most graduate programs in student affairs include at least one course in which theories are introduced. In many cases, emphasis is placed on understanding the underpinnings and structures of theories, usually one after another throughout the semester. Hence, many professionals graduate from student affairs programs having memorized Chickering and Reisser's (1993) seven vectors, for example, but lacking a clear understanding of how to employ this knowledge in practice. This problem is only exacerbated over time, as newcomers to the profession eventually become midlevel and senior professionals who forget the vectors, positions, stages, and statuses of theories learned long ago. More emphasis should be placed on socializing students in preparation programs to consciously use theory in practice. It is also important to offer continual learning about theory in student affairs divisions, as more than half of mid- and senior-level administrators do not have graduate degrees in student affairs (Harper and Kimbrough, 2005; and Winston and Creamer, 1997).

2. *Theory is boring.* Theory can lack excitement if thought of merely as something that was memorized for comprehensive exams in graduate school. However, there are many dimensions of theory that can be used to ignite deep and meaningful conversations among colleagues and students. When used as frameworks for sensemaking, theories can help clarify and untangle complex phenomena. For example, Harper, Harris, and Mmeje's (2005) theory of male misbehavior provides insights for which judicial officers in higher education have long searched. Men commit almost all of the violent behaviors and property destruction offenses on college campuses (Dannells, 1997). Harper and others' theory elucidates the reasons for this and provides an instructive lens for the development of effective interventions to curb destructive behaviors among male undergraduates. Relying on theory to make sense of and respond to long-standing institutional problems such as this could be stimulating.

3. *Practical experience supersedes theoretical insight.* Years of experience are believed to render student affairs professionals more competent and credible in their roles. Consequently, those who have worked for several years usually command more respect than recent graduates from master's degree programs. Although newcomers to the profession may be exposed to more recent technological, practical, and theoretical advancements in the profession, those who have worked longer (even in the same position, doing the exact same thing year after year) are typically deemed wiser. Although experience is important, so too is exposure to new frameworks that help explain student behaviors and improve organizational effectiveness. Much like the theory *or* practice debate, we argue here that practical experience *and* theoretical proficiency together are the best combination.

4. *Classic theories are useless in contemporary contexts.* Patton and others (2007) offered a critique of popular student affairs theories as a result of the reliance in their development on mostly male, predominantly white samples. Accepting such theories as universal truths and attempting to apply them to diverse cohorts of contemporary undergraduates without contemplation would be erroneous. Notwithstanding, there are various aspects of classic theories that remain applicable to groups beyond those from which they were originally derived. For instance, Stage 1 (basic trust versus mistrust) of Erik Erikson's (1959) theory can still do much to explain why some students are unwilling to establish close personal relationships with peers and faculty, why the director of career services micromanages staff members, or why a vice president for student affairs struggles to delegate tasks to others. Also useful are additions and new developments to classic theories. McEwen, Roper, Bryant, and Langa (1990) offered nine dimensions of African American college students' developmental experiences that had been previously overlooked in psychosocial theories. Their aim was

not to fully discredit or toss out existing theories, but instead to extend them. Thoughtful critique not withstanding (Braxton, 2000) several aspects of Tinto's (1975) theory of student departure deserve to be honored and are still useful in many ways.

5. *Simply knowing theory ensures its use in practice.* One of the biggest misconceptions is that theory automatically influences practice without much effort and consciousness. That is, once it is learned, an assumption is made that professionals will mindfully rely on it in their daily roles and responsibilities. No matter how well one has studied the Evans and others (1998) book or the latest theoretical breakthroughs published in student affairs journals, theory will not inform or enhance administrative action on its own.

An Overview of Theories That Inform Student Affairs Practice

A number of resources exist for readers interested in extensive syntheses of theories pertaining to college student development (Evans and others, 1998; McEwen, 2003; and Torres and others, 2003), campus environments (Strange, 2003; and Strange and Banning, 2001), retention and student departure (Bean, 2005; Braxton and Hirschy, 2005; Braxton, Hirschy, and McClendon, 2004; and Peltier, Laden, and Matranga, 1999), and organizations (Kezar, 2001; and Kuh, 2003). In this section, we provide a basic overview of theoretical perspectives related to college students and campus environments, and offer examples of how being conscious about them could prove useful in practice. Our coverage of theories is not intended to be exhaustive. Instead, we endeavor to illustrate how student affairs educators might use certain aspects of select theories in their work.

Psychosocial Development Theories

Psychosocial development theories attempt to explain or describe particular developmental, age- related tasks that focus on the resolution of qualitatively different crises or life moments that people experience. Strange and King (1990) explained that psychosocial theories are "cyclical periods of transition and stability, generally a function of chronological maturation, and offer opportunities for teachable moments when the learning tasks are personally relevant" (p. 15). Such theories highlight the development of external identities such as race, gender, and sexuality, and internal processes such as behavior, thoughts, and value systems. Moreover, these theories highlight the significant role of the environment in mediating the developmental process. Thus, development is not only unique to the individual but also hangs in balance with the ways in which the individual relates to others and the surrounding environment.

Psychosocial development theories focus on the substance or "content" of development (Evans and others, 1998; Miller and Winston, 1990). The content of development may include but is not limited to the construction of interpersonal or intimate relationships, selection of career interests or declaring a major, establishing a deeper understanding and definition of oneself beyond authoritative figures such as parents, and establishing a sense of confidence and autonomy to make decisions and express ones values through thought and action. According to Miller and Winston, these "developmental tasks" represent "an interrelated set of behaviors and attitudes that one's culture specifies should be exhibited at approximately the same chronological time in life by a given age cohort in a designated environment context such as the higher education setting" (p. 104). In other words, development is a continuous, cumulative, and natural process comprised of developmental tasks that are often culture specific, age related, and qualitatively different in terms of how they are experienced (that is, how people think, behave, or feel as a result of the experience). Moreover, development rests within the individuals' ability to effectively resolve the uncomfortable and challenging nature of the tasks in increasingly complex and diverse ways. These resolutions are contingent on an individual's ability to master the challenges and opportunities presented in previous tasks.

Erikson's work (1959, 1963, 1968, 1980) is commonly credited as a significant contribution to the way that student affairs educators understand and use psychosocial development theories to inform practice. Hamrick, Evans, and Schuh (2002), Evans (2003), and others have noted that while Erikson did not focus specifically on the development of college students, nevertheless, his work is significant for student affairs educators. Moreover, later work focusing on development has been significantly influenced by Erikson's work.

Numerous other theories of psychosocial development have evolved, including those of Marcia (1966), Josselson (1991, 1996), and Chickering and Reisser (1993), to name a few. Each of these theories highlights the developmental process and in some cases the development of a particular identity within the context of the broader developmental process. Chickering and Reisser's seven vectors explain how college students learn, grow, and develop. The vectors denote a change in magnitude and direction and include developing competence, managing emotions, establishing identity, moving through autonomy toward interdependence, developing integrity, developing mature interpersonal relationships. Chickering and Reisser's vectors can be used in many ways to assist student affairs educators with a diverse student body. For example, Andrea, a first-year student, must resolve feelings of fear, anger, depression, and anxiety that have emerged as a result of challenges she has faced in getting adjusted to a new campus environment and finding new friends. The work of Chickering and Reisser, specifically their articulation of the managing emotions vector, can be helpful to student affairs professionals in shaping their efforts to assist students like Andrea in understanding their emotions and in generating support programs that help those students. Understanding this vector might also be beneficial for student affairs educators when handling campus crises that result in violence, death, suicide, and loss of friends and loved ones.

Psychosocial theories also highlight the developmental process as it relates to social identities such as gender, sexual orientation, and race. The work of Cross (1991, 1995) and of Cass (1979) are examples of such theories. Cross's (1991, 1995) theory of psychological Nigrescence focuses on the development of a healthy Black identity and is among the first to specifically highlight the developmental experiences of people of color. Cross offers a five-stage model that describes the process of racial identity development among African Americans that includes: pre-encounter, encounter, immersion-emersion, internalization, and internalization commitment. It should be noted that Cross suggests that the fourth and fifth stages be collapsed into one until more research is done to support the existence of additional stages.

In explaining the process of Nigrescence, the term "race salience" is used to describe the degree of significance that race holds for individuals (Vandiver, 2001). High race salience indicates that race is central to one's self-concept, while low race salience refers to those who have a sense of, yet attribute very little of their self-concept to, being African American (Cross and Fhagen-Smith, 2001). This theory is particularly helpful in providing developmental support for African American students. For example, the first stage of the theory, "pre-encounter," refers to individuals who demonstrate low race salience. They tend to relate their experiences with a mainstream, neutral, or pro-White identity, or they are opposed to African American culture and may assume an anti-Black stance. Student affairs educators would find this theory useful in working with an African American student at a predominantly White institution. For example, Brian, an African American male who comes to campus with low race salience, would likely be unprepared to deal with being labeled with a derogatory racial slur, especially if it represents his first conscious encounter with racism. Thus student affairs educators might intervene by offering recommendations to the student, such as reporting the incident, connecting the student with an African American mentor who has experience with racism and is willing to help the student process the experience, or encouraging the student to become involved in activities or academic courses that can shed light on the African American experience and the role of this identity in society. These types of activities can help the student to gain a greater self-concept with regard to race and serve as a safe space to learn about African American culture and history in the American context.

Cognitive Development Theories

Cognitive development theories describe the varied approaches that individuals use to organize, think about, explain, and make meaning of life situations. Rodgers (1990) explained, "Cognitive developmental theories attempt to describe the increasing degrees of complexity with which individuals make meaning of their experiences with moral questions, questions of knowing and valuing, questions of faith, and questions of what is self and object" (p. 35). In addition, individuals may grapple with epistemological reasoning (Baxter Magolda, 1992) and the development of wisdom (Brown, 2004).

Cognitive development theories also describe how individuals transition toward increasingly complex ways of seeing the world and the assumptions that they use to understand the world. Simply stated, these theories attempt to explain "how" we think (Chickering and Reisser, 1993), which is somewhat different from psychosocial theories that explain "what" we think about life situations (Evans and others, 1998). As different and varied experiences emerge, individuals are challenged to think about their own viewpoints and their underlying assumptions, as well as how these viewpoints contradict or counter societal viewpoints. In doing so, cognitive dissonance occurs, pressing individuals to interpret and make meaning of these experiences.

Cognitive development theories suggest that development occurs in a sequential, predictable, hard-staged, and irreversible pattern. Thus, once individuals reach a certain point in their development, they rarely regress because development is viewed as cumulative and invariant. So an individual is not able to "unthink" a certain position, opinion, or decision, but instead may reinterpret or ascribe new meanings to these components in the cognitive development process. King (1990) shared three major assumptions to consider when examining cognitive development: 1) the meaning of experiences is cognitively constructed, 2) cognitive structures evolve, and 3) development occurs in interaction with the environment. She explains that at the heart of the process of interpreting different experiences, are "cognitive structures," a set of connected assumptions that serve as an interpretive framework and represent the logic contained in the meaning making process. In most cognitive development theories, cognitive structures represent the stages that describe the process of progressing from simplistic to complex thinking. The cognitive structures do not remain stagnant. Instead, these structures, generated through previous experiences, buttress the creation of future structures. As individuals transition into adulthood, they use more evidence or information to construct meaning. As such, foundational structures are deemed insufficient and must be revised to reflect more complex and advanced thinking. The changing or revising of cognitive structures does not exist in a vacuum. The amount of challenge and support (Sanford, 1967) offered in different environments plays a significant role in cognitive development. The interrelated assumptions used to generate cognitive structures change as individuals mature and interact with the world. Interactions within any given environment have the capacity to facilitate the necessary stimulation and challenge to move individuals toward greater cognitive complexity or to stifle development through the lack of challenge or the nonexistence of a supportive environment to address such challenges.

A number of cognitive theorists have offered perspectives on cognitive development including Perry (1999), Kohlberg (1976, 1984), Rest, Narvaez, Bebeau, and Thoma (1999), King and Kitchener (1994), Kegan (1982, 1994), Fowler (2000), Parks (2000), and Brown (2004). While explaining each of these theories is beyond the scope of this chapter, it should be noted that the work of other theorists, including Gilligan (1982), Belenky and others (1986), and Baxter Magolda (1992), provide insights about gender differences in the cognitive development process.

All cognitive development theories can be used to inform student affairs practice. For example, Perry (1999), influenced by the work of Jean Piaget, offered a scheme of intellectual and ethical development comprised of nine positions that when condensed include dualism, multiplicity, relativism, and commitment. Dualistic thinkers use a dichotomous thought pattern, which consists of viewing ideas and experiences as black and white or right and wrong. Dualistic thinkers do not acknowledge "gray areas" and see everything as having concrete meaning. Evans and others (1998) stated, "Learning is essentially information exchange because knowledge is seen as quantitative (facts) and authorities (including people and books) are seen as having and dispensing the right answers. Dualism represents concrete meaning making and belief that all questions have an answer." Student affairs educators that have familiarity with this theory can use it, for example, to assist students in a residence hall learning community in moving beyond dualistic thinking toward more complex thinking. One intervention is to invite members of the floor to participate in a "hot topics" program in which they would offer their opinions and hear opposing viewpoints. With the proper facilitation (by a faculty member or student affairs educator), students could be challenged to think about how they respond to a particular topic, how they justify their stance, and how hearing additional information and viewpoints might enhance their thinking about the topic.

In terms of later theorists who found gender differences in the way that men and women develop cognitively, Belenky and others (1986) described five epistemological perspectives, or ways of knowing, that were reflective of the women who participated in their longitudinal study. The perspectives include silence, received knowledge, subjective knowledge, procedural knowledge, and constructed knowledge. These perspectives closely resemble Perry's cognitive scheme but focus more on the unique voices of women.

One perspective that the authors describe is subjective knowledge. In this perspective, a shift occurs in how knowledge is viewed. The shift involves movement from trusting the knowledge of others to recognizing and trusting the knowledge that resides internally. Thus, women participate in the "act of choosing self over other" (Evans and others, 1998, p. 148) in how they think. An example of this perspective could be seen with Patricia, a student who has majored in chemistry, a male-dominated academic department at her institution. Up to this point, her professors have been men, who lack a true understanding of her unique experiences as a woman, particularly in this academic setting. Therefore, she may feel underappreciated, ignored, and invisible. A student affairs educator who is aware of this situation could create an undergraduate women's retreat that provides space for women students to share their experiences, how they think about the experiences, and how their views are shaped by the experiences. Through the retreat, the student from the chemistry department may feel empowered to do more self-examination of how she thinks and generate ways to maneuver through the chemistry program to be successful, such as taking a course in women's studies or using the resources at the women's center on campus for consultation.

Environmental Theories

Environmental theories explain the ways in which educational settings "attract, sustain, and satisfy students" (Strange and King, 1990). These theories focus on the manner in which the environment influences and shapes the experiences of those within them. According to Lewin's Interactionist Paradigm (1936), behavior is a function of the interaction between the person and the environment. Environmental theories focus less on development and more on individual patterns of behavior. Such theories explain the larger milieu and context in which behavior occurs and what behaviors individuals might exhibit. Strange and Banning (2001) identified four environmental perspectives to consider when working with college students: physical environments, organizational environments, constructed environments, and human aggregate environments. Physical environments comprise the tangible aspects such as buildings, the way particular environments are arranged (that is, classrooms and residence halls), and the nonverbal messages that are communicated to individuals in the environment. Organizational perspectives describe the rules that are communicated through an environment. Constructed perspectives explain the lived reality of those within an environment based upon how these individuals construct this reality. Different individuals experience the same environment in different ways based upon their background and experiences.

Human Aggregate Perspective

The remainder of this section focuses on the human aggregate perspective, or the characteristics of the individuals who comprise the environment. The human aggregate perspective suggests that individuals and the environment are mutually influential in shaping one another (Strange and Banning, 2001). The human aggregate perspective is comprised of typology theories, which focus more on predicting how individuals will act in a particular environment rather than the individuals' developmental process. Chickering and Reisser (1993) stated that such theories "are not technically developmental theories, since they do not describe the hallmarks of development, the means of measuring it, or the ways to foster it" (p. 3). Typology theories explain not simply the behavior itself but how behavior might be exhibited. Such theories acknowledge that people have individual patterns or personal styles that influence their behavior and learning preferences. Typology theories represent the unique perspectives that each individual contributes to the environment.

Typology theories include the work of Holland (1973), Myers and Briggs (Myers, 1987; Myers and McCaulley, 1985), and Kolb (1984, 1985). Each theory can be related to educational and developmental interventions for students. For example, the Myers-Briggs Type Indicator (MBTI) examines perceptual, judging, and attitude preferences. When applied, the Indicator, based upon Jung's (1971) personality theory, describes individual preferences using four dichotomized personality dimensions consisting of sensing or intuition, thinking or feeling, extraversion or introversion, and judgment or perception. The MBTI can serve as a valuable resource for student affairs educators. For example, through administering the instrument, a residence hall supervisor may find that the resident assistants working in the building have both extravert and introvert characteristics. This dichotomy describes how individuals interact with those in the environment. Extraverts derive their energy externally, while introverts produce energy internally. Thus, residence life training should consist of different activities that cater to different styles. Small-group interactions may be more comfortable for introverts, whereas large-scale activities might be more comfortable for extraverts. Similarly, the MBTI could be used in the classroom, leadership training, and career development because of its ability to help individuals assess their personality type and gain insight into how they process information and view the world.

Other Bodies of Theory Relevant to Student Affairs

Limits on the size of this chapter prohibit even a cursory review of other bodies of theory that might inform the professional practice of student affairs. Certainly a familiarity with the broad critical, postmodern, Afrocentric, feminist, indigenous, queer, or neo-Marxist theoretical frameworks can be valuable in helping student affairs professionals to interrogate the hidden curriculum of our field.

In addition, the following specific bodies of theory are often used to inform our professional work:

- Student success theories such as the Astin's (1985) theory of involvement, Tinto's (1975) theory of integration, or the work of Schlossberg, Lynch, and Chickering (1989) on mattering theory,
- Organization theories, including Senge's (1990) work on learning organizations, Mintzberg's (1979) work on organizational forms, or Bolman and Deal's (1991) four organizational frames, and
- Leadership theories, for example Bass's (1990) work on transformational leadership or Greenleaf's (1977) model of servant leadership.

As previously stated, the overview offered in this section provides a glimpse of the theories that are often used to inform student affairs practice. We offered some examples of how these theories can be used to inform practice. However, we now turn our attention to the use of reflection to bridge the gap between theory and practice.

Applying Theory to Practice: A Cross-Case Example

"Student affairs practice without a theoretical base is not effective or efficient" (Evans and others, 1998, p. 19). Upcraft (1994) argued that theory is not well known among educators and administrators and is rarely integrated into practice. Those who have worked in the profession would likely agree that student affairs administrators are always "on the go" and deeply entrenched in a wide range of institutional responsibilities—indeed, they have much to balance. In these moments, it is often difficult and unrealistic to always be diligent, explicit, intentional, and reflective about using theory to inform practice amidst more pressing day-to-day responsibilities. For example, "I used Chickering and Reisser's vectors to guide my work with a student today" probably does not come to mind during the course of a busy workday. Upcraft (1993) added, "There is an underlying suspicion, usually felt by the researchers and theoreticians in our field, that our theories are not used enough by practitioners as they develop policy, make decisions, solve problems, deliver services and programs, manage budgets, and in general do their jobs" (p. 260). We strongly advocate an intentional and reflective integration of theory into student affairs administrative practice. In this section, we provide brief illustrative examples of how one Lesbian, Gay, Bisexual, and Transgender (LGBT) Student Center director at a large university and a vice president for student affairs on a small college campus exemplify theory-minded practice.

The LGBT Center Director

Despite ongoing outreach efforts, fewer and fewer students are using the LGBT Center as a resource. In fact, it appears that the same students hang out at the center and participate in its programs on a regular basis. Reportedly, there is a large population of LGBT and questioning students at the university who hold negative perceptions of the center and its staff. Many believe the center caters almost exclusively to certain "versions" of gay and lesbian persons, and the director is perceived to be especially discriminatory toward closeted students who prefer to keep their sexual orientations undisclosed. Also, racial and ethnic minority student engagement in the center is woefully low, as many have felt pressured to privilege their sexualities above other aspects of their identities. The director was recently given this feedback by the dean of students, the person to whom she directly reports, and told that she and her staff must either reconsider their approach to attract more students or risk having the current stand-alone unit merged into the multicultural resource center on campus. Many of the negative comments came as a surprise to the director, as she had erroneously concluded that her personal efforts and the ethos of the LGBT Center were inclusive.

After the meeting, the director began to reflect on the undercurrents of barriers to student engagement. She first examined herself and the ways in which she interacts with students, the assumptions with which she and her staff plan programs, and the biases and preferences she brought to her role. As a White woman who had long publicly identified as lesbian and directed an LGBT center for the previous five years, she realized for the first time that she had actually privileged students who were at the "identity pride" stage of Cass's (1979) model of homosexual identity formation. Suddenly she recalled that some persons may never choose to engage in one of D'Augelli's (1994) identity development processes, "entering a lesbian/gay/bisexual community," as they may not want to assume the sociopolitical risks of doing so or simply do not wish to affiliate as strongly. The challenge for her was to make the center less intimidating to students who were not at that particular place in their identity development, recognizing that some could benefit from the resources and support without engaging immediately in the LGBT community.

"The character of an environment is implicitly dependent on the typical characteristics of its members" (Moos, 1986, p. 286). To this end, Strange and Banning's (2001) explanation of human aggregates was useful for making sense of why some LGBT students may have felt uncomfortable coming to the center. Specifically, if the "typical" people who hang out at the center act and behave in similar ways, characteristics are created that may not be appealing to LGBT students whose identities are positioned differently. The director also accessed the multiple dimensions of identities models offered by Jones and McEwen (2000) and Abes, Jones, and McEwen (2007) to better understand the low levels of engagement among racial and ethnic minority students. This enabled her to see how a Latina bisexual student may feel more allegiance to her ethnic community or how a Black lesbian may embrace her womanist identity more strongly (Constantine and Watt, 2002). These theories proved helpful in her reflection on issues, problems, and concerns with the center. She then began to think critically about why she and her staff approached their work in ways that were alienating to some students. Afterward, the director began to reflect on what she could do differently in the future to make the center more inviting and her own personal approach more appealing to students representing a range of sexual identities.

The Vice President for Student Affairs

The president of a small liberal arts college called an emergency meeting of her executive cabinet (all of the vice presidents) to strategically develop a response to the weeklong Black student protest on campus. At the beginning of the meeting, the president expressed confusion and frustration, as she could not understand the source of the students' discontent. Instead of jumping in immediately to offer a set of explanatory possibilities, the vice president for student affairs first took a moment to engage colleagues seated around the table—all of whom were White—in a conversation about their privileged racial positions at the college. He asked them to imagine for a moment being one of only twenty-two total persons representing their own racial group. Explicitly drawing on Critical Race Theory (see Bell, 1989 Delgado and Stefancic, 2001; Ladson-Billings and Tate, 1995; and Solórzano, Ceja, and Yosso, 2001), he suggested why some Black students are compelled to challenge the oppressive institutional ethos and racial microaggressions with which they are often forced to contend.

Furthermore, this vice president shared his own personal viewpoint that being at the "immersion-emersion" stage of William E. Cross's (1971, 1991,

1995) Theory of Psychological Nigrescence is not bad. He explained that this stage is characterized by strong, positive feelings for the Black race as well as the exploration of ethnic history, knowledge about the oppression of Black people in America and elsewhere, and the collection of artifacts pertaining to Black culture. Although the Black students were protesting, the vice president for student affairs thought it was good that they were demanding racial justice on behalf of the Black student community on campus. Despite his efforts, the president and senior cabinet members still maintained their positions that the student protest was disruptive and unnecessary.

After the meeting, as the vice president for student affairs walked back to his office, he reflected on Tinto's (1975, 1993) concept of social and academic integration, as well as Rendón's (1994) Cultural Validation Model. He understood that Black students were feeling marginalized in the classroom and socially excluded from the activities offered outside of the classroom and therefore were likely to depart prematurely if they were denied support. He was disappointed that his fellow cabinet members could not see or understand this. Notwithstanding, he felt that he had done a reasonably good job of at least attempting to expose the president and senior leaders to theoretical perspectives that explained Black student discontent on the campus. He took into account the environmental factors that complicated the acceptance of his argument and committed himself to trying a different approach in the next meeting regarding the protest. Furthermore, he recognized the value of his reflection and understood how it would compel him to become an agent and advocate for racial justice in future interactions with his colleagues.

Conclusion

There are a number of implications for using theory to inform student affairs practice. This chapter is a call to student affairs educators to be more active and conscious of the how theory can inform the work that they do and the services they provide by better helping them understand students they assist, the colleagues with whom they work, and the institutions at which they serve. This requires a certain degree of reflection, done alone or in the company of trusted others, as was the case with the president's executive cabinet at the small college. A balance between the two will likely bring forth new thinking about self and practice. We also contend that it is extremely important to challenge, problematize, and question assumptions that we hold and understand how such assumptions shape the profession and our professional practice.

This chapter served as a venue through which theory-to-practice in student affairs was promoted. However, more exploration of the relationship between theory and practice and how we promote these entities in the profession (graduate school, professional development, staff training) is warranted. As Eraut (2003) surmised, "When theories are used, their meanings are shaped both by the context(s) in which they are acquired and by the context(s) in which they are used" (p. 61). We believe that theory and practice are not separate constructs, but have an interdependent connection, which can enhance our ability to successfully handle the rigors of student affairs work in an intentional manner.

References

Abes, E. S., Jones, S. R., and McEwen, M. K. "Reconceptualizing the Model of Multiple Dimensions of Identity: The Role of Meaning-Making Capacity in the Construction of Multiple Identities." *Journal of College Student Development*, 2007, 48(1), 1–22.

Astin, A. *Achieving Educational Excellence: A Critical Assessment of Priorities and Practices in Higher Education*. San Francisco: Jossey-Bass, 1985.

Bass, B. "From Transactional to Transformational Leadership: Learning to Share the Vision." *Organizational Dynamics*, 1990, 18(3), 19–31.

Baxter Magolda, M. *Knowing and Reasoning in College: Gender-Related Patterns in Students' Intellectual Development*. San Francisco: Jossey-Bass, 1992.

Bean, J. P. "Nine Themes of College Student Retention." In A. Seidman (Ed.), *College Student Departure: Formula for Student Success*. Westport, CT: Praeger and American Council on Education, 2005.

Belenky, M. F., Clinchy, B. B., Goldberger, N. R., and Tarule, J. M. *Women's Ways of Knowing: The Development of Self, Voice, and Mind*. New York: Basic Books, 1986.

Bell, D. A. *And We Are Not Saved: The Elusive Quest for Racial Justice*. New York: Basic Books, 1989.

Bolman, L., and Deal, T. *Reframing Organizations*. San Francisco: Jossey-Bass, 1991.

Braxton, J.M. *Reworking the Student Departure Puzzle*. San Francisco: Jossey-Bass, 2000.

Braxton, J. M., and Hirschy, A. S. "Theoretical Developments in the Study of College Student Departure." In A. Seidman (Ed.), *College Student Departure: Formula for Student Success*. Westport, CT: Praeger and American Council on Education, 2005.

Braxton, J. M., Hirschy, A. S., & McClendon, S. A. *Understanding and Reducing College Student Departure*. ASHE-ERIC Higher Education Report, vol. 30, no. 3. San Francisco: Jossey-Bass, 2004.

Brown, R. D. *Student Development in Tomorrow's Higher Education: A Return to the Academy*. Alexandria, Va.: American Personnel and Guidance Association, 1972.

Brown, S. C. "Learning Across the Campus: How College Facilitates the Development of Wisdom." *Journal of College Student Development*, 2004, *45*, 134–148.

Cass, V. C. "Homosexual Identity Formation: A Theoretical Model." *Journal of Homosexuality*, 1979, *4*, 219–233.

Chickering, A. W., and Reisser, L. *Education and Identity* (2nd ed.). San Francisco: Jossey-Bass, 1993.

Constantine, M. G., and Watt, S. K. (2002). "Cultural Congruity, Womanist Identity Attitudes, and Life Satisfaction Among African American College Women Attending

Historically Black and Predominantly White Institutions." *Journal of College Student Development*, 2002, 43(2), 184–194.

Cross, W. E. Jr. "Toward a Psychology of Black Liberation: The Negro-to-Black Conversion Experience." *Black World*, 1971, 20, 13–27.

Cross, W. E., Jr. *Shades of Black*. Philadelphia: Temple University Press, 1991.

Cross, W. E., Jr. "The Psychology of Nigrescence: Revising the Cross Model." In J. G. Ponterotto, J. M. Casas, L. A. Suzuki, and C. M. Alexander (Eds.), *Handbook of Multicultural Counseling*. Thousand Oaks, Calif.: Sage, 1995.

Cross, W. E. Jr., and Fhagen-Smith, P. "Patterns of African American Identity Development: A Life Span Perspective." In C. L. Wijeyesinghe and B. W. Jackson, Jr. (Eds.), *New Perspectives on Racial Identity Development: A Theoretical and Practical Anthology*. New York: New York University Press, 2001.

D'Augelli, A. R. "Identity Development and Sexual Orientation: Toward a Model of Lesbian, Gay, and Bisexual Development." In E. J. Trickett, R. J. Watts, and D. Birman (Eds.), *Human Diversity: Perspectives on People in Context*. San Francisco: Jossey-Bass, 1994.

Dannells, M. *From Discipline to Development: Rethinking Student Conduct in Higher Education*. ASHE-ERIC Higher Education Report, vol. 25, no. 2. Washington, D.C.: George Washington University, Graduate School of Education and Human Development, 1997.

Delgado, R., and Stefancic, J. *Critical Race Theory: An Introduction*. New York: New York University Press, 2001.

Eraut, M. "The Many Meanings of Theory to Practice." *Learning in Health and Social Care*, 2003, 2(2), 61–65.

Erikson, E. H. *Identity and the Life Cycle*. New York: International Universities Press, 1959.

Erikson, E. H. *Childhood and Society* (2nd ed.). New York: Norton, 1963.

Erikson, E. H. *Identity: Youth and Crisis*. New York: Norton, 1968.

Erikson, E. H. *Identity and the Life Cycle*. New York: Norton, 1980. (Original work published 1959)

Evans, N. J. "Psychosocial, Cognitive, and Typological Perspectives on Student Development." In S. R. Komives, and D. B. Woodard (Eds.), *Student Services: A Handbook for the Profession* (4th ed.). San Francisco: Jossey-Bass, 2003.

Evans, N. J., Forney, D. S., and Guido-DiBrito, F. *Student Development in College: Theory, Research, and Practice*. San Francisco: Jossey-Bass, 1998.

Fowler, J. W. *Becoming Adult, Becoming Christian: Adult Development and Christian Faith*. San Francisco: Jossey-Bass, 2000.

Gilligan, C. *In a Different Voice: Psychological Theory and Women's Development*. Cambridge, Mass.: Harvard University Press, 1982.

Greenleaf, R. K. *Servant Leadership: A Journey into the Nature of Legitimate Power and Greatness*. Mahwah, N.J.: Paulist Press, 1977.

Hamrick, F. A., Evans, N. J., and Schuh, J. H. *Foundations of Student Affairs Practice: How Philosophy, Theory, and Research Strengthen Educational Outcomes*. San Francisco: Jossey-Bass, 2002.

Harper, S. R., Harris, F. H., and Mmeje, K. C. "A Theoretical Model to Explain the Overrepresentation of College Men Among Campus Judicial Offenders: Implications for Campus Administrators." *NASPA Journal*, 2005, 42(4), 565–588.

Harper, S. R., and Kimbrough, W. M. "Staffing Practices, Professional Preparation Trends, and Demographics Among Student Affairs Administrators at HBCUs: Implications from a National Study." *NASAP Journal*, 2005, 8, 8–25.

Harper, S. R., and Quaye, S. J. *Student Engagement in Higher Education: Theoretical Perspectives and Practical Approaches for Diverse Populations*. New York: Routledge, 2008.

Holland, J. L. *Making Vocational Choices: A Theory of Careers*. Englewood Cliffs, N. J.: Prentice Hall, 1973.

Howard-Hamilton, M. F. "Theoretical Frameworks for African American Women." In M. F. Howard-Hamilton (Ed.), *Meeting the Needs of African American Women*. New Directions for Student Services, no. 104. San Francisco: Jossey-Bass, 2003.

Howard-Hamilton, M. F. "Theory to Practice: Applying Developmental Theories Relevant to African American Men." In M. J. Cuyjet (Ed.), *Helping African American Men Succeed in College*. New Directions for Student Services, no. 80. San Francisco: Jossey Bass, 1997.

Jones, S. R., and McEwen, M. K. "A Conceptual Model of Multiple Dimensions of Identity." *Journal of College Student Development*, 2000, 41, 405–414.

Josselson, R. (1991). *Finding Herself: Pathways to Identity Development in Women*. San Francisco: Jossey-Bass, 1991.

Josselson, R. (1996). *Revising Herself: The Story of Women's Identity from College to Midlife*. New York: Oxford University Press, 1996.

Jung, C. G. *Psychological Types* (R.F.C. Hull, Ed.; H. G. Baynes, trans.). Vol. *6 The Collected Works of C. G. Jung*. Princeton, N.J.: Princeton University Press, 1971.

Kegan, R. *The Evolving Self: Problem and Process in Human Development*. Cambridge, Mass.: Harvard University Press, 1982.

Kegan, R. *In Over Our Heads: The Mental Demands of Modern Life*. Cambridge, Mass.: Harvard University Press, 1994.

Kezar, A. J. *Understanding and Facilitating Organizational Change in the 21st Century: Recent Research and Conceptualizations*. ASHE-ERIC Higher Education Report, Vol. *28*, no. 4. San Francisco: Jossey-Bass, 2001.

King, P.M. "Assessing Development from a Cognitive-Developmental Perspective." In. D. G. Creamer, and Associates (Eds.), *College Student Development: Theory and Practice for the 1990s*. Washington, D.C.: American College Personnel Association, 1990.

King, P. M., and Kitchener, K. S. *Developing Reflective Judgment: Understanding and Promoting Intellectual Growth and Critical Thinking in Adolescents and Adults*. San Francisco: Jossey-Bass, 1994.

Knefelkamp, L. L., Widick, C., and Parker, C. A. (Eds.). *Applying New Developmental Findings*. New Directions for Student Services, no. 4. San Francisco: Jossey-Bass, 1978.

Kohlberg, L. *Essays on Moral Development*, Vol. *2*: *The Psychology of Moral Development*. San Francisco: HarperCollins, 1984.

Kohlberg, L. "Moral Stages and Moralization: The Cognitive-Developmental Approach." In T. Lickona (Ed.), *Moral Development and Behavior: Theory, Research, and Social Issues*. New York: Holt, Rinehart & Winston, 1976.

Kolb, D. *Experiential Learning: Experience as the Source of Learning and Development*. Englewood Cliffs, N.J.: Prentice-Hall, 1984.

Kolb, D. A. *The Learning Style Inventory*. Boston: McBer, 1985.

Kuh, G. D. "Organizational Theory." In S. R. Komives and D. B. Woodard (Eds.), *Student Services: A Handbook for the Profession* (4th ed.). San Francisco: Jossey-Bass, 2003.

Ladson-Billings, G., and Tate, W. F. "Toward a Critical Race Theory of Education." *Teachers College Record*, 1995, 97(1), 47–68.

Lewin, K. *Principles of Topological Psychology*. New York: McGraw-Hill, 1936.

Marcia, J. E. "Development and Validation of Ego-Identity Status." *Journal of Personality and Social Psychology*, 1966, 3, 551–558.

McEwen, M. K. "The Nature and Uses of Theory." In S. R. Komives and D. B. Woodard (Eds.), *Student Services: A Handbook for the Profession* (4th ed.). San Francisco: Jossey-Bass, 2003.

McEwen, M. K., Roper, L. D., Bryant, D. R., and Langa, M. J. "Incorporating the Development of African American Students Into Psychosocial Theories of Development." *Journal of College Student Development*, 1990, 31(5), 429–436.

McEwen, M. K., and Talbot, D. M. "Designing the Student Affairs Curriculum." In N. J. Evans and C. E. Phelps Tobin (Eds.), *The State of the Art of Preparation and Practice in Student Affairs: Another Look*. Lanham, Md.: University Press of America, 1998.

Miller, T. K., and Prince, J. S. *The Future of Student Affairs: A Guide to Student Development for Tomorrow's Higher Education*. San Francisco: Jossey-Bass, 1976.

Miller, T. K., and Winston, R. B. "Assessing Development from a Psychosocial Perspective." In. D. G. Creamer and Associates (Eds.), *College Student Development: Theory and Practice for the 1990s*. Washington D.C.: American College Personnel Association, 1990.

Mintzberg, H. *The Structuring of Organizations*. Englewood Cliffs, N.J.: Prentice Hall, 1979.

Moos, R. H. *The Human Context: Environmental Determinants of Behavior*. Malabar, Fla.: Krieger, 1986.

Myers, I. B. *Introduction to Type: A Description of the Theory and Applications of the Myers-Briggs Type Indicator* (4th ed.). Palo Alto, Calif.: Consulting Psychologists Press, 1987.

Myers, I. B., and McCaulley, M. H. *Manual: A Guide to the Development and Use of the Myers-Briggs Type Indicator*. Palo Alto, Calif.: Consulting Psychologists Press, 1985.

Parks, S. D. *Big Questions, Worthy Dreams: Mentoring Young Adults in Their Search for Meaning, Purpose, and Faith*. San Francisco: Jossey-Bass, 2000.

Patton, L. D., McEwen, M. K., Rendón, L., and Howard-Hamilton, M. F. "Critical Race Perspectives on Theory in Student Affairs." In S. R. Harper and L. D. Patton (Eds.), *Responding to the Realities of Race on Campus*. New Directions for Student Services, no. 120. San Francisco: Jossey-Bass, 2007.

Peltier, G. L., Laden, R., and Matranga, M. "Student Persistence in College: A Review of Research." *Journal of College Student Retention*, 1999, 1(4), 357–375.

Perry, W. G. Jr. *Forms of Ethical and Intellectual Development in the College Years: A Scheme*. San Francisco: Jossey-Bass, 1999.

Rendón, L. I. "Validating Culturally Diverse Students: Toward a New Model of Learning and Student Development." *Innovative Higher Education*, 1994, 19(1), 33–51.

Rest, J. R., Narvaez, D., Thoma, S. J., and Bebeau, M. J. "A Neo-Kohlbergian Approach to Morality Research." *Journal of Moral Education*, 1999, 29, 381–395.

Rodgers, R. F. "Recent Theories and Research Underlying Student Development." In D. G. Creamer (Ed.), *College Student Development: Theory and Practice for the 1990s*. Alexandria, Va.: American College Personnel Association, 1990.

Sanford, N. *Where Colleges Fail: A Study of the Student as a Person*. San Francisco: Jossey-Bass, 1967.

Schlossberg, N., Lynch, A., and Chickering, A. *Improving Higher Education for Adults: Responsive Programs and Services from Entry to Departure*. San Francisco: Jossey-Bass, 1989.

Senge, P. M. *The Fifth Discipline. The Art and Practice of the Learning Organization*, London: Random House, 1990.

Solórzano, D. G., Ceja, M., and Yosso, T. J. "Critical Race Theory, Racial Microaggressions, and Campus Racial Climate: The Experiences of African American College Students." *Journal of Negro Education*, 2001, 69(1), 60–73.

Strange, C. C. "Dynamics of Campus Environments." In S. R. Komives and D. B. Woodard (Eds.), *Student Services: A Handbook for the Profession* (4th ed). San Francisco: Jossey-Bass, 2003.

Strange, C. C. "Student Development: The Evolution and Status of an Essential Idea." *Journal of College Student Development*, 1994, 35(6), 399–412.

Strange, C. C., and Banning, J. H. *Educating by Design: Creating Campus Learning Environments That Work*. San Francisco: Jossey-Bass, 2001.

Strange, C.C., and King, P.M. "The Professional Practice of Student Development." In. D. G. Creamer and Associates (Eds.), *College Student Development: Theory and Practice for the 1990s*. Washington, D.C.: American College Personnel Association, 1990.

Tinto, V. "Dropout from Higher Education: A Theoretical Synthesis of Recent Research." *Review of Educational Research*, 1975, 45(1), 89–125.

Tinto, V. *Leaving College: Rethinking the Causes and Cures of Student Attrition* (2nd ed.). Chicago: University of Chicago Press, 1993.

Torres, V., Howard-Hamilton, M. F., and Cooper, D. L. *Identity Development of Diverse Populations: Implications for Teaching and Administration in Higher Education*. ASHE-ERIC Higher Education Report, vol. 29, no. 6. San Francisco: Jossey-Bass, 2003.

Upcraft, M. L. "Translating Theory into Practice." In M. J. Barr (Ed.), *The Handbook of Student Affairs Administration*. San Francisco: Jossey-Bass, 1993.

Upcraft, M. L. "The Dilemmas of Translating Theory to Practice." *Journal of College Student Development*, 1994, 35(6), 438–443.

Vandiver, B. J. "Psychological Nigrescence Revisited: Introduction and Overview." *Journal of Multicultural Counseling and Development*, 2001, 29(1), 165–173.

Winston, R. B., and Creamer, D. G. *Improving Staffing Practices in Student Affairs*. San Francisco: Jossey-Bass, 1997.

CHAPTER NINE

MAINTAINING AND MODELING EVERYDAY ETHICS IN STUDENT AFFAIRS

Jon C. Dalton, Pamela C. Crosby, Aurelio Valente, and David Eberhardt

Janice Jenkins hung up the phone and reflected on the words of the vice president: "I need your help on this, Janice," he said. "The faculty is very concerned about student cheating, especially by athletes, and I think we need to make an example of this student. Your recommendation of disciplinary probation may be too lenient, and I would like for you to consider suspension in this case. Please get back to me on this matter by tomorrow."

Janice Jenkins, Dean of Students at Eastland College, had called her supervisor to tell him that she had completed her formal review of an academic conduct code violation by Rod Simmons, a freshman member of the football team who had been found guilty of plagiarizing an English paper from an Internet source. Based on her review, she was recommending that the student be placed on probation because of his first offense, his lack of familiarity with rules for using source material for writing assignments, and his apparent genuine remorse. She did not anticipate the vice president's disagreement with her proposed sanction.

She stared at the student's open folder before her and thought about the vice president's words, "I need your help . . . ," and "consider suspension in this disciplinary case." Janice was troubled by conflicting thoughts: Have I been unreasonable in my review of this student's conduct? Am I being consistent with what I have done in the past? How would my actions affect the well being of the student? Do I owe the vice president my loyalty when he asks for my help? Should his judgment about this situation trump my own? What will happen to me if I disagree with him? What is my duty as dean of students? For the first time since becoming dean, Janice was vacillating, unsure of what she ought to do and afraid of making a wrong decision.

Sooner or later, every student affairs professional comes to grips with a compelling ethical situation that can become a defining moment in his or her professional and personal life. Such questions are unavoidable given that the work of student affairs is steeped in ethical considerations and conflicts. Examples of common ethical questions in student affairs include:

- How do I balance punishment and forgiveness when disciplining a student?
- Is it appropriate to date a student?
- Should I side with students in a complaint against the college?
- On what grounds should I give someone "special consideration"?
- When should I intervene in the life of a troubled student?
- Can I be loyal to my supervisor and still disagree with her or him?
- Should I tell the whole truth about student binge drinking to the local television reporter?
- Was I right to suspend the fraternity?
- Should I fire an unproductive longtime employee who has several young children?
- What should I do when my conscience conflicts with institutional rules?

This chapter provides an introduction to the role of ethics in student affairs work in higher education. It identifies and discusses examples of everyday ethical issues to assist practitioners in recognizing and understanding the moral terrain of professional work. It also presents and discusses a conceptual framework for examining ethical issues and making moral decisions. We offer and discuss practical examples for applying the conceptual model in professional roles. In order to illustrate the variety of approaches to ethics that are utilized and emphasized in the profession, we review professional ethics statements of several student affairs national organizations. Finally, the chapter offers observations and recommendations to assist student affairs professionals when confronting difficult ethical issues and decisions.

What Is Ethics?

Failure to act ethically can call into question one of the most important qualities an individual can possess as a professional: personal integrity. Consequently, ethics lies at the heart of professional competence and is an indispensable trait of effective student affairs practice. Richard Niebuhr (1999) used the analogy of driving a car to describe the complexities of ethical decision making. When driving a car, he argued, one has to obey the rules of the road, keep control of the vehicle, respond to unexpected situations that may arise, avoid harming others, and still successfully manage to reach one's destination. In much the same way, moral decisions, like driving a car, have to be made in the context of dynamic circumstances in which many things are happening and one must try to keep things under control, avoid harming others, and reach a desirable outcome. While it is possible to study ethical dilemmas as isolated and static cases, real-life ethical decision making always takes place in dynamic situations in which moral decisions, like driving down the highway, must be managed in the context of some very fluid and often compelling circumstances.

Ethics is the study of how individuals ought to act in moral conflict situations where issues of right and good are at stake. Ethics centers on an examination of two moral questions. *What ought I to do? What is my responsibility?* These questions are at the heart of ethics because they require that a judgment of right or wrong, good or bad be made and that the criteria used to make the judgment be clearly evident and justified. Ethical issues arise from those situations that generate questions about the rights and welfare of individuals or of one's moral character (Callahan, 1988). The authors of this chapter use the phrase "everyday ethics" to refer to the types of ethical problems that are common to college student affairs work as well as to the application of some practical principles and strategies that can help staff to resolve ethical issues in their work.

Ethics as the Art of Making Wise and Responsible Decisions

Managing ethics is more of an art than a science. Fletcher (1966) notes that there are no formulas, prescriptions, or instructions that guarantee correct moral decisions. While guidelines and principles can help to illuminate the process of ethical decision making, they do not guarantee moral outcomes. Making wise and responsible ethical decisions depends in part upon experience, practice, and reflection in much the same way that becoming a good driver requires both considerable training and practice. Moreover, ethical decision making must be responsive to unique situations that vary from case to case so that moral maxims must be translated to ever-changing contexts. The goal of ethical decision making is, therefore, to determine how to be responsible in the midst of unique and changing circumstances involving issues of right and wrong.

The dynamic and contextual nature of everyday ethics requires regular practice, discussion, and reflection in real-life circumstances of professional practice. Aristotle (Bostock, 2000) argued that skill in moral judgment is developed through the regular exercise of making practical ethical decisions in daily life. One becomes competent in ethical decision making through practice over time in many different situations. Effective training in ethics enables one to think quickly and automatically without having to rely upon an authority to point out specific steps.

Why Be Concerned About Ethics?

There are several practical reasons for paying attention to ethics in the work of student affairs:

- Ethical conflicts represent some of the most complex and difficult situations confronted in professional life.
- Effectiveness as a professional is judged in part by one's ability to make ethical decisions in a competent, fair, and consistent manner.
- Student affairs professionals are expected to act in accordance with established professional ethics that define the moral norms of good practice.
- Personal integrity, the bedrock virtue of an individual's credibility and authenticity, depends upon the ability to maintain and model ethical reasoning and behavior.
- Finally, good ethical practice helps to ensure that all who are involved in moral conflict situations receive fair and equal consideration.

Paying attention to ethics, therefore, is an intrinsic aspect of being a capable leader, an effective professional, and a good human being.

Five Domains of Ethical Responsibility

When managing any serious ethical issue, student affairs professionals usually find themselves engaged with five different types or domains of ethical responsibility. These five domains represent critical relationships with individuals, groups, and institutions to which they have a special duty and obligation as student affairs professionals. These five domains of ethical responsibility include (1) student welfare, (2) the institution, (3) the profession, (4) the community, and (5) personal conscience. All of these domains of duty and responsibility

FIGURE 9.1 DOMAINS OF ETHICAL RESPONSIBILITY

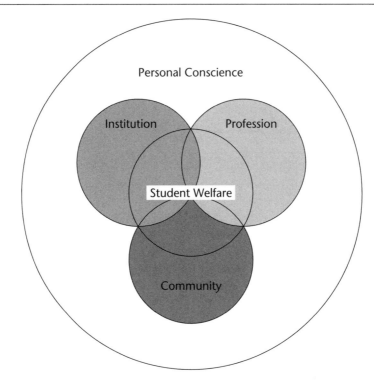

represent critical relationships in which a special ethical claim is made upon student affairs staff. These five domains of ethical responsibility are illustrated in Figure 9.1.

Each of these domains of professional work represents an area of professional responsibility and obligation. Each of them lays some claim to the ethical obligations of student affairs professionals and may at times compete and conflict in their claims. These five ethical domains are briefly described following.

The Student

The holistic welfare of students is the moral center of student affairs work. Students, as individuals and in groups, are where one begins in efforts to determine how to manage and model ethics in professional practice. While there are a number of competing priorities in professional responsibilities, the first and most important moral obligation is the welfare and development of students.

It is important to stress this moral priority, since students generally have so little power in higher education and are so transient.

Scenario. Janice, the dean of students, has an ethical responsibility to do all she can to promote the holistic welfare of Rod Simmons, the new student athlete who has violated the school's academic honor code. She must consider his needs and welfare as a student, a new student, an athlete, and a human being. She must also consider the impact of his conduct and her disciplinary sanction on the holistic welfare of other students in the university.

The Institution

The institution that employs student affairs professionals has a strong claim on their ethical responsibilities through the employer-employee relationship, but even more strongly, it can be argued, through the institution's stated mission and values. By accepting employment with a college or university, a student affairs professional affirms and agrees to promote actively the institution's mission and values.

Scenario. The dean of students must consider her responsibilities to her boss and the institution she both works for and represents. She must determine what her proper duty is to both of them and how she can fulfill those expectations in a manner consistent with the holistic welfare of the student involved.

The Profession

By joining professional associations and subscribing to their standards of ethical practice, student affairs professionals agree to be guided by the standards of conduct determined by practitioners in the field. Subscribing to a profession's ethics is one of the ways in which professionals assure the public that their occupation will be performed in accordance with certain standards (Boylan, 2000).

When they join professional associations, student affairs staff are required to consider the association's ethical principles and rules when confronting ethical problems and issues in their work. Some professional organizations have disciplinary procedures to address violations of their standards and some do not. Procedures for documenting good standing and managing disciplinary procedures are especially important in situations where licensure or certification is required for professional practice.

Some student affairs staff work in professional positions but do not join professional associations. They, too, have a responsibility to observe the ethical standards of the professional group associated with their area of work, but this responsibility is less formal and documented.

Scenario. The dean of students has an obligation to apply the standards of ethical practice endorsed by her primary professional organization that apply to situations like the one she is confronting. As a consenting member and representative of the profession association, she has made a commitment to implement their ethical standards in professional practice.

The Community

Student affairs professionals also work in the context of a community that includes a broad network of laws, rules, relationships, and mores. For student affairs professionals, this community consists of parents, local police and health officials, community service agencies, state agencies, news media, homeowners, bar owners, alumni, school officials, and a host of other individuals, organizations, and groups that are connected to the institution in a variety of different ways. This community exerts legal, moral, and political influence on student affairs professionals and can affect the manner in which ethical issues are discussed and decided. Some aspects of the community adhere to particular values and moral beliefs and expect student affairs professionals to observe them in their activities.

Scenario. The dean of students must be aware of and considerate of the moral, social, and legal standards of the community of which she is both a member and an official, particularly as these standards may relate to the situation she is confronting. Community values and standards usually have less direct influence on professional practice, but they provide an important context for moral decision making that should be considered.

Individual Conscience

In addition to the previously discussed four domains of ethical responsibility, it is important to include the fifth domain, individual conscience, in our discussion of managing and modeling ethics in professional practice. Conscience is the domain of one's most deeply held personal beliefs and convictions that are formed by life experiences and commitments. Conscience is highly individual and deeply rooted in both emotion and reason. It bridges the realms of rationality and emotion but is not entirely grounded in either. Conscience is the individual's internal court of last resort that reflects his or her deepest convictions about what is fundamentally right and wrong. Conscience is important in ethics because it provides an integrative function in ethical decision making that helps to define personal responsibility. It helps to interpret, integrate, and balance the various realms of responsibility we have previously discussed.

In deciding how to proceed with a professional ethical problem, student affairs professionals should be guided by these five domains of ethical responsibility. The first four domains of responsibility—that is, student holistic welfare, institution, profession, and community—are viewed through the lens of conscience, which provides a necessary personal context and helps one weigh priorities and claims using ethical principles guided by conscience.

Personal conscience also provides what one might call a "comfort fit" in exploring ethical responsibilities. Do I feel right about this course of action? Can I be proud of this decision? Would I feel good about explaining this decision to people I respect? Thus, conscience helps to integrate the process of moral decision making by providing a lens through which to interpret moral responsibilities and decisions.

Personal conscience can and should trump other moral considerations in certain situations. If student affairs professionals believe that a decision or action would compel them to violate a sacred personal belief or value, then they must decide whether to follow their conscience. Student affairs professionals must cultivate and use their best personal judgments when deciding how to apply stated standards of ethical practice in particular situations so as to bring about maximum benefit to all involved. However, there is no free ride in commitment to conscience. When deciding to follow one's conscience, the student affairs professional must also weigh and accept the practical consequences of acting on the basis of individual conscience.

Scenario. The dean of students tries to separate her purely personal beliefs and values as much as possible from the circumstances of the problem she is seeking to resolve. In the end, however, she knows she must be true to her deepest personal convictions about what is right and good to do in this situation. These convictions may at times run counter to what is endorsed by the institution, her profession, and her community and require courage to act on conscience and to accept the consequences of that moral stance.

Ethics in the Student Affairs Profession

To guide student affairs professionals in ethical decision making and conduct, a number of professional organizations have developed ethical standards and codes of ethics. These standards and codes are intended to do three primary things: (1) promote the interests and welfare of those who are served by professionals, (2) protect the professional, and (3) advance the profession. Ethical standards help to insure the greatest good for those who are served and to protect against self-interest and personal gain that can undermine professional credibility as well as the credibility of the profession.

The professional field of student affairs work is currently comprised of more than thirty-five different professional associations (Council for the Advancement of Standards in Higher Education, 2006). Many of these professional associations have adopted formal ethical codes of professional practice that prescribe ethical standards for their members. While there is considerable overlap in the ethical standards of these student affairs associations, there are also considerable differences. Discussion continues as to whether or not student affairs can rightfully be understood as a profession (Blimling, 2001; Carpenter, 2001), but for the purposes of this chapter it is treated as one. Certainly there is much common agreement about the ethical responsibilities of student affairs professionals, as this chapter demonstrates.

In an effort to identify ethical principles that are shared in common by the various student affairs professional associations, the Council for the Advancement of Standards in Higher Education (CAS) conducted a study of professional ethical codes. Their review identified seven ethical principles that are shared across the various student affairs professional groups in higher education (CAS Statement, 2006). These shared ethical principles include:

1. *Autonomy:* Respecting freedom of choice
2. *Nonmalfeasance:* Doing no harm
3. *Beneficence*: Promoting the welfare of others, especially students
4. *Justice*: Being fair and respectful to others
5. *Fidelity*: Being faithful to our word and duty
6. *Veracity*: Being truthful and accurate
7. *Affiliation*: Fostering community and the public good.

There are several interesting aspects about these commonly shared ethical principles. First, they encompass the five ethical principles identified by Kitchener (1985) that are widely utilized in the profession today. Second, they have the advantage of recognition by CAS as well as endorsement by all of the member professional associations that have professional ethical codes. These seven shared ethical principles do not supplant the individual ethical codes of student affairs professional groups, but they do offer a foundation of core ethical standards for the student affairs profession as a whole. The seven CAS principles are utilized in this chapter as normative ethical standards that can be useful in addressing ethical issues.

Because CAS standards must be general enough to represent the shared core values of thirty-five associations, CAS's summary of ethical principles cannot depict all of the specificity of interests and values that are unique to particular associations. As principles become more general and inclusive of diverse organizations, they necessarily become increasingly abstract, providing more silhouette and shadow and less context and detail. Following is a brief overview of the ethics statements of four student affairs organizations that are members of CAS. The overview illustrates some of the differences in approach to professional ethics and the special emphasis placed upon the importance of the holistic welfare of students in student affairs work. The ethical statements and/or core values of these four organizations illustrate the diverse ways that values or domains are structured and the many ways that students are emphasized.

ACPA's Statement of Ethical Principles and Standards

The American College Personnel Association (ACPA) is comprised of members from both public and private colleges and universities in the United States and abroad, and includes administrators and faculty who work, teach, and/or research in the areas of student affairs as well as graduate students who pursue degrees in student affairs and higher education administration.

The purpose of ACPA's *Statement of Ethical Principles and Standards* is to provide a context for thinking about ethical issues relating to student affairs practice and to assist members to acquire sensitivity to problems relating to potential ethical dilemmas. The *Statement* also clarifies expected standards of behavior and helps members to monitor their own conduct. Finally, it helps to increase an awareness of standards of behavior in others through a spirit of collegiality (American College Personnel Association [ACPA], 2006). The *Statement* is based on Kitchener's (1985) ethical principles, as noted earlier.

In contrast to the organization of CAS principles, whose standards are presented according to value statements, ACPA's *Statement* consists of four standards, each representing what has been identified in this chapter as a *domain of ethical responsibility*:

1. Professional responsibility and competence
2. Student learning and development
3. Responsibility to the institution
4. Responsibility to society (ACPA, 2006)

Subsumed under each standard are specific statements describing ethical actions that embody the standard. For example, under "Student Learning and Development" are indicator statements of moral actions including:

> 2.3 Abstain from all forms of harassment, including, but not limited to, verbal and written communication, physical actions and electronic transmissions,
>
> 2.4 Abstain from sexual intimacy with clients or with students for whom they have supervisory, evaluative, or instructional responsibility,
>
> 2.5 Inform students of the conditions under which they may receive assistance. (ACPA, 2006, p. 3)

The fact that an entire section is devoted to issues focusing on the treatment of, and interaction with, students reflects ACPA's emphasis on the importance of student growth and development, a domain central to its mission. ACPA underscores its commitment to accountability to students by stating, "Student development is an essential purpose of higher education. Support of this process is a major responsibility of the student affairs profession" (ACPA, 2006, p. 3).

NASPA's Standards of Ethical Behavior

The National Association of Student Personnel Administrators (NASPA) is a professional organization of student affairs administrators, faculty, and graduate students. NASPA describes itself as an association committed to *serving college students* by means of furthering the education of the *whole student* and advancing the integration of *student life and learning* (The National Association of Student Personnel Administrators [NASPA], n.d., p. 1). NASPA's mission is to provide support and guidance for those whose focus is on broadening the college student experience (NASPA, n.d., p. 1).

NASPA's standards of ethical behavior are markedly general, consisting of core values with no direct interpretation of how those values are to be operationalized. The core values of diversity, learning, integrity, service, fellowship, spirit of inquiry, collaboration, and access are described as essential in NASPA's active commitment to, and engagement with, students. As a result, it is clear that NASPA relies on individual institutions to apply these values to and incorporate these values into their own specific contexts and daily practice.

ACUI's Ethical Standards

The Association of College Unions International (ACUI) is a professional organization that encourages college union and student activities professionals to build strong campus communities through educational resources and programs. Its members include students as well as professionals in college student union administration who may be, for example, student union directors, program directors, or food service administrators, among others.

Similar to CAS, ACUI's ethical standards are presented as values, not domains of ethical responsibility. The purpose of ACUI's core values of unconditional human worth, joy, caring community, innovation, communication, and integrity (ACUI, n.d., p. 2), as well as their *Code of Ethics*, is to articulate the organization's expectations of members' "professional behavior" (ACUI, n.d., p. 1). Under each core value are indicator statements.

One subsection under the core value "integrity" is devoted specifically to students and is entitled, "Students as Individuals." It includes the following:

- Members view each student as a unique individual with dignity and worth, and with the ability to be self-directed.
- Members are concerned for the welfare of all students and work to provide an environment that encourages personal growth, effectiveness, creativity, and responsible citizenship.
- Members respect the rights of students and promote responsible behavior.
- Members respect the privacy of students and hold in confidence personal information obtained in the course of the staff/student relationship (ACUI, n.d., p. 2).

NODA's *Statement of Professional Ethics*

The National Orientation Directors Association (NODA) is an association of professionals in the field of orientation, transition, and new student programs in the academic community. NODA's professional standards are intended to be used as a "benchmark for ethical practice" (National Orientation Directors Association [NODA], n.d., p. 2). The purpose of NODA's *Statement of Professional Ethics* is to lend support to its members in choosing actions that will further college students' "educational outcomes" (NODA, n.d., p. 1).

NODA's *Statement of Professional Ethics* is similar to the statement of ethical principles of ACPA in that its standards are organized by domains of ethical responsibility, not by values or virtues (as is the case for ACUI and CAS). Five standards focus on the accountability of orientation directors to the following groups with whom they interact: student staff members; students in transition; parents, guardians, and families of students; faculty and staff colleagues; institutions; and corporate partners or sponsors. In addition, one standard focuses on orientation directors' general accountability as higher education practitioners.

Of the six standards, two are devoted especially to ethical decisions focusing on students: student staff members and students in transition. For example the standard that pertains to interactions with students in transition, stipulates that "Orientation Professionals shall:

- Ensure that students receive accurate and adequate information necessary for decision-making,
- Ensure that students have access to relevant materials, and that materials are available in multiple formats, including text, web resources, and other adaptive technologies when possible,
- Recognize the diversity of experiences of students in transition, and work to meet the various needs of new students, transfer students, adult learners, and other special populations." (NODA, n.d p. 7)

As the examples here illustrate, there are differences in approach and emphasis among the various student affairs professional organizations in how they articulate ethical standards and priorities. Despite these differences, they share a strong commitment to the welfare and development of college students, and this commitment forms the foundation of the profession's ethics.

The Holistic Welfare of Students as the Moral Focus of Student Affairs Work

Most professions claim a guiding moral purpose and have an ethical focus that helps to define their deepest values (Anderson, 1980). The medical profession, for example, affirms the moral principle of preserving life as central to professional practice. The legal profession emphasizes the core principle of justice, while journalists claim truth as their guiding moral purpose. These defining ethical principles serve to guide practitioners of these professions and to anchor their practice to a strong moral foundation.

The enduring central moral purpose of student affairs work has been and continues to be the holistic welfare of college students. This central and defining ethical purpose provides the basic moral foundation that guides our profession and is the beginning point for the examination of professional ethics. From the inception of the profession in American higher education student affairs, practitioners have stressed the importance of learning in the context of students' holistic needs and development.

This holistic educational focus runs deep in the profession's history and legacy and has played an important role in shaping contemporary student affairs professional practice. Bryan, Winston, and Miller (1991) note that "above all, student affairs practitioners are engaged in the business of helping students improve their lives" (p. 10). This moral focus has also been reaffirmed in various professional statements and documents (Whitt, 1997).

A professional ethics grounded in an ethic of care for students' holistic welfare emphasizes that the well-being and development of every student are a central purpose of professional practice. Starting with this core purpose provides an important moral foundation for constructing the ethics for the profession. Although the student affairs profession has grown rapidly in scope and complexity over the past century, its moral focus, its ethical center, continues to be on students and the values associated with their welfare, learning, and development.

A Multi-Lens Perspective on Managing and Modeling Everyday Ethics

Ethics is often viewed from a *top-down* perspective, in which particular normative ethical principles are identified and then applied to specific moral situations in professional work. This approach has been utilized often in the past and is examined in several recent publications on ethics in the student affairs profession (Canon and Brown, 1985; Fried, 2003; Kitchener, 1985; and Lampkin and Gipson, 1999). Kitchener's (1985) five ethical principles mentioned earlier have been especially influential among student affairs practitioners and are widely cited in student affairs literature and utilized in professional ethics statements (for example, American College Personnel Association).

Normative ethical constructions like Kitchener's have the advantage of viewing ethics from a conceptual framework of relatively fixed ethical principles that provide continuity and clarity across many different kinds of ethical issues. Using the principles-based approach is appealing to some because it provides unchanging standards or guidelines for making ethical decisions. Those who use normative ethics treat similar cases similarly and pay less attention to the particular circumstances of the individuals involved (Laney, 1990). To use the analogy of driving, ethical principles are like the rules of the road that guide our choices and behaviors while driving down the highway.

The disadvantage of normative ethics can be, however, that approaching moral conflicts from the vantage point of relatively fixed moral principles can sometimes be abstract and disconnected from the everyday ethics of professional work. Normative ethical approaches also give less recognition to some powerful human motivations that can in some ethical situations overwhelm reason. Moreover, people can interpret abstract principles so differently that professionals may make considerably different decisions in similar situations and thus not treat those affected equally. Rules of the road are less useful when one is contemplating how fast to drive in the growing dusk on a little used, unmarked, and unfamiliar side road.

At the other end of the continuum in approaches to ethics is the perspective of contextualism or situation-oriented ethical decision making. In this approach, sometimes called the *case-based* orientation (Lampkin and Gipson, 1999, p. 75) more emphasis is placed on the unique circumstances and conditions of specific moral situations that confront the professional. Considerable attention is also given to the personality and psychology of the individual facing an ethical dilemma (Laney, 1990). This perspective offers much greater flexibility and relevance in particular cases than the moral principles approach, but it has a serious downside in that there is much less continuity, uniformity, and predictability from one ethical decision to the next.

The practical work of solving everyday ethical problems in student affairs work requires both a situation-specific understanding of moral problems and decision makers and the ability to apply relevant normative ethical principles. Consequently, solving everyday ethical problems is facilitated by the use of both normative and contextual ethical approaches. The authors refer to this method of incorporating both approaches in managing ethical issues as a "multi-lens perspective" because it starts with a perspective on the individual circumstances of moral situations and also incorporates the perspective of relevant moral principles in the process of decision making in ethical situations.

Moreover, the authors argue for a *bottom-up* approach, in which one begins ethical deliberation by first examining the practical moral situations and responsibilities that student affairs professionals confront in their everyday work. As much as possible ethical deliberation should be kept as closely connected to the real ethical issues, roles, and responsibilities that student affairs professionals encounter in their everyday responsibilities.

It is also important to connect professional ethics to the broader moral and social context in which professional practice takes place. As Thompson (2007) notes, ethics tends to focus on individuals, but ethical issues are very often connected to the broader social and political environments of institutions and communities.

The Moral Landscape of Student Affairs Work

Ethical practice in student affairs work requires an understanding of the moral landscape of ethical problems that one is likely to confront in his or her professional responsibilities. In this section, some of the most characteristic everyday ethical issues that student affairs staff encounter in their work are examined. In order to ensure that this approach to ethics is grounded in the real-life experiences of student affairs staff, the authors reviewed the literature on ethics in student affairs and conducted an online survey of student affairs professionals utilizing several professional and regional Internet listservs. The survey asked student affairs colleagues to identify examples of ethical issues they had encountered in their work and the domains of ethical responsibility involved. In all, more than 150 unique ethical conflict situations were identified using this process.

Approximately half of respondents indicated they were in middle management positions, and about one third indicated they were new professionals in entry-level positions. The remaining respondents identified themselves as serving in senior leadership positions. Most respondents reported that they worked for four-year public institutions; however, community colleges, professional, and proprietary institutions were also represented among the respondents.

An important observation that can be drawn from this review of ethical issues is that many of the ethical dilemmas one encounters in the moral landscape of student affairs work are not unique to this field. The ethical conflicts that arise in the work of student affairs encompass many of the same ethical problems—such as dilemmas involving dishonesty, deception, integrity, loyalty, conflict of interest, and favoritism—that are common in other professions. What makes these issues distinctive in student affairs work are the special contexts and circumstances in which they occur and the unique moral status accorded the holistic welfare of college students.

Common Ethical Issues in Student Affairs Work

The followings ethical issues are culled from the literature and from the issues most frequently mentioned in the online survey conducted by the authors. The list is by no means exhaustive.

Institutional Alcohol Policies and Practices. One of the most common student affairs ethical dilemmas arises out of the conflict of trying to serve students' welfare on one hand while also promoting institutional rules and values on the other. This conflict can be seen especially in the area of institutional alcohol policies and enforcement. Colleges and universities generally have strict policies restricting alcohol consumption by students. Often these policies are ignored or downplayed by institutions at alumni and student events on home football game weekends or on other special college occasions. Student affairs staff thus find themselves teaching and enforcing a set of college rules and policies that students quickly learn are unevenly applied. Colleges and universities have rules and policies that prohibit underage alcohol consumption but, in practice, often look the other way when underaged students party. Inconsistent application and enforcement of institutional policies on alcohol presents a common type of ethical dilemma for student affairs staff.

Personal Relationships with Students. A pervasive ethical dilemma that challenges professionals in student affairs involves personal relationships with students. Student affairs staff are often young themselves and not far removed in age from college students. Moreover, student affairs staff probably spend more time with students than anyone else on campus (Kuh, 1991). These circumstances often lead to close personal relationships between staff and students and can sometimes cross, or appear to cross, the boundary of propriety and ethical responsibility. Ethical dilemmas easily arise when student affairs staff enter into romantic relationships with students or socialize with students in ways that seem to compromise professional standards or responsibilities. Because of their close rapport with students, student affairs staff often are seen as powerful role models and mentors, and this special relationship makes ethical conduct especially important.

Confidentiality. Another common ethical dilemma for student affairs staff involves confidentiality of student information. Institutional policies regarding confidentiality of student information are grounded in federal and state laws as well as professional codes of ethics that are intended to foster student privacy and welfare. However, when student affairs staff become aware of physical, mental, or emotional health problems of specific students, such as clinical depression, learning disabilities, or diabetes, they often feel a sense of responsibility to help these students. Yet privacy policies restrict the information that can be divulged to any other individuals. Alerting other university officials who come in contact with these students could help avert serious problems, but to do so could compromise students' confidentiality. Many student affairs staff feel conflicted about how to serve the welfare of students while observing confidentiality requirements.

Exception, Privilege, and Favoritism. Another common type of ethical dilemma presents itself when student affairs staff are asked to make exceptions to policies for students in special situations. For example, a popular or well-connected student, such as the relative of an institutional trustee, becomes involved in a disciplinary situation. The judicial affairs department receives a phone call from the president's office asking to be kept informed of the case. Student affairs officials then face dilemmas about how to proceed, how to appropriately discipline the student, and to whom to report their findings and actions once decisions are made.

A similar type of ethical dilemma is created when a staff member is asked to consider an exception to an admission denial decision. For example, an influential parent threatens to sue a college or university for denying enrollment to his son or daughter. The college dean responds by applying subtle pressure on the student affairs leader chairing the admissions appeals committee to admit the student through the appeal procedures. Since many prospective students with much stronger academic credentials have already been denied through the appeal process, the staff member faces a serious ethical decision.

Punishment. Student affairs staff are often responsible for student conduct and judicial procedures on campus and also carry responsibility for administrative operations which must be enforced through procedures and regulations. Consequently, student affairs staff frequently find themselves in situations in which they must administer sanctions and penalties for violations of one type or another. Determining the most appropriate discipline for students can be especially problematic for student affairs staff, since they are strongly oriented to the holistic welfare of students and may be uncertain about the uses of punishment.

Fairness. Many of the ethical conflicts student affairs staff face are related to situations that challenge their sense of fairness in the workplace. For example, professionals often must consider challenging policies, supervisors, or practices they may believe are not ethical in nature. When staff members feel that a departmental policy is unfair or unevenly applied, should they challenge it when doing do may compromise their professional standing? Such policies may include unfair hiring and promotion decisions, inequities in applying and distributing compensation and vacation time, and inappropriate use of departmental funds.

Finally, although practitioners generally share a common moral focus on student welfare, individuals within the same department may differ on how they view ethical issues and come to different conclusions about what is required ethically. Moreover, as student affairs staff progress through positions of increasing responsibility, they may interpret ethical issues differently depending on their experience, responsibilities, and judgment.

Deciding and Acting in Ethical Conflict Situations

The goal of ethics is to enable an individual to act on the basis of moral reflection and commitment. Using ethical principles and reason to determine ethical

TABLE 9.1 COMPONENTS OF ETHICAL DELIBERATION AND ACTION

Everyday Ethical Issues*	Domains of Responsibility	Ethical Principles	Decisions/Actions
Rules/Policies Confidentiality Relationships Punishment Fairness Truthfulness	Students Institution Profession Community Conscience	Autonomy Non-malfeasance Beneficence Justice Fidelity Veracity Affiliation	Specific actions taken in ethical conflict situations based on multi-lens approach

*Most common types of ethical issues.

responsibility in moral conflict situations must finally be affirmed in behavior in order to be judged ethical. The requirement of acting on ethical decisions is also a reminder that courage is always a necessary virtue of ethical decision making and behavior. Ethical decision making, like driving a car, requires action in order to be responsible. Failure to act in an ethical situation as well as in driving has real consequences.

A multi-lens approach to ethics consists of (1) identifying and understanding the nature of the ethical conflict with which one is presented, (2) examining the appropriate domain(s) of ethical responsibility that are entailed, (3) applying appropriate ethical principles to the moral conflict, and (4) deciding and acting on the basis of one's ethical conclusions. Table 9.1 summarizes these four components of ethical action.

Using a Moral Compass in Everyday Ethics

This chapter has examined the knowledge, processes, and skills that constitute the components of a student affairs professional's moral compass. A compass points the way to some known objective or goal and is used when one is uncertain about current position or direction. A moral compass points the way to what is right or good when one is uncertain about the right thing to do in any situation. A moral compass utilizes established ethical benchmarks and decision-making criteria to point the way to one's moral responsibility in specific situations.

While using a moral compass helps student affairs professions to navigate through ethical dilemmas, some individuals succeed and some fail when faced with tough moral choices. There are at least four common reasons or explanations that account for success or failure when confronting ethical conflicts:

First, some student affairs staff have a moral compass that helps them to recognize very early that a situation involves serious ethical considerations.

Some individuals, however, lack the moral sensitivity to recognize that an issue is ethical in nature, and this oversight can inhibit them from taking appropriate action quickly and effectively. Thus, the ability to perceive quickly that a problem has a serious ethical consideration is important for helping student affairs staff to anticipate ethical problems. The sensitivity of one's moral compass is developed by studying ethics, observing ethical role models, and managing real-life ethical conflicts.

Second, some student affairs staff develop a feeling or sensitivity for the specific domain(s) or type of ethical responsibility that is implicated in the ethical situation confronting them. Others may recognize that a situation involves ethical issues but not be able to determine which specific domains of ethical responsibility make the greatest claims on their attention and commitment.

Third, some student affairs staff are aided in acting in morally responsible ways by taking advantage of the conceptual tools of ethical analysis and reflection or, in essence, learning how to use their moral compass. Others can fail to reason clearly about the appropriate application of ethical principles in ethical situations so that principles fail to be effective guides and illuminators to understanding and decision making.

Fourth, some student affairs staff act with conviction and courage in situations that test one's moral fiber. Others lack the will or courage to act on what they determine to be the right thing to do. Self-interest, fear, and uncertainty can erode one's best intentions to do the right thing. Thus, managing and modeling ethics in student affairs require skills in perceiving, feeling, thinking, and acting in ethical situations.

Conclusion

Acting ethically keeps the professional's work on track. A moral compass points the way to what matters most in professional work. It helps one to make tough decisions and gives continuity to leadership and example. Striving to do the right thing helps keep order in the wide array of choices that one must face in professional work and makes it possible to sleep at night after agonizing over conflicts and dilemmas. Being an ethical professional makes it possible to take unpopular stands when taking the easy way is so inviting. Being ethical gives one an enduring place to stand in the midst of constant change. Ethical competency is indispensable for student affairs professionals who are both blessed and burdened with being among the most influential role models and mentors for today's students in higher education.

References

American College Personnel Association. *Statement of Ethical Principles and Standards.* [http://www.myacpa.org/au/documents/Ethical_Principles_Standards.pdf]. 2006.

Anderson, R. M. "Applied Ethics: A Strategy for Fostering Professional Responsibility." *Carnegie Quarterly,* 1980, XXVII (2&3). [Special Issue].

Association of College Unions International. *Mission of the Association.* [http://www.acui.org/content.aspx?menu_id=90&id=186&ekmensel=c580fa7b_90_0_186_1]. n.d.

Bostock, D. *Aristotle's Ethics.* Oxford: Oxford University Press, 2000.

Blimling, G. S. "Uniting Scholarship and Communities of Practice in Student Affairs." *Journal of College Student Development,* 2001, 42, 381–396.

Boylan, M. *Basic Ethics.* Upper Saddle River, N.J.: Prentice Hall, 2000.

Bryan, W., Winston, R., and Miller, T. *Using Professional Standards in Student Affairs.* New Directions in Student Services, no. 53. San Francisco: Jossey-Bass, 1991.

Callahan, J.C. *Ethical Issues in Professional Life.* New York: Oxford University Press, 1988.

Canon, H. J., and Brown, R. D. *Applied Ethics in Student Services.* San Francisco: Jossey-Bass, 1985.

Carpenter, D. S. "Student Affairs Scholarship (re?)considered: Toward a Scholarship of Practice." *Journal of College Student Development,* 2001, 42, 301–318.

Council for the Advancement of Standards in Higher Education. *CAS Professional Standards for Higher Education* (6th ed.). Washington, D.C.: Council for the Advancement of Standards in Higher Education, 2006.

Council for the Advancement of Standards in Higher Education. *CAS Statement of Shared Ethical Principles.* Washington, D.C.: Council for the Advancement of Standards in Higher Education, 2006.

Fletcher, J. *Situation Ethics: The New Morality.* Philadelphia: Westminster Press, 1966.

Fried, J. "Ethical Standards and Principles." In S. R. Komives, D. B. Woodard, and Associates, *Student Services: A Handbook for the Profession.* San Francisco: Jossey-Bass, 2003.

Kitchener, K. "Ethical Principles and Ethical Decisions in Student Affairs." In H. Canon and R. Brown (Eds.), *Applied Ethics in Student Services.* New Directions for Student Services, no. 30. San Francisco: Jossey-Bass, 1985.

Kuh, G. D. "Characteristics of Involving Colleges." In G. D. Kuh and J. H. Schuh (Eds.), *The Role and Contributions of Student Affairs in Involving Colleges.* Washington, D.C.: National Association of Student Personnel Administration, 1991.

Lampkin, P., and Gipson, E. *Mountains and Passes: Traversing the Landscape of Ethics and Student Affairs Administration.* Washington, D.C.: National Association of Student Personnel Administrators, 1999.

Laney, J. T. "Through Thick and Thin: Two Ways of Talking About the Academy and Moral Responsibility. In W. W. Ma, (Ed.), *Ethics and Higher Education.* New York: Macmillan, 1990.

National Orientation Directors Association. *NODA Statements of Professional Ethics.* [http://www.nodaweb.org/ethics.htm]. n.d.

National Association of Student Personnel Administrators. *About NASPA.* [http://www.naspa.org/about/index.cfm]. n.d.

Niebuhr, H. R. *The Responsible Self: An Essay in Christian Moral Philosophy.* Westminster: John Knox Press, 1999.

Thompson, D. "What Is Practical Ethics?" [http://www.ethic.harvard.edu/welcome_practical.php]. 2007.

Whitt, E. J. "The Student Personnel Point of View." In E. J. Whitt (Ed.), *College Student Affairs Administration.* Needham Heights, Mass.: Simon & Schuster Custom Publishing, 1997.

CHAPTER TEN

APPLYING PROFESSIONAL STANDARDS

Jan Arminio

The word *standard* was first used in western Germany in the twelfth century to describe a "flag or conspicuous object as a rallying point" (Harper, 2001, p. 1). Literally, *standard* meant to stand hard or firm. Two hundred years later, the word was used by the Anglo-French to refer to setting weights and measures. Linking from these earlier meanings, today *standard* has come to define an authoritative expectation and means for making judgments. Having standards that are inflexible measures necessitating compliance has become an important criterion for determining whether a burgeoning field of work is a profession (Miller, 1984; Paterson and Carpenter, 1989). In the historical debate on whether student affairs is a field or a profession (Penney, 1972), having standards has bolstered the argument that indeed student affairs is a profession.

Professional standards provide a mechanism against which professionals can judge the quality of their work, giving the profession a means of self-regulation. Standards also serve as guides that explain expectations to new professionals and inform professionals when initiating new programs, enhancing existing programs, and accepting new responsibilities. Taken together, standards serve as a self-regulatory means for ensuring quality practice and continual improvement.

One advantage of a profession establishing standards is that standards can eliminate or at least lessen the necessity for government intervention in professions. In fact, professions have created standards partly to avoid government regulation. Often considered interference, there is a long history of government involvement in professions. For example, Downie (2006) conjectured that during the Roman Empire government officials were intimately involved in regulating professional life, including initiating cost-cutting measures among army legion physicians. Currently, local, state, and federal governments greatly influence the work of professionals through regulation (Kaplin and Lee, 2006). At a recent meeting, a Department of Education official stated, "When the government gets involved, the two plagues always come home: bureaucratization and politicization. If we can keep this inside, we can avoid these plagues" (Miller as cited in Field, 2006, p. 15). One of the most important means of "keeping this inside" is through establishing and promulgating standards and using them as a basis on which to make decisions about how to improve professional work.

Establishing standards has become critical to the reputation and public trust of professions. Using established standards as guidelines for practice facilitates institutional accreditation and individual certification or licensure. More important, using standards creates benchmarks against which an organization can measure the quality of its programs and services. This identifies areas of and means for improvement. Note that *accreditation* "compares the observed performance of institutions against preset standards that are usually determined by the [authoritative] body" (Alstete, 2004, p. 15), whereas *certification* is granted by an institution or association to an individual indicating a level of competence. *Licensure* is granted to an individual by a government agency and typically indicates an even greater level of competence. The Web site for the National Board of Certified Counselors (NBCC) indicates that a benefit of becoming a certified counselor is that it promotes a national standard created by counselors rather than legislators (National Board of Certified Counselors [NBCC], 2007).

This chapter covers the purpose, influence, and application of standards in higher education, but most particularly in student affairs practice. Because they are probably the standards most closely associated with student affairs educators, the Council for the Advancement of Standards in Higher Education (CAS), along with their role in a comprehensive assessment plan, is discussed in some detail.

Standards in Education

There are a number of uses of standards in education. In K–12 education, curriculum-based standards dictate what students should be taught and should learn. However, recently, standards have taken on a heightened importance in the K–12 community. "Standards-based reform is a strategy that includes specifying [not only] what is to be learned, [but also] devising tests to measure learning, and establishing consequences of performance" (Betts and Costrell, 2001, p. 1). In schools where expectations for learning have been especially low, standards in

K–12 education offer incentives for improvement but also negative consequences for lack of improvement. There is great controversy over standards-based reform, as increased standards for high school graduation have served to detain some students from earning diplomas (Betts and Costrell, 2000). In addition, there has yet to be a consensus on test scores that indicate achievement (Betts and Costrell, 2000; and Wallis and Steptoe, 2007). Moreover, school districts bemoan the cost of testing required to prove or disprove compliance with standards.

Standards in Higher Education

Standards in higher education have been less controversial for several reasons. First, they have mainly served to improve educational practices rather than to impede student degree attainment. Second, attendance at higher education is not mandatory by law; hence there is less public scrutiny. Last, standards in higher education have been less controversial because higher education generally has enjoyed public approval (U.S. Department of Education, 2006). Some states and institutions have created performance standards for higher education that are tied to funding requests. The connection of these practices to increased student learning, however, has not been confirmed and has not been closely related to the learning that occurs outside of the formal classroom. What is the role of standards in learning that occurs outside the classroom in higher education?

In comparison to standards in other professions, standards related to higher education are relatively new because "there were relatively few colleges and universities, only a small portion of the population attended, and the curriculum was not of concern to many" (Alstete, 2004, p. 7). Earnest interest in standards and accreditation in higher education began in the early twentieth century due to the great inconsistency and confusion regarding the preparation necessary for college admission. Because creating a national admissions process with consistent criteria was beyond the scope of state governments and because the federal government had no authority at the time to intervene, regional intra-institution associations began to set minimal standards for accreditation of an institution (Alstete, 2004). *Accreditation* came to be defined as a systematized process for recognizing institutions that have met a prescribed level of performance by an established formalized authoritative body to engender public trust (Mable, 1991).

Also during the early twentieth century, Andrew Carnegie established the Carnegie Foundation for the Advancement of Teaching, which decided that any institution wanting to receive money from its foundation had to comply with national "minimal standards" regarding faculty, courses, and admission requirements (Alstete, 2004). It is from these beginnings that regional and national standards have mandated greater ease in students transferring from one institution to another.

Alstete (2004) offered the following timeline and eras regarding standards and institutional accreditation:

- 1880s–1900s: Admission standards formalized, postsecondary institutions defined.
- 1900s–1970s: Specialized discipline standards (such as counseling, college health) established and promulgated.
- 1970s–present: Criticism of the accreditation system intensifies.

Though accreditation served to ensure that certain national institutional standards were met, accreditation was not without its critics. Some educators disliked the notion of outsiders dictating institutional policies (Alstete, 2004). Other critics described the accreditation system as "elusive, nebulous, superficial, and meaning different things to different people" (p. 17). Still other critics disparaged the cost (in terms of time, money, and other resources) and the self-serving nature of accreditation. There is also the belief that accreditation discourages innovation and encourages competition for precious institutional resources between disciplines.

In student affairs, both the move to create and promulgate specialized standards in particular disciplines and the growing disenchantment with accreditation, led to the establishment in 1979 of the Council for the Advancement of Standards in Higher Education (CAS). CAS emphasized self-assessment rather than accreditation.

Standards in Student Affairs

There are a number of uses for standards in student affairs. These include program development, continuous improvement, self-study for accreditation or review, staff development, student development, program planning, program evaluation, acceptance of and education about student affairs services and programs, political maneuverability, budgetary assistance, ethical practice, and standardized language in functional areas (Arminio and Gochenauer, 2004; Bryan and Mullendore, 1991; Gold, 1995; Jacobs, Hayes-Harris, Lopez, and Ward, 1995; Mann, Gordon, and Strade, 1991; and Winston and Moore, 1991). In addition, they provide "criteria by which programs of professional preparation can be judged" (Miller, 1991, p. 48). This section of the chapter focuses on the role of the CAS in promulgating standards in student affairs. In addition, the role of CAS member and nonmember associations in promoting standards in student affairs is addressed.

Council for the Advancement of Standards in Higher Education

CAS is a consortium in that individuals are not members of CAS. Rather, professional associations in higher education are members. The first CAS standards were published in 1986. Subsequent standards have been published in 1997, 1999, 2001, 2003, and 2006.

Since the publication of its first set of standards, CAS has not only grown in the number of its consortium members but also has broadened its focus. Originally named the Council for the Advancement of Standards for Student Services/Development Programs, CAS changed its name to Council for the Advancement of Standards in Higher Education to acknowledge involvement by associations and functional areas sometimes found outside of traditional student affairs divisions (for example, American College Health Association, College Information and Visitor Services Association, College Reading and Learning Association, National Association of Academic Advisors).

CAS Standards. The creation of CAS standards was encouraged by two characteristics of the evolving student affairs profession. First, because establishing standards is necessary for any profession, the creation of standards in student affairs was a natural progression as student affairs continued to mature into a profession from a burgeoning field (Miller, 1984; and Paterson and Carpenter, 1989). Paterson and Carpenter stated that CAS standards represented "a major step forward in the efforts toward becoming a profession" (p. 125). Second, assessment to obtain or maintain accreditation had increasingly become a necessary part of higher education as government agencies and the public sought to hold institutions more accountable for student learning (Upcraft and Schuh, 1996). CAS standards represent the student affairs profession's will to set its own standards rather than to have others outside the profession who are possibly uninformed as to its purpose, values, and goals set them. By establishing standards, "student affairs clearly announced its determination to control its own destiny" (Byran and Mullendore, 1991, p. 29). CAS standards are "evolving documents" (p. 29) in that already established standards are revised every five to seven years and new standards are being written continuously.

CAS addresses standards across a myriad of educational programs and services in higher education including service learning, housing and residence life, undergraduate research, dining services, counseling services, and many more. The credibility of these standards is based on interassociation consensus for the purpose of establishing professional standards for student development services and for graduate school preparation of professionals entering the field of student affairs (Council for the Advancement of Standards in Higher Education [CAS], 1980).

Standards and Guidelines. According to Jacoby and Thomas (1986), CAS standards offer essential components of student affairs programs regardless of the organization's structure. Standards are written as *must* or *shall* statements for 37 functional areas (for example housing and residence life, commuter student programs and services, academic advising, campus programs, service learning, academic advising, undergraduate research, visitors services) plus master's level professional education. In order to comply with CAS standards, programs and services must meet these *must* or *shall* statements unless the review team can make a legitimate claim that the standard is met by another functional area within the institution. *Should* or *may* statements, called "guidelines," are offered as descriptors of ways to enhance program quality beyond the essential components.

Standards and guidelines are written within the following categories: mission, program, leadership, organization and management, human resources, financial resources, facilities, technology, equipment, legal responsibilities, equal opportunity, access, affirmative action, campus and community relations, diversity, ethics, and assessment and evaluation. Interestingly, the National Association of Colleges and Employers (NACE) standards are written in very similar categories (National Association of Colleges and Employers [NACE], 2006). *Standards of Good Practice for Education Abroad,* published by the Forum on Education Abroad, also highlight mission, learning, and ethics (Forum on Education Abroad, 2005). The Network Standards emphasize promulgating, assessing, and enforcing policy related to collegiate alcohol and other drug use (Network, 2007).

CAS Domains of Learning Outcomes. In 2003, in addition to identifying standards and guidelines, CAS articulated sixteen domains of learning outcomes. However, in 2008, these learning outcome domains were revised to be more congruent with learning outcomes described in *Learning Reconsidered 2* (Keeling, 2006). CAS now organizes learning in six broad categories: knowledge acquisition, construction, integration and application; cognitive complexity; interpersonal development; interpersonal competence; humanitarianism and civic engagement; and practical competence. Programs and services must identify relevant and desirable learning from these domains, assess relevant and desirable learning, and articulate how their programs and services contribute to domains not specifically assessed. CAS still offers suggestions of how to determine whether or not learning was achieved.

For example, if a user wanted to conduct a study measuring the growth of students' cognitive complexity, CAS offers illustrations of ways that students demonstrate achievement in cognitive complexity. These include (1) applies previously understood information to new situations or settings, (2) uses complex information from a variety of sources to form a decision, and (3) formulates new approaches to problems.

Self-Assessment Guides. CAS Self-Assessment Guides (SAGs) offer standards as criteria measures in an assessment rating form for conducting a self-study. They were first published in 1988. SAGs allow for easier utilization of the CAS standards (Bryan and Mullendore, 1991). The self-assessment guides "provide the perfect means to judge compliance" with standards (Gold, 1995, p. 68). Raters circle a score that indicates their belief of the degree to which a standard is being met.

Process. A CAS review is a self-assessment process in that no outside reviewers are necessary and no authority mandates that a CAS review be conducted. On the other hand, outside reviewers could be part of the process, and a CAS self-assessment can be conducted in preparation for an accreditation review. CAS suggests that organizations conducting a CAS review implement the following steps (CAS, 2006).

Establish and prepare a self-assessment team. Determining the membership of the review team is a critical first step. Because of the time commitment, it is recommended that those on the review team care about and be committed to the program or service under review. Representatives of stakeholders and users of the program or service could be included in the review team. This typically includes students, alumni, staff and faculty members as well as employees of the program or service. If possible, the director of the unit should not serve on the review committee, as he or she will be the recipient of the report generated from the review team. It would also be constructive to invite a "critic" to serve on the review process. This may be the best means to convert a critic to a supporter. Training for the review team is important and should include expectations of the group, familiarization with standards and self-assessment guides, consistency in ratings, and the interpretation of noncompliance (CAS, 2006).

Initiate self-study. Review members must be given data and other evidence that they use to complete the self-assessment guide forms. Hence, it is recommended that data be compiled systematically prior to the CAS review, instead of collecting data and other evidence solely during the year of a CAS review. Data should include assessment outcome data, survey data, and evaluation data from students, alumni, and other stakeholders. Besides data, other evidence may include mission and goal statements, publications such as manuals and program descriptions, annual reports, professional development activities, and student developmental transcripts. Units under review can offer the review team areas of emphasis on which to concentrate.

The review team's ratings indicate whether and to what degree standards are being met. The review team can either mark rating forms individually for a later comparison with other review team members or team members as a group can mark ratings through a process of consensus.

As an example, regarding the standard that programs must have "identified student learning and development outcomes that are relevant to its purpose," a reviewer could indicate that this standard was not rated (NR), meaning that there is no evidence to rate the criterion measure. A score of 4 would indicate that the standard was fully met, meaning that student learning outcomes have been identified and are relevant. A score of 3 would indicate that some outcomes have been identified or that only some are relevant, 2 that only some have been identified and only some are relevant, or 1 that learning outcomes have not been identified and are not relevant. A review team could indicate ND (not done), if another unit at the institution is held responsible for complying with that standard. In this example, however, it would be exceedingly rare for an organization in higher education to not be responsible for identifying relevant learning outcomes, including functional areas typically considered auxiliary services such as dining services, camps and conferences, and visitors' services.

Identify and summarize evaluative evidence. In this step, reviewers ensure that evidence exists that supports criterion measure ratings. It also allows team members to determine the strengths and weaknesses of the unit under review.

Identify discrepancies between practice and CAS Standards. The review committee determines areas where the program or service fails to comply with standards. Keep in mind that the purpose of self-assessment is to determine areas of weakness so that improvements can be initiated. It is the role of the review committee to highlight areas that necessitate follow-up action. There should be no embarrassment in noncompliance, only in ignoring discrepancies.

Determine appropriate corrective action. The review committee offers recommendations on what adjustments are necessary for the unit to comply with CAS standards. Subdividing corrective action into manageable tasks for corrective action can be left for the employees of the program or service. In any case, laying the groundwork for corrective action is imperative.

Recommend steps for program enhancement. In addition to determining action steps that should be implemented to correct discrepancies between practice and standards requirements, steps that would enhance the program, that is take the program from "good to great" (Collins, 2001, p. 3), should also be identified. Specific actions that enhance programs and services should be listed in order of priority.

Prepare an action plan. Employees must determine steps required to take corrective action and program enhancement as well as propose timelines and appoint people responsible for coordinating improvements. This plan should acknowledge the program's strengths and strategically use them in addressing discrepancies. Creating and completing an action plan is the most important aspect of a CAS study. If an organization is not willing to alter practice, then initiating a CAS review is purposeless.

Research on Use of CAS Standards. Research on the use of CAS standards finds that the awareness of and use of standards has increased since its inception. Also, research indicates that job title, size of institution where employed, level of education, race, and gender can influence use, satisfaction of use, and opinions on necessary training.

In 1989, Marron found that the distribution of the standards was not sufficient. Hence, only minimal utilization was found and the long-term effects were not predictable. Later, Mann and others (1991) found that 51 percent of senior student affairs officers used the standards, 33 percent did not use them, and 16 percent were unaware of the CAS standards. In the comments section of their survey, fifteen examples of specific use of the CAS standards were noted. Using a larger random sample of individuals who are members of CAS consortium associations, including new professionals as well as directors, deans, and vice presidents, Arminio and Gochenauer (2004) found that 61 percent of respondents in general and 85 percent of vice presidents and associate vice presidents had heard of CAS. Twenty-seven percent of respondents regardless of job title indicated that they had read the standards, 33 percent that they used the standards as a program guide, and 18 percent used the standards for assessment. In his doctoral dissertation, Ratcliffe (2004) found that 55.1 percent of 346 career services directors indicated a mean score rating of 5 or above on a scale of 1 (not aware of CAS standards) to 7 (very aware of CAS standards).

It appears that those with more experience and greater responsibility are more likely to have heard of CAS. Contrarily, those with fewer than five years of experience were less likely to be aware of CAS standards (Ratcliffe, 2004).

Studies (Arminio and Gochenauer, 2004; and Marron, 1989) indicate that public institutions are more likely than private institutions to use CAS standards. Also, professionals are more likely to use standards as a guide or management tool than for actual self-assessment (Arminio and Gochenauer, 2004; and Ratcliffe, 2004). There are numerous uses of standards, including program credibility, program management, and program review (Ratcliffe, 2004); they are also used for evaluating individual units, measuring achievement, and setting goals and objectives (Mann and others, 1991). Ratcliffe discovered that the level of awareness of CAS and fear of noncompliance were predictors of non-use. Staff noted lack of time and staff resources as barriers to using standards (Ratcliffe, 2004). Ratcliffe also found that as size of institutions increased, career services directors with doctorates were less likely to utilize CAS standards for program credibility. Those from midsized institutions (5,000 to 15,000 students) were the most likely to be satisfied with using CAS for program credibility.

CAS standards influence practice in a number of ways. In order of frequency, these are assessing a current program, expanding current programs, creating a mission statement and goals, justifying current programs, training students and staff, guiding new programs, and influencing budget requests (Arminio and Gochenauer, 2004). Arminio and Gochenhauer found that 27 percent of professional association members of varied job titles stated that CAS standards influence professional practice through assessment, whereas Mann and others (1991) found that fewer than one third of campus leaders in student affairs divisions surveyed perceived any changes at their institutions due to the establishment of CAS Standards. Because senior student affairs officers are more likely to know about CAS than their supervisees, this may indicate the increased use of CAS standards by professionals who are not division leaders.

In a study that dealt more with the viability of the CAS format, Cooper and Saunders (2000) surveyed 107 leaders in student affairs divisions asking if the CAS *must* statements were of importance to student affairs practice and if participants needed additional training or knowledge to comply with the CAS standards. The researchers found that all of the CAS standards *must* statements were viewed to be at least of some importance. Those *must* statements deemed most important were those of broad organizational concerns such as legal, ethical, and financial issues. However, significant differences by race and gender were found regarding the importance of individual standards. Women were significantly more likely than men to state that setting goals and selecting staff on the basis of education, work experience, and personal attributes were important standards. Women, more so than men, expressed a need for training in establishing procedures for providing appropriate professional development opportunities for staff. African American participants rated ten CAS *must* statements as significantly more important than did White participants. These included leaders must recruit, select, supervise, and develop others in the organization; evidence of effective management must include clear sources and channels of authority; evidence of effective management must include effective decision making and conflict resolution procedures and accountability systems; programs and services must establish procedures for providing appropriate professional development opportunities; degree- or credential-seeking interns or others in training must be taught and supervised adequately by professional staff members; staff members must be informed about institutional policies regarding personal liability and related insurance coverage options; staff members must use reasonable and informed practices to limit the liability exposure of the institution, its officers, employees, and agents; and the institution must inform staff and students in a timely manner and systematic fashion about extraordinary or changing legal obligation and potential liabilities.

Faculty members whose work is related to student affairs know little about the use of CAS standards. However, though they had a small sample, Arminio and Gochenauer (2004) found that faculty members were more likely to measure learning outcomes than were student affairs practitioners.

Besides functional area standards, CAS also promulgates standards on graduate education of student affairs professionals. Young and Janosik (2007) compared the perceptions of recent graduates of CAS-compliant graduate programs with those that are not CAS compliant. They found that graduates of CAS-compliant programs reported greater understanding of 48 out of 60 learning outcome measures based on the CAS master's degree program standards. None of these items were statistically significantly different. In contrast, graduates of noncompliant CAS programs reported statistically significant higher understanding of involvement theory and data variables in quantitative analysis. Obviously, more research is necessary in measuring the influence of CAS standards on student affairs graduate education.

Future Research Needed. Regardless of these initial studies, Creamer (2003) called upon the student affairs profession to study of the effects of CAS standards and guidelines on learning. The research questions he proposed include:

- What student learning and development outcomes are associated with the use of CAS standards and guidelines by practitioners within a specific functional area?
- What behaviors of staff are associated with the implementation of CAS standards and guidelines in their functional area?
- Do practitioners perceive that the use of CAS standards and guidelines effectively improves their performance?
- Do student users of selected programs and services who are guided by the use of CAS standards and guidelines perceive a benefit to their learning and development?

- Are educational programs and services that are guided by CAS standards and guidelines more effective than similar programs and services that are not guided by CAS standards and guidelines?
- How is professional behavior influenced by CAS standards and guidelines?

It is hoped that researchers and practitioners will respond to this call.

In collaborative efforts of revising CAS standards, concerns beyond the need for additional research have been frequently noted. Criticisms include that the standards are too prescriptive, are based on inputs rather than on outcomes, and are not available for free (W. Barratt, personal communication, June 5, 2002; and Love, 2000). The graduate preparation program standards have been criticized for not allowing institutional programs to express their unique nature (Love, 2000).

Using CAS Standards in Comprehensive Assessment. How do standards fit into a larger assessment plan? Several authors (Erwin and Wise, 2002; and Upcraft and Schuh, 1996) have offered components that constitute a comprehensive assessment model, of which standards are one component. (See Chapter Twenty-Seven in this volume for a more complete discussion on assessment in student affairs.) Essentially, in order to have a comprehensive assessment plan, the following types of assessments should be conducted.

User Satisfaction. This is the most common form of assessment in higher education and involves monitoring usage of service or attendance at programs, workshops, or other educational opportunities. Typically users are also asked to indicate their satisfaction with the service or program.

Outcomes. Assessing what value the program or service adds to a student's learning is becoming more imperative as government officials, trustees, parents, and students increasingly hold higher education accountable for the rising cost of tuition (U.S. Department of Education, 2006). These stakeholders want assurances that students are learning from their experiences in higher education. Providing evidence of what students are learning from their involvement in programs and services in higher education is the essence of learning outcomes assessment. This type of assessment must take into consideration what students bring to the institution in order to determine what they gain from it.

Inputs. Standards are considered an input. So, too, are *benchmarks* and *best practices*. These do not measure what students gain from their experiences but rather offer guidance of what educational experiences should entail. Their authority is based on professional consensus. Benchmarks describe the practice of comparing an institution's practices within the same institution (internal), with like institutions (competitive), or to national norms (external). They are typically concrete and quantifiable (for example, number of counselors per students at an institution). When using benchmarks, it is important that an institution's particular mission and niche be taken into consideration. Best practices are those that reflect the profession's current understanding of what is effective and efficient as indicated in the literature. Best practices are dynamic in nature, changing along with the profession's understanding of its work.

Campus Environments. Because physical and digital surroundings influence learning and opportunities, assessing perceptions of the campus environment is imperative. How do campus design, terrain, population aggregates, organizational dimensions, social climate, and campus policies and practices promote or inhibit student learning (Strange and Banning, 2001)? Campus environment assessments seek to address this question.

Student Motivation. Assuredly all educators are aware that for student learning to take place, students have to be actively engaged in the learning process. A great detractor from student learning is the lack of student motivation. Working with an unmotivated population brings particular concerns including the validity of assessment contexts (Erwin and Wise, 2002) and necessitates in response specific pedagogical skills and resources. Assessing student motivation is another important component in a comprehensive assessment plan in that it adds insight into the lack of learning achievement. For example, to what degree should a women's center be expected to have men as clients when evidence indicates that many men are not motivated to become involved?

CAS standards are an example of an assessment input that requires additional types of assessment to be conducted for there to be compliance. Other types of assessment required to meet CAS standards include collection of user and satisfaction data, student needs assessment, and an audit of the environment. A comprehensive plan that encompasses these types of assessments should be completed within a prescribed time frame, such as ten years.

Efforts of CAS Member and Nonmember Associations

In addition to CAS, a number of associations of professionals who work in higher education have created standards specific to their functional areas. Many of these associations are members of CAS and support the promulgation of CAS standards in their areas of expertise while maintaining their own standards. Those CAS members who also have created their own standards that are available to the public include the Network: Addressing Collegiate Alcohol and Other Drug Issues; the Association on Higher Education and Disability (AHEAD); the National Association of Academic Advisors (NACADA); and the National Association of College and University Food Services (NACUFS). The Association of College and University Housing Officers-International (ACUHO-I) and the National Association of Colleges and Employers (NACE) are CAS members and have their own professional standards that are available to their members. The American Association of Collegiate Registrars and Admissions Officers (AACRAO) is not a member of CAS and has professional standards available to its members. Some associations ended their standards development when they became members of CAS (for example, National Association for Campus Activities [NACA]) and as the use of CAS standards became more prevalent. Other associations, such as the Forum on Education Abroad, are not members of CAS but have standards available to the public on their Web sites. The National Intramural Recreation Sports Association (NIRSA) is a member of CAS and promotes CAS standards for generic use in recreational sports, but has established specific standards in areas such as facility management and student conduct of club members.

Case Illustrations

Because cases assist the reader in understanding practical applications, three cases follow that exemplify the varied uses of standards. After the cases is a brief analysis of how standards play a role in these cases.

Case 1

Gabrielle is an assistant director of multicultural student affairs. In this position she is responsible for advising several multicultural clubs and the events they sponsor; implementing programs her office sponsors; and conducting multicultural training, education, and development across campus. She has applied and been hired for the position of director of campus programs at the same institution. Though she has significant experience in advising student groups, programming, and conducting training, major responsibilities of her new position, she will have additional, new responsibilities as well. These include more student groups to advise (the most complex being student government), a larger budget to manage, and professional staff to supervise. Her previous experience made her a viable candidate for her new position; however, there are obvious different and increased responsibilities. What resource might she consult to guide her as she begins to negotiate these new responsibilities?

Case 2

The institution where Carlos is employed has made a concerted effort to measure learning outcomes. Carlos initiated a study attempting to uncover evidence of cognitive gains by first-year students who participated in new student orientation. He measured cognitive development using a standardized instrument during students' first semester, comparing the scores of those who participated in orientation with those who did not, holding high school grades constant. He was disappointed to learn that no significant differences were found between the two groups of students. He has tried and been unsuccessful in obtaining additional resources for this orientation program. Currently, it is a two-day event that consists of tours, one small-group discussion with orientation leaders regarding hypothetical situations new students will likely face, and an academic advising session leading to scheduling for classes. He realizes that cognitive gains may not be realized after a two-day orientation. What literature in the profession representing a professional consensus might Carlos consult so that he could better advocate for resources to enhance the orientation program?

Case 3

Most institutions are now engaging in assessment programs that encourage professionals to make data-driven decisions. With that in mind, Mark has designed a five-year plan utilizing multiple measures that assess learning. As Mark embarks upon the five-year plan and as pieces to the student learning puzzle begin to take shape, he does not know how he should begin to respond to his outcomes data. Meanwhile, his supervisor is concerned that Mark's assessment plan only incorporates learning outcomes. He asks Mark to contemplate how other types of assessment would not only complement but also improve his assessment plan. What resource might Mark consult to bolster his assessment plan and guide how he responds to learning outcomes data?

These three cases all illustrate various roles standards play in seeking to ensure the high quality of educational programs and services. All three student affairs professionals profiled would be wise to consult standards for guidance. They would likely find CAS standards as well as other standards beneficial: Gabrielle as she begins her new job responsibilities, Carlos as he begins to revise his orientation program and advocate for the resources necessary to meet its goals, and Mark as he initiates a comprehensive assessment.

Gabrielle would see that, in general, there are three aspects to campus programs: implementation of campus programs, advisement of student organizations, and implementation of training, development, and educational opportunities. Most likely she already knew this. Knowing that her office must encourage a broad scope of involvement, that every student organization must have an advisor, and that advisors must be offered training will be important as she begins to prioritize her efforts. In preparation for advising student government, she discovers that the student government association must have a written mission, indicate clear criteria for student involvement, and articulate clear financial and grievance procedures. Moreover, she must encourage student government to operate in accordance with the institution's mission. A considerable amount of her energy will be spent in offering training, education, and development opportunities for students, and staff and faculty advisors. Through standards she realizes that these opportunities must be delivered by several people in multiple ways and take into account various student development levels.

In advocating for resources to create a more comprehensive orientation program, Carlos reads that orientation programs must enhance educational experiences at the institution and that orientation must continue as a process to address, as appropriate, transitional events, issues, and needs. The orientation process must include pre-enrollment, entry, and postmatriculation services. He also reads that these could be accomplished by other entities within the institution, such as the center for service learning, learning communities, first-year interest groups, via face-to-face or Web-based seminars. Carlos begins to envision how through collaboration he can better assist new students and their families to understand the nature and purpose of the institution and enhance efforts to increase cognitive gains through orientation programs.

CAS standards require that professionals directing programs and services conduct regular assessments that employ both qualitative and quantitative methodologies to determine to what degree stated mission, goals, and learning outcomes are being met. Complemented by his outcome data and his review team, Mark is able to contrast program discrepancies with standards and determine what program standards need the most attention. Accordingly, Mark generates a list of priorities that lead to an action plan complete with time line and tasks to be accomplished.

Conclusion

Standards in higher education are relatively new compared to standards in other professions. Moreover, the establishment of standards specific to student affairs is even a more recent phenomenon. Research indicates that it has taken time for educators to become knowledgeable about standards in student affairs and for these standards to be recognized as useful. As the scenarios in the previous section reveal, there are several important reasons that standards are used to guide and improve practice and, consequently, student learning. Though measuring outcomes offers educators insight into what students are gaining from programs and services, standards are necessary to assist in determining the process to achieve outcomes, and they offer authoritative guidance on how to respond to outcomes.

References

Alstete, J. W. *Accreditation Matters: Achieving Academic Recognition and Renewal.* ASHE-ERIC Higher Education Report, Vol. 30, no. 4. San Francisco: Wiley, 2004.

Arminio, J., and Gochenauer, P. "After Sixteen years of Publishing Standards, Do CAS Standards Make a Difference?" *College Student Affairs Journal*, 2004, 24, 51–65.

Betts, J. R., and Costrell, R. M. "Incentives and Equity Under Standards-Based Reform." *Brookings Papers on Education Policy.* Brookings Institution. [http://muse.jhu.edu/journals/brookings_papers_on_education_policy/v2001/2001.1bettshtml]. 2001.

Byran, W. A., and Mullendore, R. H. "Operationalizing CAS Standards for Program Evaluation and Planning." In W. A. Bryan, R. B. Winston Jr., and T. K. Miller (Eds.), *Using Professional Standards in Student Affairs.* New Directions for Student Services, no. 53. San Francisco: Jossey-Bass, 1991.

Collins, J. *Good to Great: Why Some Companies Make the Leap and Others Don't.* New York: Harper Collins, 2001.

Cooper, D., and Saunders, S. "The Perceived Importance of the CAS Standards: Implications for Practice." *College Student Affairs Journal*, 2000, 19, 71–81.

Council for the Advancement of Standards in Higher Education. *CAS Professional Standards for Higher Education* (6th ed.). Washington, D.C.: Council for the Advancement of Standards in Higher Education, 2006.

Council for the Advancement of Standards in Higher Education. *CAS Professional Standards for Higher Education* (4th ed.). Washington, D.C.: Council for the Advancement of Standards in Higher Education, 2003.

Council for the Advancement of Standards. *By-laws.* Washington, D.C.: Council for the Advancement of Standards. 1980.

Creamer, D. G. "Research Needed on the Use of CAS Standards and Guidelines." *College Student Affairs Journal*, 2003, 22, 109–124.

Downie, R. *Medicus: A Novel of the Roman Empire.* New York: Bloomsbury, 2006.

Erwin, T. D., and Wise, S. L. "*A Scholar-Practitioner Model for Assessment.*" In T. W. Banta (Ed.), *Building a Scholarship of Assessment.* San Francisco: Jossey Bass, 2002.

Field, K. "Spellings Promises Fast Reforms in Accrediting." *Chronicle of Higher Education.* [http://chronicle.com/weekly/v53/i16/16a00101.htm]. December, 8, 2006.

Forum on Education Abroad. *Standards of Good Practice for Education Abroad.* [http://www.forumea.org/standards.cfm]. 2005.

Gold, J. A. "Criteria for Setting Allocation Priorities." In D. Woodward Jr. (Ed.), *Budgeting as a Tool for Policy in Student Affairs*. New Directions for Student Services, no. 70. San Francisco: Jossey-Bass, 1995.

Harper, D. *Online Etymology Dictionary*. [http://etymonline.com/index.php?search=standards$ searchmode=term]. 2001.

Jacobs, B. C., Hayes-Harris, M., Lopez, C. A., and Ward, J. A. "Maintaining an Ethical Balance in Student Orientation Programs." *College Student Affairs Journal*, 1995, 15, 44–53.

Jacoby, B., and Thomas, W. "Introduction to the CAS "Standards and Guidelines for Commuter Programs and Services." *NASPA Journal*, 1986, 24, 55–57.

Kaplin, W. A., and Lee, B. A. *The Law of Higher Education* (4th ed.). San Francisco: Jossey-Bass, 2006.

Keeling, R. (Ed.). *Learning Reconsidered 2: Implementing a Campus-Wide Focus on the Student Experience*. Various: American College Personnel Association, Association of College and University Housing Officers-International, Association of College Unions-International, National Academic Advising Association, National Association for Campus Activities, National Association of Student Personnel Administrators, National Intramural-Recreational Sports Association, 2006.

Love, P. *Report on the Feedback Received About the CAS Self-Assessment Guide and Process*. Unpublished manuscript, 2000.

Mable, P. "Professional Standards: An Introduction and Historical Perspective." In W. A. Bryan, R. B. Winston Jr., and T. K. Miller (Eds.), *Using Professional Standards in Student Affairs*. New Directions for Student Services, no. 53. San Francisco: Jossey-Bass, 1991.

Mann, B. A., Gordon, S. E., and Strade, C. B. "The Impact of CAS Standards on the Practice of Student Affairs." *The College Student Affairs Journal*, 1991, 10, 3–9.

Marron, J. M. "A Study of the Utilization of the Council for the Advancement of Standards for Student Services/Development Program Standards at Four-Year Undergraduate Degree-Granting Colleges and Universities." Doctoral dissertation, George-Peabody College for Teachers of Vanderbilt University, 1989.

Miller, T. K. "Using Standards in Professional Preparation." In W. A. Bryan, R. B. Winston Jr., and T. K. Miller (Eds.), *Using Professional Standards in Student Affairs*. New Directions for Student Services, no. 53. San Francisco: Jossey-Bass, 1991.

Miller, T. K. "Professional Standards: Whither Thou Goest?" *Journal of College Student Development*, 1984, 25, 412–416.

National Association of Colleges and Employers. *Professional Standards for College and University Career Services*. Bethlehem, PA: National Association of Colleges and Employers, 2006.

National Board of Certified Counselors. "Benefits of Being a Certified Counselor." [http://www.nbcc.org/whyncc]. 2007.

"The Network: Addressing Collegiate Alcohol and Other Drug Issues." *The Network Standards*. [http://www.ahead.org/about/Final%20Program%20Standards%20with%20Performance%20Indicators.doc]. 2007.

Paterson, B. G., and Carpenter, D. S. "The Emerging Student Affairs Profession: What Still Needs to Be Done." *NASPA Journal*, 1989, 27, 123–127.

Penney, J. F. *Perspective and Challenge in College Personnel Work*. Springfield, Ill.: Charles C. Thomas, 1972.

Ratcliffe, S. R. "Use of CAS Standards by Career Services Directors at Four-Year Public Colleges and Universities." Unpublished doctoral dissertation, Virginia Polytechnic Institute and State University, 2004.

Strange, C. C., and Banning, J. H. *Educating by Design: Creating Campus Learning Environments That Work.* San Francisco: Jossey-Bass, 2001.

Upcraft, M. L., and Schuh, J. H. *Assessment in Student Affairs: A Guide for Practitioners.* San Francisco: Jossey-Bass, 1996.

U.S. Department of Education. *A Test of Leadership: Charting the Future of U.S. Higher Education.* Washington, D.C.: U.S. Department of Education, 2006.

Wallis, C., and Steptoe, S. "How to Fix No Child Left Behind." *Time,* June 4, 2007, 34–41.

Winston, R. B., and Moore, W. S. "Standards and Outcomes Assessment: Strategies and Tools." In W. A. Bryan, R. B. Winston Jr., and T. K. Miller (Eds.), *Using Professional Standards in Student Affairs.* New Directions for Student Services, no. 53. San Francisco: Jossey-Bass, 1991.

Young, D. G., and Janosik, S. M. "Using CAS Standards to Measure Learning Outcomes of Student Affairs Preparation Programs." *NASPA Journal,* 2007, 44(2), 341–365.

CHAPTER ELEVEN

PROFESSIONAL ASSOCIATIONS IN STUDENT AFFAIRS

Nancy J. Evans and Jessica J. Ranero

New student affairs graduate students and professionals are almost immediately bombarded with acronyms of professional student affairs associations, both generalist in nature and specific to the functional areas in which they are employed. It can be overwhelming to determine what all these organizations do, how they are related to the work of student affairs, and which groups, if any, are worth joining. This chapter provides information about professional associations in student affairs, including their functions, history, and structure. The various types of associations are reviewed, the benefits of membership are discussed, and opportunities for involvement are highlighted.

The Functions of Professional Associations

The Web site of the American Society of Association Executives (ASAE) and the Center for Association Leadership (American Society of Association Executives and the Center for Association Leadership, 2007) explains that professional associations consist of individuals who voluntarily join the group because they share common interests and goals. The ASAE Web site lists a variety of purposes to which associations commit themselves, including (1) education and professional development of their members, (2) provision of information about the field or area they represent, (3) the establishment of ethical and professional standards, (4) a vehicle for discussion of issues and concerns in the profession, (5) volunteer and service opportunities for members in their areas of interest, and (6) the development of a community of people who share common interests for support and networking.

These purposes are reflected in the work of student affairs associations, which serve individual student affairs professionals, institutions of higher education, and the profession as a whole. An increasingly critical role of student affairs associations is lobbying government officials regarding issues and legislation important to the profession and its members. Student affairs professional associations also provide information to the general public through Web sites, media interviews, and publications (Moore and Neuberger, 1998).

The History of Student Affairs Professional Associations

As mentioned in Chapter One and discussed by Nuss (2003), professional associations started to appear in the early 1900s to provide support, professional development, and a voice for individuals in the emerging field of student affairs. As discussed in greater length in Chapter One, the deans of women and deans of men, who were the most visible student affairs professionals at this time, had little preparation for assuming their new roles and few colleagues who understood their role on campus (Rhatigan, 2007). The need to discuss the issues facing them in their new positions provided the impetus for the development of two early associations.

National Association of Women in Education

The deans of women were the first to see the value of organizing. In 1903, eighteen women deans came together informally at a meeting at Northwestern University (Bashaw, 2001a). The group formally organized in 1916 as the National Association of Deans of Women (NADW). In the early years of NADW, the organization's focus was on the role and responsibilities of deans of women, and later, on issues facing women in education and the women students they served (Hanson, 1995). In 1938, NADW began publishing a journal to disseminate research on these topics.

Over time, the role and mission of this association expanded to include a broader base of membership, starting with admission of deans of girls at the elementary and secondary levels to encourage continuity of services for women as they moved from one educational setting to the next (Hanson, 1995). In response to "demotion and dismissal" (Bashaw, 2001b, p. 263) of college deans of women during the conservative atmosphere following World War II, many questioned the need for a gender-specific association; in 1952, NADW considered combining with other student affairs organizations but decided to remain separate to ensure that ongoing equity issues in higher education and the unique needs of women educators and students were addressed (Bashaw, 2001b; Hanson, 1995). However, to better reflect the roles being played by women in education at this time, the organization's name was expanded in 1956 to the National Association of Women Deans and Counselors (NAWDC) (Hanson, 1995). To more fully achieve its goals, the association organized itself into sections based on employment setting and increased networking with other groups serving women educational professionals and students (Bashaw, 2001b; Hanson, 1995). NAWDC also partnered with the National Association of Student Personnel Administrators (NASPA) and the American College Personnel Association (ACPA) to address issues facing the student affairs profession as a whole.

In 1973, the association's name was changed to the National Association of Women Deans, Administrators, and Counselors (NAWDAC) and the association for the first time offered membership to men (Hanson, 1995). To respond more effectively to professional development needs, sections were reorganized to reflect employment and professional interests. Intentional initiatives to create a more inclusive organization resulted in the development of committees for graduate students and young professionals, women of color, disability issues, and lesbian and bisexual issues. In 1991, the association's name was changed to the National Association of Women in Education (NAWE) to better reflect its focus on issues facing women working in all educational settings (Hanson, 1995; Moore and Neuberger, 1998). Despite serving as a valued professional home for many women in student affairs and other areas of education, decreases in membership and conference attendance resulted in the decision of the leadership and membership of NAWE to dissolve the association in 2000 (Nuss, 2003).

National Association of Student Personnel Administrators

The deans of men first met at the University of Wisconsin in 1919 with six men present (Rhatigan, 2007). From that meeting until 1929, this gathering was called the Conference of Deans and Advisors of Men. In its early years, meetings of the association were held on college campuses and provided an opportunity to informally share ideas and discuss issues facing male students.

In 1929, the name of the organization was changed to the more formal National Association of Deans and Advisors of Men (NADAM) and conferences from 1929 on were held at off-campus sites (Rhatigan, 2007). In 1932, institutional membership was established, with each member school having one official representative who voted on association business. However, institutions could send additional delegates to the conference.

As the title Dean of Men disappeared on campuses, an increasing need was felt for an organizational name that reflected the broader roles of NADAM's membership (Rhatigan, 2007). In 1951, the name National Association of Student Personnel Administrators (NASPA) was adopted and new members were actively recruited to join. However, the main target audience of NASPA remained senior student affairs officers and their senior staff (Moore and Neuberger, 1998). In the 1960s, NASPA developed a system of regional meetings paralleling the national accreditation regions, with each region having a vice president who served on the executive committee of the national organization. Because of its size, Region IV was split into IV-East and IV-West; thus, there are seven NASPA regions (Rhatigan, 2007).

Although women had attended association meetings earlier, it was not until 1958 that the first woman served as an institutional representative and 1966 when a woman first served on the executive committee (Rhatigan, 2007). A women's network was established within NASPA in 1971 to encourage women to join the association and to provide a forum for addressing their issues. In 1976, NASPA elected its first woman president, Alice Manicur (Rhatigan, 2007). Between 1990 and 2007, 12 of the 18 presidents were women (National Association of Student Personnel Administrators [NASPA], 2007a), and currently 62 percent of the members are women (Evangeline Soleyn, NASPA Director of Membership Services, personal communication, July 17, 2007). Student affairs professionals of color and those working in community college settings also became more prevalent in the overall NASPA membership and in leadership positions in the late twentieth century (Rhatigan, 2007).

In 1967, a national office was established to coordinate the association's activities, and NASPA appointed its first executive director in 1975. In 1985, the national office was permanently moved to Washington, D.C. (Rhatigan, 2007). In recent years, NASPA has expanded the role of its national office with regard to member services.

With just over 10,000 members, NASPA is currently the largest student affairs organization (Evangeline Soleyn, personal communication, July 17, 2007). Its stated mission is "to provide professional development and advocacy for student affairs educators and administrators who share the responsibility for a campus-wide focus on the student experience" (NASPA, 2007a). NASPA has led the way with technology-driven services, including online publications and Web-based knowledge communities. It is also recognized for its timely response to current issues in the field (Coomes, Wilson, and Gerda, 2003). NASPA's Undergraduate Fellows Program (NUFP), the purpose of which is to increase the number of persons of colors, persons with disabilities, and/or persons who identify as lesbian, gay, bisexual, and transgender in student affairs and higher education, has been the impetus for many highly qualified and competent undergraduate students to pursue graduate education in student affairs (NASPA, 2007d). Other notable NASPA programs include the Alice Manicur Symposium for Women Aspiring to be Senior Student Affairs Officers, Institute for New Senior Student Affairs Officers, Student Affairs Benchmarking Project, the NASPA Faculty Fellows, and Multicultural Affairs Institute (NASPA, 2007b; NASPA, 2007d).

American College Personnel Association

The other generalist student affairs association, the American College Personnel Association (ACPA), began as the National Association of Appointment Secretaries (NAAS) in 1924 (Bloland, 1972; Sheeley, 1991). Appointment secretaries served as placement officers, assisting graduating students to find positions as teachers. The purpose for which NAAS was founded was to promote and develop the work of appointment offices across the United States, emphasizing cooperation, research, and service. In 1929, NAAS became the National Association of Placement and Personnel Officers (NAPPO) to better reflect the work responsibilities of its members (Bloland, 1972).

Two years later, in 1931, the name American College Personnel Association was adopted to encourage a broader membership and mission—one that included student affairs professionals with a wide variety of responsibilities. Sections, later called "commissions," were established to deal with different aspects of student affairs work, and an emphasis was placed on professional development of student affairs personnel (Evans and Powell, 2002). In the 1960s, state branches of ACPA were formed (Sheeley, 1991).

A desire to bring together the major guidance organizations led to the formation of the American Personnel and Guidance Association (APGA, later the American Association of Counseling and Development, AACD) in 1952; ACPA led this initiative and became the first division of this new association (Bloland, 1972). As the student affairs profession became increasingly complex, taking on education and administrative responsibilities as well as work with individual students, ACPA's need to focus on these changing roles became apparent (Evans and Powell, 2002; Steffes, 2001). In 1991, ACPA leaders and members voted to disaffiliate from AACD. The separation became effective in 1992 when ACPA moved into its own office space at the National Center for Higher Education in Washington, D.C., and hired an executive director (Evans and Powell, 2002). ACPA has recently reorganized its governance structure to more efficiently accomplish its goals and has added the tagline, "College Student Educators

International" to the ACPA acronym to better reflect the educational and international initiatives that have become increasingly important parts of its mission (American College Personnel Association [ACPA], 2007).

ACPA's current membership is nearly 8,000 (ACPA, 2007a). According to its mission statement, "ACPA supports and fosters college student learning through the generation and dissemination of knowledge, which informs policies, practices and programs for student affairs professionals and the higher education community" (ACPA, 2007a). ACPA's roots are in the counseling tradition of student affairs, and it has been a welcoming home for professionals in many functional areas of student affairs (Evans and Powell, 2002). Throughout its history, ACPA has been recognized for its commitment to inclusion and advocacy for underrepresented groups. Its leadership reflects this value, with executive council positions overwhelming held by women and people of color in recent years (Steffes, 2001). ACPA also has a long history of scholarship (Evans and Powell). In addition to publishing the premier research journal in the student affairs field, the *Journal of College Student Development*, many of the foundational documents of the field were generated as ACPA projects or by scholars affiliated with ACPA. The Senior Scholars and Emerging Scholars programs also help to keep scholarship at the forefront in ACPA (Coomes and others, 2003). ACPA's strong standing committees and commissions provide many educational and leadership opportunities for the association's members (ACPA, 2007c; ACPA, 2007e).

Efforts to Consolidate

Throughout their histories, student affairs associations have collaborated on programming, held joint conferences, and cooperated to address major issues facing the student affairs profession (Bloland, 1972; and Moore and Neuberger, 1998). A number of attempts have been made to consolidate or merge associations to increase visibility, respect, and effectiveness in addressing the issues facing the student affairs field (Bloland; Coomes and others, 2003; and Moore and Neuberger, 1998). However, none of the efforts to consolidate has been successful, including a recent attempt to combine ACPA and NASPA into one organization (Moneta and Roberts, 2003).

Several arguments have been presented in favor of consolidation. Coomes and others (2003) pointed out that ACPA and NASPA share many commonalities in their missions, values, and functions. Both associations have similar goals of generating and sharing knowledge, supporting diversity, promoting professional development, policy development, and supporting student learning and development. However, differences in organizational culture, management philosophy, organizational structure, and priorities are also apparent (Coomes and others).

Advocates of a combination of the associations see the differences between the two organizations as minimal. They argue that a unification of the two organizations is needed to create one vision for the field of student affairs. Furthermore, by having one national organization, both members and institutions will save money, a particularly important factor during times of financial difficulties. Those in favor of combination argue that one organization will contribute to the creation of a single professional home, fewer regional conferences and workshops, greater connections between the scholarship and practice of student affairs, and the creation of common goals (Blimling, 2003). Whether consolidation of the major student affairs associations happens in the future or not, collaboration across the field of student affairs is key for its continued growth.

Confederations

Somewhat more successful than attempts at consolidation have been confederations of organizations to achieve specific goals, starting in the 1960s with the development of the Council of Student Personnel Associations in Higher Education (COSPA), a confederation of student affairs associations designed to facilitate communication among the different associations. This group developed several position pieces related to the role of student affairs, issues facing the profession, and professional preparation (Caple, 1998; and Crowley, 1964). More recently, the Council for the Advancement of Standards in Higher Education (CAS), which has representatives from more than thirty professional student affairs associations, has developed and continuously revises standards for professional practice in a wide variety of areas of student affairs practice as well as professional preparation (Moore and Neuberger, 1998). In addition, the Higher Education Secretariat (HES), a group of more than thirty national associations that meets monthly under the auspices of the American Council on Education, and the Council of Higher Education Management Associations (CHEMA), a group of equivalent size convened twice a year by the National Association of College and University Business Officers (NACUBO), focus on collaborative initiatives and governmental lobbying related to issues relevant to member associations (Moore and Neuberger, 1998).

Specialty Associations

As the profession of student affairs grew, so did the need to have associations that represented the specific interests of particular areas within the field. In addition to the generalist higher education associations, NASPA and ACPA, there are numerous professional associations that focus on specific subdivisions of student affairs. The Council for the Advancement of Standards in Higher Education includes more than thirty different associations with a variety of specializations within the field of higher education, which are listed in Exhibit 11.1 (Council for the Advancement of Standards in Higher Education, 2007). In addition, StudentAffairs.com, an online resource, provides a list of more than seventy professional associations (StudentAffairs.com, 2006).

EXHIBIT 11.1 A SAMPLE LISTING OF PROFESSIONAL ASSOCIATIONS

American Association for Employment in Education (AAEE)
American College Counseling Association (ACCA)
American College Health Association (ACHA)
American College Personnel Association (ACPA)
American Counseling Association (ACA)
Association for Student Judicial Affairs (ASJA)
Association of College Honor Societies (ACHS)
Association of College Unions International (ACUI)
Association of College and University Housing Officers-International (ACUHO-I)
Association of Collegiate Conference & Events Directors-Int'l (ACCED-I)
Association of Fraternity Advisors (AFA)
Association on Higher Education and Disability (AHEAD)
Canadian Association of College and University Student Services (CACUSS)
Collegiate Information and Visitor Services Association (CIVSA)
College Reading and Learning Association (CRLA)
Council for Opportunity in Education (COE)
NAFSA–Association of International Educators (NAFSA)
National Academic Advising Association (NACADA)
National Association for Campus Activities (NACA)
National Association for Developmental Education (NADE)
National Association of College Auxiliary Services (NACAS)
National Association of Colleges and Employers (NACE)
National Association of College and University Food Services (NACUFS)
National Association of College Stores (NACS)
National Association of Student Affairs Professionals (NASAP)
National Association of Student Financial Aid Administrators (NASFAA)
National Association of Student Personnel Administrators (NASPA)
National Clearinghouse of Commuter Programs (NCCP)
National Clearinghouse for Leadership Programs (NCLP)
National Consortium of Directors of Lesbian, Gay, Bisexual, and Transgender Resources in Higher Education (Consortium)
National Council on Student Development (NCSD)
National Intramural and Recreational Sports Association (NIRSA)
National Orientation Directors Association (NODA)
National Society for Experiential Education (NSEE)
National Women's Studies Association (NWSA)
The Network: Addressing Collegiate Alcohol and Other Drug Issues (The Network)
Southern Association for College Student Affairs (SACSA)

Source: Council for the Advancement of Standards in Higher Education Member Associations.

Organizations such as the Association of College and University Housing Officers-International (ACHUO-I), the National Orientation Directors Association (NODA), the National Association for Campus Activities (NACA), the Association of Fraternity Advisors (AFA), the Association for Student Judicial Affairs (ASJA), and the National Academic Advising Association (NACADA) were established to focus on specific areas of student affairs. The structure and mission of each organization vary because of their specializations, but they share similar goals of disseminating information and providing opportunities for networking and professional development. In addition, state and regional associations, sometimes affiliated with national associations and sometimes independent, serve the needs of professionals in specific geographical regions.

More recently, associations focused on the needs of underrepresented and constituent groups have been established. The National Association of Student Affairs Professionals (NASAP) was founded at Howard University in 1954 by members of the National Association of Deans of Women and Advisors of Girls in Colored Schools and the National Association of Personnel Deans of Men at Negro Educational Institutions (National Association of Student Affairs Professionals [NASAP], 2005). Today, NASAP focuses on promoting research, professional development, and effective student affairs programs.

The Association on Higher Education and Disability (AHEAD) was founded in 1977 to ensure universal accessibility to higher education for persons with disabilities (Association on Higher Education and Disability [AHEAD] 2004). AHEAD accomplishes its mission through trainings, workshops, publications, and consultation. Similarly, the National Consortium of Directors of LGBT Resources in Higher Education was founded in 1997 to ensure that lesbian, gay, bisexual, and transgender members of the college community have equity and equal access to higher education (LGBT Resources in Higher Education, 2005).

The Asian Pacific Americans in Higher Education (APAHE) was established to ensure that national attention was given to the issues affecting a particular constituent group. APAHE was founded in 1987 to address discriminatory admissions policies that were directed against Asian Pacific Americans at several research universities across the country. Currently, APAHE's goal is to address issues that affect Asian Pacific American students, faculty, staff, and administrators (Asian Pacific Americans in Higher Education, 2007). The American Association of Hispanics in Higher Education (AAHHE) is a recent outgrowth of the American Association of Higher Education's Hispanic Caucus. The mission of AAHHE is to advocate for increased access for Hispanics in higher education and to increase the number of Hispanics attending and completing graduate programs in higher education (Association of Hispanics in Higher Education, 2007). The National Association of Diversity

Officers in Higher Education (NADOHE) is a recently established association that also focuses on diversity. NADOHE began with an informal meeting in 2003 of a few senior diversity officers in higher education and business sectors. Out of the meeting grew an interest in continued dialogue, which led to the official establishment of NADOHE in 2006 and its first conference in 2007 (National Association of Diversity Officers in Higher Education, 2007). The purpose of NADOHE is to create a network of senior diversity officers and multicultural experts in order to create more inclusive colleges and universities.

In addition, there are associations that focus on religious affiliations and student affairs. The Jesuit Association of Student Personnel Administrators (JASPA) was founded in 1954 to promote the mission of Jesuit higher education (Jesuit Association of Student Personnel Administrators [JASPA], 2004). In 1999, the Association for Student Affairs at Catholic Colleges and Universities (ASACCU) was founded by student affairs professionals working at Catholic institutions (Association for Student Affairs at Catholic Colleges and Universities, 2004). The Council for Christian Colleges and Universities (CCCU) was established in 1976 to "advance the cause of Christ-centered higher education" (Council for Christian Colleges and Universities, 2007). All of these associations provide their members with opportunities to share resources through conferences, workshops, Web sites, and various other activities.

Although there has been an increase in the number of organizations that focus on the needs of underrepresented populations, there are still gaps. For example, there is no association that is dedicated to the work of multicultural affairs offices on college campuses. Although NADOHE was recently established, its primary focus is on issues facing senior diversity officers, which are often different from the work of multicultural affairs offices. Conferences such as the National Conference on Race and Ethnicity in American Higher Education (NCORE) and the Creating Change Conference sponsored by the National Gay and Lesbian Task Force provide additional resources regarding diversity in higher education.

The increase of specialized student affairs professional associations presents a number of benefits. As the profession continues to grow, there is an increased need to understand the complexities of the various areas within student affairs, which these specialized associations address. The creation of new organizations has also contributed to an increased awareness of the vast needs of diverse students.

Despite these gains, there are some concerns that increased specialization in student affairs is threatening the strength of the profession. Sandeen (1998) stated that specialization contributes to professional isolation by creating challenges to communication among professionals in the field. In addition, upward mobility within the profession may become more difficult because student affairs professionals are no longer seen as having a generalist skill set, but instead are now seen as experts within a specific area. Furthermore, collaboration within and outside of student affairs may become more difficult because of competing needs (Sandeen, 1998).

In the current higher education environment, student affairs professionals must challenge themselves to be both generalists and specialists. As Sandeen (1998) stated, it is the duty of student affairs professionals to work toward the holistic development of students, which requires a general knowledge of the overall university system and the field of student affairs as well as the specific needs of student populations. To gain the necessary knowledge and skills, both generalist and specialty organizations are needed.

The Structure of Professional Associations

In addition to sharing similar functions, most student affairs associations are volunteer-based organizations. They have elected governing boards that consist of volunteers who take on leadership roles within the associations. The governing boards are charged with responsibilities that include the oversight of policies and procedures, budget management, and the development of strategic plans. Most associations also have special interest committees or task forces that focus on special interests and specific constituent groups, as well as state or regional divisions that hold their own conferences to provide additional opportunities for professional development.

There are a few associations, including ACPA and NASPA, that have central offices with paid full-time staff who are responsible for seeing that the activities of the association are carried out and who represent the association in various settings. They manage membership and conference planning, as well as the finances of the organization. Associations are primarily funded through membership dues, although grants from corporate sponsors and revenue from conferences and workshops bring in additional funding. Larger professional organizations, including NASPA, ACPA, NACA, and Association of College and University Housing Officers-International (ACUHO-I), have affiliated foundations that seek philanthropic support for association activities such as scholarships, research, innovative programs, study tours, and leadership development (ACPA, 2007; NACA, 2008; NASPA, 2007c; ACUHO-I, 2007).

Benefits of Membership in Professional Associations

Becoming involved in student affairs professional associations can be time consuming and expensive. When one considers that student affairs professionals often work more than forty hours a week at their jobs and are not highly paid, why would a person want to invest extra time and money in professional association membership and activity? For most people, fortunately, the benefits outweigh the costs. Professional organizations offer opportunities for professional development, networking, job seeking, and member discounts (ACPA, 2007d).

Membership in professional associations indicates to employers that one has a commitment to the profession beyond the institutional level. Attendance at national, regional, and/or state conferences as well as enrollment in specialized workshops or Web-based seminars involves a commitment of time and additional cost, which sometimes is covered by one's institution and sometimes not. However, it provides an opportunity for active learning and engagement.

Professional associations offer extensive opportunities for professional development. Annual conferences provide educational sessions, major speakers, and opportunities to talk with and learn from other professionals. Attending conferences is a good way to stay up to date on current issues and learn about cutting-edge practice and theory. Professional associations also offer regional, national, and Web-based seminars on specific topics of importance in student affairs. These intensive seminars allow participants to learn from experts in specific areas and to interact with other professionals interested in the same topic.

Professional associations also offer networking opportunities. Interaction among professionals at conferences and workshops fosters the exchange of ideas and the development of connections that can be helpful in career advancement. Listservs also provide opportunities for communication with other members who share similar interests or job responsibilities. Publications sponsored by professional associations offer professional development opportunities by keeping members informed about current research and scholarship in the field and also provide publication outlets for those who are engaged in scholarly endeavors. ACPA, NASPA, and many specialty associations offer on-site placement services at national and regional conferences and/or Web-based career information and job postings. Many associations offer member discounts on publications, workshops, professional insurance, and merchandise. Conference registration is significantly discounted for members.

Involvement and Leadership Opportunities

There are many levels of involvement in professional associations, ranging from passive membership to extensive involvement in leadership positions. Most student affairs associations are very welcoming of volunteer assistance, and professionals can be as involved as they choose to be. Individuals need to carefully assess their time and interests to ensure that they will be able to competently carry out any assignments they undertake, as professional reputations, both positive and negative, are often built on reliability and effectiveness in professional association activities.

Presenting at a conference is often the first level of active involvement professionals take on. This type of activity requires preparation of a proposal for a program session on a topic that the presenter believes will be of benefit to other professionals. Submitted proposals undergo review by the conference committee and the best are chosen for presentation. While it can be intimidating to present to one's peers, it is also a good way to test out one's ideas. Participation in a committee or commission is also a way to get more actively involved in a professional association. Opportunities include serving on conference-planning committees, reading program proposals, developing new initiatives, editing newsletters, maintaining Web sites, and a myriad of other possibilities.

Professional writing is another way to be involved in the profession. Submitting a newsletter article is a low-risk way to get started in this arena. Professional journals are always looking for strong research-based articles, and many associations also publish books of interest to their membership. Editorial boards of association-sponsored journals and books are usually very willing to assist new authors with the writing process. Serving on editorial boards is another way to contribute to the field.

Running for elected office is the most visible and time-consuming type of involvement, but serving as an officer of a professional association is also very rewarding. Testing the waters by serving as an elected officer of a commission, standing committee, knowledge community, or state or regional executive council is a way to determine whether being involved in governance is manageable given one's institutional responsibilities. All associations eagerly welcome individuals who wish to be involved in governance; in fact, it is often difficult to find people willing to take on this type of role.

Serious thought should be given to the type and degree of involvement a professional undertakes. Professional involvement can be seductive because of the visibility, recognition, and personal fulfillment it provides. It is easy to overcommit to activities in several associations and find that one does not have the time to devote to all of them and complete one's job responsibilities on campus as well. If one has the financial resources, being a member of a number of associations is certainly beneficial for keeping up to date on current issues in various areas of student affairs. It is generally advisable to be involved in one of the generalist associations, usually ACPA or NASPA, to stay current with the profession as a whole, and one specialty association that serves the area of student affairs in which one is working or interested in working. Involvement in an association focused on a specific identity group is also an important option for many professionals.

It is generally not possible or advisable to be deeply involved in more than one association at the same time. If a professional is holding a major office in an association, deferring extensive involvement in a second association until one's term is over is probably a good idea. In any case, discussing professional involvement responsibilities with one's institutional supervisor is important to ensure that appropriate support is available and there are no misunderstandings about how the individual is spending his or her time.

Conclusion

For any professional, professional involvement is both a responsibility and opportunity. The level and timing of such activity is a personal decision. Every professional has an obligation to stay current in the field and to continue to develop the skills necessary to be effective in her or his position. Professional associations provide many and varied opportunities for professional development, both for those individuals who maintain a minimal level of involvement as well as for those who are extensively engaged in the governance of the association.

At different points in a person's career, different types of involvement may be of interest and viable. Generally, new professionals begin their careers by joining professional associations and attending conferences. They may use the placement services associations provide to secure employment. Later, presenting and volunteering provide ways to engage with other professionals and contribute to the profession. As the individual progresses professionally, writing for publication and running for office may have appeal.

At any career stage, networking with other engaged professionals and being exposed to innovative ideas are important benefits of professional association involvement. Less obvious benefits also result. In her study of women involved in leadership in ACPA, Steffes (2001) found that the association provided critical personal and professional support for these leaders. Indeed, many of them used the word *family* to describe the association.

References

American College Personnel Association. "About ACPA." [http://www.myacpa.org/au/au_index.cfm]. 2007a.

American College Personnel Association. "ACPA Educational Leadership Foundation." [http://www.my-elf.org/]. 2007b.

American College Personnel Association. "Commissions." [http://www.myacpa.org/comm/comm_index.cfm]. 2007c.

American College Personnel Association "Membership." [http://members.myacpa.org/Scripts/4Disapi.dll/4DCGI/acpajoin/intro.html?Action=join]. 2007d.

American College Personnel Association. "Standing Committees." [http://www.myacpa.org/sc/sc_index.cfm]. 2007e.

American Society of Association Executives and the Center for Association Leadership. "Association FAQ." [http://www.asaecenter.org/AboutUs/content.cfm?ItemNumber=16309]. May 2007.

Asian Pacific Americans in Higher Education. [http://www.apahe.net/]. May 2007.

Association for Student Affairs at Catholic Colleges and Universities "ASACCU History." [http://www.asaccu.org/history.html]. 2004.

Association on Higher Education and Disability. "About Us." [http://www.ahead.org/about.php]. 2004.

Association of Hispanics in Higher Education. "Vision/Mission Statement." [http://www.aahhe.org/visionStatement.aspx]. May 2007.

Association of College and University Housing Officers—International. "Our Foundation." [http://www.acuho-i.org/OurFoundation/tabid/58/Default.aspx]. 2007.

Bashaw, C. T. "'Reassessment and Redefinition': The NAWDC and Higher Education for Women." In J. Nidiffer and C. T. Bashaw (Eds.), *Women Administrators in Higher Education: Historical and Contemporary Perspectives*. Albany: State University of New York Press, 2001a.

Bashaw, C. T. "'To Serve the Needs of Women': The AAUW, NAWDC, and Persistence of Academic Women's support Networks." In J. Nidiffer and C. T. Bashaw (Eds.), *Women Administrators in Higher Education: Historical and Contemporary Perspectives*. Albany: State University of New York Press, 2001b.

Blimling, G. S. "ACPA and NASPA Consolidation: United We Stand Together . . . Divided We Stand Apart." *Journal of College Student Development*, 2003, 44(5), 581–586.

Bloland, P. A. "Ecumenicalism in College Student Personnel." *Journal of College Student Personnel*, 1972, 13, 102–111.

Caple, R. B. *To Mark the Beginning: A Social History of College Student Affairs*. Lanham, Md.: American College Personnel Association, 1998.

Coomes, M. D., Wilson, M. E., and Gerda, J. J. "Of Visions, Values, and Voices: Consolidating ACPA and NASPA." Paper presented at the NASPA Annual Conference. St. Louis, March 2003.

Council for the Advancement of Standards in Higher Education. "Member Associations." [http://www.cas.edu/]. May 2007.

Council for Christian Colleges and Universities. "About Us." [http://www.cccu.org/about/about/asp]. 2007.

Crowley, W. H. "Reflections of a Troublesome but Hopeful Rip Van Winkle." *Journal of College Student Personnel*, 1964, 6, 66–73.

Evans, N. J., and Powell, T. "ACPA? NASPA? What's the Difference?" Paper presented at the American College Personnel Association Convention, Long Beach, California, March 2002.

Hanson, G. S. "The Organizational Evolution of NAWE." *Initiatives*, 1995, 56(4), 29–36.

Jesuit Association of Student Personnel Administrators. "About JASPA." [http://jaspa.creighton.edu/About/jaspa.htm]. 2004.

LGBT Resources in Higher Education "Mission Statement." [http://www.lgbtcampus.org/mission.html]. 2005.

Moneta, L., and Roberts, G. "Report of the Blue Ribbon Task Force on the Potential Consolidation of NASPA and ACPA." [http://usm.maine.edu/masap/063003_report.htm]. 2003.

Moore, L. V., and Neuberger, C. G. "How Professional Associations Are Addressing Issues in Student Affairs." In N. J. Evans and C. E. Phelps Tobin (Eds.), *The State of the Art of Preparation and Practice in Student Affairs: Another Look.* Lanham, Md.: American College Personnel Association, 1998.

National Association for Campus Activities. "NACA Foundation." [http://www.naca.org/NACA/Foundation/]. 2008.

National Association of Diversity Officers in Higher Education. "Welcome." [http://www.nadohe.org/index.htm]. May 2007.

National Association of Student Affairs Professionals. "What NASAP Is About." [http://www.nasap.net/NASAPorganization.html]. 2005.

National Association of Student Personnel Administrators. "About NASPA." [http://www.naspa.org/about/index.cfm?show=3]. 2007a.

National Association of Student Personnel Administrators. "Featured Events." [http://www.naspa.org/index.cfm]. 2007b.

National Association of Student Personnel Administrators. "NASPA Foundation." [http://www.naspa.org/foundation/index.cfm]. 2007c.

National Association of Student Personnel Administrators. "NASPA Programs & Initiatives." [http://www.naspa.org/programs/index.cfm]. 2007d.

Nuss, E. M. "The Development of Student Affairs." In S. R. Komives and D. B. Woodard Jr. (Eds.), *Student Services: A Handbook for the Profession.* San Francisco: Jossey-Bass, 2003.

Rhatigan, J. J. "NASPA History." [http://www.naspa.org/about.index.cfm?show=5]. 2007.

Sandeen, A. "Creeping Specialization in Student Affairs." *About Campus,* 1998, May–June, 2–3.

Sheeley, V. E. *Fulfilling Visions: Emerging Leaders of ACPA.* Washington, D.C.: American College Personnel Association, 1991.

Steffes, J. S. "The Experiences of Women in Leadership in the American College Personnel Association." Unpublished doctoral dissertation, University of Maryland, College Park, 2001.

StudentAffairs.com. "Websites-Professional Associations." [http://studentaffairs.com/web/profes.html]. 2006.

PART THREE

STUDENTS: THE REASON FOR OUR PROFESSIONAL PRACTICE

We come to our shared profession from a wealth of different backgrounds with a cornucopia of personal experiences, and we engage in student affairs professional practice in a wide array of functional areas. What binds us as a profession is that, no matter how heterogeneous our pathways to the profession, we share a solitary purpose: to support the success of our students through services and programs to foster their development and learning. This part of the handbook focuses on our students. In Chapter Twelve, George McClellan and Jim Larimore sketch the diversity of college students yesterday, today, and tomorrow. Jason Laker and Tracy Davis outline the challenges and opportunities available to us as we seek to enhance our own multicultural awareness and skills as well as to support our students and campus communities on their journey toward multiculturalism. Issues of diversity and multiculturalism have been with us since the inception of our profession. Student health, student insurance, and wellness are more modern issues that have come into the forefront of our practice in the modern era. In Chapter Fourteen, John Dunkel and Cheryl Presley present us with information on the physical and mental health of our students as well as on matters of access and affordability in student health and student health insurance. The number of online learners, including both those students who take all of their courses online and those who take some part of their full load online, has grown phenomenally over the past decade or so. Our profession, which has largely constructed its notions of engagement and community in terms of students coming to brick-and-mortar campuses, has yet to fully respond this sea change in learners. In Chapter Fifteen, Anita Crawley and Christine LeGore identify the needs of online learners, the ways in which student affairs professionals can help meet those needs, and the implications for our profession that will stem from understanding and addressing those needs.

CHAPTER TWELVE

THE CHANGING STUDENT POPULATION

George S. McClellan and Jim Larimore

The implications of the idea "Demographics are destiny" seem clear enough when thinking about *who* will enroll in college in the future. After all, understanding whom we are trying to educate has profound implications for our efforts to improve education on our campuses. However, it also seems important to keep that maxim in mind when we shift from thinking about who our students will be to thinking about who, in the future, will provide the financial support needed by institutions of higher education. Whether as taxpayers, tuition payers, philanthropic benefactors, or voters, we believe changes in the composition, views, and expectations of the American public will have important consequences for higher education. We hope this chapter will inform your thinking and whet your curiosity about some of the changes, demographic and otherwise, the future has in store.

By the time members of the class of 2010 celebrate their fortieth college reunion in 2050, non-Hispanic Whites will make up less than half the population of the United States. California, Hawaii, New Mexico, Texas, and the District of Columbia have majority minority populations (that is non-Hispanic Whites already make up less than 50 percent of the population). With minority populations in excess of 40 percent, the states of Arizona, Georgia, Maryland, Mississippi, and New York will be among the next to shift to majority minority status (U.S. Census Bureau, 2005). Other changes in student characteristics, attitudes, beliefs, and behaviors are also evident and will invariably impact higher education.

Students are undeniably at the center of student affairs professional practice. As such, the demographic and other trends discussed in this chapter will have significant implications for student affairs educators. It is our hope this chapter will help you to anticipate who will be enrolling in college in the decades to come and help you consider what we, as educators, will need to understand in order to effectively support, challenge, and serve these students. Given our traditional role in helping our institutions to change and adapt, changing demographics and the increasing internationalization of higher education will make it increasingly important for us to be well informed about these and other changes in the student body at our institutions. Harper and Quaye (2008) make an important contribution with their book on student engagement, which includes chapters on students whose experiences and identities reflect the incredible diversity that will increasingly define our society and campuses.

This chapter describes the diversity of students currently served in higher education and looks ahead at how the student body may change in the future. The discussion we offer is rooted in a recognition that the very notion of diversity is experienced in a variety of ways by student affairs professionals who practice in different locations around the world. Therefore, we also offer some thoughts about our own exploration of the meaning of "diversity" as employed in this chapter. Next, we provide information regarding the historical and contemporary diversity among students enrolled in U.S. higher education. Later in the chapter, we comment on benefits of and challenges to diversity. Finally, we conclude the chapter with recommendations for practice.

Diversity as a Global Issue in Higher Education

Moses (2002) emphasizes the importance of connecting diversity, multiculturalism, and internationalization in higher education. Indicators that reinforce this view include activities in Europe related to the development of multinational higher education accords designed to increase student mobility (International Higher Education Clearinghouse, 2007; Mooney, 2007; Weifang, 2001), and challenges confronting Chinese higher education as that nation seeks to provide greater access to higher education for its people (Chinese Education and Research Network, 2000). Policies recently enacted in Brazil to promote enrollment of persons with disabilities (Lloyd, 2006) also point to diversity and access as issues being addressed by practitioners around the world. Further evidence can be found in a review of papers presented at the Seventh International Conference on Diversity in Organisations, Communities, and Nations, which featured discussions focused on education in Australia (Braddock and Taylor, 2007), Greece (Karagianni,

Tressou, and Mitakidou, 2007), and Portugal (Fernandes, Almeida, Mourão, Estevão, Soares, and Veloso, 2007), among others.

Despite the increasing evidence that issues of diversity, multiculturalism, and internationalization are being discussed at conferences and on campuses around the world, the literature addressing diversity in student affairs practice outside of the United States remains quite limited (McClellan, Woodard, Zhou, C. Marques, Ramos, and Kwandayi, 2003). Hence, while we encourage readers to seek out information on global dimensions of diversity related to student affairs practice around the world, it is equally important that people consider ways they might contribute to the expansion and improvement of the knowledge base in this field. Therefore, in the balance of this chapter, by necessity we focus on diversity as it relates to professional practice in higher education in the United States.

Defining Diversity

Definitions of *diversity* are social constructs that reflect a variety of perspectives and experiences. A report from the American Association of State College and Universities and the National Association of State Universities and Land-Grant Colleges (2005) defines *diversity* as including "all aspects of human difference, including but not limited to, race, gender, age, sexual orientation, religion, disability, socio-economic status and status as a veteran" (p. 4). El-Khawas (2003) offers a more expansive taxonomy of diverse characteristics across two major dimensions: differences in background and situational differences. She identifies diversity of background as including characteristics such as race, ethnicity, religion, socioeconomic origin, gender, sexual orientation, age, generational cohorts, disabilities, and national origin. Diversity of situational differences includes full-time versus part-time student status, work status, degree objective, residential status, intermittent students, transfer students, swirlers (see Chapter Fifteen for more on these students), online learners, and type of institution. There is some evidence this broader definition of diversity may be more reflective of the ways in which many contemporary students construct and use the term (National Association of Student Personnel Administrators, 2000).

This chapter also makes use of broad socially constructed aggregations as a means for organizing and presenting data regarding diversity in higher education. In doing so, however, we remind the reader (as we have reminded ourselves) that using such descriptors is convenient for the purposes of presenting large data sets in limited space, but it obscures the rich diversity that exists within groups. Torres (2004), for example, encourages readers to recognize and appreciate the diversity within the Latino American community, including Mexican Americans, Puerto Ricans, Cuban Americans, Caribbean Americans, and Central and South Americans. Hune (2002) provides similar advice and insight regarding Asian American students. Tippeconnic Fox, Lowe, and McClellan (2005) highlight the importance of recognizing the importance of tribal affiliation rather than pan-Native identity in serving students who are Native American. These authors and others who explore the diversity that exists within various population groups are providing valuable insights into the complexity of identities and experiences our students bring to their college lives.

As a practical matter, when considering data related to these general descriptors, we often find it helpful to ask ourselves, "In what ways does this descriptor illuminate a dimension or aspect of a student's identity or experience—and in what ways might the particular descriptor mask or obscure other matters of importance, such as the experience(s) of a subgroup within a population group?" On balance, it seems to us better to ask these questions than to risk either relying too heavily on these descriptors or, conversely, discarding them due to their inherent limitations.

While recognizing notions of diversity, multiculturalism, and internationalization are intricately interconnected and interdependent, this chapter nonetheless attempts to differentiate among these terms, even as we have elected to limit our focus to a particular aspect of diversity. Diversity as discussed in this chapter refers to *structural diversity* (Gurin, Dey, Gurin, and Hurtado, 2003), a term that focuses on the numbers of students from particular groups. An operating assumption of structural diversity is that sufficient numbers of students, or members of a group, are needed to support the engagement of students from these groups throughout the institution. Multiculturalism and the more narrowly construed internationalism are understood in this chapter as descriptors of cognitive characteristics of individuals and institutions, and readers interested are directed to other chapters (Chapter Seven by Osfield and Terrell and Chapter Thirteen by Laker and Davis) in this volume to further explore those topics.

Yesterday, Today, and Tomorrow

This section of the chapter discusses diversity in U.S. higher education across three periods of time. Specifically, the following discussion focuses on diversity yesterday, today, and tomorrow.

Yesterday

Throughout the history of higher education in the United States, new populations of students have found their way to campus, and the subsequent changes and transitions in campus life have brought with them challenges and opportunities (El-Khawas, 2003; Rudenstine, 2001). The pace of change in the shifting composition of the student body accelerated in the latter half of the twentieth century and continues early in the twenty-first as a result of a series of societal transformations and legislative actions. The return of soldiers from World War II and the impact of the GI Bill (Bernstein, 1991; Wright and Tierney, 1991) fueled significant enrollment growth in colleges and universities during the 1940s and 1950s, and increased the presence of students of color and students from diverse socioeconomic backgrounds.

The assassination of Martin Luther King Jr. brought a sense of urgency to efforts rooted in the civil rights movement and the Civil Rights Act (Bowen and Bok, 1998; Carnoy, 1994) and led to the rapid acceleration of increases in the enrollment of Black students and students from other historically underrepresented groups in the late 1960s and early 1970s. Political action and efforts to assert tribal sovereignty in higher education led to the Tribal College Act (Stein, 1997; Houser, 1989), which promoted access to higher education for students from Native American tribal nations. Activism and a growing awareness of issues facing people with disabilities led to legislative actions such as Section 504 of the Rehabilitation Act and the Americans with Disabilities Act, which were instrumental in promoting the development and implementation of campus programs and services for the differently abled.

Growing numbers of women, adult learners, and part-time students have enrolled in college as opportunities for women to enter the labor force increased and as the nation's economy shifted over time from an emphasis on agriculture to manufacturing to service to knowledge, and as societal expectations changed regarding the standard of living. Finally, other social changes have produced changes in student enrollments as well. Examples include increasing numbers of military veterans; growing numbers of documented and undocumented immigrants; changes in societal attitudes related to gender expression, sexual identity, and sexual orientation; and efforts to improve college access for students from poor and working class families.

Today

Despite predictions to the contrary, college and university enrollments have continued to grow, in spite of an overall decline in the number of traditional college age students during the 1980s (Dey and Hurtado, 2005). In the fall of

2006 there were more than 17,000,000 full- and part-time students enrolled in institutions of higher education in the United States. Of those, 176,000 were Native American, 590,000 international, 1,100,000 Asian, 1,800,000 Hispanic, 2,200,000 Black, and 11,400,000 White. States with the most diverse student bodies included those in the West, Southwest, and southern half of the United States as well as those in the Northeast ("Enrollment," 2006).

Between 1981 and 2001, minority enrollment in U.S. higher education grew by more than 100 percent at both two- and four-year institutions (Harvey, 2003). In just ten years, between 1991 and 2001, the enrollment of students from historically underrepresented groups grew by 52 percent (American Association of State College and Universities and National Association of State Universities and Land-Grant Colleges, 2005). The 1980s and 1990s witnessed an increase in African American enrollment of nearly 60 percent, and during the same period Native American enrollment grew by 80 percent. Hispanic and Asian American enrollments both tripled from previous levels.

Enrollment growth among historically underrepresented groups has been a remarkable, positive, and long overdue development. However, it is important to note that academic achievement for members of racial minority groups generally continues to lag that of non-Hispanic Whites with regard to high school completion rates, college participation rates, and college graduations rates, though improvements in some of those rates for some minority groups have been noted (Harvey, 2003). Clearly, more needs to be done to ensure opportunities to enroll in college are accompanied by the advice, support, and resources students need in order to succeed and excel in college.

Women made up more than 57 percent of the college students enrolled in fall 2006 in the United States ("Enrollment," 2006), and the trend over the past twenty years or more has been for increases in enrollment by women to outpace increases for men. Women now earn the majority of baccalaureate and master's degrees conferred, while men continue to account for the majority of doctoral and first professional degrees (National Center for Educational Statistics, 2007).

In Chapter Five of this book, John Schuh notes that students from lower-income family backgrounds are projected to make up an increasing proportion of college-going students in the years to come. Citing data from the U.S. Census Bureau Web site, Schuh noted that in 2005, families in the top income quintile accounted for more than 50 percent of total income, dwarfing the combined incomes of the remaining 80 percent of the population. Given this enormous disparity in family wealth, colleges and universities must pay particular attention to the needs of students from lower-income families in order to overcome long-standing inequities in access to higher education and differences in educational attainment and degree completion.

Gupton, Castelo-Rodriguez, Martinez, and Quintanar (2008) examined the engagement and attainment of low-income and first-generation college students with particular attention to issues in college access and barriers to student engagement, personal development, persistence, and academic achievement. Citing work by Thayer (2000), Gupton and others (2008) defined first-generation students as those whose parents had not completed a bachelor's degree, and noted that Corrigan (2003) found that two thirds of low-income students were also first-generation college students. In developing a variety of recommendations to address the needs of low-income, first-generation college students, Gupton and others (2008) considered ways to help these students develop the social capital and networks that would help them succeed, especially in terms of creating connections to multiple sources of academic and social validation, and in ways that would affirm and build upon their existing social identities.

Among students from lower-socioeconomic status backgrounds and among students from historically underrepresented groups, the disparities in enrollment and degree attainment between women and men are the largest (Wilson, 2007). Cuyjet (1997), Tippeconnic Fox and others (2005), and Ortiz (2004) are among those who have examined the disparities in enrollment for women and men in specific groups of students and offered recommendations for practice.

Student interest and involvement in religion and spirituality has captured the attention of researchers and student affairs practitioners alike. The Higher Education Research Institute (2004) highlighted the tremendous diversity among college freshmen with regard to religious identification and spirituality and identified three profoundly distinct clusters of spirituality and beliefs regarding a wide spectrum of social issues among college freshmen in the United States. The first cluster included students who identify as Seventh-Day Adventists, Baptists, Mormons, and "other Christians." The second included Buddhists, members of the Eastern Orthodox Church, Episcopalians, Hindus, Jews, and Unitarians. The third included students who expressed no religious preference.

Given the current global political climate, the number of Muslim students and their experiences on college campuses are of timely interest and concern. Students who self-identify as Muslim account for just 1 percent of freshmen (Higher Education Research Institute, 2004), and there are more than 600 Muslim Students Association chapters at campuses in the United States and Canada with memberships ranging from 60 to 600 (Mubarak, 2007). There is little information currently available, however, regarding the experiences of these students on college campuses.

In addition to increased racial and ethnic diversity and the increase in enrollment by women, Hurtado and Pryor (2007) identified a number of trends in entering freshmen over the past forty years. Among these trends are a growing number of older students; an increase in the number of students with learning disabilities; an increase in the affluence of students' parents; and a decrease in the likelihood for students' parents to be living together.

In addition to trends related to the background characteristics noted, there have also been important shifts in situational differences. The percentage that reported having socialized with someone of another race has remained relatively flat (65–70 percent). The percentage who believe racial discrimination is not a major problem has also remained relatively stable (about 20 percent). However, the proportion who believe it is important to promote racial understanding has fallen from more than 40 percent to just under 35 percent. In terms of political orientation, students have become slightly more likely to self-identify as conservative, a change Dey and Hurtado (2005) argue might reflect "issues associated with the 1960s political and social movements are now seen as relatively mainstream issues and are no longer seen as liberal causes" (p. 324). Interestingly, the number of students reporting they are more career oriented has increased at the same time more have described themselves as altruistic.

The percentage of students with disabilities who completed high school in the United States rose by nearly a third between 1986 and 2001, when nearly 80 percent of high school students with disabilities completed their secondary education. Hall and Belch (2000) note that the broader construct of students with disabilities includes those with learning disabilities; health impairments; speech impairments; low vision; loss of hearing; orthopedic or physical impairments; and other types of disabilities as well. More than half of college students with disabilities are enrolled at public two-year institutions (Hall and Belch, 2000). Among the freshmen with disabilities, about 40 percent have learning disabilities, a tenfold increase since 1976 (Wolanin and Steele, 2004).

The changes in the college-going student body reflect the remarkable changes taking place within the general population. Since 2000, 40 percent of the nation's population growth has been a function of immigration. For the first time in the nation's history, the minority population in the country exceeded 100 million people, meaning minorities make up approximately 1 in 3 Americans. To put that number in perspective, in 1910, the total population of the United States was less than 100 million (U.S. Census Bureau, 2007).

Hispanics, who number around 44,300,000, make up the largest and fastest-growing minority group in the United States. Asian Americans are the second fastest-growing population, with Native Americans the third fastest-growing group (U.S. Census Bureau, 2007). Recent years have seen modest growth in the African American population. One particularly salient fact for those in higher education is the growth in the number of young people in minority communities (El Nasser and Overberg, 2007) where the median age is lower than that of the general population (U.S. Census Bureau, 2007).

Tomorrow

Within one decade, by the year 2015, it is anticipated as many as 80 percent of the roughly 2.6 million new students enrolled in American colleges and universities will be students from what today are considered historically underrepresented groups (American Association of State College and Universities and National Association of State Universities and Land-Grant Colleges, 2005; National Center for Educational Statistics, 2003). By 2015, African Americans are projected to make up 13 percent of enrollment, Asians 8.5 percent, and Hispanics 15.5 percent (Broido, 2004). Broido notes, however, while students on our campuses will become increasingly diverse, continued de facto residential and social segregation in American cities, towns and suburbs will likely mean that "although campuses generally will become increasingly diverse, interracial contact is likely to be a new experience for many (especially White) college students. However, this will not be the experience at all campuses. Because of the urbanization of people of color . . . rural campuses that draw their students from local regions may remain overwhelmingly White institutions" (pp. 74–75).

The trend of women making up larger and larger percentages of enrolled students is projected to continue through 2016, and it is predicted women will earn the majority of degrees of all types within the coming decade (National Center for Education Statistics, 2007). By 2010, the ratio for baccalaureate degrees earned by women as compared to those earned by men is expected to exceed 1.5 to 1 (Kellom, 2004).

In addition to the continued changes in enrollments relative to ethnicity and gender, Broido (2004) suggests it is likely enrollments will increase for multiracial students, children of recent immigrants, transgendered persons, and students from single-parent households. Bilodeau and Renn (2005) note evidence that students are coming out earlier and suggest it is therefore more likely students will enter college having already begun—or completed—the coming-out process as lesbian, gay, bisexual, or transgender.

With regard to students from multiracial backgrounds, Cortes (2000) addresses the complexity of identity in a world where intermarriage has become increasingly common. He identifies what he perceives as five patterns of identity for students from multiracial families: single racial identity; multiple racial identity; multiple racial-multiracial identity; multiracial identity; and nonracial identity. Cortes stresses the importance of distinguishing heritage from identity, supporting a student's self-determination of his or her identity, and providing support for student organizations involved in working with the growing number of multiracial students.

Benefits of Diversity

What are the benefits derived from the increasing diversity of students on college campuses? Views on this subject vary but tend to focus on the importance of diversity for social support, strengthening opportunities for educational attainment, and providing opportunities for students (and others) to examine and overcome preconceived ideas and stereotypes and to learn about people who are different from themselves within a context focused on openness, respect, and learning. Smith and Schonfield (2000) report, "The number of diverse people, or more specifically the presence of a critical mass of diverse people, creates greater opportunities for social support, role models, and mentoring. Having diversity in the population creates greater opportunities for individuals to be seen as individuals, thus breaking down stereotypes. In addition, greater diversity in numbers suggests the institution is committed to diversity—something that proves important in creating an inclusive climate" (p. 18).

Rudenstine (2001) adds, "In our world today, it is not enough for us and our students to acknowledge, in an abstract sense, that other kinds of people, with other modes of thought and feeling and action, exist somewhere—unseen, unheard, unvisited, and unknown" (p. 45). Thus, time students spend together, in and out of the classroom, is seen as having an educational purpose that has value both for individuals and, in the aggregate, for society. Given the de facto segregation that continues to affect where people live and with whom they attend school in our nation's K–12 educational systems (Glater and Finder, 2007), it seems likely college and university campuses will provide, for White students in particular, important opportunities for exposure and interaction across racial and other forms of difference.

Smith and Schonfield (2000) also identify student interest in being part of diverse communities and institutional viability as other benefits. In addition, they argue "the presence of diversity on our campus has the potential to challenge some of the underlying assumptions of our institutions in ways that can improve quality and effectiveness" (p. 22). Indeed, given the rapidly approaching demographic tipping point in the racial and ethnic composition of our nation, and given the increasing impact of global mobility, commerce, and politics on our lives, it seems imperative we prepare our students and our institutions to understand and embrace these changes. Chang, Altbach, and Lomotey (2005) have noted increased contact and interaction have changed the way campuses respond to acts of intolerance: "Gone are the days when only a handful of African American students protest alone to combat expressions of racial antipathy. When a racially hostile act is observed on campus (that is, use of racial slurs, threats to specific groups of students, promotion of negative racial images, etc.) for example, active calls for attention and redress now nearly always come from a large multiracial campus contingency of faculty, administrators, and students" (p. 518).

Challenges to Diversity

While much remains to be done, there has been notable progress in the United States in diversifying student enrollments in higher education, and a growing body of research on learning and developmental outcomes for students is shedding light on the importance of interactions with a diverse group of fellow students. Nonetheless, institutions seeking to diversify their campuses face a number of challenges. Among these are the continuing stratification of students from certain groups into particular types of institutions and within certain academic fields and degree programs (Chang and others, 2005). For example, Dey and Hurtado (2005) found Hispanics and Native Americans are more likely to be represented in two-year colleges than either African Americans or Whites. Other challenges include the lack of progress with regard to closing the gap between groups of students in terms of retention and academic achievement (National Center for Education Statistics, 2007), and the political backlash has fueled a series of legal and legislative challenges to Affirmative Action (Orfield, 2001).

With regard to challenges to Affirmative Action, the Supreme Court in recent years has consistently found a compelling interest on the part of higher educations institutions to diversify their student bodies (see *Regents of the University of California v. Bakke*, 438 U.S. 265 (1978) and *Grutter v. Bollinger et al.* 539 U.S. 982 (2003). The question of whether or not preferences in admission are permissible appears to be settled law, but questions remain about the specific details of how institutions can implement plans to advance that interest. In the K–12 arena, the prevailing and dissenting opinions expressed in the Supreme Court's recent decision concerning the consideration of race as a factor in desegregation efforts in public school districts reveals just how contentious and politically charged this topic remains (Lewin, 2007).

Noting the frequent intersection of ethnicity and social class, some have suggested a greater reliance on social class as a means for addressing these challenges. Orfield (2001), however, cautions the experiences of poverty are not the same across ethnicities or nationalities. Glater and Finder (2007) cite experiences in school districts in states as varied as California, Massachusetts, and North Carolina as evidence focusing on economic integration can have a beneficial impact on the educational attainment of lower-income students, but those advances do not necessarily equate to racial integration or increased opportunities for racial minorities. Chang and other (2005) have stated simply looking at income variation masks other important factors such as the effects of: "chronic unemployment, malnutrition, environmental hazards, inner city crime, economic downgrading of labor, and so on" (p. 518).

Recommendations

A review of the literature on diversity in higher education reveals a variety of helpful recommendations for student affairs professional practice. The following might serve as a useful foundation:

1. Clearly articulate a definition of diversity for your campus (Shireman, 2003).
2. Think expansively. "The dimensions of diversity today are more complex than several decades ago, but probably will develop further in the future" (El-Khawas, 2003, p. 46). Define specific goals related to diversity in terms of structural diversity or representation, increased interaction between students whose backgrounds differ, participation in various activities or programs, and improvements in various measures of educational attainment.
3. Articulate what your institution considers the value of diversity. One helpful framework focuses on three imperatives for embracing diversity: learning, economic, and democracy (American Association of State Colleges and Universities and National Association of State Universities and Land-Grant Colleges, 2005).
4. Develop specific diversity action plans at the departmental and divisional level. Use the specific goals mentioned in item 2 to drive the development of specific plans for action.
5. Seek to understand the multifaceted nature of personal identities. Focus on "developing and acknowledging . . . the multiplicity of identities" of students, staff, and faculty (Smith and Schonfield, 2000, p. 22)." Incorporate this knowledge into staff training and development efforts, and into student development initiatives as well.
6. Be mindful of Gates's (1996) observation: "People speak of race as something blacks have, sexual orientation as something gays and lesbians have, ethnicity as something so called 'ethnics' have" (p. 3). Raise this as a topic of discussion

and reflection on your campus, and ask people to consider ways that this dynamic shapes and/or inhibits relationships on your campus.

7. Keep in mind that the needs and experiences of first-generation and lower-income students are likely to require intensive and intentional efforts to help them understand and navigate the culture and systems of any campus. Engage faculty, staff, and junior/senior/graduate students from low-income and first-generation backgrounds in developing strategies to support and mentor new students as they negotiate the transition to college life.

8. Examine the concept of "othering" to gauge whether discussions on your campus lead various community members to feel included or excluded from discussions of diversity. Avoid "othering," which may lead to recentering of attention on the majority experience without adequate consideration of the experiences of those defined as outside the majority (Fine, 1994), and serve as a role model for exploring this topic openly in terms of its impact on your campus and in society.

9. Record and report information about diversity-related efforts on your campus. Assess the impact of these efforts and the progress made toward established goals. Use this information to take stock of current efforts and revise goals and plans as necessary.

Conclusion

If institutions are to achieve their aspirations with regard to diversity, multiculturalism, and internationalism, we must work to "create an environment that embraces diversity as one of its core values, infusing [diversity into] every aspect of campus life and purpose, and every measure of success" (American Association of State College and Universities and National Association of State Universities and Land-Grant Colleges, 2005, p. 1). In other words, as student affairs practitioners, we must rededicate ourselves to quantitative change while simultaneously committing ourselves to qualitative change in the lived experiences of our students if we are to advance the interest of assuring the success of our students and our institutions.

Structural diversity, while instrumental and important in its own right, is not solely sufficient in assuring the educational impact of multicultural and international learning communities. As Woodard and others (2000) accurately observe, "After a half century of touting changing student demographics, many campuses are still chilly climates for students of color, neglect adult learners and commuters, and act as if students in the 'middle' need less attention than their under-prepared low-ability or talented high-ability students" (p. 36).

References

American Association of State College and Universities and National Association of State Universities and Land-Grant Colleges. *Now Is the Time: Meeting the Challenge for a Diverse Academy.* Washington, D.C.: American Association of State College and Universities and National Association of State Universities and Land-Grant Colleges, 2005.

Bernstein, A. R. *American Indians and World War II: Toward a New Era in Indian Affairs.* Norman: University of Oklahoma Press, 1991.

Bilodeau, B. L., and Renn, K. A. (2005). "Analysis of LBT Identity Development Models and Implications for Practice." In R. L. Sanlo (Ed.), *Gender Identity and Sexual Orientation: Research, Policy, and Personal Perspectives.* New Directions in Student Services, no. 111. San Francisco: Jossey Bass, 2005.

Bowen, W. G., and Bok, D. *The Shape of the River: Long-Term Consequences of Considering Race in College and University Admissions.* Princeton, N.J.: Princeton University Press, 1998.

Braddock, R., and Taylor, P. A. "Diversity in Higher Education: Multiculturalism as a Challenge and an Opportunity, with Special Reference to the Case of Australia." Paper presented at the Seventh International Conference on Diversity in Organizations, Communities, and Nations, Amsterdam, The Netherlands. [http://d07.cgpublisher.com/proposals/577/index_html]. July 2007.

Broido, E. M. "Understanding Diversity in Millennial Students." In M. D. Coomes and R. DeBard (Eds.), *Serving the Millennial Generation.* New Directions in Student Services, no. 106. San Francisco: Jossey-Bass, 2004.

Carnoy, M. *Faded Dreams: The Politics and Economics of Race in America.* Cambridge, U.K.: Cambridge University Press, 1994.

Chang, M., Altbach, P., and Lomotey, K. "Race in Higher Education." In P. Altbach, R. Berdahl, and P. Gumport (Eds.), *American Higher Education in the Twenty-First Century.* Baltimore: Johns Hopkins University Press, 2005.

Chinese Education and Research Network. *Higher Education in China.* [http://www.edu.cn/20010101/21828.shtml]. 2000.

Corrigan, M. E. "Beyond Access: Persistence Challenges and the Diversity of Low-Income Students." *New Directions for Higher Education,* 2003, 121, 25–34.

Cortes, C. E. "The Diversity Within: Intermarriage, Identity, and Campus Community." *About Campus,* 2000, March/April, 5–10.

Cuyjet, M. "African American Men on College Campuses: Their Needs and Their Perceptions." In M. Cuyjet (Ed.), *Helping African American Men Succeed in College.* New Directions in Student Services, no. 80. San Francisco: Jossey Bass, 1997.

Dey, E. L., and Hurtado, S. "College Students In Changing Contexts." In P. Althbach, R. Berdahl, and P. Gumport (Eds.), *American Higher Education in the Twenty-First Century.* Baltimore and London: Johns Hopkins University Press, 2005.

El-Khawas, E. "The Many Dimensions of Student Diversity." In S. R. Komives and D. B. Woodard Jr. (Eds.), *Student Services: A Handbook for the Profession.* San Francisco: Jossey-Bass, 2003.

El Nasser, H., and Overberg, P. "Nation's Minority Numbers Top 100M." *USA Today,* May 17, 2000, p. 1A.

"Enrollment." *Chronicle of Higher Education,* August 25, 2006.

Fernandes, E. M., Almeida, L. Mourão, J., Estevão, S., Soares, A. P., and Veloso, A. L. "Inclusive College Education Viewed by the Non-Disabled Students." Paper presented at the Seventh International Conference on Diversity in Organizations, Communities, and Nations, Amsterdam, The Netherlands. [http://d07.cgpublisher.com/proposals/199/index_html]. July 2007.

Fine, M. "Working the Hyphens: Reinventing Self and Other in Qualitative Research." In N. K. Denzin and Y. S. Lincoln (Eds.), *Handbook of Qualitative Research.* Thousand Oaks, Calif.: Sage, 1994.

Gates, H. L. "The Ethics of Identity." *Pathways,* 1996, 20(3), 3–4.

Glater, J. D., and Finder, A. "School Diversity Based on Income Segregates Some." *New York Times.*[http://www.nytimes.com/2007/07/15/education/15integrate.html]. July 15, 2007.

Gupton, J., Castelo-Rodriguez, C., Martinez, D., and Quintinar, I. "Creating a Pipeline to Engage Low-Income, First-Generation College Students." In S. Harper and S. Quaye (Eds.), *Student Engagement In Higher Education: Theoretical Perspectives and Practical Approaches for Diverse Populations.* New York: Routledge, 2008.

Gurin, P., Dey, E., Gurin, G., and Hurtado, S. "How Does Racial/Ethnic Diversity Promote Education?" *Western Journal of Black Studies,* 2003, 27(1), 20–29.

Hall, L. M., and Belch, H. A. "Setting the Context: Reconsidering the Principles of Full Participation and Meaningful Access for Students with Disabilities." In H. A. Belch (Ed.), *Serving Students with Disabilities.* New Directions in Student Services, no. 91. San Francisco: Jossey-Bass, 2000.

Harper, S. R., and Quaye, S. J. (Eds.). *Student Engagement In Higher Education: Theoretical Perspectives and Practical Approaches for Diverse Populations.* New York: Routledge, 2008.

Harvey, W. B. *Minorities in Higher Education: Annual Status Report.* Washington, D.C.: American Council on Education, 2003.

Higher Education Research Institute. *The Spiritual Life of College Students: A National Study of College Students' Search for Meaning and Purpose.* Los Angeles: University of California [http://www.spirituality.ucla.edu/spirituality/reports/FINAL_REPORT.pdf]. 2004.

Houser, S. "Tribal Colleges: Underfunded Miracles." In P. Cahape and C. B. Howley (Eds.), *Indian Nations at Risk: Listening to the People.* Charleston, W. Va.: ERIC, 1989.

Hune, S. "Demographics and Diversity of Asian American College Students." In M. McEwen, C. M. Kodama, A. N. Alvarez, S. Lee, and C. T. H. Liang (Eds.), *Working with Asian American College Students.* New Directions in Student Services, no. 97. San Francisco: Jossey-Bass, 2002.

Hurtado, S., and Pryor, J. H. "Looking at the Past, Shaping the Future: Getting to Know Our Students for the Past 40 Years." Presented at the ACPA/NASPA joint national conference, Orlando, Florida, April 2007.

Institute for Teaching and Learning. *Internationalisation, Global Citizenship and Inclusivity Project.* Sydney, Australia: University of Sydney. [http://www.itl.usyd.edu.au/diversity]. 2007

International Higher Education Clearinghouse. *GATS and Bologna.* [http://www.bc.edu/bc_org/avp/soe/cihe/ihec/treaties/treaties_bologna.htm]. 2007.

Karagianni, P., Tressou, E., and Mitakidou, S. "The Diversity in the University: Student Teachers' Ideas on Disability, Race and Ethnicity Issues." Paper presented at the Seventh International Conference on Diversity in Organizations, Communities, and Nations, Amsterdam, The Netherlands. [http://d07.cgpublisher.com/proposals/233/index_html]. July 2007.

Kellom, G. (Ed.). *Developing Effective Programs and Services for College Men.* New Directions in Student Services, no. 107. San Francisco: Jossey Bass, 2004.

Lewin, T. "Across U.S., a New Look at School Integration Efforts." *New York Times.* [http://select.nytimes.com/gst/abstract.html?res=F40B17FD3C5A0C7A8EDDAF0894D F404482andfta=yandincamp=archive:article_related]. June 20, 2007.

Lloyd, M. "Slowly Enabling the Disabled." *Chronicle of Higher Education.* [http://chronicle. com/weekly/v52/i49/49a03501.htm]. August 11, 2006.

McClellan, G. S., Woodard, D. B. Jr., Zhou, Q., Marques, C., Ramos, J. E., and Kwandayi, H. "The Global Practice of Student Affairs/Services: An Exploratory International Survey." Unpublished paper, Tucson: University of Arizona, 2003.

Mooney, P. "Fast-Rising Tuition in China Limits Poorest Students' Ability to Obtain a Higher Education." *Chronicle of Higher Education.* [http://chronicle.com/weekly/v53/i22/ 22a03102.htm]. February 2, 2007.

Moses, Y. T. "Diversity, Globalism, and Democracy: Higher Education's Imperative." Washington, D.C.: American Association for Higher Education. [http://www.salzburg seminar.org/reports/AAHE_Diversity.pdf]. 2002.

Mubarak, H. (2007) *How Muslim Students Negotiate Their Religious Identity and Practices in an Undergraduate Setting.* Social Science Research Council. [http://religion.ssrc.org/reforum/ Mubarak]. 2007.

National Association of Student Personnel Administrators. *Diversity on Campus: Reports from the Field.* Washington, D.C.: National Association of Student Personnel Administrators, 2000.

National Center for Educational Statistics. *The Condition of Education 2007.* Washington, D.C.: U.S. Department of Education, 2007.

National Center for Educational Statistics. *Digest of Education Statistics.* [www.nces.ed.gov/ pubs2003/digest02/ch_3]. 2003.

Orfield, G. (Ed.). *Diversity Challenged: Evidence on the Impact of Affirmative Action.* Cambridge, Mass.: Harvard Education Publishing Group, 2001.

Ortiz, A. M. (Ed.). *Addressing the Unique Needs of Latino American Students.* New Directions for Student Services, no. 105. San Francisco: Jossey-Bass, 2004.

Regents of the University of California v. Bakke, 438 U.S. 265 (1978).

Rudenstine, N. L. "Student Diversity and Higher Learning." In G. Orfield (Ed.), *Diversity Challenged, Evidence on the Impact of Affirmative Action.* Cambridge, Mass.: Harvard Education Publishing Group, 2001.

Shireman, R. "Ten Questions College Officials Should Ask About Diversity." *Chronicle of Higher Education.* [http://chronicle.com/weekly/v49/:49/49b01001.htm]. August 15, 2003.

Smith, D. G., and Schonfield, N. B. "The Benefits of Diversity: What the Research Tells Us." *About Campus,* 2000, November/December, 16–23.

Stein, W. J. "American Indian Education." In D. Morrison (Ed.), *American Indian Studies.* New York: Peter Lang, 1997.

Thayer, P. B. "Retention of Students from First-Generation and Low Income Backgrounds." *Journal of the Council for Opportunity in Education,* 2000.

Tippeconnic Fox, M., Lowe, S., and McClellan, G .S. (Eds.). *Serving Native American Students in Higher Education.* New Directions for Student Services, no. 109. San Francisco: Jossey-Bass, 2005.

Torres, V. "The Diversity Among Us: Puerto Ricans, Cuban Americans, Caribbean Americans, and Central and South Americans." In A. M. Ortiz (Ed.), *Addressing the Unique Needs of Latino American Students.* New Directions for Student Services, no. 105. San Francisco: Jossey-Bass, 2004.

U.S. Census Bureau. "Minority Population Tops 100 Million." Press release. Washington, D.C.: U.S. Department of Commerce, May 17, 2007.

U.S. Census Bureau. *Texas Becomes Nation's Newest "Majority-Minority" State, Census Bureau Announces.* U.S. Census Bureau News Press Release, Department of Commerce,

Washington, D.C. [http://www.census.gov/Press-Release/www/releases/archives/population/005514.html]. 2005.

Weifang, M. *Current Trends in Higher Education Development in China*. Boston, Mass.: Center for International Higher Education at Boston University. [http://www.bc.edu/bc_org/avp/soe/cihe/newsletter/News22/text014.htm]. 2001.

Wilson, R. "The New Gender Divide." *Chronicle of Higher Education*. [http://chronicle.com/weekly/v53/i21/21a03601.htm]. January 26, 2007.

Wolanin, T. R., and Steele, P. E. *Higher Education Opportunities for Students with Disabilities: A Primer for Policy Makers*. Washington, D.C.: Institution for Higher Education Policy, 2004.

Woodard, D. B. Jr., Love, P., and Komives, S. R. *Leadership and Management Issues for a New Century*. New Directions in Student Services, no. 92. San Francisco: Jossey-Bass, 2000.

Wright, B., and Tierney, W. G. "American Indians in Higher Education: A History of Cultural Conflict." *Change*, 1991, 23, 11–18.

CHAPTER THIRTEEN

CONTINUING THE JOURNEY TOWARD MULTICULTURAL CAMPUS COMMUNITIES

Jason A. Laker and Tracy L. Davis

Diversity, access, and inclusion continue to be among the most pervasive and contentious issues facing institutions of higher education. The words, their meanings, and the commitments required to achieve them—even whether and at what costs they should happen—are debated by all sectors of the campus community. Indeed, it is often difficult to even identify who exactly is being discussed—who should be included, and in turn, who should not. This situation becomes even more complex when external constituents such as funding agencies, political bodies, students' families, and pundits of all persuasions invariably enter the often vitriolic debate.

Student affairs practitioners are frequently situated in the middle of these conversations, whether through relationships with students and families, demands to address particular aspects of the issue, or through their own initiative and desire to meaningfully engage where these issues are manifested on campus. Student affairs practitioners are in a potentially impactful role in this regard. First, they can influence the level of inclusiveness on their campuses for students already present. Second, they can create opportunities for students to develop in their own understanding and commitments to such issues, so that those same students can actively work for social justice in their respective future jobs, families, and communities. Third, they can influence policies and institutional structures that promote systematic organizational change that push campus diversity and equity efforts to deeper and more meaningful levels. Fostering equitable international and multicultural campus communities will require strategies that account for and address complexities related to individual developmental processes, epistemological frameworks that undergird professional practice, and often deeply embedded institutional policies and structures. This chapter, therefore, explores the ways that student affairs professionals can effectively promote equitable multicultural and international communities by challenging and supporting at the individual level, routinely interrogating static professional belief systems, and transforming cosmetic institutional diversity initiatives related to hiring, recruitment, curricula, educational programming, and climate.

This chapter, moreover, suggests some conceptual and theoretical lenses to deepen analysis of social identity issues, which is necessary for developing more complex and effective efforts to achieve more inclusive multicultural and international campus communities. The authors also suggest particular structural efforts that reflect the concepts discussed here.

Identity: A Critical Individual-Institutional Nexus

"An identity is established in relation to a series of differences that have become socially recognized. These differences are essential to its being. . . . Identity requires difference in order to be, and converts difference into otherness in order to secure its own self-certainty" (Connolly, 2002, p. 64). These words speak to the ways in which identities are co-constructed by the host of identity and the social milieu surrounding around them; and to the power relations that develop in these processes that situate identities in dynamic and hierarchical positions. Social identities are commonly discussed in student affairs circles in terms of privilege and oppression, and in particular the idea that the holders of a majority identity enjoy privilege, whereas those whose identity is in the minority experience oppression. The implication is that each person is either privileged or oppressed.

While it is critical to incorporate complexities of the co-construction of identities in the context of institutional oppression, emerging scholarship challenges the binary equation posed by such descriptions in professional discourse (for example, Kaufman, 1999; and hooks, 2004). That is, the either/or conceptualization of privilege and oppression "essentializes" identities in a manner that does not adequately address their multidimensional nature or the reality that students vary widely in terms of how deeply they identify with particular identities. Discussing identity as essentially privileged or oppressed not only fails to capture the complexity of identities, but it may also situate those with oppressed identities against those with privileged identities in some mythic binary debate that tends to close, as opposed to promote, discussion. In order to understand how to genuinely create multicultural communities we need to move beyond the frameworks that currently dominate student affairs discourse. According to Caryn McTighe Musil, AAC&U Vice President for Diversity, Equity, and Global Initiatives, speaking at the 2006 Diversity and Learning Conference, diversity education has outgrown its frameworks while practitioners hesitate to leave the structural, political, and intellectual shells they have so painfully crafted (Peltier Campbell, 2007, p. 1). Moreover, Barcelo (2007) argues that "to be effective leaders we must be willing to reevaluate the structures of knowledge, the patterns of relationships, and the organizing principles of institutional life" (p. 3).

Few would argue that we have achieved the kind of educational equity required by our missions and outlined by law in our democracy. Carnevale and Fry (2002), for example, demonstrate that college students from historically underrepresented populations have differential access to resources before college which often hinders educational attainment during college. In order to move beyond cosmetic changes that cover discrimination with a cloak of diversity, educators need to constantly question the assumptions that support our equity efforts, the meaning-making frameworks that deflect our focus toward simplistic solutions, and the assessment strategies which measure trivia. One of the purposes of this chapter, then, is to interrogate existing conceptual professional frameworks in order to explore roles and offer strategies that student affairs professionals might use in extending the journey toward inclusive and equitable international and multicultural campus communities. Accordingly, we assume that language like *community, international,* and *multicultural* connote meanings that cannot be understood in static or final ways, but rather are contextual and dynamic—and often quite personal and politically charged. Readers are encouraged to reflect upon and grapple with the ambiguous and at times contested discussion in this chapter, noting instances in which deeply held views are challenged, and remaining open to the possibility of refining these views (or ultimately reinforcing them with additional depth of understanding). This is analog to the discussions readers will be encouraged to foster at their respective institutions—moving from esoteric and frustrating to understandable and still frustrating. Finding solidarity in the experience of frustration about identity and institutional oppression offers potentially liberating opportunities for agreement and/or connection among diverse groups of people, important ingredients of inclusive communities.

Despite the ambiguity associated with learning about identities, we cannot remain moral relativists with regard to the social commitments incumbent upon institutions of higher education. Colleges and universities must forcefully enact commitments to promoting understanding, and to nurturing cross-cultural and inter-identity engagement for the purpose of underwriting a society in which all members have agency within, and access to, an education. Doing so will take action to make both epistemological and fundamental structural changes.

Pedagogical Issues at the Individual Level

So, what is a well-meaning and well-educated student affairs practitioner to do when trying to understand the meanings and implications of diversity, access, or multiculturalism and to be of use in fostering each of these? Indeed the contexts of college campuses are growing more complex. As discussed in Chapter Twelve, the demography of higher education is dynamic, increasing in complexity, and thus poses profound challenges for practitioners. Accepting and effectively engaging the challenges, however, is a professional mandate. Fortunately, there is clear evidence that the struggle pays off significant returns in terms of promoting learning and development.

There is general agreement in the literature that engagement across identities fosters cognitive development (Milem, Chang and Antonio, 2005; Pascarella, Edison, Nora, Hagedorn, and Terenzini, 1996; Smith and Associates, 1997; and Terenzini, Pascarella, and Blimling, 1996) and psychosocial growth (Antonio, 1998; Chang, 1996, Hurtado, 1997; and Smith and Associates, 1997), and that students learn more effectively in such environments. According to Gurin (2007), for example, "Complex thinking occurs when people encounter a novel situation for which, by definition, they have no script, or when the environment demands more than their current scripts provide. Racial diversity in a college or university student body provides the very features that research has determined are central to producing the conscious mode of thought educators demand from their students" (p. 2). From this perspective, fostering international and multicultural communities is quite simply an educational mandate for preparing citizens in a pluralistic democracy. We know, however, that while the rationale for creating diverse communities is clear, the work of advancing multicultural communities is anything but simple. Educational community participants' understanding of and willingness to interact with others who are different from themselves is not assured. Since engaging in the learning process is requisite, "a sustained and coordinated effort regarding diversity is necessary to increase the positive effects on student development and learning" (Chang, 2005). Educational benefits do not accrue by simply bringing together diverse groups. Research demonstrates that campuses must provide engaging coursework covering historical, cultural, and social bases for diversity and community, and there must be concurrent opportunities, encouragement, and expectations outside of the classroom for students to interact across identity differences (Milem and others, 2005).

Moreover, guiding and mediating the conflicts that naturally occur from such interactions are skills that require more than multicultural awareness and knowledge. Although awareness and knowledge about cultures and cultural differences is necessary, it is not sufficient to effectively negotiate the rocky terrain of establishing genuinely celebratory multicultural communities (Pope, Reynolds, and Mueller, 2004). An example of this complexity is evident in Jones and McEwen's (2000) original Multiple Dimensions of Identity (MDI) Model. In their model, sexual orientation, race, culture, class, religion, and gender are dimensions central to one's identity. The salience of a particular dimension to one's core identity depends on changing contexts that include current experiences, family background, sociocultural conditions, and career decisions and life planning. This model offers a template for gauging both individual interventions with, and institutional programs for, students, whether generally, or with respect to particular subpopulations.

As a practical tool for promoting multicultural understanding and development, student affairs professionals can use the MDI as a mental framework to avoid making assumptions about the individuals with whom they are working. This tool encourages professionals to consider how intersections of sexual orientation, race, culture, religion, and gender might impact a student. Moreover, the MDI offers a model for promoting discussion beyond an oversimplified dualistic conception of oppression. White, heterosexual men, for example, are presumed to hold privilege. While men with these identities generally hold racial, sexual and gender privilege (depending on cultural context), focusing on the identity intersections such as class and gender or class and race, helps to more accurately capture not only how oppression works, but also how it needs to be individually addressed in order to be effective (Reed, 2008). Fine, Weis, Addelston, and Marusza (1997), for example, in their qualitative research on men and boys in White, working-class neighborhoods, found that "white working-class men . . . scramble to reassert their assumed place of privilege on a race-gender hierarchy in an economy that has ironically devalued all workers" (p. 77). Further complicating the discussion is the need to understand that class too often goes unnamed in our multicultural discussions and it is much more complicated than just level of income. It includes language usage, dress styles, educational level, occupations seen acceptable, how leisure and social time is spent, and so on (Longwell-Grice, 2002; Reed, 2008). The very complexity of the various dimensions of identity, their diverse intersections, and the intricate contexts in which they are performed illustrates the absurdity of "essentializing" identity and the necessity of using newer critical approaches. Reinforcing this idea, Kaufman (1999) persuasively argues that "our whole language of oppression is in need of overhaul for it is based on simple binary oppositions, reductionist equations between identity and social location, and unifocal notions of self" (p. 70).

Another such model, "The Developmental Model of Intercultural Sensitivity," or "DMIS" (Bennett, 1986, 1993) focuses on individuals' reactions to cultural differences they might encounter in others. This particular model is comprised of six stages, the first three of which are characterized as "ethnocentric," making one's own cultural experience central to one's experience of lived reality. These stages include "Denial," "Defense," and "Minimization," which are described respectively as moving from an experience of one's own culture as the only true one, to the only good one, and eventually the universal one; in this latter case cultures other than one's own are objectified and imposed upon in normative actions such as correcting the other to behave according to one's cultural expectations.

The second three stages of the DMIS are described as "ethnorelative," and they focus on one's ability to see, interpret, and interact with multiple worldviews. These include "Acceptance," in which one comes to see one's own culture as one of many legitimate worldviews, "Adaptation," an ability to interpret and experience multiple cultural viewpoints, and "Integration," an ability to expand one's own worldview informed by others to move within and between cultural milieus with some ease. Readers are encouraged to seek out and review literature about this and other models in order to build interpretive and facilitation skills for use with students and staff. In addition, there is no amount of theoretical or conceptual understanding that can substitute for practitioners engaging in dialogue about multicultural issues. Multicultural awareness and knowledge need to be extended through well-exercised multicultural practice, as awkward and ego challenging as this sometimes is, in order to develop the kind of competence needed to effectively promote learning interventions and social justice (Pope and others, 2004).

Promoting multicultural and international communities at the individual level will also require patience and empathy with those who have not seriously engaged issues of human diversities and institutional oppression. Learning about issues of human diversities and systems of oppression is not simply an intellectual process, but also a profoundly emotional and psychological one. While it is understandable to be frustrated and angry at the lack of knowledge about differences and the systems that privilege some and oppress others, we should not be surprised when we encounter resistance. In fact, it is incumbent upon those of us in the educational enterprise to meet students and peers where they are and aim learning interventions at appropriate developmental levels and to do so with sensitive, thoughtful responses. Reason, Broido, Davis, and Evans (2005), for example, provide the theoretical foundation and practical strategies to effectively foster the development of social justice allies, specifically addressing pedagogical issues related to sexual orientation, gender, disability, and race. Goodman (2001), furthermore, outlines the sources and strategies for effectively meeting community members' resistance head-on in a manner that increases potential for enlisting them in the battle of social justice and equity.

More specifically, Kegan (1982) offers practical strategies to appropriately engage community members in growth-producing dialogue. In a description of learner positions and corresponding facilitative environments, Kegan suggests that we should meet the psychological position of defending with confirmation. Rather than challenging a student who has written sexist graffiti on a residence hall poster, for example, with arguments about oppression and/or exclusively punitive sanctions, student affairs professionals should meet this behavior with confirmation. According to Kegan, confirmation can take the form of identifying commonalities with the student, establishing and modeling ground rules for respectful listening, affirming that it is okay to be uninformed and confused, and identifying misinformation, stereotypes, or assumptions. Essentially, the sexism that may be at the heart of the negative behavior is met with the creation of a safe environment where defenses are more permeable. An understanding of students' development should help educational professionals further understand the need to meet sexist statements first with a strategy of confirmation. Community members feeling confirmed and understood are more likely to express emotions like confusion and fear. Once confirmation is used, students are more likely to surrender dogmatic positions, paving the way for subsequent strategies related to further growth (Kegan, 1982).

Student affairs professionals need to add to their skill set a broader and more complex understanding of the larger political and sociohistorical context in which learning and development occur. For example, there will likely always be tensions between lived identity experiences and the ability to find language to adequately describe them. Indeed, many of the conflicts that arise on post-secondary institutions' campuses relating to identity politics begin with language, whether printed or spoken, that is regarded as problematic, inaccurate, and/or offensive. Nonetheless, it is reasonable to believe that one cannot adequately engage an issue unless one can find words that are both agreeable and resonant to stakeholders and effective for the purposes of planning a substantive response. Communication and interpersonal skills, while necessary, need to be matched with fundamental questions regarding inclusion and power. Who on a campus should have the power to decide that there is indeed an issue? Who gets to decide the issue is resolved? Does resolution require that all stakeholders are satisfied with the outcome? What about those who are regarded not as stakeholders but instead as bystanders? Should their views inform answers to these questions?

By the time students arrive at college, they have been subject to at least eighteen years of supremacist ideologies along every category of identity. Whether they hold majority or marginalized identities in any one of these categories, the messages are present within their minds. Efforts to educate about and provide context for such worldviews is not a quick process, so the practitioner should understand and ideally become forgiving of the fact that both their own and their students' worldviews will not simply become free of the "isms" during the time they are enrolled or employed. This is not a call for complicity or acceptance of oppressive behaviors, but rather for approaches that incorporate understanding, respect, patience, and a willingness to stay in the conversation. We need to expect that the work of fostering inclusion will be rife with confusion, fear, guilt, shame, anger, resentment, frustration, and mistrust. Occasionally, and ideally, the work can achieve both hope and justice. However, those who do the work—and one hopes everyone in a community is doing it—must first respect the complexity and constantly evolving understanding of identities in order to put issues in perspective and to avoid indulging in either self-congratulatory or indignant stances.

The Conversation Must Become More Uncomfortable

It is well past time for holders of majority identities to work harder and to contribute more significantly to achieving inclusive campus communities. What, then, has been preventing this from happening? In relation to the earlier statement about socialization, some might argue that those who hold majority identities (typically Caucasians, men, heterosexuals, upper-/middle-class people, able-bodied people, and Christians) simply do not wish to cede the privilege and power afforded them by their identity and thus will act to affirm their positions. This argument may be extended by discussing the supremacist notions inculcated into the majority population both subtly (for example, media images, product labels depicting mostly majority identities) and overtly (for example, racist, sexist statements in the public sphere) with respect to their particular identities—in short, they believe overtly or have adopted subconsciously that it is both just and appropriate for them to be secure in their positions. This analysis is both provocative and compelling, yet it does not immediately discuss the process that perpetuates this problem, nor any hopeful alternative or solution.

One possible area for attention, albeit politically loaded, is to explore how systems of privilege and oppression might harm those in the privileged role. Consider, for instance, how hooks (1984) discusses this with respect to gender: "Men are not exploited or oppressed by sexism, but there are ways in which they suffer as a result of it. This suffering should not be ignored. While it in no way diminishes the seriousness of male abuse and oppression of women, or negates male responsibility for exploitative actions, the pain men experience can serve as a catalyst calling attention to the need for change" (p. 73). She goes on to discuss the harmful effects of rigid gender role scripts on women, but also on men. There are analogs across identities. How, for instance, does the faith of a Christian get diminished when Jews, Muslims, and other religious minorities are made invisible in its shadow or in its practice? How does White privilege interfere with a Caucasian's knowing oneself as a racial being and thus undermine the ability to form authentic relationships with people of color?

Student affairs practitioners are in an important position to help with this dilemma by raising these difficult questions. Undoubtedly, it is difficult to consider offering a majority person a compassionate ear when one is either profoundly offended by oppression or deeply wounded from it. Ironically, the authors argue, taking this time can create a mutually liberating transformation. People of majority identities generally, and student affairs staff with these identities in particular, should seriously consider the potential gains associated with being the first person to offer this to students. The old model, in which we diminish the student by demanding that he or she get in touch with their privilege, or call him or her homophobic, sexist, and/or racist, has yet to yield the change we claim to want. If we want to foster self-awareness, growth, and change, then we will need a different approach. While it may be justifiable and even valid to become enveloped in historical injuries, beliefs, personal issues, shame, guilt, and even fear, we must support each other in this difficult work and hold each other compassionately accountable in order to model the change we wish to experience.

Student affairs professionals with agent or majority identities must also learn to effectively tolerate discomfort. Rather than performing a "You got me all wrong—I'm an ally!" stance, majority members need to tolerate anger from people who have been marginalized due to targeted identities. While sometimes imprecisely directed, anger due to past experiences of marginalization and the agent/majority members' willingness to listen nondefensively can actually provide a painful but positive catalyst toward authentic relationships. Moreover, majority members' focus on "being a good one" can lead to complicity with superficial expectations and accolades for doing the work that we all should be doing for the sake of promoting development. To do otherwise risks a presumption of charity and thus reinscribes supremacy and privilege.

Language Matters

Another dimension of the constraints undermining inclusive multicultural campus communities is simply that our language tends to be too imprecise to articulate a problem accurately or convincingly. Words such as *racism, sexism,* and *homophobia* are used by student affairs practitioners and others to describe dynamics and behaviors ranging from subtle cultural misalignments in structures or policies to overt acts of hate violence. To be sure, any place along that continuum can result in deep hurt, marginalization, or exclusion of people from oppressed identities. In terms of remedying or preventing the situations, however, it is necessary to more clearly name what is happening. Given the espoused values of the student affairs profession, we should be held accountable to be more sophisticated in our analysis. For instance, words like *normative* and *centric*, whether used alone or as suffixes can be clearer. For example, an environment can be Anglocentric, referring to a space that is constructed in a manner that normalizes Caucasian imagery and its respective ethnicities' practices and customs. A hetero-normative environment thus could be described as containing images, customs, and expectations that assume heterosexual identity among its members, which in turn privileges those who enact that identity and oppresses those who do not. This particular example is especially important because it allows us to examine how heterosexual people who do not conform to the hetero-normative image can also experience oppression. When we describe such a place as homophobic, we might be missing an opportunity to recognize and respond to a dynamic that is centric but not actively hostile.

Clarity in this regard can inform the design of an effective response. For example, active hostility may require a regulatory response before programming can be effective, whereas a centric environment might perhaps be remedied by increasing sensitivity-raising programs. Someone with a majority identity who aligns (either through intentional efforts or simply being perceived to do so) with the subordinate identity or population can also be subject to social costs. This, too, is important to understand, because it means that people with privilege who wish to engage in anti-oppression work bear a cost for doing so. This can erode their resolve, cause pain and isolation, and steer them away from or undermine doing important social justice work. Student affairs practitioners can help to support people (ideally this includes fellow colleagues) in this situation in order to affirm and encourage them to continue. When we withhold this support, whether due to our own personal issues or not, we argue that practitioners become complicit in the oppressive system.

In terms of acting on this more nuanced analysis, Fried (2007) discusses the challenges of discussing privilege. In particular, she identifies the importance of dialogue which focuses on understanding rather than judgment. Such dialogue "demands the transcendence of binaries by requiring participants to focus on understanding . . . (which) involves describing assumptions that are embedded in each perspective as well as understanding the significance that each participant attaches to his or her position" (p. 4). This effort can lead to discovering areas of agreement aimed at dismantling oppressive structures and environments.

We should also interrogate the ways in which people of targeted identities are socialized to co-construct their own oppression. It is essential to acknowledge this logical extension of the social construction of identities while simultaneously being clear about the differences between privilege and oppression. In other words, just as people with agent or majority identities are socialized to see themselves as normal, preferable, and superior, so too are those who are most hurt—those with the marginalized identities. In the case of race, this is referred to as "internalized racism." Padilla (2001), discussing this process with respect to Latinos, observes, "These distress patterns, created by oppression and racism from the outside, have been played out in the only two places it has seemed 'safe' to do so. First, upon members of our own group—particularly upon those over whom we have some degree of power or control. . . . Second, upon ourselves through all manner of self-invalidation, self-doubt, isolation, fear, feelings of powerlessness and despair" (p. 1).

Thus, internalized oppression commences externally. In other words, dominant players start the chain of oppression through racist and discriminatory behavior. This behavior could range from physical violence prompted by the victim's race, to race-based exclusion, to derogatory race-based name calling and stereotyping together with capitalization on the fears created by those stereotypes. Those at the receiving end of prejudice can experience physical and psychological harm, and over time, they internalize and act on negative perceptions about themselves and other members of their own group. Consequently, as students from marginalized identities come into their own self-awareness, they may experience a profoundly shocking and painful realization that they have adopted negative conceptions of their own identity. It is important not to treat this subject as a diagnostic tool, but rather a possibility to consider. That is, if a student who holds one or more targeted or minority identities appears to be happy, engaged, and comfortable with their sense of self, and the like, or if the same student appears distressed and depressed, neither is a clear sign of internalized oppression. Without projecting our own agendas, it is critical that student affairs professionals offer resources for people to spend time examining identity-related issues in a safe setting. This might involve, for example, discussions with staff of similar identities, or dedicated spaces.

Looking Inward: Student Affairs and Identity Politics

As mentioned earlier in the chapter, serious challenges have been leveled that educators have become too complacent in accepting stagnant and self-serving mental frameworks that fail to effect change with regard to diversity. We need to apply this critique to the field of student affairs and question if we have been languishing in outdated and insular, or at least limiting, paradigms which often undermine practitioners' abilities to facilitate inclusive communities. Stier (2006), for example, challenges us to consider how much we remain emotionally distant and intellectually abstract in our engagement with others on issues of diversity when he says, "Undoubtedly, there is a thin line between being a critical observer, interculturally competent participator and a self righteous educator. In short, ambitions must not end with merely analyzing the actions and perspectives of others but must be followed by continuous scrutiny of his or her own [actions and perspectives]" (p. 5). From this perspective knowledge about various cultures and awareness of human differences is book knowledge that is by nature static. As Dewey (1938) forcefully articulated more than half a century ago, book knowledge "is taught as a finished product with little regard either to the ways in which it was originally built up or to changes that will surely occur in the future" (p. 19). Our explicit challenge in education, in general, and in diversity education, in particular, is to routinely interrogate our static mental frameworks and personal perspectives in order to "evoke curiosity and passion for new cultural experiences and knowledge that dissolves our own cultural imaginaries" (Stier, p. 8).

These are decidedly process, not content, issues. As such, process competence requires intrapersonal skills of "viewing oneself in the position of the other (empathy); acting as both insider and outsider roles (consciousness to positionality); coping with problems that arise originating from intercultural encounters; and keeping flexible and open with a receptive and mind noting cultural peculiarities without either valuing them automatically or uncritically" (Stier, 2006, p. 7). If we do not take on this critical, process-oriented frame of mind, student affairs professionals may unintentionally and continuously reproduce the very systems of oppression we aim to deconstruct.

Consider, for instance, that both authors of this chapter are Caucasian, heterosexual males, able-bodied, and middle class. During the writing of this manuscript, this elicited some skepticism among their colleagues, particularly and perhaps ironically among those with similar identities. It has, after all, become conventional wisdom in the student affairs field that holders of these majority or privileged identities are either suspect when making assertions about that aspect of identity, or are even unqualified to do so. Such a position is quite understandable, since identities influence viewpoints, access to resources, and agency over one's life. In addition, holders of majority identities are at daily risk of being unaware that they are enjoying these privileges. McIntosh (1988) articulated this with respect to racial privilege enjoyed by Caucasian people in the United States. Her article is widely used in diversity discussions and training, suggesting that people with majority identities (Macintosh is Caucasian) can contribute meaningfully to dialogue about and resolution of conflicts associated with diversity. This is worth further consideration, because discourse within student affairs may foster a notion that certain people are diverse, whereas certain people are not. Specifically, people with identities that are in the minority of a community are regarded as the diverse ones, leaving the majority identities unmarked and unexamined. This is highly problematic because it reproduces invisibility and normalcy of the majority identities and thus the privileges associated with being free of such critical examination. Johnson (2001) describes it this way: "A common form of blindness to privilege is that women and people of color are often described as being treated unequally, but men and whites are not. This, however, is logically impossible. Unequal simply means, 'not equal,' which describes both those who receive less than their fair share and those who receive more. But there can't be a short end of the stick without a long end, because it's the longness of the long end that makes the short end short. To pretend otherwise makes privilege and those who receive it invisible" (p. 131).

Consequently, framing issues of diversity around only a minority or targeted perspective ironically places further demands on those whose identities are in the minority to spend time educating majority identity holders about their privilege. Moreover, this difficult task is akin to explaining water to fish. Colleagues working in equity and identity resource offices (such as disability support services or multicultural affairs) are particularly susceptible to the disrespectful and impossible expectation that they assure comfort, satisfaction, and retention among people in marginalized identity positions without alienating those in privileged identity positions (with this latter expectation generally implicit but not uttered), while simultaneously having little authority to accompany this unreasonable responsibility. For this reason, it is necessary to revisit the question of the role that majority identity holders can and should have in discussions about multiculturalism.

Epistemological Privilege

Jagger (1989) and others have developed the idea that "oppressed people have a kind of epistemological privilege insofar as they have easier access to this standpoint and therefore a better chance of ascertaining the possible beginnings of a society in which all could thrive" (p. 161). This concept suggests that the viewpoint of people with marginalized identities holds more validity and relevance for examining and making assertions about identities and lived experiences and systems than those who hold privileged/majority identities. It is not in the purview of this chapter to argue one way or another about the veracity of this assertion, and in fact it would be highly contested and even ironic given the social identities of the authors. Instead, this concept has relevance in terms of examining discourse within the field of student affairs. Consider, for example, whether the Jewish identity of one of the authors affords more credibility to speak to these issues. Both authors have experienced and observed discussions in which an inventory is taken of the respective participants' identities, with varying levels of authority being granted to each by the others present in the conversation based on perceptions of who holds privilege and who does not.

This is a highly problematic state of affairs in identity discourse within student affairs. First, it essentializes identities into binary positions. Second, on a practical level, it implies that people with minority identities are inherently experts and that people with majority identities are inherently ignorant. At best, this pressures people in minority identities to speak on behalf of everyone with that identity and certainly gives permission to the majority to disengage. It also discards significant capacity among many majority identity holders to engage their peers in ways that might be better understood, or at least more willingly heard by the listener, not to mention the obligation to do so.

Indeed, the privilege enjoyed by those with majority identities can be used to disarm resistance among peers to grapple with new ways of understanding issues of identity. This is essentially the work of social justice allies. Allies are "members of dominant social groups (e.g., men, whites, heterosexuals) who are working to end the system of oppression that gives them greater privilege and power based on their social group membership" (Broido, 2000, p. 3). In addition, Bishop (2002) offers a six-step model that professionals can use to better understand how to support ally development. It is essential, however, that the holders of the majority identity have self-awareness about the presence of their privilege, and a grounded appreciation for ways of using the privilege to advance social justice without indulgent and diminishing haughtiness about doing so. Even if the reader adopts the concept of epistemological privilege among oppressed people, the authors believe that people with majority identities are obliged to work to dismantle oppression. One of the authors has had a significant experience that illustrates how student affairs professionals can effectively use privilege to advance multicultural values and social justice.

To Whom Much Is Given

Through a variety of circumstances, one of the authors was asked to serve as chair of a nonprofit organization that serves a particular marginalized population. The organization's executive director is a person with that same marginalized identity, and the assistant executive director at the time was a woman of color. The complexities related to epistemological privilege, multiple dimensions of identity, and other concepts alluded to earlier were activated when the author was asked to serve in this capacity. At a lunch with the two organization colleagues, the author shared candidly that he felt awkward about being a White man and serving as board president for this organization. It seemed to him that there should be people from that social identity, or at least someone with more direct connections to that identity, in the leadership of the board. However, he also shared his understanding that the various privileges that he held with respect to his racial and gender identities might be useful to advancing the organization. Perhaps more than being White and male, being a well-placed administrator at a local university could open certain doors useful to the agency. The author expressed his respect for their wisdom and experience. In sum, he understood it was his privilege more than a particular talent that might effect change, and he did not want to diminish either of them personally or give an impression of arrogance on his own part. They listened thoughtfully, and then the assistant executive director leaned in, extended her hand, and said, "If you've got cards to play, you play 'em, brother!" It was a moment of mutual liberation.

Promoting Structural Transformation

Wilkinson and Rund (2000) stated that organizational "structures should be reviewed periodically to determine their effectiveness . . . (since) the majority of campuses continue to follow the more traditional organizational constructs" (p. 592). Static organizational structures, like stagnant knowledge and mental frameworks, need to be routinely reviewed. Central to this process is reconsidering our organizational charts, recruitment processes, curricula, and ways of keeping those in leadership positions accountable.

Chief Diversity Officer

Institutions like the University of Minnesota, the University of Virginia, and the University of California-Berkeley have modeled mindful attention to the changing landscape of higher education by revisiting organizational needs and structures and appointing senior level diversity officers. As Nancy "Rusty" Barcelo (2007), the first vice president for access, equity, and multicultural affairs at the University of Minnesota, points out, by creating these positions "institutions not only illustrate their renewed commitment to diversity but, more importantly, assert that diversity will be 'at the table', informing policy in formal ways at key meetings with senior officials" (p. 2).

While establishing a chief diversity officer position holds promise, Barcelo (2007) contends that its success depends upon the following important aspects of infrastructure: "research and data management; development and grant writing; communications, public relations and a web site; a senior staff member who focuses on administrative and personnel issues, community development outreach, faculty and staff development, student outreach, and retention; a central budget that is base funded; a staff of diverse multiculturalists; and, diversity units that report to the CDO and provide direct services to their constituencies and resources to the campus and community" (p. 3). If colleges and universities are genuinely committed to promoting international and multicultural campuses, our organizational charts and staffing structures need to reflect those values.

Curricula and Co-Curricula

A recent review of the past decade of research related to diversity experiences provides consistent evidence that interactions with and about people from varying cultures and ethnic identities have positive net effects on a wide variety of cognitive and psychosocial outcomes (Pascarella and Terenzini, 2005). This analysis found, for example, that critical thinking, complexity of thought, self-concept, locus of control, civic engagement, and openness to intellectual challenge are all positively influenced by exposure to diversity experiences. While causal relations are not yet completely clear, Pascarella and Terenzini report that "the evidence is mounting that structural diversity (the racial-ethnic representation among students and faculty on campus) is a necessary if not sufficient condition for educational impact" (p. 638).

Quite simply, our in-class and out-of-class curricula must reflect the emerging needs of a global economy and multicultural world. While monocultural Western structures of knowledge are still relevant, they need to be interrogated and matched by exposure to philosophies, epistemological assumptions, and cultural ways of knowing outside of the traditional canons. For example, traditional student development interventions in the residence halls focused on large come-one-come-all programming could be replaced by funding smaller, more collaborative dialogues aimed at exploring controversial issues in the news related to cultural dynamics.

In addition, current educational offerings could be evaluated based on the following questions related to Ukpokodu's (2007) suggestions for campuswide diversity curriculum infusion. How do our interventions help prepare students to live and work in today's multicultural democracy and interdependent world? What issues of diversity, social justice, and civic engagement are infused in our out-of-class offerings and how? How inclusive are our selected materials? How do student and staff worldviews, learning styles, and teaching strategies match, and how are students' learning styles accommodated? And, how diversified are staff strategies for facilitating learning?

While offering programs that reflect attention to these questions is a first step, we must also bring diverse students together to interact across racial and other social identities. It is easier and less risky for students to gravitate to others with similar identities. According to Chang (2005), "When students retreat from the rich and complex social and learning opportunities offered by a diverse campus and settle into institutional spaces that are more homogenous, they are likely to miss out on the important benefits derived from diversity" (p. 3). It our experience that there is no substitute for sustained and meaningful (and often mediated) dialogue among people with different social identities both in terms of promoting learning about these issues and sustaining multicultural campus communities.

Effective Recruitment and Retention Processes

Given the clearly demonstrated educational benefits of learning environments that both contain diverse representation and foster active engagement across difference, it follows naturally that our recruitment and retention strategies for establishing a diverse human aggregate are critical. Traditional methods for recruiting and retaining a diverse staff and student population, like proactive advertising in diverse media, direct contact with diverse colleagues, and effective multicultural training of all staff, still need to be utilized, but we must go further. Planning for diversity tends to take on a chicken-and-egg framework—do we recruit diverse populations to achieve some critical mass that sustains diversity, or do we work on establishing programs that might then attract people not currently present on the campus? The authors argue that while both of these are important, institutions rarely invest significantly in fostering an inclusive sensitivity in the majority populations already on the campus. This is arguably a linchpin issue. Building resource centers and appointing support staff offer refuge, but from what? It is the daily reinscription of who matters and who doesn't that creates the climate. In truly multicultural places, even those in the majority population depart from the subconscious (or conscious) notion that they constitute normalcy and tread into a worldview in which there is a genuine interest and effort to know each identity present as a means of learning about life and a lens to more deeply understand any subject of interest.

To make this happen, recruiting a diverse staff is just a first step. It should be noted, though, that a critically self-aware and multiculturally competent student affairs organization will be a place in which staff can express their worldview, work style, and be safe to model authentic sharing without paying a personal cost of marginalization within the workplace. As Pope, Reynolds, and Mueller (2004) argue, addressing interpersonal and structural dynamics within the environment will help create a welcoming and nurturing environment that facilitates both multicultural retention and recruitment. From this perspective, all of the strategies we implement that effectively promote a multicultural campus are part of our retention and recruitment efforts. Effectively designed and targeted advertising or aggressive recruitment strategies aimed at developing a diverse candidate pool cannot mask an environment that does not truly welcome diverse voices, life experiences and backgrounds—for students and for the staff who work with them.

Assessment Strategies for Accountability

As mentioned earlier, one of the criticisms that has been leveled at our traditional efforts to promote inclusive and diverse campus environments is that our efforts have resulted too frequently in only cosmetic changes. We need, then, to implement effective assessment strategies that distinguish meaningful progress from superficial change. Student affairs professionals looking for checklist or purely quantitative strategies for assessing the effectiveness of our progress in creating multicultural campuses need to acknowledge that the nature of the phenomena being evaluated does not lend itself, at least for now, to simple designs. Pope (1995) suggests using a systematic Multicultural Organizational Development (MCOD) strategy for improving and assessing institutional effectiveness in eliminating social oppression and supporting socially just campus communities. Rather than viewing assessment as a static snapshot, the MCOD processes help transform organizations through questioning and evaluating underlying beliefs, routine practices, and core values. For example, the Student Affairs MCOD Template is an assessment tool that can be used by student affairs departments or divisions (Reynolds, Pope and Wells, 2002; as cited in Pope, Reynolds, and Meuller, 2004). The assessment template identifies ten key areas for multicultural intervention, including mission statement, leadership, policy review, recruitment and retention, multicultural competency in training, scholarly activities, programs and services, physical environment, assessment, and inclusiveness in the definition of multicultural. Specifically, for example, the target area of multicultural competency expectations and training focuses attention on opportunities for staff to attend diversity-oriented workshops and conferences, the supervision competencies of professional staff, professional development interventions aimed at diversity training, clarity of expectations regarding multicultural responsibilities of all staff, and annual evaluation of both individual and department diversity goals.

Another assessment strategy has been implemented recently by a team at Loyola Marymount University. This group used an equity scorecard to support their strategic plan, which aimed in part actively to promote diversity in the student body, faculty, and staff (Robinson-Armstrong, King, Killoran, and others, 2007). The scorecard was developed by Estela Bensimon's (2004) team at the University of Southern California to address the problem of measuring equity. She claims that while valued in principle, equity is not routinely measured in relation to educational outcomes for specific groups of students. Bensimon describes the scorecard as an assessment tool that can "foster institutional change in higher education by helping to close the achievement gap for historically underrepresented students" (p. 45). The scorecard essentially promotes a consultative process that values both the broad needs of an institution and the goals of specific units and programs. Attention is given to access, retention, educational excellence, and institutional viability. While quantitative data is used to assess these four dimensions, qualitative perspectives are not ignored. Educational excellence and institutional viability, for example, can be defined in a manner that accounts for contextual distinctions and other meaningful peculiarities. Data is then reviewed by local teams to develop and implement programmatic responses when necessary. Individual units, therefore, maintain control of equity initiatives and are held accountable for progress by either their supervisor or the president.

Climate studies are also often used to investigate the extent to which particular campus populations experience acts of oppression and discrimination, and they invariably point to bad news. While it is important to examine campus climate, the deficit paradigm generally utilized is highly problematic. First, such studies tend to be implemented after a critical incident, which points to an almost certainly and overwhelmingly negative outcome. By conducting such a study in the wake of an incident, administrators are likely to encounter not only politically charged reactions, but also defensive ones. In addition, when the report reveals just how bad things are, there will be people from the majority identity ready to point out the methodological flaws and thus dismiss the legitimacy of the findings. Instead, an investigation focusing on places where particular populations feel most affirmed might yield more valuable information. First, it allows for a positive and asset-based approach to the question. Second, it points to specific and potentially reproducible and/or scalable locations of institutional strength. Third, it assumes the reality that there are places that don't feel affirming and removes that question from debate. This is especially valuable since a debate about whether an experience actually happened (or is currently happening) only serves to further silence and demoralize those who have been hurt.

Conclusion

The philosophical and pragmatic challenges in this chapter do not promise quick or easy solutions. Professionals looking for shortcuts around the messy, uncomfortable, and emotionally charged discussions that need to occur in order to effectively interrogate our current models for implementing multicultural campus communities will have to look elsewhere for solutions and are sure to be disappointed. If, on the other hand, we are willing to accept the educational mandate to become multiculturally competent, we need to develop our "ability to reflect over, problematise, understand, learn from, cope emotionally with and operate efficiently in intercultural interaction situations" (Stier, 2006, p. 9).

Multiculturally diverse campus communities have significant and wide-ranging educational benefits. This is not an assumption, but a conclusion based on robust evidence. The stakes, therefore, are high and the pitfalls are legion. We must begin by critically reflecting on the assumptions with which we enter the discussion and taking inventory of our own understanding and capacity to meaningfully engage the issues discussed in this chapter. The structural suggestions offered grow out of an interrogation of these issues, but context matters. The strategies will need to be adapted to the cultural context of specific institutions. Moreover, those in leadership positions will need to understand and model the processes inherent in the journey toward truly multicultural campus communities.

Student affairs professionals, by virtue of their direct relationships with students and the eclectic nature of their responsibilities, are well positioned to address these important issues. However, the profession's capacity to do so is currently mitigated by serious limitations that require our attention. In particular, the authors contend that the current discourses in student affairs are stagnated because the binary notions of privilege and oppression have not advanced to an analysis of the nuances of lived identities, intersections between identities, ways in which individuals participate in co-constructing identities, and in turn how these influence a campus culture. In short, there are no simple or final answers to questions about diversity, access, and inclusion, yet much of the discourse is framed as if there are. It is critical, therefore, that student affairs practitioners not only become versed in the professional literature, but also in interdisciplinary scholarship (for example, gender studies, critical White studies, queer studies). Moreover, practitioners must have the courage to resist demands for cosmetic and short-term fixes and engage in more complex approaches to building inclusive campuses. In order to identify, implement, and institutionalize processes, policies, structures, programs, and services that are experienced as inclusive, practitioners need to understand critical theoretical lenses related to diversity, access, and inclusion as well as the processes associated with translating concepts into meaningful applied efforts.

References

Antonio, A. L. "Student Interaction Across Race and Outcomes in College." Paper presented at the American Educational Research Association Conference, San Diego, Calif., 1998.

Barcelo, N. "Transforming our Institutions for the Twenty-first Century: The Role of the Chief Diversity Officer." *Diversity Digest,* 10(2). [http://www.diversityweb.org/digest/vol10no2/barcelo.cfm]. 2007.

Bennett, M. J. "A Developmental Approach to Training for Intercultural Sensitivity." *International Journal of Intercultural Relations,* 1986, 10(2), 179–195.

Bennett, M. J. "Towards Ethnorelativism: A Developmental Model of Intercultural Sensitivity." In M. Paige (Ed.), *Education for the Intercultural Experience.* Yarmouth, Maine: Intercultural Press, 1993.

Bensimon, E. M. "The Diversity Scorecard: A Learning Approach to Institutional Change." *Change,* 2004, January/February, 44–52.

Bishop, A. *Becoming an Ally: Breaking the Cycle of Oppression in People* (2nd ed.) Halifax, Nova Scotia: Fernwood, 2002.

Broido, E. M. "The Development of Social Justice Allies During College: A Phenomenological Investigation." *Journal of College Student Development,* 2000, 41, 3–18.

Carnevale, A. P., and Fry, R. A. "The Demographic Window of Opportunity: College Access and Diversity in the New Century." In D. E. Heller (Ed.), *Condition of Access: Higher Education for Lower Income Students.* Westport, Conn.: Praeger, 2002.

Chang, M. "Racial Diversity in Higher Education: Does a Racially Mixed Student Population Affect Educational Outcomes?" Unpublished doctoral dissertation, University of California, Los Angeles, 1996.

Chang, M. "Reconsidering the Diversity Rationale. *Liberal Education.* [http://www.aacu.org/liberaleducation/le-wi05/le-wi05feature1.cfm]. Winter 2005.

Connolly, W. E. *Identity/Difference: Democratic Negotiations of Political Paradox.* Minneapolis: University of Minnesota Press, 2002.

Dewey, J. *Experience and Education.* New York: Collier, 1938.

Fine, M., Weis, L., Addelston, A., and Marusza, J., "In Secure Times: Constructing White Working-Class Masculinities in the Late 20th Century." *Gender & Society,* 1997, 11(1), 52–68.

Fried, J. "Thinking Skillfully and Respecting Difference: Understanding Religious Privilege on Campus." *Journal of College & Character,* 2007, 9(1), 1–7.

Goodman, D. J. *Promoting Diversity and Social Justice: Educating People from Privileged Groups.* Thousand Oaks, Calif.: Sage, 2001.

Gurin, P. "New Research on the Benefits of Diversity in College and Beyond: An Empirical Analysis." *Diversity Digest,* 10(2). [http://www.diversityweb.org/digest/vol10no2/gurin.cfm.] 2007.

hooks, b. "Men: Comrades in Struggle." In M. S. Kimmel and M. A. Messner (Eds.), *Men's Lives* (6th ed.). Needham Heights, Mass.: Allyn & Bacon, 2004.

Hurtado, S. Linking Diversity with Educational Purpose: College Outcomes Associated with Diversity in the Faculty and Student Body. Cambridge, Mass.: Harvard University, Harvard Civil Rights Project, 1997.

Jagger, Alison M. "Love and Knowledge: Emotion in Feminist Epistemology." In A. M. Jagger and S. R. Bordo (Eds.), *Gender, Body/Knowledge*. New Brunswick, N.J.: Rutgers University Press, 1989.

Johnson, A. *Privilege, Power, and Difference*. New York, N.Y.: McGraw-Hill, 2001.

Jones, S. R., and McEwen, M. K. "A Conceptual Model of Multiple Dimensions of Identity." *Journal of College Student Development*, 2000, 41(4), 405–414.

Kaufman, M. "Men, Feminism, and Men's Contradictory Experiences of Power." In J. A. Kuypers (Ed.), *Men and Power*. Halifax, Nova Scotia: Fernwood, 1999.

Kegan, R. *The Evolving Self: Problem and Process in Human Development*. Cambridge, Mass.: Harvard University Press, 1982.

Longwell-Grice, R. M. "Working-Class and Working College: A Case Study of the First Generation, Working Class, First Year, White Male College Students." Unpublished doctoral dissertation, University of Louisville, Louisville, 2002.

McIntosh, P. *White Privilege and Male Privilege: A Personal Account of Coming to See Correspondences through Work in Women's Studies*. Wellesley, Mass.: Wellesley College Center for Research on Women, 1988.

Milem, J. F., Chang, M. J., and Antonio, A. L. *Making Diversity Work on Campus: A Research-Based Perspective*. Washington, D.C.: Association of American Colleges and Universities, 2005.

Padilla, L. M. A "Dirty Mexican: Internalized Oppression, Latinos & Law." *Texas Hispanic Journal of Law and Policy*, 2001, 61–113, 65–73.

Pascarella, E. T., Edison, M., Nora, A., Hagedorn, L. S., and Terenzini, P. T. "Influences on Students' Openness to Diversity and Challenge in the First Year of College." *Journal of Higher Education*, 1996, 67(2), 174–195.

Pascarella, E. T., and Terenzini, P. T. *How College Affects Students: A Third Decade of Research*. San Francisco: Jossey Bass, 2005.

Peltier Campbell, K. "Diversity and Learning: A Defining Moment." *Diversity Digest*, 10(2). [http://www.diversityweb.org/digest/vol10no2/campbell.cfm]. 2007.

Pope, R. L. "Multicultural Organizational Development: Implications and Applications in Student Affairs." In J. Fried (Ed.), *Shifting Paradigms in Student Affairs: Culture, Contexts, Teaching and learning*. Washington, D.C.: American College Personnel Association, 1995.

Pope, R. L., Reynolds, A. L., and Mueller, J. A. *Multicultural Competence in Student Affairs*. San Francisco: Jossey-Bass, 2004.

Reason, R. D., Broido, E. M., Davis, T. L., and Evans, N. J. *Developing Social Justice Allies*. San Francisco: Jossey-Bass, 2005.

Reed, B. "Patterns of Gender Role Conflict in White Working-Class Males." Unpublished manuscript, University of Virginia, Charlottesville, 2008.

Robinson-Armstrong, A., King, D., Killoran, D., Ward, H., Fissinger, M. X., and Harrison, L. "Creating Institutional Transformation Using the Equity Scorecard. *Diversity Digest*, 10(2). [http://www.diversityweb.org/digest/vol10no2/robinson-armstrong.cfm]. 2007.

Smith, D. G., and Associates. *Diversity Works: The Emerging Picture of How Students Benefit*. Washington, D.C.: Association of American Colleges and Universities, 1997.

Stier, J. "Internationalisation, Intercultural Communication, and Intercultural Competence." *Journal of Intercultural Communication*, 2006, 11, 1–11.

Terenzini, P. T., Pascarella, E. T. and Blimling, G. S. (1996). "Students' Out-of-Class Experiences and Their Influence on Learning and Cognitive Development: A Literature Review." *Journal of College Student Development*, 1996, 37(2), 149–162.

Ukpokodu, O. N. "A Sustainable Campus-wide Program for Diversity Curriculum Infusion." *Diversity Digest*, 10(2), 1–2. [http://www.diversityweb.org/digest/vol10no2/robinson-armstrong.cfm]. 2007.

Wilkinson, C. K., and Rund, J. A. "Supporting People, Programs, and Structures for Diversity." In M. J. Barr, M. K. Desler, and Associates (Eds.), *The Handbook of Student Affairs Administration* (2nd ed.). San Francisco: Jossey-Bass, 2002.

CHAPTER FOURTEEN

HELPING STUDENTS WITH HEALTH AND WELLNESS ISSUES

John H. Dunkle and Cheryl A. Presley

The primary mission of institutions of higher education is the academic achievement and success of students. While multiple factors influence students' academic success, one variable that affects all students is health, both mental and physical. The late Ernest Boyer (1990) stated, "Wellness must be a prerequisite to all else. Students cannot be intellectually proficient if they are physically and psychologically unwell" (p. 6). Indeed, responsiveness to student health issues permits the university to maximize the educational environment and to meet the academic mission of the institution. Today, administrators are called upon to respond to a growing number of complex and challenging issues on campuses that affect both the individual student's health and the health of the broader student community.

The purpose of this chapter is to highlight several health and wellness concerns of college and university students today and to review some of the major administrative challenges facing institutions of higher education in meeting students' health needs. The chapter begins with a brief history of student health and university counseling centers. On many campuses, these two services have as their specific missions the goal of addressing and treating the health and wellness concerns of students. We believe that it is crucial to understand how these centers have evolved to reach the current state of service delivery. We acknowledge that some institutions have neither the resources nor the necessity to support college health services or counseling centers. Much of the research discussed in this chapter was implemented on both two- and four-year public and private institutions across the nation. In many instances, the information is generalizable to institutions whether they have health and counseling centers or not. Next, we discuss the key physical and mental health issues that students face. This section is followed by a discussion of some of the major administrative issues in meeting the health and wellness needs of students. The chapter ends with a summary set of recommendations for administrators.

Historical Context

The history of student health services goes back to the mid-nineteenth century; the origins of formal counseling centers date only to the early 1950s. This section of the chapter provides a brief historical overview of student health services and counseling centers in an effort to contextualize where these services are today in meeting the health and wellness needs of students. We begin with an overview of student health services' history, followed by the history of counseling centers.

Historical Context: Student Health Services

Initially, student health centers were designed as infirmaries and focused their care on students who were suffering from acute physical illnesses. Health was limited to restoration of the body and to protecting the campus from public health threats. The early centers pre-dated health insurance plans, accreditations, and other systemization and, in most cases, were funded centrally by institutional budgets (Turner and Hurley, 2002).

This model of health care remained fairly stable until the mid-1960s and early 1970s when changes in demographics and behaviors of students challenged administrators' perceptions and responses as to what constituted a healthy student. New approaches to student health emerged, with an increased emphasis upon preventing disease and disability rather than merely treating a condition.

Historical Context: Counseling Centers

Prior to the development and implementation of formal services, counseling was done by deans, faculty, and perhaps by a health service psychiatrist who would respond to a mental health issue when needed. After World War II, there was an explosion in the number of students seeking higher education in the United States. When veterans returned from the war, many needed guidance in choosing a career and finding work. As such, much of the counseling during this time period focused on vocational and educational counseling (Stone and Archer, 1990).

From the 1950s to the mid-1980s, the focus of university counseling centers evolved from primarily vocational and educational counseling to more personal counseling, group psychotherapy, and psychiatric services. From the mid-1970s to the late 1980s, university counseling center staff continued to develop their skills as individual clinicians while expanding their roles to do outreach (prevention) and consultation to the campus community.

Since the late 1980s to present day, counseling center staff and administrators have observed increasing levels of severity in students' presenting issues. Some professionals have attributed the increase in the level of severity to concomitant increases in social and economic problems as well as decreased levels of stigma associated with seeking mental health services (Archer and Cooper, 1998). Also, with the passage of the Americans with Disabilities Act (1990), some students with mental health concerns who may not have had an opportunity to attend college were able to have that opportunity. Mental health professionals have also become much more precise and accurate in the assessment and treatment of major psychiatric illnesses.

Student Physical and Mental Health Issues

To successfully address the health needs of today's students, the focus must move beyond the model of 30–40 years ago to one that is integrated into the fabric of the entire institution. Furthermore, there must be recognition that health is a vital concept, integrating the six dimensions of wellness: physical, emotional, intellectual, social, spiritual, and environmental (Hettler, 1984). While individual factors such as genetics, attitudes, values, and high-risk health behaviors are important contributors to student health, the campus, its environment, its beliefs, its values, and its culture are also influential factors in the health status of students.

This section of the chapter provides an overview of some of the leading physical and mental health issues that students face on campuses today. First, physical health concerns are discussed, followed by an overview of mental health issues.

Physical Health Issues

This section of the chapter presents some of the more pressing health concerns with which students are currently presenting and makes the assumption that awareness of these health issues enables institutions of higher education to respond according to their unique configuration and resources. It is beyond the scope of this section to provide an all-inclusive list of health challenges that students face.

Obesity and Physical Activity. Results of the American College Health Association (ACHA)–National College Health Assessment (NCHA) survey (American College Health Association [ACHA], 2006) revealed that 36.4 percent of college students reported being slightly to very overweight, and 39.3 percent reported doing no exercise or dieting to lose weight. Obesity and weight are the result of a variety of social, behavioral, cultural, environmental, and genetic factors. In the past twenty years, there has been a significant increase in obesity and obesity-related disorders, such as Type 2 diabetes, hypertension, and dyslipidemia (lipoprotein metabolism disorder) in people in their teens and twenties (Sparling, 2007). Nine out of ten students reported that they consume fewer than five servings of fruits and vegetables daily, and nearly six out of ten reported that they exercise vigorously or moderately fewer than three times per week (ACHA, 2006). The World Health Organization (WHO) reports that there are many "non-fatal, but debilitating health problems associated with obesity, including respiratory difficulties, chronic musculo-skeletal problems, skin problems and infertility" (World Health Organization [WHO], 2007, p. 2). Even though excess weight, poor nutrition, and lack of physical activity do not require emergency medical action, their long- and short-term impact on students should not be dismissed.

An emerging approach to weight management that is a contradiction to traditional medical guidelines is a perspective called "Health at Every Size" (HAES). Jon Robison, a leading researcher and major proponent of this approach, identifies three components of HAES: self-acceptance; physical activity; and normalized eating (Robison, 2005). Essentially, it advocates that people come in a variety of sizes and that the same narrow weight range typically prescribed is not necessarily maximally healthy for all individuals. Two of the strengths of this paradigm are that it promotes self-acceptance and seeks to encourage a normalization of one's relationship to food and encourages exercise as a component of an enhanced quality of life.

Alcohol and Other Drugs. Administrators in higher education have as one of their major concerns students' use of alcohol and more recently other drugs. In a nationally representative sample of college students at both two- and four-year, public and private institutions, Presley and Pimental (2006) found that 74 percent of all college students reported drinking in the past year; 41 percent of them reported that they consumed five or more drinks in one sitting. Of those, 38 percent reported that they drank on more than three occasions per week.

Given the types of negative consequences (for example, sexual assault, getting into a fight, getting into an argument, driving under the influence) that students reported, one can see that the results of substance use and abuse can influence psychological, social, academic, and physical well-being.

While alcohol remains the substance of choice for many college students, the National Center on Addiction and Substance Abuse at Columbia University reported that there was an increase in marijuana, cocaine, and other illicit drug use since its first study in 1993. In a press release, the center reported that there was an increase between 1993 and 2005 in the use of Percocet, Vicodin, OxyContin, Ritalin, Adderal, Xanax, Valium, Nembutal, Seconal, cocaine, and heroin (Duran, 2007). Ritalin, for example, is becoming one of the most abused prescription drugs. Bailey (1995) observed, "Although some students take Ritalin tablets whole, others pursue stronger stimulation by crushing tablets and snorting them" (p. 1).

From a mental health perspective, alcohol consumption increases risk associated with mental illness. For example, an individual who is diagnosed with major depression and takes psychotropic medications and who consumes alcohol would be at greater risk of suicide or accidental death than an individual who does not drink.

Efforts have been made to develop viable intervention programs on campuses. For example, Monchick and Gehring (2006) developed a program entitled *Back on TRAC* (Treatment, Responsibility, and Accountability on Campus), which incorporates several principles of public health safety models as well as the drug court model. According to the National Drug Court Institute (2007) Web site, the drug court model involves a team approach, including mental health professionals, law officials, social service officials, and others. The goal of this approach is to provide an intense regimen and monitoring of substance abuse and mental health treatment, case management, drug testing, and probation supervision for chronic substance abusers. The *Back on TRAC* movement is an effort to apply the drug court model on college campuses to aid in intervening, monitoring, and treating students with chronic substance abuse violations or problems. Other examples of intervention programs and best practices can be found at the Higher Education Center for Alcohol and Other Drug Abuse and Violence Prevention Web site.

Sexual Behavior. Exploration of sexuality is a normal developmental task. However, sexual exploration can involve potential health risks, such as sexually transmitted diseases, unintended pregnancies, and sexual assault. While these risks are not limited to the college-aged population, health care professionals find themselves particularly occupied with the consequences and the risks of sexual exploration. In 1997, *The National College Health Risk Behavior Survey* (NCHRBS) found that: 86.1 percent of the students reported having sexual intercourse in their lifetimes; 62.4 percent reported having sexual relations in the thirty days prior to the survey; 29 percent reported using a condom during their last sexual intercourse; and 35.1 percent reported that they had become pregnant or had impregnated someone else. The decisions regarding pregnancy, especially unintended pregnancy, are challenging for students who may be unprepared for the financial and emotional burden of parenthood while attending to their educations.

There are other sexuality issues as well that are emerging for health care facilities. For example, students who are undergoing chemical therapy prior to transgender operations must be monitored closely. Laboratory values must be checked routinely as well as the administration of hormone doses. The issues of finances for the student and of appropriate support and specialized training for physicians at health centers are preeminent. Sensitivity to the health concerns of lesbian, gay, bisexual, and transgender students is essential to the integrated provision of appropriate health care.

Sexual Assault. The NCHRBS (1997) revealed that as many as 1 in 5 college students have been forced to have sex. Because many studies are focused on women who have been victims of sexual assault, little attention has been given to an emerging silent minority of males who have also had these experiences. Koss, Gidycz, and Wisniewski (1987) reported that 15–20 percent of female college students and 5–15 percent of male college students had experienced forced intercourse. According to their findings, sexual assaults were the only violent crimes against students that were most likely to be committed by a person that the victim knew. Recently, Durant and others (2007) found that 5.6 percent of the males in their study reported some form of date fight victimization, while 61.7 percent of the women reported the same.

Similarly, the ACHA-NCHA data (ACHA, 2006) revealed that 15.9 percent of college students reported that they had experienced verbal threats of sex against their will, sexual touching against their will, attempted sexual penetration against their will, and sexual penetration against their will; 8.3 percent of the students were males. Because college can be an arena for dating violence, opportunities exist for primary and secondary prevention strategies such as those proposed by Carr and Van Deusen (2002). It is essential for health care providers to have referral and support services in place when these issues arise, as the fear and shame of reporting this type of crime often prevents students from dealing with the physical and emotional issues that surface.

Violence. Prothrow-Stith (2007), a nationally known public health leader, declared that violence is a health problem. Indeed, the tragedies that occurred at Virginia

Tech University, Northern Illinois University, and other campuses have brought the issue of campus violence to national attention. Carr and Ward (2006) stated, "Campus shootings; murder-suicides, homicides; hate crimes based on gender, race, ethnicity and/or sexual orientation; suicides; assaults; hazing; and arson require us to conduct fresh analyses and create new paradigms for preventing and decreasing all campus violence" (p. 381). Baum and Klaus (2005) found that college students 18–24 years of age were victims of approximately 479,000 crimes of violence, such as sexual assault, robbery, and aggravated assault. Additionally they found that "1) male college students were twice as likely to be victims of overall violence as female students; 2) 35% of acts of violence were reported to police in the period of 1995–2002; and 3) about one-quarter of students were injured as a result of the violence, but only 60% of those injured were treated for their injuries" (p. 1).

Other types of violence are also emerging on campuses. For example, research suggests that stalking victimization may be greater among female college students than in the general population (Fisher, Cullin, and Turner, 2000). In addition, hazing and celebratory violence are coming into the consciousness of the health care personnel and administrators as they struggle to provide safe environments in which students can learn.

Violence can influence students and staff in many ways. Very often students leave school and return home to recover from injuries and the psychological impact of violence. From a medical standpoint, practitioners can play a large role in assisting students who are victims of various types of violence to recover and regain their physical and psychological hardiness.

The underreporting of violence is an issue of great importance. Students indicate that some of the reasons why they do not report violence are that the incident is "1) too minor (39%), 2) a private matter (16%), and 3) not clear it was a crime (5%)" (Carr and Ward, 2006, p. 385). The *ACHA Campus White Paper* (Carr and Ward, 2006) is an excellent resource regarding issues of campus violence.

Mental Health Issues

Some authors (Kadison and DiGeronimo, 2004) have argued that mental health issues on campuses have reached a crisis level. Furthermore, many administrators are searching for the best ways to manage the concerns (Dunkle and Hollingsworth, 2004). At times, it is very difficult to tease out normal developmental issues that college students experience from major mental illness.

Kadison and DiGeronimo (2004) highlighted several normal developmental issues of students, including identity development, relationships and sexuality, and interpersonal issues. Traditional college-aged students (18–21 years) are developing a sense of self within the context of their families and peers. They are also navigating relationships with friends and romantic partners and all of the psychological and emotional issues, both positive and negative, that accompany such relationships. For the most part, students traverse these years successfully and without any major setbacks. However, it is during these years that serious mental health concerns may emerge that may complicate normal developmental processes. The average age of onset for major mental illness is during the 18–26 years age range (American Psychiatric Association, 2000). Therefore, by virtue of their age, traditional college-aged students are at risk for the development of a major mental illness.

According to the National Survey of Counseling Center Directors (Gallagher, 2006), 92 percent of the respondents reported that in recent years there has been an increase in the number of students with severe mental illness coming to their centers. Even more striking is that directors reported that 40 percent of the students who utilized their centers had severe mental health concerns and that 8 percent of the students had impairments so serious that they could not remain in school. Directors also reported that 2,368 students were hospitalized for psychological reasons in 2006 and, tragically, there were 142 student suicides during the same time period. Benton, Robertson, Tseng, Newton, and Benton (2003) investigated changes in counseling center client problem areas at a large public university over a thirteen-year period and found empirical support for the increase in severe mental illness.

Suicide and Depression. One of the most vexing issues that mental health professionals as well as higher education administrators face is suicide among students. Often, suicidal behavior is accompanied by depression and other major affective disorders, such as bipolar disorder. The Suicide Prevention Resource Center (2004) published a white paper that offers an exhaustive review of the literature on college student suicide data and prevention programs. According to the National Center for Injury Prevention and Control (National Center for Health Statistics, 2004), suicide is the third leading cause of death among individuals 15–24 years of age and the second leading cause of death among individuals 25–34 years. While females are more likely to attempt suicide, males are three times more likely to complete suicide. A thorough suicide assessment is a crucial part of any mental health assessment, and counseling center professionals continually must balance a respect for students' privacy with the responsibility to ensure students' safety.

Hollingsworth and Franke (2004) argued that the best way to prevent suicide (and to mitigate liability) for institutions is to have a systems approach on campus. A systems approach involves not only counseling center professionals but other administrators and professionals from various departments in academic and student affairs. In this way, a safety net is formed on campus, with the ultimate goal of reducing the likelihood of suicide. The Jed Foundation (2007) also embraces the idea of creating a safety net for students on campus. The Jed Foundation is a not-for-profit organization that was founded in 2000 and has as its mission to reduce the suicide rate among college and university students. The Web site for the organization offers excellent resources for administrators and staff, parents, and students.

Stress and Anxiety. The ACHA-NCHA survey (ACHA, 2006) revealed that students listed stress as the number one impediment to academic success. Symptoms of anxiety often accompany stress and may lead to difficulties in meeting academic responsibilities. Furthermore, stress and anxiety reactions can lead to physical symptoms such as headaches, ulcers, and fatigue. Some students may appear first at health services because of the physical symptoms. Once physical causes for symptoms are managed or are ruled out, timely referrals to mental health services are important. For some students, the belief that their concerns are medically related may be more palatable than entertaining the possibility of a mental health concern.

Some counseling centers have developed stress clinics to deal with the high numbers of students who present with stress and anxiety. Stress clinics are great options for institutions with limited resources, as many students can be seen in a group format at one time. Another effective and more affordable way to help students is to distribute self-help brochures, handouts, and links to Web sites. At times, stress and anxiety levels may require more intensive treatment such as psychotropic medication.

Eating Disorders. Another common presenting issue of students at counseling centers is eating concerns. At times, these concerns rise to the level of a diagnosable eating disorder. These disorders conjure up a great deal of anxiety for counseling center professionals, as well as other campus administrators, because of the potential medical complications and risk of death. On most campuses, these disorders are diagnosed more frequently with women. However, increasingly more men are meeting criteria for eating disorders, especially male student-athletes. Because of the psychological, physical, and nutritional aspects of eating disorders, many campuses have developed interdisciplinary eating disorder assessment and treatment teams that consist of professional staff from both the health service and counseling centers.

Learning Disabilities, ADHD, and Asperger's Disorder. Many students who arrive on campuses have been diagnosed with learning disabilities, attention-deficit/

hyperactivity disorder (ADHD), or other developmental disorders. In the most recent survey of counseling center directors (Gallagher, 2006), respondents indicated an increased concern regarding response to students with learning disabilities. This concern has increased in the past five years. In the case of ADHD, some students diagnosed at a very early age have been on medications for some time to help manage the attention problems. Many students have also received accommodations in their earlier academic endeavors and expect the same from colleges and universities. There also has been an increase in the number of students who have been diagnosed with Asperger's disorder who are attending institutions of higher education (Lipka, 2006). Asperger's disorder is characterized by social isolation, eccentric behaviors, impairments in social interactions, and age-inappropriate interests. These students often attract attention of others because of what appears to others to be strange and bizarre behavior. It is important that counseling center staff partner with disability services offices to ensure that students receive accurate diagnoses and appropriate accommodations.

Diversity Issues. Data indicate that the enrollment of every ethnic minority group has risen steadily since 1995, with the largest increases in the number of students identified as Hispanic, followed by those identified as African American (Chronicle of Higher Education, 2006). Also, there were nearly 600,000 international students enrolled at various colleges and universities in the United States in 2004. Mental health professionals are faced with the challenges of assisting with the unique mental health issues of these various student populations. For instance, some international students may come from cultures where the concept of mental health is very different than that of the United States. Furthermore, it is crucial that mental health professionals tease out true psychopathology from what may be cultural manifestations of normal developmental behavior.

Graduate, Professional, and Nontraditional-Age Undergraduate Students. Much of the focus in the professional literature on health and wellness issues tends to be, at least implicitly, on the traditional-age undergraduate student population, perhaps because of the greater numbers of those students on campuses. However, there is a growing number of nontraditional-age students attending institutions of higher education. Furthermore, about 15 percent of the individuals enrolled in colleges and universities are graduate or professional students (Chronicle of Higher Education, 2006). The developmental and mental health needs of nontraditional-age undergraduates and graduate/professional students require special attention. On the whole, these student populations tend to have very different developmental issues to manage compared to traditional-age undergraduate students.

For example, the former may need to balance school, family, and work responsibilities. Moreover, because of the intense and hectic training schedules of some graduate and professional programs, some students may make the choice to forego very important mental health treatment. For some training programs, such as medical schools, serious mental health impairment raises questions of fitness-for-duty in clinical rotations.

Major Administrative Issues

This section of the chapter highlights some of the major administrative issues in meeting the health and wellness needs of students. The issues discussed here are not an exhaustive list.

Accessibility, Affordability, and Accountability

In the Future of Higher Education's Commission report (U.S. Department of Education, 2006), three basic challenges were identified for higher education: (1) accessibility; (2) affordability; and (3) accountability. While the focus of the commission's report was on the whole of higher education, these challenges are specifically vexing in the higher education health care arena.

Accessibility. Societal access to affordable health care is one of the greatest challenges of our time. "There are more than 45.8 million Americans today without health insurance, a number expected to increase to 56 million within the next decade. As much as 10 percent of the uninsured population is composed of college students. Young adults make up the largest age-group of uninsured Americans" (Aetna Insurance Company, 2007, p. 1).

Timely access to health care from many entry points is crucial in the academic setting, as students typically have competing demands from their jobs, families, and academic programs. In order to be responsive, many institutions have considered a form of open access scheduling. The purest form of this scheduling is that if students call in, they are seen. Many institutions have chosen variations on that particular scheme, wherein a certain percentage of the appointments in any given day are open access and a smaller percentage are prescheduled. Accessibility to services is an equally crucial issue for counseling centers, where many directors have reported high student utilization rates and long waitlists for services (Gallagher, 2006). Some counseling centers are moving toward the implementation of triage systems to aid in decreasing the amount of time it takes to connect students to services (Rockland-Miller and Eells, 2006).

For some campuses that have very limited resources, there is a reliance on off-campus community services, for example, local hospitals and community mental health centers. The priorities of college health programs are inevitably different from those of managed care organizations, community hospitals, and private physicians. Student health and university counseling center personnel are specifically trained to manage an integrated health care system that responds to the particular needs of the population that they serve. They are not profit motivated but motivated by the academic mission of the university. Their programming and students' access to them can favorably influence retention.

Affordability. Affordability is inextricably linked with issues of accessibility. There are many ways that student health programs and counseling centers are financed. Barr (2002) offered detailed recommendations on budget and financial management in higher education, and her recommendations are very applicable to student health and university counseling centers. With shrinking resources and funding, centers are called upon to create an equitable and fair mechanism for financing that meets the criteria of affordability and that assures that all students have access to health and wellness programs. The three most common ways that student health and university counseling centers are financed are (1) an identified student health fee; (2) a fee for service collected from the student or parental insurance; and/or (3) a billing to a university-operated self-insurance plan (Keeling and Heitzmann, 2003).

It is necessary to predict the cost of operation so that services are not compromised on a year-by-year basis. For example, some institutions have implemented a mandatory health fee that has as its basic assumption that all enrolled students share a common responsibility for the health of the entire student body. In this manner, the health center (regardless of service type) operates much like a health maintenance organization (HMO). Many students are on some form of financial aid in order to pursue their degrees, and most financial aid packages will pay mandatory fees. Broader funding strategies, such as entrepreneurial efforts and grants, have become a necessity for student health and counseling centers to weather periods of fiscal difficulty.

Many institutions with limited resources may have to partner with community service providers and mental health professionals in order to provide the necessary services to students. Students may be able to access a drop-in location on campus to get self-care information or appropriate referrals for health care system entry. Brief interventions prior to referral to community health care providers may be another strategy to provide care to students in institutions with limited resources. The greater concern with these types of approaches is how students will pay for their health care when they are sent off campus for services.

There is great debate regarding insurance coverage for students. Many institutions have made decisions that students need to be insured by a policy that covers emergency care, pregnancy, surgery, and specialty care. Oftentimes, mental health coverage is very scarce, if available at all. The type of insurance policy that best fits any given institution is dictated by the scope of services on campus. The primary debate, however, remains whether the insurance fee should be mandatory, voluntary, or mandatory with a hard waiver. For the hard waiver option, students must show proof that they have a policy with coverage similar to the one offered by the university.

There is some merit and value to a mandatory insurance plan. First, actuarial tables and affordability can be calculated on the relative size of the pool and therefore can be priced competitively. Second, the university can be assured that students' academic careers will not be interrupted, perhaps permanently, by unpaid medical bills. Third, mandatory insurance can assist both the student and the community in terms of good relationships. For example, in one small town where access to medical care was a challenge, the community hospital became concerned because it was not receiving payment from students (the institution did not have a mandatory health insurance policy). Therefore, the relationship between the community hospital and the university became quite strained. Today, there exists a mandatory health insurance policy and a good relationship between the university and the hospital.

Due to rising costs of coverage, many parents of traditional-age students cannot afford to keep their children on their insurance policy. Furthermore, most students cannot afford to shoulder the burden of insurance plans on their own. In one midwestern university (Presley, 2007), for example, the average claim per undergraduate is nearly $3,000, and for graduate students is nearly double that amount annually. Having access to affordable health care and health insurance is central to keeping costs of unforeseen illnesses and accidents from preventing the attainment of educational goals.

Accountability. Accreditation is one of the best ways of assuring that the student health center is providing a defined level of quality care. The two major accrediting bodies for health service agencies are (1) the Accreditation Association for Ambulatory Health Care (AAAHC); and (2) the Joint Commission for the Accreditation of Healthcare Organizations. Nearly 1,400 institutions of higher education have health centers with varying degrees of service provision. Many of them are either accredited by AAAHC or the Joint Commission. The standards for each of the organizations address virtually every aspect of health services' operations.

For counseling centers, there are also specific accrediting bodies that will do a careful examination of services to ensure high quality of care. One such accrediting body is the International Association of Counseling Services (IACS). Also, if a counseling center offers a predoctoral internship, there is the option of seeking accreditation through the American Psychological Association (APA). APA accreditation also involves a thorough scrutiny of services and quality of care. For both student health services and counseling centers, the question of whether to seek accreditation must be weighed with institutional priorities, expectations, and resources.

Administrators in health and counseling services can also avail themselves of the standards recommended by the Council for the Advancement of Standards in Higher Education (Council for the Advancement of Standards in Higher Education [CAS], 2006). The CAS standards are a comprehensive set of guidelines for evaluating and developing various services on campus. Chapter Ten also discusses the application of professional standards and would be a great resource for administrators in health and counseling centers. CAS offers a self-assessment tool for administrators to complete, guiding them through the various components of health and counseling services (CAS, 2006). Additionally, Benton and Benton (2006) outline effective and proven strategies that counseling centers may employ for meeting mental health needs on campus.

Finally, another way that health and counseling centers ensure quality of services is by tracking national and local data trends. Two good examples of national data sources were discussed previously: (1) the ACHA-NCHA survey; and (2) the National Survey of Counseling Center Directors. In addition, there is a national college student mental health research effort developing out of Pennsylvania State University (Locke, 2007) that involves the collection of national data on college students visiting counseling centers. While national data trends are crucial for many reasons, it is equally important to collect local data about the health and wellness needs of students on a specific campus. Dunkle (2005) discussed the importance of tracking local data and outlined eight steps for developing, maintaining, and summarizing a local database. Local data can serve as a fixed beacon to guide strategic planning, policy and procedure development, and assessment of services.

Ethical and Legal Issues

Student health and counseling center staff and administrators deal with many vexing ethical and legal issues as well as very serious safety concerns of students. This section offers highlights of the various issues. Readers are referred to Kaplin and Lee (2007) for a much more in-depth analysis.

Confidentiality and Privacy. Confidentiality and privacy are the most significant ethical and legal concerns with which health care professionals deal in their work. Student health service and counseling center treatment records are covered by very strict confidentiality laws that are typically codified in state laws. In recent years, however, federal laws have emerged, including the Health Insurance Portability and Accountability Act (HIPAA; Public Law 104–191, 1996). Williams (2007) states that "the HIPAA privacy and security regulations are intended to provide national standards for the privacy and security of medical records" (p. 10). All health care facilities were required to be in compliance with HIPAA by 2003. Most institutions across the country have conferred with attorneys and other consultants to determine how HIPAA affects the work of their student health services and university counseling centers.

Administrators must also wrestle with questions of how confidentiality laws interact with other laws, like the Family Educational Rights and Privacy Act (FERPA; 20 U.S.C. § 1232g, 1974). FERPA, also known as the Buckley Amendment, is a federal law that protects the confidentiality of students' educational records, including records maintained on students' conduct and disciplinary proceedings. There are very specific and narrow circumstances under which health care professionals can breach confidentiality of a student-patient, including, but not limited to, an imminent danger to self or others. While there is a similar clause under FERPA, the exclusion for breaching confidentiality under mental health law is much stricter. The criterion under FERPA leaves more room for administrators to respond to student situations based on the student's behavior. At times, this distinction can cause tensions between health care professionals on campus and other administrators.

Disturbed and Disturbing Students. One of the major issues that arises for administrators and health care providers is health issues of students that also involve disruptive and, perhaps, dangerous behavior. The most extreme example of such behavior was the Virginia Tech University tragedy in 2007. That incident has re-raised questions of how to balance privacy rights with the responsibility of institutions to protect the community. Lake (2007) cogently discussed what the future legal issues may entail for colleges and universities in the aftermath of the Virginia Tech shootings.

In her seminal monograph, Delworth (1989) offered a framework for conceptualizing the type of case just described. Delworth proposed that there may be students who are disturbing, those who are disturbed, and those who are both disturbed and disturbing. She described disturbing students as individuals who engage in immature and manipulative behaviors that disrupt the campus community but do not fall too far out of the range of developmental inappropriateness. Most, if not all, of these types of student situations can be managed by student conduct procedures. Disturbed students are those who experience patterns of actions that are markedly out of sync with other students, typically indicative of a serious mental health concern. The students who are both disturbed and disturbing tend to be most challenging and problematic for administrators.

The crux of the dilemma in these types of situations is differentiating the mental health component from the conduct issue. There may be concern on the part of student affairs professionals that they may push the student over the edge if they attempt to intervene or to initiate disciplinary proceedings for the disruptive behavior. For health care professionals, there are concerns for confidentiality and not being put in the role of disciplinarian. Dunkle and Hollingsworth (2005) proposed that two simultaneous response tracks must occur. One track must involve an assessment and intervention around the student conduct, typically done by a conduct officer. The other track would involve a consultation with and assessment by a health care professional. Within these tracks, student affairs administrators and health care professionals have specific roles and responsibilities. It is crucial all parties be aware of those roles and responsibilities and they collaborate and communicate within the parameters of laws and ethics to ensure student safety. Finally, the Virginia Tech Review Panel Report (2007) delivered to the governor of Virginia recommended that institutions consider developing and implementing threat assessment teams on their campuses with the charge of detecting, monitoring, and intervening with disturbed and disturbing students.

Parental Involvement. Related to the complexity surrounding confidentiality and privacy issues is the increasing number of parents who request and, at times, demand information about their students. Indeed, parental involvement has been increasing in all areas of higher education in recent years, in part because of the characteristics of the current generation of students and their parents (Howe and Strauss, 2003). Parents of traditional-age college students are accustomed to access to information about their children in primary and secondary schools. However, once the students reach higher education and majority age, significant changes occur in parents' rights and responsibilities. This is especially true with regards to students' health care, in general, and with their mental health treatment, more specifically. For example, most state mental health laws prohibit releasing even the fact that an individual is in treatment to a third party without the consent of the patient or client. This reality can be eye-opening to some parents who believe, because they pay their children's tuition, that they have a right to the treatment information. This is not to say that student health and counseling center professionals do not want parents involved at all in students' care. In fact, there are times when partnering with parents would be in the best interest of the students. In such cases, health care professionals work to obtain written consent from students in order engage the parents.

Medical Withdrawal. Another major ethical and legal issue involves institutional medical withdrawal procedures. At times, students' health issues cause such serious impairment that they must take a medical withdrawal from school. In most cases, students, in consultation with their families, agree to take a withdrawal voluntarily. It is crucial that medical withdrawal procedures be written clearly and that students be educated concerning the specific steps to complete a withdrawal and the steps for their potential reentry into the institution.

There are some situations, however, when students would be best served by taking a medical withdrawal, but they (or their parents) do not wish to take that action. Some institutions have developed involuntary medical withdrawal procedures to manage these types of student situations. Involuntary withdrawal procedures are developed based on the notion that if students refuse to take a withdrawal voluntarily, they may pose a danger to self or others if they remain on campus. There are differing viewpoints on involuntary withdrawal procedures. On one hand, in an interview with the *Chronicle of Higher Education* (Hoover, 2006), Pavela pointed out that involuntary leave policies for medical or psychological reasons may be wrought with ethical and, potentially, legal problems. He argues that these types of policies ipso facto focus attention on the medical or psychological condition *only*, when the focus should be on behavior. He recommends, instead, that institutions have interim suspension policies that focus on student behaviors. While involuntary medical withdrawal policies may be appealing on the surface from a legal and risk management perspective, they could potentially expose the institution to claims of discrimination based on disabilities.

On the other hand, several institutions have consulted with their legal counsel and have implemented involuntary withdrawal policies that are used in extraordinary circumstances (United Educators, 2006). More recently, some administrators have reviewed and rewritten involuntary withdrawal policies in light of letter rulings issued from the U.S. Department of Education Office of Civil Rights (OCR) to various institutions of higher education (Office of Civil Rights Letter to Bluffton University, 2004; Office of Civil Rights Letter to Guilford College, 2003; Office of Civil Rights Letter to DeSales University, 2005). In the letter rulings, the OCR has provided university administrators with specific steps that institutions must take before placing a student on involuntary withdrawal status, including determining whether the student poses a direct threat to self or others. The decision to implement an involuntary withdrawal policy should be done in consultation with an institution's legal counsel and should follow the specific steps outlined by the OCR.

Finally, it is important health care administrators have access to legal counsel, either in-house counsel or off-campus special counsel, who have an expertise in the various ethical and legal issues in student health and counseling center worlds. It is equally as important that risk management officers on campuses fully understand the specific risks associated with student health and counseling centers and best practices for managing those risks.

Information Technology

Increasingly, student health services and university counseling centers are utilizing information technology solutions to meet students' health care needs. One reason for making use of technology is to keep current with students' worldviews; students today are connected very much to technology and expect services that utilize technology. Furthermore, technology offers administrators the opportunity to deliver services and reach students in ways never before available. For example, some student health services and counseling centers are offering students the option of registering online for appointments and for other programs. The use of technology assists with the accessibility issue discussed previously, as students may feel more comfortable accessing services online as opposed to calling or walking into a center. Many student health and counseling centers have moved or are moving toward electronic medical record management systems and scheduling software.

One major downside of information technology, of course, is the financial burden that is entailed in implementing and maintaining it. For example, some software programs can cost thousands of dollars to purchase, on top of the costs for the hardware that is needed to run the programs. Administrators must also factor in technology support needs to provide trouble-shooting assistance and for training of professional staff in the use of software and hardware. Technology support personnel also can assist in making sure that all software and hardware are up to date, secure, and in compliance with ethics and law. Technology can be either a blessing or a nightmare, depending on how it is conceptualized, implemented, maintained, and financially supported.

Conclusion

While no one can accurately predict what the next five or ten years will bring to the tapestry of academic life, the importance of student health services and counseling centers in the academic setting will continue to grow and change. In conclusion, we would like to offer some general recommendations for administrators to consider in addressing the health and wellness issues of students on their campuses. These recommendations are not meant to be an exhaustive list of the issues, rather just a starting point.

Institutions should give consideration to the scope of services that can be offered and the missions of their student health and counseling services. In Chapter Two of this volume, Joan Hirt discussed the importance of an institutional mission; a mission statement is as equally important at the departmental level. Careful analyses by administrators should be conducted of the resources on their campuses to determine what physical health and mental health services they can and should offer. For institutions with limited resources, it is recommended that administrators explore off-campus options for services and begin forming partnerships with them.

Administrators should take advantage of the numerous resources available to assist in developing their health and wellness services on campus, such as the AAAHC, the Joint Commission, CAS, IACS, and APA. It is also important that student health and counseling centers collect data on the students who utilize their services in order to capture the local nuances of their specific student populations.

Administrators should work to factor in issues of accessibility, affordability, and accountability, and the numerous and complex ethical and legal issues. It is also important to conduct a thorough review of policies around student insurance to ensure that all students are covered adequately for both physical and mental health issues. Administrators should also consider how much of a role information technology will play in the services that they offer and should provide adequate support for implementing and maintaining the technology and for complying with ethics and laws.

Departments in student affairs and academic affairs should collaborate in meeting the health and wellness needs of students. By partnering and collaborating across departments, a safety net can be formed for students that could potentially save lives. The collaboration must comply with confidentiality and privacy laws and must allow for adequate communication to ensure safety of students. It is also crucial in a collaborative system to make sure that the roles and responsibilities of all staff and administrators are clearly articulated.

Adequate resources should be allocated to professional development for staff and administrators to stay current with the ever-changing physical and mental health care fields. Other student affairs administrators and staff should be educated also about health care issues and challenges.

Student health and counseling center administrators should have access to legal counsel and risk management officers who have a specific expertise in the ethical and legal issues in health care. Such access can be helpful in mitigating liability for institutions as well as increasing quality of care for students.

The overall health of a campus community is very much reliant on the health and well-being of the members of that community. Competing demands for funding, competing demands for accurate determination of the real needs of the students, and also competing values regarding what constitutes the real purpose and obligations of institutions of higher education make focused and adequate health care service delivery one of constant challenges. It is clear that some services must be provided to supplement the needs of students, but what they are and what they should be must be placed into the context of the geography, the mission, and the available resources of the institution.

References

Aetna Insurance Company. "The Uninsured: College Students." [http://www.aetna.com/about/aoti/aetna_perspective/uninsured_college_students.html]. 2007.

American College Health Association. *American College Health Association-National College Health Assessment: Reference Group Executive Summary Spring 2006.* Baltimore: American College Health Association, 2006.

American Psychiatric Association. *Diagnostic and Statistical Manual of Mental Disorders* (4th ed., text rev.). Washington, D.C.: American Psychiatric Association, 2000.

Americans with Disabilities Act, H. R., Pub. L. 101–336, 1990.

Archer, J., and Cooper, S. *Counseling and Mental Health Services on Campus: A Handbook of Contemporary Practices and Challenges.* San Francisco: Jossey-Bass, 1998.

Bailey, W. J. *Ritalin.* Bloomington, Ind.: Prevention Resource Center (IPRC). [http://www.drugs.indiana.edu/drug-info-ritalin.html]. 1995.

Barr, M. J. *Academic Administrator's Guide to Budgets and Financial Management.* San Francisco: Jossey-Bass, 2002.

Baum, K., and Klaus, P. *Violent Victimization of College Students, 1995–2002.* (NCJ Publication No. 206836). Washington, D.C.: U.S. Department of Justice, Office of Justice Programs, Bureau of Justice Statistics, 2005.

Benton, S. A., and Benton, S. L. (Eds.). *College Student Mental Health: Effective Services and Strategies Across Campus.* Washington, D.C.: National Association of Student Personnel Administrators, 2006.

Benton, S. A., Robertson, J. M., Tseng, W. C., Newton, F. B., and Benton, S. L. "Changes in Counseling Center Client Problems Across Thirteen Years." *Professional Psychology: Research and Practice,* 2003, 34(1), 66–72.

Boyer, E. L. *Campus Life: In Search of Community.* Princeton, N.J.: Carnegie Foundation for the Advancement of Teaching, 1990.

Carr, J. L., and Van Deusen, K. "The Relationship Between Family of Origin Violence and Dating Violence in College Men." *Journal of Interpersonal Violence,* 2002, 17(6), 630–646.

Carr, J. L., and Ward, R. L. "ACHA Campus White Paper." *NASPA Journal,* 2006, 43(3), 380–409.

Chronicle of Higher Education. *Chronicle of Higher Education Almanac 2006–2007,* vol. 53, 2006.

Council for the Advancement of Standards in Higher Education. *CAS Professional Standards for Higher Education* (6th ed.). Washington, D.C.: Council for the Advancement of Standards in Higher Education, 2006.

Delworth, U. "The AISP Model: Assessment-Intervention of Student Problems." In U. Delworth (Ed.), *Dealing with the Behavioral and Psychological Problems of Students.* New Directions for Student Services, no. 45. San Francisco: Jossey-Bass, 1989.

Dunkle, J. H. *Building a Local Clinical Database: Let Your Local Data Be Your Guide in Developing Effective Mental Health Services.* National Association of Student Personnel Administrators Professional Development Series, Newport, R.I., January 2005.

Dunkle, J. H., and Hollingsworth, K. R. *Dealing with Disturbed and Disturbing Students: What's an Administrator to Do?* Paper presented at the National Association for Student Personnel Administrators Conference, Denver, Colo., March 2004.

Dunkle, J. H., and Hollingsworth, K. R. *Dealing with Disturbing and Disturbed Students: A Pre-Conference Workshop on Best Practices and Their Application.* National Association for Student Personnel Administrators Conference, Tampa, Fla., March 2005.

Duran, L. R. "Wasting the Best and Brightest." Press Release. National Center on Addiction and Substance Abuse at Columbia. [http://www.casacolumbia.org/absolutenm/templates/PressReleases.aspx?articleid=477&zoneid=65] 2007.

Durant, R., Champion, H., Wolfson, M., Omi, M., McCoy, T., D'Agostino, R. B., Wagoner, K., and Mitra, A. "Date Fighting Among College Students: Are They Associated with Other Health Risk Behaviors?" *Journal of American College Health,* 2007, 55(5), 291–296.

Family Educational Rights and Privacy Act, 20 U.S.C. § 1232g, 1974.

Fisher, B. S., Cullin, F. T., & Turner, M. G. *The Sexual Victimization of College Women* (NCJRS Publication No. 182369). Washington, D.C.: U.S. Department of Justice, National Criminal Justice Reference Service, 2000.

Gallagher, R. P. *National Survey of Counseling Center Directors.* Alexandria, VA: International Association of Counseling Services, 2006.

Health Insurance Portability and Accountability Act, Public Law 104–191, 1996

Hettler, B. "Wellness: Encouraging a Lifetime Pursuit of Excellence." *Health Values,* 1984, July–August 8(4), 13–27.

Hollingsworth, K. R., and Franke, A. *Preventing Suicide and Mitigating Liability; Dealing with Students in Crisis: A Systems Approach.* National Conference on Law and Higher Education, Stetson University College of Law, Clearwater Beach, Fla., February 2004.

Hoover, E. "Giving Them the Help They Need: The Author of a New Book on Student Suicide Says Colleges Need to Think About a Lot More Than Liability." *Chronicle of Higher Education,* May, 19, 2006, 52(37), A39.

Howe, N., and Strauss, W. *Millennials Go to College.* Washington, D.C.: American Association of Collegiate Registrars and Admissions Officers and Life Course Associates, 2003.

Jed Foundation. [http://www.jedfoundation.org/index.php]. 2007.

Kadison, R., and DiGeronimo, T. F. *College of the Overwhelmed: The Campus Mental Health Crisis and What to Do About It.* San Francisco: Jossey-Bass, 2004.

Kaplin, W. A., and Lee, B. A. *The Law of Higher Education* (4th ed.). San Francisco: Jossey-Bass, 2007.

Keeling, R. P., and Heitzmann, D. "Financing Health and Counseling Services." In J. Schuh (Ed.), *Contemporary Financial Issues in Student Affairs.* New Directions for Student Services, no. 103. San Francisco: Jossey-Bass, 2003.

Koss, M. P., Gidycz, C. A., and Wisniewski, N. "The Scope of Rape: Incidence and Prevalence of Sexual Aggression and Victimization in a National Sample of Higher Education Students." *Journal of Consulting and Clinical Psychology*, 1987, 55, 64–170.

Lake, P. F. "Higher Education Called to Account: Colleges and the Law After Virginia Tech." *Chronicle of Higher Education,* June, 29, 2007, 53(43), B6.

Lipka, S. "For the Learning Disabled, a Team Approach to College: A Growing Program Helps Students with Asperger's and Other Disorders Pursue Higher Education." *Chronicle of Higher Education*, December 15, 2006, 53(17), A36.

Locke, B. *Center for the Study of College Student Mental Health.* [http://www.sa.psu.edu/caps/research_center.shtml]. 2007.

Monchick, R., and Gehring, D. *Back on TRAC: Treatment, Responsibility, and Accountability on Campus.* National Conference on Law and Higher Education, Stetson University College of Law, Clearwater Beach, Fla., February 2006.

National Center for Health Statistics. *National Vital Statistics System.* National Center for Injury Prevention and Control, Center for Disease Control. [http://webappa.cdc.gov/sasweb/ncipc/leadcaus10.html]. 2007.

National College Health Risk Behavior Survey. MMWR, 1997, 46, 55–56.

National Drug Court Institute. [http://www.ndci.org/courtfacts.htm]. 2007.

Office of Civil Rights. Letter to Bluffton University. U.S. Department of Education. OCR Complaint #15–04–2042. December 22, 2004.

Office of Civil Rights. Letter to Guilford College. U.S. Department of Education. OCR Complaint #11–02–2003. December 16, 2005.

Office of Civil Rights. Letter to DeSales University. U.S. Department of Education. OCR Complaint #03–04–2041. February 17, 2005.

Presley, C. Unpublished financial report. Carbondale: Southern Illinois University Student Health Center, 2007.

Presley, C., and Pimental, E. "The Introduction of the Heavy and Frequent Drinker: A Proposal Classification to Increase Accuracy of Alcohol Assessments in Post Secondary Educational Settings." *Journal of Studies on Alcohol*, 2006, 67(2), 324–331.

Prothrow-Stith, D. "Making Campuses Safer." *Journal of American College Health*, 2007, 55, 300–303.

Robison, Jon. *Health at Every Size: Toward a New Paradigm of Weight and Health.* [http:medscape.com/viewarticle/506299]. 2005.

Rockland-Miller, H.-S., and Eells, G. T. "The Implementation of Mental Health Clinical Triage Systems in University Health Services." *Journal of College Student Psychotherapy*, 2006, 20(4), 39–51.

Sparling, P. B. "Obesity on Campus." *Prevention Chronic Disease* [serial online]. [http://www/cdc/gov/pcd/issues/2007/jul/060142.htm]. 2007.

Stone, G. L., and Archer, J. "Counseling and University Counseling Centers in the 1990s: Challenges and Limits." *Counseling Psychologist*, 1990, 18, 539–607.

Suicide Prevention Resource Center. *Promoting Mental Health and Preventing Suicide in College and University Settings.* Newton, Mass.: Education Development Center, 2004.

Turner, H. S., and Hurley, J. L. "The History and Development of College Health." In H. S. Turner and J. L. Hurley (Eds.), *The History and Practice of College Health.* Lexington: University of Kentucky Press, 2002.

United Educators. *Administrative Leave and Other Options for Emotionally Distressed or Suicidal Students.* Risk Research Bulletin: Student Affairs. April 2006.

U.S. Department of Education. *A Test of Leadership: Charting the Future of U.S. Higher Education.* Washington, D.C.: U.S. Department of Education, 2006.

Virginia Tech Review Panel Report. *Mass Shootings at Virginia Tech: Report of the Review Panel Presented to Governor Kaine.* Commonwealth of Virginia, 2007.

Williams, C. R. "FERPA, GLBA, and HIPAA: The Alphabet Soup of Privacy." National Association of College and University Attorneys Publication Series. Washington, D.C.: National Association of College and University Attorneys, 2007.

World Health Organization. "Obesity and Overweight." [http://www.who.int/dietphysicalactivity/publications/facts/obesity.en/]. 2007.

CHAPTER FIFTEEN

SUPPORTING ONLINE STUDENTS

Anita Crawley and Christine LeGore

Three interrelated trends—the changing student population (see Chapter Twelve), increasing access to computers by current and potential students, and continuing enhancements to educational software and computer-mediated communication—have led to rapid increases in online enrollment in higher education during the past ten years, which in turn has significantly shaped higher education. The three trends and the resulting increases in online enrollment will continue to be dynamic forces for change in the foreseeable future, and student affairs professionals have the opportunity to play a vital role in the success of this new form of higher learning and of the students it attracts.

This chapter describes the tremendous growth of online learning in the United States and some of the factors and trends supporting that growth. It also examines the unique preferences and needs of online learners and swirling students, as well as a broad array of innovative student affairs practices that support these learners. While most of the studies and examples that inform this chapter are from the United States, the lessons learned are relevant to educators worldwide. The chapter concludes with the authors' vision of how the role of the student affairs professional must evolve to respond to the needs of new learners.

The Explosive Growth of Online Learning

Since the late 1990s, the number of students taking online courses has increased geometrically. One and a half million students were enrolled in online courses and programs in the fall of 2002. By fall 2005, that number had exploded to nearly 3.2 million. From 2004 to 2005 the growth rate was 35 percent, and there are no signs that the rate is slowing (Allen and Seaman, 2006; and Eduventures, 2007). Online learning is no longer an experimental or fringe movement. In fact, 58.4 percent of more than 2,200 chief academic officers who responded to a 2006 Sloan Consortium survey agreed that online education is a critical component of their long-term strategic plan. Students taking at least one online course represent almost 17 percent of the 17 million higher education students in the United States. Online courses are offered by more than 80 percent of all doctoral and research institutions, 70 percent of all associates degree-granting institutions, and 40 percent of all baccalaureate degree-granting institutions. A majority of doctoral and associate institutions offer entire degree programs online (Allen and Seaman, 2006).

Changing Enrollment Trends

Because more than half of all online learners are studying at two-year institutions (Allen and Seaman, 2006), the Community College Survey of Student Engagement (CCSSE) may provide a window into the needs of online students. CCSSE learned several things from their 2006 cohort of 250,000 students, representing 447 institutions in 46 states:

- 61 percent were enrolled part time,
- 57 percent worked more than twenty hours per week,
- 34 percent spent eleven hours or more per week caring for dependents, and
- 21 percent spent 6–20 hours per week commuting to and from class (Allen and Seaman, 2006).

Data from the National Survey of Student Engagement (NSSE), given to students at four-year institutions, looks very similar and is described in detail in the next section.

Student affairs professionals face enormous challenges in trying to find ways to reach out to and interact with the busy part-time students described in these surveys. These challenges are heightened even further when one considers the complexity of dealing with *student swirl*, a term that was coined by Alfredo de los Santos and Irene Wright in 1990 to describe irregular enrollment patterns (Borden, 2004). Victor Borden summarizes eight attendance patterns of swirling students that were first identified by Alexander McCormick: trial enrollment, special programs enrollment, supplemental enrollment (for example, a summer course at another school), rebounding enrollment (usually between two schools), concurrent enrollment (also called "double dipping"), consolidated enrollment (collecting courses from several institutions), serial transfer, and independent enrollment (for professional development, mostly) (Borden, 2004).

Alan Sturtz, a researcher for the Connecticut State University (CSU) System, wanted to better understand the student swirl phenomenon in his own system. He tracked the attendance patterns of the fall 2002 entering classes for each of the four CSU institutions. Of the original cohort of 4,340 first-time, full-time, first-year students, by fall 2004 more than 1,130 (26 percent) had left to attend elsewhere (mostly out of state or at community colleges), and 119 of them had attended more than one institution after leaving CSU. Sturtz also looked at the influx of transfer students into the CSU system. A survey of the graduating classes of 2003 and 2004 showed that only 53 percent had started their higher education career at the CSU school from which they had graduated (Sturtz, 2006). Similarly, Borden discovered in the late 1990s that two thirds of the students at the large, public, urban commuter campus where he worked had started their careers at a different college or university, and this was in a state with no community college system (Borden, 2004).

Borden encourages higher education administrators to question whether or not they are addressing the reality of their large, swirling student populations. "Do they know where their students come from and at what point they are in their academic careers? Do they orient transfer students to their particular curriculum? Do they assess incoming students for prerequisite knowledge, skills and abilities? Do they send students off, regardless of when they leave, with evidence of their level of proficiency in generally accepted outcome domains?" (Borden, 2004, p. 16) The availability of thousands of online courses, for students any time, anywhere, makes it easier than ever for students to search beyond their home institutions for courses that help them progress toward their degrees.

As online enrollments grow, one may safely predict that the population of swirling students will increase, as well. Over the coming decades, colleges and universities will need to pay greater attention to the needs of swirling students if they are to remain competitive. Sturtz encourages the academy to recognize that "swirl is not a leakage in the pipeline to educational attainment. It promotes access because it provides *many points of entry* as well as educational options to students" (Sturtz, 2006, p. 158). He goes on to say, "Policy-makers must recognize that non-linear attendance is a legitimate way of experiencing college and meeting educational objectives. New definitions, measures and guidelines are needed that address the realities of higher education's diverse student body and the way they go to college" (p. 157).

Higher education professionals must respond to the new paradigm that defines today's students and how they are choosing to learn. Increasing access to online courses from thousands of institutions throughout the world and increasing numbers of part-time students with extensive family and work demands and swirling enrollment patterns are the future of higher education. In light of this new learning paradigm, traditional student affairs professional practice, which has long emphasized notions of community (in no small part defined in geographic terms) and has relied on extensive and extended interactions with students, must be revisited, reaffirmed at some points, and revised at others to help assure that all students are being well served.

A Closer Look at the Online Learner

With huge numbers of students turning to online learning for a portion or all of their higher education coursework, student affairs professionals must gain a deeper understanding of today's online learners. This section describes these students' characteristics, where they live, how they currently like to communicate, and some of the traits they have in common with today's on-campus students, most of whom were born in the 1980s and 1990s.

In 2006 the National Survey of Student Engagement examined data about online learners for the first time. Nearly 4,000 students (1,279 first-year students and 2,615 seniors) indicated that they were taking all their courses online during the then-current academic term. Researchers discovered that:

- Half of them were enrolled part time (compared to 10 percent of other students),
- Half worked more than thirty hours per week, and
- 70 percent were caring for dependents.

These 100 percent online learners have been labeled "distance education students" by NSSE. They were more likely to be first-generation students (63 percent compared to 42 percent of others), and they tended to be several years older:

- 25 percent versus 18 percent for the first-year group, and
- 32 percent versus 22 percent for the seniors (NSSE, 2006).

In published studies of why students choose online learning, the overwhelming majority of students responded that convenience played a major role

(Dare, Zapata, and Thomas, 2005; NSSE, 2006; and Walker, 2007). For adults, online learning means no commuting or hiring of babysitters. Because their students have so little time for school, colleges dealing with this population must rethink all of the services they offer: orientation, study skills workshops, opportunities for informal communication among students, faculty advising, student leadership opportunities, service learning, and career services, to name a few. Universities engaged in strategic planning must consider the needs of these students in all phases of their planning: Is the current mix of services relevant, or even accessible, to these students, and how should the university allocate its resources to meet their needs?

It may be surprising to learn that a 2007 Eduventures survey of more than 25,000 students showed that approximately two thirds of online students live within the geographical region of their awarding institution, and more than one third live within fifty miles of their online provider (Eduventures, 2007). Although many online learners live within commuting distance of their campuses, most are quite comfortable conducting their university business, as well as their courses, from a distance. In 2003, nearly 800 distance learners at North Carolina State University (NCSU) revealed their campus commuting habits on a survey conducted by Leslie Dare and colleagues:

- 40.9 percent never came to campus,
- 31.8 percent came once or twice a semester,
- 18.2 percent came monthly,
- 6.3 percent came weekly, and
- 2.8 percent came daily.

They came to campus, for the most part, to take exams and purchase textbooks and supplies (Dare and others, 2005).

Dare and her colleagues also queried the students about their preferred mode of communication with North Carolina State. It is interesting that the top two preferred modes for the 1,962 on-campus students and 778 distance learners were identical. E-mail was the first choice and conventional mail was the second choice for both groups. Instead of asking, "How are distance and online learners different from on-campus students?" student affairs administrators should ask, "How are distance and on-campus learners alike, and how should we restructure our services to meet the needs of all learners?"

While older students with family and work obligations are flocking to online learning for the sake of convenience, younger students are attracted to online learning because the milieu is comfortable for them. Carol Scarafiotti and Martha Cleveland-Innes (2006) summarize the challenges of serving recent high school graduates: "This group will adjust rapidly to online learning environments and welcome the opportunity to use well-developed competencies in the learning environment. Likewise this group will be frustrated by outdated online learning milieus such as text heavy online courses which merely replicate the content in a textbook or by faculty who refuse to use technology enhanced communication in their courses" (p. 36).

Regardless of age, students expect technology to be woven into everything they do. Banks, bookstores, travel agencies, and other businesses have used technology to make their services accessible to their customers 24/7. To be relevant and accessible to students, we need to familiarize ourselves with the technologies they prefer.

Is Online Learning the Real Thing?

As millions of students flock to online learning, student affairs professionals may question the value of an online learner's experience. Skeptic Robert Zemsky proclaims, "What the Web provides are merely correspondence courses distributed electronically" (Zemsky and Massy, 2004), but faculty and students report that they are experiencing something much richer.

Mark Kassop (2003), a sociology professor who has taught more than 1,200 students in fifty online course sections, identifies ten areas in which he believes online education either matches or surpasses face-to-face learning (see Table 15.1). Kassop's enthusiasm is shared by thousands of professors at conferences and workshops sponsored by leading distance education organizations like the Sloan Consortium and Western Cooperative for Electronic Telecommunications (WCET) and in regularly published research (Allen and Seaman, 2006).

Students' self-reported experiences in online courses are equally powerful. Seniors who identified themselves as online learners on the 2006 NSSE reported significantly greater educational gains and levels of satisfaction than their campus-based peers in several areas: level of academic challenge, supportive campus environment, higher-order learning, reflective learning, gains in practical competence, gains in personal and social development, and gains in general education. First-year online students gave higher rankings than their on-campus counterparts to level of academic challenge, student faculty interaction, enriching educational experience, reflective learning, gains in practical competence, and gains in personal and social development. In fact, of the twelve areas that were compared, the online students scored lower than their on-campus counterparts in only one area: active and collaborative learning (NSSE, 2006).

Washington State University's (WSU) Office of Distance Degree Programs (DDP) found similar results when it surveyed its alumni. Although distance and

TABLE 15.1 STRENGTHS OF ONLINE LEARNING

Student-centered learning	On-demand interaction and support services
Writing intensity	Immediate feedback
Highly interactive discussions	Flexibility
Geared to lifelong learning	An intimate community of learners
Enriched course materials	Faculty development and rejuvenation

Source: Adapted from Kassop (2003).

on-campus learners gave very similar answers to most questions, DDP alumni outstripped their campus counterparts in reporting greater satisfaction with WSU's contribution to their growth in three areas: learning independently, understanding differing philosophies and cultures and their interactions, and understanding the interaction of society and the environment. In a separate question that was asked of DDP alumni only, students responded disappointingly to the category "working collaboratively with others." Only 52 percent of the group reported being "very satisfied" or "considerably" satisfied. As a result, DDP now demands that all new online courses include activities that require students to work collaboratively (Kendall and Pogue, 2006). Student affairs professionals might use their group process expertise to assist faculty in integrating more collaborative learning experiences into their online courses.

Eight hundred North Carolina State (NCS) distance learners and 2,000 on-campus students rated the importance of a sense of connection with students in their courses, students in general, their instructor, their academic advisor, their academic department, faculty in general, and NCS. Distance students assigned a significantly higher level of importance than their on-campus counterparts to every interaction, except for the connection with their instructor. In rating their satisfaction with these interactions, distance learners again outscored the on-campus students, reporting significantly higher levels of satisfaction with their connections to students in general, their instructor, their academic department, faculty, and NCS (Dare and others, 2005).

Critics of online learning state that distance learners are exposed to fewer full-time faculty than are on-campus learners. However, chief academic officers responding in 2005 to a survey by the Sloan Consortium reported that their universities were using the "same mix of core and adjunct faculty for their online courses as they were for their face-to-face courses" (Allen and Seaman, 2006).

Are Online Degrees Credible?

The education community is assessing whether potential employers view online degrees favorably. For a January 2007 issue of the *Chronicle of Higher Education*,

Dan Carnevale interviewed people from a range of institutions and businesses. Although many employers viewed an online degree as "less than" a traditional degree, Jennifer Schramm of the Society for Human Resource Management contends that the "name recognition of the college matters more than whether the degree was earned online" (Carnevale, 2007). In an April 2007 issue of *Diverse* magazine, Benjamin Akande of Webster University says, "We've had no issues whatsoever with employers discounting the online knowledge . . . I think that employers nowadays are doing their due diligence, and they are recognizing that online education is probably a little bit more challenging than in-class education" (Nance, 2007). Carnevale mentions that several companies, like Johnson & Johnson, partner with online institutions to provide professional development programming for their employees. It is reasonable to predict that as more employers observe the benefits of online learning for their employees, the question about the value of an online degree will become a moot point.

Distance learning is here to stay. It has made huge inroads in a majority of our institutions of higher learning, and continues to grow annually at double-digit rates. Faculty, students, and institutions agree that the online learning experience is not only as good as, but is often better than, traditional face-to-face learning. Huge numbers of today's higher education students are swirlers who find online learning a perfect solution to the challenges of their busy, demanding lives. Sally Johnstone and Kurt Larsen deftly summarize the trend: "It seems that U.S. students are acting like consumers of education. They are shopping for the best deals or the approach to teaching that matches their needs. Most institutions did not anticipate this new, consumer-oriented approach to course-taking that has been adopted widely by today's college students and enabled by e-learning opportunities (Johnstone and Larsen, 2006).

The second half of this chapter examines how the student affairs community is responding to these rapid changes in higher education. An array of best practices in online services for distance, online, and swirling students is presented, followed by a new vision of the role of student affairs professionals in the evolving e-culture.

Online Students: Whose Responsibility?

The U.S. Department of Education (2006) suggests a role for student affairs in supporting online learners when it notes that services for online learners are of a lower quality when provided by personnel from offices other than those who specialize in delivering student services. Student affairs professionals have played a significant role in implementing technological innovations such as student information systems, online application, and registration (Kretovics, 2003), yet these same professionals have sometimes been less involved in developing remotely delivered services that support online learners. It is tempting to think that, for online learners who are willing and able to come to campus, traditional on-campus services are appropriate and sufficient to meet their needs. However, student affairs professionals must be able to communicate the unique demands of online coursework and help students become successful online learners. For students living in geographically remote locations our experience tells us that online learners not only expect student support services equivalent to those available to on campus students, but want those services to be delivered using the same technology as their courses. Meeting these expectations is a key challenge for the next decade.

In 2000, the National Association of Student Personnel Administrators (NASPA) established a distance learning task force that identified four issues that are directly relevant to the support of distance learners. Student affairs needs to:

1. Learn who the distance learners are and assess their support needs,
2. Determine what services can be delivered using traditional means and what services need new methods of delivery,
3. Assess online student motivation and what services they need to achieve academic success, and
4. Provide online students opportunities for community and affiliation even though these students may never come to campus (NASPA, 2004).

Despite the encouragement from NASPA, implementation of the agenda within the student affairs profession has not kept up with the growth of online courses. At the Joint Meeting of NASPA and American College Personnel Association (ACPA) in 2007, the largest student affairs conference ever held, there was only one breakout session devoted to supporting online students (ACPA-NASPA Joint Meeting, 2007).

It is understandable that student affairs practitioners may be hesitant to become actively involved in supporting online learners. Student affairs professionals are busier than ever. They may have concerns about the quality of remotely delivered services and the loss of personalized interaction with students. Additionally, they may have fears about job security if services can be delivered more efficiently at a distance. Student affairs personnel may also wonder if they can master the skills needed to deliver student services effectively at a distance (NASPA, 2000). While these are reasonable concerns, today's on-campus and online students expect to access a wide range of services from the convenience of their homes or residence halls. Colleges must respond or risk losing their swirling and online students to colleges and universities that offer programs and services in formats that better fit students' busy lives.

All regional accrediting bodies in the United States mandate that institutions provide services to online students. Best Practices for Electronically Offered Degree and Certificate Programs (WCET, 2001) states, "The institution recognizes that appropriate services must be available for students of electronically offered programs, using the working assumption that these students will not be physically present on campus." The 2006 Council for the Advancement of Standards in Higher Education (CAS) reaffirms the mandates of the regional accrediting commissions and provides explicit details about the importance of delivering services that assure understanding of curriculum, course and degree requirements, technical competence of students, and access to academic and educational support services (Miller, 2007). Many of these functions are primary responsibilities of student affairs. These standards provide opportunities and guidelines for student affairs professionals to transform their services for online students.

What Roles Might Student Affairs Professionals Assume?

While much has been written about supporting online students, little research has been conducted about the student affairs role in these efforts. Kretovics (2003) identifies four areas of support to be addressed by student affairs:

1. Offering services via the Web
2. Creating communities of online learners
3. Providing a leadership role in the development of distance learning programs, and
4. Training student affairs graduate students by incorporating online learning into graduate programs (Kretovics, 2003).

Dare and others (2005) provide the following seven recommendations for student affairs professionals:

1. Understand the administration of distance learning programs.
2. Understand the vocabulary of distance learning.
3. Understand the funding of distance learning programs.
4. Be prepared to advocate for the role of student affairs in distance learning and to educate others about the mission, function, and objectives of student affairs units.
5. Advocate for equal services for students who take courses online and on campus.
6. Develop programs to meet the unique needs of online students.
7. Establish positions with duties focused entirely on the needs of online students.

The fact that online students need online services has been clearly articulated, and possible roles for student affairs professionals have been described. The following sections describe online student services and provide examples of good practices.

What Is the Scope of Online Student Services?

As part of a Fund for the Improvement of Postsecondary Education (FIPSE) grant, WCET developed a graphic that has been widely used to illustrate the scope of services that might be provided to students via a college Web site. Some services are best delivered from the public Web site and others from behind a password-protected student portal. The WCET spider web portrays five service suites: administrative core, communications, student communities, personal services, and academic services.

Colleges frequently begin by providing services from the administrative core. Once students are able to apply to the college, apply for financial aid, register for courses, pay bills, and receive grades online, they want to be able to accomplish more at a distance. College Web sites range in sophistication from static information pages to interactive decision-making tools that use artificial intelligence to assist students wherever (an Internet connection is all that is required) and whenever (24/7) they need assistance.

Electronic delivery of student services provides challenges as well as opportunities. One such challenge is how to create remotely delivered services while retaining the high-touch qualities that characterize student services. WCET has provided guidelines to assist colleges in this endeavor (WCET, 2003).

Best Practices in Online Student Services

With the needs of online students as a focal point, it is helpful to explore the specific needs of these students as they progress through the various stages of the enrollment process. Some services overlap, but using a model that associates typical services needed at each stage of enrollment may be helpful in developing comprehensive online services. Floyd and Casey-Powell's (2004) five-phase matriculation model provides a good basis for examining colleges and universities that have developed online student services that are considered best practices (Floyd and Casey-Powell, 2004). This section highlights several college and university programs, including some that have been recognized for awards by the National Academic Advising Association (NACADA) or WCET.

FIGURE 15.1 STUDENT SERVICES FOR ONLINE LEARNERS

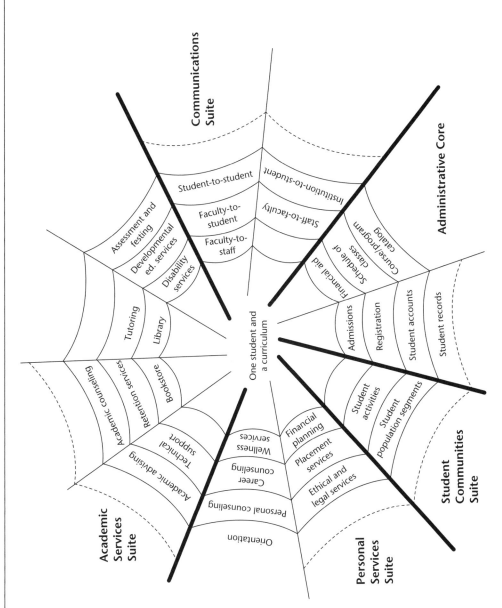

Communications Suite

Administrative Core

Student-to-student

Institution-to-student

Faculty-to-student

Staff-to-faculty

Faculty-to-staff

Assessment and testing

Developmental ed. services

Disability services

Financial aid

Schedule of classes

Course/program catalog

Tutoring

Library

Admissions

Registration

Student accounts

Student records

Academic counseling

Retention services

Bookstore

Student activities

Student population segments

Technical support

Academic advising

Wellness services

Financial planning

Placement services

Ethical and legal services

Career counseling

Personal counseling

Orientation

One student and a curriculum

Academic Services Suite

Personal Services Suite

Student Communities Suite

Source: Shea and Blakely (2002).

Learner Intake Phase

The Floyd and Casey-Powell model begins with the learner intake phase. During this phase, students need information about the demands of online learning, admissions, online programs, placement testing, contact information, financial aid, scholarships, and orientation to the college. The main task for students is to determine whether or not online learning is appropriate for their learning style, level of motivation, and personal needs. Students can best prepare for online learning by participating in an ungraded online learning experience. The Ohio Learning Network (2007) provides a free online course facilitated from within the learning management system. The course provides information about online learning and gives students an opportunity to "test drive" online learning and the learning management system tools. At Northern Arizona University (2007), students have an enrollment guide and checklist that details the key steps to enrolling in a distance learning class. At Northern Virginia Community College, students participate in a remotely delivered, synchronous orientation to online learning. A Web-based live classroom using Wimba software allows students to participate from their computer (no additional software required), view and listen to a PowerPoint presentation, take a tour of the course management system, and ask questions of the session facilitators. Those who cannot attend the live session can view and listen to the recording online. The presentation becomes an on-demand tutorial either for review or for initial viewing by those who could not participate in real time.

Learner Intervention Phase

The learner intervention phase begins with the student's first online course. During this phase, students learn how to become independent and effective online learners. They discover how to contact the student help desk, develop technology skills, buy books, use the online library, and select and register for courses. This information is often a part of orientations to online learning. Orientations come in many formats. Some are text based with no interactivity; others incorporate interactivity by including audio and video as well as assessments to measure learning outcomes.

Some orientations are facilitated, but most are self-paced. Metropolitan State College (2007) has developed a self-paced orientation that welcomes students to the university, provides academic planning, and teaches strategies for online success. Students are required to pass a quiz hosted in the university's course management system. This orientation was originally created to help students prepare for online learning but is now also used as an orientation to the college.

At Capella University (2007), students participate in a required, instructor-facilitated orientation that includes many features:

- An orientation to the learning management system,
- Tips on how to purchase books,
- Information about policies and procedures,
- Opportunities to practice using the discussion board,
- Expectations about academic honesty,
- Strategies for learner success, including use of the online writing center, library, career center, disability support services, academic success center, and
- Lessons about time management targeting the needs of online learners.

Students are expected to actively participate by posting to the discussion board, taking quizzes to measure learning, and submitting assignments, all of which provide practice using the learning management system tools. By the time students begin their first online course, they are ready to focus on course content (Capella University, 2007).

A third example of services needed during the learner intervention phase comes from the University of Washington (2007). Online learners need technology skills ranging from basic skills to high-end technical abilities, depending on the course. Catalyst, the name of the University of Washington's online help center, provides how-to guides for a wide variety of technical skills.

Learner Support Phase

During the learner support phase, which covers the rest of the academic term, students develop additional skills that lead to successful course completion. Those skills are acquired with the help of academic advising and instructional support. Students may be provided information about time management and organizational skills, both of which are crucial for online student success. Students learn how to use the online library, purchase books, and access disability support services. Sometimes these elements are included in orientation services prior to a student's first online course.

No matter when these services are first provided, students must be able to continue accessing this information on an as-needed basis throughout the term. The University of Maine System's (2007) off-campus library services Web site offers a rich array of resources for off-campus students. On this Web site, students have live chat, text messaging, e-mail, 1-800 telephone access to reference librarians, and an array of research tutorials. Particularly worth noting are the course Web sites that library staff have created for specific distance courses. These Web sites lead students to the databases and resources that are most relevant to their courses, narrowing the dizzying array of information to a manageable size.

At Montgomery College, Maryland, online learners receive information through an online student success center located on the college web site and from a virtual counseling and advising center: an online companion, which is facilitated by a distance learning counselor inside the learning management system (Montgomery College, 2007). Along with career and academic planning resources called for in the learner transition phase, the online companion provides information about several online success skills. Students have easy access to various professionals, including online faculty and a student support specialist, through the discussion board. The intent of this resource is to provide information and establish an online community of learners.

San Diego Community College (2007) offers remotely delivered academic and career counseling. This service uses a WebEx virtual classroom with audio, text, whiteboard, file, and Web site sharing capabilities for live interactions with counselors or advisors to help students make academic and career decisions. Students sign up for e-workshops or e-appointments, or they participate in e-counselor walk-in appointments or chat sessions. These live interactions provide opportunities for developmental advising, something that is difficult to achieve when communication is only text based and asynchronous, such as e-mail advising.

Penn State World Campus (2007) provides comprehensive online student services. The student portal, eLion, has a variety of tools, including one that uses artificial intelligence to help students make decisions about whether to drop a course. Penn State offers online career workshops and study sessions conducted inside the course management system. The goals are to teach content and to build community. Modules are available for independent study and self-improvement, while professionals are available to answer questions through the course management communication tools.

Student government at Washington State University (WSU) is not just for on-campus students (Washington State University, 2007). The Associated Students of WSU Distance Degree Programs is a fully developed student activities program with online meetings, a committee structure, a constitution, by laws, and more. WSU's student government model provides valuable opportunities for distance learners, with the help of their student government advisors, to practice and develop leadership skills.

Learner Transition Phase

During the learner transition phase, students need career counseling and academic advising to help them achieve their educational goals. The Life Map at

Valencia Community College (2007) is designed to accompany all students—both distance and on campus—throughout their enrollment at Valencia and beyond. Life Map is a comprehensive developmental advising system that is organized around a five-stage model: transition to college, introduction to college, progression to a degree, graduation transition, and lifelong learning. The goal is to develop self-directed learners. To this end, Life Map provides interactive tools to help students develop an educational plan, a career plan, a portfolio, job prospects, and a long-term financial plan.

Health and wellness, personal counseling, and disability support services are examples of services that students may need during any of the phases discussed. The University of Chicago (2008) has a Web site that addresses health and wellness issues important to college students. The site includes Virtual Pamphlets, as well as self-assessment tools and guidelines for faculty and staff.

Remotely delivered personal counseling certainly poses unique challenges. ReadyMinds, an organization that trains distance learning counselors to deliver both personal and career counseling, believes this is a viable service if done responsibly. "A total of 313 individuals have been awarded Distance Credentialed Counselor recognition through the Center for Credentialing and Education, Inc., an affiliate of National Board of Certified Counselors" (National Board of Certified Counselors, 2007).

It is essential to provide services to online students with disabilities. Burgstahler (2006) advocates being proactive by creating online courses and Web sites using principles of universal design and reactive by providing accommodations to enrolled students with disabilities. This article identifies criteria for designing courses and Web sites for each of the following groups: current and potential students with disabilities, distance learning course designers, distance learning instructors, and program evaluators. Accessibility issues should be included in online teacher training. Distance learning Web sites should include information for how students with disabilities can request accommodations for distance learning courses. The distance learning program should communicate a clear commitment to providing equal access for all students.

Measurement Phase

During the measurement phase, the institution looks at the effectiveness of its online student services by assessing retention, graduation, and persistence rates (Floyd and Casey-Powell, 2004). University of Maryland University College (UMUC), through careful research, identified risk factors for students who were less successful in online courses, then piloted specific interventions designed to increase student success (University of Maryland University College,

2007). UMUC targets students who register after the start of classes, are in high-enrollment entry courses, have taken fewer than 45 credits, are taking courses in mixed formats, or are taking their first online course. Pilot programs include an e-mentor program for one-to-one contact and an early intervention program for high-risk populations, an orientation course for newer students, an online tutoring program for high-enrollment entry courses, and learning coaches for discipline-specific enrichment. Long-term tracking of participants began fall 2006; early results were positive (Hrutka and Davis, 2006).

The Floyd and Casey-Powell model provides a useful chronological approach to developing and delivering online student services that respond to student needs at various stages of enrollment and matriculation. A rich and varied menu of online services gives colleges and students opportunities to engage in meaningful relationships. These relationships are critically important for the online learner and, as Judith Boettcher (2007) reminds us, "Support and advising systems provide a competitive edge for institutions by helping to develop a lasting relationship between eLearner and school" (p. 1).

Conclusion

This chapter has emphasized the fact that the higher education landscape has changed dramatically in the past ten years. The typical higher education student is no longer eighteen to twenty-two years old, but older than twenty-five. More students are working part or full time, caring for dependents, taking longer than four years to complete a baccalaureate degree, swirling among institutions, and commuting to class. For many of these students, convenience is the first priority in selecting a course, a program of study, or an institution of higher education. Online learning, with convenient, accessible services, suits their lifestyle and their needs.

At the same time, a new generation of tech-savvy students has arrived on our campuses, with expectations that they can do just about everything online. Colleges and universities must adapt their student services to this new population to remain competitive in the marketplace. Being neither at the beginning nor at the end of this transformation, many in the academy may feel in limbo. Higher education is too far into the online education movement to turn back, yet there is still a collective memory of how things used to be. It is normal for student affairs professionals, who take great pride in providing high-touch, individualized services, to be cautious, and sometimes reluctant, about using technology to deliver services to online and commuter students. On the other hand, these same professionals possess excellent communication and leadership skills and are well equipped to lead the needed transition.

While this chapter has focused on the needs of students who are unwilling or unable to come to campus, it is clear that services on campus will remain the cornerstone of most student affairs offices. However, online, primarily self-services will continue to grow as an attractive alternative delivery method. Online services will vary from static Web pages to interactive, on-demand tutorials, to live, remotely delivered sessions. Student affairs professionals will be challenged to match students with the modality that best meets their needs. As more students take advantage of self-service opportunities, student affairs professionals will have time to work with those students who have the most complex and demanding needs.

These ideas will require a shift in resources. Many colleges and universities provide technical support, tutoring, call centers, and library services 24/7. Some purchase these services, while others participate in a consortium with others or contract with their own staff to provide coverage beyond normal business hours. The decision to develop resources in-house or to partner with a vendor is complex and beyond the scope of this chapter. The process of selecting vendors and developing resources is an excellent opportunity to bring together all university staffs who work with students. This provides a chance for student affairs to take the lead in serving today's changing student population.

So what are some first steps for leaders eager to move their area forward? First, student affairs leaders might develop a plan for managing change. Because change is difficult for most people, leaders should consider the impact new expectations may have on the staff.

Second, as described in Chapter Twenty-One, it is critical for student affairs to forge strong partnerships with academic affairs in the development and delivery of online student support. Both groups can build on their successful collaborations in the areas of learning communities, student leadership, service learning, and academic advising. At Cerro Coso Community College in California (2007), counselors are working with online instructors on an early warning system that identifies online students at risk of not succeeding.

Third, if the skills and resources that are needed to effect change are not evident on campus, the college may decide to enlist the assistance of an outside consultant. The Center for Transforming Student Services (CENTSS), a recognized leader in the development and delivery of online student services, has developed an audit tool to assess a school's online student services, set goals, and plan improvements based on the audit results (Center for Transforming Student Services, 2007). The twenty student services included in the audit provide the opportunity to bring both student and academic affairs professionals to the table to discuss a seamless approach to improving online services for all students. Choosing an external facilitator provides the advantage of a neutral person leading the discussion.

An approach used by many colleges and universities is to participate in a consortium to deliver online student services. Some examples include:

- Illinois Virtual Campus (2007) supports test proctoring and academic advising services for colleges throughout the state. Online students can receive these services from their local community colleges even if their courses are from a different institution in the state.
- Connecticut Distance Learning Consortium (2007) provides a central point of access to a variety of services, including tutoring, help desk, and e-portfolio, for its member institutions.
- University of Texas Telecampus (2007) facilitates online student business services and provides free online tutoring services, digital library resources and services, 24/7 technical support, and a call center for prospective and current students (University of Texas Telecampus).
- Minnesota State Colleges and Universities (2007) make a multimedia electronic portfolio available to all Minnesota residents.
- Kentucky Virtual Campus (2007) provides extensive resources to help students conduct scholarly research.

These are a few examples of online student services designed to reach students from more than one college or university.

Similar to their faculty counterparts, student affairs professionals who have implemented support programs for online learners have been enthusiastic about the opportunities created for on campus, as well as online students. Developing online student services provides a forum to rethink many of the college's connections: to students, among students, among faculty and students, and among faculty and staff. This is an exciting time for student affairs professionals to lead their institutions in the delivery of innovative student services.

References

American College Personnel Association-National Association of Student Personnel Administrators. *Our Power and Responsibility to Shape Education.* ACPA-NASPA Joint Meeting, Orlando, Fla., March 31–April 4. 2007.

Allen, I. E., and Seaman, J. "Making the Grade, Online Education in the United States, 2006." Needham, Mass.: Sloan Consortium. [http://www.sloan-c.org/publications/survey/pdf/making_the_grade.pdf]. 2006.

Boettcher, J. V. "Serving the Online Learner." *Campus Technology.* [http://campustechnology.com/articles/46400/]. 2007.

Borden, V.M.H. "Accommodating Student Swirl." *Change,* 2004, 36(2), 10–17.

Burgstahler, S. "Ten Indicators of Distance Learning Program Accessibility to Students with Disabilities." Huntersville, N.C.: Association on Higher Education and Disability. [http://www.ahead.org/publications/alert/2006/alertjuly06.php]. 2006.

Capella University. [http://www.capella.edu]. 2007.

Carnevale, D. "Employers Often Distrust Online Degrees." *Chronicle of Higher Education,* 53(18), A28. [http://chronicle.com/weekly/v53/i18/18a02801.htm]. January 5, 2007.

Center for Transforming Student Services. *Consulting Services.* [http://www.centss.org/consult.cfm]. 2005.

Center for Community College Survey of Student Engagement. *Act on the Fact: Using Data to Improve Student Success.* [http://www.ccsse.org/publications/CCSSENationalReport2006.pdf]. 2006.

Cerro Coso Community College. [http://cconline.cerrocoso.edu/]. 2007.

Community College Survey of Student Engagement. *Connecticut Distance Learning Consortium.* [http://www.ctdlc.org/]. 2007.

Dare, L. A., Zapata, L. P., and Thomas, A. G. "Assessing the Needs of Distance Learners: A Student Affairs Perspective. In K. Kruger (Ed.), *Technology in Student Affairs: Supporting Student Learning and Services.* New Directions for Student Services, no. 112. San Francisco: Jossey-Bass, 2005.

Eduventures, Inc. *Geography Matters in Online Higher Education.* [www.eduventures.com/about/press_room/03_28_07.cfm?print_version=yes&mpid=&tid=]. 2007.

Floyd, D. L., and Casey-Powell, D. "New Roles for Student Support Services in Distance Learning." In B. L. Bower and K. P. Hardy (Eds.), *From Distance Education to E-Learning: Lessons Along the Way.* New Directions for Community Colleges, no. 128. San Francisco: Jossey-Bass, 2005.

Hrutka, M. E., and Davis, C. *Supporting the First-Time Adult Learner.* Paper presented at WCET 16th Annual Conference, Portland, Ore. [http://conference.wcet.info/2006/presentations/Davis,Cynthia_AdultLearner.swf]. November 2006.

Illinois Virtual Campus. [http://www.ivc.illinois.edu/]. 2007.

Johnstone, S., and WCET Associates. *Advancing Campus Efficiencies: A Companion for Campus Leaders in a Digital Age.* Bolton, Mass.: Anker, 2007.

Johnstone, S., and Larsen, K. "Consumer Protection in Cross-Border E-Learning Delivery: A White Paper to Guide Discussion for the International Seminar Regulation of E-Learning: New National and International Policy Perspectives." Berkeley, CA: University of California, Berkeley. [http://cshe.berkeley.edu/research/regulation/documents/consumer-protection.pdf]. 2005.

Kassop, M. "Ten Ways Online Education Matches, or Surpasses, Face-to-Face Learning. *Technology Source.* [http://technologysource.org/article/ten_ways_online_education_matches_or_surpasses_facetoface_learning/]. May/June 2003.

Kendall, J. R., and Pogue, K. "Survey of Alumni from Distance Degree and Campus-Based Baccalaureate Programs." *Quarterly Review of Distance Education,* 2006, 7(2), 15–164.

Kentucky Virtual Campus. [http://www.kyvu.org/]. 2007.

Kretovics, M. "The Role of Student Affairs in Distance Education: Cyber-Services or Virtual Communities. *Online Journal of Distance Learning Administration,* 6(3). [http://www.westga.edu/~distance/ojdla/fall63/kretovics63.html]. 2003.

Metropolitan State College. [http://www.metrostate.edu/orientation/portal/index.html]. 2007.

Miller, T. K. *The Book of Professional Standards for Higher Education*: Washington, D.C.: Council for the Advancement of Standards in Higher Education. 2007.

Minnesota State Colleges and Universities. [http://www.mnscu.edu/]. 2007.

Montgomery College. [http://www.montgomerycollege.edu/Departments/studevgt/onlinsts/]. 2007.

Nance, M. "Online Degrees Increasingly Gaining Acceptance Among Employers." *Diverse,* April 5, 2007.

National Association of Student Personnel Association. "Distance Learning and Student Affairs: Defining the Issues." [http://www.ed.gov/about/bdscomm/list/acsfa/distnaspa.pdf]. 2000.

National Board of Certified Counselors. CCE and Readyminds Offer Training for Distance Credentialed Counselors and Facilitators." [http://www.readyminds.com/about/ncc_vol23_no1_winter07.pdf]. 2007.

National Survey of Student Engagement. "Engaged Learning: Fostering Success for All Students." Bloomington, IN: Indiana University. [http://nsse.iub.edu/NSSE_2006_Annual_Report/docs/NSSE_2006_Annual_Report.pdf]. 2006.

Northern Arizona University. [http://www.distance.nau.edu/start/enrollment.aspx]. 2007.

Northern Virginia Community College. [http://enova.nvcc.edu/main/index/jhtml?default=true]. 2008.

Ohio Learning Network. [http://www.oln.org/discover/e4me.php]. 2007.

Penn State World Campus. [http://www.worldcampus.psu.edu/StudentServices.shtml]. 2007.

San Diego Community College. [http://www.ecounselsdcity.net/index.htm]. 2007.

Scarafiotti, C., and Cleveland-Innes, M. *The Times They Are A-Changing.* Needham, Mass.: Sloan Consortium. [http://www.sloan-c.org/publications/jaln/v10n2/pdf/v10n2_3scarafiotti.pdf]. 2006.

Shea, P., and Blakely, B. "Designing Web-based Student Services—Collaboration Style." In D. Burnett and D. Oblinger (Eds.), *Innovation in Student Services: Planning for Models Blending High Touch/High Tech.* Ann Arbor, MI: Society for College and University Planning, 2002.

Sturtz, A.J. "The Multiple Dimensions of Student Swirl." *Journal of Applied Research in the Community College,* 2006, 13(2), 151–158.

University of Chicago. [http://counseling.uchicago.edu/resources/virtualpamphlets/wellness.shtml]. 2008.

University of Maine. [http://www.learn.maine.edu/ocls/]. 2007.

University of Maryland University College. [http://www.umuc.edu/online_ed.shtml]. 2007.

University of Texas Telecampus. [http://www.telecampus.utsystem.edu/]. 2007.

University of Washington. [http://catalyst.washington.edu/help/index.html]. 2007.

U.S. Department of Education. *Evidence of Quality in Distance Education Programs Drawn From Interviews with the Accreditation Community* [http://www.itcnetwork.org/Accreditation-EvidenceofQualityinDEPrograms.pdf]. 2006.

Valencia Community College. [http://portal.valencia.cc.fl.us/cp/home/loginf]. 2007.

Walker, B. "Adult Learners Demand Education on Their Terms: Eduventures Explores the Scheduling and Format Preferences of Adult Learners." *eMediaWire.* [http://www.prweb.com/pingpr.php/Q3Jhcy1QaWdnLUhhbGYtU3VtbS1NYWduLVplcm8]. March 6, 2007.

Washington State University. [http://aswsu-ddp.wsu.edu]. 2007.

Western Cooperative for Educational Telecommunications. "Guidelines for Creating Student Services Online." [http://www.wcet.info/services/studentservices/beyond/guidelines/]. 2003.

Western Cooperative for Educational Telecommunications. "Best Practices for Electronically Offered Degree and Certificate Programs." [http://wcet.info/services/ publications/ accreditation/Accrediting_BestPractices.pdf]. 2001.

Zemsky, R. and Massy, W. *Thwarted Innovation: What Happened to E-Learning and Why*. University of Pennsylvania: Learning Alliance for Higher Education. [http://www.irhe. upenn.edu/WeatherStation.html]. 2004.

PART FOUR

HUMAN RESOURCES IN PROFESSIONAL PRACTICE

Supporting our students is the primary purpose of our profession, and staff are our primary resource in pursuing that purpose. The organization, recruitment, selection, supervision, and development of human capital, including our own capital, is an essential endeavor for the successful practice of student affairs. Chapter Sixteen by Linda Kuk offers an overview of traditional and cutting-edge organizational models for student affairs. Next, Michael Jackson, Larry Moneta, and Kelly Anne Nelson discuss staff management in Chapter Seventeen. The unique role of the middle manager is the focus of Chapter Eighteen by Don Mills. Through comparing and contrasting the role of the middle manager with those of the entry-level professional and senior student affairs officer, he also offers a portrait of the ways in which roles change over the full span of a career in our field. Chapters Nineteen and Twenty chart a host of options for student affairs professional development. In the former, Susan Komives and Stan Carpenter present a model for guiding professional development and describe a variety of professional development activities. In the latter, Mary Howard-Hamilton and Randy Hyman address questions related to pursuing doctoral education as a part of professional development in student affairs.

CHAPTER SIXTEEN

THE DYNAMICS OF ORGANIZATIONAL MODELS WITHIN STUDENT AFFAIRS

Linda Kuk

Student affairs is well established as an organizational unit within higher education, and its role has become an integral link to both student and institutional success. The foundation for the role of student affairs in higher education was laid many years ago. (See Chapter One for an extended discussion.) The specific components associated with this role and the organizational structures of student affairs units have continued to evolve and change. As student affairs has developed, its mission and purpose have evolved to focusing on serving the needs of students, fostering the academic success and personal development of students, and creating campus environments that support the educational mission of collegiate institutions. Over time, the structural issues of which units should constitute student affairs, how these units should be organized, to whom they should report, and how they should be managed have continued to evolve.

Today, student affairs organizations constitute a wide variety of operating units, programs, and services within nearly every higher educational institution in the United States. This growth and complexity was initially propelled by the tremendous growth in the number, diversity, and needs of students accessing higher education after World War II. From the late 1950s into the mid-1970s, higher educational institutions created separate student services structures to more specifically address the needs of students (Knock, 1985). Campus unrest, civil rights, and court cases challenging institutional *in loco parentis,* and First Amendment speech issues led to additional responsibilities and services from student affairs and increased its organizational complexity (Manning,

Kinzie, and Schuh, 2006). In recent decades, this growth and complexity has been sustained by the demands of consumer-oriented students and their families for greater access, greater educational and service amenities, and more individualized programs and services. In order to compete, higher educational institutions have added services, programs, and facilities to lure and retain students and to maintain and enhance the organizations' educational reputations.

The world around American higher education and the student affairs organizations within it are changing. Throughout higher education, there is increasing pressure for institutional accountability and for resources to align with the goals and mission of the institution (see Chapter Six). As we look to the future, there is a growing need to focus on how student affairs might more effectively reorganize programs and services to serve the changing needs of students and other constituent groups, in addition to addressing institution and student affairs division strategic goals. This chapter focuses on organizational design issues within student affairs organizations, common student affairs organizational models, and research and theory in the area of student affairs organizational design. It also offers several pertinent considerations for adopting a systemic approach to crafting student affairs organizational models in the future.

Organizational Design Issues in Student Affairs

Most student affairs organizations within American higher education institutions have historically been structured functionally. In recent decades, these structures have grown more complex and have evolved to address the specific needs of the students and the institutions they serve. As the needs for services and programs have grown, units were created and added to the existing organizational structures. Most of the student affairs organizational models utilized today are the result of institutional history, institutional type, state law, and institutional financial policies, as well as the individual preferences of institutional leadership.

For many, the concept of organizational models or structures has traditionally been captured in a rigid and static organizational chart. However, student affairs organizations are becoming increasingly more dynamic and process oriented. While there are current similarities in organizational models based on organizational mission and types of institutions, organizational design and structures within student affairs are not and cannot be fixed and permanent, especially in light of the ever-changing demands on student affairs programs and services. Most student affairs organizations have retained their functional characteristics in terms of structure. At the same time, committees, task forces, work groups, and other cross-functional teams have increasingly been used to enhance communication and to work more collaboratively across unit and department boundaries, especially in relation to faculty and academic affairs administrators. Unfortunately, most of these structures are short lived and are not imbedded into the fabric of the organization.

While there are a number of similarities in both organizational structure and process among student affairs organizations, there are also some distinct differences in what service and support units are a part of student affairs at various institutions. Most organizational portfolios include student activities, student programming, student clubs and organizations, student leadership programs, student volunteer and civic engagement programs, student counseling, student health, residence life, student recreation, multicultural student services and services for students from special populations with special needs, student conduct, and student mediation and advocacy services. Some student affairs organizations also include enrollment management, career services, student union management, alcohol and drug education programs, TRIO programs, retention programs and learning centers, and general student advising services. To a lesser extent, student affairs organizations include campus police and athletics.

The ongoing issue of what constitutes student affairs as an organizational unit on a given campus is not directly related to any obvious organizational factor other than organizational history and the desires of institutional leadership. Shuffling of units within, and in and out of, student affairs is a common occurrence and is reportedly the most common organizational change process impacting student affairs organizations (Kuk, 2007).

Where student affairs fits organizationally within the larger institution continues to be a critical issue facing student affairs divisions and their leadership. As institutional growth and complexity has increased, the relationship of student affairs to institutional decision making has tended to change and become increasingly merged within the academic organizational units of institutions. While these changes have been in line with philosophical changes in institutional foci, the direct impact on student affairs programs and services and the students they serve is unclear and remains a critical concern to student affairs organizations.

Like other areas within higher education, many student affairs organizations have suffered from decreased resources, and they have not always been able to restore resources that have been lost to budget reduction. Many student affairs leaders live in dread of when the next resource cuts will come, or how they will stretch the existing resources to best serve the increasing numbers and diverse needs reflected in their student populations. As a result, many student affairs organizational models reflect a patchwork of making do with the resources, both human and fiscal, that the organization has at its disposal.

In a recent survey (Kuk, 2007), which was part of a more comprehensive study related to student affairs organizational design, Senior Student Affairs Officers (SSAOs) reported how they conceptualized their current student affairs structures and issues of structural change. The results are summarized in the next section.

Organizational Structures

In examining the organizational models utilized by student affairs divisions across a variety of institutional types, the models selected were essentially functional in nature, with distinct functional units reporting through a varied number of hierarchical levels. While the specific individual functional units within a given student affairs division varied greatly, the organizational structures themselves looked very similar no matter what type of collegiate institution they were in. All of the structures were hierarchical and pyramid shaped in design. No other variations in organizational structure were reported as being used within student affairs.

Some of the larger organizations appeared to have a form of a *matrix* or *lateral* structure integrated across their primary functional structures, but these structures were not a prominent part of the organization's design, and the existence of this aspect of the structural model was not consciously noted by any respondent. It is likely that these structures were added to enable increasingly complex and specialized organizations to communicate across the existing organizational units and to create greater efficiency in commonly used resources and services. The smaller organizations appeared to address the communication and efficiency issues by having staff assume some generalist and cross-over responsibilities among functional areas and by having a flatter, less complex structure. Most of the smaller organizations had directors of functional units reporting directly to the SSAO, while the larger organizations had at least one layer of management in between the SSAO and unit directors. The directors of functional units reported through these management layers to the SSAO.

The smaller student affairs organizations appeared to have more generalists engaged in a variety of responsibilities, while the larger and more complex organizations had more specialists. As a result, the larger organizations appeared more complex, with more hierarchical layers and staff performing more specialized functions, resulting in more overall units in the organization. The organizations differed in which units reported to which higher level within the structure and how many hierarchical levels were represented in the organizational structure.

In addition to the wide variation in which functional units were included in student affairs, the biggest differences in structural design across all types of institutions appeared in the areas of span of control and hierarchical levels. The number of staff directly reporting to SSAOs varied greatly, spanning from four to seventeen people, and the number of levels within the organizations also varied. Most of the organizations appeared to have at least three hierarchical levels within the student affairs division, but many had four or five levels of hierarchy.

The variation in types of units, the span of control within the divisions, and the number of hierarchical levels within a division did not appear to be directly related to organizational type. For example, having large spans of people reporting at various levels or having three or four levels of hierarchy was not directly related to the type of institution. Differences in which institutional units reported to student affairs and which did not were found across all types of institutions. There was no pattern of what constituted student affairs by institutional type or size of institution.

However, the perceived and/or real availability of resources may be a factor that has influenced the design of student affairs organizations, especially in relation to levels of hierarchy and spans of control. Kuk (2007) found that the SSAOs' perceptions about the amount and quality of existing human resources within their organization in relationship to their perceived level of need may have influenced both their organizational spans of control and the number of levels within the organizational hierarchies. Where the SSAO respondents expressed concern about the shortage of or need for more staff within their organization, the student affairs organizations appeared to be flatter, and the SSAOs and their directors appeared to have more units reporting directly to them. In most of these cases, the SSAO also expressed concerns about having too many direct reports, or no resources to hire a desired associate or assistant senior-level staff person. Also, in most of these cases, the directors of the organization reported directly to the SSAO without a level of management in between. This relationship between structure and perception of resources was present in all types of institutions regardless of institutional size or type.

Organizational Change and Redesign

In the Kuk study (2007), only a small number of the respondents indicated that they had redesigned their current student affairs organizational structure at some time during their time as the SSAO. Most reported that these changes occurred when the SSAO first assumed the role at his or institution. It was also reported that the organizational changes that were made were very modest changes, such as shifting reporting lines among various units.

The majority of SSAOs indicated that they were happy with their organizational structures and/or did not intend to make any major organizational changes in the near future. Only two SSAOs respondents reported conducting major organizational audits and implementing major organizational changes when they first took over as the SSAO at their institutions. Some SSAOs reported that, although they desired to make changes in their organizational structure, they believed that the political consequences were too great or they needed to wait for some of their staff to retire before they could make desired changes.

When asked about reasons they had or would use for deciding to redesign the student affairs division, the responding SSAOs identified five reasons they used for making organizational changes. They included (1) to address financial concerns; (2) to meet strategic priorities; (3) to enhance efficiencies and effectiveness; (4) to promote teamwork and collaboration; and (5) to reduce hierarchical approaches to decision making. None of the SSAOs indicated they would redesign the organization to work differently or to collaborate differently. No one indicated that they were thinking about an organizational model that was different than the hierarchical, functional structures they were presently utilizing.

Common Student Affairs Organizational Models

Hirt (Chapter Two) discusses the importance of institutional mission as it relates to higher education. Current student affairs organizational structures appear to be closely aligned with their mission, and organizational type (Hirt, 2006; Kuk, 2007). In recent years, institutions have sought out best practices based on institutional types and comparable missions, and this may have enhanced the similarities in student affairs organizational structures. The following are summaries of common organizational models used within student affairs organizations based on organizational mission and type (Hirt, 2006; Kuk, 2007).

Baccalaureate Colleges

The student affairs organizational structure of most baccalaureate and liberal arts colleges are modest in scope and hierarchical depth. These organizations have few professional staff that serve a primarily small-scale residential student body. These organizations are usually led by a dean of students or vice president for student affairs, with assistants and associates who both manage functional units and also serve in a generalist capacity. While the assistants and associates may have functional responsibility for a particular area, such as housing, student activities, or counseling, the levels within the organization are not very deep, and staff often cross over various student affairs service areas. For example, a residence hall director may be responsible for a residence hall and also advise student groups or provide advising and/or counseling to the general student population. These student affairs organizations may have closer formal and informal ties with the academic units within the college. In some cases, student affairs may report through a dean of the college or an academic dean to the president, or they may report directly to the president and be part of the college's executive management team.

Master's Colleges and Universities

These institutions are generally larger and have more complex student affairs organizations than baccalaureate colleges with more defined hierarchical and functional units. At the same time, they may still retain a level of generalist responsibilities within functional units. These organizational structures are generally not very hierarchical or deep with regard to numbers of staff in each unit. As a result, the staff within these functional units may have a breadth of responsibilities and serve a more generalist role covering many responsibilities within the unit. For example, residence life personnel may serve as residence hall directors and housing assignment personnel and handle student conduct or other administrative or student development functions within their operation. Student activities personnel may work with student organizations, advise the campus programming board, and conduct student leadership activities.

These organizations, while functional in structure, often are served by centralized budgeting and human resource operations and receive resource services from other institutional units such as facilities, maintenance, and security. If auxiliary units do exist, they are likely to report, wholly or in part, to the finance or administrative division and collaborate with student affairs where the two divisions overlap, such as in the administration of housing or college unions operations. The specific functional units within student affairs organizations vary among institutions, with public institutions more frequently including enrollment service areas and private institutions having a separate enrollment management unit or division. Student affairs organization leaders in these types of institutions more frequently report directly to the president and serve as a member of the cabinet or executive team of the institution.

Research and Doctoral Granting Universities

Student affairs organizations at research and doctoral granting institutions are generally the most complex among higher educational institutions. Serving large numbers of students, these organizations are more hierarchical and specialized within their functional units than other types of organizations. Staff responsibilities are likely to be very specialized. For example, an individual staff member's exclusive role may be to provide training for residence hall staff or to advise the university programming board.

A vice president for student affairs or an associate provost generally leads these organizations. In addition, there may be a number of associate or assistant vice presidents or provosts managing the day-to-day responsibilities of a number of functional units. This added layer of organization is seldom found in other types of student affairs organizations. The breadth and complexity of these organizations require a number of layers and may at times have other *matrix* organizational structure overlays, such as division committees or budgeting and technology units that provide for organizational coordination and divisionwide services to all functional units.

These organizations are also more likely to have auxiliary and fee-funded areas that operate as decentralized units that generate their own revenue and expend their resources within their own areas. The organizational structure of these units is often influenced by state and/or institutional financial laws and regulations that govern the use and accounting of auxiliary operational funds. Because of the auxiliary nature of these units, the complexity of these organizations is often increased with the inclusion of accounting, maintenance, custodial, service, commercial sales and marketing, and security personnel that are not generally found in student affairs organizations at other types of institutions. While these types of student affairs organizations have more decentralized control of their programs and services at the unit level, their complexity, multiple organizational layers, and specialization often provide for less financial flexibility and staff mobility within the student affairs organization as a whole.

In recent years, student affairs organizations at research institutions have increasingly been shifted to report to the provost or senior academic officer or senior vice president of the institution and not directly to the president. In most cases, the student affairs leader retains a voice on the executive team or cabinet but does not meet directly with the president on a regular basis. At some institutions enrollment management is part of the student affairs organization, and at others enrollment management is a separate division within the institution.

Associate's Colleges

Student affairs at associate's colleges, also known as community colleges, is a relatively newer organizational entity than at other types of institutions. Student affairs at most community colleges consists of providing student services and academic support services focused on enhancing student success. These organizations may include enrollment service units, counseling, academic advising, transfer services, and student activities, as well as other student engagement and leadership-related campus services and programs.

Community colleges generally serve local and/or regional student populations and have not traditionally provided student services for campus residential students, such as residence halls, health centers, and recreation centers. As a result, they have not had these types of functional units as part of the student affairs organizational portfolio. Since these institutions are not residentially focused, they may provide services for students who take evening classes, but since students leave campus at the end of their day, these student affairs organizations are not required to organize their programs and services to cover a 24/7 operation. However, some community colleges are building residence halls and recreation centers and essentially are becoming residential colleges. With the addition of these facilities and service units to the student affairs portfolios, the mission and organizational foci of these units will likely change.

At community colleges, student affairs may report to a vice president or a dean responsible for both academic and student affairs, or they may report directly to the campus president or campus chief executive officer (CEO). In either case, student affairs is more closely tied to academic units within the institution and is generally not viewed as being as separate and distinct, as may be the case in other institutional types.

Theory and Research Related to Organizational Design

Unfortunately, there has not been a great deal of research devoted to understanding organizational design and structural models within student affairs organizations. While early references to student personnel services were descriptive of the type of services and programs that should be provided, these efforts did not clearly discuss what organizational structure or reporting lines should be used to organize and provide these programs and services. Most assumed that functional structures were the only way to organize student affairs, and the many past discussions focused on variations of this basic organizational paradigm. More recent student affairs literature (Allen and Cherrey, 2000; Hirt, 2006; Love and Estanek, 2004; Manning and others, 2006; Strange and Banning, 2001) has offered several more diverse general philosophical models and guiding principles related to organizational design issues and strategies. However, many of these models do not specifically deal with organizational structural design issues, and they also do not provide practical application of how these philosophical orientations are orchestrated to produce student affairs organizational structures.

Birnbaum (1988) applied the concepts of systems and used five typological models of organizational functioning to describe the various ways collegiate organizations function. These models included (1) the collegiate institution, (2) the bureaucratic institution, (3) the political institution, (4) the anarchical institution, and (5) the cybernetic institution. Kuh (1989) identified four conventional models for examining different organizations. These models included (1) the rational model, (2) the bureaucratic model, (3) the collegiate model, and (4) the political model. These models closely resemble the four organizational frames of theory and research outlined by Bolman and Deal (2003).

Ambler (1993) conducted a survey of more than one hundred student affairs divisions and found a wide variety of unique and different organizational structures. Ambler (2000) later repeated the distribution of the survey to the same sample of student affairs programs and found that many had experienced institutional changes that impacted their divisions' structures. Some of these changes included the adoption of the provost model, establishment of an executive officer for enrollment management, increased use of technology, and the privatization of some services. He found that despite these changes, four basic models of management structures for student affairs remained in the institutions he surveyed. These included (1) the revenue source model, (2) the affinity of services model, (3) the staff associates model, and (4) the direct supervision model.

The *revenue source model* was found in institutions that utilize an auxiliary services funding model. In these types of organizations, their own revenue streams funded the auxiliary units. The student affairs organizational structure that existed reflected the number of such units and size of the units within the organization as well as the financial requirements of the institution or state. Within the *affinity of services model*, the functional units were clustered by their common or like purposes. This model was most common in larger complex organizations with a large number of functional units. The *staff associate model* was often used to provide technical or specialized services within a division of student affairs through the use of staff personnel that provided specific services to the division as a whole. These divisionwide services might have included budgeting, personnel, staff development, and research. The *direct supervisory model* was usually found in smaller organizations where the SSAOs had all the line, functional directors reporting directly to them.

In *Systematic Leadership*, Allen and Cherrey (2000) applied the ideas of systems and learning organizations to student affairs organizations, leadership, structures, and student affairs practice. They discussed the idea of fragmentation and its application to traditional hierarchical organizations. They offered the idea of connectivity and networking as a more systems-focused view of how student affairs organizations could become more effective. They discussed a vision based on new ways of relating, new ways of influencing change, new ways of learning, and new ways of leading. Allen and Cherrey also argued that student affairs practitioners' thinking needed to change in several ways in order to integrate these new dimensions of organizing and implementing student affairs practice.

Strange and Banning (2001) created a comprehensive model for student-friendly and learning-supportive environments. They focused on the dimensions of organizational environments, the organization's structural anatomy, dynamics, and the relationship to these environmental dimensions that created effective learning environments within college campuses.

In their work on rethinking student affairs practice, Love and Estanek (2004) used organizational development theory and new science ideas to challenge student affairs practitioners to think differently about their work, student affairs structures, and processes, and to adopt new models for change.

Hirt (2006) focused on understanding the professional life of student affairs practitioners at six different types of higher educational institutions. This portrait depicted the distinctive differences in how student affairs work is carried out at different types of institutions and what differing skills and understanding are needed to be effective practitioners. While her work does not directly address issues of organizational structure, it makes a strong case for viewing institutional type and the context of student affairs work as critical factors in creating unique organizational designs and structures, strongly aligned with the institution's mission and goals.

Manning and others (2006) discussed the organization of student affairs work based on a study of twenty high-performing colleges and universities. This work highlighted the history of student affairs organizations as well as contemporary issues that have an impact on organizational structures within student affairs. They suggested that there are three approaches to student affairs work that influenced the organization of student affairs: (1) student services, (2) student development, and (3) student learning. Manning and others build a strong case for asserting that the structure of student affairs should be closely shaped and aligned with the mission of the institution.

From their analyses of the interviews and their review of student affairs literature, they identified eleven student affairs organizational models. Six traditional models were developed through an analysis of the student affairs literature, and five new innovative models grew out of the Documenting Effective Educational Practices (DEEP) Project they conducted. Tables 16.1 and 16.2 summarize the two sets of models.

TABLE 16.1 TRADITIONAL MODELS OF STUDENT AFFAIRS PRACTICE

Models	Description	Assumptions
Extracurricular Model	Organized to provide student life and student development	Student affairs is entirely separate from academic affairs
Functional Silos Model	Organized to operate from a management and leadership approach rather than student development	Units perform their functions and services as discrete entities, and integration and communication is achieved through loose coordination
Student Service Model	Organized to operate from a management and leadership perspective. Services often cluster together with the focus on providing quality programs and services, with close coordination of like units	There is minimal if any integration of programs with academic units
Competitive/ Adversarial Model	Student affairs units operate independent of academic units	Student affairs and academic affairs units are concerned with what students learn and how they grow, but there is little acknowledgement of the contribution of the other
Co-Curricular Model	Student affairs and academic affairs have complementary, yet different missions, and each acknowledges the contributions of the other to student learning	Both student affairs and academic affairs units are concerned with student learning
Seamless Learning Model	Student learning experiences are conceived as integrated and continuously happening across all aspects of the student experience and campus life.	Every member of the institution and the student affairs organization can contribute to learning; the mission of the institution and all its units are dedicated to the total student learning experience

Source: Adapted from Manning and others (2006).

Manning and her colleagues (2006) concluded that there is more than one way to practice student affairs work and that there is no single best organizational model for student affairs practice. "Rather careful consideration of the campus culture, hard work, thoughtful reflection, and a clear understanding of how student affairs can facilitate student success are essential ingredients in developing student affairs organizations that truly are effective" (p. 34). This work provides a sound philosophical framework for linking student affairs organizational design to the educational focus and strategic mission and goals of student affairs organizations, but it does not provide any guidance or models on how to restructure organizations to ensure the creation of this vital link.

TABLE 16.2 INNOVATIVE MODELS OF STUDENT AFFAIRS PRACTICE

Models	Description	Assumptions
Student-Centered, Ethic of Care Model	Center on care and relationships; fundamental response to address what students need to be successful; goal of facilitating student success through the integration of service, policies, and programs	All practices are centered on the ethic of care; focuses on students who have the most need of support
Student-Driven Model	Student involvement and leadership serve as core operating principles, and valuing students as integral members of the community. Students have a strong voice in governing the organization. Students drive campus activities and make key decisions about campus life.	Student learning is enhanced by greater student involvement and engagement, and identification with the institution contributes to student persistence and success
Student Agency Model	Students assume as much responsibility as possible in the development of their learning experiences by managing campus life and helping to design curriculum; students serve as workers in providing a wide range of student services and programs	Students have the primary role and responsibility for their learning and their education; are completely responsible for student life, and they perform as full and equal partners with faculty and staff in these efforts
Academic-Student Affairs Collaboration Model	Student affairs and academic affairs emphasize mutual territory and combine efforts to engender student engagement and success; work is supported with tightly coupled student affairs structures and philosophies that support student learning and success	Student affairs and academic affairs units place student learning at the center of their goals and activities and create institutional coherence about student success; assumes seamless collaboration between student affairs and academic affairs units on a routine basis
Academic-Centered Model	Organized around the academic core and promotes the academic experience over co-curricular activities; student affairs serves as a support to the academic focus of the institution and is almost invisible in the academic focus	Student affairs and academic units place student learning at the center of their goals and activities; both share responsibility for student success

Source: Adapted from Manning and others (2006).

Kuk's (2007) survey of senior student affairs officers asked respondents to ascertain which of the philosophical practice organizational models (Manning and others, 2006) they utilize within their student affairs organizations. The most frequently used model was reported to be the co-curricular learning model. In this model, student affairs and academic affairs have complementary yet different missions, and each acknowledges the contributions of the other to student learning. Another third of the respondents indicated that their organizational structure was reflected in the seamless learning model, in which student learning experiences are conceived as integrated and continuously happening across all aspects of the student experience and campus life.

When asked which model they would choose if they could redesign their division to reflect a new model, nearly half of the respondents indicated that they would not pick a different model. Other SSAOs responded that they would change to one of three models, the seamless learning model, the academic-student affairs collaboration model, or the co-curricular learning model. The other models were not indicated.

Student affairs organizations, especially in larger public institutions, appear to have retained the complex hierarchical, functional structures that have evolved over the past several decades, and there is little indication of a desire to change these structures very much, if at all. Yet, the philosophies and perceptions of organizational models being used by student affairs divisions to define their practice seem to have shifted away from the extracurricular and administrative organizational models that were traditionally used within student affairs operations (Manning and others, 2006) to philosophical models that are learning and academic-centered.

It is unclear whether student affairs organizations will be able to adapt their current functional structures to effectively implement the new philosophical models they have adopted, or if they can recreate new organizational structures to be effective in addressing the changing demands being placed on student affairs organizations. Most of the recent research and theory about organizational viability and survival being conducted within the business sector would suggest that such shifts are not generally possible (Ashkenas, Ulrich, Jick, and Kerr, 2002; Galbraith, 2002; and Hesselbein, Goldsmith, and Beckhard, 1997). It is clear that additional research needs to occur about student affairs organizations to better understand their changing dynamics and to determine how they might craft their organizations to better accomplish their changing missions and goals.

New Approaches to Organizational Design and Structure

Research and experience has demonstrated that there is no single correct way to structure student affairs organizations (Ambler, 2000; Barr, 1993; and Sandeen and Barr, 2006). But this does not mean that there is not a need to engage in structural change and organizational redesign. In fact, student affairs organizations should be structured to address the strategic mission of the institution and the division they serve. At the same time, the structure should fit with the needs of the institution and the surrounding external environment in which it exists. This means that as the institution's priorities or directions change, or the environment surrounding the institution changes, the student affairs organization must be willing and able to change as well.

In today's student affairs world, organizational structures and models do not have to be silo grounded and functionally fixed. In fact, the current approach may not be the most effective way to organize student affairs organizations in the future. New research and theory on organizational design suggest modern organizations need to be flexible, responsive, collaborative and adaptive (Ashkenas and others, 2002; Galbraith, 2002; and Hesselbein and others, 1997).

Fluidity and adaptability are key characteristics in future organizational designs (Galbraith, 2002; Hesselbein and others, 1997; Senge, 1990, 2006). Organizational structure is concerned with how individuals, groups, and systems organize their time, energy, and resources to accomplish goals. Adaptive organizations continually align resources and strategies to address institutional and divisional strategic goals and attempt to become more efficient and effective in the allocation and deployment of resources, especially human resources. Fluidity, in this regard, refers to being able to adapt easily, changing priorities, strategies, and resources in the midst of shifting organizational direction. The notion that structure assumes a fixed or stationary position for indefinite periods of time is no longer realistic. New types of organizational structures must be aligned to meet institutional goals and at the same time be fluid enough to be able to change as goals and strategies change.

Different types of institutions may have different environmental, political, and economic issues that impact the design and structure of student affairs. These differences will likely be reflected in the institution's mission and strategic goals and should be evident in the organizational structure as well. The goal of any design process should be to craft an organizational structure that best fits the environmental needs of the institution and most effectively promotes the strategic goals of the organization. Student affairs divisions should have a strategic plan that is aligned with the institutional strategic plan and that is used as the guiding vision for its organizational redesign and resource allocation process. Many student affairs organizations do not have a strategic plan (Kuk, 2007).

Efforts to design effective student affairs organizations should also take into consideration the needs and challenges presented by the diversity among the students and other constituent groups it serves. For example, residential campuses might create a very different structure than would a commuter-oriented student affairs organization. Institutions with large numbers of underserved populations or disadvantaged populations may create different structures than organizations that will serve more traditional or economically advantaged students. Urban institutions may have different structural needs than more rural institutions. As student needs change and the demographic dimensions of students shift, the organizational structure of student affairs will need to adjust to these changes. Simply adding more specialty functional units that serve very distinct populations is not likely to remain the preferred response to changing demands. Given the restraints on new resources and increasing accountability, the student affairs organizations of the future will more likely be asked to restructure existing resources to serve changing needs and new student demands instead of receiving new allocations.

Technology, and its integration into higher education teaching, learning, and service delivery processes, will continue to grow and change the way student affairs does its work. As a result, technology will have a key impact on student affairs organizational models. Student demands for one-source service locations and anytime, any place access will be greatly aided by advances in technology. At the same time, these expectations for anytime technology access will likely place greater demands on those areas and needs that cannot be easily served by technology. Student affairs organizations will likely be asked to adjust to the demands for 24/7 real-time services, individualized to meet the needs of each student, and also to provide continuity of individual service from orientation to graduation and beyond. These types of service and accompanying resource demands will likely influence how services are structured and, as a result, influence the larger student affairs organization.

A Systematic Approach to Organization Structural Design

Student affairs leaders and their staffs may want to step back and assess their current organizational structures in terms of organizational effectiveness. Are the current functional silos that permeate the organizational structures of most student affairs units really the most effective way to realize the institutions' and divisions' strategic missions and goals? Do emerging assessment plans adequately provide for assessing organizational design and structural effectiveness? What is on the horizon that will demand new ways of providing student focused programs and services, and how will student affairs adapt to these demands and expectations? How can student affairs leaders think differently about how to organize, deliver, and coordinate their services and programs?

Not many senior student affairs officers have the opportunity to start from scratch as they craft the organizational structure for their division. Most inherit an organizational model, and they are clearly limited by available resources, both human and fiscal. Neither of these factors, however, need become a deterrent to making necessary and effective changes. In fact, limitations on resources may present a sound and compelling reason for a student affairs organization to undergo an organization redesign process. Applying an effective change strategy that is well thought out and includes securing staff and organizational buy-in is critical to the success and sustainability of any redesign process. The following are points for consideration as plans for organizational assessment and redesign are contemplated. These include creating a strategic plan; focusing on organizational strengths, priorities, and resources within the organization; crafting the leadership role; considering alternative organization structural elements; and building into the change process assessment for organizational effectiveness.

Strategic Plan

Student affairs leaders might want to create or update their strategic plan and ensure that it is in line with the institution's mission and strategic goals. This plan provides the basis and guiding map for examining and redesigning an organizational structure. An organization's structures should grow out of its strategic priorities.

Organizational Strengths

It is critical to conduct and maintain a thorough and comprehensive assessment of resources (human, financial, facilities, and so on). It is essential that the leadership within student affairs determine the strengths of the organization and the individuals within the organization. Uncovering and building on the strengths of an organization is a productive way of securing buy-in and of helping to dispel negative fears and threats to change. Too often leaders focus on the negative or on problems and miss opportunities to build on strengths that allow them to create new learning opportunities for individual staff and the entire organization.

Priorities and Resources

Successful redesign requires first a realistic determination of what needs to be done to accomplish the strategic plan. Second, it requires a careful alignment of resources to address the strategic priorities. This process should not be defined or held hostage by what an organization does not have in terms of new resources. A common mindset that change can only happen by adding more resources often inhibits the ability to make constructive and creative change. It is easy to become paralyzed by the notion that there are not enough resources.

Organizational redesign and structural changes can very successfully be accomplished with no or very little additional resources. What is required is getting people in the organization to think differently about what they do and how they do it. This process requires a willingness to reconfigure organizational resources and approach establishing institutional and division priorities openly and honestly. More fundamentally, it requires leaders to think very differently about how work is done, who does it, and how it is rewarded. This type of redesign might require an investment in professional development, retooling, and cross-training of staff. But these costs can usually be recaptured through realignment and rethinking work, structure, and organizational priorities.

Leadership

The student affairs leadership should be responsible for crafting the agenda of what needs to be redesigned within the organization and will likely want to involve the various divisional units in the process. It is easy for such a process to get sidetracked or derailed without a clear and consistent focus. The leadership may want to secure the assistance of an outside consultant to help frame the difficult and important issues that need to be faced in regard to matching and reallocating resources and in setting priorities and helping to steer the change process. Having a neutral, guiding perspective can help the process retain its integrity and its focus.

Consideration of Structural Options

Once the desired roles within the organization are defined and aligned to work responsibilities, a variety of organizational philosophical and structural models might be considered and appropriately adopted to align the roles to work effectively together. It is critical to think creatively. It is at this point that organizational structure takes shape and should reflect the changing nature and requirements of the student affairs organizational goals and expectations. Structures and/or structural elements other than silo, functional structures should be strongly considered and integrated into the design as appropriate.

Assessment

As the student affairs leaders consider the elements of redesigning they might also consider how they want to assess the organization's ongoing effectiveness. How will effective performance and progress toward achieving the mission and goals be measured and rewarded? How will the change process be managed, and who will be assigned accountability for various elements within the change process and the implementation of the final plan? Assessment is a very critical component of the design process in that it enables the organization to both gauge its effectiveness and to know when and how it needs to adapt to change in the future.

Organizational structure and design is dynamic. It should be about creating organizational environments that maximize opportunities for creativity and achievement of goals and strategies. It should be about being able to adapt to change and to ensure that resources are efficiently allocated in the interests of students and the institution's mission. At its core, organizational structure is about being effective!

Conclusion

Student affairs organizations have evolved over the past century to be a major complex organizational unit within most American colleges and universities. Their growth has fostered the development of complex functional organizations that have served students and their institutions well. In their current form, student affairs organizational models are functional in form and most closely are aligned with the institutional mission and type. These models continue to reflect a number of unresolved concerns and issues around what units should be included in student affairs, how student affairs organizations should be designed to serve the changing needs of students and institutional goals, how student affairs should be aligned within the greater institution's organization, and how student affairs leaders should respond to the changing dynamics within their organizations. Given the changing nature of student affairs work and the greater societal pressures for accountability and individualized services, student affairs organizations may need to adapt new organizational models in order to become more effective in achieving the strategic goals and missions of the institutions and the students they serve.

Over the years, not much attention has been paid to research and the development of theory related to student affairs organizations. Student affairs scholars have more recently begun to explore the dimensions of organizational structure and design and have proposed changes, philosophical practices, and organizational models that might advance the development of student affairs' organizational structures to meet emerging needs. In the future, organizational design and structure should be viewed as a dynamic process within the student affairs organization and critical to its ability to be effective.

References

Allen, K. E., and Cherrey, C. *Systemic Leadership: Enriching the Meaning of Our Work*. Lanham, Md.: American College Personnel Association and the National Association for Campus Activities, 2000.

Ambler, D. "Organizational and Administrative Models." In M. J. Barr and M. K. Desler (Eds.), *The Handbook of Student Affairs Administration* (2nd ed.). San Francisco: Jossey-Bass, 2000.

Ambler, D. A. "Developing Internal Management Structures." In M. J. Barr (Eds.), *The Handbook of Student Affairs Administration* (1st ed.). San Francisco: Jossey-Bass, 1993.

Ashkenas, R., Ulrich, D., Jick, T., and Kerr, S. *The Boundaryless Organization: Breaking the Chains of Organizational Structure*. San Francisco: Jossey-Bass, 2002.

Barr, M. J. "Organizational and Administrative Models." In M. J. Barr (Ed.), *The Handbook of Student Affairs Administration* (1st ed.). San Francisco: Jossey-Bass, 1993.

Birnbaum, R. *How Colleges Work*. San Francisco: Jossey-Bass, 1988.

Bolman, L. G., and Deal, T. E. *Reframing Organizations: Artistry, Choice and Leadership* (3rd ed.). San Francisco: Jossey-Bass, 2003.

Galbraith, J. R. *Designing Organizations: An Executive Guide to Strategy, Structure and Process*. San Francisco: Jossey-Bass, 2002.

Hesselbein, F., Goldsmith, M., and Beckhard, R. *The Organization of the Future*. New York: Jossey-Bass, 1997.

Hirt, J. B. *Where You Work Matters*. Lanham, Md.: University Press of America, 2006.

Knock, G. H. "Development of Student Services in Higher Education." In M. J. Barr and L. A. Keating and Associates (Eds.), *Developing Effective Student Services Programs: Systemic Approaches for Practitioners*. San Francisco: Jossey-Bass, 1985.

Kuh, G. D. "Organizational Concepts and Influences." In U. Delworth and G. R. Hanson (Eds.), *Student Services: A Handbook for the Profession* (2nd ed.). San Francisco: Jossey-Bass, 1989.

Kuk, L. "Designing Student Affairs Organizations." Unpublished raw data, 2007.

Love, P. G., and Estanek, S. M. *Rethinking Student Affairs Practice*. San Francisco: Jossey-Bass, 2004.

Manning, K., Kinzie, J., and Schuh, J. *One Size Does Not Fit All: Traditional and Innovative Models of Student Affairs Practice*. New York: Routledge, Taylor and Francis Group, 2006.

Sandeen, A., and Barr, M. J. *Critical Issues for Student Affairs: Challenges and Opportunities*. San Francisco: Jossey-Bass, 2006.

Senge, P. M. *The Fifth Discipline: The Art and Practice of the Learning Organization*. New York: Doubleday/Currency, 1990.

Senge, P. M. "The Leader's New World: Building Learning Organizations." In J. V. Gallos (Ed.), *Organization Development*. San Francisco: Jossey-Bass, 2006.

Strange, C. C., and Banning, J. H. *Educating by Design: Creating Campus Learning Environments That Work*. San Francisco: Jossey-Bass, 2001.

CHAPTER SEVENTEEN

EFFECTIVE MANAGEMENT OF HUMAN CAPITAL IN STUDENT AFFAIRS

Michael L. Jackson, Larry Moneta, and Kelly Anne Nelson

The goal of this chapter is to provide information on recruitment, selection, supervision, professional development, and retention of student affairs professionals. It will assist senior-level student affairs leaders in improving existing programs and practices. New and midlevel professionals will also find it useful since the information discussed will help them better understand what institutions and the profession of student affairs can provide them as they navigate their careers. Ultimately, however, this chapter hopes to reinforce the idea that human capital is the greatest asset of any student affairs division.

Producing a fairly brief body of commentary focused on the human resource needs of a student affairs organization has complexities that make the task difficult, if not impossible. For example, are recruitment issues comparable for institutions in major market, urban areas versus those in rural parts of the country? Do private institutions have advantages (particularly financial ones) that influence staff retention and career development? Since smaller institutions tend to offer broader role definition and generalist cross-training, is this of preference to some candidates? Conversely, does the specialized nature of jobs at large universities advantage them in the recruitment and selection process?

Clearly, these questions address but a minute segment of all the issues associated with institutional type, geographic distinctions, size and wealth, and the many other characteristics that distinguish American colleges and universities from one another. Even among student affairs divisions themselves, we find organizational diversity that challenges our capacity to offer generalizable assertions (Manning, Kinzie, and Schuh 2006). Institutional reporting structures, degrees of autonomy, and scope of authority and oversight all, to some degree, influence the relative attractiveness of a particular role and position and can, despite comparability in prospect recruitment and job rewards, influence the likelihood of winning candidate acceptance of a particular job offer.

Perhaps most important are the distinctions found within the field of student affairs and the substantially different role definitions and requirements associated with the many subprofessions that comprise student affairs. When we speak of student affairs, are we making reference to the generalist jobs found in deans' roles at smaller colleges, senior student affairs positions at universities, departmental roles and functions, or all of the above?

With smaller institutions increasingly resembling the specialized constructs of larger colleges and most universities, the issue of function diffusion and fragmentation is increasingly universal. Student affairs has evolved into a label defining a collection of student (but not only student) services focused primarily (but not exclusively) on the human and developmental dimension of college students, both undergraduate and graduate or professional.

The process of finding, hiring, and keeping competent managers of the overall entity is quite daunting. As we look beyond the "top-down" staffing needs of student affairs, we discover a far more challenging environment. Are the human resource approaches identical for career centers and women's centers, for religious life programs and student activities offices, for judicial affairs and enrollment management? All of these are commonly found within student affairs portfolios, as are quite often units distinctive to one campus or another. For example, oversight of the golf course at the University of Maryland is in student affairs. Student affairs at Indiana University oversees both parking and transportation services. Many student affairs deans, particularly at smaller schools, supervise athletic programs, and we certainly recognize the unique challenges in hiring, retaining, and, often, firing coaches.

All of this is offered to highlight the difficulty in presenting in one chapter valid, pertinent, and generalizable information regarding the human resource needs of student affairs. Yet, with this disclaimer in place, more can be said regarding differentiation. Human resource management of entry-level, middle management, and senior positions require differing strategies that in subsequent sections are acknowledged.

Recruitment

As noted previously, prospect pools will differ widely for various roles and functions. Some may be local and others national (and occasionally international).

Historically, many student affairs professional roles, particularly at the entry and middle management levels, were filled through recruitment efforts at two national conferences: National Association of Student Personnel Administrators (NASPA) and American College Personnel Association (ACPA). Additionally, there are other smaller, more focused job-matching gatherings that supplement the large conference-supported placement events. These approaches remain important and viable, perhaps more so with a 2007 announcement of a comprehensive partnership between NASPA and the Association of College and University Housing Officers-International (ACUHO-I), in concert with other professional associations, to create an even more substantial student affairs career enterprise.

A survey of recruitment practices (Winston, Torres, Carpenter, McIntire, and Peterson, 2001) examined the frequency of use of several methods for announcing entry-level and midlevel vacancies. The authors found that word of mouth (supplementing the required public listing) was the most common way of announcing a position, used for 85 percent of entry-level and 87 percent of midlevel vacancies. Additionally, it was reported that positions were listed on a professional association Web site or listserv (51 percent entry level, 63 percent midlevel), at a student affairs placement conference (53 percent entry level, 58 percent midlevel), in the *Chronicle of Higher Education* (40 percent entry level, 86 percent midlevel), and in publications that target underrepresented populations (37 percent entry level, 51 percent midlevel). However, the diversification of roles as described earlier, coupled with the profession's continued commitment to diversification, suggest that new and more creative approaches may be necessary. These approaches include expanded advertising in print publications, the use of search firms, recruitment through various professional associations and conferences, online methods, and informal networking.

Print publications include newspapers (for example, the *Chronicle of Higher Education* and the *New York Times Careers in Education*), professional newsletters, and various magazines. Generally these sources will be most useful for specialized roles that can be featured in job-specific publications. It is also important to remember that print publications that require paid subscriptions vary in the size of their subscriber base. Print publications, some of which also offer online editions, can vary in price quite significantly and, depending on publication frequency, may take several weeks to print a posting.

The use of search firms has historically been limited to senior student affairs positions and rarely used for jobs below the level of dean or assistant vice president. Increasingly, however, search firms are available with specialty practices associated with various professions. These include health and counseling specialties, residence life and housing, career services, and more. The role of a search firm can be limited to market development and initial qualification of candidates or management of the job fulfillment role from start to finish. A search firm can be a good option for an organization that does not have the time or staff to conduct a thorough search, as a comprehensive search typically takes several months to complete. Good search firms should also be able to identify candidates that may have been overlooked or had not previously considered your position. However, search firms generally charge one third to one half of the annual salary for the position for their comprehensive services, so it is important to consider the budgetary implications of using this recruitment method.

The substantial array of professional associations representing the expanding field of student affairs provides various staffing services. Some simply provide listing opportunities for candidates and employers, while others offer more extensive opportunities for in-person interviews. Those with large, national conferences, such as NASPA and ACPA, often include job placement functions in concert with professional development sessions.

Online recruitment has progressed rapidly over the past years. Increasingly, student affairs jobs can be found on commercial sites such as Monster.com and Jobs.com. Web sites such as StudentAffairs.com and HigherEdJobs.com are dedicated to the profession and include position listing and matching services. Online postings are relatively inexpensive and, in part because the posting is typically immediate, can be very useful when a position comes open outside of the traditional job search season.

Many job placement Web sites do not charge a fee for candidates to access the position listings or to upload copies of their résumés. It has become increasingly more acceptable to submit an electronic version of a résumé and cover letter, particularly for entry-level positions. For a candidate who is unable to attend one of the large placement conferences, these Web sites can be a very affordable way to conduct a search.

The proliferation of online job placement services may serve as a mixed blessing. On the one hand, what could be more convenient than to list openings with numerous online sources and for candidates to "drop" résumés through these agencies for jobs that seem remotely of interest? On the other hand, there's evidence (Gowan, 2007) that all this has done is populate cyberspace with excessive information both from job seekers and employers and that response rates are exceedingly low. Thus, online search utilization needs to be strategic, targeted, and limited to appropriate positions and online services. Undoubtedly, online recruiting will continue to grow as a major part of the hiring landscape but, it is hoped, with ever more sophisticated job sorting and candidate screening tools. We should also anticipate growth in the use of technology for distance-based interviews and other strategies to reduce the cost of candidate and employer travel.

Finally, many positions are advertised via informal communications among colleagues. The proliferation of online networks representing communities of practitioners provides intimate, fast, and productive ways to disseminate information about job openings and obtain nominees from trusted parties. While word of mouth is a very popular recruiting tool, it should not be the only method used to advertise a vacancy.

These various options notwithstanding, successful recruitment is dependent upon an institution's capacity to make a position sufficiently attractive to the marketplace of prospects. The attractiveness of a position begins with the quality of the role as portrayed by the job announcement and the detailed job description. Assuming the availability of an accurate and desirable role, the challenge will be to sell the program, the institution, and, perhaps, the local environment. Attractive program features will include direct compensation as well as a variety of tangible and intangible benefits. Professional development opportunities, leadership options, and even social activities may all help to seal the deal.

All this suggests that person-institution fit is critical to successful recruitment. That fit requires that both candidate and institution accurately portray themselves and that the selection process provide a genuine opportunity for discovery by both parties.

Selection

Once an adequate pool of qualified prospects has been assembled, the process of differentiating among the candidates to discover individuals most likely to match the job characteristics begins. Institutions deploy various forms of search committees to undertake this endeavor. On some occasions, hiring authorities may choose to dispense with a formal committee and conduct interviews and make employment offers without such input. While most expeditious, this process may alienate others who have vested interest in the role and preclude alternate and valuable perspectives on the viability of the candidates.

Most often a committee of stakeholders is created to review résumés, conduct interviews, and develop a preferred list of acceptable candidates from which the hiring authority can make a choice. Search committees will vary in size, scope, and authority, and the precise composition for any such committee will be dependent on the level of authority of the role, the breadth of stakeholder interest, the political climate of the campus (and of the job), the size of the candidate pool, and other characteristics local to each campus. Some public institutions are bound to obligatory public procedures by state and system governance rules.

It is increasingly common, especially for senior-level positions, to use an outside agency to market the position, collect résumés, and conduct an initial screening for basic compliance with the education and experience requirements. The prescreened pool of candidates may then be conveyed to the search committee for further review and interviews.

It may appear to be a small matter, but hiring authorities may prefer to receive an unranked list of acceptable hires with strengths and weaknesses identified. A selection can be made without appearing to ignore the singular preference of the search committee.

One tension experienced by those with hiring responsibility is the competition between internal candidates seeking promotion and external candidates looking for new opportunities. In filling a variety of roles, a senior administrator will attempt to balance the placement of new personnel with a combination of internal and external hires. Organizational strength is generally advanced by a balance of infusion of the fresh perspective of outside hires with the institutional memory and familiarity of the inside promotion.

It is also important to ensure opportunities for career mobility within the organization to motivate and reassure employees of the investment being made in them. Absent any confidence in promotional opportunities, an organization is likely to suffer from low morale and confidence, potentially contributing to more frequent staff turnover. Conversely, excessive dependency on internal promotions may inhibit creativity and foster a sense of mediocrity and repetition.

The final selection of a new employee may be more art than science. Rarely will a candidate's portfolio of experiences exactly match the desired background, and personality attributes are exceedingly difficult to assess. That a measure of the selection process is based on supervisor instinct should neither surprise nor frighten. One hopes that that instinct has been honed by past practice, effective recruitment, and screening and vetting of the candidates with trusted and experienced colleagues.

Once the preferred candidate is identified, the challenge becomes one of obtaining an acceptance of the offer. Many elements may influence this phase of the process. They include compensation, working conditions, and various personal needs.

Presumably, the search process narrowed the field of candidates to those already expecting the position's salary range and basic benefits package. What remains, then, will be a negotiation for starting salary and personalized benefits subject to various limitations. Public institutions, for example, may have rules limiting hiring authority flexibility to adjust initial offers. Compression and equity pressures also affect salary negotiation opportunities. *Compression* and *equity* refer to the salary distinctions between various levels of staff. For example, one would expect a reasonable difference in pay between an entry-level staff member in a student activities office and a middle manager in that same unit. However, if the market for career center staff requires that entry-level employees engaged in employer relations must be paid more in order to obtain qualified employees, how will that distinction be justified? This form of compression is becoming increasingly of concern, as various student affairs roles are harder to fill than others.

Occasionally, the market prices—that is, industry standards for a particular field—may push salary levels higher than standard inflation rates such that a long-term employee who has been getting average raises annually may be earning far less than a new hire with far less experience. That form of equity conflict also requires regular review and adjustment. Thus, it is critical that hiring authorities be familiar with market trends and regional variations of salary levels. Such data is available through multiple sources, such as Towers-Perrin for chief housing and health staff, NASPA for various student affairs roles, College and University Professional Association for Human Resources (CUPA-HR), and other professional associations for their specific personnel. Often, compensation experts within an institution's human resources department can provide a salary equity analysis to help guide compensation offers.

It is important to recognize that all these issues have significant financial implications. A commitment to annually review equity and compression requires careful budgeting. Inevitably, inequities will be uncovered that require market adjustments. These can often be quite sizable adjustments, which will require ongoing financial commitments.

Before an offer is made, there are several legal issues to consider. Institutional policies vary, but many now require background checks, credit checks, and/or transcript verification. It is important to follow the policies and procedures of an institution's human resources department. If the institution does not have a policy about background checks, credit checks, or transcript verification, consider working with human resources before screening candidates with these tools. Prior to conducting a background check, an office or department should have a set of working guidelines around what will be done if something comes back from the reporting agency. What if a candidate received a citation for driving under the influence? What if it was while they were a student? What if the citation was fifteen or twenty years ago? What if it was last year? What if the candidate did not disclose the information about the citation during the interview process? Setting guidelines in advance helps ensure that the information will be handled in a fair and equitable way.

Social networking sites bring a somewhat thorny ethical dilemma to the recruitment and selection process. There are widely varied opinions on whether sites such as Facebook and MySpace should be used in the selection process. Some institutions, such as the University of Southern California and Cornell University, are working toward developing related protocols for student selection processes as well as staff selection processes. Should a department choose to screen candidates' postings on a social networking site, it is a good idea to first check with the human resources department to make sure that any preexisting policies are followed. As with the background and other checks mentioned, standards by which the candidates' profiles are judged should be established to create an unbiased process.

It is not uncommon that the decision to accept a job offer includes consideration for a partner or spouse who may also need to find suitable employment. Accommodating a trailing partner may pose an additional challenge in the effort to solicit a job offer acceptance. Institutional responses can include a formal program of partner job support (more common at senior-level positions), but even when such formal possibilities are not available, being sensitive to partner concerns may make a difference in obtaining the preferred outcome.

Other considerations may include relocation advising and support, travel reimbursements (particularly when a family will follow at some later date), matching previous employer's benefits (for example, tuition expenses, automobile allowances, and even private club memberships) and home purchase support (for example, loan options). All this is to suggest that higher education and student affairs are in a competitive market for candidates, thus requiring recruitment and compensation practices generally presumed to be associated with corporate environments.

Supervision

An exemplary supervisory relationship is built on a foundation of clear and mutually agreed-upon expectations. Those expectations begin to be expressed in the written job description that, if appropriately constructed, carefully and concisely articulates the responsibilities, functions, and performance measures associated with the position. Unfortunately, well-crafted job descriptions may be the exception rather than the rule. Keeping job descriptions current and updated is vital to maintaining clarity of expectations.

The provision of a meaningful job description enables the likelihood of a positive and productive supervisory relationship. A frequent need to review and negotiate the terms of this contract suggests a poor or deteriorating relationship.

The job description communicates in writing functional roles and performance expectations, but effective supervision depends on frequent, consistent, and candid communications. Such communications are enabled by regular meetings between supervisor and staff member, an organizational culture that promotes performance feedback and discourages unsubstantiated criticism, and management training designed to improve supervisor and employee competencies.

Student affairs as a profession and collection of professions should manifest such a culture, but personal experience over more than three decades at more than a half-dozen institutions suggests that this is not always the case. Supervisors of counselors, deans, programmers, and bookkeepers share the strengths and weaknesses of employees of any organization. That student affairs is recognized as a helping profession comprised of caring staff does not necessarily mean that those with supervisory responsibility have innate managerial competence. They, too, require instruction, practice, feedback, and experience to be effective and well-regarded supervisors.

Various student affairs roles require unique forms of supervision. For example, supervision of therapists in a counseling center is guided by practice standards associated with formal credentialing obligations and protocols. The same is true for other staff, such as health center clinical medical practitioners and others with licensing or credentialing requirements.

Live-in staff, such as those employed in residence life, may have other supervisory conditions. Here, clarity of role distinctions, expectations regarding time on duty and time off duty, spouse and partner expectations, and more are critical. Live-in staff are, generally, relatively new professionals and are most in need of role clarity and persistent supervision, especially given the immersive nature of their jobs.

The around-the-clock nature of student affairs work poses additional challenges to effective supervision. Staff with formal, assigned, on-duty responsibilities often earn extra compensation in the form of dollars or compensatory time. However, often such staff will have worked far beyond negotiated expectations, leaving the supervisor to determine how best to recognize the quality and quantity of work performed.

Staff Awards and Recognition

It is important for supervisors, department heads, and upper administration staff to acknowledge employees for their work. This acknowledgment can take a variety of forms: a short conversation in the hallway letting someone know that they did a great job organizing a retreat; an e-mail, with a copy to his or her supervisor, praising the way a staff member helped a student; a handwritten note telling a new professional that the memo he or she prepared for a meeting was well written; or praise in the monthly directors' meeting of an office that did a particularly good job developing a student leadership activity. Each of these acknowledgments makes those cited for mention and others feel valued and encouraged to keep up the good work. As supervisors make a habit of such activities, positive feelings are generated throughout the organization.

When recognition of good effort is done within the context of an organized staff development process and part of the work of a divisionwide staff development committee, it takes on added symbolic meaning for those recognized and those who help determine who is recognized. Recognition of staff during an organized process reduces ambiguity about what is valued, reinforces the goals of the organizations, and provides direction (Bolman and Deal, 2003).

In addition, when a student affairs staff development committee is comprised of people from different levels within the organization, there is more opportunity for creativity in the development of formal award categories. Traditional awards might include New Professional of the Year; MidLevel Professional of the Year; and Most Outstanding programs. In addition, fun awards can also be given for categories like staff guru of the year (for the person who was a great mentor to younger staff); graduate student of the year award (for short-term community service projects); the above-and-beyond-the-call-of-duty award (for the residence coordinator who had a particularly busy year with residents); watchman of the year award (for the new professional in the recreation department who supervised nighttime basketball intramurals during spring semester); or the most spirited award (for the staff person who started the staff choir when no one thought it could be done). Ultimately, there are lots of fun ways to recognize staff in front of their peers.

Another interesting feature of giving out awards that have unusual or humorous titles is that those who are reviewing nominations can be creative and have enriched conversations about what is important in the service of students and the institution. They have more flexibility in making awards. They also spend time thinking about how the awards may inspire them and other staff in the organization and make them feel good about their own work.

Helping Staff Manage Their Time

One aspect of supervision that is often overlooked is whether or not individual staff know how to organize and prioritize their work. It is assumed they do, based on reviewing their college backgrounds and previous work experience.

However, it is often the case that new professionals, in particular, have never sat down with someone to review how they work, organize their time, set priorities, use data to help them make decisions, and how to make informed decisions in a timely manner.

It is important that supervisors meet with new professionals to discuss:

- Their work styles,
- How they approach getting tasks accomplished,
- Their understandings of work priorities and how to set them,
- What is important to the functioning of an office,
- Why schedules are important and how they should be organized,
- How the employees' work fits into the context of their offices and the divisions of student affairs in which they serve,
- The resources available to help them accomplish their job responsibilities,
- How effective they are in accomplishing their job responsibilities,
- How to evaluate whether their job has been done well, and
- When and to whom they should go for help when they have questions and if they feel insecure about their performance.

Meetings

Meetings are a powerful tool, often misunderstood and misused. A key area that is often overlooked is teaching staff how to manage meetings. Effective meetings can be modeled for staff, but in the course of supervision, meetings might also be an appropriate topic for discussion. It is frequently assumed that just having a meeting means that it was successful. This approach does not recognize the fact that most meetings are organized to share information and make decisions. The reality is that if a specific agenda was not developed and if the most important items on the agenda were not reviewed, time was probably wasted. There are, of course, different types of meetings, and this should also be clear to those who will attend and participate. For example, meetings can be used to discuss a particular topic; report on the progress of a project; develop a plan of action for collective and individual work; evaluate the effectiveness of a program or response to a big issue on campus; convey news about a new initiative; or discuss budget planning and spending priorities for the coming academic year. The key is that whoever is organizing the meeting understand its purpose, who should attend and what their roles are, and which topics will be addressed and by whom.

There are a number of strategies to help assure that meetings are effective. Here are some simple guidelines:

1. Start on time and end on time.
2. Have an agenda and be clear about the purpose of the meeting. Is it designed for information sharing, planning, and/or decision making?
3. What is the context for the meeting? Is its purpose and agenda tied to some larger project or process?
4. When possible, let others help develop the agenda.
5. Maintain a running agenda of recurring items and topics so participants can keep track of ongoing initiatives.
6. Provide opportunities for others to lead the discussion.
7. Help less experienced staff learn how to facilitate discussions in meetings to increase likelihood of successful results.
8. Cancel meetings if there is no useful agenda.

If a meeting is to be held primarily to report out, find fun ways to do it so as to break up the monotony and formality, particularly when you meet often with the same people.

Fundamentally, supervision can be narrowly viewed as simply providing formal job definitions and oversight, or more broadly as providing guidance, competency development, and feedback to optimize the professional development of an employee. Though the latter is preferred, pitfalls exist in this form of supervisory relationship as well. A supervisory relationship carried to excess, with far too much familiarity and social engagement, can be problematic.

The key, of course, is finding good balance between personal and professional relationships with staff. In its ideal, effective supervision is characterized by modest intimacy, a commitment to mentorship, pride in employee achievement, and sensitivity to the unique challenges associated with the multiple and varying roles and functions associated with student affairs work.

Staff and Professional Development

There are several aspects to creating a comprehensive staff development program. These include developing a guiding philosophy for professional development, recognizing the mutuality of individual and organization needs, promotion of staff development by the organization' s leaders, determining what staff want and need, taking advantage of opportunities available through professional associations, and considering professional publications as a form of

professional development. In addition to these traditional avenues for professional development, Chapter Nineteen discusses additional pathways to pursue.

Guiding Philosophy

Ultimately, all staff members are responsible for their own professional development. They must be entrepreneurial in the way they approach their careers.
However, sometimes they are so busy carrying out their responsibilities and
helping students and fellow staff be successful that they forget to reflect on their
work and ask themselves some basic questions. Employees in student affairs
should frequently ask themselves:

- Do I like what I am doing?
- Am I good at what I am doing? If not, what do I need to do to get better? If
  so, what are my strengths and how can I enhance them to become an even
  stronger professional? In which skill and knowledge areas must I improve?
- Do I have the skills and experience I need to move ahead in my career?
- Do I have mentors who will talk straight with me and tell me what else I can
  do to become a stronger student affairs professional? If not, how do I get the
  honest feedback I need about my skills and work?
- Do I have an educational philosophy that provides vision, guides my work, and
  keeps me grounded in my decision making, risk taking, and support of others?

Staff development starts from within. Professionals must be self-motivated
and open to external influences that can inspire and help them change and
improve. If not, they will stagnate, be less satisfied with their work, and miss new
opportunities for improvement and increasing levels of responsibility, thereby
stunting their personal and professional growth and career advancement.

Mutual Interests and Mutual Needs: Organizations and Individuals

While it is true that individuals are responsible for their own professional development, the organizations in which they work can have a powerful influence on
their development. If they are fortunate enough to work in an organization that
pays attention to their professional development, they will have more opportunities to learn how to become better leaders in student affairs. If the work environment in which they work is not supportive of the development of the group and
individual staff members, it will be harder, though not impossible, to improve.

The incentives for the organization and its staff members to develop
and maintain a robust professional development program are very powerful.

Employees who see senior leadership invest time and resources in the development of the organization and its staff will generally be more motivated, dedicated, and willing to put extra effort into helping the organization accomplish its mission and goals. Employee satisfaction is enhanced, esprit de corps is infused into working relationships, and staff are motivated to identify activities for themselves and others that can improve individual and group performance. The entire organization, while fulfilling its institutional role, is simultaneously focused on improvement, learning, and quality service.

Professional development can also be seen as a way to retain outstanding employees. Given the lack of opportunities for upward mobility that can occur in student affairs, offering additional professional development may encourage staff members to stay at an institution and can provide them with new challenges that will help keep them engaged.

What Leaders Must Do to Promote Professional Development

Senior student affairs leaders must explicitly state that the professional development of staff is part of the mission and strategic focus of the organization and offices they lead. Discussions about organizational development and individual professional development should be held on a regular basis. Staff outside the senior leadership should be involved in these discussions and in the development of divisionwide professional development programs.

Ritscher (1985) says there are key elements to what leaders must do to create esprit de corps within organizations to help maximize collective effectiveness and a sense of shared commitment. He offers the following qualities that he says are "easier to talk about than to practice":

- Create a shared vision.
- Maintain a high level of individual and organizational integrity. Keep agreements.
- Create an organizational culture that values service, excellence, dedication, contact with the customer, and action over personal advancement and personal gain.
- Create cooperation, communication, and community.
- Create a supportive environment for the individual.
- Create an organizational culture that supports personal growth (p. 43).

If these overarching tenets can be combined with several other of Ritscher's individually focused qualities—like clarity of mind, low ego, high results, trust and openness, and skill in creating people structures—a very powerful and compelling staff development ethos and environment can be more effectively nurtured and developed.

What Do Individuals Want and Need?

The development of staff is actually a very straightforward enterprise. There are, of course, a variety of ways to help staff become better professionals and leaders in student affairs and higher education. However, some basic conditions must be in place to provide the greatest opportunity for success. Staff at all levels need to know they are:

- Respected as professionals and individuals who are striving to do their best,
- Asked to carry out responsibilities that are within their knowledge, experience, and skills to accomplish,
- Given appropriate resources and guidance to perform their jobs,
- Compensated fairly and reasonably given their workload and what others of similar rank and experience are asked to do,
- Confident that strong performance can lead to advancement within the organization or externally, if they decide to seek employment at another institution,
- Able to get regular and clear feedback about their work and what they can do to improve,
- Able to give feedback to supervisors about how they are working together and what the supervisee needs in order to be more successful,
- Helped with expanding their networks of professional contacts,
- Given appropriate opportunities to participate in campus-based and external professional development programs sponsored by professional associations and educational institutions, such as the Harvard Management Development Program or Bryn Mawr Summer Institute for Women in Higher Education, and
- Acknowledgement for their efforts to balance professional and personal lives.

Professional Development Programs Sponsored by Associations

One important area that each of us must never overlook is the wide variety of conferences, workshops, retreats, and other professional development programs offered by student affairs and other related associations. There are a number of very prominent, well-organized, and well-funded associations with strong traditions of helping professionals expand their skills and knowledge within the specific areas of student affairs, broaden their national networks of contacts, help them learn about the wide variety of colleges and universities at which they could work, and provide a common language and understanding of issues and trends that affect their work. They provide staff at all levels the opportunity to learn from experts about specific areas within student affairs as well as focus on developing specific skills. Involvement with professional organizations is discussed in greater detail in Chapter Eleven of this book.

Publications as a Form of Staff Development

One of the most economical ways to promote and sustain staff development is to make publications available to staff on a regular basis. There are a number of first-rate publications that provide information on the latest research about student behavior, administrative strategy, reviews of publications about student affairs issues, and analyses of how certain students of different ethnicities, socio-economic status, and college attendance history perform in different types of institutions. The number of topics covered is nearly endless, and there are publications to suit all levels of experience, interests, and specializations within the field of student affairs.

A great way to use publications in in-house staff development programs is to assign publications to certain staff to read and review at staff meetings on a regular basis, so that there is a collective understanding that staying current in the field helps advance the overall effectiveness of the staff.

Another way to take advantage of publications is to cull articles that a director or the staff development committee believes are timely and pertinent to current activities on campus, share the articles, and discuss them at a staff meeting. Many of the following publications are available only for subscribers, individual or institutional, but they are all potential selections for staff development readings.

About Campus. *About Campus* is a "magazine designed to serve as a catalyst for educators in colleges and universities to thoughtfully examine a variety of issues, policies, and practices and how they affect the quality of undergraduate education and students' learning" (American College Personnel Association, 2007). It is published by Wiley.

Business Officer. *Business Officer,* a publication of the National Association of College and University Business Officers (NACUBO), is a monthly magazine that "addresses current challenges and emerging trends in strategic planning and budgeting, accounting, finance, technology, facilities, student financial services, leadership, and other areas of higher education administration. The magazine presents experiences of chief business officers, analysis of NACUBO research, and practical tools that can be applied in enhancing the efficiency and effectiveness of institutions of all sizes and classifications" (NACUBO, 2007).

Change. *Change* is an opinion magazine that examines "contemporary issues in higher education, spotlighting trends, providing new insights and ideas, and analyzing the implications of educational programs, policies and practices" (*Change*, 2007). The Carnegie Foundation for the Advancement of Teaching provides editorial leadership for this publication. *Change* is published bimonthly in print and online formats and is available only by subscription.

The Chronicle of Higher Education. The *Chronicle* is a general weekly publication that covers faculty, research, government and politics, money and management, information technology, students, and careers in higher education. The print version of the *Chronicle* is "published in three sections: the news section; The Chronicle Review, a magazine of arts and ideas; and Careers, with career advice and hundreds of job listings" (*Chronicle of Higher Education*, 2007). The online version of the *Chronicle* is published every weekday and "features the complete contents of the latest issue; daily news and advice columns; thousands of current job listings; articles published since September 1989; vibrant discussion forums; and career-building tools" (*Chronicle of Higher Education*, 2007). Some of the online content, although not all, can be accessed without a subscription.

Journal of College Student Development. The *Journal of College Student Development (JCSD)* is a "leading scholarly journal and the largest empirical research journal in the field of student affairs and higher education" (ACPA, 2007). Published by ACPA, *JCSD* is available in both print and online. Article abstracts from recent *JCSD* issues are available on the ACPA Web site.

Leadership Exchange. Published by NASPA, *Leadership Exchange* is a "quarterly management and leadership magazine that is tailored specifically for Senior Student Affairs Officers. It features columns from industry experts and stories on the most current issues in student affairs" (National Association of Student Personnel Administrators [NASPA], 2007).

Inside Higher Ed. *Inside Higher Ed* is a free online source for news, opinion, and jobs for all of higher education. The publication is geared to all levels of staff with "breaking news and feature stories, provocative daily commentary, areas for comment on every article, practical career columns, and a powerful suite of tools to help higher education professionals get jobs and colleges identify and hire employees" (*Inside Higher Ed*, 2007).

NASPA Journal. The *NASPA Journal* is a refereed "publication outlet for contemporary scholarship in student affairs administration, research, and practice" (NASPA, 2007). It is published quarterly and is available only online.

NetResults. *NetResults* is a "bi-weekly magazine that contains a feature-length story and four columns: Research, Assessment, Alcohol and Drug Issues, and Building Blocks: Issues for New Professionals" (NASPA, 2007). It is published by NASPA.

NASPA Forum. The *NASPA Forum* is a "monthly online newsletter that offers news about NASPA programs, conferences, workshops, and members, and features messages from the executive director and president, as well as a list of upcoming events" (NASPA, 2007). It is another NASPA publication.

The American Council on Education (ACE), one of the most prestigious higher education associations, also produces many fine publications for leaders in higher education, particularly those who aspire to become presidents, provosts, vice presidents, and deans in colleges and universities. The range of topics on which ACE publishes is quite broad; examples include distance education, financial aid, minorities, transfer students, women in higher education, lifelong learning, international education, leadership and institutional effectiveness, and teacher education (American Council on Education [ACE], 2007).

The Association of American Colleges and Universities (AAC&U) is another flagship umbrella association that produces several excellent publications that can help one learn more about higher education from different perspectives. *Liberal Education* "expresses the voices of educators, faculty and administrators in colleges and universities nationwide who are working to enrich liberal learning and undergraduate education" (AAC&U, 2007). *Peer Review* "provides a quarterly briefing on emerging trends and key debates in undergraduate liberal education" (AAC&U, 2007). *On Campus with Women* "is a quarterly online newsletter designed to provide readers with the most up-to-date information about women in higher education, focusing on issues and trends affecting academic leaders, faculty members, staff, and students" (AAC&U, 2007). *Diversity Digest* "is specifically designed to broadly illuminate the scope, accomplishments and educational value of the campus diversity movement; and help practitioners learn to effectively communicate the educational value and success of their local diversity initiatives" (AAC&U, 2007).

Staff development committees, directors, and other senior leaders may also develop a reading list of special books that are read and discussed as a group. For example, staffs on many campuses have read *Learning Reconsidered* (Keeling, 2004) and *Learning Reconsidered 2* (Keeling, 2006). *Learning Reconsidered* argues for the integration of all of higher education's resources in the education and preparation of the whole student. This landmark publication builds upon historical student affairs statements that focus on student affairs as a profession

(NASPA, 2007). *Learning Reconsidered 2* is a blueprint for action. It shows how to create the dialogue, tools, and materials necessary to put into practice the recommendations in *Learning Reconsidered* (NASPA, 2007).

Staff should also be encouraged to publish their own research, best practices, and ideas. The publications listed here vary in their publication requirements, but there is a forum for a wide variety of topics and writing styles. Publication is not simply a beneficial professional development activity; it also makes a vital contribution to our field.

Continuing Education of Staff

Most divisions of student affairs promote continuous educational advancement and learning among staff, particularly if there is a graduate school of education on campus or nearby. One of the more common ways this is expressed in staff development terms is to encourage professionals, regardless of where they rank in the organizational hierarchy, to earn an advanced degree, generally a master's degree (M.A. or M.Ed.) or a doctorate (Ph.D. or Ed.D.). In some cases, an individual will be working to complete his or her bachelor's degree.

When helping an employee manage the pursuit of an advanced degree, it is helpful to:

- Explicitly encourage staff to pursue advance degrees,
- Talk with staff during annual performance reviews about their plans,
- Discuss whether or not the institution can help pay for the advanced degree,
- Discuss when the staff person might not be able to work regular hours because he or she must attend class, work on a special project, or travel with the class on a required trip, and
- Discuss whether earning the advanced degree will result in higher pay, a promotion, or a change in job responsibilities.

Getting permission and support to earn a degree while working full time and requesting some modification of one's work schedule (and possibly duties) is a privilege, not a right. However, the benefits to both individuals and institutions are immense. For a more detailed discussion of earning an advanced degree, please refer to Chapter Twenty.

Vision, Creativity, and Commitment

Professional development can come in many forms: conference attendance, reading and writing for publication, and formal education. Personal reflection and conversations with mentors are critical components of professional development. While the ultimate responsibility for professional development lies with the individual, organizations do have a shared responsibility to create a culture that supports and values this development. Student affairs leaders must see this effort as integral to the accomplishment of the mission student affairs is asked to carry out on their campuses. When staff are given opportunities to develop personally and professionally, they are more satisfied with their work, feel respected, and are more likely to work even harder to help students and the institution be more successful.

Staff Retention

A discussion on employee retention presumes, of course, a desire to retain particular staff. This is most often the case with senior staff, including department heads and those in dean and central student affairs administration roles. As an agency devoted to individual and community development, student affairs generally celebrates staff achievement, including promotion to higher levels. The nature of the profession is such that frequently promotion is obtained by moving to a new college or university.

Retention of an individual staff member requires options unique to that situation. But a student affairs organization that avoids unnecessary and frequent turnover will be attentive to staff needs in a variety of ways. Such an organization considers the needs of staff in a deliberate and thoughtful way.

Appropriate compensation, reasonable benefits, and informative feedback are all critical to retention of key staff. But so are opportunities for professional development, a voice in departmental and divisional governance, and generally, the capacity to feel needed and effective in assigned and extended areas of responsibility.

Retention also depends on various personal accommodations, including flextime, flexibility to support children and aging parents, and various educational opportunities, including postgraduate degree attainment, specialized institutes, and seminars.

Another fairly new retention (and management development) option is the provision of executive coaching to key staff. Coaching is widely used in the corporate world and has only recently been deployed on college campuses as a way to strengthen the skill sets of essential personnel. Several student affairs organizations (Duke University, for example) are using coaching services effectively to support and empower middle and senior leaders.

Finally, in our ever-growing globalization movement, international experience is no longer a mere luxury. International exposure, such as attending a conference abroad, working with shipboard education, or getting involved with international students at one's home institution, would be a good thing for staff even if only as a retention attraction. Clearly, the cultural currency such as travel provides is an essential requirement of effective contemporary student affairs practice.

Conclusion

The recruitment, selection, supervision, professional development, and retention of student affairs staff can, in many respects, resemble the characteristics of any complex human services organization. The staff of such organizations react to stimuli and detractors in ways common to most such agencies. Opportunities to make a difference, earn competitive and respectable salaries, acquire new skills, and meet personal as well as professional obligations all serve to incentivize prospects and current staff. Absent some or all of these attributes, organizations find unwanted and unnecessary employee attrition.

Student affairs organizations require additional considerations to satisfy their unique human resources expectations. Student affairs leaders and hiring authorities must adjust tactics and techniques to accommodate the unique conditions associated with the remarkably varying employment sectors associated with the differing service units that comprise student affairs.

Finally, contemporary management practices in student affairs should include creative accommodations including flexible work hours, exposure to coaching and other support structures, and international exposure. Future generations of student affairs staff and leaders will bring far more diverse and challenging expectations. Fortunately, we are a profession and a set of professions accustomed to adaptive environments and practices. With thoughtful planning and novel management approaches, the future of student affairs human resources is bright.

References

American College Personnel Administrators. [www.myacpa.org]. 2007.

American Council on Education. [http://www.acenet.edu//AM/Template.cfm?Section= Home]. 2007.

Association of American Colleges and Universities. [http://www.aacu.org/]. 2007.

Bolman, L. G., and Deal, T. E. *Reframing Organizations: Artistry, Choice and Leadership* (3rd ed.). San Francisco: Jossey-Bass, 2003.

Change. [http://www.heldref.org/change.php]. 2007.

Chronicle of Higher Education [http://chronicle.com/]. 2007.

Gowan, M. "Find the Right Job Online." *PCWorld*. [http://www.pcworld.com/article/id,36584-page,7-c,techindustrytrends/www.idgconnect.com]. 2007.

Inside Higher Ed. [http://www.insidehighered.com/]. 2007.

Keeling, R. P. (Ed.). *Learning Reconsidered: A Campus-Wide Focus on the Student Experience*. Washington, D.C.: American College Personnel Association and National Association of Student Personnel Administrators, 2004.

Keeling, R. (Ed.). *Learning Reconsidered 2: Implementing a Campus-Wide Focus on the Student Experience*. Various: American College Personnel Association, Association of College and University Housing Officers-International, Association of College Unions-International, National Academic Advising Association, National Association for Campus Activities, National Association of Student Personnel Administrators, National Intramural-Recreational Sports Association, 2006.

Manning, K., Kinzie, J., and Schuh, J. *One Size Does Not Fit All: Traditional and Innovative Models of Student Affairs Practice*. New York: Routledge, 2006.

National Association of College and University Business Officers. [http://www.nacubo.org/x199.xml]. 2007.

National Association of Student Personnel Administrators. [http://www.naspa.org/pubs/index.cfm]. 2007.

Ritscher, J. A. "Spirituality in Business." *IN CONTEXT: Living Business*. [http://www.context.org/ICLIB/IC11/Ritscher.htm]. Autumn 1985.

Winston, R. B., Torres, V., Carpenter, D. S., McIntire, D. D., and Peterson, B. "Staffing in Student Affairs: A Survey of Practices." *College Student Affairs Journal*, 2001, 21, 1, 7–25.

Recommended Reading

Ackerman, R. L. (Ed.). *Mid-Level Managers*. Washington, D.C.: National Association of Student Personnel Administrators, 2007.

Allen, D. *Getting Things Done: The Art of Stress-Free Productivity*. New York: Viking, 2001.

Amey, M. J., and Reesor, L. M. *Beginning Your Journey*. Washington, D.C.: National Association of Student Personnel Administrators, 2002.

Blimling, G. S., Whitt, E. J., and Associates. *Good Practice in Student Affairs: Principles to Foster Student Learning*. San Francisco: Jossey-Bass, 1999.

Gabarro, J. J., and Kotter, J. P. "Managing Your Boss." *Harvard Business Review*, 1993, 71(3), 150–157.

Henry, N. B. *The Fifty-Eighth Yearbook of the National Society for the Study of Education*. Chicago: National Society for the Study of Education, 1959.

Lakien, A. *How to Gain Control of Your Time and Your Life*. New York: Signet, 1973.

Miller, T. K., Winston, R. B., and Mendenhall, W. R. *Administration and Leadership in Student Affairs: Actualizing Student Development in Higher Education*. Muncie, Ind.: Accelerated Development, 1983.

Nelson, H. B. *Personnel Services in Education*. Chicago: National Society for the Study of Education, 1959.

Sandeen, A., and Barr, M. J. *Critical Issues for Student Affairs: Challenges and Opportunities*. San Francisco: Jossey-Bass, 2006.

Winston, R. B., and Creamer, D. G. *Improving Staffing Practices in Student Affairs*. San Francisco: Jossey-Bass, 1997.

CHAPTER EIGHTEEN

MIDDLE MANAGERS

Roles and Responsibilities Spanning the Student Affairs Professional Career

Donald B. Mills

A newly appointed middle manager may walk into work the first day and wonder exactly what it is she has agreed to do. Advice flows freely both from above and below. Middle managers frequently have significant responsibility but may not have final authority. They implement policy but may not always feel an integral part of the decision-making process. They often supervise other staff, but final decisions about staffing levels and compensation may be made by others. They are expected to empower students but may feel powerless themselves. They may have training in a professional specialty but not training for a broader supervisory role. Even with these limitations, the middle manager plays a vital role in the student affairs function on the campuses of institutions of higher education. The middle manager's role, because of its position in the organization, provides good insight into the challenges facing all levels of management in student affairs.

This chapter discusses the middle management role in student affairs and how it relates to roles at other points in the span of a career in student affairs, especially entry-level positions. It addresses generational challenges as well as mobility and professional development challenges. The chapter concludes with recommendations for effective practice.

Management in Student Affairs

A precise definition of what constitutes a middle manager proves to be as elusive as an exact definition of middle age. Clearly, there are differences between entry-level staff managers and executive-level administrators. Where do the middle managers fit, and what do they do?

The simple answer is that middle managers manage people, money, information, and programs. A starting place is to examine an organizational chart. Figure 18.1, the organizational chart of a fictional university, indicates where the middle resides at that institution. Institutional differences reflect differences in title, breadth of responsibility, and programmatic offerings.

Young (2007) indicates that middle managers provide support services and other administrative duties linking vertical and horizontal levels of an organizational hierarchy. A middle manager provides supervision of programs (White, Webb, and Young, 1990). Student affairs midlevel managers must balance the transactional realities of work while attempting to implement the transformational goals of student affairs (Young, 2007). Byrnes (2005) maintains that middle managers should focus half of their energies on structuring the work of their departments and coaching their subordinates' performance and half on activities that require coordination with other middle management colleagues.

As the title indicates, the work of a middle manager bridges that of the entry-level professional and the senior student affairs officer (SSAO). Entry-level staff positions vary in their specific duties, but virtually without exception these staff have the most consistent interaction with students. Entry-level positions typically focus on a specialized area within student affairs (for example housing, Greek life, or multicultural affairs), and the responsibilities include routine tasks, programming, and projects within that specialty while supervising student paraprofessionals. Senior student affairs officers, on the other hand, hold a broader view of the span of the student affairs profession, and their daily activities focus on divisional and institutional priorities while supervising a limited number of direct reports.

Because of their position in the organizational hierarchy, middle managers implement and interpret policy but may not create it. Policy decisions are generally the prerogative of executive-level administrators. Middle managers most often have influence, however, in those decisions directly influencing their area of expertise and responsibility. Positions in student affairs that would be classified as middle management include directors and associate directors of functional departments, facilities, and programs such as admissions, residence life, counseling center, student center, alcohol education, and recreation.

FIGURE 18.1 SAMPLE STUDENT AFFAIRS ORGANIZATION

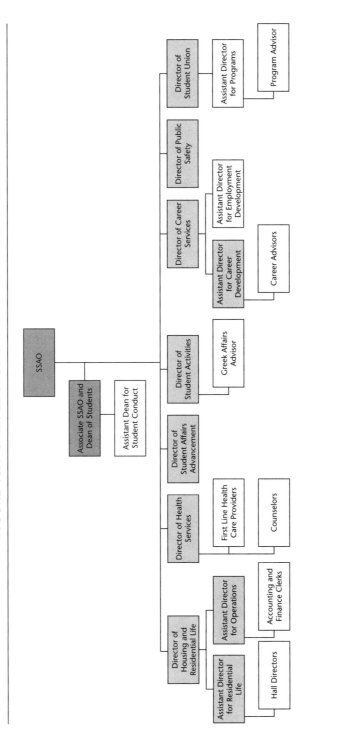

Managing Information and Money

As institutions of higher education have grown increasingly complex, gathering and interpreting information has become more important. Both research programs and assessent programs improve the quality of programs, promote effective use of resources, and enhance the student experience. The effective manager, whether a middle manager, entry level, or senior executive, develops systems to routinely collect and interpret information and makes decisions based on an appropriate interpretation of such information.

Perhaps the most obvious use of information is involved in managing funds. As funds become more scarce or have more stringent accountability requirements, managers must not only understand changing conditions but must also develop alternative means of supporting programs. The budget is the basic document the middle manager uses to implement plans and to develop strategies to achieve objectives. (For a general discussion of budgeting, please refer to Chapter Twenty-Five.) The process of creating an annual budget requires setting programmatic priorities, evaluating staffing needs, and determining levels of material support necessary to accomplish objectives. These priorities, staffing levels, and necessary support are determined in conjunction with the executive-level supervisor but with consideration of the impact on the work of entry-level staff and must be consistent with institutional priorities and strategic plans.

Influencing the Culture

The culture of an organization is composed of its mission and value system. In the face of rapid change, these relieve potential stress on the organization. The mission keeps a focus on doing the right thing. Values define the culture. The manager understands both and is comfortable in the particular institutional setting. The question is not only what does a person know, but what are the values, decision-making styles, and methods of adapting to changing conditions compatible with the institution (Hanaka and Hawkins, 1997)?

At the center of the culture of higher education is the academic enterprise. The astute middle manager develops positive and fruitful relationships with the faculty. Even though the institutional culture has an academic core, managers in student affairs are in a unique position to understand that culture and to impart it to students and other staff. By their nature, academic programs are composed of particular knowledge and fields; by contrast, administrative functions are more specific to the institution. In addition, interaction with staff and students places student affairs professionals in a unique position to hear institutional myths and to shape institutional traditions. Kuh and Whitt (1988) provide valuable insight in understanding the complexity of the culture of institutions of higher education, and student affairs professionals at all career levels will profit from reading their work.

Role Issues for Management

The middle manager must resolve many issues to function effectively within the organization, including scope of authority, supervision responsibilities, planning, and the importance of staff development. These functions must be dispatched in an ethical and credible manner.

Authority

Questions of power and authority are inherent for the middle manager. What can the middle manager decide, and what must receive approval from a higher authority? Should decisions be approved before implementation, or is notification of them appropriate? These questions are especially difficult to resolve when the middle manager has recently been appointed to the position.

Drucker (1974) indicates that an efficient organization demands clear decision-making authority. The participants in the process must agree on what determinations can be made and at what level. Unless authority for them is precisely articulated, confusion will result. The responsibility for clarifying questions rests with both the middle manager and senior-level management. However, experience indicates that the clarification should be initiated by the middle manager, as the results are more critical to his or her performance. Clarification of authority is also vital to entry-level professionals, given their subordinate role in the organizational structure.

The authority issue is complicated by the development of teams. One management implication of the team approach is that individuals must learn to work simultaneously in different organizational structures. "We are now evolving toward structures in which rank means responsibility but not authority. And in which your job is not to command but to persuade" (Drucker, 1999, p. 115). Teams provide opportunities for entry personnel to display their understanding of a situation and creativity in finding solutions. The middle manager must learn to work in an environment of ambiguity that team approaches and project management create.

Supervision of Staff

Managing clerical and professional staff is a critical element of the middle manager's responsibility. Although it is never an easy task, it is frequently the most rewarding. As stated previously, entry-level staff members work primarily with student paraprofessionals, but the middle manager probably works most closely with staff. The ability to manage staff successfully is one important determinant of success for the middle manager. In acting as a supervisor, the middle manager must be more than a manipulator; he or she must be a leader. The middle manager must develop the skills of motivation, delegation, performance appraisal, and staff selection. Chapter Seventeen includes a more comprehensive discussion of these issues.

Performance Appraisal

The middle manager has the responsibility to assure that staffs have the ability to accomplish what is expected. A technique that has gained currency is the supervisor as coach, with the manager adopting a style of guiding rather than dictating. The manager is able to supervise more staff, create a more flexible workforce by providing employees the tools to be self-reliant, and enhance employee job satisfaction by encouraging greater individual responsibility (Gendron, 1998a). Brown (1988) recommends that performance appraisal be approached the way a coach views working with a player or a mentor with a student. It is designed to improve performance and to enhance an individual's skills. Lack of a formal, consistent approach to performance appraisal leads to a system that does not improve morale, appears biased, and may be considered ineffective. A successful program provides the manager with information that can be used to improve performance, determine goals, and evaluate progress (Brown, 1988). The coaching style serves as an important model for staff. In the coaching environment, entry-level staff are able to understand expected outcomes but are offered the freedom to achieve them based on individual skills. Entry-level staff should never discount the value of effective performance appraisal and coaching for student paraprofessionals as well.

Planning

Gendron (1998a) states that middle managers can play important roles in the strategic planning process. The middle manager acts as strategy ambassador bringing information about institutional strategy to front-line workers and bringing front-line knowledge back to executives. The cascade of information in this paradigm flows both downward and upward. When the middle manager is involved in the planning process, several important benefits accrue to both the middle manager and the organization. The middle manager assumes a sense of ownership and is motivated by the challenge to provide critical, useful information, while the organization benefits because of the improved quality of information.

The form planning takes will vary depending on the culture of the particular institution. Mintzberg (1987), however, maintains that strategic plans can take forms other than a deliberate, structured plan. Plans can also *emerge*. In emergent planning environments, the learning that occurs as the plan is implemented is recirculated into the plan. So the plan is continually being reworked and rewritten. The middle manager is key in this environment.

Entry-level staff may be the first to recognize when existing strategies or processes no longer are effective. For example, an admissions counselor or residence hall director may first recognize changes in student culture that would necessitate changes in institutional plans. Or a financial aid director recognizes changes in governmental policy that will impact institutional plans. When the middle manager recognizes that changes have occurred in the operating environment, it is appropriate that middle managers develop a response to the challenges.

Staff Development

Staff development programs designed to improve skills and challenge individuals intellectually and philosophically are necessary aspects of the middle manager's work. Staff members must sense that they are not stagnating but are continuing to grow. This is an especially important workplace value for younger staff. Staff development can occur through formal programs, individual mentoring, performance appraisals, and self-directed learning (Bryan and Mullendore, 1990).

The middle manager should consider encouraging staff to continue formal education. The development of communication and critical-thinking skills, involvement in research, and exposure to a breadth of knowledge provides valuable support to the middle manager (Young, 1997). The value placed on scholarship within the academy translates into an improved image of the division of student affairs when educational levels of staff members increase. While staff development may enhance skills, the focus should be on skill or knowledge enhancement that improves the learning outcomes for students.

Ethics and Credibility

"First, do no harm." The famous admonition from Hippocrates forms the basis of all ethical systems. For the middle manager, having a solid value system and behaving in an ethical manner is critical to achieving success. The responsibilities of the middle manager create ethical challenges. Sometimes the proper course of action is prescribed by law, and generally there are institutional policies and ethical codes of conduct to define appropriate behavior. However, some ethical issues can never be fully codified. The key question in ambiguous situations is always, "What is the right thing to do?" Chapter Nine provides more on professional ethics.

Essentially the manager manages through a variety of techniques, but at root is the sense that a person is honest, fair, credible, and can be trusted. Kouzes and Posner (1993) maintain that leadership is a relationship, "a reciprocal relationship between those who choose to lead and those who decide to follow" (p. 1). Credibility has a significantly positive impact on the performance of the individual and the organization. Service to the institution and the people of the institution, values consistent with the values of the institution, competency, honesty and fairness are qualities found in the successful manager.

The Generational Challenge

For the first time in American history, four generations of workers are present simultaneously in the workplace. Each generation has been formed by events and circumstances surrounding their formative years, resulting in a multidimensional workplace. Each generation has identifiable characteristics related to leadership style, desired supervisor direction, work ethic, attitudes toward work, and workplace values. An understanding of these characteristics provides guidance to supervisors of middle managers and for middle managers in their relationships with others—the SSAO, other middle managers, and entry-level staff. Table 18.1 provides a summary insight into some factors at work as a result of the interplay between generations (Anand, 2007).

For supervisors it is important to recognize the unique generational values, attitudes, and work ethic. The Baby Boomer executive supervising a Generation X (Gen X) manager should recognize that performance evaluation, life/work balance, and organizational leadership are essential to Gen X satisfaction. It is vital that the Gen X middle managers be given the rationale for decisions. They are unlikely to merely accept direction but seek an understanding of the why as well as the what from supervisors. Generation X middle managers have less respect for "paying dues." The important value for them is one of competence, and if they seemingly possess greater competence, they should be rewarded for it with leadership positions. Decision making by Baby Boomer leaders is often accomplished through a process of consensus. It is more useful, in the Gen X

TABLE 18.1 GENERATIONAL WORKPLACE CHARACTERISTICS

	Traditionalists 1925–1945	Baby Boomers 1946–1964	Generation X 1965–1983	Millennials 1984–2002
Leadership Style	Hierarchy	Consensus seeking	Competence based	Team; everyone pulls together
Feedback Desired	No news is good news	Annually, much documentation	Will ask how they are doing	Instant feedback requested
Work Ethic	Work hard; save money	Work hard, play hard; worry about money	Work hard if it doesn't interfere with play	Work should be fun; let others pay
Loyalty	To organization	To work	To self	Resume always ready
Attitude Toward Work	Get it done	Is it meaningful?	Pays the bills	Is it fun?
Values	Dedication/sacrifice/loyalty/ hard work repaid with responsibility Deferred gratification	Personal growth/ health/ wealth Work hard and be noticed Looking for personal path	Life balance Think globally Self-reliant	Cross-cultural, multi-tasking Emphasis on doing/achieving Sense of entitlement Team oriented

view, to simply let the person with the ability have autonomy to perform the task without involvement of others.

The reverse effect is also true. A Generation X supervisor must consider the needs of a Baby Boomer, Millennial, or Traditionalist subordinate. Understanding the needs, motivations, and morale of employees is an important trait of any supervisor. It makes sense, then, for any supervisor to provide an environment that considers the unique generational values of middle managers, supervisors, and other employees. Effective mentoring of Generation X middle managers requires a balancing act. While Generation X managers desire frequent and direct feedback regarding what is to be accomplished, successful mentoring encourages creativity and provides real autonomy in determining how it is to be accomplished. It is important that Generation X managers understand their working relationships as being colleagues rather than as supervisor and employee. The supervisor must be committed to helping the Generation X student affairs professional learn new skills (remember the Generation X person places a high value on employability, and the career path is quite flexible). Generation X middle managers in student affairs will work best when given the desired outcome and allowed to determine the most effective means of achievement on their own (Thielfoldt and Scheef, 2005). Of course, if the supervisor is Generation X and the middle manager is a Baby Boomer or Traditionalist, then other mentoring techniques would be appropriate. For example, a Baby Boomer would be more interested in determining means and having the supervisor as part of the decision process. The use of consensus rather than autonomy provides a more comfortable environment for the Baby Boomer middle manager. Likewise, feedback that is direct and frequent works well for the Generation X middle manager but would pose a threat to the Baby Boomer.

In interviews with middle managers and supervisors, it became evident that the middle managers were mostly interested in knowing expected results and then being provided with the freedom to achieve those results without interference. Process was of little interest, especially meetings that did not seem to add to the ability to get things done. Interestingly, there was near unanimity in the desire to have mentoring from supervisors. Generation X middle managers were blunt in their assessments of performance of supervisors, and most stated that they were very willing to be direct with their supervisors about their frustrations. Said one, "I expect (my supervisor) to provide the training and mentoring I need for my career. What interests me is how I can do a better job and prepare for the next one. I left my last job because my boss wanted to tell me what to do. I would leave this job, too, if I wasn't learning and if I didn't enjoy the work." Some of those interviewed discussed the common perception of Baby Boomers and Traditionalists that a person was expected to "pay their dues" as part of a career path. Baby Boomers saw "dues paying" as part of the job; recognition of their commitment to work would be rewarded with pay and promotion. Generation X managers, however, frequently stated that this was an outmoded means of evaluating performance and, in fact, might cause some to look for positions at other institutions. The implication for collaborative work is plain. The successful supervisor needs to point out the beneficial outcomes and benefits to students of collaboration. It is especially difficult when middle managers of different generations suffer a workplace values collision. Said one Baby Boomer middle manager about a Generation X middle manager, " [He] is new and hasn't the experience to know how things are done. [He] doesn't see that collaborating would be better and he should be using the expertise of those who have been here longer. He hasn't paid enough dues to ignore us." It is a clear that one has placed a high value on collaboration, while the other on values of autonomy and individual competence.

Generational differences are significant factors in the supervision and mentoring of middle managers. The conflict of workplace values and attitudes could result in challenges to effective outcomes. Yet these same potential conflicts, when approached creatively, can result in a workplace that is more creative and more outcomes-base than a workplace with a uniformity of values and attitudes. Many, perhaps most, entry-level staff are Millennials. It is important as part of professional growth for Millennial staff to understand the challenges of generational differences. It is of considerable value to understand generational contexts to make best use of performance appraisals and outcome expectations.

Other Supervisory Concerns

Generational differences pose unique challenges. Means may be adjusted to accommodate generational differences, but traditional elements of successful management remain in place. Determination of levels of authority (where decisions are made) must be clarified, and recognition that decisions made at a higher level must be implemented, frequently, by the middle manager.

Both the middle manager and the entry-level manager must have effective means of communication with the supervisor. Both formal and informal means are important, as is providing data and information from across the institution and division. The manager should continually be involved in an environmental scan and provide the information to the more senior officer. An effective manager will communicate both the status of present conditions and future goals, issues, plans, and their implications.

It is especially useful for the manager to provide information about issues not directly related to student affairs. An effective student affairs division interacts with units across campus, and keeping senior student affairs officials informed about these relationships is most important. There must be continual communication between the middle manager and the SSAO. Avoiding surprises to supervisors should be a goal. Even though unforeseen problems will develop, middle managers must try to keep the supervisor up to date. It is equally true that the SSAO should work to keep middle managers well informed about issues being discussed at the executive level, while middle managers should share what is appropriate with entry-level staff.

All managers must be accountable to a variety of constituents, including students, supervised staff, the SSAO, colleagues, and the institution itself. These competing groups and individuals require differing levels of accountability, which essentially requires that the middle manager set priorities. It may not be possible to please all constituencies, but acting responsibly toward the institution and supervisors will generally assure that other constituencies are properly treated.

Managing Up (and Down) the Organization

A critical part of leadership is *managing up*, providing assistance to supervisors. Managing up is not undermining the position of the executive, but rather it is providing support in a beneficial way. Managing up provides insights or suggests changes in direction before mistakes are made. Managers must have the courage to confront a supervisor, even when the confrontation is unwelcome, and the self-confidence to listen to subordinates when they have suggestions. Managing up requires fortitude and perseverance. Supervisors should also build a culture that encourages people to share openly concerns and ideas that may prevent a blunder or generate an important initiative (Useem, 2002).

Useem (2002) has developed guidelines for leading up in an organization that are instructive for all levels of managers and executives:

1. Subordinates must be bold in challenging superiors when it appears the superior is making a mistake; superiors should insist that managers challenge assumptions and programs. The bond between managers and senior officials is enhanced by frank interactions between them.
2. Managers must learn from past mistakes and not be paralyzed by them. Therefore, accuracy and the ability to communicate well are critical elements of successfully leading up in an organization. Supervisors should listen sensitively to determine exactly what is being expressed.
3. When required, middle managers must possess the courage to assume leadership and the persistence to move the division forward. Senior student affairs officers should assure that principles, goals, and strategies are clear, so that middle managers are successful when assuming leadership functions.

Mobility

For many managers, both middle and entry level, respect from superiors is a highly significant aspect of their positions. However, almost equally significant is a career commitment and a desire to assume to more responsible positions. White and others (1990) state that most middle managers expect to relocate to achieve advancement. Movement to another institution seems to be required for many student affairs middle managers with fewer than ten years of experience who wish to advance. For younger managers, mobility is the norm, the resume is always up to date and ready to use. For Generation X members, the average job is held for only two and a half years. Willingness to move is not a problem for most. Consistently demonstrating that one is broadly informed, professional in all settings, has the courage and willingness to inform upper management of both bad news and good, and is trustworthy to both upper management and lower-level staff make a middle manager attractive for more senior-level jobs. While these capabilities do not replace the knowledge requirements, without them advancement is more difficult.

Entry-level managers need to be careful about rapid movement between jobs. While this may seem to be positive to a member of Generation X or a Millennial, a Baby Boomer considering hiring may not see rapid movement as an asset. Remember that it takes at least a year for a person to understand institutional culture and become fully productive.

Not every person in middle management will want to move up the organizational ladder. Many reach professional fulfillment in middle management positions and find the contributions to students and institutions to be uniquely satisfying. Successfully developing the professional and personal attributes necessary for advancement also provides a foundation for professional satisfaction and growth for those whose heart remains in middle management positions.

Professional Development

The middle manager must seek means to develop new skills and competencies. Although these are key to advancement, Drucker (1974) argues that they are important for performance as well. He maintains we need "manager development precisely because tomorrow's jobs and tomorrow's organization can be assumed, with high probability, to be different from today's job and today's organization" (p. 424). The effective middle manager will make new skills a priority, a priority that blends nicely with the workplace values of younger managers.

Professional associations can be critical for the mobility of middle managers. Not only do associations provide opportunities to increase knowledge, develop new abilities, and learn of professional developments, but they can also be used to build networks with colleagues across the country or within a region. It is rare that the middle manager will face a challenge that has not been faced by someone, somewhere. A network can identify those who have faced similar problems and provide the voice of experience to the manager seeking a solution. Middle managers should be active in professional associations for several professional reasons, but forging links with colleagues is a major one. (See Chapter Eleven for a more comprehensive discussion of professional associations.)

Some Career Issues

During midlife, many adults examine careers and career aspirations, take a closer look at family and those relationships, and search for a sense of meaning to life (Schlossberg, Lynch, and Chickering, 1989). These issues are particularly relevant to the middle manager, especially one who has been in a position for several years. Middle managers examine their relationships to employing institutions as they might ties to family. The meaning of a position, and ultimately a career, has its roots in the fundamental relationship between the manager and the institution. Failure to find a satisfactory answer to the quest for meaning in the relationship often causes persons to seek career opportunities outside student affairs (White and others, 1990). Buford (2007) maintains that those who find the most significance in the latter part of their career are resistant to stereotypes, characterized by freshness, do not let things grow stale, enjoy relationships that endure, have personalities that remain stable, and are continually finding ways to move forward and continuing to make a difference, perhaps in new and different ways.

Conclusion

The role of manager in student affairs is difficult to define. The nature of student affairs virtually assures ambiguity about the exact nature of the work. However, middle managers can adopt several approaches to aid in achieving success:

1. Clearly define the position, its authority, and its accountability.
2. Commit to providing the best supervision of staff possible to meet institutional goals and objectives.
3. Adopt a management style that helps staff while enabling the manager to meet performance expectations.
4. Create a relationship with the SSAO or other supervisor that is open and designed to enhance the middle manager's role in the institution.
5. Assume responsibility for personal development of new skills and competencies.
6. Be involved in professional associations to create a network of colleagues for assistance and support.
7. Establish a personal career path, with contingencies, to keep professional decisions in focus.
8. Analyze what provides job satisfaction and create situations where those factors can be exploited.

Entry-level staff has its set of ambiguities as well, but a careful look at the list presented will inform those staff of the requirements necessary to be successful in entry-level positions as well as those in middle management.

Supervision of managers is complicated by generational differences in the workplace. Differing values, leadership styles, attitudes toward work, work ethic, and values require creative approaches that may breathe new life into an institution and hasten needed organizational change. They may also cause difficulties if not handled properly.

The middle manager has a unique function in a student affairs program. Midlevel managers must select, train, and develop staff. They must implement policy and programs. They must furnish communication both up and down the organizational ladder. They may provide direction to a specific functional program and yet are expected to have an institutional view on issues. Middle managers may be asked to provide direct assistance in institutional planning and organization reengineering.

Robert Ackerman's work, *The Mid-Level Manager in Student Affairs* (2007), expands on many of the topics discussed in this chapter. For those interested in a fuller discussion of the middle manager in student affairs, this work provides an in-depth look at the challenges and opportunities for the midlevel professional.

Even with the ambiguities and seeming contradictions inherent in their positions, middle managers provide the leadership of functional areas that form the basis of student affairs programs. They are the knowledge professionals of student affairs programs and have an important influence on each student's development and that of staff members who will be the professional leaders of the next generation. Entry-level staff carry the responsibilities of being frontline staff, engaging students with the institution, and providing direction for student growth. Sandeen (1991) offers insight to the aspiring chief executive officer: Know yourself, have a philosophy, pay your dues, be willing to move, select your institution, and love the students. These insights are good advice for other student affairs managers as well.

References

Ackerman, R. L. (Ed.). *The Mid-Level Manager in Student Affairs*. Washington, D.C.: National Association of Student Personnel Administrators, 2007.

Anand, R. *The Campus of Today and the Future*. Presentation at Sodexho Campus Services Client Symposium. Austin, Texas, May 2007.

Brown, R. D. "The Need for the Purpose of a Performance Appraisals System." In R. D. Brown (Ed.), *Performance Appraisal as a Tool for Staff Development*. New Directions for Student Services, no. 43. San Francisco: Jossey-Bass, 1988.

Bryan, W. A., and Mullendore, R. H. "Professional Development Strategies." In R. B. Young (Ed.), *The Invisible Leaders: Student Affairs Mid-Mangers*. Washington, D.C.: National Association of Student Personnel Administrators, 1990.

Buford, B. "Finishing Well: How Pathfinders Transform Success to Significance." *Leader to Leader*, 43, 2007, 37–43.

Byrnes, J. "Middle Management Excellence." In *Working Knowledge for Business Leaders* online newsletter. Cambridge, MA: Harvard Business School, December, 2005.

Drucker, P. F. *Management: Task, Responsibilities, Practices.* New York: Harper Collins, 1974.

Drucker, P .F. "The Shape of Things to Come." In F. Hesselbein, and P. Cohen, (Eds.), *Leader to Leader.* San Francisco: Jossey-Bass, 1999.

Gendron, M. "Keys to Retaining Your Best Managers in a Tight Job Market." *Harvard Management Update,* 1998a, 3(6), June.

Gendron, M. "Strategic Planning—Why It's Not Just for Senior Managers Anymore." *Harvard Management Update,* 1998b, 3(5), May.

Hanaka, M. E., and Hawkins, B. "Organizing for Endless Winning." In F. Hesselbein, M. Goldsmith, and R. Beckhard (Eds.), *The Organization of the Future.* San Francisco: Jossey-Bass, 1997.

Kouzes, J. M., and Posner, B. Z. *Credibility.* San Francisco: Jossey-Bass, 1993.

Kuh, G. D., and Whitt, E. J. *The Invisible Tapestry: Culture in American Colleges and Universities.* ASHE-ERIC Higher Education Report, no. 1. Washington, D.C.: Association for the Study of Higher Education, 1988.

Mintzberg, H. "Crafting Strategy." *Harvard Business Review,* July–August 1987.

Sandeen, A. *The Chief Student Affairs Officer.* San Francisco: Jossey-Bass, 1991.

Schlossberg, N. K., Lynch, A. Q., and Chickering, A. W. *Improving Higher Education Environments for Adults: Responsive Programs and Services from Entry to Departure.* San Francisco: Jossey-Bass, 1989.

Thielfoldt, D., and Scheef, D. "Generation X and the Millennials: What You Need to Know About Mentoring the New Generations." *Law Practice Today,* November 2005.

Useem, M. "Mastering People Management: The Ups and Downs of Leading People." *Mastering People Management.* [http://www.itstime.com/feb2002.htm]. 2002.

White, J., Webb, L., and Young, R. B. "Press and Stress: A Comparative Study of Institutional Factors Affecting the Work of Mid-Managers." In R. B. Young (Ed.), *The Invisible Leaders: Student Affairs Mid-Managers.* Washington, D.C.: National Association of Student Personnel Administrators, 1990.

Young, R. B. *No Neutral Ground.* San Francisco: Jossey-Bass, 1997.

Young, R. B. "Still Leaders! Still Invisible?" In R. L. Ackerman (Ed.), *The Mid-Level Manager in Student Affairs.* Washington, D.C.: National Association of Student Personnel Administrators, 2007.

CHAPTER NINETEEN

PROFESSIONAL DEVELOPMENT AS LIFELONG LEARNING

Susan R. Komives and Stan Carpenter

A few years ago, Illinois Wesleyan University sent an invitation to alumni weekend with the bold announcement, "Your Degree is Now Obsolete!" The same could be said for all of our undergraduate and graduate degrees. In this information age, the half-life of information is shortening; it requires our continued learning to stay updated, competent, and visionary. Indeed, "workers and practitioners in virtually all industries and disciplines must remain students for life to stay current in their skills and knowledge" (Cantor, 2006, p. 28).

Although grounded in bodies of knowledge from our formal study in higher education, student affairs, or student development, today's times require that professionals acquire new information to approach contemporary challenges. Vaill (1991) affirms that in these rapidly changing times, we must become comfortable being beginners again and again as we face new situations. He wrote, "It is not an exaggeration to suggest that everyone's state of beginnerhood is only going to deepen and intensify so that ten years from now each of us will be even more profoundly and thoroughly settled in the state of being a perpetual beginner" (p. 81). Professionals may not need competency skills for this kind of lifelong learning, but they do need comfort with incompetency skills—acknowledging what we do not know or know how to do with the confidence that we know how to learn. These may be the skills of being effective beginners (Vaill, 1996). Paradoxically, we build our capacity when we admit we do not know something and we have the efficacy to know we can learn it.

In the sections that follow, we assert the need for lifelong professional learning and identify the complexity of skills and competencies needed in the field. We advance a notion of professional development, propose a model for thinking about individual and group professional development, offer some suggestions about how to implement a comprehensive professional development plan, and share some exemplary professional development activities.

Lifelong Professional Learning

The complexity of problems student affairs professionals face daily, the rapid influx of new information, the need for knowledge management (Cantor, 2006), the nature of evolving technologies, and the importance of examining diverse frameworks and perspectives clearly signal that no individual ever has enough information or personal skill to address such complexity. For these and many other reasons, professional student affairs administrators and student development educators are obligated to a personal commitment to socialization and regeneration (Carpenter, 2003), especially initial preparation and lifelong learning (Carpenter, 1991). The juxtaposition of knowledge and skills necessary for the practice of any profession, together with the complexity of the student affairs practice, leads to a discussion of the knowledge and learning requirements for lifelong professional education.

Professional Competencies

To illustrate the complexity of student affairs work, it is useful to consider several recent projects that examine necessary competencies, areas of emphasis or study that define professional practice. Pope, Reynolds, and Mueller (2004) identified competencies in the areas of:

1. Administration and management,
2. Multicultural awareness, knowledge, and skills,
3. Helping and advising,
4. Assessment and research,
5. Teaching and training,
6. Ethics and professional standards, and
7. Translation and use of theory to guide practice.

In a study for the National Association of Student Personnel Administrators (NASPA), Janosik (Janosik, Carpenter, & Creamer, 2006) proposed the following competency groupings:

1. Student development, characteristics, environment, and learning,
2. Assessment and research practices,
3. Culture, diversity, and multiculturalism,
4. History, values, and philosophy of the profession,
5. Administration, management, technology, and organization development, and
6. Law, legislation, and policy.

In recent years, the American College Personnel Association (ACPA) has convened a group to consider what areas might be used to construct a curriculum for organizing professional development that parallel the other two efforts mentioned:

1. Advising and helping,
2. Assessment, evaluation, and research,
3. Ethics,
4. Legal foundations,
5. Leadership and administration/management,
6. Pluralism and inclusion,
7. Student learning and development, and
8. Teaching (ACPA Steering Committee on Professional Competencies, 2007).

The Council for the Advancement of Standards in Higher Education (CAS) published the first standards for master's preparation in student affairs and higher education in the early 1980s. Many graduate preparation programs use these standards for their program design and are in voluntary compliance with this approach to professional preparation. Table 19.1 outlines the key areas presented by CAS (Council for the Advancement of Standards in Higher Education [CAS], 2006c), foundational studies, professional studies, and supervised practice. Bodies of knowledge for each area are identified in this table.

TABLE 19.1 THE CAS CURRICULUM

Areas of Study	Specific Curriculum
Foundational Studies	Historical higher education and student affairs foundations
	Philosophical higher education and student affairs foundations
Professional Studies	Student development theory
	Student characteristics and effects of college on students
	Individual and group interventions
	Organization and administration of student affairs
	Assessment, evaluation, and research
Supervised Practice	Practica and internships covering two different experiences

Source: Adapted from CAS (2006c), p. 350.

Clearly, each of the areas cited in these attempts at defining the necessary knowledge and skills for the field are complex in and of themselves. They sum to quite a daunting whole. These lists also represent a remarkable convergence of needed skills and competencies in professional student affairs practice. These competencies are complemented by the general and personal qualities advanced by CAS in their document, "Characteristics of Individual Excellence for Professional Practice in Higher Education" (CAS, 2006a), which are clustered as general knowledge and skills, interactive competencies, and self-mastery. This compilation is available on the CAS Web site and serves as a useful self-assessment to guide a personalized professional development plan.

Student affairs has the distinct challenge of comprising professionals from diverse backgrounds (for example, health care, accounting, recreation, counseling) working together in a student affairs division. Blimling (2001) applied the idea of communities of practice to student affairs, noting that we do not have one culture and literature to pay homage and attention to, but perhaps several. Respecting each of these communities and studying the interesting ways in which they intersect and interact are necessary for contemporary student affairs practice. *Learning Reconsidered* (Keeling, 2004) recognized that many professionals contribute to student learning who may not have formal preparation in student affairs. The authors wrote:

> While the educational preparation of student affairs professionals must focus on in-depth knowledge of these topics, it is equally important that other members of the academic community understand the context of higher education, theories of student development and learning, factors that contribute to student success and retention, and characteristics and needs of diverse student populations. Since many academic administrators and advisors do not receive formal education in these areas, institutions of higher education must provide professional development to assist them in gaining this knowledge base. (p. 25)

With the quantity and complexity of information needed and the personal qualities required, it is no wonder that we feel like continual beginners! Clearly, the question really is not whether one should engage in professional development, but how can one stay truly ready? The answer lies, as most things in education do, in a commitment to lifelong learning.

Defining Professional Development

Carpenter and Stimpson (2007) explored scholarly practice, professionalism, and professional development, concluding that intentional practice (research, peer review, and experience driven) demands career-long learning. Further, such learning should be reflective of the best thinking in the field. Student affairs work has a proud history of scholarship interacting with practice. Hence, there is an imperative for professionals to participate in lifelong learning and reflection, organized according to the standards of the profession.

In addition, professionals need to identify their basic orientations to their work roles. Komives (1998) explored this notion of a continuum, including "practitioner-practitioner; practitioner-scholar; scholar-practitioner; and scholar-scholar" (p. 179), suggesting that either extreme is suboptimal. The *practitioner-practitioner* has no theoretical grounding and operates without regard to applications of theory and research to his work. Likewise, the *scholar-scholar* is solely interested in theory and the generation of research without connection to practice and the policy and student development questions that need understanding. The *practitioner-scholar* leads with her skill in application but is informed and understands the theoretical and research bases of practice. The *scholar-practitioner* is motivated by advancing theory and research from the context of practice and actively studies and assesses practical outcomes and experiences. Understanding the range of these orientations to professional work is useful for the group to design appropriately targeted professional development programs.

One way to look at professional development is to compare it to identity formation. Miller and Carpenter (1980) took this tack, reasoning that professional development ought to conform to human development principles, and derived five propositions (Table 19.2) that clearly support (indeed, demand) a commitment to learning from the beginning of one's career to the end.

Carpenter (2003) later modified the model derived from these propositions to consist of the formative, application, and additive stages, mileposts along the way to professional identity, each with characteristic behaviors, attitudes, and developmental tasks. The *formative stage* is characterized by a more external locus

TABLE 19.2 THE NATURE OF PROFESSIONAL DEVELOPMENT

1. Professional development is continuous and cumulative in nature, moves from simpler to more complex behavior, and can be described via levels or stages held in common.
2. Optimal professional development is a direct result of the interaction between the total person striving for professional growth and the environment.
3. Optimal professional preparation combines mastery of a body of knowledge and a cluster of skills and competencies within the context of personal development.
4. Professional credibility and excellence of practice are directly dependent upon the quality of professional preparation.
5. Professional preparation is a lifelong learning process.

Source: Miller and Carpenter (1980), p. 84.

of control, as the young professional looks to more seasoned ones to guide her training and orientation into the field. We might think of the dominant activity in this stage as *learning*. The *application stage* features a transition from external to internal locus of control, as the professional trusts himself and his judgment more and more, always continuing to learn new information and skills, of course. This stage is concerned mostly clearly and concisely with *doing*. Similarly, the *additive stage* professional is in a position of *contributing* to student affairs practice in any number of ways: humane and informed supervision, role modeling, the creation of policy, professional association leadership, scholarly productivity, and other exemplary activities. These stages, then, represent macro-versions what Carpenter (2003) called the "cycle of professional development—learning, doing, and contributing" (p. 582). Perhaps an even more interesting way to look at this cycle is in a micro way. The learning, doing, and contributing motif is a good way to think about every aspect of practice, almost as if this simple sequence operates as a kind of fractal, describing and guiding everything from the smallest structures of our daily interactions with colleagues and students to the largest aspects of organizational and scholarly productivity, hearkening back to our earlier discussion of continual beginnerhood. We are what we learn, do, and contribute to clients, colleagues, the profession, and society!

This more fundamental and complex way of looking at professional development is consonant with recent scholarship in the field of continuing and professional education. Departing from what Cervero (2000) suggested was a sort of pause in the progress of continuing professional education in the 1990s, Dirkx, Gilley, and Gilley (2004) argued for a much more subjective and contextual view, decrying a narrow focus on "simple" skill and competency development, presumably especially when "transmitted in a didactic fashion and offered by a pluralistic group of providers (workplaces, for-profits, and universities) that do not work together in any coordinated fashion" (Cervero, p. 4). To Dirkx and others (2004), professional development is mediated by experience and vice versa. The practice and personal contexts are mutually interactive with content and process, so that no particular skill or knowledge set is appropriate or even advisable from person to person. Knowledge and skills, as well as needs for further development, evolve for each professional.

Such a broadened conception of formal professional development means that it becomes a much more integral part of professional practice and identity than has heretofore been thought. Carpenter (2003) and Carpenter and Stimpson (2007) reinforce the notion that professional development, as any other area of practice, should be intentional, research based, peer reviewed, and carefully evaluated.

In the next section of the chapter, we explore a model that reflects these characteristics. If professional development programs are to flourish, a "continuum of professional practice" (Knox, 2000, p. 16) must be adopted that views professional education as a lifelong process. Knox views the continuum being an organized, coordinated effort that focuses on "goals, learning activities, providers, resources, context, and negotiation" (p. 17) concerning the aspects of professional development. Professional development activities should ideally begin where professional preparation programs leave off and respond to needs thereafter. In the student affairs profession, this is even more complex because practitioners enter from a wide variety of rich backgrounds, making appropriate content a moving target on both ends. Professional development activities should be application focused (which helps with the differential preparation issue), without losing sight of theory. Encouraging professionals to apply what is learned is a natural and appropriate extension of professional development. Finally, professional development activities should receive support from all parties concerned with professional improvement, including administrators, learners, and policymakers (Knox, 2000).

In this information age, in our networked world, Allen and Cherrey (2000) advocate that we need new ways of relating across the organization, new ways of leading, new ways of changing, and new ways of learning together. It is not sufficient to think that individuals will bring adequate knowledge with them to solve complex problems, but it is encouraging that there is a growing recognition that together we can learn and change our processes to function as a learning organization (Senge, 1990). Staff development enables a group with shared purposes to expand the collective capacity of the group (Bandura, 1997). Teams that attend a shared experience (for example, faculty and student affairs teams attending an assessment institute) become change agents in their shared learning. Organizational learning often changes the culture of the organization and makes it possible to address complex issues and accomplish transformative change.

A Model of Professional Development

Given the considerations discussed, modern professional development in a student affairs work context should have certain characteristics, whether designed for individual learning or group and unit development, captured here in a mnemonic fashion. Professional development activities should be:

> *Purposeful, intentional, and goal related.* Professional development should result from a felt need, a desire to get better at particular aspects of practice. Professionals and groups should continually strive to improve and understand that this will usually require more learning.

Research, theory, and data based. Appropriate professional development, like any other professional activity, should have a rational basis in theory and ideally will have been demonstrated to have value through disciplined inquiry. Using techniques or approaches that are not theory and research based is risky, at best, and may be wasteful or even harmful.

Experience based. Less experienced professionals should take opportunities to learn from more experienced ones. This dictum applies to both content and mode. This guideline is not age related; for example, very young professionals may have technological expertise to bring to a division or team. Many mechanisms of professional development are fairly well known and available. Likewise, in student affairs, there is a variety of ways to learn new things and practice new skills. Professionals should take advantage of these established avenues, perhaps with occasional individual changes for context. At a minimum, readily accessible wisdom, in the form of proven modes, is the place to start when considering ways to learn.

Peer reviewed. An underutilized resource in student affairs is peer review. In the context of professional development, it is particularly important to get some "organized help" in the form of individual opinions and analysis, committee efforts, departmental or divisional programs, professional association curricula or models, or one of many other methods. It is unnecessary and inefficient to ignore the judgment of other professionals when considering one's own professional development, and it seems especially unwise when mechanisms for doing so are readily available.

Assessed. Taking all the preceding factors into account, one must still check out the feasibility, likely cost and benefit(s), likelihood of achieving the purpose, level of challenge, and availability of needed resources, including time and energy. Simply stated, is the proposed activity going to result in the desired learning? It should go without saying that this assessment should be done in advance.

Reflected upon and reflected in practice. Every professional development activity, as any other educational endeavor, requires reflection to complete the learning loop. Schön's (1991) conception was that one's practice should include a significant amount of reflection, that continual reexamination, learning, and even intuition are necessary elements in any profession. Time and methods should be built in for thinking about and carefully applying lessons learned.

Evaluated. Did the activity result in what was expected? If not, was the result better or worse, and how can the former be maximized and the latter minimized in the future? If the needs or goals were not met, the professional should fold that knowledge into the ongoing plan for professional development. Similarly, if the goals were met, what is the next step? Again, this is analogous to all areas of professional practice.

The notion here is that it is necessary to PREPARE throughout the entire career. One is never finished learning, and the part of learning that follows formal preparation needs to be just as organized, just as carefully thought out, as any academic program ever was. In fact, in keeping with the notion that professional preparation is actually akin to identity development and is constructivist in nature, even the formal preparation is subject to the same considerations as traditional professional development. For example, a formative stage professional, engaging in a formal academic program, would also be involved in heavily supervised practice activities in the form of an assistantship or practicum (Carpenter, 2003). The overall program and every aspect of the experiences could be analyzed using the PREPARE framework. Formative stage individuals not in a formal preparation program are equally dependent upon supervision and mentorship for a period of time. Obviously, the considerations of the model would need to be evaluated and analyzed by someone with a fair amount of experience in the field—people new to the profession could not be expected to do so with any accuracy or comprehensiveness.

In the application stage (Carpenter, 2003), the professional would take more and more ownership for his or her own professional growth and development path, still asking for and getting help and guidance from mentors and supervisors, in addition to responding to professional associations and literature. The application stage person also grows in the ability to understand that professional development interacts with practice in often unpredictable ways. Reflection, with the help of a colleague or alone, can lead to great insight. In the additive stage (Carpenter, 2003), one is usually responsible not only for personal professional development decisions but also for creating environments that facilitate the development of others, whether the student affairs division, the institution, or profession-wide. A great way to add or contribute to the profession is to participate in designing and delivering high-quality professional development experiences on one's campus and beyond.

The professional development activities that would be subject to the considerations detailed in the simple model represented here would ideally be part of a larger context. One's personal plan should be as detailed and long term as possible, given one's experience and knowledge, which will obviously grow with time. Similarly, the employing institution should offer a carefully thought-out and extensive professional development plan that encompasses all levels of professional development for a wide variety of student affairs generalists and specialists, with the hallmark being individual responsibility and intentionality. There should be, in short, a long-term plan for a whole career, changing as necessary, as well as shorter-term goals, as in any practice setting or job.

A full program of professional development entails several considerations. Professional development activities can be short term, long term, or incidental. For example, one might participate in a training workshop focusing on intercultural awareness (short term) as a part of a larger plan to learn more about significant subcultures on campus (long term). Along the way, one might become more aware of positive and negative interaction styles through a conversation with a person of another culture (incidental). The latter activity could only be placed in the PREPARE framework after the fact, but it can clearly form the basis for future growth. Table 19.3 illustrates how sample professional development activities can be framed as intentional, developmental experiences.

Several examples of innovative and excellent programs are mentioned later in this chapter. The real key is not single activities but organized programs, encompassing individual and group plans and activities, on-campus and off-campus activities, formal and informal programs, as well as opportunities to participate in association leadership at the state, regional, and national levels. Student affairs divisions, especially, have a responsibility and obligation to provide opportunities and encouragement to individual practitioners and to work unit learning. Professional development has many benefits to the individual, clearly, but it benefits the organization and the clientele (students) even more by fostering an ever more accomplished workforce.

Winston and Creamer (1997) captured this triple benefit idea best in their book on staffing practices in student affairs, proposing "a radically different perspective on supervision . . . a helping process, which is designed to support staff as they seek to promote the goals of the organizations and to advance their professional development" (p. 194). Their model of "synergistic supervision" (p. 194) features a growth orientation, a focus on competence, a focus on job/position/unit needs and expectations and personal ones; joint effort in supervision activities, requiring strong two-way communication; a focus on competence rather than deficits, implying the need for professional development to gain competence; a growth orientation; proactivity to spot problems and challenges early and deal with them; goal-based activities reflecting both institutional and personal and professional perspectives; systematic and ongoing processes; and a holistic view of the employee as both a person and a professional.

The PREPARE model offers a way to frame the plans and conversations necessary for synergistic supervision to occur. With this mindset, it is easy to see

TABLE 19.3 SAMPLE PROFESSIONAL DEVELOPMENT ACTIVITIES AND THE PREPARE MODEL

Dimension of Quality	Research Teams/ Writing Groups	Internships/Job Sharing/ Job Swapping	Book Clubs	Institute Attendance
Purposeful	Advance knowledge in the field; build personal research/ writing skills; product oriented	Support career goals or skill-building goals	Identify books that relate to campus needs or individual needs and interests	Support job needs or professional development plan
Research/Theory Based	Grounded in review of scholarship	Learn scholarship that applies to new functional areas of interest	Provide new scholarly understanding to apply to practice	Institute should make theoretical frames transparent
Experience Based	Follow guidelines of successful projects in the past	Seek guidance from supervisors, mentors, and colleagues about how to gain maximum benefit	Discuss with peers to make application	Immersion experience for 2–3 days of institute; plan transference; vetted by professional association
Peer Reviewed	Involvement of peer debriefers; submitted for formal peer review	Might use application process for selection; guidelines for program created by committee of colleagues	Peer process on choice of books assures quality of books; books have undergone some peer review process in order to be published	Quality is implied through sponsoring organizations
Assessed	Work pace important to writing time commitments; identify skill deficits (for example, analysis methods)	Check fit, willingness, meaningful involvement; make it time limited	Use criteria for book selection	Justify fit with personal goals and organizational needs
Reflected	Process experience with team	Provide developmental supervision on site	Expect application of material to work context	Require debriefing, report, or presentation upon return to campus
Evaluated	Team evaluated; productivity identified	Use 360-degree feedback strategies (that is, supervisor, peer, subordinate); process with regular supervisor	Evaluate learning after each reading cycle	Require institute impact to be addressed in annual review

how professional development benefits both the person and the organization, which means that students are better served. Taking this notion one step further and combining it with the ideas of Dirkx and others (2004) that professional development and practice contexts are interactive, we arrive at the fundamental position that professional practice, done properly, is, in some sense, professional development and vice versa. Professionals need to be intentional, theory based, cognizant of history, responsive to peer review, reflective, and evaluative in *all* that they do, whether working with students or sharpening their knowledge and skills.

There is no limit to creative opportunities for specific professional development activities. In addition to activities individuals or offices might design for themselves, Cantor (2006) identifies four distinct categories of common sources for professional continuing education (PCE), often in competition in the marketplace for the training dollar. These four categories are professional associations, commercial vendors, proprietary schools and colleges, and not-for-profit organizations. Using a revised version of Cantor's taxonomy, Table 19.4 presents examples of the range of professional development opportunities in the student affairs or higher education fields:

TABLE 19.4 EXAMPLES OF CONTINUING PROFESSIONAL DEVELOPMENT BY PRIMARY SOURCES OF DELIVERY

Category of Sources	Sample Activities
Professional associations (see Chapter Eleven)	Attend and present at international, national, regional, and local conferences (CEU credits often are possible)
	Become involved in diverse associations (broaden into new specialties including those outside student affairs)
	Attend and present at special institutes and workshops (for example, ACUHO-I's National Housing Training Institute (NHTI); NASPA's Richard Stevens Institute for Senior Student Affairs Officers; ACPA's Donna M. Bourassa Mid-Level Management Institute; NCLP, ACPA, NACA and NASPA's Leadership Educators Institute)
	Experience e-learning courses; webinars; teleconferences
	Participate in international study tours
	Read and write for publications (for example, journals, magazines)
	Develop mentors/sponsors/peer supports/networks through associations
	For lists of higher education associations see http://www.cas.edu; www.naspa.org/

Commercial vendors	Explore the portfolios of such e-vendors as Magna, PaperClip, studentaffairs.com
	Hire consultants and consulting firms
	Work with a personal coach
	Enroll in Web-based short courses and seminars
Not-for-profit organizations	Identify programs and involvement in:
	• Chamber of Commerce
	• Public libraries
	• American Red Cross
	• Faith-based organizations
	• Heritage-based organizations
	• Service learning
	• Specialized institutes like the Social Justice Training Institute: http://www.sjti.org/
Colleges and universities	Participate in campus-based opportunities such as:
	• Individual graduate courses
	• Select undergraduate courses
	• Certificate programs or degree programs [see Chapter Twenty]
	• Office of Human Resources/Personnel programs
	• Center for Teaching Excellence programs
	• Office Technology programs (using of SPSS or Blackboard)
	• Seminars and institutes
	• Internships, postgraduate fellowships, and sabbaticals
	• Job exchanges or cross-training
	• Teaching courses
	• Book groups or case study groups
	• Reading groups (perhaps use syllabi from outstanding courses)
	• Research teams
	• Short courses (for example, Harvard institutes)
	• Alternative Spring Break programs
	• Mentors and peer supports
	• Proprietary college programs in management, technology, or human services
International experiences	Become more globally minded through such experiences as:
	• Semester-at-Sea (http://www.semesteratsea.com/jobscareers/index.html)
	• The ScholarShip (http://www.TheScholarShip.com)
	• Fulbright appointments (http://exchanges.state.gov/education/fulbright/)
	• Peace Corps (http://www.peacecorps.gov/index.cfm?shell=learn.howvol)

Exemplary Practices

Some institutions have developed outstanding professional development programs that provide examples to emulate. The ones mentioned here are the result of a quick poll the authors conducted of a very limited group of professionals from several listservs, with no pretense of comprehensiveness. No slight of any institution not mentioned is intended.

Texas A&M University annually holds the Academy for Student Affairs Professionals (ASAP), which is a weeklong workshop aimed specifically at student affairs division employees who do not have a traditional student affairs background or preparation, including everyone from medical professionals to administrative assistants. The topics are developed by surveys of professionals of all levels as well as graduate faculty members. Participants learn about the history and philosophy of higher education, student development and learning theory and practice, organizational politics, current issues, and a host of other topics delivered in a concentrated format. Evaluations indicate that ASAP graduates have new appreciation for the aims and goals of the student affairs profession, regardless of their previous training or background.

The University of South Carolina has an extensive professional development program that requires each professional to have a plan on file with the division that responds to development in one or more core competency areas and to be evaluated on it annually. Salary increases and travel funds, among other things, are contingent upon success with the plans, which can include attendance at the speaker series hosted by the division, conference and association attendance and leadership activity, formal coursework, service to the community, cross-training, and a variety of other activities. Just about any activity could be sanctioned if an employee makes a good case that it is needed for professional development. This pervasive process of professional development provides a good example of what is called for in this chapter.

The University of North Carolina-Wilmington has a Fellows program involving five to seven Fellows working in departments other than their own for up to five hours a week, with host mentors providing help and supervision. This is a wonderful way to build community as well as cross-train and orient professionals who might want to check out a new area or simply learn more about an office that they work with but with which they have little familiarity. Experiences are reported on annually in the Fellow's Symposium. The host office gets some help, but more important, a fresh eye to help make changes that might not be obvious to an insider.

The Association of College and University Housing Officers-International (ACUHO-I) has a long-standing annual institute for professionals with three to five years full-time housing experience, built on a set of fifty competencies identified and refined over the years by housing professionals. This institute, the James C. Grimm National Housing Training Institute (NHTI), brings midlevel professionals into intense work with faculty who are seasoned housing and general student affairs professionals and faculty.

Other programs that were suggested in this very informal poll included:

- Reading and writing support groups and clubs of various kinds,
- International opportunities, including the student affairs-oriented Fulbright Program for International Administrators to Germany, Korea, and Japan,
- Very structured programs aimed mostly at newer and midcareer professionals, involving heavy mentoring and extra help with travel and formal preparation,
- Senior staff (vice president and associates, directors) trip to another university to give them an intensive look at how functions are accomplished in another venue,
- A best practices/worst mistakes program to encourage sharing throughout the division,
- Programs focusing on administrative staff involving personal enrichment activities off campus, and
- Intern programs in which one person a year is picked to be a half-time assistant in the vice president's office in order to get the bigger picture of student affairs administration.

Each of these programs exists within a larger context, of course, but would be excellent parts of an overall plan.

Conclusion

In a review of ethics statements by the Council for the Advancement of Standards in Higher Education of its thirty-five member associations, associations concurred that as a dimension of professional autonomy, it is an ethical practice to "engage in continuing education and professional development" (CAS, 2006b). By implication, not to do so would be unethical. Both ACPA and NASPA advance professional development in their ethics statements. The ACPA (2006) statement explicitly asserts that professionals must "maintain and enhance professional effectiveness by continually improving skills and acquiring new knowledge."

Developing professionally must be viewed as a daily activity of learning and applying new perspectives as a way of being. One should have a clear and active plan, and so should one's unit, department, division, and institution. Ultimately, however, Kruger (2000) is absolutely right that professional development is the responsibility of each individual practitioner. It is ethical and desirable for individual offices and student affairs divisions to support, expect, and promote continuing education in diverse forms, but even if the employer does not provide reasonable supports to make that happen, individual professionals must ensure their own capacity building and renewal.

Professional development is the responsibility of individuals, units, and divisions, and also of professional associations. Moreover, professional development is so intertwined with appropriate, intentional student affairs practice that the two can be thought of as mutually constructed—it makes little sense to talk about one without the other. So, the question becomes not whether one engages in professional development, but how well, and the answer dictates the quality of practice. Knowing this changes our conversations in fundamental ways.

References

American College Personnel Association. "Professional Competencies: A Report of the Steering Committee on Professional Competencies." [http://www.myacpa.org/au/governance/]. 2007.

American College Personnel Association. *Statement of Ethical Principles and Standards.* [http://www.myacpa.org/au/documents/EthicsStatement.pdf]. 2006.

Allen, K. E., and Cherrey, C. *Systemic Leadership: Enriching the Meaning of Our Work.* Lanham, Md.: University Press of America, 2000.

Bandura, A. *Self-Efficacy: The Exercise of Control.* New York: Freeman, 1997.

Blimling, G. S. "Uniting Scholarship and Communities of Practice in Student Affairs." *Journal of College Student Development,* 2001, 42, 381–396.

Cantor, J. A. *Lifelong Learning and the Academy: The Changing Nature of Continuing Education.* ASHE Higher Education Report, no. 32(2). San Francisco: Jossey-Bass, 2006.

Carpenter, D. S. "Professionalism." In S. R. Komives and D. Woodard Jr. (Eds.), *Student Services: A Handbook for the Profession* (4th ed.). San Francisco: Jossey-Bass, 2003.

Carpenter, D. S. "Student Affairs Profession: A Developmental Perspective." In T. K. Miller, R. B. Winston, Jr., and Associates (Eds.), *Administration and Leadership in Student Affairs.* Muncie, Ind.: Accelerated Development, 1991.

Carpenter, D. S., and Stimpson, M. "Professionalism, Scholarly Practice, and Professional Development in Student Affairs." *NASPA Journal,* 2007, 44(2), 265–284.

Cervero, R. M. "Trends and Issues in Continuing Professional Education." In. V. W. Mott and B. J. Daley (Eds.), *Charting a Course for Continuing Professional Education: Reframing Professional Practices.* New Directions for Adult and Continuing Education, no. 86. San Francisco: Jossey-Bass, 2000.

Council for the Advancement of Standards in Higher Education. "CAS Characteristics of Individual Excellence." [http://www.cas.edu/]. 2006a.

Council for the Advancement of Standards in Higher Education. "CAS Statement of Shared Ethics." [http://www.cas.edu/]. 2006b.

Council for the Advancement of Standards in Higher Education. "Master's Level Student Affairs Administration Preparation Programs." In CAS Professional Standards for Higher Education (6th ed). Washington, D.C.: Council for the Advancement of Standards in Higher Education, 2006c.

Dirkx, J. M., Gilley, J. W., and Gilley, A. M. "Change Theory in CPE and HRD: Toward a Holistic View of Learning and Change in Work." *Advances in Developing Human Resources*, 2004, 6, 35–51.

Janosik, S., Carpenter, D. S., and Creamer, D. "Beyond Professional Preparation Programs: The Role of Professional Associations in Ensuring a High Quality Work Force. *College Student Affairs Journal*, 2006, 25(2), 228–237.

Keeling, R. P. (Ed.) *Learning Reconsidered: A Campus-Wide Focus on the Student Experience*. Washington, D.C.: National Association of Student Personnel Administrators and the American College Personnel Association, 2004.

Knox, A. B. "The Continuum of Professional Education and Practice." In V. W. Mott and B. J. Daley (Eds.), *Charting a Course for Continuing Professional Education: Reframing Professional Practice*. New Directions for Adult and Continuing Education, no. 86. San Francisco: Jossey-Bass, 2000.

Komives, S. R. "Linking Student Affairs Preparation with Practice." In N. J. Evans and C. E. Phelps Tobin (Eds.), *The State of the Art of Preparation and Practice in Student Affairs*. Washington, D.C.: American College Personnel Association, 1998.

Kruger, K. "New Alternatives for Professional Development." In M. J. Barr, M. K. Desler, and Associates (Eds.), *The Handbook of Student Affairs Administration* (2nd ed.). San Francisco: Jossey-Bass, 2000.

Miller, T. K., and Carpenter, D. S. "Professional Preparation for Today and Tomorrow." In D. Creamer (Ed.), *Student Development in Higher Education*. ACPA monograph series. Washington, D.C.: American College Personnel Association, 1980.

Pope, R. L., Reynolds, A. L., and Mueller, J. A. *Multicultural Competence in Student Affairs*. San Francisco: Jossey-Bass, 2004.

Schön, D. A. *The Reflective Practitioner: How Professionals Think in Action* (2nd ed.). London, U.K.: Ashgate, 1991.

Senge, P. M. *The Fifth Discipline: The Art and Practice of the Learning Organization*. New York: Doubleday, 1990.

Vaill, P. B. *Learning as a Way of Being: Strategies for Survival in a World of Permanent White Water*. San Francisco: Jossey-Bass, 1996.

Vaill, P. B. *Permanent White Water: The Realities, Myths, Paradoxes, and Dilemmas of Managing Organizations*. San Francisco: Jossey-Bass, 1991.

Winston, R. B. Jr., and Creamer, D. G. *Improving Staffing Practices in Student Affairs*. San Francisco: Jossey-Bass, 1997.

CHAPTER TWENTY

DOCTORAL EDUCATION AND BEYOND

Mary F. Howard-Hamilton and Randy E. Hyman

Imani has been an assistant director of the Ida B. Wells Black Cultural Center at My University for ten years. She advises the student gospel choir, Sister Circle Book Club, and Black Action Leadership Society, in addition to supervising programs and projects throughout the year. However, recently she has been seeking new challenges and would like to learn more about the financial and administrative structure of higher education. The director of the Wells Cultural Center has been encouraging Imani to begin exploring the possibility of enrolling in a higher education doctoral program.

Imani has enrolled in a few graduate classes for fun at My University, and this has been intellectually empowering. Imani conducted several informational interviews with higher education administrators and faculty on campus about the doctoral process and discovered that there are two traditional degrees offered in education, the Ed.D. and Ph.D., along with several classroom options for persons who want to work full time or attend school full time. There are also various teaching methods such as online programs, distance teleconference classrooms, cohort-structured programs, and the traditional full-time process with required courses and a broad selection of electives. Once she receives the degree, there is also the option to teach at the collegiate level. The challenge for Imani is choosing an institution that is compatible with her personal and professional goals and objectives. How does Imani make this life-altering educational decision?

Faculty, administrators, and mentors have been asked by individuals who have completed their master's degrees, "How do I choose a doctoral program and how do I know it is the right time to go?" This chapter connects Imani's doctoral decision, which is a typical scenario for most administrators in student affairs, with practical advice on the process of selecting an institution that offers a terminal degree in higher education or student affairs. The chapter is written from the perspective of those pursuing a terminal degree in the United States; other international educational systems rely less on earned doctorates and more on practical experience. Particular attention is given to when to pursue a doctoral education, selecting an Ed.D. or Ph.D. degree, steps to enhance your matriculation in the doctoral program, and choosing a career after the degree has been completed. The chapter concludes by expanding upon the opportunities available once the doctoral degree has been conferred.

Why a Doctorate?

The decision to pursue a doctorate is difficult because the process typically means interrupting your life for three to seven years, depending on whether or not you are enrolled continuously full time or choose to read, write, and attend class part time while you work full time. Since 1967, the time to complete a doctoral degree has increased by as much as two years (de Valero, 2001). The length of time to obtain a doctorate varies by academic discipline; however, "the median time spent enrolled as graduate student has increased from 6.6 years in 1983 to 7.1 in 1993" (de Valero, 2001, p. 341). The process is exacerbated even further when you are making decisions about marriage or a permanent partnership, child bearing or child rearing, and the possible physical as well as intellectual distancing from family and friends (Howard-Hamilton, 2004). Conversely, you will be among the educationally elite: "In 2000 a mere 1 percent of the nation's adult population—approximately 1.5 percent of the men and 0.6 percent of the women eighteen years and older—had earned a doctoral degree" (Nettles and Millett, 2006, p. 10). The National Center for Education Statistics (2007) indicates that there were 52,600 doctoral degrees conferred in 2004–05, with the largest number in education at 14.6 percent (7,700), followed by engineering at 12.5 percent (6,600), then the health professions, 11.1 percent (5,900).

Imani's doctoral decision allows her an opportunity to reflect on the time she has spent as a full-time student affairs administrator and what her vision is for the future. She has worked for ten years after the completion of her master's degree, which is within the decision-making range for individuals in education. Education majors tend to be older than other doctoral students; they make the decision to start their degree progression around the age of thirty, compared to other disciplines in which prospective students decide in their twenties (Nettles and Millet, 2006). The authors also found that the average age for

African American doctoral students in education is thirty-seven years (slightly older), compared with thirty-five years for other racial ethnic groups.

Without a doctorate, many administrators remain in entry- or midlevel positions and will often make lateral moves rather than advance to positions with authority over budgets, policies, and a large staff. There are some institutions that allow administrators with master's degrees to teach courses such as residence advisor workshops, leadership seminars, or training programs for orientation counselors. Komives and Taub (2000) observe, "A current job could be retained without the doctoral degree, and promotions from within are one way that someone without a doctorate can advance" (p. 509). However, according to Komives (1993), many middle management and upper management positions at most institutions will be less available to those without the doctorate. Student affairs practitioners may feel pressure to acquire a doctorate merely to retain their present positions (Townsend and Mason, 1990).

Entering a doctoral program takes commitment and sacrifice, because students will change intellectually and oftentimes psychosocially forever. As a result, however, there are career opportunities that may allow administrators to transform the institutional environment as well as the faculty and staff around them.

There are numerous benefits of acquiring the "three magic letters" (Nettles and Millett, 2006, p. 1). In Imani's case, she is pondering careers in the professorate, administration, and consulting. These are all viable options, since the doctorate does open the door to teaching in student affairs or higher education administration preparation programs. Moreover, Imani has worked in one functional area for ten years and is no longer challenged by the day-to-day assignments. Doctoral students have the opportunity to acquire advanced educational administrative skills (Komives and Taub, 2000), leadership skills, and engage in active research with faculty as well as individually through the dissertation process.

Where to Go?

According to the American College Personnel Association (ACPA) directory of graduate programs (Collins and Barratt, 2007), there are approximately 134 colleges and universities across the country offering master's, specialist, and doctoral degrees in student affairs or higher education. Imani has many options from which to choose. However, Eberly (2000) stated that "fortunately or unfortunately, few prospective doctoral students have the option to go anywhere they might choose—they are bound by elements of time, finances, and proximity" (p. 1). Eberly further notes that it is imperative that prospective students visit the institutions they are most interested in, spend time with the faculty, talk to the current doctoral students, and, if at all possible, talk to program alumni.

Traveling to several institutions may be cost prohibitive, so Imani decides to use the American College Personnel Association's Web site to peruse the directory of graduate programs. The directory provides a wealth of comprehensive, comparable information about each program, including program mission, admission requirements, curricula, student demographics, and individual faculty areas of specialization, as well as the percentage of faculty time devoted to the program. Even though there is an outline of information provided in the ACPA directory, there are several other environmental and institutional fit or cultural and personal adjustment issues Imani needs to consider.

A recent study of faculty members teaching in higher education and student affairs preparation programs provided a demographic profile of full-time faculty and those serving in faculty roles who hold primary responsibility as administrators (Amey, Dannells, Lovell, and Heinmiller, 2006). Respondents were predominantly White, with slightly more males than females, and two-thirds were married. The same percentage of women and men were tenured. Full-time faculty spend 50 percent of their time on teaching, about 25 percent on research and scholarship, and 25 percent on institutional and professional service.

The results of the study demonstrate that faculty in these programs devote considerable time and energy toward professional service above and beyond the traditional expectations of teaching, research, and institutional service. Professional service is identified, specifically, as additional time spent recruiting and advising students and supervising field experiences.

Studies involving students of color indicate that several factors influence decisions to attend higher education doctoral programs. These include academic quality, academic infrastructure, institutional sensitivity to students of color, and positive interaction with faculty. Academic reputation and faculty friendliness were also noted as particularly important features of higher education doctoral programs by students of color (Poock, 1999). These are a few of the issues Imani should consider when evaluating doctoral programs.

The graduate experiences of more than 4,000 doctoral students from twenty-seven universities and representing eleven arts and sciences disciplines are reflected in the Survey of Doctoral and Career Preparation Web site (Golde and Dore, 2001). The information provided can help prospective doctoral students reflect on the process of selecting a program, and prospective students can read about other students' experiences through quotes and sage advice.

Overall, the importance of fit with the institution and program is a primary issue emphasized by numerous authors (Golde, 2000; 2005; Gonzalez and Marin, 2002; Nettles and Millett, 2006; and Poock, 2002). Searching for a doctoral program is a reflective process for Imani. She uses the framework described by Barratt (2005) to help her narrow her choices. She begins to ask herself a series of questions as she evaluates and reviews each academic program. Some questions relate to her apparent fit with the institutions she is considering, whereas other questions are more practical. Some of her questions include:

- Is there a diversity component in the mission statement?
- How diverse is the faculty?
- Are there enough faculty to accommodate the number of students in the program?
- What are the research interests of the faculty, and how broad are their areas of expertise?
- Will they likely be interested in my dissertation topic?
- Are the faculty actively engaged in professional organizations, consultations, and other visible activities in the field?
- Are there paid assistantships, internships, and fellowships available?
- What is the program's reputation, and how important a factor is that for me?
- Will the faculty assist with postgraduation employment contacts?

The next set of questions Imani asks regard the students in the program:

- How diverse are the students currently in the program?
- Do full-time students seem to finish their degrees in a timely manner?
- Is the program cohort-based or individually structured?

Another important issue is the campus and community Imani may become part of for three to seven years. She asks whether or not there are cultural outlets in the area. If there is not a sizable cultural or ethnic group in the area, is there another community or support system available?

Having addressed these questions, Imani begins reviewing the various program coursework requirements and degree completion steps. Most doctoral programs in the field require that students take coursework in higher education administration, organizational theory, finance, higher education law, qualitative and quantitative statistics, history or philosophy of higher education, diversity or multicultural education, as well as student development theories. Many programs transfer graduate course credits in to satisfy some program requirements. Dissertation credits can constitute considerable coursework toward graduation.

There is also a written qualifying or preliminary exam taken after all coursework is completed, followed up with an oral exam. Students are then directed how to prepare their dissertation proposal; the proposal may vary in length from a prospectus to the first three chapters, or even a rough draft of the final dissertation. Most programs specify the number of years in which a student must complete the dissertation process, normally ranging from seven to ten years. Therefore, it is important to ask the program faculty what the average length of time it takes for students in their particular program to complete the doctoral process.

Imani has begun to choose a doctoral program by identifying those that she feels validate her identities (gender and racial/ethnic) and provide ample opportunities for her to meet current as well as prospective students through campus visits and orientation programs. One other important consideration for Imani is whether she will choose to pursue a Doctor of Education (Ed.D.) or a Doctor of Philosophy (Ph.D.)

Ed.D. or Ph.D.?

The oldest and most recognized degrees in education are the Doctor of Philosophy, or Ph.D., and the Doctor of Education, or Ed.D. degrees. Yale University established the first Ph.D. degree in 1860, and the first Ph.D. in education was granted in 1893 at Teachers College, Columbia University (Nettles and Millett, 2006). Harvard University conferred the first Ed.D. in 1920, followed by Teachers College in 1934. The degrees were created to present clear lines of demarcation between the preparation of administrative leaders in education, the Ed.D., and the preparation of researchers, university teachers, and scholars in education, the Ph.D. (Carnegie Initiative on the Doctorate, 2003). Concomitantly, the dissertation requirements for the two programs should be distinctively different; however, in most programs today they are strikingly similar, with the research questions and techniques mirroring each degree. Imani's mentors include a professor in higher education with an Ed.D. and her direct supervisor, the vice president of student affairs, with a Ph.D. The latter is also an adjunct professor in student affairs.

According to the Summary of the Doctoral Education Literature (Carnegie Initiative on the Doctorate, 2003), there is an inconclusive battle over the prestige and academic rigor applied to the Ph.D. as compared to the Ed.D. Imani is attempting to decide which institution to attend based in part upon the type of degree offered; she should carefully review the difference between the coursework requirements and ultimately understand that upon completion of either degree her title will be "Doctor" (Eberly, 2000). Carpenter (2006) noted that

95 percent of the Ph.D.s in higher education are practitioners and the remaining 5 percent enter into the professorate or research areas. Position postings for available jobs usually do not state a preferred degree, such as Ph.D., Ed.D. or J.D. In fact, "most state that an earned doctorate or terminal degree is preferred or required" (Howard-Hamilton, private e-mail message to Kandace Hinton, 2004, p. 8). Imani should now focus on finding a group of faculty members who will provide a rich and engaging research experience so she can publish and make presentations at professional conferences. She should also consider programs that have a practicum or internship so she can explore administrative career options and add depth to her curriculum vitae.

Area of Program Emphasis

Imani is considering which academic program would provide the best background and experience for her as she considers future career options. She wants to be prepared to lead a complex organization and possibly to become a college president. In addition to the student affairs professionals with doctorates she has known, she has also known some administrators who have law degrees. While doctoral degrees in higher education or student affairs are common pathways to senior administration, several studies suggest consideration of other academic areas. Mason and Townsend (1988), in examining the careers of higher education doctoral recipients, found that a substantial number of higher education doctoral recipients believe they made a poor choice in selecting higher education as a field of study. A recent study of senior student affairs officers at four-year institutions (Hyman, Lovell, and Stringer, 2007) indicated that about two thirds of the respondents held doctoral degrees, although not always in either higher education or student affairs. The results of another study examining the value of a higher education doctorate among senior administrators (Townsend and Wiese, 1992) revealed that 47 percent of the respondents indicated a higher education doctorate is preferable to one in an academic discipline. Community college administrators valued the doctorate in higher education more than administrators in four-year institutions.

The Doctoral Study Journey

Imani realizes that the decision to pursue a doctorate is an important part of her professional journey. She knows that some students start but do not complete doctoral programs, and she wants to be sure that does not happen to her. It is important that she consider the issues of persistence and graduation.

Persistence

Forty to 60 percent of students who begin doctorates do not earn their degrees (Bair and Haworth, 1999; and McAlpine and Norton, 2006). Attrition rates vary widely according to the field of study and the program of study. Bair and Haworth found evidence that departmental culture and difficulties with the dissertation can dramatically affect student persistence. Student financial support, familial support, peer support, faculty support, chairperson support, and student motivation represent factors that contribute most significantly to degree completion (Pauley, Cunningham, and Toth, 1999). Students' involvement in their respective program, especially with the faculty, has a direct influence on students' intent to earn the degree (Faghihi and Ethington, 1996). Institutional factors such as financial aid and the presence of academic support service are most likely to influence degree persistence among Latino(a) and African American students (Gonzalez and Marin, 2002; Nettles and Millett, 2006; and Poock, 2002). Nettles and Millett have observed challenges to doctoral student persistence in two areas: faculty advisor issues (unexpected faculty departures, conflicts with a mentor) and academic issues (difficulty in making the transition to an independent scholar, loss of confidence, loss of interest in the dissertation topic, and changing academic interests and current programs not meeting their needs).

Finishing the Program

Imani knows that the final step is writing a dissertation, but she does not know exactly how this document comes to fruition. She has also noticed individuals who have verbalized or placed in writing that they are *ABD*, which stands for "all but dissertation." Imani's mentor advised her that the phrase *doctoral candidate* has more meaning in the academic world than ABD. Faculty members on doctoral committees should emphasize the importance of using the correct terminology when a student has completed the various stages of the program and completed the steps involved to reach candidacy. A clear explanation from faculty at the qualifying exam phase and dissertation proposal defense stage helps to demystify the language protocol for doctoral students or candidates and encourages them to use scholarly terminology before they begin the job search process.

Perlmutter and Porter (2005) have indicated that "being a doctoral student, and then a job candidate, is not a hiatus before the proper academic employment begins" because "the career track starts immediately" (p. C4). Perlmutter and Porter also offer the following advice:

- Choose the direction of your dissertation when you begin the program.
- Begin the publication process by coauthoring with a mentor. Insist on working with your professors, initiate projects, or join a writing group. Offer to write first drafts, literature reviews, or search for articles.
- Attend conferences and build relationships with scholars in the field.
- Review the position announcements so you can enhance your qualifications while in the doctoral program.
- Be open to looking at various locations for positions upon completion of the degree.
- Be well prepared for the interview. "Faculty members will respect your CV, but they will hire you" (Perlmutter and Porter, p. C4).

Completing the dissertation can be a daunting task if you are accustomed to seeing your classmates regularly, because the writing process is an individual endeavor. You may not connect with another doctoral student or faculty member face to face while collecting data and writing. Some doctoral programs have established structured support groups for academic credit, such as the Dissertation Academy at Indiana State University (Howard-Hamilton, private e-mail message to Kandace Hinton, 2007). The Dissertation Academy allows doctoral candidates who have completed their preliminary exams an opportunity to meet periodically throughout the semester during a specific time and date to discuss their proposal, proofread each other's work, and participate in a mock defense. A faculty member in the higher education program is assigned to the Dissertation Academy as the primary instructor so that there is consistency and each student is held accountable for attending the classes. Structured programs such as the Dissertation Academy can be beneficial in expediting the writing process and keeping the candidate task oriented.

Career Paths After the Doctorate

The doctorate opens up additional career possibilities for those who complete the degree. They automatically meet the educational requirements for positions that are listed as doctorate required. It is reasonable to assume that most graduate students consider changes in their professional lives once they complete their doctoral degree (Krueger and Peek, 2006; and Talbot, Maier, and Rushlau, 1996). However, the aspirations of some students for senior-level administrative positions may be unrealistic (Daddona, Cooper, and Dunn, 2006). Several studies (Baker, Wolf-Wendel, and Twombly, 2007; Coomes, Belch, and Saddlemire, 1991; and Schuh, 1989) have indicated that 80 percent of doctoral candidates pursue administrative careers, while 20 percent aspire to be faculty members. Daddona and others (2006) found that half of the respondents in their study aspired to higher-level administrative positions in higher education, while a third of their population wanted to remain in their current positions. This supports earlier observations of Komives (1993) and Townsend and Mason (1990) in that many doctoral students are pursuing terminal degrees to hold current positions, not for professional advancement.

Further study is needed of the utility of the doctorate in higher education. While the demand for the doctoral degree has increased (Coomes and others, 1991), with increasing numbers of student affairs professionals pursuing the doctorate, many doctoral graduates may be resigned to mid-level administrative positions for which they are over-prepared in terms of research knowledge, yet under-prepared in terms of practical experience (Saunders and Cooper, 1999). Previous studies (Coomes and others, 1991; and Johnson, 1982) have determined the need for substantive administrative experience before beginning doctoral work. Johnson observed that most doctoral programs require doctoral students to have had previous higher education experience.

Faculty Positions

Doctoral students who aspire to a faculty role must consider several important issues as they determine whether (or not) this role is in their best interests. They should be able to identify a line of research about which they feel passionate, which may be the subject of their dissertation.

Aspirants to faculty positions should carefully examine the type of institution in which they would seek an appointment. The advantages and disadvantages of working in a public university environment must be weighed and considered against those in a private institutional setting. Applicants must invest energy in studying the culture of the institution and the unit or department to assess whether their own values will be compatible. Careful consideration should be given to the nature of the academic program. Is it primarily focused on preparing master's students, or does it include doctoral programs? Is it administratively focused, counseling based, or a blended model? What is the profile of prospective faculty colleagues? Are your research interests likely to be compatible? Could these individuals be supportive colleagues? A careful study of the program and departmental Web sites may yield rich insights in response to several of these important questions. Students' initiative to consult with others via phone, e-mail, and in face-to-face conference encounters will be important to establish a thorough understanding of the faculty environment.

There is no substitute for ambitious networking on students' part to obtain the most complete picture possible of the culture and climate at any institution and program where they might pursue a faculty post. Other doctoral student colleagues are a rich resource of support to learn more about institutions where candidates might choose to work. An online listserv for higher education faculty, CSP (College Student Personnel) Talk, provides an active forum for lively exchange about a multitude of topics, including unique institutional practices, curricular expectations, program requirements, and faculty qualifications, and it serves as a vehicle for program faculty to alert their national colleagues of faculty position openings at their respective institutions. The National Association of Student Personnel Administrators (NASPA's) Faculty Fellows and ACPA's Commission on Professional Preparation support the efforts of their respective associations in providing conference programs, coordinating publications, seminars, institutes, and other initiatives that serve the needs of aspiring and current faculty members.

New faculty members encounter substantive challenges in navigating the promotion and tenure (P and T) process. It is in this regard that most realize the value of their lines of research. A new faculty member must develop a research agenda early, as the annual P and T review process will likely result in careful scrutiny of his or her scholarship, consistent with that agenda. Exercise caution in the negotiation process before hiring to ensure an assigned course load that will permit time to focus on a research agenda. Be familiar with the local ground rules and expectations that surround the P and T timetable. New faculty must demonstrate evidence of successful progress toward tenure on an annual basis. Understand what the specific departmental and collegiate expectations are for performance in terms of scholarship (research and publications), teaching, and service. A new faculty member will do well to balance her time so that she can accomplish her annual goals in each of these three important areas.

Administrative Positions

Careful scrutiny of potential employing institutions is also warranted for doctoral students who aspire to administrative posts after they complete their degrees. The type of administrative position pursued will likely be a reflection of previous full-time experience in higher education, graduate assistantship experience, and exposure to role models and mentors. Those aspiring to administrative positions should ask themselves several key questions. What are their career goals? Do they aspire to be the senior student affairs officers? Are they interested in academic administration, university development, institutional research, system administration, professional association, or foundation work? Are they inclined to retain current administrative appointments or pursue similar positions at other institutions?

Career administrator aspirants must be familiar with the differences among multiple university environments. Administrative duties and responsibilities will likely vary with the institutional setting (community college, state university, private college, residential or urban campus). However, in every postsecondary setting, administrators must demonstrate competence as leaders and managers. Additionally, they must be creative and visionary fund and friend-raisers for their assigned administrative areas. As mentioned earlier in the chapter, administrators can also accept faculty appointments. Being visible in the classroom and on campus provides students with a model that administrators are also researchers and scholars. Whether faculty member or administrator, there are some "threads of experience" that are common to both roles. Regardless of specific responsibilities, all faculty members and administrators are educators. They ought to be committed to best practices in the performance of their assigned duties. They should value scholarship and the contributions the literature makes to the accumulated wisdom of good educational practice.

Implications for Best Practice in Doctoral Education

Maki and Borkowski (2006) offer a foundation for faculty and academic leaders of doctoral programs to promote inquiry into the educational practices that define their programs and contribute to graduate students' learning. Good practice in doctoral education means that consideration of students' career expectations and goals should begin at the time students are considering a doctorate (Daddona and others, 2006). Furthermore, doctoral faculty will maintain information about recent graduates regarding location, job level, and salary to enable improved understanding of current hiring practices and career trends (Daddona and others, 2006). Doctoral admission criteria should include requiring all applicants to have had at least some prior full-time administrative experience prior to entering the doctoral program (Coomes and others, 1991). Finally, good practice means carefully considering the following questions (Nettles and Millett, 2006): What experiences should all doctoral students have? What broad skill sets should graduates have and be able to use? How well do we understand what entering graduate students expect from their graduate programs? How can we exploit the differences students bring to improve their graduate experience?

Over the past few years, the doctoral colloquium at the NASPA annual conference has provided numerous doctoral students with the opportunity to network, learn, and explore issues and concerns around their programs of study and their futures as professionals in higher education. Carpenter (2006) has shared powerful advice with this audience based on his accumulated wisdom, working with numerous doctoral students over many years. Carpenter admonishes students to appreciate what they have in the environment they're in. They should acknowledge their freedom to learn, the opportunity to use amazing resources, and the exposure to guided reflection and collegiality. He encourages students to be as productive as possible, treating their work as important. Moreover, at the end of the doctoral experience, there is a bounce in one's step, a feeling of pride, a deep and abiding humility, a powerful feeling of accomplishment, the knowledge that you have the discipline to do anything, and a shiny new title (but don't wear it out).

References

Amey, M., Lovell, C., Dannells, M., and Heinmiller, K. *Identifying Issues of Individual Commitment and Generating strategies for Collective Action.* Paper presented at the annual meeting of the National Association of Student Personnel Administrators. Washington, D.C., March 2006.

Bair, C. R., and Haworth, J. G. *Doctoral Student Attrition and Persistence: A Meta-Synthesis of Research.* Paper presented at the annual meeting of the Association for the Study of Higher Education. February 1999. (ERIC Document Reproductions Service No. ED 437008).

Baker, B. D., Wolf-Wendel, L., and Twombly, S. "Exploring the Faculty Pipeline in Educational Administration: Evidence from the Survey of Earned Doctorates, 1999 to 2000." *Educational Administration Quarterly,* 2007, 43(2), 189–220.

Barratt, W. "Selecting a Student Affairs Graduate Program." [http://www.myacpa.org/c12/selecting.htm]. June 2005.

Carnegie Initiative on the Doctorate. "Summary of the Doctoral Education Literature in Education." [http://www.ed.uiuc.edu/cid/Summary.pdf]. May 2003.

Carpenter, D. S. *Moving On: There Is Another End to the Tunnel.* Paper presented at the annual conference of the National Association of Student Personnel Administrators. Washington, D.C., March 2006.

Collins, D., and Barratt, W. (Eds.). *American College Personnel Association Directory of Graduate Programs.* [http://www.myacpa.org/c12/directory.htm]. July 2007.

Coomes, M. D., Belch, H. A., and Saddlemire, G. L. "Doctoral Programs for Student Affairs Professionals: A Status Report." *Journal of College Student Development,* 1991, 32, 62–68.

Daddona, M. F., Cooper, D., and Dunn, M. S. "Career Paths and Expectations of Recent Doctoral Graduates in Student Affairs." *NASPA Journal,* 2006, 43(2), 203–215.

de Valero, Y. F. "Departmental Factors Affecting Time-to-Degree and Completion Rates of Doctoral Students at One Land-Grant Institution." *Journal of Higher Education*, 2001, 72(3), 341–367.

Eberly, C. "Selecting a Doctoral Program in Student Affairs." [http://www.naspa.org/communities/kc/uploads/npgskc_selectingadoctoral.pdf]. 2000.

Faghihi, F., and Ethington, C. A. *The Effect of Doctoral Students' Background, Involvement, and Perception of Growth on Their Intent to Persist.* Paper presented at the annual meeting of the Association for the Study of Higher Education., Memphis, Tenn., November 1996.

Golde, C. M. "The Role of the Department and Discipline in Doctoral Student Attrition: Lessons from Four Departments." *Journal of Higher Education*, 2005, 76(6), 669–700.

Golde, C. M. "Should I Stay or Should I Go? Student Descriptions of the Doctoral Attrition Process." *Review of Higher Education*, 2000, 23(2), 199–227.

Golde, C. M., and Dore, T. M. *At Cross Purposes: What the Experiences of Doctoral Students Reveal About Doctoral Education.* [http://www.phd-survey.org]. Philadelphia: Pew Charitable Trusts, 2001.

Gonzalez, K. P., and Marin, P. "Inside Doctoral Education in America: Voices of Latinas/os in Pursuit of the PhD." *Journal of College Student Development*, 2002, 43(4), 540–557.

Howard-Hamilton, M. "ISU Dissertation Academy." May 5, 2007.

Howard-Hamilton, M. F. "Considering the Doctorate: Introduction." In K. A. Renn and C. Hughes (Eds.), *Roads Taken: Women in Student Affairs at Mid-Career.* Sterling, Va.: Stylus, 2004.

Hyman, R. E., Lovell, C., and Stringer, J. *The Essential Knowledge of Student Affairs: What NASPA Voting Delegates Think.* Paper presented at the annual conference of the National Association of Student Personnel Administrators. Orlando, Fla., April 2007.

Johnson, J. A. *A Profile of Faculty of Doctoral Programs in the Study of Higher Education in the United States.* Paper presented at the annual conference of the Association for the Study of Higher Education. Washington, D.C., March 1982.

Komives, S .R. "Advancing Professionally Through Graduate Education." In M. J. Barr (Ed.), *Handbook of Student Affairs Administration* (1st ed.) San Francisco: Jossey-Bass, 1993.

Komives, S. R., and Taub, D. J. "Advancing Professionally Through Doctoral Education." In M. J. Barr and M. K. Desler (Eds.), *The Handbook of Student Affairs Administration* (2nd ed.). San Francisco: Jossey Bass, 2000.

Krueger, P. M., and Peek, L. A. "Figuring It Out: A Conversation About How to Complete Your Ph.D." *College Student Journal*, 2006, 40(1) 149–157.

Maki, P. L., and Borkowski, N. A. *The Assessment of Doctoral Education: Emerging Criteria and New Models for Improving Outcomes.* Herndon, Va.: Stylus, 2006.

Mason, S. O., and Townsend, B. K. *Graduates of Doctoral Programs in Higher Education: Demographics and Career Patterns.* Paper presented at the annual meeting of the Association for the Study of Higher Education. February 1988. (ERIC Document Reproduction Service No. ED 303073).

McAlpine, L., and Norton, J. "Reframing Our Approach to Doctoral Programs: An Integrative Framework for Action and Research." *Higher Education Research and Development*, 2006, 25(1), 3–17.

National Center for Education Statistics. [http://nces.ed.gov/programs/coe/2007]. July 2007.

Nettles, M. T., and Millett, C. M. *Three Magic Letters: Getting to Ph.D.* Baltimore: Johns Hopkins University Press, 2006.

Pauley, R., Cunningham, M., and Toth, P. "Doctoral Student Attrition and Retention: A Study of a Non-Traditional Ed.D. Program." *Journal of College Student Retention*, 1999, 1(3), 225–238.

Perlmutter, D. D., and Porter, L. "Thinking Beyond the Dissertation." *Chronicle of Higher Education*, December 16, 2005, pp. C1 & C4.

Poock, M. C. "Graduate Student Orientation: Assessing Needs and Methods of Delivery." *Journal of College Student Development*, 2002, 43(2), 231–245.

Poock, M. C. "Students of Color and Doctoral Programs: Factors Influencing the Application Decision in Higher Education Administration." *College and University*, 1999, 74(3), 2–7.

Saunders. S. A., and Cooper, D. L. "The Doctorate in Student Affairs: Essential Skills and Competencies for Midmanagement." *Journal of College Student Development*, 1999, 40(2), 185–191.

Schuh, J.H. *Selected Characteristics of Students Enrolled in Doctoral Programs in Student Affairs.* Paper presented at the annual meeting of the American College Personnel Association. Washington, D.C., April 1989.

Talbot, D., Maier, E., and Rushlau, M. "Guess Who's Coming to Doctoral Programs: Factors Influencing Potential Students' Choices of Doctoral Programs in Student Affairs." *College Student Affairs Journal*, 1996, 16(1) 5–15.

Townsend, B. K., and Mason, S. O. "Career Paths of Graduates of Higher Education Doctoral Programs." *Review of Higher Education*, 1990, 14(1), 63–81.

Townsend, B. K., and Wiese, M. "The Value of a Doctorate in Higher Education for Student Affairs Administrators." *NASPA Journal*, 1992, 30(1), 51–58.

PART FIVE

INTERPERSONAL DYNAMICS IN PROFESSIONAL PRACTICE

Given that our primary purpose is serving students and our primary resource for doing so is staff colleagues, it should come as no surprise that interpersonal dynamics play a pivotal role in the successful practice of student affairs. Part Five of the handbook includes chapters addressing various dimensions of those dynamics. Chapter Twenty-One by Adrianna Kezar is focused on the importance to student learning of the development of active and vital partnerships between student affairs professionals and colleagues in academic administration and academic departments. Next, in Chapter Twenty-Two, Jeremy Stringer describes the political dimensions of student affairs professional practice, an area of activity for which those new to the profession often feel ill prepared and from which they may feel estranged. Shannon Ellis shares strategies for developing effective relationships on campus and in the community in Chapter Twenty-Three. Because people and interpersonal interactions are at the heart of our daily activities understanding and managing conflict must be second nature to student affairs professionals. Dale Nienow and Jeremy Stringer provide an overview of various approaches to conflict and strategies for addressing it in Chapter Twenty-Four.

CHAPTER TWENTY-ONE

SUPPORTING AND ENHANCING STUDENT LEARNING THROUGH PARTNERSHIPS WITH ACADEMIC COLLEAGUES

Adrianna Kezar

Partnering with academic colleagues might have been considered a controversial and difficult activity in the past, but it has now become relatively commonplace on college campuses across the country (Kezar, 2001). In 1999, Kuh noted that, historically, collaboration has been more espoused than enacted. However, the landscape has changed, and national surveys have documented that partnerships between academic and student affairs are happening at thousands of varying institutions and across institutional types and sectors (Kezar, Hirsch, and Burack, 2001; and Kolins, 1999). A seachange has occurred during the past decade, in large measure a result of national conversation begun by the American College Personal Association (ACPA) and the National Association of Student Personnel Administrators (NASPA). The dialogue became more active in 1994 with the publication of *The Student Learning Imperative* (American College Personal Association [ACPA]), in which student affairs professionals were challenged to create a seamless learning environment by bridging organizational boundaries and forging collaborative partnerships with faculty and other educators to enhance learning. The report writers noted that students perceived their educational process as a set of disjointed, unconnected experiences. The authors of the *Imperative* were responding to research on learning that demonstrated that students' cognitive and psychosocial learning is intertwined, in contrast to our organizational structures, which are fragmented. Furthermore, the report's authors were concerned with criticism by higher education leaders such as Ernest Boyer (1987) and reports such as *An American Imperative* (Wingspread Group on Higher Education, 1993). These criticisms suggested higher education had lost its sense of community and wholeness, and the fragmented experience was hurting students. An unhealthy separation between academic and student affairs had developed and needed to be addressed.

Perhaps the most well-known document articulating the benefits and need for collaboration is *Powerful Partnerships: A Shared Responsibility for Learning* (American Association for Higher Education [AAHE], ACPA, and National Association of Student Personnel Administrators [NASPA] 1998). The report makes the case that "only when everyone on campus—particularly academic and student affairs staff—shares responsibility for student learning will we be able to make significant progress for improving it." The *Powerful Partnership* authors also note that "only by acting cooperatively in the context of common goals, as the most innovative institutions have done, will our accumulated understanding about learning be put to best use" (p. 1).

Learning Reconsidered: A Campus-Wide Focus on the Student Experience (Keeling, 2004) also identified partnerships as critical for developing integrated or transformative learning necessary within our current society. As the report boldly states, "No single arena of experience is solely responsible for producing these college outcomes. All areas of college engagement provide opportunities for student learning and development" (p. 30).

What is exciting to the profession of student affairs is that the field has moved from describing the importance of partnerships and discussions of obstacles (which dominated the discourse of the 1980s and 1990s) to examining the best strategies for developing partnerships and understanding some of the best models for collaboration.

This chapter synthesizes the literature and research about partnerships spawned by *The Student Learning Imperative*. The chapter is aimed at helping practitioners by shedding light on barriers, benefits, strategies, and promising practices for partnerships. It begins with four reflections that set a foundation to understand the current context around collaboration. The reflections are followed by action steps on ways to create and sustain collaborative partnerships.

Before getting started, it is important to consider definitions. People use the words *collaboration, partnerships, cooperation,* and *coordination* interchangeably. There is a distinction that is important to keep in mind. Coordination or cooperative arrangements typically involve sharing information or working on tasks together but usually do not fundamentally alter the work itself (Hagadoorn, 1993; Lockwood, 1996). On the other hand, partnership or collaboration involves joint goals, a reliance on each other to accomplish those goals, joint planning, and often power sharing. In order to be considered collaboration, it is key that there be an interactive process (relationship over time) and that groups develop shared rules, norms, and structures, which often become their first work together. When practitioners talk about partnerships, they are usually referring to either coordination or collaboration. This process usually begins with coordination and then, if it makes sense, there is an effort to move toward collaboration. These terms are used generically in the chapter, as practitioners typically do; this distinction is made within the research literature.

Reflection 1: Remember History

In the past, the discussion about collaboration was dominated by student affairs practitioners who felt that they were second-class citizens to academic affairs practitioners. The former felt that the latter looked down on their profession and that their work did not contribute to the institution or student learning. Smith (1982) notes that student affairs has been stereotyped as anti-intellectual and not part of the central mission of the institution. Hyman (1995) explains that most faculty had little understanding of what student affairs staff do, and student affairs staff had little if any relationship with faculty and academic administrators on campus. In 1997, Bloland noted that collaborations had been difficult in the past because of inferiority complexes that student affairs practitioners held, and that "they need to be challenged to set aside their traditional feelings of inferiority and isolation and seek interaction with faculty in a straightforward, confident posture of equality" (p. ix).

Bourassa and Kruger (2001) have suggested that *The Student Learning Imperative* helped to change the discourse because student affairs practitioners began to see their connection to the core mission of learning in and outside the classroom. This recent history is important for staff members and leaders to be aware of if they encounter resistance by other colleagues, whether they be in student or academic affairs, to partnering. Past experiences can adversely affect willingness or belief in the ability to partner. Understanding the difficult relationships between academic and student affairs that existed in the past (and still exist on many campuses) helps to overcome this perspective. If you are on a campus that is still struggling with its past, it might be important to have people on campus read *Learning Reconsidered*, *The Student Learning Imperative*, or *Powerful Partnerships* in order to understand the important role that both student and academic affairs play and to also help address biases that people may hold about student affairs work. One promising strategy might be to form a campus reading group. Research on reading groups has demonstrated that if cross-campus teams read articles and information in common and then have discussions on this material, they are more likely to develop a shared understanding of each other, to share cognitive frameworks, and to move toward change and better working relationships (Eckel, Kezar, and Lieberman, 1999).

Reflection 2: Logic Overcomes Barriers

Schroeder (1999c) and Knefelkamp (1991) describe how college and university campuses have evolved into structures in which collaboration is difficult. For example, the hierarchical, bureaucratic organizational structure, specialization of knowledge, fragmentation of campus work, and deterioration of work into separate silos makes educators less able to participate in partnerships. As Schroeder (1999b) notes, "These vertical structures, while often effective at promoting interaction within functional units, create obstacles to interaction, coordination and collaboration between units" (p. 137). Historically, one significant obstacle to collaboration and partnerships appears to have been specialization. This occurs when people focus increasingly on a very specific issue related to student learning or organizational functioning. As a result of specialization, professionals may become more and more distanced from each other, sharing fewer and fewer values and goals. These different values systems create distinctive cultures on campus, and the result is that student and academic affairs administrators have difficulty communicating and relating or understanding each other's work. Faculty members have tremendous pressures to publish and have less time for students or for collaborating with staff on campus. Thus, they are not even able to participate in collaborative activities. In addition, academic and student affairs are often in competition for funding, which also prevents them from collaborating on goals. Schroeder (1999b) summarizes the barriers by saying, "Universities are characterized not by a sense of community, but rather by a constellation of independent principalities and fiefdoms, each disconnected from the others and from any commitment to institutional purpose or transcending values" (p. 9).

These many barriers were the focus of discussion throughout the 1990s. The dialogue helped people to recognize why collaboration might be difficult and why careful planning was needed. However, there was also an underlying sense that, due to the formidable challenges, such collaboration just might not be possible.

One way to overcome these barriers is to create a compelling logic for collaboration and to help student affairs educators to see their connection to the academic mission. A host of texts and reports beginning in the 1990s helped underscore the importance of collaboration and why it was critical for student affairs to form partnerships (AAHE, 1998; Engstrom and Tinto, 2000; Fried, 2000; Hyman, 1995; Kezar and others, 2001; Keeling, 2004; Martin and Murphy, 2000; Potter, 1999; and Schroeder, 1999a, 1999b). Partnerships have the capacity to create a seamless learning environment—settings where in-class and out-of-classroom experiences are mutually supporting and where institutional resources are marshaled and channeled to achieve complementary learning outcomes. Partnering can improve student outcomes, enhance service, better capitalize on resources, create better decisions, improve graduation rates, enhance retention, revive undergraduate education, improve institutional communication, create a culture of trust and better campus relationships, increase student satisfaction, and improve organizational functioning and service, for example, more effective advising (Engstrom and Tinto, 2000; Schroeder, 1999a, 1999b; and Schuh and Whitt, 1999).

While the logic has been developing for years, we now have much greater research support and evidence that partnerships actually live up to their suggested benefits. For example, recent research by Kuh, Kinzie, Schuh, and Whitt (2005) found that shared responsibility for educational quality and student success is related to stronger levels of student engagement. While earlier research was suggestive that collaborations and partnerships would increase student learning, we now have research that has found a relationship between the use of partnerships and higher levels of student engagement, which is a proxy for student learning. Also, a variety of studies have been conducted on specific types of programs and partnerships that academic and student affairs work on together. For example, research on learning communities—a collaboration between academic and student affairs administration—demonstrates they produce improved learning outcomes and improve retention (Smith and McCann, 2001; and Westfall, 1999). First-year interest groups help to improve retention (Schroeder, Minor, and Tarkow, 1999). Programs designed jointly between academic and student affairs to retain special populations such as African American or low-income students have shown greater success than programs designed by one unit (Jackson, Levine, and Patton, 2000; and Williams and Wilson, 1993). This research is extremely important, as it provides evidence for the logic that has been advanced in *Powerful Partnerships* and *The Student Learning Imperative*.

Much attention has been given to the way collaborations improve student outcomes, but there is also research about its organizational benefits. One of the most important studies, conducted by Bensimon and Neumann (1993), found that working collaboratively in cross-functional teams creates cognitive complexity, innovation, and learning between units and improves organizational functioning. Cognitive complexity relates to the ability of decision makers to come up with better decisions because they have more perspectives to bring to bear on an issue. In their research, campuses that drew on the expertise across units that typically do not work together were able to make better decisions that increased the organizational functioning of the campus. These teams also use the expertise from diverse areas to inform each other, creating organizational learning and improving functioning on other tasks and activities. This learning (a result of bringing together perspectives that are not usually coalesced) also led to innovation within in the partnership itself as well as innovation on a campus more generally.

Another outcome or benefit of collaboration is that it creates better service within a college (Schroeder, 1999a). While organizations set up individual units to handle and manage a discrete set of activities, processes cut across organizational units. Because information is shared among offices and communication is open, each office has a better chance of serving the students and helping them understand what other office they need to interact with to resolve the problem. This also helps to address student concerns more quickly, creating greater efficiency as well as effectiveness. It is important to create a strong customer service environment, especially in light of calls for greater accountability on campus. See Chapter Six for a discussion of pressures for greater accountability in higher education.

Knowledge of the recent research in support of collaboration can be helpful on any specific campus. In fact, one of the most cited reasons for successful collaboration is leaders who are knowledgeable and can articulate the benefits of partnerships (Schroeder, 1999b; and Westfall, 1999). Recognizing that many campuses have overcome these formidable challenges and engage in multiple partnerships between academic and student affairs should provide inspiration to those campuses early in their journey to collaboration. Also, research results demonstrate that one successful collaboration leads to others (Kezar, 2001). You may have skeptical colleagues on your campus who resist collaboration between student affairs and academic affairs or who have been involved in unsuccessful attempts at collaboration between the two. However, sharing the compelling logic of collaboration and the recent research evidence with colleagues can help even those who have had a negative experience to envision a different outcome and to try again.

The barriers and important benefits of collaboration are also important to remember if your campus is experiencing the typical breakdowns in communication and misunderstanding based on differing values. The barriers remind us to check our processes, and the benefits keep us moving forward in the face of conflict and poor interpersonal dynamics. National survey data uncovered that a focus on student learning helped campuses to keep moving forward and to be successful in partnerships (Kezar, 2001). The survey also revealed that leaders did not believe that institutional obstacles or barriers prevented them from creating partnerships. They noted that the obstacles existed, but that logic of collaboration, models for collaborating such as learning communities, and the successful strategies they used help them to overcome these barriers. The research evidence cited previously can also be used in reading groups and cross-functional teams on campus to help provide encouragement to continue their work, knowing many benefits that lie ahead.

Reflection 3: Fortuitous Timing

Culture is never static. As student affairs leaders have been focusing on how their work can relate more directly to student learning and the importance of partnering, faculty and academic affairs leaders have also been engaged in a variety of changes that makes them much more amenable to partnerships. For example, faculty are involved in a variety of teaching and research activities that are more collaborative, such as interdisciplinarity, team teaching, service learning, action or participatory research (in which faculty partner with other groups such as community members to conduct research) (Kezar, Chambers, and Burkhardt, 2005). Also, academic administrators are trying to determine ways to create greater collaboration among faculty members through research institutes, interdisciplinary departments, and multidisciplinary teaching configurations. Academic leaders have also been reading about the importance of cross-functional teams and reconfiguring operations to have deans and department chairs work together more on an ongoing basis. Many of the recent publications and books for academic administrators have challenged the siloed organization of college campuses and advocated for more collaborative forms of work (Ferren and Stanton, 2004). Incentive and reward systems are changing on some campuses to encourage more collaboration and cooperative endeavors (Diamond, Bronwyn, and Adam, 2004).

It is important for student affairs leaders to be familiar with these changes, as they provide leverage to create and sustain partnerships with academic affairs. The more that student affairs administrators are familiar with collaborative work in academic affairs and recent publications that academic affairs leaders are reading, the better prepared they are to persuade academic affairs leaders to engage in collaborative work.

Reflection 4: Collaboration Is Deepening

In the past, most partnering occurred around orientation or advising and was limited in scope (Kezar, 2001). For example, campuses recognized the need to coordinate services for first-year students. Staff from both academic and student affairs broke traditional work boundaries and partnered to offer orientation programming and worked together to develop the overall program. More recently, student affairs has played a partnership role in important curricular programs, including first-year experience seminars, learning communities, living and learning environments, service learning, senior capstone, citizenship education, intergroup dialogues, and leadership. All of these curricular innovations have been demonstrated to improve student learning and are gaining in popularity on campuses across the country. This section of the chapter details three of these curricular programs: first-year seminars, service learning, and learning communities. More detail on these curricular innovations can be found in a variety of texts (see Jacoby, 1996; Kezar, 1999; and Schuh and Whitt, 1999).

On many campuses, first-year experience seminars emerged exclusively in either student or academic affairs. If they emerged in student affairs, it was often in the form of a noncredit course that was offered optionally and that focused on issues of time management, becoming socially involved, and study skills. First-year seminars that emerged in academic affairs focused on a particular content area, such as understanding human experience, and brought in content from psychology, sociology, and anthropology. They also included information relevant to first-year students, such as evaluating the status of their own psychosocial development during their first year of college. More recently, a variety of campuses are recognizing the need for academic and student affairs to partner and offer the course jointly, utilizing the expertise of both groups. Often these courses are team taught by both the student affairs staff member and a faculty member. The course tries to combine goals from both models of first-year experience seminars such as the purpose of a liberal arts education, general education and majors, career exploration, study skills, psychosocial development, and life skills in college, such as financial education. *Powerful Partnerships* provides the example of the College of New Jersey's collaboration between faculty and student life to offer a novel first-year experience program.

Another example of a curricular partnership that is being institutionalized on many campuses is service learning. Similar to first-year experience programs, service learning programs have evolved on some campuses exclusively within student affairs (usually taking more of a volunteerism approach) or academic affairs (tied more directly to the curriculum). However, on campuses that have recognized the power of collaboration, student affairs staff work directly with faculty members to offer service learning. Student affairs staff work with academic affairs providing training on reflection, helping establish relationships with community agencies, leading sessions in the residence halls connecting the service work to their life experiences, working on transportation and logistics, helping connect faculty members across campus who are conducting similar work, and bringing together faculty to share techniques. Faculty work with student affairs staff to amend their curricula, develop new syllabi, learn reflection and journaling activities, and connect students with other types of service activities beyond their specific class. These partnerships enhance the service learning experience for the student, as students have a better opportunity to connect the curricular experience with their co-curricular and life experiences. As a result, service becomes more prevalent throughout their learning experience. *Powerful Partnerships* offers an example of this type of successful collaboration in service learning, noting the program at the Community College of Rhode Island.

Learning communities are another curricular innovation that student affairs is creating jointly with academic affairs. Learning communities take a variety of forms, but their essential feature is that they intentionally group students together (by matched schedules, living and learning environments, or linked courses with common themes) so that students have the opportunity to work with the same group over time and engage in out-of-classroom conversation and activities. Campuses that partner to offer learning communities often incorporate a residential component. Students enroll in a set of similar courses, and faculty encourage students to extend the conversation into the dining hall or residence hall to create a seamless intellectual experience. In addition, faculty often attend social events or dinners within the residence hall and connect with students outside of class time and in more informal settings. Residential staff become familiar with the content of the courses, offer programming within the residence halls that relates to class topics, and invite faculty to social and programmatic events. A synergy between the learning in and out of classroom creates an extremely powerful learning experience. The College Park scholars program at the University of Maryland, also described in *Powerful Partnerships*, is an example of a learning community that relies on both academic and student affairs expertise.

Another critical finding in the literature on partnerships is that specific recommendations are specific to the type of curricular program being developed. For example, developing a partnership in service learning will be slightly different from developing a partnership in learning communities (Kezar, 2001; Schuh and Whitt, 1999). Therefore, reading the literature on the specific type of partnership to be created is important. For information on creating a service learning partnership, read Jacoby (1999).

After reading the specific literature, identify model programs or institutions and contact them for advice. As Westfall (1999) notes, "Talk with colleagues engaged in similar work at sister institutions. This helps identify potential landmines, provides practical examples of success and broadens the range of realistic options open to your campus" (p. 60).

The need to obtain information cannot be underscored enough. Most campuses still coordinate service rather than collaborate, because true partnerships require intensive planning and fail without careful coordination. So, conducting some background work can make the process much easier. There are now hundreds of models to examine. Senior administrators should take their staff on field trips to other campuses. Staff members should be encouraged to conduct Internet research and talk to people on other campuses. All staff and faculty should read about partnerships they are interested in creating. Knowing key areas of collaboration that have worked at hundreds of colleges and universities across the country to create seamless learning helps leaders to determine where to focus their efforts.

Action Step 1: Start with a Problem and Success Area

Various scholars (Hirsch and Burack, 2001; and Schroeder, 1999b) with experience working on collaboration or helping campuses to form partnerships, such as the New England Resource Center for Higher Education (NERCHE), have noted the importance of beginning the process of collaboration by identifying a problem to be solved that crosses traditional organizational boundaries. These problems become opportunities to bring people across campus to work together because they represent fundamentally different challenges that are difficult for an individual unit to resolve. Schroeder (1999b) describes his experience scouting for problems to be solved at his institution that become opportunities for collaboration: achieving general education outcomes, improving graduation rates, developing learning communities, responding to institutional accrediting agencies' mandates, fostering civic leadership, or enhancing the success of special populations. The problem also becomes a common reference point and helps to create a shared vision for undergraduate education or institutional problems (Schroeder, 1999a). NERCHE identified the following areas in their work with academic and student affairs leaders across the New England region: assessment, technology, changing student population, student retention, and general education. A few of the issues are reviewed next to demonstrate ways academic affairs and student affairs can create dialogues.

One critical area for partnering is assessment. As Hirsch and Burack (2001) note, assessment is difficult to conduct without both academic and student affairs input: "Providing evidence of student learning and of the value added by a college education requires collaboration and coordination across traditional campus boundaries" (p. 54). Instruments such as the National Survey of Student Engagement provide measures important to both academic and student affairs practitioners, and these groups can work together to administer, review, and develop recommendations from the assessment (Kuh and others, 2005). Both academic and student affairs have expertise in this area, and there is, typically, not an existing institutional body to conduct this work.

Student affairs practitioners are valued by their academic affairs colleagues for their expertise on the changing student populations and in student retention. Developing cross-campus teams to examine these issues and to jointly develop programs or interventions is becoming an important trend on campuses (Hirsch and Burack, 2001; Kezar, 2001; and Schroeder, 1999b). Many campuses collect detailed data about students through their institutional research offices, and astute student affairs officers will ask their institutional research offices to develop student profiles and to look at trends and changes in the student body. In addition to quantitative data, student affairs staff also talk with and are closely attuned to the student experience. Student affairs leaders have become well versed in changes within the student body. This qualitative data becomes extremely valuable for campuses trying to develop programs or interventions for students.

Technology will increasingly become important; today's students spend much of their time playing video games, browsing the Internet, or instant messaging their friends. Technology is a key area for academic and student affairs to develop partnerships and to work in cross-functional teams. Most campuses will not be able to make accurate decisions about technology in ways that can be used to enliven the curriculum and enhance community life unless they draw upon the expertise of people across campus. Technology is also an extremely expensive area; if mistakes are made the costs are very high. Campus leaders are realizing that cross-functional teams can develop the greatest cognitive complexity so that resources are not squandered.

Research also demonstrates that beginning with programs or activities in which there has been a history of some coordination, such as orientation or first-year programs, can be a very successful strategy (Kezar, 2001). Kezar's (2001) national survey found that campuses were most successful with partnerships when they began with an area that already had some coordination of service. The survey also found that areas of coordination differed by institutional type. Community colleges leaders are much more likely to coordinate on academic advising, while academics in private four-year institutions are working with student affairs on community service learning. Areas where there is already some common work provide a platform for moving to more and deeper partnerships.

Action Step 2: Leadership for Success

Over the past few decades, much energy has been put into providing a vision for what collaboration can look like, but strategies for getting there have been overlooked. Recent research suggests a variety of proven principles for helping to initiate and sustain partnerships on campus (Kezar, 2001). What strategies can be used to facilitate change and assist in academic and student affairs collaborations? Not surprisingly, institutional leadership from both academic and student affairs is necessary to ensure that partnerships are successful (Kezar, 2001). Senior administrators provide resources, a sense of priority, staffing, capacity to hire new staff, and philosophical support. Leaders also help to initiate the various strategies (described in the next section) that initiate and sustain partnerships. Thus, developing senior administrative support is a first critical step. If calls for collaboration are not coming from the top, then staff members need to meet with and garner senior administrative support (usually the chief student affairs and academic affairs officers). Without this support, success can be very difficult. However, leadership does not just entail senior administrative support but also requires champions who will work to nurture and sustain the partnership over the years (Schroeder, 1999a & b).

What exactly do senior leaders do to support partnerships and collaboration? First, it is often important for leaders to examine their own assumptions about collaboration in order to develop a vision or philosophy related to collaborative work. If leaders have not thought through the advantages of collaboration and when collaboration works best, motivating others to work collaboratively can be difficult. As mentioned earlier, for leaders who are in the process of developing a vision or philosophy related to collaborative work can employ ideas such as reading groups and key documents.

Collaboration often involves a shifting of resources and at times additional resources. Groups on campus can only get so far if they do not have the appropriate resources to initiate the partnership activities. On many campuses you hear stories about well-meaning senior administrators who talk about their support for the collaboration, but when it comes time for the budget process do not allocate appropriate funding. Leaders need to make sure that the resources exist for partnerships to succeed (Schroeder, 1999b).

Senior administrators can also establish rewards and incentives for staff to engage in partnerships and collaboration (Keeling, 2004). Many campuses that are successful at collaboration have modified their employee evaluation forms to include involvement in collaborative projects. In addition, bonuses and merit increases are tied to supporting new collaborative initiatives. Leaders also create motivation by signaling partnership as a priority. At campuswide and divisional meetings, senior administrators should discuss the importance of collaboration and partnerships to let people know they take this seriously. Last, motivation can be created through evaluation processes in which leaders set expectations about how roles and responsibilities are structured. In these meetings, they can stress the importance of collaborative work and help to brainstorm ways to be successful in this work.

Leadership also has the ability to hire new staff (Kezar, 2001). On many campuses with successful partnerships, one or two strategic hires were critical to help move the partnership forward. These new employees may come from a campus that has already been successful with partnerships or are individuals who have enthusiasm for collaborative work. The experience and energy of new individuals can provide motivation to other staff. In general, leaders can reallocate human resources in ways that can provide support for partnerships. An example of reallocating human resources is moving a staff member to a new learning community program from an area of lower priority.

Furthermore, senior administrators can be open to various restructuring plans that might emerge from staff that can better support collaborative endeavors (Keeling, 2004). Senior student affairs officers can also create joint and cross-functional teams that can problem-solve institutional problems and issues as well as work on collaborative programs and projects. Often leaders are afraid to restructure units because of the political ramifications; people often resist change in routine, and restructuring typically results in modification of work. But partnerships may fail if leaders are not courageous enough to make needed changes. In a national survey conducted of student and academic affairs officers, academic affairs officers were more likely than student affairs administrators to describe the importance of providing incentives or rewards and restructuring units to ensure collaboration (Kezar, 2001). This difference in perspective may be related to the fact that student affairs staff are motivated by the desire to work cooperatively and do not feel they need incentives or structural support. However, they need to be aware that other members of the institution may not have the same motivations or perspective and that providing rewards or restructuring positions may be the only way to successfully obtain commitments from other staff.

Senior administrators are also pivotal in making sure that partnerships and collaborative efforts are assessed. As many scholars have pointed out, if partnerships are not assessed and their value established, they will be subject to losing funding in times of tight resources (Bourassa and Kruger, 2001; Keeling, 2004; Kezar, 2001; Schuh, 1999; and Schroeder, 1999b). Increasingly, campuses are examining their processes of measuring student outcomes. The good news is that many campuses are conducting outcomes assessment of academic and student affairs collaboration; in fact, 45 percent of the campuses polled nationally were conducting some form of outcomes assessment; most assessments focused on institutional effectiveness, but some also examined student learning and development. We need more data on specifically how collaboration improves student learning and development to ensure that it will be supported in the future in light of funding constraints and accountability. (See Chapters Five and Six of this volume.)

Action Step 3: Attend to Culture, People, and Planning

In addition to identifying a problem or issue and providing leadership, there are a variety of strategies that can be used to initiate partnerships between academic and student affairs. Key strategies identified in the literature and research include encouraging cross-institutional dialogue, setting expectations, generating enthusiasm, creating a common vision, promoting staff development, hiring new people committed to collaboration, examining personalities, choosing the right people as partners, and planning (Kezar, 2001; and Kuh, 1996). Underlying these various strategies are three main principles: attend to culture and values, get the right people, and be intentional in planning.

Attend to Culture and Values

Campuses that have successful collaborations between academic and student affairs create opportunities for cross-institutional dialogue (Hirsch and Burack, 2001; Kezar, 2001; Kuh, 1996; and Schroeder, 1999a & b). The cross-boundary work described earlier (in areas such as technology, changing student demographics, assessment, general education, and student retention) represent areas that interest individuals across campus and can be used as opportunities for cross-campus dialogue. In addition, the areas noted as benefits of collaboration (such as creating seamless learning or improved service) and research demonstrating the success of collaborations are also issues that can be used to begin dialogue among groups that can result in collaboration. Dialogue leads directly into the next two strategies: creating a common vision and generating enthusiasm for collaboration. Cross-campus dialogue helps people to understand each other's values and work toward a shared vision of seamless learning. Often it is helpful if someone writes a concept paper outlining the goals and benefits of a particular collaboration, helping people to see more concretely the direction to head. These dialogues also generate enthusiasm and create champions or change agents for the initiative that help to provide buy-in from others.

As noted earlier, leadership and the presence of change agents are critically important factor for enabling collaboration.

Attend to People

After discussion, creation of a common vision, and the development of champions, the next step is to get the right people in place or to work with existing staff to develop the skills to collaborate effectively. As mentioned earlier, campuses successful in developing partnerships often hired new people who are committed to collaboration to lead one or more efforts. While this strategy can be used by senior administrators, it can also be used at other levels of the organization to generate enthusiasm for a collaborative effort. Since the new staff already understand the importance of collaboration, they help other employees to develop a shared vision. However, the opportunity to hire is not always available, so staff development can be another option. Sending staff to NASPA, ACPA, American Association of Colleges and Universities (AAC&U), and other conferences that describe the importance of collaboration can open their eyes to new ways of doing work. In addition, human resources offices on campus sometimes offer leadership training that emphasizes collaboration.

Collaboration also requires establishing committees to initiate the partnership. In creating these cross-functional committees, careful attention needs to be paid to the personalities and experience of the people involved. A single individual can upset the best-laid plans. Therefore, composition of committees needs to be carefully considered: Does this person have experience with collaboration? Does this person share in the common vision of the project? Has the person been involved with cross-campus dialogues? Is this person likely to generate more enthusiasm and talk to others about the project? Are there any historical or political circumstances that would make the appointment of this person problematic?

Attend to Planning

Last, even with discussion, enthusiasm, and the right people on board, without intentional and careful planning and implementation, partnerships often fail (Kezar, 2001; Schroeder, 1999b; and Schuh and Whitt, 1999). Members of the planning team need to move from a shared vision to specific goals, strategies, and an implementation plan. Habits are extremely hard to break, and a planning process reminds people on an ongoing basis that the nature of work is changing. Dialogues can assist people in reconsidering their values, but the hard work of changing day-to-day work and responsibilities is better enabled by a planning process (tied to evaluation and merit pay) that holds people accountable for new behaviors. Therefore, planning is only as effective as the accountability structures and expectations that are put in place to follow up on goals.

Action Step 4: Sustaining Partnerships

Once the collaboration is up and going, a leader's work is not complete; leaders need to evaluate, provide feedback mechanisms, and be observant of group dynamics. Campuses need to make sure that they provide mechanisms to sustain and institutionalize the partnership. One of the key strategies for ensuring that partnerships are successful is to evaluate the effort (Schuh, 1999). Evaluation should examine both the process and outcomes. In terms of the process, evaluations should examine whether the right people are included, whether there are clear decision-making structures, whether there are appropriate feedback mechanisms and communication channels, whether they have the appropriate structure and resources (both financial and human), whether both student affairs and academic affairs are involved, and whether there is a balance in perspective between academic and student affairs. Through these evaluations, leaders and senior administrators can provide necessary resources and direction to continue the success of the partnership. An evaluation should examine student learning outcomes. In particular, questions should determine whether the students' learning process appeared seamless and if the specific goals that were developed for the partnership were met.

Evaluation is one form of obtaining feedback, but less formal processes can be used as well. Some examples include reflection on the work through online surveys or pulling aside a few members to obtain their input on the process. As Fuller and Haugabrook (2001) note, "Much of the actual work of collaboration boils down to team building and attending to the individual relationships beyond the larger partnerships. A member of a collaborative team's unaddressed concerns can stall the whole project if not dealt with effectively. Mechanisms for feedback need to be part of the system and stakeholders should feel that they have opportunities to express their ideas or take the lead in aspects of the project for which they have particular expertise" (p. 85).

One of the major areas that can destroy collaborations and partnerships is the formation of dysfunctional group dynamics. Several resources on intergroup dynamics should be given to chairs or facilitators of partnerships to ensure that they have skills in mediating intergroup dynamics and conflict (Bensimon and Neumann, 1993; and Parker, 1990). Evaluation, feedback, and attention to intergroup dynamics ensure that communication channels are open, helping to avoid collisions of culture between student and academic affairs. Also, if a staff member leaves a partnership, leaders may need to step in to attend meetings until the position is filled. Once the replacement is hired, leaders can also help the new person to transition onto the team. Many partnerships fall apart when key staff leave and interpersonal dynamics become strained, partly because trust is low when new people join the group. Leaders need to be aware that these are key times to step in and be more involved.

Conclusion

While this chapter has focused on reviewing literature and research that can provide strategies for initiating and sustaining the partnerships, it is important to understand that every campus varies in its openness to and history with collaboration. In other words, campus culture matters. Some campuses have had success in the past and will need much less planning, evaluation, and hiring of new people, as they already have had experience and understand the value of collaboration. Campuses with a history of failed collaborations will need to spend more time on understanding the benefits, developing a shared vision, hiring new people, and generating enthusiasm in order to move forward. Each campus faces unique challenges with student and academic affairs collaboration. Therefore, an important step when starting any partnership is to examine the culture of the campus and determine which of the collaboration strategies described will work best for the institution. Kuh and Whitt (1988) and Schein (2004) both offer suggestions for how campuses can conduct cultural audits that can be used to understand how to approach collaboration on campus.

While Barr (1997) reminds us that collaboration has been part of the student affairs field since its origin, marked change in philosophy and practice has occurred in recent years. Student affairs sees itself as an equal partner in student learning and development. Thousands of individual partnerships exist, and models continue to be developed on campuses and replicated on other campuses. Partnerships between academic and student affairs are no longer a passing fad or hope; they are now an organizational reality with hundreds of different examples. However, many of the existing partnerships involve coordination rather than deeper forms of collaboration, which is still relatively rare. The models of deep partnerships, as highlighted in documents such as *Powerful Partnerships*, continue to evolve. These deep partnerships require careful leadership and attention; otherwise, they fail or do not manifest the anticipated benefits. While coordination is helpful, true collaboration is transformative for students. We need more courageous leaders who will make collaboration a priority, knowing it is best for students.

Collaboration is not only transformative for students but also for student and academic affairs divisions themselves. As academic and student affairs work together more closely, their values and philosophy will likely be changed. Deans of academic units often start to question the "sink or swim" approach to education and "weeder" courses after working closely with student affairs. They begin to set up peer-mentoring programs or faculty and student affairs social hours to create better relationships between the groups. Other deans of students, after working more closely with academic affairs, examine the learning outcomes of their co-curricular programs or try to incorporate ideas from the book assigned by academic affairs to all incoming students into leadership programs. Both academic and student affairs can be transformed into units that are more aligned to the overall goal of supporting student success in learning.

References

American Association for Higher Education, American College Personnel Association, and National Association of Student Personnel Administrators. *Powerful Partnerships: A Shared Responsibility for Learning.* Washington, D.C.: American Association for Higher Education, American College Personnel Association, and National Association of Student Personnel Administrators, 1998.

American College Personnel Association. *The Student Learning Imperative: Implications for Student Affairs.* Washington, D.C.: American College Personnel Association, 1994.

Barr, M. J. *Student Affairs Collaborations and Partnerships: Our Future Challenges.* Greensboro, N.C.: ERIC Counseling and Student Services Clearinghouse, 1997.

Bensimon, E. M., and Neumann, A. *Redesigning Collegiate Leadership: Teams and Teamwork in Higher Education.* Baltimore: Johns Hopkins University Press, 1993.

Bloland, P. A. *Strengthening Learning for Students: Student Affairs Collaborations and Partnerships.* Greensboro, N.C.: ERIC Counseling and Student Services Clearinghouse, 1997.

Bourassa, D. M., and Kruger, K. "The National Dialogue on Academic and Student Affairs Collaboration." In A. J. Kezar, D. J. Hirsch, and C. Burack (Eds.), *Understanding the Role of Academic and Student Affairs Collaboration in Creating a Successful Learning Environment.* New Directions for Higher Education, no. 116. San Francisco: Jossey-Bass, 2001.

Boyer, E. L. *College: The Undergraduate Experience in America.* New York: Harper & Row, 1987.

Diamond, R. M., Bronwyn, S., and Adam, E. "Balancing Institutional, Disciplinary and Faculty Priorities with Public and Social Needs: Defining Scholarship for the 21st Century." *Arts and Humanities in Higher Education,* 2004, 3(1), 29–40.

Eckel, P., Kezar, A., and Lieberman, D. "Learning for Organizing: Institutional Reading Groups as a Strategy for Change." *AAHE Bulletin,* 1999, 25(3), 6–8.

Engstrom, C. M., and Tinto, V. "Developing Partnerships with Academic Affairs to Enhance Student Learning." In M. J. Barr, M. K. Desler, and Associates (Eds.), *The Handbook of Student Affairs Administration* (2nd ed.). San Francisco: Jossey-Bass, 2000.

Ferren, A. S., and Stanton, W. W. *Leadership Through Collaboration: The Role of the Chief Academic Officer.* Westport, CT: American Council on Education/Praeger Publishers, 2004.

Fried, J. *Steps to Creative Campus Collaboration.* Washington, D.C.: National Association of Student Personnel Administrators, 2000.

Fuller, T. M. A., and Haugabrook, A. K. "Facilitative Strategies in Action." In A. J. Kezar, D. J. Hirsch, and C. Burack (Eds.), *Understanding the Role of Academic and Student Affairs Collaboration in Creating a Successful Learning Environment.* New Directions for Higher Education, no. 116. San Francisco: Jossey-Bass, 2001.

Hagadoorn, J. "Understanding the Rationale of Strategic Partnering: Interorganizational Modes of Cooperation and Sectoral Differences." *Strategic Management Journal,* 1993, 14, 371–385.

Hirsch, D. J., and Burack, C. "Finding Points of Contact for Collaborative Work." In A. J. Kezar, D. J. Hirsch, and C. Burack (Eds.), *Understanding the Role of Academic and Student Affairs Collaboration in Creating a Successful Learning Environment.* New Directions for Higher Education, no. 116. San Francisco: Jossey-Bass, 2001.

Hyman, R. E. "Creating Campus Partnerships for Student Success." *College and University,* 1995, 72(2), 2–8.

Jackson, B., Levine, J., and Patton, J. *Restructuring for Urban Student Success: Essay Collection.* Indianapolis: Restructuring for Success, 2000.

Jacoby, B. *Service-Learning in Higher Education: Concepts and Practices.* San Francisco: Jossey-Bass, 1996.

Jacoby, B. "Partnerships for Service Learning." In J. H. Schuh and E. J. Whitt (Eds.), *Creating Successful Partnerships Between Academic and Student Affairs.* New Directions for Student Services, no. 87. San Francisco: Jossey-Bass, 1999.

Keeling, R. P. (Ed.). *Learning Reconsidered: A Campus-Wide Focus on the Student Experience.* Washington, D.C.: National Association of Student Personnel Administrators and the American College Personnel Association, 2004.

Kezar, A. "Organizational Models and Facilitators of Change: Providing a Framework for Student and Academic Affairs Collaboration. In A. J. Kezar, D. J. Hirsch, and C. Burack (Eds.), *Understanding the Role of Academic and Student Affairs Collaboration in Creating a Successful Learning Environment.* New Directions for Higher Education, no. 116. San Francisco: Jossey-Bass, 2001.

Kezar, A. (Ed.). *Early Intervention for College Programs: A Collection of Research to Inform Policy and Practice.* Advances in Education Research, no. 4. Washington D.C.: Government Printing Office for the National Library of Education, 1999.

Kezar, A., Chambers, T., and Burkhardt, J. (Eds.). *Higher Education for the Public Good: Emerging Voices from a National Movement.* San Francisco: Jossey-Bass, 2005.

Kezar, A., Hirsch, D., and Burack, C. (Eds.). *Understanding the Role of Academic and Student Affairs Collaboration in Creating a Successful Learning Environment.* New Directions for Higher Education, no. 116. San Francisco: Jossey-Bass, 2001.

Knefelkamp, L. L. *The Seamless Curriculum: Is This Good for Our Students?* Washington, D.C.: Council for Independent Colleges, 1991.

Kolins, C. A. "An Appraisal of Collaboration: Assessing Perceptions of Chief Academic and Student Affairs Officers at Public Two-Year Colleges." Unpublished doctoral dissertation, University of Toledo, 1999.

Kuh, G. D. "Guiding Principles for Creating Seamless Learning Environments for undergraduates." *Journal of College Student Development,* 1996, 37(2), 135–148.

Kuh, G. D. "Setting the Bar High to Promote Student Learning." In G. S. Blimling and E. J. Whitt (Eds.), *Good Practice in Student Affairs.* San Francisco: Jossey-Bass, 1999.

Kuh, G. D., Kinzie, J., Schuh. J. H., and Whitt, E. J. *Student Success in College: Creating Conditions That Matter.* San Francisco: Jossey-Bass, 2005.

Kuh, G. D., and Whitt, E. J. (1988). *Invisible Tapestry: Culture in American Colleges and Universities.* ASHE-ERIC Higher Education Reports (vol. 1). Washington, D.C.: Association for the Study of Higher Education, 1988.

Lockwood, A. T. *School-Community Collaboration.* Washington, D.C.: Office of Educational Research and Improvement, 1996.

Martin, J., and Murphy, S. *Building a Better Bridge: Creating Effective Partnerships Between Academic Affairs and Student Affairs.* Washington, D.C.: National Association of Student Personnel Administrators, 2000.

Parker, G. *Team Players and Teamwork.* San Francisco: Jossey-Bass, 1990.

Potter, D. L. "Where Powerful Partnerships Begin." *About Campus,* 1999, 4(2), 11–16.

Schein, E. H. *Organizational Culture and Leadership* (3rd ed.). San Francisco: Jossey-Bass, 2004.

Schroeder, C. C. "Collaboration and Partnerships." In C. S. Johnson, and H. E. Cheatham (Eds.), *Higher Education Trends for the Next Century: A Research Agenda for Student Success.* Washington, D.C.: American College Personnel Association, 1999a.

Schroeder, C. C. "Forging Educational Partnerships That Advance Student Learning." In G. S. Blimling and E. J. Whitt (Eds.), *Good Practice in Student Affairs.* San Francisco: Jossey-Bass, 1999b.

Schroeder, C. C. "Partnerships: An Imperative for Enhancing Student Learning and Institutional Effectiveness." In S. A. McDade and P. H. Lewis (Eds.), *Developing Administrative Excellence: Creating a Culture of Leadership.* New Directions for Higher Education, no. 87. San Francisco: Jossey-Bass, 1999c.

Schroeder, C. C., Minor, F. D., and Tarkow, T. A. *Learning Communities: Partnerships Between Academic and Student Affairs.* Greensboro, N.C.: ERIC Counseling and Student Services, 1999.

Schuh, J. H. (1999). "Guiding Principles for Evaluating Student and Academic Affairs Partnerships." In J. H. Schuh, and E. J. Whitt (Eds.), *Creating Successful Partnerships Between Academics and Student Affairs.* New Directions for Student Services, no. 87. San Francisco: Jossey-Bass, 1999.

Schuh, J. H., and Whitt, E. J. (Eds.). *Creating Successful Partnerships Between Academics and Student Affairs.* New Directions for Student Services, no. 87. San Francisco: Jossey-Bass, 1999.

Smith, B. L., and McCann, J. (Eds.). *Reinventing Ourselves: Interdisciplinary Education, Collaborative Learning and Experimentation in Higher Education.* Bolton, MA: Anker, 2001.

Smith, D. G. "The Next Step Beyond Student Development—Becoming Partners Within Our Institutions." *NASPA Journal,* 1982, 19(4), 53–62.

Westfall, S. B. "Partnerships to Connect In- and Out-of-Class Experiences." In J. H. Schuh and E. J. Whitt (Eds.), *Creating Successful Partnerships Between Academic and Student Affairs.* San Francisco: Jossey-Bass, 1999.

Williams, J., and Wilson, V. C. "Project C.A.R.E.: A University's Commitment to African-American Student Retention." *College Student Affairs Journal,* 1993, 13(1), 48–57.

Wingspread Group on Higher Education. *An American Imperative: Higher Expectations for Higher Education.* Racine, Wisc.: Johnson Foundation, 1993.

CHAPTER TWENTY-TWO

THE POLITICAL ENVIRONMENT OF THE STUDENT AFFAIRS ADMINISTRATOR

Jeremy Stringer

Politics is deeply engrained in higher education; yet, new professionals are frequently dismayed by the politics of their positions. They like their students and their institution, but they can't seem to avoid political situations. Unfortunately, new administrators are frequently unprepared to deal with overtly political environments (Marshall and Mitchell, 1990). They are thrust into intensely political situations they frequently do not understand or appreciate. Newer professionals sometimes seem surprised that decisions in the academy are not always the result of rational, even scholarly give and take.

A study of senior student affairs officers (Herdlein, 2004) found that "knowledge of politics" was one of the three management skills most critical for successful practice. Similar to other types of organizations, the "goals, structure, technology, job design, leadership style, and other seemingly formal aspects of organizational functioning" of colleges and universities all have a political dimension (Morgan, 2006, p. 203). Senior student affairs officers may wonder, "Why can't graduate preparation programs do a better job of preparing new professionals to understand and succeed in political situations? Theory is nice, but we need staff who can navigate in political waters or their theories are useless to them."

Since educational leaders consistently describe their roles as political (Ball, 1987; Blase, 1991; Bolman and Deal, 2003; and Ellis, 2003), student affairs administrators who want to operate effectively need to find ways of integrating political principles into their administrative skill sets. This chapter is intended to be a resource for student affairs administrators who want to understand and effectively utilize political concepts. It begins with a discussion of the university as a political system, addresses political behavior as a concern for student affairs, reviews traditional political concepts within the academy, presents emergent political strategies and values deemed especially relevant to student affairs practice today, and concludes with a discussion of the limitations of the political metaphor.

The University as a Political System

For purposes of this discussion, all organizations are regarded as *political systems*. Each college or university is a political system, as is each division and each department. In addition, committees, task forces, and groups, both formal and ad hoc, are political systems. All members of a political system are *political actors*. Some actors participate fully in their political environment, while others do not. Some potential political actors can remain dormant within the system for a long time, only to have a tremendous impact once they decide to participate. One has only to consider the 1960s to recognize the impact when the relatively passive student bodies of the decade earlier evolved into ones who decided to become politically active.

The focus of this chapter is on college and university *micropolitics*: the political behavior of campus individuals and groups. Laurence Iannacone is considered to be the person who coined the phrase "micropolitics of education" (Scribner, Aleman, and Maxcy, 2003). He used it to describe the interaction among administrators, faculty, and students within a school setting. A more inclusive definition of micropolitics was offered by Blase (1991): "Micropolitics refers to the use of formal and informal power by individuals and groups to achieve their goals in organizations. In large part political action results from perceived differences between individuals and groups, coupled with the motivation to use power to influence and/or protect. [A]ny action, consciously motivated may have 'political significance' in a given situation. Both cooperative and conflictive actions and processes are part of the realm of micropolitics" (p. 11).

Bacharach and Mundell (1995) added, "Micropolitics can occur on numerous levels such as the department, school, and district levels. Micropolitics is not defined by its context, but rather by its nature. That is, micropolitics (at all levels) involves the strategic contests among interest groups over different logics of action" (p. 432).

This chapter does not address the broad political environment of higher education (the macropolitical environment). However, it is important to remember that the organizational politics of a department are a subset of a larger political system, such as a campus division; the division, in turn, is part of a larger college or university political system. The institution itself may be a part of a larger system within the region or state. And, in the case of some online institutions, boundaries may transcend geography altogether. Macropolitics can and does play an important role in shaping the substance and the tone of conversations at the micropolitical level.

The culture of higher education varies dramatically from one institution to another. An institution's culture establishes "an 'envelope' or range of possible behaviors within which an organization usually functions" (Birnbaum, 1988, p. 73). Birnbaum presents four models of organizational cultures within the academy. The types he describes are the *collegial institution,* where the sharing of core values permeates the institution and results in a sharing of power among various campus components; the *bureaucratic institution,* in which classic bureaucratic characteristics, such as a hierarchy of decision-making authority, prevail; the *political organization,* where competition for resources among various constituencies results in necessary bargaining and coalition building to accomplish subunit goals; and the *anarchical institution,* where it is sometimes difficult to discern overall institutional goals and decision making is diffuse and uncoordinated. His models illuminate archetypes, and it would be rare, if not impossible, to see a university that did not have characteristics of several of them. Community colleges tend to lean more toward the bureaucratic and the political models (Cohen and Brawer, 2003, p. 105). Birnbaum's description of *political* organizations does not just apply to some institutions; all colleges and universities can be described in political terms, regardless of which of Birnbaum's archetypes seems to best describe them.

Another taxonomy that is helpful in understanding the political nature of higher education is the frame structure articulated by Bolman and Deal (2003). They posit four frames through which political behavior in an institution may be viewed. Bolman and Deal's frames are useful ways of viewing the core tendencies of administrators within higher education. The frames they discuss are the structural, the human resource, the political, and the symbolic.

The *structural* frame emphasizes the importance of organizational structure, established goals, and clear roles and responsibilities. Those who see organizations predominantly through this frame frequently believe that the solution to an organization's problems will often be found through analysis and restructuring. The *human resource* frame posits that organizations exist to serve human needs (not the reverse). Those for whom this frame is dominant stress the importance of a good fit between individuals and their organizations in order to both fulfill human needs and accomplish the organization's goals. Many professionals in student affairs, and certainly most new ones, lean heavily toward the human resource frame.

The *political* frame views organizations as "living, screaming political arenas that host a complex web of individual and group interests" (Bolman and Deal, 2003, p. 186). Because resources in a political system are limited, coalitions of individuals compete with each other for them by jockeying for power and influence, frequently utilizing the strategies of bargaining and negotiating. The final frame presented by Bolman and Deal is the *symbolic*. The symbolic frame underscores the importance of understanding organizational culture. Because events may have multiple meanings and interpretations, people who lead from this frame create symbols to "resolve confusion, increase predictability, find direction, and anchor hope and faith" (Bolman and Deal, p. 242). Leaders in this frame create symbols, rituals, and stories to help understand and prosper in organizational life.

Consider a hiring situation faced by a community college dean of students as an example of how utilizing Bolman and Deal's four frames can enrich decision making. The dean is responsible for a large and complex group of departments. Two associate deans report to him, and each of them manages large numbers of staff and has a substantial budget. The dean and two associate deans are White males. One is primarily responsible for a cluster of offices that might fall under the heading of enrollment services: admissions, financial aid, registrar, and academic advising. When this position becomes vacant, a search is conducted. Three very different finalists emerge: a White male with a doctorate who has experience managing a similar cluster of departments at a four-year university in another state; a White woman with a master's degree who has worked her way up at the college for fifteen years, serving most recently as director of advising; and an African American woman from outside higher education who has a master's degree and some doctoral work and has run a successful nonprofit agency in the local community.

After the candidates all interview on campus, each has strong support, but for different reasons. The dean of students decides to analyze each of the finalists utilizing Bolman and Deal's frame structure. The candidate from the four-year university is appealing from the perspective of the structural frame. He understands all of the job functions and has some great ideas about how the area could be restructured in order to be more efficient. If the dean looked at this situation primarily through the structural frame, he might hire this candidate. As someone from outside the state and outside the community college network, though, the candidate has no political allies at the college.

And symbolically, hiring him might send an unintended message that qualified women will not be considered for promotion in his area. The director of advising has strong political support on campus. As director of advising, she has pockets of support in many academic departments and in the registrar's office that she would supervise. From the perspective of the human resource frame, promoting her would foster trust and loyalty and provide an incentive for other ambitious people in the system to work hard. Looking at the hiring decision primarily from the human resource frame, he would be tempted to hire her. However, she lacks direct experience managing a comparable structure, and she would not bring the new ideas he would expect from the other two. The candidate from the nonprofit agency has tremendous ties to the local community. Her success in the community would be respected, and she would bring a valuable outside perspective. Looking through the political frame, her community coalitions would be a big asset to the college, outside the dean's area as well as inside it. Since there are no administrators of color in the higher levels of his organization, he knows that hiring her would send a symbolic message of the importance of a diverse administration. Hiring her might give his area (and him) a big boost in the communities of color on campus and off. Since both he and the other associate dean are White males, he is also concerned about what symbolic message not hiring her (or the other woman) would send.

The most capable leaders develop an ability to shift their focus (or reframe) from their usual, or preferred frame(s), to see other ways in which an issue might be considered. Regardless of the dean's choice in the hypothetical scenario described, would it be fair to consider the decision as "political"? Perhaps, but only to the extent that political ramifications were among those factors he considered. Whichever person the dean hires, he knows he has tried to look at the situation objectively from all four frames. There are advantages to selecting each candidate, and there are consequences for not hiring each of them, as well. One of the consequences will no doubt be political. Since this chapter is largely concerned with the political frame, it is our contention that student affairs leaders can enhance their effectiveness by learning how to consider issues through the political frame.

Morgan (2006) urges caution in the use of the political metaphor for organizational decision making. He suggests, "When we analyze organizations in terms of the political metaphor it is almost always possible to see signs of political activity. This can lead to an increased politicization of the organization, for when we understand organizations as political systems we are more likely to behave politically in relation to what we see. We begin to see politics everywhere and to look for hidden agendas even where there are none" (p. 205). This caveat serves as an important caution to not overdo the political metaphor. It is one of several ways of viewing organizational life (Bolman and Deal, 2003), but it is fundamental to a realistic understanding of administrative functioning (Baldridge, 1971; Birnbaum, 1988; Bolman and Deal, 2003; and Moore, 2000).

Political Behavior as a Concern for Student Affairs

Early textbooks in student affairs (then known as student personnel work) did not include the importance of political behavior. Hill and French (1967) were among the first to explore the political dimensions of university life, but Baldridge (1971) gave the political model for higher education full explication. Baldridge introduced theories of conflict, power, and interest groups as vital elements in university functioning and laid the foundation for later writers (Appleton, 1991; Love and Estanek, 2004; Moore, 1991, 2000; and Smith, 1991) who would apply concepts of political theory to student affairs practice.

By the late 1980s, the topic of politics was beginning to find its way into the field's lexicon. George Kuh (1989) described the political model that acknowledged "the uneven distribution of power within increasingly pluralistic colleges and universities" (p. 219). He indicated that "faculty and student affairs staff who think of their institution as a community of equals may reject or feel threatened by actions described in the assumptions of the political model. Conflict and competition are antithetical to the traditions of collegial decision-making and governance processes. Some associate campus politics with Machiavellian behavior and ruthless self-interest. . . . [Nevertheless], acknowledgement of the political nature of colleges and universities is essential to identifying the relevant actors both on and off the campus, and to maximizing the potential benefits of conflict resolution and policy-making" (p. 220).

The Importance of Context

Context is vitally important in political systems. Although useful models exist for trying to understand institutions in a general way, like Birnbaum's discussed earlier and those mentioned in Chapter Three on governance, the reality is that every college or university is unique. Every institution has its own mission, history, traditions, culture, and ways of operating. Many administrators have belatedly discovered that it is difficult to automatically transfer what might have worked in a previous institution to their new one. Administrators moving to new institutions profit from trying to get a good read on their new environment as quickly as possible.

Political Map

A useful exercise to help student affairs leaders understand their political environment is to construct a political map. A political map is a visual representation of the political terrain of an individual in her or his current position. Included on the map are all the people the role incumbent is in a position to influence or be influenced by in any political situation. To illustrate how this works, let's develop a map for a hypothetical senior student affairs officer at a land-grant institution in a small state.

Dr. Sylvia Ramirez has been vice president at Superlative State University for eight years. She is an alumna of Superlative and returned to assume her current position of vice president after receiving her Ph.D. in higher education and working as associate vice president at a comparable land-grant university. Superlative is located in the state capitol, a midsized community with no heavy industry where the state and the university are the major employers. She sees people she knows nearly everywhere she goes. It is not unusual for her to run into alumni from Superlative, faculty members, and elected officials during the evening or on weekends. As one of the most visible women leaders at the university, and the only Hispanic vice president, she is frequently asked to speak to both campus and community groups. Although her job at Superlative is very demanding, she finds time to be involved with several nonprofit organizations and feels strongly that she should give back to the larger community.

A map describing Dr. Ramirez's political terrain is presented in Figure 22.1. She is at the center of her map, surrounded most closely by people she sees or could see *daily*. This group includes her office staff, direct reports (assistant or associate vice presidents and/or department directors), the president, other vice presidents on the campus and their direct reports, and student leaders. Spanning out from this nucleus are people with whom she has *regular contact* (but usually not daily), both on and off-campus. This group includes academic deans, leaders of the faculty senate, the department chair in the department in which she teaches one course a year, the assistant attorney general that handles the university's legal issues, the city councilpeople for both the area in which the university is located and the one for her residential area, directors and other board members from the nonprofit groups with which she is involved, senior student affairs officers at other regional institutions and at comparable institutions nationally, and students (other than student leaders) she has gotten to know.

Dr. Ramirez's political map is not limited to those she sees daily and regularly. It also includes those she sees or could see *periodically*. This group could include any student, faculty, staff, or administrative member of the Superlative community; it certainly includes all members of the board of regents, with

FIGURE 22.1 POLITICAL MAP FOR A SENIOR STUDENT AFFAIRS OFFICER

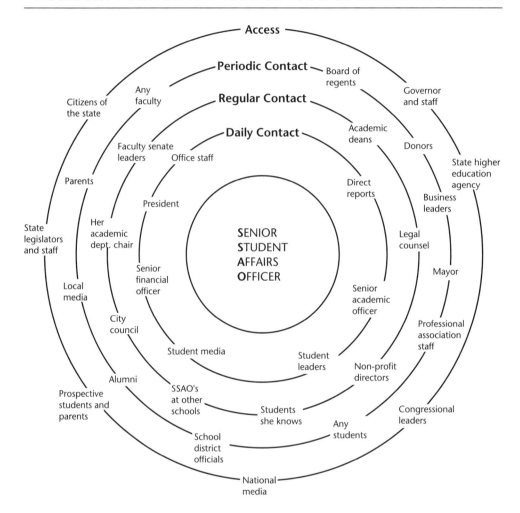

whom she meets quarterly; it includes alumni of the institution, parents of students, the local media, and other members and the executive staff of the local, regional, and national professional associations to which she belongs. It includes business leaders, many of whom are alumni or donors to the university, teachers and administrators in the district where her children go to school, the mayor and other elected officials in the city, and the officials, both elected and appointed, who are involved with higher education at the state level. The final group consists of those to whom she has *access* or who have access to her. This includes prospective students and their parents, citizens in the community and state, as well as the governor and other state politicians, staff of the state higher education agency, congressional leaders, and the local and national media.

There are literally thousands of people represented on Dr. Ramirez's political map. Because of her position and her passion for community involvement, her map may be more comprehensive than most. She usually does not think about the influence she has or the number of people who are in a position to influence her, but when confronted with major decisions that have political ramifications, she systematically thinks through how the decision might affect different political actors involved with the university. That way she knows with whom she has to consult in advance, what their concerns are likely to be, and how to shape a decision to mitigate against potentially negative political consequences for either her institution or herself.

An important consideration in creating a political map is the geographic location of the institution. As Tucker and Bryan (1998) point out, "Urban universities are inevitably caught up in city politics, and many times the urban university can find itself in danger of becoming the focus point of savage municipal political wars" (p. 15). And universities located in less urban areas may find that, as the only game in town, their activities are magnified to the local community in a way they would not be in an urban center.

Ethical Considerations

Some believe that in order to be a successful navigator of an organization's political waters, administrators must check their ethics at the door. On the contrary, in higher education a deep appreciation for ethics and ethical principles is essential to successful administrative functioning. Therefore, ethical considerations are important to mention in a discussion of political behavior within student affairs. *Ethics,* as used here, is that set of principles and beliefs that guides the moral actions of college administrators. Two parts are important: the principles and beliefs, and the fact that they are used to guide action. A study (Cranston, Ehrich, and Kimber, 2006) of educational leaders found that ethical dilemmas were widespread; they were so ubiquitous they were the "bread and butter" of leaders' lives (p. 106). Another study (Dempster, Carter, Freakley, and Parry, 2004) found that school principals, though well meaning, did not display consistent knowledge of major ethical theories. They seemed to lack a "reliable system of analysis" for making ethical decisions (p. 461).

Although little empirical research about ethical dilemmas has been reported in the student affairs literature (Janosik, Creamer, and Humphrey, 2004), the student affairs profession has well-articulated and helpful standards for professional behavior. See Chapter Nine for an excellent discussion of ethics in student affairs. Frequently, decisions student affairs administrators have to make do not involve relatively easy questions of right versus wrong; rather, they pose difficult choices between two right alternatives (Cranston and others, 2006). Then, the choices are all ethically appropriate. When this occurs, decisions fall into the political arena.

Traditional Political Concepts

Concepts are important ideas used in theory building (Kezar, Carducci, and Contreras-McGavin, 2006). Several traditional concepts are important to understanding the university as a political system. They are authority, power, interest groups, conflict, communication, and coalition building. These concepts cannot be fully understood in isolation from each other. They interact powerfully with one another in any political environment.

Authority

Leaders in higher education have several sources of authority available to them. Sergiovanni and Starratt (2007) highlight four broad sources of authority: bureaucratic, personal, professional, and moral. *Bureaucratic authority* is generally available to supervisors. It consists of the perquisites shared by those in bureaucracies, including job descriptions, rules, regulations, and the expectation of evaluation. Bureaucratic authority is more strongly associated with the administration than the faculty. This type of authority places a heavy emphasis on external accountability (Sergiovanni and Starratt, 2007, p. 27). The Center for Creative Leadership invited thirty-six American college presidents to participate in a forum on leadership in American universities. Possibly because bureaucratic authority in a university is polycentric (Walker, 1979), participants noted that the exercise of hierarchical power was less effective in a university than it might be in the corporate world (Ponder and McCauley, 2006, p. 214*). Personal authority* varies by individuals and includes their personal leadership qualities and personality characteristics. Embedded in this type of authority is the assumption that what gets rewarded gets done. Core technologies of this type of authority are the supervisors' leadership styles and motivational techniques (Sergiovanni and Starratt, 2007, p. 29).

Professional authority combines the experience, education, and expertise of the individual. This type of authority is not externally derived but rather is formed by "professional socialization and internalized knowledge and values"

(Sergiovanni and Starratt, 2007, p. 32). Administrators with this type of authority as their core source may believe that their authority as a professional supercedes the knowledge base of the student affairs profession.

Finally, *moral authority* derives from the values, ideals, and ideas shared by those within the institutional and larger communities. This type of authority is well suited to learning communities that are characterized by agreed-upon commitments. The norms and values of the organization are substituted for direct supervision as administrators become increasingly self-managing.

Power

Those with authority have power. Power is inherent in any political system and is at the heart of the discussion of politics within the academy. A typical definition is that offered by Birnbaum (1988): power is "the ability to produce intended change in others, so that they will be more likely to act in accord with one's own preferences" (p. 13). Love and Estanek (2004) observe that student affairs professionals frequently disdain the use of power as "unsavory" (p. 33). This is a mindset that is limiting and potentially career ending. Various forms of power are available to all student affairs professionals, and the adroit exercise of power will occasionally be very necessary.

Several forms of power exist in higher education. French and Raven (1968) provide a useful introduction to the bases of social power. Among the forms of power they identify are coercive power, expert power, and referent power. Morgan (2006) adds several additional sources of power; included among these are the control of scarce resources, the control of technology, and the control of the "informal organization." Another form of power is collegiality. Each of these is briefly described.

Coercive power stems from the expectation that individuals or groups may be punished if they fail to conform to an attempt to influence them. It suggests the explicit or implicit use of force or intimidation. It is likely this form of power that is most strongly resisted by student affairs professionals. Student affairs administrators who rely on this form of power too often will diminish their credibility and effectiveness.

Expert power is bestowed upon those with specialized knowledge. Expertise is highly valued in higher education, suggesting that student affairs professionals can utilize this form of power to great advantage. As students of students, student affairs professionals should possess a vast reservoir of expertise about student development theory and practice, in general, and about the students on their campuses, in particular. This information, when kept current and informed by the literature in the field, is a significant source of expert power in the academy. French and Raven (1968) point out that expert power is limited to specific cognitive areas, and this form of power will be "limited to these areas, though some 'halo effect' might occur" in some instances (p. 268).

Referent power has its basis in the strong identification of one social agent (person or group) with another. By "identification" with the person or group, French and Raven (1968) mean "a feeling of oneness," or a "desire to become closely associated" (p. 266). The stronger the association felt, the greater the referent power. Referent power may be in play in the choice of social organizations by students, their choice of majors, or even their choice of careers.

In organizational settings, *access to and control of scarce resources* is a key form of power. Morgan (2006) points out that this type of power is dependent on two things: the resource in question being in short supply and others' dependence on its availability. Colleges and universities have a large percentage of their budgets tied up in ongoing personnel costs. Managers whose budgets appear large may actually have very little budgetary flexibility for operations. Therefore, those who have access to pools of discretionary money to spend may have strong organizational power. This power often extends to those who are the gatekeepers of the ultimate decision makers as well as the budget managers themselves.

An increasingly vital form of power within the academy is *control of technology*. As technology infrastructure consumes an ever-increasing share of institutional budgets, those administrators who control the technology are increasingly powerful. In just a short period of time, the position of "chief information officer" has become ubiquitous within the academy, with role incumbents sometimes serving as very powerful campus administrators. Particularly relevant to student affairs professionals, technology is also a significant source of student power. Students are able to send text messages to each other at lightning speed, upload videos of compromising situations, and post powerful messages (both positive and negative) on social networking sites that can reach thousands of people instantaneously. So, while the control of an institution's technology infrastructure may yield traditional organization power, the "democratization" of technology and its skillful use by students may also present political challenges for administrators. Although technology providers still have considerable power, so now do the users of the technology themselves.

Leadership in the *informal organization* is also a distinct source of power. All organizations have informal networks of people who are drawn to each other for various reasons. Coworkers may meet on a regular basis for lunch, sports events, or social activities. They may share the same religious or ethnic backgrounds, have children of the same age, or be enrolled in graduate classes with each other. The leaders of these informal networks can have a strong influence on the more formal organization.

A final source of power is *collegiality*. Hardy (1996) points out that collegiality, long a hallmark of our perception of higher education at its best, involves the use of power; to her, collegiality is "a particular use of power that avoids conflict" (p. 204). Collegiality, like any of the forms of power available to student affairs administrators, is neutral until utilized and can be abused as well as positively employed.

Interest Groups and Conflict

In his explication of the relevance of the political model to higher education, Baldridge (1971) borrowed from sociological conflict theory. Applications he highlighted are the fragmentation of social systems into smaller interest groups, each with specific goals; the interaction of interest groups, and especially the manner in which one group tries to prevail over others; the clustering of groups around divergent values; and the centrality of change, for change is to be anticipated in a social system characterized by differing interest groups, with potentially opposing values, each trying to gain advantages over the others.

Much of higher education today is polycentric. Although a central administration usually maintains titular control over major decisions, the day-to-day functioning of the academy is diffused throughout a panoply of departments, centers, divisions, and colleges. Schools and departments "exercise centrifugal force and distribute sources of influence," which renders hierarchical authority impossible, according to Thomas Hearn, president of Wake Forest University (Ponder and McCauley, 2006, p. 214). This dispersion of control gives rise to voluminous interest groups, many of which are in competition with each other for scarce institutional resources. And, for public institutions, this competition may be intensifying as their share of the public funding pie continues to shrink.

Baldridge (1971) discusses four types of active interest groups. They are anomic interest groups, partisan-dominated cliques, authority-dominated cliques, and associational interest groups.

Anomic interest groups present the type of spontaneous activity expressed in riots, mutinies, and strikes. This type of activity was a regular feature on many campuses in the 1960s and early 1970s and may manifest itself on particular campuses when conditions there allow for large-scale mobilization of political actors.

Partisan-dominated cliques have no formal group status and are usually much less visible; their characteristics are stability over time, informal leadership, a low degree of organization, and intermittent political activity. Examples of these cliques might include student groups that get together to protest large hikes in the cost of tuition; administrators concerned about the failure of the institution to appoint qualified women to positions of institutional leadership; or a group of faculty and students concerned about vestiges of institutional racism. Although these groups have no official group standing within the institution, they can frequently be mobilized into political activity by the right (or wrong) combination of events.

Authority-dominated cliques develop when an authority within the institution decides to rally supporters for a cause or issue. This might be occasioned by an issue where the ultimate authority for the decision resides elsewhere, such as reorganization efforts affecting that person's area, or a conflict with another division over which one will supervise a particular administrative function. These groups display the same general characteristics as partisan-dominated cliques except that they are gathered together by authorities within the institution.

In contrast to the first three types of interest groups, *associational interest groups* are formally organized and continuously active despite fluctuating membership and regularly evolving goals. They are designed to support and protect the interests of specific campus or extracampus groups. Examples might be a staff association on a particular campus, a student club, or a professional association, such as the National Association of Student Personnel Administrators. Unlike the other three types, associational interest groups may be consulted by the hierarchy in advance about potential campus decisions; like them, they may decide to become politically active when their interests warrant it.

Communication

Administrators in higher education have sometimes been accused (Manning, Kinzie, and Schuh, 2006) of operating in functional silos. When this occurs, interest group conflicts can become exacerbated. Successful political activity cannot occur when administrators operate in isolation from one another. In any political system, political actors know what they and their interest groups are doing, but they cannot know about the activities of all others. This is why communication is fundamentally important. Effective political activity requires discussion and problem solving among people and groups whose natural interests may be different. However, "even if the various groups understand each other perfectly, they will continue to view the world differently, to define problems and solutions differently, to protect different interests, and, at times, to pursue different objectives" (Hardy, 1996, p. 8). Even the most effective communication will not remove the probability of conflict.

Conflicting paradigms are common in the academy. Particularly when resources are scarce, individuals in the system will struggle with each other. Two courses of action present themselves to student affairs administrators. Either they must work with others to create a common vision and enroll others in attempting to achieve it, or they must be prepared to battle with opponents if conflict arises. Sandeen and Barr (2006) note that communication tools such as Web pages, e-mail, and Web logs (blogs) have increased the politicization of higher education. Technology brings conflicts and debates that were once confined to a particular campus "into the purview of others" (p. 21). If administrators are unsuccessful at finding common ground for agreement with those who think differently on their campus, their dispute (or one version of it) may be electronically available worldwide.

Coalition Building

Higher education has a "fragmented system of influence" (Baldridge, 1971, p. 183) in which no single part of the institution dominates everything. Another way of looking at this dispersed authority is to view each functional area as a potential power center. In order to accomplish organizational objectives, including the enhancement of student learning, student affairs administrators must occasionally (if not frequently) unite individuals from various power centers to pursue common goals.

The ability to build a successful coalition is critical to the success of any administrator in higher education. Ponder and McCauley (2006) point out that, for many leaders outside of higher education, their "drive to forge partnerships emanates from a desire for financial gain, for competitive advantage, or to feed a competitive spirit" (pp. 217–218). But since higher education values "human development over monetary gain" (p. 218), coalition building serves the larger goal of commitment to the purpose of education. They say that "while on the surface the act of coalition building may appear similar to the politicking engaged in by other leaders, effective university [leaders] firmly anchor these relationships in the ethical standards, values, and mission of their university" (p. 218). Mandating change is not an effective political strategy in higher education; the diffuse power centers of a university require effective leaders to build bridges across divisions of the institution in order to affect positive change. The most effective leaders, according to university presidents assembled by the Center for Creative Leadership, are ones who display a commitment to open dialogue and engagement, ones whose personal values align with those of the institution, and ones who "stand ready to adopt principled, value-driven stands when necessary" (Ponder and McCauley, p. 218).

Emergent Political Concepts and Values

There are several emergent political concepts and values that should supplement the traditional political concepts already discussed, especially for student affairs practitioners. These include broadening participation, boundary spanning, team orientation, and critical and postmodern paradigms. Each of these is rooted in the values of the student affairs profession. They are utilized by exemplary practitioners across a wide spectrum of institutional types.

Broadening Participation

When discussing political participation within educational environments, Lopez (2003) argues that trumpeting the usually accepted descriptions of success within political systems ignores the fact that the power pendulum tips heavily toward White, middle-class men. Lopez says typical micropolitical theories "fail to address why certain individuals fail to participate in the political process altogether and/or how and why the 'democratic' process itself marginalizes and silences diverse peoples, their actions, and their perspectives" (p. 75). In addition to the lack of participation of some diverse populations, their ability to benefit from the political process has also been questioned. Willis Hawley stated, "Political scientists have been more interested in studying the political *processes* than they have been in studying who receives what benefits from the political process" (quoted in Lopez, 2003, p. 75).

The student affairs profession strives to honor people of all backgrounds. As our student communities as well as our profession continue to become more diverse, ways of broadening participation in the political systems of our campuses must be a priority. In addition to opening up processes of participation, we must be attentive to the impact of the political procedures of our campuses on people of color, the working poor, the disabled, gays/lesbians/bisexuals/transsexuals, non-native speakers and other potentially marginalized populations. Student affairs professionals are generally committed to empowering others rather than exercising power over others.

Boundary Spanning

The existence of various discrete cultures within higher education is almost axiomatic. William Bergquist and Kenneth Pawlak (2008) provide a helpful model. They advance six cultural archetypes: the collegial culture, the managerial culture, the developmental culture, the advocacy culture, the virtual culture, and the tangible culture.

The *collegial culture* is an extension of faculty life in the colonial colleges. Faculty are discipline based but also concerned about the transmission of values. Faculty members are the dominant group adhering to this culture.

The *managerial culture* believes that colleges should have clearly established goals and priorities, strategic planning, and outcomes assessment. Frequently, legal affairs, business affairs, and human resources personnel are staunch advocates of the advantages of viewing an institution through this cultural lens.

The *advocacy culture* appeals to those with a traditional view of micropolitical activity inside the academy. The origins of this culture are found in the competition among various factions for scarce institutional resources. Community colleges frequently have negotiating cultures, perhaps because of the strong foothold unions have on many campuses. Larger universities are also fertile ground for advocacy cultures to develop; the sheer size of many universities has created conditions in which some members of the campus community seem estranged from the type of collegiality that might characterize collegial culture participants.

The *developmental culture* "finds meaning primarily in the creation of programs and activities furthering the personal and professional growth of all members of the collegiate community" (Bergquist, 1992, p. 5).

The *virtual culture* has emerged as a twenty-first-century phenomenon. Proponents of this culture value "the global perspective of open, shared, responsive educational systems" (Bergquist and Pawlak, 2008, p. 147). They envision educational institutions as a part of a global learning network, attempting to bring a sense of order to the chaotic postmodern world. They "find and create meaning in the global knowledge economy" (Bergquist and Pawlak, 2008, p. 245).

Those who identify with the *tangible culture* find meaning in its roots, values, and "spiritual grounding" (Bergquist and Pawlak, 2008, p. 185). As it exists today, the tangible culture is based on strong institutional identity, a shared sense of community, and grounding in religious versus secular values. Those aligned with this culture value the physical space of a college campus and the face-to-face relationships they have with colleagues and students in real time.

Across institutional types, it seems that most faculty are comfortable in the collegial culture, most business affairs officers in the managerial culture, and most student affairs practitioners in the developmental culture. However, these should be thought of as general tendencies and not absolutes. For instance, many faculty are fully ensconced in the developmental culture, and many student affairs practitioners almost wholly in the managerial culture. There are tensions among proponents of the various cultures; for instance, those in the collegial culture highly value autonomy; developmentalists regard collaboration more highly.

Increasingly, student affairs professionals are called to center their activities on student learning. As the student learning movement becomes more ubiquitous, it promises to redefine traditional faculty and student affairs roles as well as the cultural assumptions that undergird them. This creates a need for student affairs professionals to reach out to faculty and others within the collegial culture and recenter activities in support of learning. Student affairs practitioners are ideally positioned to bridge the various cultures of the academy. This is because the nature of their work requires regular and effective communication with all parts of the institution. Successful student affairs boundary spanners may "permeate and reform" (Heifetz, 1994, p. 119) boundaries between existing university cultures. They may create a "political commons" (Terry, 1993, p. 258) where the educational needs of students and their learning leads to a new and vital culture that crosses traditional organizational and cultural boundaries.

Team Orientation

Political activity in higher education is sometimes thought of as a characteristic of individual political actors, such as a charismatic president. Increasingly, though, we are aware that political success is the result of highly effective teams working together to accomplish common goals. An important political skill for contemporary student affairs professionals is creating a highly functioning team. The team may consist of an intact group, like department directors, or it may be an ad hoc group brought together for a single purpose. Bensimon and Neumann (1993) point out both the promises and pitfalls of working with teams. Teams can assist creative problem solving, facilitate cognitive complexity, provide peer support, and increase accountability; but they can also become isolated, fall into groupthink, silence opposing viewpoints, and become excessively time consuming. Several aspects of effective team functioning are highlighted here: fostering cognitive complexity, avoiding isolation, and encouraging the expression of opposing points of view.

Neumann (1989) found that cognitive complexity (the ability to view situations through multiple lenses) was rare among college presidents. It is assumed that other role incumbents face the same limitations. However, a carefully constructed team might overcome this by employing a variety of thinking strategies to address political situations. Thinking is usually considered an individual characteristic, but it applies to teams as well. Bensimon and Neumann (1993) describe the following "thinking roles" of cognitively complex teams: defining the team's reality; analyzing issues from diverse angles and against larger contexts; interpreting how those outside the team might see and understand issues; advocating opposing points of view; and synthesizing the work done by the team.

All of these roles are politically significant. Student affairs leaders and their teams must be very clear about who they are and what priorities they hope to accomplish. In any political system, there are always more potential issues to work on than time will allow. Carefully setting priorities as a team allows for multiple voices to be heard as priorities are assembled and should lead to greater support from the team itself. Analyzing issues from multiple perspectives is vital to the team's campus credibility. If possible, people outside the team itself should be asked for their perspectives on critical issues. Insular teams can blunder into groupthink (Janis, 1972) by assuming people outside the team agree with them when in reality they do not. A very useful team role is advocating opposing viewpoints. This allows for the faults of a proposed plan to be identified; after weaknesses of a proposed idea are surfaced, the idea can be modified or a strategy developed to minimize its limitations. Critics inside a team offer vital intellectual challenge and diversity; and they may be verbalizing what others outside the group are saying. Bensimon and Neumann's (1993) research on presidential teams discovered that cognitively complex teams had fewer turf issues, met more often, were more open and tolerant, and integrated new members more effectively; however, they also brought more chaos and were more difficult to manage.

Critical and Postmodern Paradigms

Scholars in the late twentieth century and early twenty-first century have introduced new paradigms relevant to the political environment of higher education. *Paradigm,* as used here, refers to a set of underlying assumptions that together form a discrete worldview. In particular, the critical and postmodern paradigms offer alternative views about political activity in the academy. The *critical paradigm* critiques and questions "the class-based society that currently exists" (Kezar and others, 2006, p. 21). The interests of critical theorists intersect with political analysis in their efforts to deconstruct hidden assumptions, such as power relationships within society. Kezar and others state about critical theorists: They might ask questions such as "Are hierarchical arrangements between leader and follower merely socially constructed and not natural or inherent? And are they used to disempower or privilege certain groups?" (p. 21).

Critical theory is important in the context of the political environment within higher education. Student affairs administrators need to be aware of its basic thrust; it helps to provide an intellectual foundation for efforts to level the playing fields of political activity on campus. Particularly as our campuses become increasingly diverse, issues of power and privilege can be expected to intensify, not fade away. Critical theorists can be important allies for student affairs professionals who are concerned about how issues of gender, race, and class affect students and others who may feel marginalized within the academy.

The *postmodern paradigm* has been applied to a wide variety of disciplines within the academy. Postmodernists reject the linear worldview in which individuals are able to exert control over their own destinies (Kezar and others, 2006, p. 23). They are far more open to fluidity, chaos, and ambiguity. Postmodernists would seem to be comfortable in political environments in which participants move in and out of conversations (like faculty frequently do), where outcomes are not predetermined, and where power and participation are diffused. Some of the implications of postmodernist thought on the politics of the academy include the value of listening to individual voices, a rejection of traditional strategic planning, and the importance of deconstructing the values that undergird decision making. Administrators who endeavor to form coalitions involving postmodernists should be aware that the postmodernists' worldview might cause them to reject active involvement and even to question the need for a coalition in the first place.

Limitations of the Political Metaphor

The purposes of this chapter have been to foster a greater understanding of the political nature of higher education organizations and to assist student affairs administrators to prosper within their political systems. Before concluding, it is important to underscore the limits of the political metaphor. Political analysis is only one way of looking at organizational life. It is part of the administrator's tool kit for understanding and effectively participating in the practical world of student affairs.

In any organization, some individuals wield more power than others. Although every political actor who chooses to participate within a political system has sources of power available, "ultimate power rests with the people or forces that are able to define the stage of action on which the game of politics is played" (Morgan, 2006, p. 206). Morgan discusses that radical critics of pluralist politics, such as Marx and Weber, suggest that organizational reality is strongly related to the ability of the dominant class to control the lives of its workers. They view organizational structures as instruments of "social domination" (p. 293). While *domination* may be too strong a word to apply to even the most autocratic leaders in a college setting, vestiges of class privilege are certainly present in the academy. Although there is a veneer of egalitarianism inherent in contemporary higher education, we should not dismiss the claims that some within the academy are less than equal partners. Particularly within the administrative arena, sometimes a hierarchy of authority trumps the hierarchy of ideas. Accepting this as a valid perspective makes it even more important for student affairs professionals to gain a thorough understanding of colleges and universities as political systems.

While the political metaphor has its limitations, administrators in student affairs must understand their political environments in order to be successful in their roles. Although not all administrative situations require political analysis, an informed political perspective is essential for effective student affairs practice.

References

Appleton, J. R. "The Context." In P. L. Moore (Ed.), *Managing the Political Dimension of Student Affairs*. New Directions for Student Services, no. 55. San Francisco: Jossey-Bass, 1991.

Bacharach, S. B., and Mundell, B. L. "Organizational Politics in Schools: Micro, Macro, and Logics of Action." *Educational Administration Quarterly*, 1995, 29, 423–452.

Baldridge, J. V. *Power and Conflict in the University*. New York: Wiley, 1971.

Ball, S. J. *The Micropolitics of the School: Towards a Theory of School Organization*. London: Methuen, 1987.

Bensimon, E. M., and Neumann, A. *Redesigning Collegiate Leadership: Teams and Teamwork in Higher Education*. Baltimore: Johns Hopkins University Press, 1993.

Bergquist, W. H. *The Four Cultures of the Academy*. San Francisco: Jossey-Bass, 1992.

Bergquist, W. H., and Pawlak, K. *Engaging the Six Cultures of the Academy*. San Francisco: Jossey-Bass, 2008.

Birnbaum, R. *How Colleges Work*. San Francisco: Jossey-Bass, 1988.

Blase, J. (Ed.). *The Politics of Life in Schools: Power, Conflict, and Cooperation*. Newbury Park, Calif.: Sage, 1991.

Bolman, L. G., and Deal, T. E. *Reframing Organizations: Artistry, Choice and Leadership* (3rd ed.). San Francisco: Jossey-Bass, 2003.

Cohen, A. M., and Brawer, F. B. *The American Community College* (4th ed.). San Francisco: Jossey-Bass, 2003.

Cranston, N., Ehrich, L. C., and Kimber, M. "Ethical Dilemmas: The 'Bread and Butter' of Educational Leaders' Lives." *Journal of Educational Administration*, 2006, 44(2), 106–121.

Dempster, N., Carter, L., Freakley, M., and Parry, L. "Conflicts, Confusions and Contradictions in Principals' Ethical Decision Making." *Journal of Educational Administration*, 2004, 42(4), 450–461.

Ellis, S. *Dreams, Nightmares and Pursuing the Passion: Personal Perspectives on College and University Leadership*. Washington, D.C.: National Association of Student Personnel Administrators, 2003.

French, J. R. P. Jr., and Raven, B. "The Bases of Social Power." In D. Cartwright and A. Zander (Eds.), *Group Dynamics: Research and Theory* (3rd ed.). New York: Harper and Row, 1968.

Hardy, C. *The Politics of Collegiality: Retrenchment Strategies in Canadian Universities*. Montreal: McGill-Queen's University Press, 1996.

Heifetz, R. A. *Leadership Without Easy Answers*. Cambridge, Mass.: Belknap Press, 1994.

Herdlein, R. J. III. "Survey of Chief Student Affairs Officers Regarding Relevance of Graduate Preparation of New Professionals." *NASPA Journal*, 2004, 42(1), 51–71.

Hill, W. W., and French, W. L. "Perceptions of the Power of Department Chairmen by Professors." *Administrative Science Quarterly*, 1967, 11, 548–574.

Janis, I. L. *Victims of Groupthink*. Boston: Houghton-Mifflin, 1972.

Janosik, S. M., Creamer, D. G., and Humphrey, E. "An Analysis of Ethical Problems Facing Student Affairs Administrators. *NASPA Journal*, 2004, 41(2), 356–374.

Kezar, A. J., Carducci, R., and Contreras-McGavin, M. *Rethinking the "L" Word in Higher Education: The Revolution of Research on Leadership*. ASHE Higher Education Report, vol. 31(6). San Francisco: Jossey-Bass, 2006.

Kuh, G. D. "Organizational Concepts and Influences." In U. Delworth and G. R. Hanson (Eds.), *Student Services: A Handbook for the Profession* (2nd ed.). San Francisco: Jossey-Bass, 1989.

Lopez, G. R. "The (Racially Neutral) Politics of Education: A Critical Race Theory Perspective." *Educational Administration Quarterly*, 2003, 39(1), 68–94.

Love, P. G., and Estanek, S. M. *Rethinking Student Affairs Practice*. San Francisco: Jossey-Bass, 2004.

Manning, K, Kinzie, J., and Schuh, J. *One Size Does Not Fit All: Traditional and Innovative Models of Student Affairs Practice*. New York: Routledge, 2006.

Marshall, C., and Mitchell, B. "The Assumptive World of Fledgling Administrators." Paper presented at the annual meeting of the American Educational Research Association, Boston, April 1990.

Moore, P. L. (Ed.). *Managing the Political Dimension of Student Affairs*. New Directions for Student Services, no. 55. San Francisco: Jossey-Bass, 1991.

Moore, P. L. "The Political Dimensions of Decision Making." In M. J. Barr, and M. K. Desler (Eds.), *The Handbook of Student Affairs Administration* (2nd ed.). San Francisco: Jossey-Bass, 2000.

Morgan, G. *Images of Organization*. Thousand Oaks, Calif.: Sage, 2006.

Neumann, A. "Strategic Leadership: The Changing Orientations of College Presidents." *Review of Higher Education*, 1989, 12, 137–151.

Ponder, K. M., and McCauley, C. D. "Leading in the Unique Character of Academe: What it Takes." In D. G. Brown (Ed.), *University Presidents as Moral Leaders*. Westport, Conn.: Praeger, 2006.

Sandeen, A., and Barr, M. J. *Critical Issues for Student Affairs: Challenges and Opportunities*. San Francisco: Jossey-Bass, 2006.

Scribner, J. D., Aleman, E., and Maxcy, B. "Emergence of the Politics of Education Field: Making Sense of the Messy Center. *Educational Administration Quarterly*, 2003, 39(1), 10–40.

Sergiovanni, T. J., and Starratt, R. J. *Supervision: A Redefinition* (8th ed.). New York: McGraw-Hill, 2007.

Smith, D. G. "Small Colleges and Religious Institutions: Special Issues." In P. L. Moore (Ed.), *Managing the Political Dimension of Student Affairs*. New Directions for Student Services, no. 55. San Francisco: Jossey-Bass, 1991.

Terry, R. W. *Authentic Leadership: Courage in Action*. San Francisco: Jossey-Bass, 1993.

Tucker, A. and Bryan, R. A. *The Academic Dean: Dove, Dragon and Diplomat*. New York: MacMillan, 1998.

Walker, D. E. *The Effective Administrator*. San Francisco: Jossey-Bass, 1979.

CHAPTER TWENTY-THREE

DEVELOPING EFFECTIVE RELATIONSHIPS ON CAMPUS AND IN THE COMMUNITY

Shannon Ellis

There is a secret to being a successful leader *and* administrator in higher education, and the profession of student affairs knows what it is. It's the key to attaining professional goals (Bryson, 1995), achieving outcomes (Snyder, 2002), transforming organizations (Kouzes and Posner, 2002), assessing effectiveness (Schuh and Upcraft, 2001), and sustaining an inclusive institutional culture (Harper, 2008) where learning occurs throughout the educational community. This approach to managing programs and services for college students is revolutionary only in its simplicity amidst today's complexity. It does *not* require the latest technology or an enormous budget. In fact, it requires neither machinery nor money. It *does* require the most precious assets of all—an administrator's time and attention—along with humility, commitment, and honesty. Described by Allen and Cherrey (2002) as networked systems, by Freire (1970) as true generosity and dialoguing, by Kouzes and Posner (2002) as deeper connections, and Kotter (1990) as thick networks, it is also known as support systems, teams, partnerships, coalitions, cooperatives, and alliances. All of these things are forms of the root of it all: relationships. Peggy Barr once observed, "Relationships are our legacy" (Roper, 2002, p. 24).

This chapter explores developing effective relationships on campus and in the community. It opens with a discussion of the importance of relationships. Next, various types of relationships are described. Then consideration is given to developing relationships at the level of both individuals and constituent groups. Following that, the chapter addresses how relationships are formed and the role of conflict in relationships before moving on to concluding remarks.

The Importance of Relationships

Relationships are essential to the accomplishments of student affairs professionals. In *Learning Reconsidered 2* (Keeling, 2006) the first of three primary skill areas identified for achieving success is "sustained collaborative efforts" (p. 60). Through this, "the group must develop relationships built on trust and open communication" (McDonald and Associates, 2002, p. 170). Because of *other people, we* achieve and succeed.

"There is no such thing as an unimportant or insignificant relationship. Every person and every interaction matters" (Roper, 2002, p. 12). It is when student affairs administrators are without relationships that they fail to achieve their goals. "In the absence of specific goals or plans for developing partnerships, whatever good intentions there might be to foster seamless learning can languish unfulfilled" (Schuh and Whitt, 1999, p. 1).

The lesson is to develop a multitude of good relationships *with* people and *among* people. Kotter (1990) points out why such relationships are important: "These thick networks of informal relationships help coordinate leadership activities in much the same way as formal structure coordinates managerial activities. The key difference is that thick informal networks can deal with the greater coordinating demands associated with non-routine activities and change. The multitude of communication channels and the trust among the individuals connected by those channels allow for an ongoing process of accommodation and adaptation regarding who will play what role" (p. 90). Wheatley (1992) points out that where organizational change has been realized, it has been the result of successful relationships. Thus, in *Learning Reconsidered 2* (Keeling, 2006), the authors conclude, "Similarly, successful learning happens in relationship—relationships with new ideas, new people, and new ways of achieving" (p. 14).

Types of Relationships

The types of relationships developed with others are influenced by organizational structure, campus culture, issues to be addressed, and the personalities and professional style of individuals and groups (Bolman and Deal, 2003). For the student affairs practitioner, relationships come in many forms, with individual students and student groups, colleagues, supervisors, other administrative units and constituencies within the institution, as well as those outside the organization.

Student Affairs Practitioner-Student

Opportunities for relationships with students abound in the campus setting. Faculty and administrators are agents of influence (Love, 1995; Pascarella and Terenzini, 2005). They create powerful learning environments through these relationships. Advising students on academic coursework, career planning, or leadership development can have great impact on a college student's life through the relational system they create—"the ways in which students interpret and respond to the people, conditions, and institutions in their external world" (Pascarella and Terenzini, 2005, p. 213).

Advisor-Advisee. "The advising relationship is a wonderful opportunity to facilitate the development of students" (Love, 2003, p. 511). Richard Light (2001) believes that "good advising may be the single most underestimated characteristic of a successful college experience" (p. 81). Love (2003) warns, "While the advisor may indeed have more knowledge and experience than the advisee and be aware of the 'bigger picture,' the goal of advising is to generate learning, growth, and self-determination in addition to sharing information, opinion and one's accumulated wisdom" (p. 507).

Teacher-Learner. A core value of student affairs is to serve as educators and fulfill a teaching role (Roper, 2003). While teaching is often described as a transformative activity, instruction is embedded in relationships and involves connectedness among the teacher, the subject, and students (Palmer, 1983). Teachers must create "knowledge communities" through the learning in others (Moore, 2007; Twale and Sanders, 1999). "Those who work in student affairs are keenly aware that teaching is not merely a role, but an activity and process that involves relationships and community-building" (Roper, p. 470).

Developer/Enforcer-Community Member. Student affairs professionals hold the dual responsibility of helping students mature and develop competencies while holding students accountable for behavioral standards established by society and the institution (Cooper and Schwartz, 2007). Relationships are at the forefront as colleges and universities approach student discipline as an opportunity to reinforce and integrate community values (Dannells, 1997). The positions of Greek Affairs coordinator (Strayhorn and Colvin, 2006), resident advisor (Blimling, 2003), and judicial officer (Dannells, 1997) fulfill this most difficult assignment and are at the vanguard of the field of student development. Building community through successful relationships depends upon the abilities to understand and work with students while also resolving conflict and managing crises.

Mentor-Mentee. Laurent Daloz (1990) defines the mentor as a "trusted guide rather than a tour director" (p. ix). If mentors have, as he asserts, "something to do with growing up, with the development of identity" (p. 19), then it is a perfect role for professionals in the field of student affairs. It is important to understand what the process of mentoring entails so that one knows when to ask the hard questions, when to encourage, and when to simply let things be (Kouzes and Posner, 2002).

Student Affairs Practitioner-Colleagues and Constituencies

Experience proves that the achievement of institutional initiatives (that is, student success) is not guaranteed by its righteousness but rather by one's ability to build effective partnerships, coalitions, and alliances (Snyder, 2002; Sockett, 1998). The art of "building authentic relationships with diverse others" (Rogers, 2003, p. 460) demonstrates truly collaborative leadership characterized by dialogue in which all voices are valued and power is shared. Internal and external relationships with individuals and groups are keys to success. The form of these relationships will vary by motivation, duration, and desired outcome.

Powerful Partnerships. Partners share a joint interest and work together to accomplish a common goal with a shared sense of purpose and sharing responsibility for the outcome (Jackson and Maddy, 2008). Each is an agent for the other. Powerful partnerships engage in a mutual enterprise, sharing its possibilities and its risks (Dietz and Enchelmayer, 2001; Schuh and Whitt, 1999). Leaders are confident of the shared purposes that the partnership has established and believe in the power of the collective process. "You succeed by finding ways to capitalize on who you are, not trying to fix who you aren't. If you are blunt on one or two important areas, try to find a partner whose peaks match your valleys" (Buckingham and Coffman, 1999, p. 171). A partnership among educators from pre-school through higher education to prevent dropout and ensure academic preparedness results in increased college-going rates, especially among underrepresented populations.

Alliances and Allies. An alliance is an association entered into for mutual benefit as opposed to a partnership formed around the risks and possibilities of a common interest. "The basic point is simple: as a manager you need friends and allies to get things done. To get their support, you need to cultivate relationships" (Bolman and Deal, 2003, p. 210). Allies know that one person's success is also their own success. Administrators who seek to be an ally to others on campus in their efforts will quickly develop allies for their own agenda. One succeeds in a career by cultivating allies along the way who are relied upon time and again in pursuing personal and professional goals (Patterson, 2001). Student affairs professionals may be simultaneously involved in several different forms of alliances, such as with academics to embed diversity studies across the curriculum, with development officers to raise money for scholarships, and with the campus neighborhood to pass city council ordinances that would hold landlords accountable for tenant behavior.

Coalitions. Viewing student affairs work in the higher education organization as a coalition questions many traditional views (Bolman and Deal, 2003). Coalitions imply a temporary alliance of varied, sometimes, opposing factions during which they cooperate in joint action, each in their own self-interest (Croteau and Hicks, 2003; Tarrow, 1998). A coalition may form in a time of crisis or scarce resources. "Individuals and groups have their insular objectives and resources, and they bargain with other players to influence goals and decisions" (Bolman and Deal, p. 190). At such times, student affairs professionals may need to join with a wide variety of those with whom they would not otherwise engage: employee unions and student government around campus safety concerns; and Democrats, Republicans, Libertarians, and the Green party to create a level playing field for all views to be expressed. The arrangement allows distinct people or entities to pool resources and combine efforts to arrive at solutions to carry out a plan and/or to effect change.

Cross-Constituent Committees. These long-term committees comprised of a range of stakeholders serve to give all perspectives a voice in the dialogue about an issue and recommended future action. Commonly utilized in strategic planning or search committees, such teams present diverse needs as well as specific opinions and expertise on facets of the organization (Bryson, 1995; Finn, 1995). The relationships formed among committee members are influenced by the charge given by its convener. By getting outside the student affairs "groupthink" (Janis, 1972) that is inevitable, there is the benefit of other viewpoints and broader all-campus and community buy-in.

Relationships with Individuals and Constituencies

The many types of relationships that exist in the workplace include those with staff, a supervisor, the community, students, public officials, institutional governing boards, donors, alumni, parents, and faculty. These relationships are significantly influenced by who these people are and what they expect.

Staff

The employee-manager relationship has a direct impact on work-life happiness, productivity, and retention. Don't underestimate how great an influence a supervisor is on employee performance and their motivation to rise to their greatest potential (Pardee, 2008). Staff members are a precious resource. Understand and value their contributions. Most people truly desire to commit to the organization for which they work. Steven Sample (2002), President of University of Southern California, asserts that people should "work hard for those who work for you" (p. 121).

Supervisor

Over time a quality relationship with a supervisor will be the most important one a professional develops in a career (Hawkins and Shohet, 2000; Scaife, 2001). Supervisors have a lot invested in an employee's success. In turn, employees have a role in helping their supervisor achieve his or her goals and vision for the organization. Dalton and McClinton (2002) reflect that "loyalty is the glue of friendship between leaders and followers.... Leadership is a lonely business, and loyalty is one of the important ways in which bosses recognize trust and goodwill and build upon it important professional relationships" (p. 18).

Community

Every higher education institution resides in a community where, at any given time, support, apathy, or hostility can exist toward the resident school. Local officials, elected council members, neighborhood advisory groups, and businesses are just a few of the constituents that define the term *community* (Grace, 2002). Less obvious may be K–12 education, local churches, law enforcement, communities of color, and cultural arts organizations (Bonsall, Harris and Marczak, 2002). A sense of being part of the external community may be achieved when there is "a vision of shared purpose" (McDonald and Associates, 2002, p. 7). The key is not to avoid conflict as much as to establish relations founded on open lines of communication, leading to shared values that guide all actions.

Students

Building a relationship with students and among students, faculty, and staff is the core of student affairs work (Astin, 1993; Pascarella and Terenzini, 2005; Tinto, 1993). A student affairs professional is best served when brokering opportunities for relationship building between students and others on campus and in the community. In describing conditions that matter to student success, Kuh and others (2005) state, "Colleges and universities with supportive campus environments are characterized by high-quality student relationships with other students, faculty, and the institution's administrative personnel" (p. 260).

Public Officials

Public officials influence funding and policies related to the institution regardless of public or private status (Henkel and Little, 1999). A gateway to this world is the institution's external relations officer responsible for legislative affairs (Ellis, 2003). It is important to avoid the role of lobbyist but rather to embrace the role of educator by offering information related to student issues. During a career, this can run from how financial aid is awarded to retention and graduation rates and the implications of unfunded mandates such as the Americans with Disabilities Act. What is important to remember is that public officials are often looking for information on an issue they can champion.

Institutional Governing Boards

At some point in his or her career a student affairs professional will conduct business with board members who govern the institution. Typically this would be around student issues such as approval of fees, policies affecting students, and possibly capital projects such as the construction of a residence hall (Bumba, 2002; Richardson, Bracco, Callan, and Finney, 1999). The job is to inform, gain their understanding, and secure approval. Try to establish a connection through attendance at mutual campus functions, serving on joint committees, and listening carefully to them at meetings. By understanding board members' values and reasons for their service, it is possible to help promote their vision.

Donors

Student affairs and development professionals should have relationships that are positive and cooperative (Fygetakis and Dalton, 1993; Penney and Rose, 2001). Everyone is in the business of cultivating long-term donor relations. As funding for higher education continues to be constrained on both public and private campuses (see Chapter Five), donors are an excellent source of revenue. Think of this work as "friend raising." Cultivate a relationship now for payoff later.

Alumni

While alumni may also be donors to the institution, it is important to develop relationships to sustain connections to the institution, preserve history, celebrate traditions, and cultivate volunteers for a variety of institution-related events (Jablonski, 2000; Singer and Hughey, 2002). Everyone can benefit from bringing students and alumni together, which is often through a student affairs and alumni relations connection. Alumni are important people with whom a student affairs professional can create an alliance of old and new students.

Parents

Today's parents of college students have an increased level of involvement that is best addressed through an alliance or partnership. By partnering with parents, student affairs staff can create understanding about one another's role in a student's educational experience (Mullendore, Banahan, and Ramsey, 2005). Parents do not view a college or university as an organizational chart, so they are likely to contact someone with whom they have established a relationship (Kepplar, Mullendore, and Carey, 2005). Begin with consistent communication through e-mail distribution lists, newsletters, Web pages, and on-campus events such as parent orientation and parent or family weekend.

Faculty

Partnerships with academic colleagues should focus on the academic mission. Major inroads can be made by aligning the values and expectations of both groups, lessening the notion of working at cross-purposes (Kezar, Hirsch, and Burack, 2002). Cooperative possibilities abound, resulting in collaborative strategies that achieve common goals such as restructured organizations that resolve competition for resources and that allow seamless learning. Spend time with faculty, understand their fields of study, and look for areas of interest related to students. These opportunities often include issues of academic integrity in the classroom, a student who needs tutoring or counseling, or helping a student get financial aid.

How Relationships Are Formed

Relationships form when people's interests meet up and are complementary and compatible. They grow in depth and increase in strength over time as the mutual benefits are realized. Seek to structure enviable and sustainable partnerships, collaborations, alliances, and collegial friendships.

Connect

There is no substitute for personal, face-to-face contact. Max Depree's (1992) book, *Leadership Jazz*, begins with the story of his premature granddaughter who required his surrogate father skills to tell her over and over that he loved her as he rubbed her body and legs and arms with the tip of his finger. He said this is the best description of a leader. "At the core of becoming a leader is the need always to connect one's voice and one's touch" (p. 3). In this day of fewer "in-person" and voice-to-voice conversations, there is great value placed on a phone call and face-to-face time with people.

Use e-mail, instant, and text messaging consciously—to send reminders, set up appointments, follow up to phone conversations or meetings, or to send concise and clear messages, preferably in the subject line. Before writing the message, ask whether the job would be done better in a phone conversation or face-to-face communication (Kling, 1996). Certain types of messages should never be delivered via computer. These include anything confidential, anything requesting clarification of an earlier written message, delivery of bad news, or attempting to resolve conflict.

Find Common Ground

Groundbreaking works such as *Learning Reconsidered* (Keeling, 2004) and *Learning Reconsidered 2* (Keeling, 2006) placed learning at the center of the institution and for all who work there, in and out of the classroom. The shared work of creating a learner-centered campus brings academic affairs and student affairs particularly close from often-estranged corners of campus. It is possible to find one thing in common with anyone. Do it and use it as the basis or introduction to cultivating a relationship.

Map Your Relationship Landscape

Relationships change over time as circumstances arise and players change. This is particularly true when new leadership arrives in the form of a new president or vice president of student affairs. Additionally, colleges and universities possess different institutional cultures where decision makers and influencers are unique to that campus. Frequent analysis of the campus and community landscape will take an accounting of the health of relationships and those that still need to be established.

Develop an Action Plan

Plans help to create, sustain, fix, refresh, and end relationships. Working effectively through great relationships is not like getting into shape. It is like staying in shape. Following up on relationships ensures their sustenance and growth. This is particularly true when it comes to alliances that form quickly in the face of crisis. Continuing to cultivate familiarity, common procedures, and frequent communication provides ongoing success.

Become Interdependent

Four years after Max Depree's premature granddaughter was born, he confirms that they have a very special relationship, saying, "These days, her voice and touch are as important to me as my voice and touch were to her" (Depree, 1992, p. 5). In the American culture of rugged individualism, it can be hard to surrender to the influence of others, but in doing so, the objective is achieved with integrity. Student affairs professionals realize this when giving much power and decision-making authority to students.

Create a Trustworthy System

Kouzes and Posner (2002) write that part of creating trust is "getting to know the people you work with" (p. 10). Spend a lot of time with employees and other constituents to engage in trust building. Making the time and focusing on a person without distraction strengthen trust. Allow people to get to know you so they know what kind of leader or manager they are following. Coming through on commitments and promises completes the never-ending cycle of building trust.

Engage in an Honest Self-Critique

In the end, the only person you can change is yourself. Don't be surprised when the problem or part of the problem in a stalled or negative relationship is you.

The level of self-appraisal modeled by Dalton and McClinton in *The Art and Practical Wisdom of Student Affairs Leadership* (2002) creates awareness that "there are elements of our dealings with others that may not serve us well. Whether it is the manner in which we speak our truth or the standards we use to determine to whom we will accord respect, we all need to work consistently on getting better at how we relate to others" (p. 18).

See the Other Person's Point of View

Stephen Covey urges: "Seek first to understand then to be understood" (2004, p. 235). This requires a commitment of attention and time. Roper (2002) writes, "when we enter into conversations with others we must be fully present to them. Being present means that we are tuned into the needs and feelings of the other person and willing to respond appropriately" (p. 15).

Be on the Other Person's Side

This is something slightly different from seeing the other person's point of view. In providing praise or criticism, it is important to let people know we are doing it because we want them to succeed. A professional has the ability to support others while still disagreeing. The important skill to exercise is to intensify lines of communication with such colleagues so that relationships are intact over the longer run (Roper, 2002).

Develop the Skill of "Awaiting"

Parker Palmer (2000) says that *awaiting* means to be attentive—to listen—which helps us arrive at a common spot, then, *wait* for the moment when you truly hear what is being said to you. Wait to respond until it is understood how one's values relate to the situation at hand. Only then can an effective professional respond in a meaningful way and bridge the gap instead of widening it.

Devise a Support System

Buckingham and Coffman (1999) advise, "Be part of a team that complements and needs your strengths and that compensates for your weaknesses" (p. 168). As team leader, manage around employees' weaknesses so that they can spend time focusing on their strengths. Draw the best out of people.

Share Common Values and a Linked Vision

Shared values and vision help to bind people together (Blanchard and O'Connor, 1997). When conflict occurs, it is these shared values that can help resolve the conflict. "Perhaps most important, this process of dialogue and accommodation can produce visions that are linked and compatible instead of remote and competitive. Relationships are heavily value-laden. They involve honesty, trust, integrity, and faith" (Kotter, 1990, p. 91).

Take Care of Other People and Manage Their Reputations

Helping others build a respected reputation is easily done when things are going well. Praising an employee in front of his or her supervisor or nominating a colleague for recognition can lead to good feelings between people. The true test is when one has an opportunity to damage a person's reputation because of something he has done or not done. Stop and think about the long-term consequences of criticizing him in front of others. Instead, take the time to meet and express concern and the desired outcomes (Roper, 2002).

Relationships in Conflict

Parker Palmer writes of "creating a community of truth in which conflict enhances understanding and competition diminishes learning" (1983, p. xii). Inevitably, conflict will arise in even the best relationships. Conflict can be useful and often indicates a need for change and growth. It is important for successful relationships that professionals learn to discuss conflict from a more positive perspective. Understanding and learning to manage conflict effectively can greatly enhance one's ability to accomplish goals.

One of the most useful models of conflict management was designed by Thomas and Kilmann (1974). They identified two underlying dimensions to conflict-handling behavior: (1) cooperativeness, the attempt to satisfy the other person's concerns, and (2) assertiveness, the attempt to satisfy one's own concerns. These two dimensions define five specific methods of dealing with conflict: avoiding, accommodating, competing, collaborating, and compromising. These are discussed in more detail in Chapter Twenty-Four. While each style is useful in some situations, collaborative conflict management may be the most conducive to continuing a relationship. Trust and openness must exist between the parties in conflict. Everyone must be equally invested in his or her own satisfaction with the outcome and in the other party's true satisfaction.

Five core skills can be useful to student affairs practitioners to better deal with conflict. They include:

1. *Direct communication.* "In personality clashes and misunderstandings, it is often good practice to encourage parties to speak directly with each other. . .

discussing contentious issues in a manner that is not accusatory and... focusing on the common ground of the participants" (Gunsalus, 2006, p. 184).

2. *Nothing personal.* Think of conflict as being about a situation and not about anyone personally, regardless of what someone says. The attack may really mean, "The way this situation was handled didn't work for me personally. I don't like how that was done, and I'm taking it out on you."

3. *Inquire and listen.* Ask the person to explain his or her perception of the problem. Conflict cannot be resolved without understanding the root of it. Taylor (2003) cites six root causes of conflict: differences in values, differences in style and goals, scarce resources, organizational or environmental conditions, role ambiguity, and cultural differences. Asking questions and listening to answers allows time to think and breathe and helps to understand the entire situation from the other person's point of view. In addition, these are great strategies for getting emotions under control.

4. *Explain the situation the way you see it.* Discuss how the conflict is affecting your relationship.

5. *Agreement engenders trust.* Bolman and Deal (2003) believe a professional's approach to conflict should be directed by the answers to two questions: "How much opportunity is there for a win-win solution?" and "Will I have to work with these people again?" Agreement by all parties is a good solution, and the tactics used should engender trust and good will (Deutsch, 1973; McFarland, 1992). Once all parties agree on the problem, it is possible to discuss solutions and what each person will do to contribute to the solution. Professionals who are perceived to be manipulative and self-interested find it difficult to build the relationships needed for the future.

Conclusion

In the end it is how *each of us* acts that defines the success of our relationships and our effectiveness as student affairs professionals. As Peggy Barr has noted, "Our relationships are our legacy" (Roper, 2002, p. 24), and the work to create and sustain them is well worth the investment of time and effort.

References

Allen, K., and Cherrey, C. *Systemic Leadership: Enriching the Meaning of Our Work.* Lanham, Md.: University Press of America, 2002.

Astin, A. W. *What Matters in College? Four Critical Years Revisited.* San Francisco: Jossey-Bass, 1993.

Blanchard, K., and O'Connor, M. *Managing by Values*. San Francisco: Berrett-Koehler, 1997.

Blimling, G. *The Resident Assistant: Applications and Strategies for Working with College Students*. Dubuque, Iowa: Kendall Hunt, 2003.

Bolman, L. G., and Deal, T. E. *Reframing Organizations: Artistry, Choice, and Leadership*. San Francisco: Jossey-Bass, 2003.

Bonsall, D. L., Harris, R. A., and Marczak, J. N. "*The Community as Classroom*." In M. B. Snyder (Ed.), *Student Affairs and External Relations*. New Directions for Student Services, no. 100. San Francisco: Jossey-Bass, 2002.

Bryson, J. M. *Strategic Planning for Public and Nonprofit Organizations*. San Francisco: Jossey-Bass, 1995.

Buckingham, M., and Coffman, C. *First Break all the Rules*. New York: Simon & Schuster, 1999.

Bumba, R. "State Systems of Coordination: A Primer for Student Affairs." In M. B. Snyder (Ed.), *Student Affairs and External Relations*. New Directions for Student Services, no. 100. San Francisco: Jossey-Bass, 2002.

Cooper, M., and Schwartz, R. "Moral Judgment and Student Discipline: What Are Institutions Teaching? What Are Students Learning?" *Journal of College Student Development*, 2007, 48(5), 596–607.

Covey, S. R. *The Seven Habits of Highly Effective People*. New York: Free Press, 2004.

Croteau, D., and Hicks, L. "Coalition Framing and the Challenge of a Consonant Frame Pyramid: The Case of a Collaborative Response to Homelessness." *Social Problems*, 2003, 50(2), 251–272.

Daloz, L. *Effective Teaching and Mentoring*. San Francisco: Jossey-Bass, 1990.

Dalton, J. C., and McClinton, M. (Eds.). *The and Practical Wisdom of Student Affairs Leadership*. New Directions for Student Services, no. 98. San Francisco: Jossey-Bass, 2002.

Dannells, M. *From Discipline to Development: Rethinking Student Conduct in Higher Education*, ASHE-ERIC Higher Education Report, 25(2). Washington, D.C.: George Washington University Press, 1997.

Depree, M. *Leadership Jazz*. New York: Dell, 1992.

Deutsch, M. *The Resolution of Conflict: Constructive and Destructive Conflict*. New Haven, Conn.: Yale University Press, 1973.

Dietz, L. H., and Enchelmayer, E. J. (Eds.). *Developing External Partnerships for Cost-Effective, Enhanced Service*. New Directions for Student Services, no. 96. San Francisco: Jossey-Bass, 2001.

Ellis, S. *Dreams, Nightmares and Pursuing the Passion*. Washington, D.C.: National Association of Student Personnel Administrators, 2003.

Finn, C. B. *Utilizing Stakeholder Strategies to Ensure Positive Outcomes in Collaborative Processes*. Minneapolis: University of Minnesota, Hubert Humphrey Institute of Public Affairs, 1995.

Freire, P. *Pedagogy of the Oppressed*. New York: Continuum, 1993.

Fygetakis, E.C., and Dalton, J. "The Relationship Between Student Affairs and Institutional Advancement Offices in Educational Fundraising." In M. C. Terrell and J. A. Gold (Eds.). *New Roles for Educational Fundraising and Institutional Advancement*. New Directions for Student Services, no. 63. San Francisco: Jossey-Bass, 1993.

Grace, G. "Student Affairs Collaborations and Partnerships." In M. B. Snyder (Ed.), *Student Affairs and External Relations*, no.100. San Francisco: Jossey-Bass, 2002.

Gunsalus, C. K. *The College Administrator's Survival Guide*. Cambridge, Mass.: Harvard University Press, 2006.

Harper, S. R. (Ed.). *Creating Inclusive Campus Environments.* Washington, D.C.: National Association of Student Personnel Administrators, 2008.

Hawkins, P., and Shohet, R. *Supervision in the Helping Professions.* Milton Keynes: Open University Press, 2000.

Henkel, M., and Little, B. (Eds.). *Changing Relationships Between Higher Education and the State.* Philadelphia: Kingsley, 1999.

Jablonski, M. R. "Collaborations Between Student Affairs and Alumni Relations." In J. A. Feudo (Ed.), *Alumni Relations: A Newcomer's Guide to Success.* New York: Council for the Advancement and Support of Education, 2000.

Jackson, D., and Maddy, W. "Fact Sheet on Coalitions." [http://ohioline.osu.edu/bc-fact/0001.html]. 2008.

Janis, I. L. *Victims of Groupthink.* Boston: Houghton Mifflin, 1972.

Keeling, R. (Ed.). *Learning Reconsidered.* Washington, D.C.: American College Personnel Association and National Association of Student Personnel Administrators, 2004.

Keeling, R. (Ed.). *Learning Reconsidered 2: Implementing a Campus-Wide Focus on the Student Experience.* Various: American College Personnel Association, Association of College and University Housing Officers-International, Association of College Unions International, National Academic Advising Association, National Association for Campus Activities, American College Personnel Association, and National Intramural-Recreational Sports Association, 2006.

Kepplar, K., Mullendore, R., and Carey, A. (Eds.). *Partnering with Parents of Today's College Students.* Washington, D.C.: National Association of Student Personnel Administrators, 2005.

Kezar, A., Hirsch, D. J. and Burack, C. (Eds.). *Understanding the Role of Academic and Student Affairs Collaboration in Creating a Successful Learning Environment.* San Francisco: Jossey-Bass, 2002.

Kling, R. *Computerization and Controversy.* East Lansing, Mich.: Morgan-Kaufmann, 1996.

Kotter, J. P. *A Force for Change: How Leadership Differs from Management.* New York: Free Press, 1990.

Kouzes, J. M., and Posner, B. Z. *The Leadership Challenge.* San Francisco: Wiley, 2002.

Kuh, G., and others. *Student Success in College.* San Francisco: Jossey-Bass, 2005.

Light, R. J. *Making the Most of College: Students Speak Their Minds.* Cambridge, Mass.: Harvard University Press, 2001.

Love, P. "Advising and Consultation." In S. Komives and D. Woodard Jr. (Eds.). *Student Services: A Handbook for the Profession.* San Francisco: Jossey-Bass, 2003.

Love, P. "Exploring the Impact of Student Affairs Professionals on Student Outcomes." *Journal of College Student Development*, 1995, 36, 162–170.

McDonald, W. M., and Associates. *Creating Campus Community.* San Francisco: Jossey-Bass, 2002.

McFarland, W. P. "Counselors Teaching Peaceful Conflict Resolution." *Journal of Counseling & Development*, 1992, 71, 18–21.

Moore, E. L. (Ed.). *Student Affairs Staff as Teachers.* New Directions for Student Services, no. 117. San Francisco: Jossey-Bass, 2007.

Mullendore, R., Banahan, L., and Ramsey, J. "Developing a Partnership with Today's College Parents." In K. Kepplar, R. Mullendore, and A. Carey (Eds.), *Partnering with the Parents of Today's College Students.* Washington, D.C.: National Association of Student Personnel Administrators, 2005.

Palmer, P. *Let Your Life Speak.* San Francisco: Jossey-Bass, 2000.

Palmer, P. *To Know as We Are Known*. San Francisco: Harper Collins, 1983.

Pardee, D. "Those Who Have Left: The Value of Building Employee Relationships." [http://www.talentmanagement.com]. 2008.

Pascarella, E., and Terenzini, P. *How College Affects Students*. San Francisco: Jossey-Bass, 2005.

Patterson, G. "Playing the Alliance Game in Higher Education." [http://dx.do.org/10.1080/13603100150505190]. 2001.

Penney, S., and Rose, B. *Dollars for Dreams*. Washington, D.C.: National Association of Student Personnel Administrators, 2001.

Richardson, R. C. Jr., Bracco, K. R., Callan, P. M., and Finney, J. E. *Designing State Higher Education Systems for a New Century*. Phoenix, Ariz.: Oryx, 1999.

Rogers, J. L. "Leadership." In S. Komives and D. Woodard Jr. (Eds.). *Student Services: A Handbook for the Profession*. San Francisco: Jossey-Bass, 2003.

Roper, L. "Relationships." In J. C. Dalton and M. McClinton (Eds.). *The Art and Practical Wisdom of Student Affairs Leadership*. New Directions for Student Services, no. 98. San Francisco: Jossey-Bass, 2002.

Roper, L. "Teaching." In S. Komives and D. Woodard Jr. (Eds.). *Student Services: A Handbook for the Profession*. San Francisco: Jossey-Bass, 2003.

Sample, S. *The Contrarians Guide to Leadership*. San Francisco: Jossey-Bass, 2002.

Scaife, J. *Supervision in the Mental Health Professions: A Practitioners Guide*. Hove, U.K.: Brunner-Routledge, 2001.

Schuh, J., and Upcraft, M. L. *Assessment Practice in Student Affairs*. San Francisco: Jossey-Bass, 2001.

Schuh, J., and Whitt, E. *Creating Successful Partnerships Between Academic and Student Affairs*. New Directions for Student Services, no. 87. San Francisco: Jossey-Bass, 1999.

Singer, T. S., and Hughey, A. W. "*The Role of the Alumni Association in Student Life*" In M. B. Snyder (Ed.), *Student Affairs and External Relations*. New Directions for Student Services, no. 100. San Francisco: Jossey-Bass, 2002.

Snyder, M. B. (Ed.). *Student Affairs and External Relations*. New Directions for Student Services, no. 100. San Francisco: Jossey-Bass, 2002.

Sockett, H. "Levels of Partnership." *Metropolitan Universities*, 1998, *8*, 75–82.

Strayhorn, T. L., and Colvin, A. J. "Assessing Student Learning and Development in Fraternity and Sorority Affairs." [http://www.fraternityadvisors.org/uploads/Public/Documents/Oracle_vol2_iss2_Strayhorn.pdf.]. 2006.

Tarrow, S. *Power in Movement: Social Movement and Contentious Politics*. Cambridge, U.K.: Cambridge University Press, 1998.

Taylor, S. "Conflict Resolution." In S. Komives and D. Woodard Jr. (Eds.), *Student Services: A Handbook for the Profession*. San Francisco: Jossey-Bass, 2003.

Thomas, K. W., and Kilmann, R. H. *Thomas-Kilmann Conflict Mode Instrument*. Woods Road, N.Y.: Xicom, 1974.

Tinto, V. *Leaving College: Rethinking the Causes and Cures of Student Attrition*. Chicago: University of Chicago Press, 1993.

Twale, D., and Sanders, C. S. "Impact of Non-classroom Experiences on Critical Thinking Ability." *NASPA Journal*, 1999, 36(2), 133–36.

Wheatley, M. *Leadership and the New Science*. San Francisco: Berrett-Koehler, 1992.

CHAPTER TWENTY-FOUR

UNDERSTANDING AND MANAGING CONFLICT

Dale Nienow and Jeremy Stringer

Higher education institutions are maelstroms of conflict, and student affairs administrators at all stages of their careers need to understand and navigate through these turbulent waters. For example, residence hall staffs spend countless hours trying to resolve lifestyle differences and roommate conflicts. Student activities staff may be caught between student leaders who want to challenge university policies and higher-level administrators who want to maintain the status quo. Midlevel managers may have to resolve differences between department directors whose animosity for each other has threatened the effectiveness of their work group, and senior student affairs officers may be faced with critical disagreements among members of the executive team or with the president. The manner in which these conflicts are addressed will go a long way toward determining how effective these administrators are able to be in their positions.

Because conflict in higher education is inevitable, student affairs professionals must understand themselves and their dispositions regarding conflict as well as how others typically choose to deal with it. They must also have an understanding of the value of positively dealing with conflict in order to develop and maintain a healthy organization. This chapter discusses varying approaches to conflict and reviews various types of conflict interventions. It reviews both internal and external responses to conflict. It presents a positive approach to conflict by suggesting how a healthy approach to conflict resonates with developmental theory and social and emotional intelligence. Last, it presents the concept of *gracious space* as an important method of developing a healthy organization that will make destructive organizational conflict less likely.

Understanding Our Differing Approaches to Conflict

It is important to understand the meaning of *conflict*. In addition, we have different preferred approaches to conflict. Recognizing our proclivities, as well as those of our colleagues, provides an important opportunity to develop a positive approach to conflict.

Conflict Defined

Conflict has multiple formal definitions. Ury (2000) describes three different meanings of the term. The first refers to an underlying *conflict of interests* (needs and desires); the second is a *conflict of positions* (demands based on the underlying interests); and the third refers to a *struggle for power* (p. 41). Derived from the Latin word, *conflictus*, conflict literally means, "to strike together."

William Wilmot and Joyce Hocker (1998) offer a useful approach to defining interpersonal disagreements. They indicate that conflicts represent a struggle between the parties, that the parties are somehow interdependent, and that they perceive interference from the other in accomplishing their objectives. As an example, suppose that a senior student affairs officer (SSAO) is concerned about the job performance of a member of her staff who reports to one of her department directors. She thinks that the director should begin to document in writing all of the conversations the director has with the staff member in order to build a strong paper trail in case the staff member needs ultimately to be dismissed. The department director, however, resists, feeling that the staff member will be demotivated and his performance will then get worse instead of better, leading to a self-fulfilling prophecy virtually guaranteeing his dismissal.

This situation meets all of the criteria of Wilmot and Hocker's (1998) definition. The parties are strongly interdependent, they have a struggle about the right thing to do regarding the staff member, and they both feel that the other person is interfering in how each would prefer to solve the problem. How the SSAO and the director approach this conflict will be determined, at least partially, by their varying approaches to conflict.

Varying Approaches to Conflict

In a situation like the one described, it is important to understand the predilections toward conflict we all possess. Kenneth Thomas (1992) discusses various approaches to conflict, based on behavior across two dimensions: assertiveness and cooperativeness. Considering these two spheres together, Thomas (1992) defines five basic methods individuals use to deal with conflict. The five methods are competing, accommodating, avoiding, collaborating, and compromising.

The *competing* mode is assertive and uncooperative. This is a power-oriented mode, and the person utilizing it is unwavering in the attempt to "win" an argument or get her way. This mode produces clear winners and losers.

The opposite of the competing mode is *accommodating*. The person who employs this mode is unassertive and cooperative, and willingly accedes to the other person's arguments without attempting to compete. The person may exhibit a self-sacrificing demeanor by yielding when he would really prefer not to.

Individuals may exhibit a pattern of *avoiding* conflict. This mode typically describes those who are unassertive and uncooperative. A person may postpone dealing with a conflict until a more opportune time, secretly hoping it will go away (it rarely does).

The opposite of avoiding is *collaborating*. Individuals demonstrating this approach are both assertive and cooperative. They search for a solution to a conflict that will satisfy both parties. It may mean creating a new alternative solution instead of the resolution both sides may have originally had in mind.

Finally, *compromising* individuals search for an intermediate solution that will at least partially satisfy both parties. Compromising individuals address conflict situations but may not spend as much time or energy searching for creative solutions. Compromise solutions may be reached more quickly than collaborative ones. This may be crucial when time is short to reach a resolution, but it may not be as satisfying as a true collaborative agreement.

There are times in organizational life when any of these conflict behavior modes will be most appropriate. The competing mode might be employed when an unpopular course of action, such as cutting the budget, has to be employed. Accommodation might be utilized when avoiding disruption is more important than the outcome of the issue being discussed, or when a party realizes she is wrong. Avoidance might be practiced in order to let people "cool down," or when one might do more damage than good by confronting a situation. Collaboration might be sought when integrative solutions are required and all parties have the time to deal with differences in depth. And compromise might be the best option when the parties are intractable and there are immediate time pressures to reach a conclusion.

In the example given, the SSAO could use the competing mode. As the supervisor of the director, the SSAO has the most power in their relationship and might insist that the director begin to document all conversations with his staff member in writing, even if the director is opposed. Alternatively, the director might be accommodating to the SSAO even if he feels she is wrong. In all likelihood, the best approaches will be to either seek a compromise or to collaborate on a solution. We favor collaboration in this situation, as both the SSAO and the director have a strong investment in their relationship as well as the staff member's need to improve. They should try to see if they can create a positive course of action they can both support. Only if time is short should they settle for a compromise.

Successful student affairs leaders have to be comfortable resolving conflict in more than one mode. A valuable instrument for assessing differing approaches to conflict in a work setting is the Thomas-Kilmann Conflict Mode Instrument (Thomas and Kilmann, 1974). This instrument can be administered within a given unit and scored very simply. It measures a person's behavior across the two dimensions of assertiveness and cooperativeness. Taking the Thomas-Kilmann Conflict Mode Instrument will help a leader identify her dominant modalities for dealing with conflict as well as those that are utilized infrequently.

Another tool available to help staffs understand approaches to conflict is the Myers-Briggs Type Indicator (MBTI) (Myers, 1998). This instrument can be interpreted to understand the impact of preferences on conflict. Damien Killen and Danica Murphy (2003) provide a model for managing conflict based on the Myers-Briggs. Completing one of these instruments as a staff, particularly before difficult conflicts arise, will allow the staff to discuss the tendencies each person has when dealing with conflict and subsequently discuss as a team how they can work together effectively when faced with tough situations.

Types of Conflict Interventions

Understanding differing approaches to conflict is valuable. But despite the work they do in advance to anticipate how to resolve difficult problems, leaders in student affairs need to be skilled in a variety of conflict interventions. They will need to utilize various conflict-handling modes in their own relationships, and they may need to conduct or arrange for third-party interventions. The four most common types of interventions student affairs professionals will need to understand are *facilitation, negotiation, mediation,* and *arbitration.*

Facilitation

Student affairs leaders will sometimes be called upon to facilitate conversations between two parties (individuals as well as groups) who are at odds with each other. Facilitators provide an even playing field for the parties to discuss issues of immediate concern as well as long-term goals. It is usually helpful if the facilitator is a neutral party to whatever dispute is being discussed. Sandra Cheldelin and Ann Lucas (2004) describe several steps in a typical facilitation process. They include "ensuring all members have an equal opportunity to speak and to be heard; clarifying goals and agendas; keeping the group focused; helping them to accomplish their tasks; and 'walking the talk' in terms of demonstrating capacities to listen, paraphrase, reframe, and otherwise model nonconflictual ways of working together" (p. 81). The facilitator is the *guardian* of the process. Although supervisors may feel they are totally objective, they may not always be perceived as such by other parties. Because of this, it is useful to consider asking someone outside the organization with good group process skills to conduct the facilitation.

Negotiation

Negotiation is different from facilitation. Whereas facilitation tends to be process oriented, negotiation is outcomes orientated (Cheldelin and Lucas, 2004). Roger Fisher and William Ury (Fisher, Ury, and Patton, 1991) provide a useful framework for negotiated agreements. Drawing on the work of the Harvard Negotiation Project, they advocate a method called *principled negotiation* designed to produce agreements "efficiently and amicably" (p. 10). The four parts of principled negotiation are separate the people from the problem; focus on interests, not positions; invent options for mutual gain before deciding what to do; and insist that the result be based on some objective standard. Each of these aspects of principled negotiation is discussed in turn.

Separate the People from the Problem. Fisher and Ury (Fisher and others, 1991) advocate structuring a negotiation so that solving difficult problems is separated from discussing the interpersonal relationships between the negotiators. They advise negotiators to "protect people's egos from getting involved in substantive discussions" (p. 37). They suggest that building a solid working relationship will make a negotiation easier. Sitting side by side with an antagonist may help competing parties to think of themselves as partners in search of an equitable solution instead of adversaries out to defeat the other side.

Focus on Interests, Not Positions. The second of Fisher and Ury's (Fisher and others, 1991) principles is to focus on interests instead of positions. While positions are concrete and out in the open, the underlying interests may be more unexpressed and difficult to discern. But a skillful negotiator will realize that figuring out the other side's interests is at least as important as expressing her own. The negotiator might use probing questions to better comprehend the other's interests. In searching for a person's dominant interests, one might remember the power of basic human needs. A negotiation over money, for instance, might really be more about respect or recognition than the actual dollar amount.

Fisher and Ury (Fisher and others, 1991) admonish negotiators to be specific about their interests and to articulate them to the other party. They warn that sometimes people fall into a pattern that resembles a negotiation, but it serves only to perpetuate disagreement. People go back and forth to score hurtful points or to confirm their preexisting biases. Hurt feelings can get in the way of reaching agreement. It is only when they are able to put past offences (real and imagined) behind them that they can focus on resolving their differences and moving forward. Fisher and Ury advise, "Be hard on the problem, soft on the people" (p. 54).

Invent Options for Mutual Gain. Searching for a single right answer is often a barrier to reaching a decision that will satisfy all parties. Identifying several solution options may pave the path to a creative solution, perhaps one even better than the parties had expected. Participants need to guard against premature criticism, as well as premature closure, in order to find meaningful solutions. They should look for opportunities to make each party gain from the exchange rather than forcing a situation where one side wins and the other side loses.

Insist on Using Objective Criteria. Fisher and Ury's final principle (Fisher and others, 1991) is that effective negotiators will insist on using objective criteria. This requires preparation in order to identify what criteria exist and to apply them to the case at hand. For example, in a discussion about salary, one might propose that the salary be set by comparing the position's compensation to that at comparable schools in the region, or to comparable positions whose mean salaries are available from the College and University Professional Association for Human Resources (CUPA-HR). Fisher and Ury suggest that participants "reason and be open to reason as to which standards are most appropriate and how they should be applied" (p. 88).

Mediation

Mediation is considered an extension of the negotiation process. It involves helping the parties reach an agreement by "problem solving, transforming the relationship, or some combination of the two" (Cheldelin and Lucas, 2004, p. 22).

A mediator is not party to the dispute. A student affairs professional who serves as a mediator should help the parties "communicate more clearly with each other, identify misunderstandings or misconceptions, sort out multiple issues related to the conflict, and assist them to agree on which issues need attention" (Taylor, 2003, p. 532).

In a litigious society a party who perceives he has been wronged may be quick to file a lawsuit in order to seek justice. However, senior student affairs officers may want to see if a dispute can be mediated instead of going to court. As Cheldelin and Lucas (2004) affirm, mediation is less costly than court settlements, takes less time, and has a higher rate of compliance with the outcomes. It allows a party to express his emotional hurt and to get a less costly impartial hearing of the grievance. Particularly when the threat of a lawsuit is present, student affairs administrators would be wise to consider engaging a professional mediator to conduct the process.

Arbitration

Like mediation, arbitration is an alternative to a court hearing. It may be binding on the parties or nonbinding. More formal than many types of dispute resolution, an arbitrator hears evidence and issues rulings in the dispute. Student affairs professionals who work with unions might have occasion to deal with arbitration, but others in the field would be unlikely to be involved with arbitration. Still, it is a type of dispute resolution that could be considered should the situation warrant it.

Internal and External Responses to Conflict

There are several different ways to improve our ability to manage conflict. Some of these are responses that individuals must make, others involve the work they must undertake with others or in organizations. They include personal reflection, changing individual behavior, developing a more positive organizational culture, and changing systems and structures.

Personal Reflection

It is important to build individual reflection into the work of higher education (Schön, 1990). This is especially true of conflicts with others. When interpersonal conflicts occur, it may be easy to blame the other person or to dismiss her ideas outright. It is harder to look at our own role in the situation, but that may be just what is needed.

In any conflict, individuals need to look at their own part in creating and maintaining it. For instance, consider a supervisor who is about to terminate the employment of a student worker because the student is not meeting expectations. This supervisor has had a series of people come into the same position, not work out, and then leave, voluntarily or otherwise. Perhaps the supervisor should stop and ask, "Is there a pattern here I need to look at?" Another viable question might be, "What am I doing or not doing that contributes to the situation?" The individual reflection we conduct may show us a path to developing more positive and healing relationships.

Cultural Development

A positive and supportive organizational culture can make a critical difference in conflicts. People shape the cultures of their organizations. The culture we ultimately create will strongly influence the behavior of its members. Cultural development requires taking a long-term view versus one focused on a quick fix. Student affairs divisions need to develop norms and spirit over time by asking themselves key questions. "What values will guide our work together? What kinds of relationships does the group want to have? What culture will we create?" These conversations need to be shared by everyone in the group to avoid building the norms in separate informal conversations.

Think of the range of different work environments. An open and honest working environment helps people discuss and work through challenges. Contrast this with a hit-and-run culture in which it is okay to drop a bomb of disruption into the room and let others deal with the aftermath. Or consider a culture of gossip in which gossip is the fuel that reinforces conflicts and disruptive behavior. Culture can be intentionally established or created by default— there is a choice. Whenever we are tempted to let it happen on its own we should ask if our culture is as positive as it can be or if it can be strengthened.

Changing Individual Behavior

Although we all have different preferences for dealing with conflict, each individual has a choice of how to behave in conflict situations. The action taken can continue the conflict, add to it, or move toward positive developments or resolution. It is easy to get locked into an unproductive impasse of egos and righteousness. It is harder to take a step that will invite others to higher levels of behavior.

What risks and first steps are we willing to take in our organizations to create an opening for others to remember their highest and best behavior? It is easy to expect the other party in a conflict to change. It is harder to try to change ourselves. However, this may be the most important key to resolving a conflict.

Changing Systems and Structures

Student affairs leaders may need to attempt to change the systems and structures that harbor unhealthy conflict. Systemic change may be required to provide support so individuals do not have to engage in heroic acts of courage just to do their jobs. When the conflict is personally threatening, or too big for an individual, we need to have supporting structures and processes. Institutional authority needs to be used to shape the way the institution operates. This applies to developing hiring practices to select people capable of bringing out the best in others and also to creating systems capable of effectively handling complaints about unfairness or abuses of power.

Those in charge of the systems and structures should be looking at what supports are needed. Does conflict have an outlet in the institution's departments, programs, or divisions? Are people stuck in unproductive patterns? Do current repertoires for handling conflict in the organization work or seem inadequate?

Conflict Resolution Scenario

In conflict situations we usually want to see or bring about a change—in behavior, someone's position on an issue, or in the level of tension in a situation. The approaches described earlier cover individual and group behavior and both internal and external work. For change to be effective and lasting, we need to be aware of all of the possible approaches. Let's consider a hypothetical scenario.

In a student affairs department an employee is increasingly viewed as disruptive to healthy interpersonal relationships. While basically competent in his primary work assignment, he creates high drama and disruption in working with others and is developing a pattern of taking projects off task. Colleagues are beginning to work around him, complaining frequently in private but avoiding direct confrontation. These problems and issues are routinely passed on to the person's supervisor. She raises the issues in a positive, conversational manner, but she is so subtle that the employee often misses the point. When the supervisor gets too close to forthright confrontation, the employee lashes out in an aggressive, defensive response. The supervisor is becoming fatigued with serving as referee to the dynamics around this staff member.

This is a situation that must be addressed, but how? The supervisor reflects on what part of the difficulty with this conflict she is perpetuating. Has she learned avoidance, hoping the problem will go away? Does she rationalize that sugar-coating negative feedback is somehow more kind to the employee than presenting honest and direct descriptions of his disruptive impact? The staff member seems to be assertive and uncooperative whenever she tries to confront him, signs of a competing approach. Should she be more assertive? Is she too accommodating? What message is she sending to her other staff by accepting handoffs from them of problems they are experiencing?

The supervisor can act on these reflections by trying different behavior. For example, she could engage the employee in a conversation about what he is trying to accomplish and explore options for approaches that might be more effective. This could shift the focus from assigning blame to looking for ways to positively alter his behavior. She might try to facilitate a conversation between the employee and others in the department who are complaining. Most human resources departments have established procedures for supervisors to use when dealing with dysfunctional employees. They usually involve leaving a paper trail that will support future disciplinary action and/or termination. When following these guidelines, which often have a strongly legalistic flavor, the key is to do it in a way that does not dispirit those involved.

Perhaps treating the employee as a problem the supervisor needs to fix has been part of perpetuating the situation. Perhaps she needs to work to reshape the organizational culture so that the other members of the organization accept more responsibility. This might take the form of bringing together those who have complained along with the employee to discuss openly the patterns of behavior that are not working for the group. She might suggest a process of mediation or negotiation through which the staff in the department can explore together the different roles they are playing in creating an unhealthy dynamic. The supervisor could also engage the group in getting new agreements for their shared roles in clearing up disputes. For instance, group norms might include not working around others when there is an issue, taking responsibility for speaking up at the moment issues surface, and not trying to shift all responsibility for problem solving to the supervisor.

Thinking of the department's systems and structures suggested by the scenario, the supervisor could work to build into the expectations for all employees the responsibility to bring out the best in others and to address issues directly when they arise. This builds mutual responsibility into the system. She might also introduce a mentoring program or a coaching support network for people experiencing challenging situations.

Reviewing the approaches taken in the scenario, the supervisor utilized personal reflection to assess what role she might be unwittingly playing in perpetuating the problem in the department. She considered what role her approach to conflict was playing and how it seemed to differ from the approach the staff member was taking. She then considered several possible interventions, including facilitating dialogue between the employee and other staff members and mediating or negotiating new group norms. Regardless of the path(s) the supervisor chooses in this situation, a strong understanding of conflict and the various approaches available will shape her approach.

Moving Beyond Conflict Management

Poor conflict management can turn highly functioning organizations into toxic ones. Well-handled conflict can stimulate an organization's creativity and innovation (Kotter, 1985). Conflict management has long been regarded as a core skill of effective student affairs practitioners (Moore, 2000; Pope and Reynolds, 1997; and Sandeen, 1991).

Conflicts may result from the need to resolve new challenges that cannot be addressed by expert knowledge and routine management techniques. Ronald Heifetz (1994) indicates that leaders need to distinguish between situations that require *technical* responses and those that require *adaptive* ones. A typical technical situation facing a student affairs leader might be the selection of a food service vendor for the campus. It is a situation for which several viable alternatives can be identified and analyzed and a decision-making process smoothly set in place. Adaptive challenges are very different. Both the problem and the alternative solutions may be unclear. Once the problem is defined, potential solutions may still be uncertain. An example of an adaptive challenge is the matriculation of Muslim students at a traditionally Christian university. The university may struggle with how to meet the needs of these students within the institution's mission and historical context. Adaptive challenges (Heifetz, 1994; Parks, 2005) require individuals and organizations to exhibit a new kind of behavior. These difficult issues may require "changes of heart and mind—the transformation of long-standing habits and deeply held assumptions and values" (Parks, p. 10).

Heifetz believes that sometimes surface conflicts over procedures, lines of authority, and organizational structure may serve as proxies for deeper, underlying conflicts. Quite possibly, people engaging in destructive conflict may be trying to respond to an adaptive challenge to the status quo. Individuals are advised to step back from the immediate conflict and ask a deeper set of questions about the nature of the conflict and how it might be resolved.

It is important to have approaches that can minimize the amount of conflict at key moments and to resolve conflicts that emerge. These are foundational elements of student affairs practice. We need to move beyond simple approaches to more intentionally build into our work the productive role of conflict, the creative and energizing holding of tensions, and the liberating movement forward past "stuck" patterns of interaction.

Lee Bolman and Terrence Deal (2003) point out that organizational conflict is likely to occur at the boundaries of organizational life, such as interfaces between departments or divisions. Cultural conflict may also occur among groups with varying religious, political, racial, and cultural traditions and lifestyles. The university is not a sanctuary from the tensions that exist in society at large; frequently, conflicts in the academy mirror those in the larger society. Tannen (1998) posits that an "argument culture," characterized by habitually aggressive and adversarial discourse, has developed. It is easy to see the manifestations of this culture, where nuanced arguments give way to sound bites and put-downs of the points of views of others by those who would have us believe that the Truth is whatever they want us to believe at the moment. Conventional wisdom often undervalues less confrontational tactics "even if they work well, favoring more aggressive tactics even if they get less favorable results" (Tannen, p. 23). We suggest a different perspective on conflict, one that allows individuals to interact with others with respect and appreciate the gifts different perspectives can bring to conflict resolution.

Gracious Space

Even experienced administrators can be challenged to find a way to work through conflict with others positively and productively. Doing so is critical to building a healthy student affairs organization. This can require stretching beyond personal comfort with closely managing the process to exploring processes that draw on deeper goodwill and collective wisdom of members of the community, present even among those experiencing conflict. This is where belief in whole person development and drawing on student development theory can be an asset.

Some administrators seem more adept at building trusting relationships and working through social dynamics. In their human development model, Chickering and Reisser (1993) include two components, managing emotions and developing interpersonal competence, that are particularly relevant to work with conflict. Goleman (1995, 2006) highlights the importance of emotional and social intelligence. Emotional intelligence involves *self-awareness* and *self-management,* evidenced in being able to "persist in the face of frustrations, control impulse and delay gratification, regulate one's moods and keep distress from swamping the ability to think, to empathize and to hope" (1995, p. 34). Social intelligence is "being intelligent about relationships" (1995, p. 11). There are two main elements: *social awareness,* "what we sense about others," and *social facility,* "what we do with that awareness" (2006, p. 84).

Administrators who intentionally work on development of their own emotional and social intelligence will create different possibilities for those involved in the conflict. They can know what to do with emotions that have been triggered and can choose wisely how to address the relationship messages sent. This can transform the spirit of the conflict. With less developed social and emotional intelligence, negative emotions and social interactions can be given back to the sender or transferred to others. As social and emotional intelligence increase, the administrator can transform negative interactions into something more helpful. This can better position the administrator to draw out the emotional and social intelligence of others in the conflict—to tap into their best energy and ideas. This accumulated emotional and social intelligence will create greater likelihood of handling conflict productively and of building healthy student affairs organizations.

An innovative approach, developed by the Center for Ethical Leadership (Hughes, 2004), draws on the emotional and social intelligence of community members in building strong relationships that can address conflicts positively. It is called creating *gracious space,* defined as a spirit and setting where the stranger is welcome and learning in public is embraced. This method can help student affairs administrators change the way they interact, particularly around conflict. It is illustrated in the following vignette.

At an advisory board meeting for a graduate program, the program director presents the dilemma of the cohort of students not getting along and behaving unprofessionally. He asks the board for suggestions. A number of thoughtful ideas are suggested: one is to confront the students behaving unprofessionally and give them notice of shaping up or leaving the program. Another is "tell the students they have to sit down and work it out." A third suggestion is to invite them to a day of creating gracious space and discussing what matters most to them.

The director chooses the creating gracious space option. As students in the graduate program gather, they are invited to hold two questions throughout the day: What kind of professional do you want to be? What kind of profession do you want to inhabit? Students go through a core values exercise to identify the values that most centrally guide them in their lives. They are taught the concept of gracious space. After learning the concepts, they are invited to create an opening for a different relationship dynamic by assuming goodwill and suspending their judgments. Through storytelling and dialogue they get to know each other more fully and begin to have the difficult conversations they need in order to create their professional norms and begin acting in the way they want to engage professionally. The culture of the graduate program begins to shift.

As illustrated in the foregoing example, creating gracious space involves intentionally integrating the following elements into the group's interaction: spirit, setting, welcoming the stranger, and learning in public.

Spirit

Participants are encouraged to bring a positive spirit to their work. We all have conversations in our heads as we deal with others. What are you bringing into the work with others? Judgment? Fear that others' inadequacies will limit your own productivity? Preparing to bring positive spirit into the interaction requires changing an internal conversation that dreads the interaction to one that looks for the gifts the other can offer to the relationship.

Setting

It is important to create enough time and an inviting physical space to enable people to open up to relationship building and deeper dialogue. It does not work to schedule a difficult conversation in an uncomfortable setting squeezed into a busy day.

Welcoming the Stranger

The concept of welcoming the stranger means intentionally building into the interaction those factors that make others feel that they belong, that they matter, and that you want to get to know them. It can help to invite group members to remember a time when they were outsiders and made to feel welcome. As they tell their stories and identify together the conditions that made them feel welcome, the welcoming environment becomes more explicit.

Learning in Public

Learning in public means allowing others to provide feedback and receiving it as constructive, not being defensive and argumentative. It means being open to the ideas and perspectives of others, and not critical of the person offering comments. Can you make yourself vulnerable in a public setting? Exceptional educators are able to make their own behavior part of the learning of the group (Parks, 2005). Demonstrated vulnerability opens the space for greater learning.

It creates room for the wisdom of others. Are you willing to be influenced by another? Are you willing to not be the expert, but to ask the question that draws out others?

Learning together can be a powerful tool for change. Peter Senge and his colleagues (Senge, Scharmer, Jaworski, and Flowers, 2004) have created *Theory U*, which describes the movement of letting go, opening up to collectively seeing the world, and creating new patterns together. It is important to "not impose preestablished frameworks" and "mental models" in this process (Senge and others, 2004, p. 88). They stress that it is important to determine what we need to unlearn together before we can open up to new ideas.

In the concept of social intelligence, "a mood can sweep through a group with great rapidity" (Goleman, 2006, p. 48). Intentionally building gracious space through these four elements helps create a safe, supportive, and open field of energy that can sweep through the group in a positive way. This can lead to conversations that are open, honest, and *safe* rather than open, honest, and *destructive*.

Gracious space does not stop at basic civility. It breaks through the limits of surface civility to create space in which conflict can be productively engaged in order to move people into deeper relationships of shared purpose. It transforms the violent energy that can sometimes come out in conflict. Parker Palmer (2004) defines this violence as "violating the identity and integrity of another person" (p. 169). Sometimes our instincts with conflict are to turn down the temperature or remove the tension as soon as possible. In reality it may be much more effective to act as the thermostat that turns up the heat and holds it there. Gracious space can allow the heat to be turned up long enough to help the group break through to the other side of superficial politeness, peaceful coexistence, or shallow support. It can offer an alternative to approaches that seek to fix others, remove the offender as though cutting out the cancer, or acting on righteous indignation. It allows participants to remember who they are at their core and to act on what they most care about and allow others the space to do the same.

Conclusion

Conflicts will occur in higher education. Regularly denying and suppressing conflicts is a form of self-deception. Conflict is something to be respected, not feared. Bennis (1989) indicates that leaders should see conflict as an opportunity, indicating that once they embrace that perspective, conflict becomes a challenge, not a threat. He writes that true leaders "are not deterred by hard times. That is perhaps, finally, what makes them leaders" (p. 159).

References

Bennis, W. *Why Leaders Can't Lead*. San Francisco: Jossey-Bass, 1989.

Bolman, L. G., and Deal, T. E. *Reframing Organizations: Artistry, Choice, and Leadership* (3rd ed.). San Francisco: Jossey-Bass, 2003.

Cheldelin, S. I., and Lucas, A. F. *Academic Administrator's Guide to Conflict Resolution*. San Francisco: Jossey-Bass, 2004.

Chickering, A. W., and Reisser, L. *Education and Identity* (2nd ed.). San Francisco: Jossey-Bass, 1993.

Fisher, R., Ury, W., and Patton, B. *Getting to Yes: Negotiating Agreement Without Giving In* (2nd ed.). New York: Penguin, 1991.

Goleman, D. *Emotional Intelligence: Why It Can Matter More Than IQ*. New York: Bantam, 1995.

Goleman, D. *Social Intelligence: The New Science of Human Relationships*. New York: Bantam, 2006.

Heifetz, R. A. *Leadership Without Easy Answers*. Cambridge, Mass.: Belknap Press, 1994.

Hughes, P. *Gracious Space: A Practical Guide for Working Better Together*. Seattle: Center for Ethical Leadership, 2004.

Killen, D., and Murphy, D. *Introduction to Type and Conflict*. Palo Alto, Calif.: Consulting Psychologists Press, 2003.

Kotter, J. P. *Power and Influence: Beyond Formal Authority*. New York: Free Press, 1985.

Moore, L. V. "Managing Conflict Constructively." In M. J. Barr and M. K. Desler (Eds.), *The Handbook of Student Affairs Administration* (2nd ed.). San Francisco: Jossey-Bass, 2000.

Myers, I. B. *Introduction to Type*. Palo Alto, Calif.: Consulting Psychologists Press, 1998.

Palmer, P. *A Hidden Wholeness: The Journey Toward an Undivided Life*. San Francisco: Jossey-Bass, 2004.

Parks, S. D. *Leadership Can Be Taught*. Boston: Harvard Business School Press, 2005.

Pope, R. C., and Reynolds, A. L. "Student Affairs Core Competencies: Integrating Multicultural Awareness, Knowledge, and Skills." *Journal of College Student Development*, 1997, 38, 266–277.

Sandeen, A. *The Chief Student Affairs Officer: Leader, Manager, Mediator, Educator*. San Francisco: Jossey-Bass, 1991.

Schön, D. A. *The Reflective Practitioner: How Professionals Think in Action*. New York: Wiley, 1990.

Senge, P. M., Scharmer, C. O., Jaworski, J., and Flowers, B. S. *Presence: Human Purpose and the Field of the Future*. Cambridge, Mass.: Society for Organizational Learning, 2004.

Tannen, D. *The Argument Culture: Moving from Debate to Dialogue*. New York: Random House, 1998.

Taylor, S. L. "Conflict Resolution." In S. R. Komives and D. B. Woodard Jr. (Eds.), *Student Services: A Handbook for the Profession* (4th ed.). San Francisco: Jossey-Bass, 2003.

Thomas, K. W. "Conflict and Negotiation Processes in Organizations." In M. D. Dunnette and L. M. Hough (Eds.), *Handbook of Industrial and Organizational Psychology* (2nd ed.). Vol. 3. Palo Alto, Calif.: Consulting Psychologists Press, 1992.

Thomas, K. W., and Kilmann, R. H. *Thomas-Kilmann Conflict Mode Instrument*. Woods Road, NY: Xicom, 1974.

Ury, W. *The Third Side*. New York: Penguin, 2000.

Wilmot, W. W., and Hocker, J. L. *Interpersonal Conflict* (5th ed.). Boston: McGraw-Hill, 1998.

PART SIX

SKILLS AND COMPETENCIES OF PROFESSIONAL PRACTICE

The field of student affairs comprises a wide array of functional areas, and each of these areas has skills and competencies unique to it. Still, there are a number of skills and competencies that are common across student affairs. A number of those are presented for consideration in this section of the handbook. In Chapter Twenty-Five, Peggy Barr shares information on common budgeting pitfalls, common categories of expense and revenue, several budgeting models, and the annual budget cycles. Beverly Ledbetter outlines select legal issues in Chapter Twenty-Six. Marilee Ludvik Bresciani discusses the crucial skill of assessment in Chapter Twenty-Seven. Michael Cuyjet and Sue Weitz present, in Chapter Twenty-Eight, a useful model for the planning and implementation of single events and for ongoing programs. In Chapter Twenty-Nine, Jerry Price describes the facilities planning and development process, with an emphasis on including students at all stages. In Chapter Thirty, Kevin Kruger provides an update on technological innovations and implications for students' lives and hence for student affairs practice. In Chapter Thirty-One, Keith Miser and Cynthia Cherrey share their lessons learned as well as the lessons learned by other student affairs colleagues in preventing and responding to campus crisis, a topic much on the minds of student affairs professionals given the events of recent years.

CHAPTER TWENTY-FIVE

BUDGETING AND FISCAL MANAGEMENT FOR STUDENT AFFAIRS

Margaret J. Barr

At any student affairs professional meeting, discussions can be heard about the need for sufficient budget support for programs and services in support of students. Adequate fiscal resources are critical for the success of student affairs programs and services. As competition for funding increases both within and without higher education, it is clear that student affairs administrators must be good fiscal managers and excellent stewards of financial resources. Fiscal management skills, however, are often learned on the job. This chapter seeks to accelerate that process by providing basic information on budgeting and fiscal management.

The chapter provides a brief review of the larger fiscal environment of higher education (see Chapter Five for a more extended discussion), identifies sources of funds to support the student affairs enterprise, highlights concerns related to some sources of funds, discusses the types of budgets in higher education, and presents common budget models. The focus then shifts to identifying the differences between budget and financial management in public and private institutions. The purposes of budgets are discussed as are the budget cycle and the responsibilities of student affairs administrators within that cycle. The chapter concludes with a presentation of practical ideas on how to maximize resources and deal with unexpected budget cuts. Although this chapter focuses on public and private (independent) institutions, the budgeting and fiscal management information is equally applicable to those working in proprietary institutions.

The General Fiscal Environment for Student Affairs

Higher education institutions, whether public or private, are experiencing great challenges in identifying and capturing needed fiscal resources to support the work of the institution. A first step in sound fiscal management for student affairs professionals is increased understanding of the broader fiscal context of higher education. That broader context sets very real constraints on what can and cannot be accomplished at any college or university.

External Issues

There are a number of issues external to the institution that can influence the fiscal management of student affairs. These include increased competition for resources, increased concerns from legislative bodies and the general public regarding the costs of attending higher education, paying for unfunded mandates and increased regulation from government at the state and federal levels, the cost of technology, the rising costs for other goods and services, and the increase in competition for qualified students, faculty, and staff. Schuh's chapter (Chapter Five) discusses these issues and others in greater detail, and the reader is urged to read that chapter to fully understand the external context of higher education.

Internal Issues

Just as there are external issues that can influence fiscal management, so too are there internal issues. Several such issues are discussed in this section.

Internal Competition. Student affairs units must compete with other parts of the institution for support for their programs and services. There are always more requests for budget support than there are funds to support such requests. Mayhew (1979) said in part that "budgets are really a statement of educational purpose phrased in fiscal terms" (p. 54). Some items seem not to be debatable on the surface but often can be examined from a different perspective. An increase in the cost of utilities provide one good example that could be looked at either as a "given" or as an opportunity for conservation. There are some financial issues, however, that are genuinely not debatable, such as a settlement in a lawsuit or an unfunded mandate from the federal government. Competition for the available dollars from within the institution will continue to be major issue for student affairs.

Linking Student Affairs to the Mission of the Institution. Success for the division of student affairs in securing adequate resources depends on the ability of managers within the division to directly link student affairs programs and services to the educational purposes of the institution. It is relatively easy for the English Department to link a budget request to the educational purpose of the institution. For student affairs to be successful in capturing financial resources, budget managers must be able to link unit programs and services, in a concrete way, to the educational mission of the institution.

Being Overly Optimistic. In general, student affairs professionals are optimistic souls and look for the best in most situations. However, those professionals with budget responsibility must learn to curb optimism and not make assumptions that any areas are "safe" during the budget process. For in any given year it is possible that student affairs will have to reargue the case for support in light of other competing requests for support. Prudent budget managers learn to curb their enthusiasm and be prepared for any contingency.

Understanding the larger fiscal environment of higher education and the pressures within the institution is important in successful fiscal management. The next step is an increased understanding of the sources of funds to support the institution and any limitations that exist regarding the expenditure of those funds.

Sources of Funds

A number of sources support both public and private institutions of higher education. However, the emphasis and dependence on a specific source of financial support will vary across institutional types, although current trends seem to indicate that those distinctions are becoming more blurred in the changing fiscal environment of higher education.

State Appropriated Funds

Funds from the state government are the primary source of income for most public colleges and universities. At a community college, such income may be also supplemented by direct support from the county or municipality where the institution is located. In addition, tribal colleges receive financial support from their sovereign nations, and the level of that support will vary from nation to nation.

Some states use formula funding based on the number of full-time, part-time, graduate, and undergraduate students, with different funding formulas provided for each student category. In other states, formula funding is based on a rolling average of credit hours at the undergraduate and graduate level generated over the past three to five years by the institution. In many states, legislative review of each institutional budget is extensive and may even involve line item review of all budget items. Some states use a combination of formula funding (overseen by the higher education agency of the state) and extensive legislative review of new requests and capital budgets. Finally, a limited number of institutions in eleven states are constitutionally autonomous (not subject to the regulation of other state agencies) and are treated in the budget process the same as other state agencies.

The role of state appropriation for private (independent) institutions is much more narrow than for their public counterparts. State appropriations for private colleges and universities are usually limited to support for specific programs that meet state priorities or interests such as working with the physically challenged, or dental education. In addition, state support for private institutions may come in the form of capital budget support (see "State and Federal Capital Budgets" section later in chapter) or direct financial aid to students that can be used at any public, private, or proprietary institution.

Tuition

Undergraduate tuition is the engine that drives much of higher education in the private sector and is becoming more important in the public sector as state support for higher education diminishes. The cost of tuition can be calculated on the basis of each credit hour and the level of enrollment (undergraduate or graduate), or it can be calculated on a full-time enrollment basis.

For private institutions, tuition is an extremely important component of the institutional budget. In smaller institutions, enrollment (and thus tuition dollars) can be the difference between meeting budget expectations and going into the red. Attracting and retaining students is critical to maintaining the sound fiscal base in both public and private institutions, and student affairs plays a central role in that task.

Public institutions often have statutory restrictions regarding the amount of tuition that may be charged to in-state residents. Usually there are no such restrictions on out-of-state tuition rates or on student fees.

Graduate tuition does not begin to pay the cost of graduate education. Exceptions to this rule include specialized graduate degree programs, usually at the master's level, offered on a full-time basis for full-tuition-paying students or specialized executive M.B.A. programs. Doctoral programs are very expensive, and tuition does not offset the cost associated with doctoral education.

Professional school programs provide similar budgetary challenges to the institution. While graduate doctoral programs are essential to the core functions of teaching and learning, they are not moneymakers or contributors to the funding stream for any institution.

Mandatory Student Fees

At public institutions, and increasingly at private institutions, mandatory student fees have been used as one means to obtain needed revenue without raising tuition. In the politicized context of higher education, mandatory student fees are used as a way to avoid confrontations with the legislature or the public on the volatile issue of tuition. Such fees are usually charged on a term basis and are assessed from, at least, all undergraduate students. Examples include building use fees, technology fees, bond revenue fees, laboratory fees, breakage fees, student services fees, and student activity fees. Such fees are usually dedicated as support for a specific building or program and must be reserved for those uses. To illustrate, a steady stream of mandatory fees from all undergraduates provides the financial foundation for many campus recreation centers and student centers.

The process of allocating general mandatory fees, such as a student service fee, also varies from institution to institution. In some colleges and universities, mandatory fees are routinely allocated to support units as part of the general budgeting process. In others, a committee with student representation allocates the fees after holding budget hearings with departments and agencies. In most cases, mandatory student activity fees are solely allocated by student government groups under the general supervision of an office in student affairs. Working effectively with such allocation processes is clearly a key task for student affairs professionals.

Private institutions are often much less likely than their public counterparts to adopt the use of mandatory student fees as a strategy to generate money. Many of the programs supported by student fees (recreation, health services, disability services) at public institutions are funded by tuition income at private institutions. This is particularly true of programs such as student centers or recreation facilities that serve all students. Mandatory student fees, in addition to high tuition, are not seen as a positive recruitment tool for expensive private institutions.

Special Student Fees

Two types of special student fees are used as a means of budget support: one-time fees and fees for services. Such fee structures are present in both public and independent institutions.

One-time fees are assessed for participation in a specific program or activity. Examples of one-time fees include study abroad fees, loan-processing fees, and commencement fees. The income from the fee helps offset the cost of the program and reduces the dependence of the program on general revenue funds of the institution.

Fees for service are growing phenomena in higher education and are usually linked to psychological services, health care, or the ability of students to attend popular intercollegiate athletic events. To illustrate, at many counseling centers students seeking help are provided a limited number of therapy sessions but must provide some copayment for continued therapy. The impact of this approach to funding mental and physical health services on students needing help has not been clearly evaluated. For example, it is not clear if charging for some psychological services discourages students most in need of help from seeking such help. But as the debate continues, the use of fees for services continues to expand in higher education. Reliance on special mandatory student fees for central services in student affairs may make the unit particularly vulnerable to rapid changes in enrollments or higher demand for services.

Endowment Income

The institutional endowment is a major source of budgetary support for private institutions. Overall fiduciary responsibility for managing the endowment rests with the institutional governing board, although day-by-day management decisions are the responsibility of institutional staff or investment managers. Prudent institutions do not use all of the income generated by the investment of the endowment for current operations. Instead, spending rules are adopted by the governing board, regarding the percentage of the endowment income that may be spent on operations in any fiscal year. Such spending limits accomplish two goals: providing a relatively steady income stream to the institution and reinvesting a portion of the income in the endowment to help it grow.

Currently, most public institutions have much more modest endowments than their private counterparts. That is likely to change in the future as state support for public higher education erodes and alternate sources of income are needed. At some public institutions, independent foundations have been established to raise money and invest it for the good of the institution. While any foundation must meet the requirements of state statutes and regulations of the state where the foundation is located, the organization and control of foundations at public institutions will vary. For example, some foundations have institutional representatives on the foundation governing board and some do not. Some are absolutely independent, and some receive office space, clerical, and accounting support from the institution. When an independent foundation exists, the institutional officers face the challenge of convincing the decision makers in the foundation to first support institutional priorities over projects of interest to major donors. Control of an important segment of institutional funding is vested in such circumstances in an outside source not under direct institutional control.

Fund Raising

Acquiring private financial support for the institution is becoming increasingly important at both public and private institutions. Identifying potential donors, cultivating them, and providing opportunities for them to financially support the programs, services, and offerings of the institution is a major task. Two equally important types of fund raising are essential to higher education: annual giving and long-term campaigns for programs and facilities.

For most private institutions, annual giving is a critical revenue source for the operating budget of the institution. Revenue goals are set for the development office based on past performance, and usually revenues from annual giving become a source of funds for the general budgeting process of the institution. At times, however, donors designate some annual gifts for specific units or programs. Such gifts are usually not incremental for the unit but instead provide budget relief for the institution as the new designated funds are merely used to replace current institutional dollars allocated to the unit.

In addition, many institutions engage in campaigns to fund both buildings and programs. In recent years, such campaigns have evidenced a greater emphasis on program support, such as undergraduate scholarships, endowed chairs, and professorships or athletics. Still other institutions do not engage in formal campaigns but continually raise money for programs and buildings relying on an in-depth knowledge of donor interests and matching those interests to donor needs.

Student affairs has, on the whole, been a passive rather than an active contributor to such fund raising activities. The expectations, however, for student affairs to actively participate in fund raising on many campuses are growing, and the ability to attract resources to support programs will become more important to student affairs in the future. (See Chapter Five for a further discussion.)

Grants and Contracts

The research enterprise at most institutions is primarily funded by grants from the federal government, state agencies, business and industry, and private foundations. In addition to providing direct support in terms of salaries and operating costs of the specific research activity, grants to the institution are also required to recapture some of the indirect costs related to the grant. Indirect costs include, for example, services provided by the institution such as payroll, accounting, purchasing, space renovation, maintenance, utilities, and administration. The federal government indirect cost rate is negotiated between the institution and the federal government and applies to all federal research grants. Indirect costs are also assessed on grants from other sources. Charges for indirect costs do not accrue to the unit budget but are considered part of the general revenue stream of the institution.

Contracts are time-limited arrangements with business, industry, or the government whereby the institution provides a direct service in return for payment. Examples of contracts include providing training for a state agency, teaching an academic course for the employees of a specific company, or providing technical support for a computer project being completed by local government. Overhead rates are established for such contracts to cover some of the same costs as grants.

Most institutions have a centralized approval process for grants and contracts to assure that appropriate charges are being made and that the proposed grant or contract is congruent with the institutional mission. Finally, grants and contracts offices supervise fund disbursement to the unit and assure that all reporting requirements of the grant or contract are met.

Auxiliary Services

Auxiliary services usually do not receive any institutional support and are expected to generate sufficient income to cover all operating expenses (including maintenance) as well as long-term facility rehabilitation and repair costs associated with the enterprise. Auxiliary services must adhere to the same institutional rules regarding compensation, purchasing, and human resources as other units. Each institution defines what programs and activities will be designated as auxiliaries. Examples include student housing, food services, student unions, recreation buildings and, on occasion, intercollegiate athletic programs. Auxiliary enterprises are, for many student affairs divisions, a major part of the total budget of the division.

Special Programs

Such programs may be one-time events, such as a department-sponsored seminar for which entrance fees are charged to cover the cost of the event. Or special programs may be recurring ventures, including sports camps or conferences that return to campus each summer. In either case, the program must be self supporting unless specific institutional permission has been given to have expenses exceed income. The unit to offset expenses usually retains the revenue from the program. The goal for most special programs is to break even at the end of the year. Sometimes, however, if revenue exceeds expectations, modest reserve funds can be established to cover the unit for an unanticipated shortfall in revenue in another fiscal year.

Contracted Institutional Services

In both public and private institutions, functions such as food services, bookstores, and custodial services are increasingly being outsourced to private enterprise. Through competitive bidding processes, service contracts become a source of funds to support both operations and capital expenditures such as facility repair and renovation, new construction, and program enhancements. Negotiations for service contracts may include yearly lump sum payments for capital expenses in addition to a regular income stream from sales. In recent years, this concept has been expanded to include exclusive contracts for certain soft drinks, telephone service, washer and dryer services, and so on, whereby the institution receives a percentage of the gross sales in return for the privilege of providing services or a specific product on campus.

Church Support

Church-supported or church-related private institutions of higher education may also rely on denominational financial support. Such support usually carries with it the requirement for representation on the governing board of the institution and institutional support for the values of denomination.

State and Federal Capital Budgets

Most public institutions must go through a separate budgeting process in order to receive funds for new construction or massive facility renovation. That process is separate from the regular state budgeting process. At times, private institutions can access state capital funds if the project meets a pressing state priority, such as medical research.

If the new facility is consistent with a federal priority and there is support for the facility in the federal appropriation process in Congress, then federal dollars for facility construction may be available to both public and private institutions for facility construction. This avenue is long, complicated, and very political.

Other Sources of Income

There are a number of miscellaneous sources of income used to support programs and facilities in higher education. Facility rental fees, rental fees for specialized equipment, and sales of athletic paraphernalia are examples of other revenue sources. The privilege of parking on campus generates revenue through a parking fee that helps support parking facilities. Although individually such sources of support are small, in the aggregate such income sources are essential to the financial health of the institution's various units.

Implications of Fund Sources for Student Affairs

Budgeting and financial management in student affairs requires understanding of the sources of funds that directly support the various units under the auspices of student affairs. First, it is critical that the budget manager and directors of units understand where the money is coming from and what the restrictions are (if any) on the use of the money.

Second, if mandatory student fees are part of the revenue budget, then the responsible administrator must have a clear understanding of the annual and long-term processes used by the institution to access those funds. For example, must a budget be first submitted to a fee committee and receive approval from the committee before it can become a part of the overall division of student affairs budget?

Third, if a division of student affairs has auxiliary enterprises such as housing and food services, what are the construction bond obligations for those units? What is the long-term plan for repair and replacement of existing buildings and equipment? How are new structures funded? What new regulations regarding health and safety need to be accounted for in the operating budget and/or the capital budget? These are but a few of the questions that must be asked by those responsible for managing auxiliary budgets and reserve funds to operate those units.

Fourth, if supervision of any contracted institutional services such as housekeeping or food service is part of the responsibility of the division, is there a clear understanding of what the institutional responsibilities are under the contract and what the mechanisms are for enforcement of the contract? It is imperative to identify who in the institution must be involved in contract review and who has authority to sign the contract on behalf of the institution.

Fifth, has the division of student affairs clearly defined the opportunities for fund raising that exist within the division? Have those opportunities been communicated to colleagues in development and elsewhere in the institution?

Understanding the sources of funds supporting student affairs units and the implications related to those fund sources is an essential step in sound financial management practices. Another important step in understanding budgeting and budget management in student affairs is recognizing the implications of public versus private control of the institution.

Public Versus Private Financial Issues

In the past, funding for higher education differed markedly between public and private institutions. Currently those distinctions are becoming increasingly blurred with regard to the sources of funds used to support higher education. Both public and private institutions may be actively engaged in fund raising, may have endowments, and may receive support from the state. The financial distinctions between public and private institutions are based on the amount of funds received from any single source and the degree of control on financial matters exercised beyond the campus. For example, well-endowed private institutions have, compared to public institutions, a much larger part of their operating budget covered by interest income from the endowment, a higher portion of their budget from tuition, and a lower portion of their budget from state support. The differences also extend to the control exerted on the institution beyond the campus.

Controls and Approvals

While both types of institution must conform to applicable state law, in private institutions, financial policies, investment strategies, and institutional policies are controlled either through the governing board or through other campus-based governance and administrative bodies. This approach provides greater degrees of freedom in using resources to meet unexpected needs or problems. For example, rising energy costs can be met through campus-based reallocation at many private institutions, while their public counterparts often are required to seek permission from a state coordinating board or other oversight body to respond to unexpected cost changes.

Policies

Fiscal policies at private institutions are likely to be less cumbersome, permitting transfers of funds for reasonable purposes without many approvals or other bureaucratic barriers. The budget manager is, however, held accountable for assuring that at the end of the fiscal year there is no deficit.

In public institutions, usually the institutional budget office must grant permission for line item transfers over a certain dollar amount. Sometimes, for certain categories of expenditures, the governing board or the supervising state agency must also approve such transfers.

Purchasing

Both public and private institutions have regulations regarding the purchase of goods and services. For many public institutions, purchasing of goods and services is complicated by state regulations, required low-bid acceptance, and overarching state contracts for certain goods and services. When a state contract is in place for a certain product, the budget manager must provide a viable justification to purchase the item from a vendor other than the one on the state contract.

Usually, at private institutions, purchasing requirements are less rigid and are not complicated by state contracts. In fact, at many private institutions, purchasing for some items is highly decentralized, with the unit budget manager taking responsibility to seek bids and then making the decision on the purchase. Whereas on the surface such freedom can be very attractive, it also requires that each budget manager exercise due diligence to assure the institution is getting the most for its purchasing dollar.

Audit Requirements

Audit requirements exist at both public and private institutions. An external audit provides an independent review of the financial and management decisions made by a unit. Both financial and management reports are issued at the conclusion of the audit, and the budget manager and other administrative officials review the reports and agree to needed changes in policies and procedures. A scheduled follow-up is then conducted to assure that the needed changes have been made. Sometimes such audits are conducted by outside auditors, and sometimes there is an internal audit office.

If the institution has an internal audit office that regularly conducts audits of all offices, policies and procedures can be strengthened rather rapidly because less time is spent bringing an outsider auditor up to date on institutional policies. New budget managers should also ask the internal audit office to conduct an initial audit of office accounts to identify problems or issues that could be improved.

Public institutions often have the added complication of audits from an independent state agency. State auditor general offices conduct such audits and the outcomes are public records. A negative audit finding, though minor in nature, can result in negative publicity and institutional embarrassment.

Human Resource Issues

Both types of institutions have complex human resources issues including compliance with state and federal law, unions, compensation benefits, position classification, and other variables. While in some ways it may seem that human resource management may be easier in the private institution, do not be misled. Personnel issues are complicated, and the prudent administrator seeks help early and often from those who know more about policies and procedures than he or she does.

The Purposes of a Budget

There are many purposes for a budget in higher education. Maddox (1999) defines five general purposes of a budget: putting business strategy into operation, allocating resources, providing incentives, providing control, and providing a means of communication both within and without the institution.

Putting Business Strategy into Operation

Although it is difficult for many student affairs professionals to think of higher education as a business enterprise, in a very real sense that is what it is. Like any business, income comes into the institution for services rendered or promised, and invoices for goods and services must be paid. Higher education is usually a not-for-profit enterprise (the exception being proprietary schools). Any excess income over expenses at the end of the fiscal year is used to help finance the future of the institution, meet pressing operating costs, construction, or infrastructure needs, or in some public institutions reverts to the state (Barr, 2002).

The institutional budget reflects the plans, priorities, goals, and aspirations that drive the institution. The budget is the fiscal blueprint of what is important. For example, if the institution has adopted the goal of having the number one business school in the country, the budget will reflect substantial investment over multiple years in that unit. Or if the institution is committed to keeping access open to low-income students, the student financial aid budget will rise in direct proportion to any increases in tuition, room and board, and fees. Each institution has unique and sometimes conflicting priorities and goals, and the informed budget manager understands those goals as requests are made for financial support.

Sometimes the budget is not goal directed but instead is focused on identifying resources to cover unexpected increases in costs such as utilities. In other words, the institution does not have a strategic goal of paying higher utility costs, but it must do so in order to provide basic educational services. Some institutional priorities simply involve keeping the doors open, the water flowing, and the heat and lights turned on.

A careful examination of the budget of the unit and the institution can help student affairs budget managers understand both the problems faced by the institution and the priorities held by the board and the central administration. With this base of understanding, it becomes much easier to present budget requests that comport with institutional priorities.

Allocating Resources

The reality is that no institution of higher education has unlimited resources and the ability to meet all the needs and wants of all budget units within the institution. Decision makers in the budget process must make clear distinctions between needs and wants. On one hand, a *need* is an essential element of the service, program, or instructional unit that must be funded in order to meet institutional expectations and priorities. For example, if English is required for all entering freshman and the freshman class is larger than expected, then the English Department may need additional instructors. Other alternatives should be explored prior to making such a commitment. Examples of alternatives might include increasing the size of each section of freshman English or rescheduling some sections into peak demand times for students; if an analysis reveals that such changes still will not provide English instruction for all freshman, then the institution is faced with two choices: adjust the budget to increase the resources to the English department or modify the requirements regarding freshman English. Either decision has consequences (intended and unintended) that must be understood by decision makers.

A *want*, on the other hand, is something desired by the unit or an individual member of the unit. A want may have the potential to move both the unit and the institution forward, but it is not essential to either the operation of the unit or the institution. For example, an administrator might want all staff members in the unit to have cell phones but does not have a compelling reason to support the request. At times, wants are simply amenities that might make life easier but are not essential to either the institution or the unit. An effective institutional budget assures that the general funds of the institution are used to support the highest priorities and the greatest needs of the entire institution.

Providing Incentives

Sometimes the institutional rules governing budgets are structured in ways that work against sound fiscal management. For example, at the end of the fiscal year there often is a frenzy of spending. Supplies are ordered in bulk or computers are purchased in order to use up funds allocated to the unit. This activity is usually caused by budgeting rules that require excess funds in a unit to revert back to the control of the central administration or to the state. A better approach to budgeting might be to provide an incentive for budget managers to keep tight control of expenses. One method is to allow the unit to retain some, if not all, of the money left in the unit budget at the end of the year. This money then could be placed in a reserve account to support major equipment purchases or facility renovation or could be carried forward to fund some *wants* of the unit in the next fiscal year.

Exerting Control

The most traditional role of the budget is to exert fiscal control within the institution (Maddox, 1999). There are two basic approaches to budget control: highly centralized and unit centered. In the highly centralized approach, a central budget authority approves all changes and modifications to the budget and the planned expenditures. Under the decentralized model, each unit budget manager is held responsible for using fiscal resources in a prudent and responsible manner. Most institutions have developed a hybrid approach, incorporating elements of both the centralized and decentralized models. Most routine decisions are made at the unit level, and central budget control is exercised for large fund expenditures. This combination approach seems to work quite well, providing some degree of institutional control yet permitting some degree of freedom for those who are closest to the problems and issues within the unit (Barr, 2002).

Means of Communication

Mayhew (1979) indicated that the budget was a tool for communication to a variety of publics about the goals, priorities, and aspirations of an institution of higher education. When a decision is made to allocate resources to a particular program or activity, it signals the importance of that program or activity to the overall mission of the institution. For example, if retention of faculty is an important institutional goal, then the merit increment pool for faculty members may be larger than that for other members of the institutional workforce.

In public institutions, the budget is usually an open document and provides evidence to the legislature and state agencies of the priorities of the institution. Private institutions are more apt to consider budget documents private information, and no requirement exists that they be made public. Budget information does, however, need to be made available for review by foundations and agencies providing funding to the institution. Finally, the budget is the primary means for the institutional administration to convey to the governing board the real priorities and needs of the institution.

Types of Budgets

Generally there are three major types of budgets on any campus: operating capital, and auxiliary. In some cases, affiliated hospitals or other service providers may also have a separate budget. For purposes of this chapter, the discussion is limited to the operating budget and the capital budget.

Operating Budget

The operating budget is the core budget of the institution for the fiscal year (Woodard and von Destinon, 2000). An operating budget reflects all income from all sources (including funds restricted to specific purposes), as well as all approved expenditures for the fiscal year (Meisinger and Dubeck, 1984). The fiscal year will vary from institution to institution and is generally governed by the academic calendar. Each institution has specific rules governing the movement of money within the operating budget, and the astute student affairs administrator both understands and complies with those rules.

Capital Budget

Capital budgets reflect the money set aside to improve the physical plant, finance new construction, purchase major pieces of equipment, replace vehicles, or for expenses that must be paid over several fiscal years. All capital expenses are not automatically funded by the capital budget. Replacement of personal computers in offices, for example, is often funded as part of the operating budget. Sometimes available funds in the capital budgets are not sufficient to meet construction needs. When that occurs, an institution sometimes sells bonds to potential investors and has a plan to pay the investors through the operating budget of the institution through one of the sources of funds previously discussed. The bond rating assigned to the institution at the time of selling the bonds reflects the general fiscal health of the institution.

Budget Models

There is more than one correct way to develop a budget. This section reviews some of the common budget models used in American higher education.

Incremental Budgets

An incremental budget is based on the assumption that both needs and costs vary only a small amount from year to year. It also assumes that the budget from the previous fiscal year is accurate and fairly reflects the yearly expenditures of the unit. Both of these assumptions may be false. The budget for the current year becomes the base budget for the next fiscal year. Under an incremental budget model, all units of the institution receive the same percentage increases for the same line items within the budget. Those increases are based both on the amount of money available and often reflect some index for inflation, such as the *Higher Education Price Index* (Research Associates of Washington, 2005). There is no strategic examination of the expenditure patterns of the total institution or of individual budget units.

Incremental budgeting models minimize conflicts within the institution because every unit is treated in the same way. Such budget models also avoid examination of past commitments to determine whether or not they are meeting the current needs of the institution. Maddox (1999) indicates, "A unit that has a generous budget will only get better off relative to other units—its extra budget grows on that budget excess, whereas another unit treads water as essential funding is increased just (or not) enough to keep pace with cost increases" (p. 16). Formula budgeting is another version of incremental budgeting and is used by most states to allocate money to state-supported institutions of higher education (see earlier discussion on sources of funds).

Redistribution

At times institutions will combine incremental budgets with a redistribution process. This approach provides a general budget increase for operations but permits the budget manager to redistribute the dollars within all line items within the budget. The new budget cannot be increased more than the allocation provided through the budget increment. While an improvement, redistribution still does not address inequities between units. That problem can be partially addressed by providing the percentage increment to all budgets within an administrative unit such as a division of student affairs. The dean or vice president can then address within-division inequities between units that have developed as a result of incremental budgeting.

Zero-Based Budgeting

The zero-based budgeting model requires that each item in the budget be justified and that nothing is assumed to be guaranteed in the budget. Incremental funds are not distributed to units; instead each budget manager must justify every expense in his or her budget request. A zero-based budgeting model has the advantage of enabling careful review of all institutional expenditures and requires that all expenditures be linked to the strategic goals of the unit and the institution. Although effective, zero-based budgeting is labor intensive and time consuming.

Some institutions have developed a modified version of zero-based and incremental funding. Incremental funding is provided for all but a few line items; those line items then must be justified using the zero-based budgeting model.

Cost or Responsibility Center Models

Though slightly different, these two alternative budget models are grouped together for purposes of this discussion. Under a strict cost-centered approach, each part of the organization is responsible for generating revenue to meet expenses and is expected to stand on its own bottom line. Although this works for auxiliary enterprises, the model does not adapt itself to instructional, academic support, and student support units.

Responsibility-centered budgeting has been adopted by many institutions as a means to extend decision making for budgeting beyond the central administration (Woodard and von Destinon, 2000). Each unit is responsible for management of its enterprise, and if the unit incurs a deficit in any fiscal year, that deficit must be made up the following fiscal year from allocated budget resources to the unit. If the unit has excess income over expenditures, the unit is permitted to carry forward the surplus for reallocation or support of new projects. Responsibility-centered models in budgeting provide incentives and greater flexibility to meet changing priorities (Stocum and Rooney, 1997). It has the disadvantage of concentrating on unit goals to the exclusion of institutional goals and objectives.

The Budget Cycle

The two major elements of any budget are revenue and expenses. The key to successful budget management is to be able to closely predict the revenue and assure that expenses do not exceed available funds.

Identifying Revenue

The first step in budgeting is to identify all sources of funds that support the enterprise, including general revenue support, reimbursed costs for services provided, grants, contracts, fees for certain programs and activities, and, if the unit is lucky, income from a designated endowment to support the program. Each revenue source should be classified as to whether it is ongoing or a one-time source of funds.

Identifying Expenses

Expenses vary from year to year dependent on the activities of the unit. Some are *required* or *fixed costs* such as telephone, data service, and postage. For auxiliary enterprises, there are also fixed costs set outside the unit for utilities and maintenance of facilities. Even though such costs are fixed, they should be examined to see if there is not a more cost-effective way to conduct business.

Discretionary costs include travel, registration fees, library acquisitions, publicity, office supplies, and program promotion. Some discretionary costs are directly related to special programs and should be budgeted so that expense does not exceed revenue.

The astute budget manager in student affairs understands these elements of the budget prior to the beginning of the institutional budget cycle.

Institutional Parameters

Development of institutional guidelines is not an easy process and requires financial staff to analyze past performance of the institution, including both fixed and discretionary costs and the influence of the greater environment on the financial health of the institution. Although the environmental scan may be rigorous in some institutions and less so in others, each institution seeks to understand the outside forces that impinge on the financial operation of the college or university.

At the same time, large variances in the prior year budget are examined in detail. Problem units or line items are identified and must be accounted for in any institutional rules. Budget guidelines and parameters reflect the assumptions of the planners regarding enrollment, demand for services, opportunities and problems facing the institution. Each unit budget manager should try to understand the assumptions and beliefs that drive the budget parameters.

Timetables

Institutional budget instructions include the timetable(s) for the submission of all budget documents. Each unit budget manager then must establish earlier deadlines to make sure the unit can meet the required submission deadline. If there are problems meeting the deadline, then the unit budget manager should immediately discuss those issues with their administrative superior. The important thing is not to ignore budget timelines, for such actions can adversely affect the budget of the unit.

Developing Unit Budget Requests

There at least ten specific steps that can assist a unit budget manager in organizing and submitting the unit budget request. Some steps can occur simultaneously, and others proceed in a sequential order.

Step 1. Take the time to analyze previous unit budget performance and understand what happened and why.

Step 2. Share information: budgeting should not be a secret process. Information regarding the parameters established by the institution should be shared widely within the unit.

Step 3. Establish an internal process for development of the budget request. The process should be clear and unambiguous, and once it is established it should be followed. As part of the unit budget process, additional internal guidelines may be set for all program areas.

Step 4. Listen carefully and listen to everyone. It is essential that the members of the organization have an opportunity to present their ideas and concerns as the budget is developed. Depending on the size and complexity of the unit, informal hearings or informal conversation could be held. It is important that members of the unit have an opportunity to share their goals and aspirations for their programs. Remember that the process of listening to aspirations does not have to wait until formal budget guidelines are issued.

Step 5. Establish internal guidelines and timetables and provide an opportunity for those responsible for submitting budget requests to understand those guidelines and timetables.

Step 6. Review proposals for new or increased funding from programs or departments. Such proposals should be clearly linked to the plan and goals of the larger unit and the institution. The following questions are useful as proposals are reviewed at the unit level:

a. What is the rationale for the proposal, and can others easily understand it?
b. What change will occur if this funding request is granted?
c. Are any anticipated savings in the proposal accurate and supportable?
d. Does the proposal rely on transferring a program or service to another unit or agency? Are they prepared to take it on?
e. Is the basic arithmetic of the proposal correct? Arithmetical errors occur frequently and should be identified and corrected prior to budget submission, and
f. Finally, have the routine inflationary increases been examined to assure that they are really needed or if savings could be realized?

Step 7. Prior to submitting the budget proposal, all available options for funding should be reviewed and tested, including limiting or eliminating a current program in order to fund a new venture. The reader is referred to *Prioritizing Academic Programs and Services* (Dickeson, 1999) for a well-developed discussion on how to prioritize programs within the academy.

Step 8. Feedback to those who developed budget requests should be provided, both for those requests supported by the unit and those not forwarded as part of the budget process. Improvement in the quality of requests and the accuracy of budget documents will occur only if specific feedback is provided to staff that developed the proposal.

Step 9. Prepare the final budget submission for the unit. Be clear, concise, and accurate as budget documents are prepared. As part of the final budget proposal to the central administration, clearly identify the implications of the request beyond the current fiscal year being reviewed.

Step 10. Approval of the budget request is an iterative process. The work is not completed when the request is submitted, and the budget manager or others in the unit must be prepared to answer questions and concerns. Once the institution agrees upon the budget, it is submitted to the governing board for approval. Final approval of the budget only occurs after the ongoing process of information sharing and decision making by the administration, the board, and the various committees of the governing board.

Monitoring Performance

After the budget is approved and the fiscal year begins, monitoring of the budget must occur on a regular basis. The diligent budget manager monitors budget performance each and every month. For that activity to be productive, the budget manager must understand the ebb and flow of expenditures and the institutional rules governing accounting and charges, including encumbrances (funds commited but not yet expended).

Adjusting the Current Budget

If there is a revenue shortfall, then expenses, where possible, should be adjusted downward to cover at least part of the projected deficit. If there are uncontrollable costs being faced by the unit, those costs should be identified and clearly communicated to appropriate administrative and budget personnel.

Closing

When the current budget is closed, no more charges can be made against that budget year or no new revenue can be added to a prior fiscal year. Invoices for goods and services not paid by the time of closing will be charged to the next fiscal year. This has the effect of starting the new fiscal year in debt. The budget manager must understand the closing dates used by the budget office and plan for those dates in their year-end fiscal planning.

Analyzing the Results

When the budget cycle for the fiscal year is completed, the results must be analyzed. Earlier it was noted that the first step in the budget cycle was to analyze past performance. Such analysis is also the last step in the process of budget management. If variances from the budget plan occurred, then the reasons why those variances occurred must be uncovered. Such information will assist in the planning process for the next fiscal year. Remember, the unit budget manager is always dealing with three budgets: understanding what happened in the prior fiscal year, monitoring the current fiscal year budget, and planning for the next fiscal year.

Dealing with Budget Cuts

Two levels of decisions govern the response to budget cuts. The first is the response from the institution, and the second is the response from the unit.

Institutional Strategies

There are four common strategies employed by an institution facing a budget cut: a freeze, across-the-board cuts, targeted reductions, and restructuring. A *budget freeze* is not really a budget cut, but it is perceived as one by faculty and staff members. Under a budget freeze, new hires are postponed and major purchases are postponed. A budget freeze is a good way to get the attention of faculty and staff regarding the serious nature of the financial problem faced by the institution.

Across-the-board cuts are the easiest, most expedient way to manage a budget reduction. Funds captured from such cuts are used to offset budget reductions. *Targeted reductions* occur when selected line items are earmarked for savings. Travel, honoraria, and new equipment purchases are often the line items chosen in the initial phase of a budget reduction. A more draconian measure involves *restructuring* the way the institution does business through combining programs, instituting new fiscal rules, and reorganizing reporting relationships to reduce overhead. Whatever the choices made at the institutional level, the individual unit budget manager can also take steps to respond.

Unit Reduction Strategies

Rumors abound when the institution faces fiscal concerns, so it is first important to share information with those within the unit. Second, ask for suggestions on how to curtail costs; faculty and staff have a number of good ideas that can be considered. Third, use contingency funds (resources set aside for unforeseen expenses) as a primary resource in responding to budget cuts—it may be labeled as a contingency line or could be an equipment replacement line—no matter what the label, use those funds first.

Ask for voluntary cutbacks and some interesting ideas may surface. If members of the unit understand the dimensions of the problem, they may come up with new ideas, such as a change in a position from twelve months to nine months or even a solution as simple as charging for office coffee when it has been provided at no charge. A number of little steps can result in substantial savings.

Sometimes outsourcing is a valuable strategy, as costs may be less expensive if an outside vendor is used for certain functions. This strategy may have implications beyond the unit and should be discussed with decision makers prior to seeking proposals from vendors. Sharing resources is a viable strategy for units in close proximity to each other where shared equipment (fax, copy machine) or personnel (receptionists) may reduce costs.

Conclusion

Sound fiscal management at all levels of the organization is necessary for an institution of higher education to succeed. The financial health of the institution is predicated on the aggregate financial health of all the units within the institution. The ability to translate information to those within a unit and to decision makers within the institution is a key factor in the success of budget managers. Four simple rules should guide your professional practice in budgeting and financial management:

1. *Be honest and trustworthy.* Do not try to cover up mistakes or be less than forthcoming with decision makers about problems and issues in the unit.
2. *Be consistent.* This rule is a corollary to the first rule. Consistency is a virtue in budget management.
3. *Be creative.* Within the rules and regulations of the institution, think creatively about possible solutions to problems.
4. *Be fair.* Treat all members of the organization with dignity and respect, and do not provide special budget benefits to one part of the organization without a rationale to support such a decision.

Good budgeting and financial management requires attention to detail, a curious mind, and a willingness to persist while seeking answers to questions. The art of budgeting and financial management can be mastered with time and energy.

References

Barr, M. J. *Academic Administrators Guide to Budgets and Financial Management.* San Francisco: Jossey Bass, 2002.

Dickeson, R. C. *Prioritizing Academic Programs and Services: Reallocating Resources to Achieve Strategic Balance.* San Francisco: Jossey-Bass, 1999.

Maddox, D. *Budgeting for Not-For-Profit Organizations.* New York: Wiley, 1999.

Mayhew, L. B. *Surviving the Eighties: Strategies and Procedures for Solving Fiscal and Enrollment Problems.* San Francisco: Jossey-Bass, 1979.

Meisinger, R. J., and Dubeck, L. W. *College and University Budgeting: An Introduction for Faculty and Academic Administrators.* Washington, D.C.: National Association of College and University Business Officers, 1984.

Research Associates of Washington. *Higher Education Price Index.* Washington, D.C.: Research Associates, 2005.

Stocum, D. L., and Rooney, P. M. "Responding to Resource Constraints: A Departmentally Based System of Responsibility Centered Management." *Change,* 1997, 29(5).

Woodard, D. B. Jr., and von Destinon, M. "Budgeting and Fiscal Management." In M. J. Barr, M. K. Desler, and Associates (Eds.), *The Handbook of Student Affairs Administration* (2nd ed.). San Francisco: Jossey-Bass, 2000.

CHAPTER TWENTY-SIX

LEGAL ISSUES IN STUDENT AFFAIRS

Beverly E. Ledbetter

The relationship between an institution of higher education, whether public or private, and a student is one of great importance to society. The relationship exists within a complex legal framework that is continually under the courts' review and that continues to evolve. It is increasingly important that student affairs practitioners be familiar with the evolving body of law influencing student affairs work.

University legal obligations and potential for liability to students are derived from three common law principles that are reviewed in this chapter: (1) breach of an express or implied contract between the university and the student to provide both education and living arrangements; (2) negligent failure to meet general standards of care for student safety and well-being required of universities under tort law; and (3) failure to meet heightened standards of care required by the existence of a special relationship that may exist between a university and a particular student. Beyond these common law principles that create obligations and potential liability for university student affairs offices, the chapter reviews state and federal statutes and regulations that also constrain the manner in which universities interact with students. This chapter also addresses public universities' liability for violations of the state and federal constitutional law protections enjoyed by students in those institutions, in particular the right to free speech, due process, and freedom from unreasonable searches and seizures.

The author wishes to acknowledge the assistance of James M. Green (deputy counsel), Pamela Collet (executive assistant), and Stephen Imondi (legal assistant), all colleagues from Brown University, in helping to prepare this chapter.

The University's Contractual Responsibilities to Students

It is well established that there is a contractual relationship between a student and his or her university. A student claiming that a university breached its contract with the student must show that there was a valid contract, that the university breached its duties under its contractual agreement, and that the breach caused the student damage. Even in the absence of all of the legal formalities of a contractual agreement between the student and the university, the courts will permit a student to reasonably rely on a promise, offer, or commitment by the university (*Guckenberger v. Boston University*).

Publications and Communications

Since most universities do not enter into a formal contract with their students, courts look to university publications and communications to determine the obligations and responsibilities of the student and the university. College catalogues, academic and disciplinary codes, student handbooks, and admission brochures, enrollment forms, and tuition agreements are all common sources relied upon to establish the specific terms that bind the parties. Various provisions may be alleged to be terms of an "express contract." Administrators should review these documents annually to ensure that they correctly set forth the expectations that the university has of the students and the obligations of the university.

A university will not only be held to the promises made in its documents, but ambiguities will be construed against the institution as the drafter of the documents. Sometimes the precise nature of the agreement and the scope of the institution's obligations are made difficult by the sheer number of documents relating to the subject area. Care must be taken to ensure that documents that are intended to set forth institutional obligations are reviewed and promulgated by authorized officers of the university and not by students or individuals and groups that lack the authority to bind the university. Miscellaneous information disseminated through institutional channels may be relied on by others to the detriment of the school.

Themes

There are several themes that are repeated in claims by students and their parents that a university has breached its contractual obligations. These include allegations that the university misrepresented its offerings, resources, and program at the time of admission. In *Guckenberger*, students sued Boston University (BU) after BU declined to extend certain accommodations for the students' learning disabilities. The court declined to decide whether there was an enforceable contract under Massachusetts law based on BU brochures. Instead, the court found an enforceable contract based on specific promises BU faculty made to the students and their parents concerning the accommodation of the students' learning disabilities.

In the 2005 case *Shin v. Massachusetts Institute of Technology* (MIT), the court rejected the claim by the parents of an undergraduate who committed suicide that they had an express or implied contract (or both) with MIT, supported by adequate consideration, to provide necessary and reasonable medical services to their daughter. The court concluded that representations made in the MIT medical department literature were merely generalized representations and were not definite and certain and were too vague and indefinite to form an enforceable contract.

The conduct of the institution in its interactions with the student may form the basis for an "implied contract," one that is not the result of written or express communications. A decision to drop programs, courses, or activities referenced in documents that might be relied on by students at the time of the admissions decision may create a detrimental reliance by the students if such programs or activities are discontinued without adequate notice or provision of reasonable alternatives. Students may challenge their separation or dismissal for lack of academic progress or disciplinary reasons as being contrary to the institution's own expressed rules or as contravening standards of fundamental fairness. A Florida federal trial court allowed a law student expelled from a private university for threatening and physically intimidating law school community members to proceed with his claim that the university breached the terms of an implied contract with the student by not affording him the procedural protections of the university's academic code, including the right to know the allegations against him, the right to have those charges investigated by a disciplinary committee, and the right to make a statement at the opening and closing of a disciplinary hearing on his own behalf (*Jarzynka v. St. Thomas University of Law*).

The University's Noncontractual Obligations to Students

Absent a contractual obligation to a student, a university may still face liability if it wrongs students in a way that the law forbids. A tort is a civil, not a criminal wrong, other than a breach of contract, for which a lawsuit may be brought. The remedy is generally monetary damages that compensate an individual for the harm they have suffered and/or that punish them for the harm caused. Thus, damages can be either compensatory or punitive.

Both the right to sue and the right to recover damages may be negated by doctrines that take into account whether the actions of the injured party contribute to the injury. A finding that the injured party's actions contributed to the injury is usually sufficient, under the *doctrine of contributory negligence*, to bar recovery of damages. Some states permit a comparison of the fault of the plaintiff and that of the defendant and allow proration of the damages accordingly. Similarly, a person who willingly puts himself in a position of danger may be barred from recovery under the doctrine of *assumption of risk*.

Negligence

There are several torts that might impose liability on educational institutions, but negligence is most commonly relied on to impose institutional liability and thus deserves special comment. *Negligence* is defined as "the failure to exercise the standard of care that a reasonably prudent person would have exercised in a similar situation" (Black and Garner, 1999, p. 1056). Another way of stating this is that negligence is the doing of something one is legally obligated not to do or not doing something one is legally obligated to do.

Negligence requires proof of four elements. They are (1) a legal duty or obligation to conform to a certain standard of conduct for the protection of others; (2) failure to conform to the required standard; (3) a reasonably close casual connection between the conduct and the resulting injury (proximate cause); (4) and a resulting actual loss or damage (Prosser, 1971).

In *Heller v. Consolidated Rail Corporation*, a federal trial court in Pennsylvania in 1982 held that a university had no duty as either a university or a landowner to prevent a student from injuring himself by climbing atop a railroad box car temporarily stopped on tracks that crossed the university's property. Where there is no duty, there is no liability.

In the 1987 case *University of Denver v. Whitlock*, the Colorado Court held that the university had no duty to Whitlock to eliminate the private use of trampolines on its campus or to supervise its use. A student injured his neck jumping on the trampoline, which was owned by a recognized campus fraternity and was kept on the fraternity house lawn. The fraternity house was leased to the fraternity by the university, and the university was responsible for maintaining the fraternity building and its surroundings. The university was aware of the presence and use of the trampoline. Over the years, several individuals were injured as a result of using the trampoline. Some of these injuries were reported to university security, and some individuals were treated by the university student health clinic. The court concluded that the lease, and the university's actions pursuant to its rights under the lease, provided no basis upon which a special relationship could be found, and the university was under no duty to take affirmative action to assure the safety of recreational equipment such as a trampoline.

In another case, a college providing a makeshift athletic field on its property owed the participants the duty to use reasonable care to inspect the field for defects. When the plaintiff slipped into a concealed depression, the facts established a prima facie case of negligence (*Lamphere v. State of New York*). However, in a similar case, the university did not breach its duty to participants, when a dangerous condition was visible to participants and thus the participants assumed the risk of participation (*Scaduto v. State of New York*).

Special Relationship

In analyzing the relationship between the students and the institution, courts will look at the degree of control vested in the institution. A greater degree of control will result in greater institutional responsibility and a corresponding duty. The student's level of maturity may also be a factor in determining a reasonable standard of care. Students who are under the age of majority, that is, minors, recognized by the state where the institution is located may be subject to a different standard than those of majority age. This is not a factor in most cases involving students matriculating at the college level even when the student is still technically a minor. However, secondary school students attending summer or special programs require a higher standard of care, generally in the form of more supervision and stricter parietal rules. For instance, high school students may be subject to a curfew consistent with that of the local or state laws. Occasionally, a duty arises to an individual that is demonstrably different from the duty owed to other students. This is usually the result of a finding of a *special relationship*. Most courts have not held that either the enrollment relationship or the landlord-tenant relationship is a special relationship.

A *duty* is "a legal obligation that is owed or due to another and that needs to be satisfied; an obligation for which somebody else has a corresponding right" (Black and Garner, 1999). Generally, "there is no duty to control the conduct of a third person so as to prevent him from causing physical harm to another unless:

(a) a special relation exists between the actor and the third person which imposes a duty upon the actor to control the third person's conduct; or

(b) a special relation exists between the actor and the other which gives the other a right to protection." (Restatement (Second) of Torts § 315, 1965)

Even if the relationship does not impose a duty to control or protect, a college or university may be liable if it voluntarily assumes responsibility for some aspect of the student's life. At common law, a duty once it has been assumed must be performed with reasonable care (Restatement (Second) of Torts § 323). Whether the institution has assumed responsibility and what responsibility it has assumed may present a gray area in terms of potential liability for the acts of students.

In *Shin v. Massachusetts Institute of Technology*, the trial court denied summary judgment to the MIT medical professionals who treated the student who committed suicide and the MIT administrators with knowledge of her suicidal tendencies. The court found that the doctor-patient relationship imposed a duty on the medical professionals. The court found a "special relationship" between Shin and MIT's dean of counseling and a dormitory housemaster imposing a duty on them to exercise reasonable care to protect her from harm. "The Plaintiffs have provided sufficient evidence that [the administrators] could reasonably foresee that Elizabeth would hurt herself without proper supervision."

In *Rabel v. Illinois Wesleyan University*, a student was injured by another student who, under the influence of alcohol, and as a fraternity party prank, forcibly grabbed the plaintiff, threw her over his shoulder, and ran with her through a crowd until he tripped and fell, injuring the plaintiff. The court rejected the plaintiff's argument that the university assumed the duty to control the actions of its students by its handbook regulations and policies, and that having assumed the duty failed to carry it out with due care. The court stated that the university's responsibility to its students, as an institution of higher education, is to properly educate them, and declined to impose the additional role of custodian over its adult students.

An all-female college was found liable in *Mullins v. Pine Manor College* when a student was raped by an unknown assailant in her dormitory room. This case rejected what had been the majority rule that an institution does not have a duty to protect its students from the intentional, criminal, or negligent acts of third parties without the existence of some special relationship. The court reasoned that the college voluntarily undertook providing its students with protection in the dormitories, and that since both the student and her parents relied on the college's protection in deciding to attend this particular college was enough to impose a duty to act reasonably on the college. The court found that the college breached this duty and was liable to the plaintiff for her injuries. Over the past decade, courts have continued to find that the protection of students in a dormitory setting requires special safeguards.

Duty as Landlord

Plaintiffs may claim that an institution has the duty to protect its students from harm because it provides the student with housing. Thus the institution may be sued in its capacity as landlord.

In *Miller v. State*, the plaintiff student was confronted in the laundry room of her dormitory by an assailant who brought her to a dormitory room and raped her. Notwithstanding the university's knowledge of numerous crimes in the dormitory, including one other rape, the doors of the dormitory were kept unlocked even though each door had a locking mechanism. The court held that the state college in its role as a landlord had a duty to protect students from reasonably foreseeable criminal assaults by outsiders and breached this duty by allowing the doors to remain unlocked, and so was liable to the student for her injuries.

The court in *Rabel* supra refused to find the university liable as landlord for the student injured in the fraternity prank, holding that the landlord-tenant relationship does not in and of itself create a duty on the part of the landlord to protect its tenants from the intentional, criminal, or negligent acts of others. Nor did the landlord-tenant relationship constitute a special relationship under the theory of the Restatement (Second) of Torts §315, under which the landlord would have the duty to control and be liable for the acts of its tenants or protect its tenants from the acts of others.

The court in *L.W. v. Western Golf Association* noted that whether or not the defendant owes a duty to the plaintiff depends upon the relationship between the parties, and that once a duty exists, the duty is to exercise reasonable care under the circumstances—the duty never changes. However, the standard of conduct required to fulfill that duty varies according to the particular circumstances.

Even when an institution is not in a landlord-tenant relationship, it has responsibility and liability for property it owns or controls. *Pitre v. Louisiana Tech University* illustrates the scope of responsibility an institution has as a landowner. Pitre, a twenty-year-old student, was injured while sledding down a campus hill on a large trash can cover that hit a light pole in the parking lot below. The court held that the university had no duty to warn the students of the risks of sledding or to protect them against injury. Furthermore, the risk that sledders might collide with objects in the sledding path is an obvious risk, and the light pole that the claimant hit was in the middle of the path and visible to the those sledding. This case demonstrates in part how the obligation of a landowner differs for patent or apparent defects and latent or hidden defects.

Colleges and universities must also be conscious that they have a duty to students when they have notice of a potentially dangerous situation. In *Sharkey v. Board of Regents,* the campus police were informed that a male student was harassing a female student but took no action. The female student's husband, also a student, was stabbed when he confronted the alleged harasser.

Following the April 2007 tragedy at Virginia Tech, lawyers for the shooting victims are considering a lawsuit against the college. Seung Hui Cho killed two people at a Virginia Tech dormitory the morning of April 16, 2007. About two and a half hours later, at an academic building, Cho shot and killed thirty students and faculty members before shooting himself. If a lawsuit is brought, the victims may very well rely on the findings of a government-appointed review panel that concluded that lives could have been saved had the university alerted students sooner about the shooting in the dormitory and canceled classes because the gunman had not been caught.

Respondeat Superior

In order to find a person vicariously liable for the acts of another under the doctrine of *Respondeat Superior,* one of four special relationships must exist between the parties: (1) employer-employee; (2) principal-agent; (3) joint enterprise; or (4) family purpose. If an institution's relationship with its student can be characterized as any of these, then the institution can be held liable for the tortious or criminal acts of its students. State laws may also define special relationships on which a duty is predicated. Although attempts have been made to expand the list of special relationships, the college/university-student relationship has never been added to the list.

A university can be held liable for acts of its students if they are found to be acting as agents for the university. In *Brueckner v. Norwich University,* the court held a military college liable for the actions of upper-class cadets hired by the school for "indoctrinating and orienting" plaintiff." Brueckner was mistreated verbally and physically by the cadets. The university was found to be "directly liable for damages resulting from negligent supervision of its agents" as well as "vicariously liable for tortious conduct of its agents."

In Loco Parentis

Under the theory of *in loco parentis,* an institution is seen as a surrogate parent. Until the mid-1960s, colleges and universities functioned much like parents, exercising extensive control over students and their behavior. Challenges to the broad exercise of authority and control led to a reduction in the institution's power and thus to the demise of *in loco parentis* as a basis of liability for colleges and universities.

More recent cases that have addressed the claim that an institution acts *in loco parentis* have unanimously held that the principle does not apply to college or university students (see, for example, *Bradshaw v. Rawlings, Beach v. University of Utah, Smith v. Day*). Because of this overwhelming consensus, it is unlikely that *in loco parentis* is a viable theory for imposing liability on institutions for students' actions.

In jurisdictions that have addressed the issue, the general rule is that a modern American college is not an insurer of the safety of its students (*Bradshaw*). The rationale for this rule is that the authoritarian role of institutions has greatly diminished in recent decades.

In *Bradshaw*, the court declined to hold a college liable for injuries to a student resulting from another student's drunk driving accident returning from an off-campus class picnic, which was planned, in part, by the class advisor who also signed the check for funds used to purchase beer. The court held that the college's anti-alcohol regulations and sanctions, alone, were insufficient to create a special relationship between the college and its students and refused to impose a duty on the college to control its students' actions. (See also *Albano v. Colby College.*)

Another court rejected *in loco parentis* as the basis for holding a college liable for a freshman's abduction and rape. "The in loco parentis doctrine is outmoded and inconsistent with the reality of contemporary collegiate life" (*Johnson v. State of Washington*). The same court allowed the litigation to proceed against the college because it found that the rape victim was a business invitee on the college's premises and was owed a duty of care for that reason.

In rejecting *in loco parentis,* a number of courts make note of the difference between elementary and high schools, which with minor students are both educational and custodial, and colleges and universities, which are educational but not custodial institutions (*Graham v. Montana State University, Beach v. University of Utah*).

College students are considered to be adults in almost every phase of institutional life. A beginning student is usually at least eighteen years of age and is no longer a minor. The expectation that an institution can control the actions of its students is unrealistic. The additional costs of expecting an institution to exercise such control are great in that the exercise of control would contravene a primary goal of higher education, that is, the maturation of the students, and would infringe upon an institution's academic freedom. Such exercise of control would be inconsistent with the nature of the relationship between the student and the university in that it would produce a repressive and inhospitable environment, largely inconsistent with the objective of a modern education. Institutions are now being permitted to regulate student life without being held responsible for injuries resulting from violations of regulations (*Beach v. University of Utah*).

Responsibility for Criminal Acts of Students

Institutions are generally not liable for their students' criminal acts unless the institution has a special relationship duty to the victim to protect against crime, has assumed the obligation to protect, or has fostered an atmosphere increasing the risk of injury due to crime. Unless student behavior is foreseeable, it is unlikely that the college or university will be held liable for the criminal acts of its students.

In *Smith v. Day*, the plaintiffs argued that the breakdown in the enforcement of the university's rules and regulations prohibiting illegal conduct proximately caused their injuries. Rejecting the plaintiff's arguments, the court found that neither the university's exercise of a large degree of control over its students' activities nor the existence of stringent student life rules and regulations imposes a duty upon the university to control its students' volitional criminal acts for which it had absolutely no reasonably foreseeable notice.

In *Eiseman v. State*, the trial court found the State University College at Buffalo liable for the rape and murder of a student by a second student who was an ex-convict with an extensive criminal record and a history of psychiatric problems who had been admitted under a program for economically and educationally disadvantaged students. The court held that once the university decided to accept incarcerated felons, it assumed a duty to establish rational criteria for screening such applicants in order to protect its students. The court of appeals reversed the decision finding that the college had no legal duty requiring it to respond in damages for student's rape and murder. The court added that "while hindsight has a peculiar clarity and wisdom, the fact remains that the contemporaneous, nonrenewable judgments by which the College's actions must be evaluated were that Campbell, upon his release, needed no psychiatric care or other treatment, and further that he had a potential for success in college."

Dram Shop and Social Host Liability

Many states, under Dram Shop statutes, hold persons who negligently furnish liquor to minors vicariously liable for minors' acts. Institutions could be liable to third parties for its students' acts if the university furnishes liquor or authorizes the serving of liquor to minors.

Besides Dram Shop statutes, colleges may also face liability under the developing common law theory of social host liability. It has been recognized as a viable theory of third party liability (see *Ely v. Murphy*, in which a social host was held liable for injuries caused by a minor to whom the social host served liquor; and *McGuiggan v. New England Tel and Tel Co.*, in which a parent who held a graduation party that a minor attended was held liable for injuries to a third party as a result of furnishing liquor to a minor).

Plaintiffs have argued that inaction on the part of an institution with knowledge that its students are drinking alcohol is in effect furnishing or authorizing the serving of liquor for the purposes of imposing social host liability on the institution. Although this is a tenable argument, many courts have held that an institution's knowledge of student drinking and its failure to prevent it is not an affirmative act that can constitute furnishing of alcohol. In *Alumni Ass'n v. Sullivan*, the court ruled that a university was not liable for damages caused by a minor student who was served alcoholic beverages at a party held in his freshman dormitory under the theory that the university should have known that alcohol would be served to minors. The court held that social host liability extended only to persons who knowingly furnished alcohol to a minor, and that there was no indication that the university was involved in planning parties or serving, supplying, or purchasing liquor.

Since the institution of a new minimum drinking age of twenty-one, there have been a number of highly publicized cases that assert that institutions, particularly those that are residential, have a duty to act to minimize the risks to the health, safety, and welfare of students due to either their own drinking or that of others. The institution may be alleged to have been on notice as to the number of student violations of the minimum drinking age in residential facilities, at or before athletic events, at social events on campus, or on property owned or controlled by the institution. Although most cases are civil cases seeking monetary damages for personal injuries or wrongful death, state prosecutors are also beginning to take an interest in these matters, and they may become the subject of criminal indictments.

Higher Education and the Constitution

The U.S. Constitution, particularly in the Bill of Rights, limits the ability of government, whether federal or state, to control the actions of individuals. The constitutions of the individual states also confer rights and limit what government may do. College students are protected individuals under the federal Constitution and state constitutions, and publicly supported schools and colleges are considered part of government. Public colleges must, therefore, gauge whether their actions violate any of their students' constitutional safeguards. Private institutions are not limited in their actions by the Constitution. Many private schools confer certain procedural protections to their students (akin to those required of public universities), but they are not mandated to do so by the Constitution.

Most claims against universities under the Constitution fall into three categories of law. Those are (1) the free speech protections of the First Amendment, (2) the right to due process of law under the Fourteenth Amendment, or (3) the protections against unreasonable searches and seizures of the Fourth Amendment.

Due Process

Due process is a constitutionally protected right under the Fourteenth Amendment. Accordingly, it is most likely to be asserted against public universities. It is a guarantee of fundamental fairness and includes the right to notice and an opportunity to be heard before a decision is made that would deprive the individual of a protected liberty or property right. An interest in pursuing an education is a protected property interest. These constitutional due process requirements are not mandatory for private institutions, but they are often afforded to students by the private institutions, explicitly or by inference, out of the private institutions' sense of fundamental fairness (*Jarzynka v. St. Thomas University of Law*).

A person in danger of losing a protected right should have the opportunity to challenge the prospective loss by presenting information and witnesses in support of the individual's case. This is possible only if the student has timely notice of the offending conduct and a fair opportunity to respond to the allegations. Notice is *actual notice*, but questions regarding the timing and adequacy of the notice are more prevalent when the notice is oral rather than written. The "opportunity to be heard" is often misunderstood as requiring judicial-like trappings, particularly with respect to a proceeding designed to allow both sides to present information and support for their positions. In fact, such an opportunity for hearing can be extremely informal.

Written policies and procedures that clearly set forth the rules and the process for review of allegations of violations, including any appeals process are essential. The policy and procedures should reflect the objectives of the institution. Practices should be aligned with the policies and procedures so that they reflect both the culture of the particular institution as well as the resources available. Care should be taken to review the policy and procedures annually to insure that they are up to date and consistent with current practices.

Free Speech

Among its many protections, the First Amendment to the Constitution prohibits government from infringing on the right of free speech, free press, and free assembly. Public colleges and universities must afford students, faculty, and others these rights. At private institutions, students and faculty are usually afforded free speech rights as part of a right of academic freedom, or they gain the right because the private institution has held itself out as a public forum.

Both the First Amendment and academic freedom rest on an understanding that the community benefits from a robust exchange of ideas. Certain governmental limitations on speech are permitted by the First Amendment provided they relate to the time, manner, and place in which speech is made and are content neutral. Colleges and universities, as they have become increasingly diverse, have had to face the challenge of balancing the right to free speech with the right of students to be free of harassment because of gender, race, religion, or sexual orientation. Many colleges have instituted speech and behavior regulations that attempt to limit certain expressions and words that are designed to harass rather than express a viewpoint. While recognizing that certain types of speech, such as *fighting words* (words that are "likely to produce a clear and present danger of a serious intolerable evil that rises above mere inconvenience or annoyance" (*Terminiello v. Chicago*), are not protected by the First Amendment, courts give these speech codes the strictest of reviews, and many have been overturned. The student affairs practitioner must be vigilant in making sure that anti-hate policies do not become anti-speech policies.

The First Amendment also protects individuals from government interference in the exercise of their religious beliefs while prohibiting the establishment of a government-endorsed religion. In *Rosenberger v. Rectors and Visitors of the University of Virginia*, the U.S. Supreme Court held that the university could not withhold a share of student activity fees to a student organization "whose purpose was [t]o publish a magazine of philosophical and religious expression." The Court held that withholding funds constituted viewpoint discrimination and threatened to create an attitude of hostility to religion in violation of the establishment clause.

Reasonable Searches and Seizures

The Fourth Amendment to the Constitution limits governmental ability to search and seize citizens and their property. Public university administrators who engage in searches and seizures are considered governmental officials, and students at public institutions have Fourth Amendment protection. The Fourth Amendment requires that governmental searches be reasonable. A significant development in this area is the advent of statutes mandating certain types of searches in the educational sphere, including drug testing and weapon control.

Federal and State Statutes and Regulations

Federal and state laws and regulations are responsible for the majority of the legal obligations imposed on institutions during the past three decades. Laws are enacted by Congress or state legislatures. Departments or agencies within the executive branch implement the laws through regulations they issue and enforce. Often, guidelines are also published to provide useful guidance. The regulations have the force of law; guidelines do not.

Although most laws impose legal duties on the institution rather than on individuals, some do provide for fines or criminal sanctions (or both) against individuals. Some regulations provide a private right of action, allowing those who enjoy its protections to bring legal actions to enforce the law through court action. Others provide redress only through the governmental entity responsible for its enforcement.

State regulations are applicable only to the institutions within the state and influence public institutions most often. Federal regulations are based on the federal government's power to regulate interstate commerce and to provide for the general welfare as well as contractual relations within the institutions, such as those relating to receipt of federal funds. Although institutions of higher education may be subject to federal laws that also apply to employers and businesses that are neither nonprofit or education, several federal regulations relate directly to higher education institutions and affect their relationship with students and require continuing oversight and compliance.

Compliance with legislative requirements cannot be the responsibility of one or just a few administrators or staff members. University policies and practices, vetted through the university's legal counsel, must set forth the requirements of the regulations as they are to be addressed by responsible staff members, no matter where they are located.

Several of the hundreds of federal regulations that have an impact on the day-to-day operations of the institution are so uniquely related to the responsibilities of student affairs administrators that all staff within the office should have a working understanding of the regulations. In addition to Titles VI and IX, the Family Educational Rights and Privacy Act (FERPA) and the Jeanne Cleary Disclosure of Campus Security Policy and Campus Crime Statistics Act (Campus Security Act) require special mention.

Discrimination

Several well-known statutes prohibit discrimination in programs or activities at educational institutions that receive federal financial aid. Pell grants would be one example of such aid. The best known of these nondiscrimination laws are Title VI of the Civil Rights Act of 1964 (prohibiting race, color, and national origin discrimination), Title IX of the Education Amendments of 1972 (prohibiting sex discrimination), and Section 504 of the Rehabilitation Act of 1973 (prohibiting disability discrimination). The Americans with Disabilities Act (ADA) of 1990 prohibits discrimination against qualified individuals with a disability in both public and private institutions, whether or not they receive federal funding. Title II of the ADA covers state and local governments, including public colleges and universities, while Title III of ADA covers all public accommodations that include private higher education institutions.

Title VI, Title IX, and Section 504 established a national priority against discrimination in the use of federal funds, authorized the federal Department of Education (DOE) to establish standards of nondiscrimination, and provided for enforcement by withholding of funds from funded entities or "by any other means authorized by law." The duty to enforce the educational provisions of Title VI and Title IX resides with DOE's Office for Civil Rights (OCR). OCR investigates complaints of discrimination and initiates enforcement actions against entities that refuse to comply. OCR is also permitted to refer these cases to the U.S. Department of Justice for enforcement. The courts have also recognized a private right of action to enforce these laws. Enforcement of the ADA (Titles II and III) is the responsibility of the Justice Department.

Title VI states that "no person in the United States shall, on the ground of race, color, or national origin, be excluded from participation in, be denied the benefits of, or be subjected to discrimination under any program or activity receiving federal financial assistance" (41 USC 2000(d)). Title VI has been interpreted by court decisions as covering all programs and activities at the institution, not just the program or activity receiving or administering the funds. Thus, in addition to the offices responsible for admissions and/or financial aid, other programs such as academic enrichment, special retention programs, and student services are affected.

The majority of cases alleging Title VI violations focus on race and ethnicity and university practice that either promotes or limits access based on race or ethnicity. Many colleges and universities have adopted affirmative action policies to increase the racial diversity of their student populations. When these policies are challenged on constitutional grounds or under Title VI, reviewing courts subject them to strict scrutiny and find them unlawful unless they serve a compelling institutional interest and are narrowly tailored to meet that interest. Affirmative action programs may be found by the courts to be sufficiently compelling when they are designed to remedy the present effects of past discrimination or to promote diversity. An affirmative action program is narrowly tailored if it has been designed and implemented in the narrowest way possible to advance the goal of diversity without unnecessary infringement on the rights of other prospective students. Many affirmative action initiatives in education have been unable to pass muster under strict scrutiny (see, for example, *Regents of the University of California v. Bakke, Grutter v. Bollinger, Gratz v. Bollinger*).

Northwestern University was sued under Section 504 when it rejected a student with a disclosed heart condition's request to play basketball. A federal trial court ruled that Northwestern was in violation of the Rehabilitation Act, "which protects 'otherwise qualified individuals' from discrimination on account of disability" and issued an injunction allowing the student to play basketball. The court said that playing college basketball qualified as a major life activity under the act. The Seventh Circuit Court of Appeals *Knapp v. Northwestern University* reversed the trial court, concluding that the student was not disabled under the Rehabilitation Act since his condition was not a "continuing disability." The student was "only disabled when his heart stops." The appellate court also refused to define "major life activity" in such a way that the act would apply whenever someone wishes to play intercollegiate athletics.

Family Educational Rights and Privacy Act

The Family Educational Rights and Privacy Act of 1974, 20 U.S.C. §1232, provides students with access to their personal information as maintained in the institution's "education records" and, subject to specific exceptions, prohibits disclosure without the student's prior consent of the student's personally identifiable information to persons other than those within the institution with a need to know. Universities must provide annual notice to students of their rights under FERPA and the university's policies and procedures relating to the act. Specifically, a student must be given the opportunity to inspect the education record, to amend the record if the student believes it is inaccurate, misleading, or in violation of rights of privacy.

Although a student must be granted access to information within forty-five days of a request, there are certain records, such as law enforcement, employment records, and medical records, that under certain circumstances are excluded from the definition of education records. These exceptions recognize other legitimate relationships that extend beyond the educational relationships of the parties and may therefore be subject to other valid constraints. For instance, access to medical records is also governed by state law providing certain access to confidential medical information and the federal Health Insurance Portability and Accountability Act (HIPAA). HIPAA protects personally identifiable medical information from unauthorized disclosure, but its applicability to students is limited because its privacy provisions are not applicable to education records that are subject to FERPA and treatment records that are exempted from FERPA. It should be noted, however, that those treatment records may still be subject to a state's medical records laws regarding access and disclosure.

FERPA also creates numerous exceptions under which an institution can disclose student education records without a student's consent. These disclosures without consent exist for a wide range of purposes, such as health and safety emergencies, lawfully issued subpoenas, disclosures to authorized government agencies, and disclosures to other school officials in the institution with a legitimate educational interest.

There are broad categories of information ("directory information") that FERPA allows, but does not require, institutions to release without the student's consent. This is information that would not generally be regarded as harmful to the student, such as name, address, enrollment status, major field of study, participation in recognized activities, and honors and awards. The student may "opt out" from having such information released.

There has been much misunderstanding both within and outside higher educational institutions as to the extent that FERPA's exceptions permit the institution to release information to parents, professional personnel, and law enforcement and to meet the obligations imposed on the institution by other legislation. Some institutions have declined to provide parents or guardians with information that they could otherwise provide in accordance with one of the enumerated exceptions. Although some reluctance may be attributed to confusion about the applicability of the exceptions or conflicts in interpretation, others may relate to the particular institution's sense that the individual student should be entitled to more privacy protection than required by the act. In the past decade, additional exceptions and/or clarification to the disclosure provisions have been added to address subject areas, including violation of alcohol and drug policies and violence, that schools felt reluctant to address in disclosures to parents and guardians and to clarify that such disclosures are permitted, as well as certain public disclosure regarding information that might relate to the safety and welfare of the university community (Cleary Act).

In the wake of highly publicized tragedies at Virginia Tech and other institutions, state and federal governments reexamined their privacy policies to ensure that they did not unduly inhibit the flow of information to those with a need to know, regardless of whether they were within or outside the institution. In October 2007, the DOE issued a brochure highlighting exceptions under which student education records may be disclosed to parents or others without a student's consent. In addition to FERPA issues, the brochure also contains information on the release of student health information, disciplinary records, law enforcement records, and releases relating to the Campus Crime and Reporting Act (Cleary Act) and Student and Exchange Visitor Information System (SEVIS).

Disciplinary records are considered education records under FERPA. However, disciplinary actions may be disclosed without the student's permission to the alleged victim of any crime of violence or nonforcible sex offense once a decision has been rendered. Final results of a disciplinary hearing may also be disclosed to the university community regardless of whether the student was found to be in violation of the institution's rules and regulations.

The act is replete with particulars that define the circumstances that permit disclosure. In March 2008, the Department of Education issued proposed guidelines that clarify and update matters relating to the privacy of student records and the exceptions under which student information may be disclosed. Among the updates and clarifications are that Social Security numbers and student ID numbers cannot be disclosed as directory information; parents are appropriate parties to whom a disclosure can be made in a health and safety emergency; an institution must use reasonable methods to ensure that school officials obtain access only to those education records in which they have legitimate educational interests. The department also removed language that would have limited disclosures for health and safety purposes to those that were strictly necessary to address the specific health or safety emergency and added a provision that an institution may take into account the totality of the circumstances pertaining to a threat to the safety or health of a student or other individuals. If the institution determines that there is an specific and significant threat to the health or safety of a student or other individuals, it may disclose information from education records to any person whose knowledge of the information is necessary to protect the health and safety of the student or other individuals.

When institutions use third parties rather than their own personnel to provide certain services, then the institution may allow the third parties to have access to education records under the same conditions that access is permitted to school officials, namely, when there is a legitimate educational interest to disclose. The outside parties must operate under the direct control of the institution and have procedures in place that limit further disclosure of student education records.

Violations of FERPA are addressed through complaints to the Family Policy Compliance Office (FPCO) at the Department of Education. Findings of violations may result in sanctions ranging from reprimand to loss of federal funding. There is no private right of action by individuals for alleged institutional violations of FERPA. The Family Policy Compliance Office has responsibility for oversight and enforcement of FERPA and has promulgated a model notice along with other information that is available to provide technical assistance to institutions.

Jeanne Cleary Act

The Jeanne Cleary Act was named for a Lehigh University freshman who was raped and murdered in 1986 while asleep in her dormitory room. After Jeanne's parents learned that the university had not told students about thirty-eight violent crimes in the three years preceding her murder, they joined with others to lobby for federal reporting requirements. In 1990 Congress passed the Crime Awareness and Campus Security Act of 1990, which has come to be known as the Cleary Act.

The law requires universities to notify the campus community of certain criminal activity and includes a provision giving individuals who bring sexual assault complaints access to information regarding the institution's findings. When a crime takes place on or near its campus that the school believes presents a threat to students and employees, the act requires a timely notice to the campus community of the threat to aid in the prevention of similar crimes. This is a significant aspect of the statutory requirements, and universities must decide on the form these notices will take and the level of detail they will contain. These determinations are most often made by campus police and security working in conjunction with student affairs officials. Allegations of violation of this particular provision are often made in the wake of campus tragedies.

Universities are required to keep a daily log of and annually report to the campus community a number of serious crimes reported to local police agencies or to a campus security authority: criminal homicide; sex offenses, forcible or nonforcible; robbery; aggravated assault; burglary; motor vehicle theft; manslaughter; arson; and arrests for liquor law violations, drug-related violations, and weapons possession.

Universities must also record and report other crimes involving bodily injury to any person in which the victim is intentionally selected because of the actual or perceived race, gender, religion, sexual orientation, ethnicity, or disability of the victim that are reported to campus security authorities or local police agencies. In addition to reporting arrests for liquor and drug law violations and illegal weapons possession, the act also requires recording and reporting referrals for campus disciplinary action for liquor law violations, drug law violations, and illegal weapons possession. The annual statistical report must cover three years of information and advise the campus community where the state maintains registered sex offender notices.

The university must record and report those crimes or referrals occurring on campus, on public space near campus, and on off-campus locations that are related to the school. The report must provide a geographic breakdown of crimes in those three categories.

Liability for Internet Use

The federal Digital Millennium Copyright Act (DMCA) limits the liability of Internet service providers (ISPs) such as colleges and universities for inadvertent Internet copyright infringement by providing space for infringers or providing access to infringed materials. ISPs are required to comply with demands from copyright holders to remove infringed material from their servers and have a policy of excluding repeat infringers.

Conclusion

As Donald Gehring (2000) noted, "The law has definitely arrived on campus. It permeates every program, policy, and practice of the institution" (p. 371). This is particularly true in the relationship between the college or university and its students. Student affairs professionals must be aware in general of the legal issues discussed in this chapter and can find additional information concerning legal issues related to higher education from professional associations of student affairs administrators. Administrators must also be prepared to seek legal advice from their college counsel when needed. The proper course of conduct for the university in a particular situation will depend on the specific facts, the current state of the ever-evolving law, as well as the public or private nature of the institution. Legal counsel for the university can guide the student affairs professional through this legal thicket.

References

Black, H. C., and Garner, B. A. (Eds.). *Black's Law Dictionary* (7th ed.). New York: West, 1999.

Gehring, D. D. "Understanding the Legal Implications of Student Affairs Practice." In M. J. Barr, M. K. Desler, and Associates (Eds.), *The Handbook of Student Affairs Administration* (2nd ed.). San Francisco: Jossey-Bass, 2000.

Prosser, W. L. *Handbook of the Law on Torts*. St. Paul, Minn.: West, 1971.

Cases Cited

Albano v. Colby College, 822 F. Supp. 840 (1993).

Alumni Ass'n v. Sullivan, 572 A.2d 1209 (Pa. 1990).

Beach v. University of Utah, 726 P. 2d 413 (1986).

Bradshaw v. Rawlings, 612 F. 2d 135 (3rd Cir. 1979).

Brueckner v. Norwich University, 730 A. 2d 1086 (1999).

Eiseman v. State, 489 N.Y.S. 2d 957 (1985).
Ely v. Murphy, 540 A. 2d 54 (Conn., 1988).
Graham v. Montana State University, 767 P. 2d 301 (1988).
Gratz v. Bollinger, 539 U.S. 244 (2003).
Grutter v. Bollinger, 539 U.S. 306 (2003).
Guckenberger v. Boston Univ., 974 F. Supp. 106 (D. Mass. 1997).
Heller v. Consolidated Rail Corporation, 576 F. Supp. 6 (E.D. Pa. 1982).
Jarzynka v. St. Thomas University, 323 F. Supp. 2d 660 W.D. Pa. 2004).
Johnson v. State of Washington, 894 P. 2d 1366 (Wash. App. 1995).
Knapp v. Northwestern University, 938 F. Supp. 508 (1996).
Knapp v. Northwestern University, 101 F. 3d 473 (3rd Cir. 1996).
Lamphere v. State of New York, 91 A. 2d 54 (1982).
L.W. v. Western Golf Association, 675 N.E. 2d 760 (1997).
McGuiggan v. New England Tel and Tel Co., 496 N.E. 2d 141 (Mass., 1986).
Miller v. State, 478 N.Y.S. 2d 829 (Ct. App. 1984).
Mullins v. Pine Manor College, 449 N.E. 2d331 (Mass. 1983).
Pitre v. Louisiana Tech University, 661 So. 2d 454 (1998).
Rabel v. Illinois Wesleyan University, 514 N.E. 2d 552 (Ill. App. 1987).
Regents of the University of California v. Bakke, 438 U.S. 265 (1978).
Rosenberger v. Rectors and Visitors of the University of Virginia, 515 U.S. 819 (1995).
Scaduto v. State of New York, 86 A.D. 2d 682 (1982), aff'd 56 NE 2d 281 (1982).
Sharkey v. Board of Regents, 615 N.W. 2d 889 (Neb. 2000).
Shin v. Massachusetts Institute of Technology, 19 Mass. L. Rptr. 570 (Mass. Super. 2005)
Smith v. Day, 538 A. 2d 157 (Vt. 1987).
Terminiello v. Chicago, 337 U.S.1 (1949).
University of Denver v. Whitlock, 744 P.2d 54 (1987).
Whitlock v. University of Denver, 712 P. 2d 1072 (Col. App. 1985).

Federal Laws and Regulations Cited

Americans with Disabilities Act of 1990 (ADA) (42 USC §12101)
Crime Awareness and Campus Security Act of 1990 (Cleary Act) (20 USC §1001)
Digital Millennium Copyright Act (DMCA) (17 USC 101)
Family Educational Rights and Privacy Act (FERPA) (20 USC §1232)
Health Insurance Portability and Accountability Act (HIPAA) (42 USC §1320d-2)
Jeanne Cleary Disclosure of Campus Security Policy and Campus Statistics Act (Campus Security Act) (20 USC §1092e)
Rehabilitation Act of 1973, Section 503 (29 USC 793), Section 504 (29 USC §794)
Student and Exchange Visitor Information System (SEVIS) (6 USC §252)
Title VI of the Civil Rights Act of 1964 (41 USC §2000 d)
Title IX of the Education Amendments of 1972 (20 USC §1681)

CHAPTER TWENTY-SEVEN

IMPLEMENTING ASSESSMENT TO IMPROVE STUDENT LEARNING AND DEVELOPMENT

Marilee J. Bresciani

Conversations about outcomes-based assessment appear to be everywhere, thanks in part to increased pressure from regional accreditors, state legislators, and the Commission on the Future of Higher Education (U.S. Department of Education [DOE], 2006). However, outcomes-based assessment is not a new idea—not in the least. Having at its core the inquiry-based notion of "How well are we doing what we expect to accomplish?" outcomes-based assessment has been around in various versions for some time (Bresciani, 2006; Ewell, 2002; Maki, 2004; Palomba and Banta, 1999; Suskie, 2004; Upcraft and Schuh, 1996). In its earliest form and in regard to student learning, outcomes-based assessment dates back to A.D. 1063 at the University of Bologna, where outcomes-based assessment of student learning was known as "juried reviews" (Carroll, 2005; cited in Bresciani (2006).

> Here, the master teacher quizzed the student about what faculty expected the
> student to have learned. In a window above the testing platform, another profes-
> sor would stand, ensuring that the quality of the line of questioning was sound
> and that the student's responses were, in fact, acceptable for the level expected.
> In the jury in front of the student sat the professors who taught the student,
> expecting to see in the student's responses, the information they delivered to the
> student in their teachings. This early form of inquiry was passed from academy

to academy and today, we see its historical presence in university structures at the University of Bologna and at the Universidad de Salamanca. This method of internal accountability for ensuring quality learning has continued in some form or another into the present day. (Bresciani, 2006, p. 7)

Student affairs practitioners are confused about what is meant by outcomes-based assessment and how it may differ from previous self-reflection practices (Bresciani, Zelna, and Anderson, 2004; Maki, 2004; Suskie, 2004; Upcraft and Schuh, 1996). Perhaps it is because outcomes-based assessment has existed for many years in various forms, known in those forms by terms such as *institutional effectiveness (IE), TQM (total quality management),* and *continuous quality improvement (CQI).* It may be that the lack of readily available evidence of contributions to student learning and development from student affairs practitioners is not because of a lack of evaluation practice, but because of a lack of a shared conceptual framework and common language for the self-reflection practice.

This chapter provides a brief historical overview, discusses the need for assessment, and explores three common approaches to assessment. In addition, it illustrates the importance of student affairs practitioners' ability to evaluate their contributions to student learning and development through these varied approaches. Finally, the chapter concludes with some suggestions for implementing assessment.

Historical Overview

Identified as TQM, Six Sigma, CQI, IE, or other well-known acronyms, the notion of exploring whether what you are doing is working in the way you had intended remains a consistent theme no matter what it is called or how it is systematically implemented (Bresciani, 2006; Ewell, 2002; Upcraft and Schuh, 1996). Regardless of its organizational model, the idea of investigating whether what we expect to accomplish is truly what we are accomplishing has historically been most often identifiable in the business industry (Bresciani, 2006; Ewell, 2002; Upcraft and Schuh, 1996). As such, those student affairs professionals attentive to business practices found themselves readily adapting such inquiry and evaluation processes as their own, particularly in the area of evaluating the effectiveness of their services. However, professionals still found it challenging to address their units' contributions to student learning and development.

Some student affairs practitioners are unsure of how to respond when asked to describe how what they are doing contributes to student learning and development. The American College Personnel Association (ACPA) and the National Association for Student Personnel Administrators (NASPA) have published many helpful documents to stimulate student affairs practitioners in their thinking about their contributions to student learning and development. The *Student Learning Imperative* (American College Personnel Association [ACPA], 1996) was one of the most influential documents in the area of evaluating student learning and development within student affairs. Since then, other documents from ACPA, NASPA, and the National Research Council (2001) have stimulated continued discussion among student affairs professionals to consider just how they contribute to student learning and development.

Recent publication of several helpful "how-to" documents (Bresciani and Gardner, in press; Bresciani and others, 2004; Suskie, 2004; Upcraft and Schuh, 1996) on implementing outcomes-based assessment has been instrumental in many co-curricular professionals refining the evaluation of their services; however, legislators and others are still demanding more evidence regarding how student affairs contributes to student learning and development. The following section illustrates the reasoning behind the increase in demand for evidence of these contributions to student learning and development.

Evaluating Contributions to Student Learning and Development

Since 1985, several regional accrediting organizations have steadily increased their demand for institutions to articulate and evaluate student learning outcomes. This is a direct result of increased pressure from the federal government. As a part of this requirement, some regional accreditors, such as the Southern Association of Colleges and Schools (SACS), Middle States Commission on Higher Education, and Western Association of Schools and Colleges (WASC), have articulated clear and rigorous expectations that student support services document their contribution to student learning and development. Such accreditation requirements have appeared to raise the awareness among many professionals that their role in learning and development is recognized; now all they need to do is to provide evidence of their role through outcomes-based assessment.

The Student Learning Imperative (ACPA, 1996) is considered by many to be a pivotal piece that highlights the role of student affairs in the support of student learning and development; it is filled with research that generated questions and challenges for student affairs professionals. The characteristics describing learning-oriented student affairs practitioners outlined in the preamble of this document were designed to stimulate ideas and connections illustrating a variety of ways that student affairs service practitioners contribute directly and indirectly to student learning and development. The ideas presented in this document appear to be designed to generate discussion, planning, and action for many divisions. While the *Student Learning Imperative* is packed with provocative ideas and challenges, it is not evident how many student affairs practitioners have adopted its visionary thought and put those inventive ideas into practice.

In concert with the Higher Education Re-authorization Act conversations of 2002, regional accreditors pressed colleges and universities to articulate their contributions to student learning and development. For example, the Council of Regional Accrediting Commissions (CRAC) came together in 2003 to establish good practices in the assessment of student learning. In these documents (Council on Regional Accrediting Commissions [CRAC], 2003), CRAC emphasized the importance of the institution holistically evaluating the capacity that it has to contribute to enhanced student learning and development. The CRAC document authors posit guidelines and questions that invite the collaborative exploration of how every aspect of the academy is fostering student learning and development and how it knows that it is.

The Commission on the Future of Higher Education published its final report in September 2006 (U.S. Department of Education, 2006). In this report, the commission called for more accountability in higher education and transparency in institutional achievement of student learning. Interesting to note is that earlier drafts of the report appeared to accuse student affairs professionals of spending large amounts of money with no apparent contribution to student learning and development. Later versions of the report seemed remiss in acknowledging student affairs contributions in assisting with issues of access, affordability, and quality.

Current conversations surrounding the demand for evidence of student learning and development cut across political party lines and across state and federal thresholds. At the time of publication, states are being asked to carry the burden of demanding evidence of student learning and development from all components of the academy and from all institutional types. Representatives of disciplines are being asked to demonstrate how they know students are learning what they expect students to learn regardless of institutional organization. This is an opportunity for student affairs professionals to come together to articulate the contributions of their services. For example, the discipline, if you will, of career services could articulate shared learning and development outcomes for students it serves, as could the disciplines of residence life, academic advising, health and wellness, and financial aid.

Learning Reconsidered: A Campus-Wide Focus on the Student Experience (Keeling, 2004), a joint ACPA and NASPA document, was published in 2004. This document seemed to command practitioners' attention more than the documents that preceded it, possibly due to increasing accreditation requirements. Timely in its publication, *Learning Reconsidered* highlighted much of the previous research in student development and learning and emphasized the importance of evaluating student learning and development within student affairs and in partnership with academic colleagues.

The National Survey of Student Engagement (NSSE) Documenting Effective Educational Practice (DEEP) Project (Kuh, Kinzie, Schuh, and Whitt, 2005a, 2005b) builds upon earlier work and offers practitioners a tremendous amount of practical advice in how to collaboratively evaluate student learning and development. Kuh and his colleagues illustrate twenty colleges and universities that collaborate across division lines to identify how they are improving student learning and development in addition to providing questions that any institution can adapt and investigate on their campuses.

The intent of the NSSE DEEP Project (Kuh and others, 2005a, 2005b) is to provide guidelines for reflection and conversation across departmental and division lines, so that student learning centeredness can be collaboratively planned, delivered, and jointly evaluated. Its purpose is similar to *Learning Reconsidered*, the *Student Learning Imperative*, and the Council for the Advancement of Standards in Higher Education's *Frameworks for Assessing Learning and Development Outcomes* (2006).

Assessment Approaches

If we become convinced that there is a need to evaluate student learning and development, then we may only need to learn how to do it. If that is the case, there are a variety of assessment approaches that could be employed, depending on the intent of the practitioner, to gather much needed assessment data to address the concerns of how student services and student affairs practitioners contribute to student development and learning, The aforementioned resources, along with many others (Allen, 2003; Bresciani and others, 2004; Palomba and Banta, 1999; Suskie, 2004; Upcraft and Schuh, 1996) are designed to assist academic and instructional services and student affairs professionals with the steps and guidelines to implement meaningful and manageable outcomes-based assessment.

There are a number of approaches to implementing assessment. Each may be different in its intent and purpose and produce information that leads to various decisions or conversations about the quality of education. For simplicity, these approaches may be categorized as follows:

- Preassessment, student satisfaction, utilization data, and needs assessment,
- Outcomes-based assessment, and
- Astin's (1993) Inputs-Environment-Outcomes (IEO) model.

Resources cited in the sections that follow more fully illustrate the details of each approach.

Preassessment, Student Satisfaction, Utilization Data, and Needs Assessment

This group of assessment approaches produces helpful data that can inform the planning of services and educational support activities (Upcraft and Schuh, 1996). Utilizing data gathered from these methods allows student affairs practitioners to more purposefully plan their programs, outreach, services, and activities with student attributes in mind.

For example, *preassessment* data is collected on students prior to their entering the collegiate experience. One purpose of preassessment data is to understand who the students are who are entering the programs so that student affairs practitioners can more intentionally design programs that will meet the needs of students. For example, preassessment data gathered from such instruments as the Cooperative Institutional Research Program ([CIRP], 2007) may inform faculty and administrative expectations about who the students are as they design their classes and programs for incoming students. The College Student Expectations Questionnaire (College Student Experiences Questionnaire Research Program, 2007) and other related instruments can help inform faculty and administrators about student expectations and be used for assisting in students' transitions to college. Similarly, instruments such as Sedlacek's noncognitive variables (2004) can be instrumental in informing specific interventions to assist students to address noncognitive challenges instrumental to their academic success.

While preassessment data is very helpful in informing the preparation of programs and services, it is not helpful in indicating whether a planned program has accomplished what it was intended to accomplish on its own. However, preassessment data, if used intentionally, may be very helpful in articulating outcomes and planning their delivery so that those outcomes can later be evaluated with outcomes-based assessment practices.

Student satisfaction instruments are very useful when evaluating how satisfied students are with services and programming (Bresciani and others, 2004; Palomba and Banta, 1999; Upcraft and Schuh, 1996). Many administrators and constituents simply want to know if students are happy with services and programs; therefore, practitioners often engage in this type of evaluation. However, such data rarely provides information that can meaningfully identify what is "wrong" if a student is unsatisfied. For example, if 80 percent of first-year students report that they are satisfied with financial aid counter staff, what would the financial aid office do with that information? Would the financial aid staff be happy or disappointed? If they wanted to improve that 80 percent satisfaction rate, what would they do? This method of assessment did not give them the kind of detail needed to inform specific decisions.

Utilization data can be very useful for understanding how much or how little services are used, by whom, and when (Upcraft and Schuh, 1996). This data assists managers with staff scheduling, with providing explanations to students as to when and why service response declines, and with resource reallocations and budgeting. Utilization data is often used in outcomes-based assessment to supplement an understanding of why an outcome was met or not met. For example, if the quality of learning certain outcomes in standard substance abuse peer-advising sessions declines, the decline may be attributed to the fact that peer advisors are shuffling through students quickly in order to ensure that the students do not wait longer than one hour. In moving students through so quickly, the peer advisors may not have time to teach students all they want them to know in their one-on-one appointments and may have no time to find out whether their students understand what they were taught. In this example, the office utilization data can support the interpretation in the decline of learning. Similarly, if students report low satisfaction with student health during the time when there was increased utilization of student health services, the utilization data can support the interpretation and possibly the explanation of the satisfaction findings.

Needs assessment data is collected so that students' needs can be identified empirically (Upcraft and Schuh, 1996). Program coordinators can gather needs assessment data to assist with planning activities and programs that students report they need. Outcomes-based assessment, however, can require that students draft their own outcomes for programs they request, thus asking the students to clarify their needs in a manner in which they identify the end results of a requested activity. Such an exercise allows the students to differentiate between requesting an activity for an activity's sake versus desiring and then intentionally planning for the end result of the activity. Student affairs professionals can spend time learning about what their students need by the students self-reporting. This can have great value. Another approach is for student affairs professionals to discover students' needs through the students' articulation of outcomes generated from the students' desire for a particular activity or program.

Outcomes-Based Assessment

Outcomes-based assessment has many definitions (Palomba and Banta, 1999). Regardless of which scholar's definition you choose to utilize in your practice, you will notice that many of these definitions have in common the notion of continuous improvement (Allen, 2003; Banta, 2002; Bresciani and others, 2004; Maki, 2004; Palomba and Banta, 1999; Suskie, 2004). Continuous improvement means there is an assumption of purposeful planning for the delivery and evaluation of intended end results. In addition, the evaluation process is designed so the information gathered can be used to inform meaningful decisions about how the intended outcomes or end results can be met at a greater level of quality for the group that was included in the evaluation.

In outcomes-based assessment, the professional intends to evaluate the end results of the "doing" in a manner that specifies what she wants to have accomplished, how she plans to deliver it, how she plans to evaluate it, and then later report on what she has learned about what she intended to accomplish in a manner that allows her to make decisions to specifically improve the "doing." In outcomes-based assessment, the professional is simply asking and answering the following questions:

- What are we trying to do and why? *or*
- What is my program supposed to accomplish? *or*
- What do I want students to be able to do and/or know as a result of my workshop/orientation?
- How well are we doing it?
- How do we know?
- How do we use the information to improve the delivery of doing or celebrate successes?
- Do the improvements we make work? (Bresciani, 2003, p. 15)

In order to answer these questions, cause-and-effect methodology is not used. Contrary to many research epistemologies, outcomes-based assessment is not used to "prove" that learning and development are occurring; rather it embraces Papert's (1991) epistemology of situational constructionist learning. In this epistemology, the notion of discovery and response to that discovery is paramount. Papert posits that the more we learn about how well we are delivering what we hope students will be able to know and do within a certain situation, the more we will refine our delivery so that we see more evidence of student learning and development in that specific situation for those specific students.

This epistemology highlights the iterative nature of outcomes-based assessment. The end result of outcomes-based assessment is not intended to be considered research or inform how practices should be done for all students. Using this epistemology, the intended end result of outcomes-based assessment is to engage in a systematic self-reflection process where one uses the findings to inform refinements in how programs are delivered and evaluated, as well as to inform how resources are reallocated, policies improved, and organizational values clarified. The self-reflection process is necessary as an effort to improve the underperforming student and her situation that is specific to her current institution or program within that institution.

Practitioners commonly draw upon research to determine what proven intervention could address a concern that the professionals have for a certain group of students when planning to deliver their outcomes. Research may also help articulate what the end results of that activity should be. Research findings often assist the professional with her interpretation of the outcomes-based assessment results for that purposefully planned program. However, the results of most outcomes-based assessment cannot be considered research, for often the methodology used in the process is not one that would hold up to the rigor of many established research methodologies. In addition, often the sample or population being evaluated is simply not generalizeable to other populations.

The point in all of this is to clarify that outcomes-based assessment is not intended to be research. Outcomes-based assessment is designed to be a systematic self-reflection process that provides the practitioner with information on how to improve his planning and delivery processes. While findings from this process are most likely not generalizeable to other settings, the data gathered can be instrumental in demonstrating accountability. Merriam-Webster defines *accountability as* "the quality or state of being accountable; *especially*: an obligation or willingness to accept responsibility or to account for one's actions" ("Accountability," 2007). Used in this manner, outcomes-based assessment exemplifies accountability because it demonstrates responsibility for purposeful planning and the use of information derived from systematic evaluation to illustrate what is needed to improve student learning and development.

Some may choose to apply research rigor as they engage in outcomes-based assessment. When that occurs, we may very well be discussing another approach, such as Astin's (1993) Inputs-Environment-Outcomes model.

Astin's Inputs-Environment-Outcomes Model

Astin's (1993) IEO model focuses on assessing the characteristics of incoming students, their interactions with the institution, and their characteristics when departing. In this model, *I* stands for inputs, in that an institution would thoroughly evaluate what skills and attributes a student is bringing into a program. *E* indicates environment, which is that which an institution can account for in delivering the learning and development that occurs while a student is at the institution. *O* illustrates outcomes, meaning the end results of student learning and development that the student would possess when leaving the institution.

In Astin's model, more rigorous methods of research can be employed, for one is evaluating how well prepared the student is at entrance into the program, cognitively and affectively. Then, the purposeful planning ensues to deliver the appropriate experience or intervention to heighten learning. Finally, the evaluation of the outcomes ensues, so it can be determined what was gained during the educational experience. Cause-and-effect research may still be elusive, because controlling for variables that may intervene from outside the learning environment is nearly impossible. However, with the Astin IEO model, the types of pre- and postevaluation that informs value-added conversations are within reach and should be explored by those programs that have the resources to do so.

Inputs. Input indicators in higher education have traditionally been centered on those that are easy to measure, gather, compare, and report (Astin, 1993). Studies summarized by Pascarella and Terenzini (2005) indicate a multitude of inputs that may prove more illustrative in understanding how well prepared students are to enter college and therefore can inform the design of a more successful college experience. Such input indicators include evaluating student's readiness to learn, such as understanding their motivation for learning, their commitment to taking responsibility for their own learning, and the support that they have in place to enhance their learning (Pascarella and Terenzini, 2005). Sedlacek (2004) adds to these variables positive self-concept or confidence, realistic self-appraisal, understanding of and agency for diversity, preference for long-term planning over short-term goals or immediate needs, availability of strong support persons, successful leadership experience, demonstrated community service, and knowledge acquired in a field.

Institutional leadership would evaluate these complex input variables prior to a student's matriculation into the institution. In so doing, the leadership would better understand how the student is prepared to succeed and would gather additional information at the level of detail that could influence planning curriculum, programs, and interventions in order to contribute to the student's success.

Environment and Outputs. Pascarella and Terenzini (2005), along with Astin (1993) and others (Kuh and others, 2005a; Manning, Kinzie, and Schuh, 2006), emphasize that if it is understood how a student enters college, and a supportive educational experience is designed with intended learning outcomes, then a student should be able to be successful in his or her educational endeavors, given all foreseeable variables. There are many unforeseeable variables in life and in the life of the adult learner; however, the process of mindfully designing a student's learning experience seeks to work within what is known and thereby improve the student's ability to learn (Bresciani, 2006; Papert, 1991).

Therefore, it must be clearly understood how students enter into college, how the college is designed specifically to contribute to that student's success, and how the college intends to evaluate the student's success. Given all this complexity, one can quickly see the need for collaboration and intentional planning that cuts across reporting lines or programs and departments. This is an opportunity to try to shape the collegiate environment to achieve desired student learning (outputs). It is also an excellent opportunity to develop partnerships and relationships across the institution, as discussed in Chapters Twenty-One and Twenty-Three.

Portfolio assessment is an example of the evaluation of a comprehensive learning and development experience. Such an output measure of the value added by the collegiate environment requires a great deal of communication so that the collaborative ways in which students learn specific outcomes can be identified and agreed upon by all the players in the educational experience. In addition, the criteria for evaluating that learning across the demonstrated domains must also be discussed and agreed upon. Many institutional leaders may feel they do not have the time or the means to even host such collaborative discussions, as it can be a very time-consuming process. In addition to the discussion in Chapters Twenty-One and Twenty-Three about developing collaborative partnerships and relationships, models for establishing such collaborative, rich reflections of value-student learning can be found in the research of Mentkowski (2000), the National Research Council (2001), Maki (2004), and Huba and Freed (2000).

Implementing Assessment

Because the need for engagement in outcomes-based assessment of student learning and development is real, and because there appears to be little chance that the need will dissipate, the challenges facing student affairs officials in preparing to competently engage in outcomes-based assessment must be addressed. The American College Personnel Association (2006) published the *Assessment Skills and Knowledge Content Standards for Student Affairs Practitioners and Scholars* to respond to the growing need to make sure student affairs professionals are prepared for outcomes-based assessment. The standards recommend that practitioners know the many facets of implementing and managing assessment, from being able to articulate outcomes to knowing how to benchmark data to being able to educate others on the value of outcomes-based and other forms of assessment.

Student affairs practitioners should understand how what they do daily contributes to enhancing the learning and development of the students with whom they interact and how to responsibly engage in assessment practice. Furthermore, there are other aspects of institutionalizing outcomes-based assessment in an effective, efficient, and enduring manner that are also important to consider.

The following guidelines, adapted from Bresciani (2006), shares some practical suggestions for addressing the concerns facing student affairs practitioners as they prepare to engage in outcomes-based assessment.

1. *Make assessment a priority.* Take the time to reflect and plan for your program's contribution to student learning and development. It is often said that we spend time on what we value or what we are told to value. If leadership emphasizes the importance of setting aside time to plan for how each unit directly or indirectly contributes to student learning, each unit may be able to better articulate how they intend to support and contribute to student development and learning. As such, each unit would then be able to better plan for the evaluation of their contributions to learning and development. In addition, if the college or university states that it is committed to collaborating across departmental and division lines to improve student learning, then it would follow logically that leadership would provide opportunities for such collaborative dialogue, planning, and action to occur. If assessment is not made a priority, or if leadership does not provide opportunities for learning to be improved, it simply will not occur (Allen, 2003; Banta, 2002; Bresciani, 2006; Maki, 2004; Palomba and Banta, 1999; Suskie, 2004).

2. *Reallocate time to engage in assessment.* Student affairs practitioners need to reallocate time from their doing to the reflection on their doing (Bresciani and others, 2004). There is no such thing as more time. There is only a certain amount of time, and if we allocate time according to what we value or what we are told to value, then we must reallocate from our doing to the reflection and evaluation of our doing. (See Chapter Eight for further discussion on the value of reflection in practice.) We must shift our mentality from programming "more" to simply planning and evaluating what we are doing in order to improve or completely revise what we are trying to accomplish.

   In considering the re-allocation of time to implement assessment, consider reallocating time for each of the following steps (excerpted from Bresciani and Gardner, in press):

   a. Identify the alignment of the program's values or goals with the institutional, division, or statewide goals and the professional standards, if applicable. Goals are broad, general statements of (1) what the program wants students to be able to do and to know, or (2) what the program will do to ensure what students will be able to do and to know. They are often derived from the program, division, or institutional mission statement.

b. Articulate the primary outcomes for the program. (Select the outcomes that represent theoretical or programmatic priorities.) Outcomes are detailed and specific statements derived from each goals. Outcomes are specifically about what the end results are intended to be. In other words, what will the student know and be able to do as a result of the one-hour workshop, series of workshops, one-hour individual meeting, or Web site instructions? Outcomes are not planning steps of how you intend to deliver the end result, rather they use action verbs that help identify how well the student knows and can do that which is expected.

c. Identify the ways in which students will be provided all of the opportunities to learn that which is expected of them (for example, outcomes). Outcomes are often derived from the theories that undergird practice. Therefore, it is important to ensure that students are provided with opportunities to learn what they are expected to learn and at the level that they are expected to learn (for example, Bloom's (1956) taxonomy, which includes the components of knowledge, comprehension, application, analysis, synthesis, and evaluation). Literally mapping out the opportunities for students to learn also provides an opportunity to identify embedded opportunities to evaluate the learning and development.

d. Select evaluation methods, tools, and criteria to assess each outcome. Selecting one tool or method for each outcome is a great beginning. As habits of reflection are developed, more tools and methods can be added. Ensuring that the criteria used for evaluation are aligned with the theory that informed the practice and the outcomes will assist with the analyzing of the data and interpretation of results.

e. Analyze the results utilizing any expert help available to you, if necessary.

f. Interpret the findings, using national literature and expert opinion, if applicable. Involving colleagues and students in the interpretation of the findings may also prove beneficial.

g. Make decisions and/or recommendations to improve the opportunities for student learning and development, refine the assessment process, outcomes, or evaluations tools and criteria.

h. Follow up at the appropriate time (for example, next semester or three years later) to determine whether the decisions made contributed to improved student learning and development.

3. *Purposefully plan for what will work at your institution.* Resist the urge to adopt a "plug 'n' play" approach. As we have discussed, the meaningful engagement

in assessment is not intended to be an activity that is checked off a list of things that must be done; rather, it is intended to be purposeful reflection of how well the end results were accomplished. The pitfall of not allocating time for reflection and evaluation is that the evaluation process itself becomes another task, rather than an intellectual reflection of how the program is contributing to enhancing student learning and development. It is important for student affairs practitioners to resist this; assessment is an opportunity to reflect on why and how student learning and development are being promoted through every aspect of their work. Such intentional reflection includes resisting the urge to adopt a set of outcomes published by another group. Rather, professionals need to engage in collaborative conversations across departmental and division lines in order to find meaning and value in the intended end results that inform planning, delivery, and evaluation processes. In some cases, it may be best for some student affairs or services units to begin this conversation internally before inviting academic colleagues into their conversation. However, in an effort to educate the whole student, academic colleagues should ultimately be included in the conversation.

4. *Create the opportunities to learn assessment.* We would never expect one of our students to try to mediate an argument among her peers without first being provided an opportunity to learn how to mediate. Why is it then that we ask our colleagues to quickly draft assessment plans demonstrating their programs' contributions to student learning and development without ever having been taught how to do so? While several professional preparation programs around the country teach research, how many teach students how to design and implement meaningful and manageable outcomes-based assessment plans, particularly in regard to student learning and development? We need to continue to provide student affairs staff with opportunities and time to learn how to engage in effective, efficient, and enduring outcomes-based assessment practices. The *Assessment Skills and Knowing* (ASK) document (ACPA, 2006) is a good start toward articulating the competency expectations for all student affairs practitioners. Professional organizations and individual colleges and universities across the country provide many professional development opportunities for student affairs professionals to learn the ASK competency expectations.

5. *Learn the theoretical underpinnings of what you do.* Many student affairs staff members have never had the opportunity to learn the theory, such as the developmental theories that inform leadership development models or engagement theories that inform intervention programming. Moreover, those who learned the theories may not have been provided opportunities to discover

new identity development hypotheses and groundbreaking notions such as Bensimon's (2006) deficit-minded decision-making model. We need to commit to reinforcing a scholar-practitioner model within our profession. This may include a commitment to continuing education, such as (a) providing and participating in professional development opportunities at conferences or internally within our divisions/department, (b) establishing mentoring programs or train-the-trainer concepts, and (c) participating in collaborative research and evaluation.

6. *Align theories to planning and the evaluation of the planning.* Once the theoretical models have been learned, practitioners need to commit to articulating them as the underlying reasons for their models for programming and service. Similarly, such models can inform the manner in which these professionals engage in the assessment of their programs, informing methodology as well as criteria for evaluation. When one has colleagues who are unclear about how they directly or indirectly contribute to student learning and development, it may be because they are not aware of the theories that support the very existence of their service provision. Helping colleagues understand the professional literature (for example, engagement theories, student departure theories, identity development theories, models of wellness) will allow them to focus on evaluating their services while drawing on the professional literature to provide the framework that binds their services to learning and development. For example, if dining services staff do not understand how they connect to student learning and development, ask them if they are aware of the research on body image and wellness and how a student's identity contributes to his or her ability to learn. Once they have learned this body of knowledge, staff can better conceptualize how to teach students about proportions, nutrition charts, and food combinations in order to show how dining services is contributing to student learning and development. Such purposeful planning, delivery, and evaluation of direct and indirect contributions to student learning begins with the knowledge of student learning and development theories and hypotheses as well as the knowledge of how to engage in outcomes-based assessment.

7. *Consider whether you can soundly engage in Astin's IEO Model.* Consider whether you have the resources to try to "prove it." In this age of accountability, some practitioners get lost in thinking they need to prove that their program is accomplishing that which they say it is. Attempting to prove that one program can solely develop a student or be the one reason that learning was improved is simply not possible, unless you construct a rigid experimental control group. The practice of student affairs is not often afforded the luxury of controlling variables to allow for the inference of cause and

effect. Further, to try to design a clinical experience in which a practitioner would withhold an intervention or program that they believed to be beneficial to a student would most likely be considered unethical by a human subjects review board. Thus, it is important for practitioners to understand that what they are doing by engaging in assessment is not trying to prove cause and effect; rather they are engaging in systematic purposeful reflection where they state what they intend to accomplish (for example, outcomes), plan the program intended to meet those outcomes (for example, planning), evaluate to what extent the outcomes were achieved (for example, assessment), and use the information to further improve the program (for example, accountability). If the program is sophisticated enough and practitioners are able to collaborate with others to design a rigorous Astin (1993) IEO model for evaluation, do it. The profession will no doubt benefit from the discovery.

8. *Don't try to evaluate everyone and everything.* Another reason that student affairs practitioners become overwhelmed with the outcomes-based assessment challenge may be that they try to program for the entire student body when their constituent base may be much smaller. In realizing who your constituents are, practitioners can begin their evaluation with just those students.

Similarly, if services are delivered only in a one-on-one capacity, consider whether everything needs to be evaluated. For example, the effectiveness of certain types of one-on-one interventions can be evaluated rather than the effectiveness of every one-on-one interaction with every student. Finally, remember to use samples of the student population; not every student has to be evaluated.

9. *Involve the students.* Students themselves can be incredibly helpful in the students affairs practitioners' realization that too much learning is expected of them, given the mechanisms available to deliver the learning. Students can assist in illustrating that they cannot be expected to synthesize the wellness decision-making model in a one-hour workshop; rather, a more reasonable goal might be to have them identify the steps of wellness decision making in a case study. Students are incredibly helpful in critiquing student learning and development outcomes, in identifying means to evaluate the outcomes, and in articulating criteria that will evaluate the outcomes. If staff understand how the student development and learning theories they learned in school feed into the design and evaluation of their programs, they can better articulate this to students, allowing students to better understand themselves and the role they play in their own learning. Likewise, students will be able to better facilitate the connection from their classroom learning

to their co-curricular learning, because student affairs is facilitating the self-evaluation of their learning and development (Kuh and others, 2005a, 2005b; Mentkowski, 2000).

10. *Collaborate, collaborate, and collaborate.* Many student affairs practitioners make the mistake of articulating student development and learning outcomes in isolation from their student affairs colleagues and from their academic colleagues. If we truly desire more connectedness in the total student learning and development experience, then we must make ourselves vulnerable to enter into conversations with our faculty colleagues about how their classroom work could be reinforced or emphasized in the out-of-classroom experience. Student affairs professionals should take the initiative to learn about what faculty are teaching, so student affairs programs can be offered as opportunities for co-curricular learning laboratories. This kind of collaboration does take time and it takes relationship and trust building. However, if we truly desire to embody the teachings from the *Student Learning Imperative* (ACPA, 1996), *Learning Reconsidered* (Keeling, 2004), and the NSSE DEEP Project (Kuh and others, 2005a, 2005b), we will reallocate our time to designing integrated learning opportunities.

Finally, to employ the exemplar Astin's (1993) IEO model of assessment, consider evaluating the entire educational experience at the institution rather than evaluating just one program. While the Commission on the Future of Higher Education (U.S. Department of Education, 2006) recommended that all student affairs practitioners be required to engage in value-added assessment, it is this author's understanding that we would ask questions that identify the value that has emerged as a result of a student's engagement in the entire undergraduate or graduate experience, not just within one program. If we keep this broader goal in mind, it may further encourage us to engage in collaborative discussions about the very essence of our profession: exploring and improving the whole student learning and development experience through outcomes-based assessment.

References

Accountability. *Merriam-Webster On-Line Dictionary.* [http://www.m-w.com/dictionary/accountability]. 2007.

Allen, M. J. *Assessing Academic Programs in Higher Education.* Bolton, Mass.: Anker, 2003.

American College Personnel Association. *Assessment Skills and Knowledge Content Standards for Student Affairs Practitioners and Scholars.* Washington, D.C.: American College Personnel Association, 2006.

American College Personnel Association. *The Student Learning Imperative: Implications for Student Affairs*. Washington, D.C.: American College Personnel Association, 1996.

Astin, A. W. *Assessment for Excellence: The Philosophy and Practice of Assessment and Evaluation in Higher Education*. Phoenix, Ariz.: Oryx, 1993.

Banta, T. W. *Building a Scholarship of Assessment*. San Francisco: Jossey-Bass, 2002.

Bensimon, E. M. *The Underestimated Significance of Practitioner Knowledge in the Scholarship of Student Success*. Presidential address for the Association for the Study of Higher Education Annual National Conference. Anaheim, Calif., November 2006.

Bloom, B. S. (Ed.). *Taxonomy of Educational Objectives, the Classification of Educational Goals. Handbook I: Cognitive Domain*. New York: McKay, 1956.

Bresciani, M. J. "Expert Driven Assessment: Making It Meaningful to Decision Makers." *ECAR Research Bulletin*, 21. Boulder, CO: EDUCAUSE, 2003.

Bresciani, M. J. *Outcomes-Based Academic and Co-Curricular Program Review: A Compilation of Institutional Good Practices*. Sterling, Va.: Stylus, 2006.

Bresciani, M. J., and Gardner, M. M. (in press). *Demonstrating Student Success in Student Affairs*. Sterling, Va.: Stylus.

Bresciani, M. J., Zelna, C. L., and Anderson, J. A. *Techniques for Assessing Student Learning and Development: A Handbook for Practitioners*. Washington, D.C.: National Association of Student Personnel Administrators, 2004.

Carroll, M. Keynote at the Association of Institutional Research National Conference. San Diego, Calif., 2005. As cited in Bresciani, M. J., *Outcomes-Based Academic and Co-Curricular Program Review: A Compilation of Institutional Good Practices*. Sterling, Va.: Stylus, 2006.

College Student Experiences Questionnaire Research Program. *About the College Student Experiences Questionnaire*. [http://cseq.iub.edu/csxq_generalinfo.cfm]. 2007.

Cooperative Institutional Research Program. *CIRP Freshman Survey*. [http://www.gseis.ucla.edu/heri/freshman.html]. 2007.

Council for the Advancement of Standards in Higher Education. *Frameworks for Assessing Learning and Development Outcomes*. Washington, D.C.: Council for the Advancement of Standards in Higher Education, 2006.

Council of Regional Accrediting Commissions. *Regional Accreditation and Student Learning: Principles of Good Practices*. Washington, D.C.: Council of Regional Accrediting Commissions, 2003.

Ewell, P. T. "An Emerging Scholarship: A Brief History of Assessment." In T. W. Banta (Ed.), *Building a Scholarship of Assessment*. San Francisco: Jossey-Bass, 2002.

Huba, M. E., and Freed, J. E. *Learner-Centered Assessment on College Campuses: Shifting the Focus from Teaching to Learning*. Needham Heights, Mass.: Allyn & Bacon, 2000.

Keeling, R. P. (Ed.). *Learning Reconsidered: A Campus-Wide Focus on the Student Experience*. Washington, D.C.: American College Personnel Association and National Association of Student Personnel Administrators, 2004.

Kuh, G., Kinzie, J., Schuh, J. H., and Whitt, E. *Student Success in College: Creating Conditions That Matter*. San Francisco, CA: Jossey-Bass, 2005a.

Kuh, G., Kinzie, J., Schuh, J. H., and Whitt, E. *Assessing Conditions to Enhance Educational Effectiveness*. San Francisco, CA: Jossey-Bass, 2005b.

Maki, P. *Assessing for Student Learning: Building a Sustainable Commitment Across the Institution*. Sterling, Va.: Stylus, 2004.

Manning, K., Kinzie, J., and Schuh, J. H. *One Size Does Not Fit All: Traditional and Innovative Models in Student Affairs Practice*. New York: Routledge, 2006.

Mentkowski, M. *Learning That Lasts: Integrating Learning, Development, and Performance in College and Beyond.* San Francisco: Jossey-Bass, 2000.

National Research Council. *Knowing What Students Know.* Washington, D.C.: National Academy Press, 2001.

Palomba, C. A., and Banta, T. W. *Assessment Essentials: Planning, Implementing, and Improving Assessment in Higher Education.* San Francisco: Jossey-Bass, 1999.

Papert, S. "Situating Constructionism." In I. Harel and S. Papert (Eds.), *Constructionism.* Cambridge, Mass.: MIT Press, 1991.

Pascarella, E. T., and Terenzini, P. T. *How College Affects Students, Volume 2. A Third Decade of Research.* San Francisco: Jossey-Bass, 2005.

Sedlacek, W. E. *Beyond the Big Test: Noncognitive Assessment in Higher Education.* San Francisco: Jossey-Bass, 2004.

Suskie, L. *Assessing Student Learning: A Common Sense Guide.* Bolton, Mass.: Anker, 2004.

U.S. Department of Education. *The Commission on the Future of Higher Education Draft Report of 8/9/2006.* [http://www.ed.gov/about/bdscomm/list/hiedfuture/reports/0809-draft.pdf]. 2006.

Upcraft, M. L., and Schuh, J. H. *Assessment in Student Affairs: A Guide for Practitioners.* San Francisco: Jossey-Bass, 1996.

CHAPTER TWENTY-EIGHT

PROGRAM PLANNING AND IMPLEMENTATION

Michael J. Cuyjet and Sue Weitz

The development and implementation of programs is a central activity for student affairs professionals. In its broadest sense, a *program* is a cohesive arrangement of information, activities, services, or resources that supports the educational and developmental aims of the institution. Whether the program is a major new initiative, a one-time event, or a series of events, the ability to plan and implement effective programs is essential for effective service delivery. Barr and Keating (1985) identified three essential elements in planning and implementing any program: the context, the goal, and the plan (p. 3). This model, although more than twenty years old, continues to serve as a viable basis for a wide range of programming endeavors. In this chapter, we offer the Barr and Keating model, with a few refinements and the addition of a fourth component, as an outline for student affairs professionals to use for successful program development.

The chapter begins with an explanation of the basic Barr and Keating (1985) program planning model. An example of application of the model with regard to major initiatives follows. The chapter then focuses on the one-time activities or series of activities and programs that take much time and effort on the part of student affairs professionals, and we provide examples of applications

The authors wish to acknowledge the contributions of Joan Claar, who coauthored the chapter on program planning and implementation in the second edition of this handbook, from which this chapter is adapted.

545

of the model and specific steps for success in program planning: particularly, we discuss a demonstration of the fourth element of the model, the implementation stage. Next, the chapter offers suggestions for practice that should assist student affairs professionals in improving their skills and competencies in the art of program planning and implementation, followed by a case study of a one-time activity. The chapter concludes with a diagram of program planning steps to provide a clear visualization of the program development model.

The Model

Three assumptions underlie the Barr and Keating (1985) model of program development and implementation. First, the student affairs professional must understand and be able to apply a variety of theories to the task of program development. Second, there are three equal elements involved in program development: the context, the goal, and the plan or method. A third assumption is that all three program elements must be congruent in order for the program to succeed (Barr and Keating, 1985, p. 3). While we have added a fourth element—implementation—to the model in order to broaden its potential use to a wider range of applications, this does not alter the three basic assumptions. Each of the four elements is essential and interdependent, and this interdependence is critical to program success. These are displayed in Figure 28.1. As the following discussion illustrates, successful program planning is both a skill and an art.

Planning and Implementing Major Initiatives

The components of context, goal, plan, and implementation apply to the planning process whether a new program is being created, an existing program is being enhanced, or a program is being eliminated. The process applies equally to major events and to single activities. We are defining a major programming initiative as an activity that is more than one event and may include the addition or deletion of an office or function or significant enhancement of an existing program, such as orientation.

Context

A major initiative must be planned with consideration for the culture of the college or university, the need for and possible benefits of the program within the institution, external issues or concerns, interested constituencies, the resources

FIGURE 28.1 TYPICAL PROCESS OF PROGRAM PLANNING AND IMPLEMENTATION

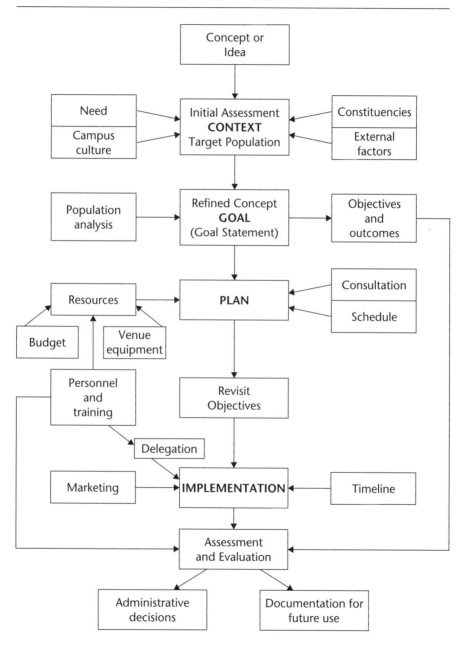

required, availability of human and fiscal resources, and timing. Failure to address these issues of context can result in the failure of an otherwise well-planned program. In the alternative, actively building positive cultural traits into programming can foster student success in numerous ways by exposing program participants to elements of the campus culture with which they may have had little or no experience.

The culture of a campus "is the collective pattern shaped by the combination of institutional history, mission, physical setting, norms, traditions, values, practices, beliefs, and assumptions that guide the behavior of individuals and groups in a college or university" (Kuh and Whitt, 1988, p. 37). Campus culture "can bring a measure of coherence to campus life that helps people make meaning of events. Moreover, student success is advanced when the culture values talent development, academic achievement, and respect for human differences" (Kuh, Kinzie, Schuh, Whitt, and Associates, 2005, p. 273).

Developing a program that is contrary to the prevailing institutional culture is likely to generate a considerable amount of resistance despite any potential value. For example, changing a lounge in a residence hall with a traditional-aged population to a facility to attract nontraditional-aged commuter students to stay on campus after attending classes may be highly beneficial for the improvement of nontraditional students' experiences at the institution. However, the potential for opposition by current residents who use the lounge in its current configuration and consider it their "turf" must also be considered and addressed as part of the planning if the change is to be successful.

The need for a proposed program within the institution also must be considered. No matter how good the plan for an initiative or program may be, if it is not needed or if the identified need is being successfully met in another way or through another program, the new initiative should not go forward. Sometimes the realization that the needs are being met in other ways does not occur until after the plan has been implemented and similarities become clear.

When analyzing or assessing needs, perceived need as seen through the eyes of particular constituencies can be as compelling as real need determined by empirical data or reliable anecdotal evidence. Student affairs professionals become adept at honoring the perceptions of groups and individuals as being real to them regardless of whether the perceptions are accurate, appropriate, or in line with campus culture. Perceived need will drive the understanding and response of a distinct group to the addition, deletion, or modification of an existing program or the introduction of a new program or event. Sincere consideration of the perceptions of impacted groups or individuals can dispel the appearance of unilateral or biased decision making and may broaden buy-in from the community.

Program planning sometimes requires consideration of factors external to the institution before a new program is undertaken. If the institution purchases a large home for the purpose of creating a new multicultural living unit for students and then discovers that the city requires a specific number of parking spaces for multiple dwelling residences, implementation of the new program in that location may not be possible unless the parking problem can be solved. Even if city regulations provide no obstacle, the attitudes and concerns of the other homeowners in the surrounding neighborhood may need to be evaluated and addressed.

The availability of institutional fiscal resources is a reality that has a direct influence on program planning and implementation. Resource needs for the program include the budget for any new staff required, facilities, and direct programming money. The addition of a separate office to serve the needs of gay/lesbian/bisexual/transgendered (GLBT) students may be desirable, but if the budget is frozen and vacant positions are not being filled, development of the office may have to be delayed. It may be possible, however, to reorganize existing programs and resources to begin providing some new GLBT services immediately, or there may be ways to achieve the outcomes desired without the creation of a new office. All options should be explored.

Goal

Providing a clearly articulated goal that can be understood and embraced by interested constituencies is critical for building understanding and support for a new program. The program goal must be consistent with the mission of the institution, and there should be widespread agreement within the campus community that the goal is desirable. When eliminating a program, it is important to inform others, especially those who are directly involved with the program, whether the goals of that program will continue to be met when the entity no longer exists.

When developing a goal statement, language that is understandable to all should be used, and terms that confuse and frustrate those who are not in student affairs should be avoided. Frustration can result in creating the suspicion or belief that the language is being used to artificially elevate the importance of the program and that the need for the program is questionable. A goal statement also helps determine if there are other programs on campus with similar or related activities. Faculty and staff involved in those established efforts might see the proposed program as taking over their territory. If there is a possibility of that response, the proposed program should be discussed with appropriate persons from the other area before planning begins.

When developing a major initiative and establishing the goal, consideration should be given to how successful achievement will be determined. The act of establishing a program, function, or office does not guarantee success. How will you and others know if the program has fulfilled the goal and how will that goal contribute to the welfare of student constituents? Specific suggestions for effective goal setting and establishing measurable learning outcomes are addressed later in this chapter.

Plan

When creating or eliminating an office or function, having a plan is essential. The plan should include the goal, consultation and involvement with others, a preliminary schedule, a proposed budget, facility needs, an outline of the program (including a goal statement), and an evaluation mechanism. When ending a program, consultation and involvement are essential, and a thoughtful and articulate goal or reason for the program's demise is essential. Frequently, when a program is eliminated, it is done in order to make resources available to add a function or office in an area with higher priority. The plan, goal, and rationale must be well conceived and well communicated to concerned constituents.

Case Example: Changing the Culture in a Residence Hall

The following case example helps illustrate the complexity of developing and implementing major program initiatives. Specifically, it offers an example of a programmatic intervention to bring about a more positive culture in a residence hall.

The Context

A small, traditional, residential liberal arts college in the Midwest is located in a small rural community. Almost all students live in college housing, which remains predominately single-gender residence halls. Although approximately one third of the students are affiliated with the local fraternities and sororities, no Greek housing exists, and affiliated students live in the residence halls. One of the men's halls has long been the building of choice for athletes because of its extra large rooms and its location across the street from the athletic facilities. This hall has had, for more than twenty years, a well-earned reputation as an "animal house." Students were generally resigned to behaviors of the men living in the hall because they saw the administration taking no action and felt that "this is just the way it is here."

The Goal

The new dean of students had been at the college for a year and observed that much of what was negative in the out-of-class environment of the college could not be changed until the residence life experience was significantly modified. The goal was to make the residence life experience more positive by making more halls coeducational. The men's hall in question was one of those targeted to become coed. A key to the successful fulfillment of the goal was modifying the unacceptable behavior in the men's hall.

The Plan

The final decision about the changes in residence halls had to be made prior to room selection in the spring. The plan included the following steps:

1. Notifying all students about the proposal and setting up opportunities for them to discuss it with residence life staff,
2. Meeting with the coaches of men's sports to obtain their support and discussing the proposal, reasons for needing change, and potential advantages for men's athletics,
3. Presenting the proposal to the student life committee of the faculty,
4. Notifying the chair of the student affairs committee of the board of trustees,
5. Keeping the president's cabinet informed about the status of the proposed changes, and
6. Making the decision using the information gathered and making appropriate modifications in the proposal.

The dean of students sent a letter to all students, announcing the proposed changes, enclosing a copy of the proposal, and reporting that the residence life staff would hold an open meeting in each of the eight residence halls on campus. As students discussed the issues in the meetings, many became highly supportive of the plan. They were favorable about the increase in coeducational living opportunities and became increasingly outspoken about the physical and behavioral conditions in the men's hall in question. Some of the men in the hall to be changed were irate and started a campaign to defeat the proposal. Others living in the hall that did not like the environment gave the plan quiet, behind-the-scenes support.

After securing support across campus, the change of the men's hall to a coeducational hall was made. Some of the men who were opposed started rumors suggesting that women who moved in would not have a pleasant experience, and women students were concerned about moving into that environment. The residence life staff designated that hall as a leadership and service learning hall and required all students interested in living there to complete an application committing themselves to involvement in leadership and service learning activities. Those who had serious disciplinary problems were not permitted to live in the hall.

Assessment and Evaluation

The change in the environment in the residence hall was dramatic, and it became one of the preferred living options on campus. Vandalism and damage in the building were significantly diminished. This result was possible through careful, comprehensive planning and deliberate action. Good communication, both with administrators and campus constituencies, contributed to the positive outcome.

Planning and Implementing Specific Activities

Many student affairs professionals spend much of their time and effort developing and implementing specific activities and programs such as concerts, plays, and lectures. Success of these programs is also dependent on understanding the context, goal, and plan. In practice, some event programmers may not think of applying a general programming model to the development of events. They just do the program: scheduling the facility, contacting the participants, using the local campus media to inform the audience, and cleaning up afterward. Although this method may work for some, developing and consistently employing a model has several advantages including training of new staff, reduction of trial-and-error mistakes, establishing greater consistency in the entire programming process across different events, and providing a mechanism for evaluating and improving the program development process. The primary benefit of using a program model is to provide an opportunity to lay an adequate contextual and theoretical foundation for each program before just jumping in and doing it.

The programming endeavor can be a powerful teaching tool for new professionals and students. Even community colleges, smaller four-year schools, or graduate schools within a large university have numerous events that must be developed and presented. These events offer an opportunity to new professionals to hone skills that they will ultimately find necessary in more complex contexts later in their careers. Engaging students in the programming endeavor creates a sense of ownership and connectedness that might be missing from events carried out solely by administrators and professional staff.

Fresh eyes may be the greatest benefit that a new professional or student can bring to the process. The neophyte is often not burdened with the same assumptions that longer-term staff may have. Questions about why things are done a certain way, alternative ways to accomplish the intended goal, and clarifications about campus culture can offer a different perspective on routine tasks. Of course, certain parameters must be respected for organizational efficiency. Despite this, proper mentoring and supervision can result in new approaches.

Context

The Barr and Keating model (1985) calls for consideration of context on three levels: the higher education context as it relates to the greater society, the contextual elements of one's particular college or university, and finally, the assessment of the environment within the student services unit of the campus. Contextual assessment for event programming focuses on the latter and mandates narrowing that focus from student affairs as a single entity to the unique characteristics of a student affairs agency or possibly a subunit of such an agency. For example, a counselor at a community college considering the context for a program she is contemplating for second-year students to begin planning for transfer to four-year schools must be aware of any general programming parameters of the counseling center and the mission of the student affairs division, as well as any influences the target population's demographics may have on program implementation. Moreover, contextual elements of the students—their awareness of baccalaureate opportunities, their aspirations to continue their education, their class and/or work schedules, the ways in which they tend to interact—are also prime considerations in the planning of any successful activities for this specific population.

Goal Setting

The Barr and Keating (1985) model recommends three general goals for programming on the campus: to provide essential institutional services, to teach life management skills, and to provide links for the integration of knowledge between the curriculum and the co-curriculum. This perspective provides an important starting point for the activities programmer, but there are more detailed elements of the goal-setting process that must be considered. A first step might be to select one or more of these three major goals as a starting point (recognizing that only the more complex events and activities might successfully address more than one goal), and then determine exactly which institutional service, life skill, or element of knowledge is to be the specific focus of the program or activity.

Population Analysis. Further refinement might include an assessment of the targeted population to determine their specific goals. For example, a career counselor might set out to design a program with the general institutional service goal of providing career planning skills to a group of students. Without further refinement of this goal, the program is likely to be inappropriate for a portion of the potential audience or to miss the mark altogether. In this case, class rank of potential participants might influence whether the goal was long-range career planning activities for freshmen or short-term strategies for seniors. The major field of study of participants, as well as whether they are in undergraduate or graduate programs, might cause a shift in planning strategies. Other characteristics, such as gender or ethnicity or age, could also alter the goals for the program, as would the longevity of the program itself—a one-time program would have different expected outcomes than a series of sessions over an extended period of time.

Objectives. Because broad-based goals are difficult to assess, specific, measurable objectives should be used to facilitate evaluation and to help determine the success of a program. Objectives for the career program might include attracting a minimum number of participants, having those participants schedule a certain number of follow-up visits, or reaching a satisfaction level as measured by a summary written evaluation completed by participants. Each of these objectives can be measured in a tangible way.

Outcomes. It is important to articulate carefully the desired outcomes of the program. Be clear about what you expect to accomplish and what you expect participants to achieve. As the relationship between student services and the academic units of the institution become more and more collaborative (Manning, Kinzie, and Schuh, 2006), there are increasing expectations that the outcomes anticipated for student participants in our programs be part of their holistic learning, providing them with usable skills and knowledge. For example, learning outcomes for a career development workshop for freshmen might include students will demonstrate familiarity with the location of the career development center and the resources available there; students will establish early contact in the first year with career center staff who can help them throughout their enrollment; students will demonstrate familiarity with lesser-known career options; students will demonstrate understanding of the correlation between minimum skills for particular careers and academic courses to acquire them; and students will demonstrate the ability to use this acquired knowledge to make informed decisions about their career paths after leaving the institution.

Plan

Barr and Keating (1985) advise that "whatever planning techniques are employed, whatever the size or complexity of the ultimate program endeavor, a systematic, time-delineated program plan must be developed if the student services program is to succeed" (p. 9). The program planner in search of a model to follow will have no lack of choices from which to select. A series of models developed in the 1970s are reviewed by Styles (1985) and include Lewis and Lewis's Schematic for Change (1974), the Aulepp and Delworth Ecomapping Model (1976), Drum and Figler's Outreach Model (1973), Morrill, Oetting, and Hurst's Cube (1974), and Moore and Delworth's Training Model (1976), which arose from work with the Western Interstate Commission for Higher Education (WICHE) and focused on a systematic development of training programs. Many of these models are interrelated: Moore and Delworth's work for WICHE is based on the Cube from Morrill and others, which emphasizes that good programmatic interventions include attention to the target, the purpose, and the method of intervention. These three components are precursors to the three elements of the Barr and Keating model. All can still be useful tools for programmers. Several more recent models might also be helpful for programmers seeking a blueprint to follow. Included in this group would be the Barr and Cuyjet (1991) program planning model and Cuyjet's (1996) later adaptation of it. Regardless of which model one chooses to follow, there are a number of essential elements that should be incorporated into the planning stage of the process.

Revisit Objectives. As the planning for the program begins, reconsider the goals and objectives and carefully identify the initial intent of the program. Is this a one-time event, a pilot program, a possible precursor to one or more subsequent programs, or a part of a clearly defined series? Are all of the objectives clear at the onset, or is it possible that components may be added to the program in the process of program development? The planning process will need to be much more flexible if links to other programs need to be established or if consideration needs to be made for program components to be added as the event begins to unfold.

Resources. Probably the most critical component of the planning process in program development is the identification of the necessary resources. No matter how innovative the idea or how admirable the goals and objectives, if the resources are not available, the program cannot succeed. Among the resources usually required for a viable program are personnel to carry out the production tasks, a suitable venue for the event, adequate equipment for each aspect of the program, and ample funding (which requires a realistic budget for clear identification and effective distribution of those funds).

Personnel. Another important consideration is the staff who will be involved in the program. The event actually requires two teams, a planning team and an implementation team. Although these groups often consist of the same people (particularly at small schools), it is sometimes convenient to think of them as two discrete operations in order to better track progress and accomplishments. Thus, the completion of the planning stage of the event should signal a point at which some formative assessment of the event's elements is made and any additional planning elements are added as the actual program is undertaken. Most program planning and implementation teams work best if comprised of a small but effective group that is able to function together as a unit and whose members, collectively, possess all the skills necessary to perform the tasks required. Particular skills that may be important for at least one member of the group to have might include the following:

- Ability to coordinate administrative functions in order to manage the team itself,
- Clerical ability in order to maintain good records and process correspondence and other written communications,
- Artistic or design skills for creating publicity materials,
- Knowledge of facilities management for selecting and preparing the site of the program,
- Budgeting and financial management skills,
- A knowledge of local resources,
- Ability in resource procurement; that is, someone with the appropriate contacts for soliciting and securing necessary items,
- Representation or firsthand knowledge of the target population or others affected by the program, particularly if the target is not a mainstream group,
- Ability to anticipate issues related to institutional requirements, risk management, and professional and organizational relationships and effectively deal with those issues,
- Aptitude in effective coordination of program assessment, and
- Evaluation of assessment data as it applies to future programming activities.

Another important factor related to staffing is the training provided to the team members. Some general orientation to the goals of the program and the target population usually is needed. Remember that training requires both information and resources, so be sure to allow for both in the planning of the event.

Budget. Another important part of the planning process is the identification of necessary resources to implement the program. The budgeting process generally has two components. First, the programmer determines the actual amount of money necessary to complete the program, including all costs for personnel, materials, space, marketing, assessment and evaluation, telecommunications, postage, food, transportation, and equipment. Second, after a total budget figure is determined, a realistic source of revenue needed to cover these expenses must be identified. Revenues may come from a single source, such as an allocation from a small school's dean of students' budget from general college funds to provide resume writing workshops for seniors. On the other hand, the budget for a major music concert at a large, urban university may rely on an elaborate web of support from a variety of sources, including ticket sales, revenues from related merchandise, student activities fees, grants and gifts, and profits from other student-sponsored entertainment events.

Venue. Prepare the location you have selected for the program. Whenever possible, the site should be barrier free, highly visible, and easy to find. If the only available venue is *not* easy to find, additional efforts, such as added marketing and/or special transportation to the location, may be desirable. Parking, accessibility for those with mobility impairments, aesthetics, and proximity to related programs are additional considerations to be taken into account. If the program consists of a series of events, using a consistent place, day, and time is usually recommended.

Equipment. Be certain adequate amounts of all needed materials and devices are on hand and in good working order. If trained personnel, such as lighting, sound, or computer technicians or interpreters for the hearing impaired are required, make sure they are available and that you provide all the materials they will need.

Theoretical Foundation. An often-overlooked step in the planning of events or programs is to identify a theoretical basis for the program. Initiatives such as *A Perspective on Student Affairs* (National Association of Student Personnel Administrators, 1989) and the *Student Learning Imperative* (American College Personnel Association, 1996) have focused attention on the need of all forms of student affairs programming to support the academic mission of the institution by contributing to the comprehensive development of students within the academic community. *Learning Reconsidered* (Keeling, 2004) affirms that all we do on the campus, including event programming, is part of students' learning experience, and *Learning Reconsidered 2* (Keeling, 2006) instructs us to identify measurable learning outcomes for all of our programmatic endeavors. Programmers may also look to other models, such as critical theory that reflects the influence of social, political, economic, ethnic, and gender factors on students' reality; and constructionist theory, which incorporates experiences and perceptions of individuals and groups as they influence the concept of reality (Guba and Lincoln, 1994). That the community and interpersonal interaction occurring in many programs has been found to enhance retention (Astin, 1984; and Tinto, 1993) provides yet another theory-based incentive for sound program planning.

Timeline. Planners need to consider two aspects related to the timing of the event. First, because programs do not occur in a vacuum, planners need to be aware of other events scheduled on the campus. This includes other similar programs that may be redundant or provide some of the same service or information and, therefore, split the target audience. However, timing also means avoiding other significant events and programs in the campus community. Certainly, the academic significance of midterm or final examinations precludes many other events from occurring during those periods. Timing also dictates that events celebrating significant campus traditions (for example, Founder's Day, homecoming, or commencement) should be respected. Dates of significant community holidays celebrated by major religious traditions should be noted and avoided, if possible.

The second aspect of timing relates to the establishment of a timeline for the program. The successful programmer identifies the date of the program, identifies all of the tasks that need to be accomplished in order to bring the event to fruition, and then works backward from the target date to establish a realistic, week-by-week activity plan.

Shared Resources. In addition to the scheduling issues mentioned in the section on timing, event planning should include consideration of how an event fits into the bigger picture on the campus. Seeing a program as part of the comprehensive offerings of the campus community not only gives a common purpose to the event, but also provides opportunities for collaboration and the sharing of personnel, funds, and materials. With the ever-present concern for the efficient use of resources, complementary programming with other agencies should be considered. To illustrate, different floors in a residence hall could cosponsor a lecture by a guest speaker or agree to support each other's programs by their mutual attendance. As another example, a community college programming board and a local community service agency that seem to share a target audience (for example, single-parent students with children) could agree either to advertise each other's programs or to cosponsor a single event.

Academic units should also be considered as program collaborators. For example, lecture or film series offerings sponsored by a club, organization, or the student activities office might be discussed in a classroom setting with credit for attending the event. There is much synergy to be created in a partnership of academics and student affairs, particularly in a service-learning context.

Implementation

The last step in the planning phase of the model refers to the actual program or event itself. To get to that end product, there are two more steps to the process: implementation and evaluation. The following are several important considerations for the implementation phase.

Delegation. Getting any of the implementation steps accomplished begins with delegating tasks and responsibilities to the members of the program planning team and identifying clear lines of accountability, reporting relationships, and deadlines. Backup responsibilities to cover all tasks in case someone fails to carry out an assignment will provide an additional margin of safety for program completion.

Marketing. Those charged with marketing should develop and initiate a marketing plan well in advance of the program itself, using a variety of media to catch the attention of both the target group and any peripheral audience that can help pass information to that target group. For example, a workshop on developing better research skills among new graduate students could also be publicized to faculty who may then encourage their students to attend. The key is to identify those who might be interested in the topic and to discover the optimal ways to reach them.

Assessment and Evaluation

Upcraft and Schuh (1996) describe assessment as "any effort to gather, analyze, and interpret evidence" (p. 18) and evaluation as "any effort to use assessment evidence to improve . . . effectiveness" (p. 19). Thus, assessment is the process of collecting feedback from program participants (and planners), and evaluation is the use of those data for making decisions about subsequent programming.

Collect evaluative responses from as many program participants as is feasible. Use a variety of media, including written forms, face-to-face interviews, Web sites, e-mails, suggestion cards, or telephone calls. Because you will want to gather evaluative data on the process (how the planning and implementation went) as well the content (the elements contained in the program itself), be sure to solicit evaluative data from members of the planning and implementation team, too. See Chapter Twenty-Seven for suggestions for use of assessment and evaluation in practice.

Analyzing how the planners and workers interacted with the process should be an important consideration. The assessment and evaluation of the personnel and training aspects of the endeavor can be seen as distinct from that of the objectives and outcomes aspect. Each program can serve as a reality check on the efficiency of the process for the people involved. It is too cumbersome? Are steps repeated for different offices depending on the specific needs of that office? Can steps be streamlined without losing proper oversight or due diligence? Complex organizations do not necessarily require complex processes in order to function. When new professionals or students are involved, there is potential for creating a fatigue or discouragement factor if the planning and implementation process is perceived as too burdensome. This hinders the teachable moment and creates disincentives to undertake future programs.

Administrative Decision. After examining all the information compiled in the evaluation phase, decide on one of three actions for the future of the program: continuation, modification, or abandonment. Continuation decisions should specify a definite period of time and include provisions for ongoing review. Modification decisions should delineate very carefully the changes recommended and the reasons for them. Abandonment decisions should offer compelling reasons and offer suggestions of possible alternate approaches to meet the goals that will be unmet when the program is abandoned. Even if the program was a one-time event, do not omit this step. Instead, make a determination as to which of the three actions you would recommend in case the program is considered for presentation again in the future. For events occurring infrequently, such as an annual program, make sure evaluation data will be readily available when the next planning team begins the process again.

Case Example: Providing a Nonalcoholic Activity Night

How might the model be applied to the development of a specific activity? The following case study offers an example of developing a nonalcoholic activity night.

The Context

A medium-sized faith-based university in the Northwest is located in an urban area that is surrounded by large expanses of rural land. The students are generally Caucasian, middle- to upper-middle-class, and eighteen to twenty-two years of age. The men's basketball team is very successful, and all home games are sold out. A regular occurrence for many students was attending private postgame parties off campus at which large amounts of alcohol are provided and consumed. There were no other organized activities offered at this time. A significant number of students used and abused alcohol at these gatherings, and the impact on academics, health, relationships, and crime was apparent. The influence was particularly noted in the residence halls occupied by first- and second-year students, all less than twenty-one years of age. Incidents in the halls typically spiked three to four hours after the game ended and students returned to their rooms. Disruptive behavior of all sorts, vandalism, assaults, and alcohol poisoning cases strained the resources of the residence hall staff, security department, and the peaceful nature of the community.

The Goal

The student activities office partnered with the wellness office to present a program that filled the niche of late-night activities for students and provided a nonalcoholic alternative to the postgame parties. The program consisted of one activity night after the last home game of the men's basketball season. Success would be gauged on participation, student reaction (through an on-site survey), any reduction in the level of disruptive late-night activity in the residence halls, and the efficiency of mounting the program.

The Plan

A committee of three organizers met for six weeks prior to the event. The committee consisted of a staff member of the wellness office, a staff member from the activities office, and a professional residence director from the housing office. Each of these persons had student staff available to assist him or her. Budgetary resources were obtained from the three offices, and the committee members also secured funding from athletics and the student life office. In-kind donations were obtained from local merchants.

The committee consulted with various campus groups and organizations to determine what would be most appealing to a student with a choice of drinking at a party or trying a nonalcoholic alternative event. The residence hall association conducted an informal poll by floor and building. The student senate provided data from a previous survey of upper-class students on programming. The wellness office already had data from alcohol intervention programs (assigned as a sanction for alcohol violations) about students' perceptions of parties, alcohol, alternative activities, and drinking habits. Once this information was assimilated, a revised goal was articulated: the objective would be to reduce illegal and problem drinking after a home basketball game by providing an alternative activity. The outcome would be to improve the living-learning experience of students, particularly in the residence halls, as well as to normalize nonalcoholic events as a viable ongoing alternative to parties.

The program was planned to coincide with the last home basketball game, so the date was firm. Data from the consultation phase was used to determine the hours most likely to appeal to the target audience. The venue for the event was selected based on foot traffic patterns around the athletic facility and residence halls. At an initial meeting, a timeline was established for completion of certain tasks (for example, major aspects of the marketing plan, procurement of prizes and donations, recruitment of event night volunteers), and achievement of benchmarks. The timeline was crucial even though not all the other pieces were in place, and in fact, most of the subcommittee assignments were not yet developed or assigned. Each committee member assumed a number of tasks and delegated work to student volunteers. As the project moved forward delegated tasks were added, removed, or modified based on conditions encountered by the committee. For example, risk management was not initially a specific task, but it became apparent that some of the planned activities, such as the mechanical bull ride, could entail some potential for injury. A marketing plan was developed to serve two purposes: normalize the nonalcoholic alternative and promote the specific event. The wellness office took the lead on this task and used current best practices related to social norms that were already utilized in other wellness initiatives.

Assessment and Evaluation

After the event, the committee met to formulate a list of questions that were later presented to the larger group of student volunteers and others that worked on the event. These data assisted the committee in understanding if those directly involved perceived the program as successful, as well as identifying areas that were problematic or could be improved. Student participant data were also analyzed, as were statistical data from the security department and personal observations by the residence hall staff of postgame incidents. The assembled data were then presented to the dean of students and other decision makers who approved several activity nights for the next basketball season. Included among the recommendations was a suggestion to approach managers of local off-campus apart-

Recommendations for Practice

Program planning and implementation is a process, but it is also an art. The same skill set needed to mount a major campus initiative is needed for a one-time program in order to produce a successful outcome. The following recommendations for practice may provide assistance to program planners.

1. Do not underestimate the importance of both timing and process. In a controversial program proposal, inadequate attention to either process or timing can result in it, instead of the actual program content, becoming the central issue.
2. Involve students in planning programs and listen to them. Student involvement, especially from the target constituency, can result in a program that is more relevant to students, and students can do a great deal to encourage attendance.
3. Communicate with other concerned constituents early in the planning process.
4. Identify the individual with responsibility for leading the initiative and provide support for that person.
5. Do everything possible to succeed, but be willing to fail and to learn from that experience.
6. Be prepared to make adjustments in the plan as needed.
7. Try to engage as many people as possible in the planning and implementation of programs—there is a great deal of expertise on any campus.
8. Enjoy the process of planning and implementing programs and use the process as an opportunity to teach students and staff.
9. Remember that the context, goal, and plan are important, but that the most important element is a committed and interested staff member. People do make the difference.

References

American College Personnel Association. "The Student Learning Imperative: Implications for Student Affairs." *Journal of College Student Development*, 1996, 37(2), 118–122.

Astin, A. W. "Student Involvement: A Developmental Theory for Higher Education." *Journal of College Student Personnel*, 1984, 25(5), 297–308.

Aulepp, L., and Delworth, U. *Training Manual for an Ecosystem Model.* Boulder, Colo.: Western Interstate Commission for Higher Education, 1976.

Barr, M. J., and Cuyjet, M. J. "Program Development and Implementation." In T. K. Miller and R. B. Winston Jr. (Eds.), *Administration and Leadership in Student Affairs: Actualizing Student Development in Higher Education* (2nd ed.). Muncie, Ind.: Accelerated Development, 1991.

Barr, M. J., and Keating, L. A. "Introduction: Elements of Program Development." In M. J. Barr and L. A. Keating (Eds.), *Developing Effective Student Service Programs*. San Francisco: Jossey-Bass, 1985.

Cuyjet, M. J. "Program Development and Group Advising." In S. R. Komives and D. B. Woodard Jr. (Eds.), *Student Services: A Handbook for the Profession* (3rd ed.). San Francisco: Jossey-Bass, 1996.

Drum, D. J., and Figler, H. E. *Outreach in Counseling.* New York: Intext Educational Publishers, 1973.

Guba, E. G., and Lincoln, Y. S. "Competing Paradigms in Qualitative Research." In N. K. Denzin and Y. S. Lincoln (Eds.), *Handbook of Qualitative Research.* Thousand Oaks, Calif.: Sage, 1994.

Keeling, R. P. (Ed.). *Learning Reconsidered: A Campus-Wide focus on the Student Experience.* Washington, D.C.: National Association of Student Personnel Administrators and the American College Personnel Association, 2004.

Keeling, R. (Ed.). *Learning Reconsidered 2: Implementing a Campus-Wide Focus on the Student Experience.* Various: American College Personnel Association, Association of College and University Housing Officers-International, Association of College Unions-International, National Academic Advising Association, National Association for Campus Activities, National Association of Student Personnel Administrators, National Intramural-Recreational Sports Association, 2006.

Kuh, G. D., Kinzie, J., Schuh, J. H., Whitt, E. J., and Associates. *Student Success in College.* San Francisco: Jossey-Bass, 2005.

Kuh, G. D., and Whitt, E. *The Invisible Tapestry: Culture in American Colleges and Universities.* ASHE-ERIC Higher Education Report, no. 1. Washington, D.C.: Association for the Study of Higher Education, 1988.

Lewis, M. D., and Lewis, J. A. "A Schematic for Change." *Personnel and Guidance Journal,* 1974, 52(5), 320–323.

Manning, K., Kinzie, J., and Schuh, J. *One Size Does Not Fit All.* New York: Routledge, 2006.

Moore, M., and Delworth, U. *Training Manual for Student Service Program Development.* Boulder, Colo.: Western Interstate Commission for Higher Education, 1976.

Morrill, W. H., Oetting, E. R., and Hurst, J. C. "Dimensions of Counselor Functioning." *Personnel and Guidance Journal,* 1974, 52(6), 354–359.

National Association of Student Personnel Administrators. *Points of View.* Washington, D.C.: National Association of Student Personnel Administrators, 1989.

Styles, M. H. "Effective Models of Systematic Program Planning." In M. J. Barr and L. A. Keating (Eds.), *Developing Effective Student Service Programs.* San Francisco: Jossey-Bass, 1985.

Tinto, V. *Leaving College: Rethinking the Causes and Cures of Student Attrition* (2nd ed.) Chicago: University of Chicago Press, 1993.

Upcraft, M. L., and Schuh, J. H. *Assessment in Student Affairs: A Guide for Practitioners.* San Francisco: Jossey-Bass, 1996.

CHAPTER TWENTY-NINE

FACILITIES PLANNING AND DEVELOPMENT

Jerry Price

The impact of facilities on student affairs work cannot be overstated. Along with personnel and financial resources, facilities are the one of the main tools we have as professionals to achieve our programmatic goals. As the term implies, facilities *facilitate*. They facilitate our programs and services, student interactions, interactions among members of the campus community, and the institutional culture. They also facilitate our programs and services by providing comfortable, welcoming, well-equipped spaces. Few things are more central to the student experience than quality peer interaction (Astin, 1993), and comfortable, inviting spaces in the student union, residence hall, and recreation center can go a long way toward facilitating such interaction. Strategic use of facilities also can promote other types of desired interactions. If it is desired to have student government leaders interact more frequently with student affairs professionals or faculty senate officers, then you can locate their offices in the same area. Likewise, if you want to encourage student-faculty interaction outside of the classroom, perhaps you can create office space for the business fraternity in the same location as business faculty offices (Kuh, Kinzie, Schuh, Whitt, and Associates, 2005; and Tinto, 1987).

Such interactions are important because experiences and interactions facilitate student learning. The concept of campus ecology focuses on an institution's student characteristics, environmental characteristics, and the transactional relationship between the two (Banning, 1978). Indeed, an institution's environments, including its physical characteristics, impact student learning (Kuh, Arnold, and

Vesper, 1991), including the informal learning—that which occurs outside of the formal classroom setting—that is a vital part of the student's total college experience (Banning, 1995).

Facilities also facilitate communication of the institution's culture and values. Abundant space for student posters and flyers suggests the institution values free speech and encourages student involvement. Prominent displays recognizing student honors and awards suggest an institution that values and celebrates student achievement. Of course, the opposite is also true: facilities that are not wheelchair accessible or have no Braille signage suggest a campus that is not inclusive of persons with disabilities. The condition of facilities themselves can send a clear yet unintended message. If a prospective student visiting campus for the first time sees facilities that are unclean and in disrepair, what inferences will that student likely make about the institution's academic programs and services?

Overall, student affairs facilities have an enormous impact on the quality of the institution's learning and work environments. As such, facility planning and development must be a critical component in our planning. This chapter offers a framework for such planning, focusing on the development of a strategic plan, including the importance of goal setting, the user, and campus culture; development of an operational plan, including the budget; and facility development, from the initial needs assessment process through final construction.

Developing a Strategic Plan

When planning a new facility project, the institution must consider countless variables. In both the planning and operation of any student affairs facility, the fundamental question should be, "What is the mission of this facility?"

Prioritizing Goals

Of course, most facilities have multiple goals and purposes. For example, if the primary purpose of a new recreation facility is to promote wellness, then perhaps the facility will assign more space to cardio and weight equipment and allocate more staff time to aerobics and nutrition classes. On the other hand, if the primary goal is to provide interactive recreation opportunities, then space and staffing priorities may focus on facilities conducive to intramural and club sports.

The extent to which various features are included in a facility should be guided by a well-developed strategic plan for the facility. This strategic plan will incorporate all of the potential goals and purposes of the facility and prioritize them according to the primary mission. Once the plan is established, it will guide both daily and long-term decisions regarding the facility.

Considering the User

The next phase of the strategic plan is to identify all of the potential users of the facility. While the most frequent users of a facility are students, faculty, and staff, a facility may also need to consider outside users, such as prospective students and other community members. In some cases, the key users of a facility may be other campus departments. Once the users have been identified, the list needs to be prioritized into primary and secondary users.

Focusing on the needs of the primary users does not mean the needs of secondary users cannot be incorporated into facility design and operation. While a food service operation's main users may be students, it would do well to try to design services that also are attractive to employees as well. On the other hand, you don't want to design a student union that will impress corporations as potential conference customers just to have it feel cold and impersonal to students, who are the primary users. The needs of the primary users, as identified within the strategic plan, should not be compromised to meet the wishes of others. Fortunately, with careful planning, a facility usually can meet the needs of primary users and still address many of the needs of secondary users as well.

Desired Experiences and Interactions

Student affairs staff often think about their work in terms of their own activities. Student union staff plan programs. Financial aid staff offer information and advice. Career services staff provide interviewing workshops. While developing the facility's strategic plan, it helps instead to think in terms of the desired experiences of the user. What do we want the user to experience in this facility? What interactions do we want to take place?

For example, if our goal is to have students interact more with their friends in the student union, we will include more comfortable furniture and a large game room; however, if we want them to be exposed to new ideas and concepts, we may focus on developing exhibits on diversity or the arts. The motivation is not on what we as professionals want to provide, but on what we want students and other users to experience.

Campus Culture

Facilities both reflect and create campus culture (Kuh, Schuh, Whitt, and Associates, 1991). They send messages—both intentional and unintentional—to students, faculty, staff, and visitors. The next question for the facility's strategic plan is, "What are the messages we want to send?"

If the goals of the facility represent the what of our strategic plan, campus culture represents the how. Some financial aid offices design their facilities to resemble a bank lobby rather than a student services office; the message to students in this design is that this is serious business: students are making important financial decisions. Similarly, a career services office may develop a corporate look in their facilities to underscore that the staff expects professional attitudes and behavior from students.

Some of the messages sent by facilities relate more to the institution's values. A large display in the student union featuring students on the dean's list communicates a value for academic excellence, while a display with payment deadlines encourages students to take care of their financial business. Academic excellence and financial responsibility are both legitimate values to communicate. The question is, "What specific message is the priority?"

However, if we are not careful we can send negative or mixed messages. If students see that the vending machine in the wellness center sells soft drinks and candy bars, what message will they receive about the institution's attitude toward their wellness? Are these products there because they will bring more revenue to the institution than will healthy snacks? Or is it simply that the institution has given little thought to the vending machine contents? At best this is a missed opportunity to send a message that reinforces the mission of the wellness center. If the housing office disciplines students for propping open exterior residence hall doors yet takes weeks to fix an exterior door that won't close properly, how seriously will students take the message that securing exterior doors is important to their safety? Or, worse, will they wonder how concerned the housing office is about their safety at all? Facilities send powerful messages to students and other users, so it important to know what messages you want to send and understand how effectively you are sending them.

Putting the Strategic Plan Together

Several questions important to developing a strategic plan for student affairs facilities follow. What are the goals for this facility? Which goals should be primary? Which facility users will be our priority? What user experiences and interactions are desired? Finally, what aspects of the campus culture do we want to convey or reinforce through our facility? The answers to these questions will vary from institution to institution and even facility to facility. How do you determine what the answers should be for your facility? While student affairs professionals certainly should tap into their own expertise in developing the strategic plan, they should not rely on this expertise alone. Other sources of information also should inform the plan.

First, there may be larger institutional goals that are relevant to this facility that might guide some of the answers to these questions. Is there an aspect to the institutional mission or culture that can and should be incorporated into the facility? If an institution is known for promoting the arts, then perhaps the student union might want to create a gallery for student art, or have excerpts of dance or theater performances in the common areas during the lunch rush. Some institutions identify a theme for each academic year; certainly most facilities could identify ways in which to incorporate the theme into their programming or environment.

Researching best practices from other institutions also can help inform your facility's strategic plan. How are similar institutions designing and managing their facilities? What does the literature say about trends in various facilities? Many student affairs functions have regional and national conferences with program tracks specifically for facilities issues. However, no assessment of a facility's needs and priorities is complete without gathering the insights and perspectives of the users directly. This kind of assessment involves more than just user surveys, although user surveys can be powerful and should be implemented; it is also valuable simply to track user usage: who is using the facility? New students? Upper-class students? Faculty? Are there groups that are not using the facility? What specific services and programs are being used? What particular time of day? Day of the week? (Schuh and Upcraft, 2001). These questions along with the other resources discussed can be valuable when you are developing your strategic plan for the facility.

Developing an Operational Plan

If the strategic plan articulates the mission of the facility, the operational plan answers the question, "How do we implement the mission?" Using the mission as a guide, the operational plan should address facility programs and services, the facility environment, and facility care and maintenance.

Establishing a Budget

The relationship between a facility's operational plan and its budget is like the proverbial chicken-and-egg scenario. Do you start with the resources available and then develop an operational plan that fits within those resources? Or is it best to develop the plan first and then identify the resources needed to implement the plan? This is particularly relevant to facilities whose budget comes from a designated fee. For example, do you establish operating hours in the recreation center based upon what the current revenue will allow, or do you identify the desired operating hours and increase the fee accordingly to generate the needed revenue? Likewise, if a child care center could meet significant unmet demand for services if it had more teachers, do you increase rates to fund these teachers? Or do you stay within the existing budget and keep the rates lower?

Establishing an operation plan considering only existing resources can lead to a program that is stagnant and does not change to meet the needs of its users. However, a facility that is quick to raise fees to fund new programs and services may put a significant financial strain on those paying the fees. Typically, the answer to this budgeting challenge is a combination of both philosophies. One approach is to create an ideal operational plan following the question, "How would we operate this facility if we had no limitations?" This question frees staff to think purely in terms of the mission and desired outcomes of the facility. Once this ideal plan is established, it is time for a reality check: How does this plan compare to the resources now available to us? Using the strategic plan to guide our prioritization, the plan can be modified and adjusted to fit more in line with the current resources. Perhaps components of the plan that are central to the mission but not immediately feasible can be phased in, or deferred until a later stage of the plan. In a successful operational plan, there should be a little tension—but ultimately a balance—between the desire to meet as many goals of the strategic plan as possible with need to minimize the financial strain on the users.

Components of the Operational Plan

There are several typical components of an operational plan that often drive the budget for a facility. Those components are briefly discussed in this section.

Staffing. One of the largest parts of a facility's budget is personnel costs. How much and what kind of staff is needed to implement the operational plan successfully? This will depend in great part on the scope of programs and services articulated in the operational plan. Does the recreation center want simply to provide open recreation opportunities for its users, or does it also want to offer wellness programming and special events? Does the residence hall want to provide a computer lab and other academic resources, or just focus on the basics of student housing? The kinds of programs and services we want to offer, as well as the scope of these programs and services, will have a major impact on facility staffing.

The staffing plan must consider not only the programs and services offered but the amount of availability of these programs and services as well. To what extent will the facility be open on weekends? Late at night?

In most student affairs facilities, the staffing plan includes professionals, support staff, and student employees. Student employees often are a key element of the plan for several reasons. First, many facilities need monitors in various locations throughout the hours of operation; hiring full-time staff to cover these hours would prove very expensive. Second, student employees often give a facility its flavor, especially in facilities with heavy student traffic; when students see other students working in a facility it reinforces the notion that the facility is for them. Finally, in many facilities the staffing plan includes tiered employment opportunities, with students having the chance to aspire to leadership positions. Many residence halls, student unions, and recreation centers rely on resident assistants, graduate assistants, or student managers to supervise the facilities during the evening and weekend hours; these positions not only enable staff to offer more services over more hours, but they provide excellent leadership development opportunities for students.

In addition to professional, support, and student staff, some facilities also utilize contracted services in their staffing plan. Student unions very frequently contract for the food service portion of their operation. Health and counseling services often contract with outside agencies to supplement their on-campus services. Recreation centers may contract with resources in the community to provide aerobics classes, massage services, or nutritional workshops. These contracted services can be a cost-effective way of enhancing the operation of the facility without committing ongoing staffing resources.

A comparatively small but important part of the staffing budget is staff training and development. How are we going to prepare the staff to implement the operational plan? The staffing plan should articulate expectations for staff involvement in professional development activities. The plan also should address training needs for the student staff, particularly those students who serve in leadership roles within the facility. These students' training typically is accomplished in house—that is, by the professional staff in the facility. Careful thought and planning should be given to the quality, scope, and timing of these trainings. Finally, the training and development of the support staff that provide day-to-day stability in the facility should not be overlooked.

Equipment, Furnishings, and Supplies. Equipment, furnishings, and supplies are another significant consideration in the facility's operational plan and budget. Not surprisingly, the costs of these vary widely depending on the facility and its mission. A residence hall will spend hundreds of thousands of dollars initially furnishing its facility and will need to budget funds for upgrades and replacements on a regular basis. On the other hand, a counseling center will have few equipment and needs beyond the routine operational needs of the office and staff. Although the type of facility will dictate many of the equipment, furnishings, and supply needs, it also is important to consider needs as determined by the goals in the strategic plan.

Technology is both a very important and very challenging consideration in the operational plan. Computers, printers, fax machines, photocopiers, and other technology have become staples of nearly every campus office; offices such as student health services and disability support services will have significantly greater technology needs. Today's users are increasingly expecting to be able to conduct their business easily and conveniently through Web sites and other technology. Providing these services requires investing not only in these technologies but also in the staff to design, operate, and maintain them. Furthermore, rapid advances in technologies require us to incorporate frequent upgrades into the budget plan.

Facility Maintenance. In some facilities, the cost of facility maintenance is significant, even exceeding personnel expenses. Utility costs, in particular, need careful planning, as external factors can result in rates changing very quickly. The utility budgets in residence halls, recreation centers, student unions, and other large facilities can absorb a large portion of the overall budget. Finding successful ways to control these costs could free up significant funds for other priorities.

Daily cleaning and maintenance needs are also a critical part of the operational plan. While these are routine for most facilities, some have specialized needs. Recreation facilities have expensive exercise equipment, and the investment in them must be managed through regular cleaning and maintenance. Swimming pools have specialized equipment with unique maintenance and chemical needs, and failure to attend to these could lead to major problems in pool operation.

Planned Maintenance. In addition to the daily cleaning and maintenance, the facility plan also should address planned maintenance needs. Planned maintenance refers to those foreseeable facility needs that are regular but less frequent. This could include replacing carpet, painting, washing exterior windows on higher floors, and cleaning or replacing filters in the facility's heating and air conditioning system. The operational plan should identify how often these issues need to be addressed. Facilities with high user traffic will need to budget carpet replacement more regularly. Likewise, facilities like health centers with specialized equipment will have greater planned maintenance costs. Having an operational plan that ensures that these needs are addressed on a planned cycle of maintenance will reduce the risk of more costly expenses later.

At times budgetary constraints and other facility priorities can lead managers to delay or defer some planned maintenance items. While some of this is unavoidable and manageable, care should be taken not to let the deferred maintenance list grow too long, as it can accumulate quickly and require a much larger investment in the future.

Unplanned Maintenance. Even if a manager pays careful attention to the daily and planned maintenance schedules, unexpected facility problems still occur. Unfortunately, these problems—such as malfunctions with the boilers, plumbing, electrical system, or the heating, cooling and ventilation system—can be very costly to remedy and diminish our ability to operate facility programs and services effectively. A leaking roof is another common facility concern that can be particularly problematic; not only may the leak be costly to repair, but also the leaking water may damage parts of the facility interior. These problems cannot be anticipated, but management must be prepared to address them when they occur. Ideally, the operational plan should include sufficient facility reserves so repair funds can be made available when such problems occur.

Debt Service. For some facilities, another major budgetary consideration is repayment debt—that is, repayment of the funds borrowed to construct the facility. Depending on the scope of the project, the debt repayment can be as much as half of the facility's budget.

Facility Partners

The operational plan should recognize the interconnected nature of facilities on campus. While a facility may be under one division and one manager in an organizational sense, there are other campus departments that play a significant role in the operation and maintenance of that facility.

Campus Facilities Office. Student affairs facility managers need to coordinate closely with the campus's facilities office. In essence, the facilities office and the facility manager share responsibility for the maintenance of the facility. This shared relationship can take several forms. On some campuses the responsibilities are clearly divided: student affairs assumes responsibility for the programs and services within the facility, and the facilities office assumes responsibility for the maintenance of the physical facility. In such situations, there are usually two separate and distinct budgets: one for the physical facility managed by the facilities office, and one for the programmatic and service aspects managed by student affairs. If a problem arises with the physical facility, student affairs staff work with facilities staff to identify and assess the problem, but the responsibility for implementing and funding any repairs falls to the facilities office. On other campuses, funds for all of the facility's needs—both physical and programmatic—are included in one comprehensive budget. While this budget usually is managed by student affairs, the facilities office usually retains responsibility for identifying and implementing the appropriate method of repairs.

There are advantages and disadvantages to this shared approach to facility maintenance. The primary advantage is that it draws upon the expertise of both facilities and student affairs professionals; while the student affairs professional managing the facility may be an expert on the programs and services involved, he or she may not have the same level of expertise in regard to the physical facility. Staff in the facilities office can provide such expertise. To work most effectively, this shared responsibility requires a great deal of communication and coordination. First and foremost, it is important that both parties involved be on the same page in regards to the facility's mission and goals. For example, student affairs' goal for a residence hall may be an environment that facilitates trust, respect, and responsibility among its residents. The facilities staff, however, may believe an environment of strong discipline and control will keep the facility cleaner and reduce incidents of damage. Or a student union director may take pride in a union that has many student organization flyers and banners throughout the facility in promotion of campus life, while the facilities staff may take pride in a union that looks orderly and free of clutter. Strong communication between the leaders of these departments can help develop a shared sense of purpose and avoid the development of distrust and misunderstandings.

Communication is particularly important when major physical problems occur. The facilities staff may be best suited to assess the problem and identify solutions, but it is the student affairs staff who knows how these solutions might impact the mission of the facility. Who ultimately decides which solution is appropriate? If the assessment of a ventilation problem in the recreation center reveals two possible courses of action—a relatively inexpensive solution that probably will last a few years, and a much more extensive and expensive solution that will solve the problem long term—how is the decision made as to which solution to pursue? The facilities office may prefer the long-term solution; however, the recreation director may feel this solution is overkill and will unduly drain the facility's reserves that are earmarked for upgrading exercise equipment. There is no easy solution to these kinds of dilemmas, but the early establishment of a strong working relationship between the departments will make reaching consensus on these issues much easier.

Campus Security. Another important partner in the management of a student affairs facility is the campus police or security department. Campus police officers or security guards often are responsible for the unlocking and locking of facilities as well as ensuring the facilities are secure during hours not in operation. As with the facilities office, communication is the key to working with security. If there is a change in the hours of operation or an after-hours special event is planned, it is the responsibility of the student affairs staff to make sure the security staff is aware of these changes. At the same time, the security staff is responsible for making sure the facility manager and facilities office are aware of any problem that arises during off hours. Again, there must also be dialogue regarding how decisions related to facility security and safety will be managed. For example, if a group of students is planning a demonstration in the student union lobby in protest of a controversial speaker, who decides where the protesters are permitted to assemble? In protection of students' free speech interests, the union director may prefer the students be permitted to gather as close as possible to the site of the program without disrupting the event; however, the security staff may feel a distance farther from the event may be more appropriate. In situations with health and safety considerations, the opinion of security usually takes precedence; a good working relationship between student affairs and the security staff often will result in a mutually agreed upon solution.

Other Departmental Stakeholders. Some facilities develop partnerships with specific campus departments because of the nature of their programs and services. Food services is a common example of such a relationship, as they usually have a close working relationship with the housing office and the student union due to the large food service needs of these departments.

Facilities also can present valuable opportunities for student affairs staff to collaborate with faculty and academic units. The student union can collaborate with the art department to create a space to exhibit student art. The recreation center staff may designate time in its facility for the kinesiology or recreation science department to offer occasional classes. The child care center may work with education faculty to provide practicum and internship opportunities for students in early childhood education or similar academic programs. The student health center can be a resource to faculty and students in a number of academic units, such as nursing and pharmacy. These and other academic-student affairs partnerships can have a significant, positive impact on the experiences of students in these programs.

Additional Operational Plan Considerations

There are a number additional issues to consider in developing the operational plan for a student affairs facility. Several are discussed in this section.

Facility Environment. As mentioned earlier, the facility is a communicator of the campus culture, and the facility environment should reflect the culture and values the staff wishes to project. This is particularly important for facilities with heavy student traffic, such as student unions, residence halls, recreation centers, financial aid offices, registrar's offices, and other key services and programs. The messages desired will vary from institution to institution and facility to facility, but should be articulated in the operational plan; however, all facility environments should communicate an ethic of inclusiveness. Photos and displays within the facility should accurately reflect the institution's student body and workforce. Services and programs should be equally accessible to persons of diverse abilities. Subtle messages such as these communicate to users of the facility that the institution values all members of the campus community.

Legal Considerations. Facility managers are responsible for being up to date on liability and other legal issues that may arise through use of the facility. The maintenance of the physical environment itself is a significant liability issue. Are there conditions within the facility that could potentially create a hazard to users or staff? Is there furniture or equipment restricting access to fire exits? Is the cleaning staff sufficiently identifying wet floors in the lobby or restrooms? It is the facility manager's responsibility to watch for such conditions and take immediate steps to remedy them.

Likewise, the facility manager should be familiar with any risks related to the programs and services within the facility. What is the liability of an acrobatic group performing on the student union stage? What are the required credentials for swimming pool lifeguards? How do we respond if a parent fails to pick up a child at the child care center hours after closing? Each facility raises its own unique set of liability issues, and each facility manager is responsible for being fully informed on applicable laws and codes. The manager also is responsible for knowing institutional policies and procedures and how they relate to this specific facility and its programs. Operating in violation of published institutional policies—even unintentionally—can put the institution in a more vulnerable position should there be an accident or injury.

Managing risks includes financial risks as well as physical risks. Are money-handling procedures clear and being followed properly? How secure is the combination to the safe, and how often is it changed? Just as scheduling regular fire drills can alleviate safety risks in a facility, conducting regular audits can reduce financial risks.

Assessment. Having an assessment component within the facility's operational plan outlines how you are going to evaluate whether the facility is meeting its goals and objectives. Surveys and focus groups of users are common assessment tools; however, many professional associations—such as the Association of College Unions International, the Association of College and University Housing Officers-International, and the National Intramural and Recreational Sports Association—provide user satisfaction instruments designed for their specific facilities. These associations also provide opportunities for their institutional members to contribute to and benefit from benchmarking data on their facilities, programs, and services (Association of College Unions International, 2007; Association of College and University Housing Officers-International, 2007; National Intramural and Recreational Sports Association, 2007). In addition, there are educational planning associations with resources that may prove beneficial to student affairs facilities planning. The Facilities Performance Indicators Survey by APPA (formerly the Association of Physical Plant Administrators) examines a variety of facility factors, including operating costs, staffing levels, and space costs and usage (APPA, 2007). Another tool is the Campus Facilities Inventory from the Society of College and University Planning; this instrument collects comprehensive data about the physical size and growth patterns of campus facilities (Society for College and University Planning, 2007). Using such instruments reduces the need to develop your own and also allows you to compare your assessment data with those from similar institutions.

Relationship Development. As discussed earlier, facility management requires considerable collaboration with the facilities office, campus security, and many other campus departments and staff. The quality of these departmental partnerships will have a major impact on the effectiveness of the facility. As a result, it is prudent to include a communications and relationship development plan as a part of your larger operation plan. How are you going to develop positive relationships with key departments and their staff? What can you do to enhance the likelihood of regular, effective communication with those staff? While not as tangible as physical facilities or budgets, relationship development issues such as these can have just as great an impact on the facility's ability to achieve its mission.

Facility Development

The prospect of creating a new facility that is tailor-made for your programs and services is as challenging as it is exciting. Facilities projects have thousands of variables to consider, and the consequences of making poor decisions are high. Therefore, careful thought and planning must be invested in every facility project.

Of course, this thought and planning would be incomplete without purposeful involvement of the primary users: students. It is critical to solicit meaningful input from students throughout the process, from large-scale issues of facility design and function to smaller-scale amenities such as furniture and color schemes. Involving students helps ensure the finished facility will meet their needs and expectations and can also help develop early student excitement and ownership in the facility.

Assessing the Existing Facility

Many facility projects are intended to enhance or replace an existing facility. When considering a new facility, the first step should be to assess the existing facility. Is it sufficient to meet the program's goals and objectives? If not, how close does it come to doing so? If the program is only a moderate priority and the existing facility meets most of the program's goals, then perhaps resources should be reallocated to a higher priority project.

Renovation Projects

If it is determined that the program is a high priority and the existing facility is not sufficient, the question becomes to what extent the existing facility, if renovated, can achieve the program's mission. One key consideration in this exercise is the facility's location. The location of a program's facility is often a major factor in its effectiveness. The advantages of constructing a new facility specifically designed for the program may be outweighed by moving the program to a less effective location. If the program already is in an ideal location, then renovation of the existing facility should be the first consideration. It is important to keep in mind that the renovation of an existing facility does not provide the same flexibility as a new construction project; as a result, institutions usually have to make some design compromises to accommodate limitations of the existing facility.

Another consideration when weighing a renovation project is the potential impact on existing programs and services. Can the programs continue to operate in the same location during the renovation? Often this is not the case, so the programs will need to relocate temporarily—although, depending on the scope of the project, "temporarily" may mean a few weeks or a year or more. Another important factor is downtime—that is, will there be a time in which the program or service will not be available at all? Some services, such as security and food services, are needed daily and the institution cannot afford any downtime. For most programs and services, however, there are times of the year when activity is slower, and thus a short downtime can be managed.

Of course, a major consideration in deciding whether to renovate is the cost of the project. What resources are available for the project, and are they sufficient to create a facility equipped to meet the goals and objectives of the program? Renovation projects are very expensive, and in some cases can cost almost as much as new construction projects of the same size and scope. Ultimately, those involved with the facility project must weigh the value of any potential savings—along with the advantages of the existing facility's location—when determining whether to renovate or construct a new facility.

New Construction

There are several factors to consider when weighing whether new construction is the best approach to solving the institution's facility needs. The first consideration is whether there is sufficient and appropriate space available for a new facility. While there may be plenty of land available a mile from campus to build a new residence hall, does being that far removed from the main campus diminish the advantages of living in a residence hall? Or will the land adjacent to a busy street make a good location for a child care center? Is its location a convenience for pickup and dropoff, or a potential safety concern for children and parents? The location of a facility has a great impact on its ability to accomplish its mission.

The availability of space to construct often is a particular challenge for urban institutions. Most of the time the available adjacent land is limited, if available at all; even when there is land available, it often is very expensive or the buildings occupying the land have significant environmental hazards that must be addressed (Hornfischer, 2007). As a result, these institutions sometimes have to tear down an existing facility and build a new one on the same site. This approach comes with the added cost of razing the existing facility and the challenge of finding space for the programs and services currently housed in the facility being razed. Both of these complications can add time to the project schedule and cost to the project budget.

Project Authorization

Once the decision has been made to pursue either renovation or new construction, the institution will need to request authorization to proceed. At independent universities, this process usually involves securing approval from a board of trustees. At public universities, the first step typically is to submit the project to a campus facilities committee of the institution's board of regents. From there the project, perhaps with revisions, is forwarded to the full board of regents for approval. Of course, a major consideration in the authorization process is the project's funding.

Project Budget and Financing

Establishing the budget for a new construction project once again introduces the chicken-and-egg scenario: Do budgetary limitations drive the facility design, or do the needs of the facility drive the project budget? Certainly there will be budgetary limitations that must be acknowledged; on the other hand, it makes little sense to invest in a major project if the budget is not sufficient to create a facility that will meet the needs of the program and its mission. The ultimate resolution to this dilemma will be a balance of both considerations. Again, a well-established mission for the facility will guide the development of priorities for the project.

Another factor that will affect the project budget is the anticipated life of the facility. Does the institution expect the facility to be in use in twenty years? Thirty? Fifty? The anticipated life of the facility influences the type of construction and materials to be used in the project, which in turn impacts the cost of construction.

Finally, the available sources of funding also impact the cost of the project. Funding for construction projects can come from a variety of sources.

Government Allocation. Some campus projects, primarily at public institutions, receive their funding from government appropriations, usually from the state legislature, although occasionally Congress will earmark funds for specific higher education facilities. Since state and federal appropriations tend to be reserved for academic purposes, securing funding from government sources for student affairs facilities can be very difficult.

Gifts. Some institutions are able to secure private gifts to fund part or all of a new facility. These gifts may come from alumni and friends of the institution as well as from corporate partners. Many private institutions pursue private gifts for their projects, as they cannot rely on financial support from the government.

Bonds. Financing construction through the issuance of bonds is a common method for funding student affairs facilities. Typically, the bond debt is repaid through revenue generated by a facility fee that either is charged to all students or charged directly to users for the facilities' services (McClellan and Barr, 2000). Recreation centers, student unions, and health centers are examples of facilities that often repay their debt through charging a designated fee, while residence halls and child care centers are examples of facilities that repay their debt through revenue generated by charging users for the facility's services.

Business Partnerships. Some campus housing projects can be financed with help from a corporate partner. Such partnerships also may enable the project to be completed on a faster pace than traditional projects (Sabo, 2006). Although the partnership specifics vary from campus to campus, usually it involves the corporation providing funding for the project (often on a site owned by the institution) in exchange for a share of the room and board revenue. In many cases student affairs staff manages the facility itself as if it were an institution-owned housing facility.

Project Design

Once the funding question has been resolved, it is time to consider the design phase of the project. Issues to be addressed during this phase are discussed in this section.

Project Programming. Before the project design comes a process known as *facility programming*, which entails determining all of the elements to be included in the facility as well as the scope of these elements. Naturally, the facility's strategic plan should be the primary guide for this process. It also is important to solicit the perspectives of the potential users of the facility. Sometimes the institution's president or other leaders also have ideas or preferences they want considered.

Selection of the Project Architects. The selection of the project architects is a critical decision in the success of the project. The architects not only will be the primary designers but also will be key links in the communication chain with all other stakeholders involved in the project. Sometimes the architects also will take a leadership role in the programming of the facility. When considering architectural firms, it is helpful to examine the firm's experience with other projects, especially those similar to the one being designed. However, it also is beneficial to look for firms that seem to "get" your project, ones that understand what you are trying to accomplish with this facility. Good architects are mindful of the institution's preferences yet, when needed, will assert their own expertise and experience to help the institution avoid making major mistakes.

Design Considerations. Many, many variables factor into the facility's design. First, is there an institutional style or look that must be followed in this project? Is there a regional or cultural style to which campus facilities adhere? Some institutions are part of a university system that has its own design expectations and preferences. Another design issue is whether there is sufficient flexibility to respond to the new program or service needs of the future. In some cases, the institution is anticipating future expansion of the facility, so ideally the design will be one that considers the potential for that expansion.

Another consideration is how the choice of design and materials can impact the facility's ongoing operating costs in the future. For example, are the materials used in high-traffic areas easy to clean? Does the design allow for the efficient monitoring of facility users by the staff? With the volatile rates of utilities, it is important to ask how the facilities' heating, ventilation, and air conditioning systems will affect future utility costs.

Green Facilities. A growing number of institutions are considering sustainability issues in regard to facility construction or renovation. In addition to helping the environment, institutions report that "going green" can reduce facility costs in the long run through energy-saving technologies (Akel, 2006). More institutions also are pursuing Leadership in Energy and Environmental Design (LEED) certification (Akel, 2006). The LEED rating system is a "nationally accepted benchmark for the design, construction, and operation of high performance green buildings" (U.S. Green Building Council, 2007). Under this system, facilities are awarded a Certified, Silver, Gold, or Platinum certification based upon the extent to which they perform in five key areas: sustainable site development, water savings, energy efficiency, materials selection, and indoor environmental quality (U.S. Green Building Council, 2007). Associations such as the U.S. Green Building Council, the Association for the Advancement of Sustainability in Higher Education, and the Campus Consortium for Environmental Excellence strive to help institutions improve their sustainability efforts (Association for the Advancement of Sustainability in Higher Education, 2007; Campus Consortium for Environmental Excellence, 2007; and U.S. Green Building Council, 2007).

Of course, sustainability and other design issues affect the cost of the project. There are correlations between the cost, quality, and scope of the project. If the institution wants to increase the quality of the materials, then it must either increase the project budget or reduce the scope of the project. Likewise, if there is a need to reduce the project budget, there must be a corresponding reduction in quality, scope, or both.

Project Construction

Once the design is complete, the construction of the project can begin. The following are important components of the construction process.

Selection of the Construction Manager. Just as with the project architect, the selection of the firm to serve as the project's construction manager, or CM, is a critical decision. Of particular importance is the individual within the firm who is to serve as the project manager, as this person will provide the day-to-day supervision of the project.

Project Schedule. The CM will oversee a project schedule that projects when each phase and component of the project will be started and completed. If the project falls behind schedule, it can put pressure on the project budget; furthermore, a project that is not completed on schedule can result in the costly deferral of anticipated fee revenues.

Budget Challenges. It is not unusual for the cost estimates from the initial design to exceed the funds budgeted for the project. When this occurs, the project stakeholders usually engage in a process known as value engineering. Through this process, the architects, CM, and institution all explore—and ultimately agree upon—cost-saving alternatives to the original design (Mills, 2003). Once the estimates are within budget, the construction can proceed. However, surprises inevitably arise during the construction process, which calls for more difficult decisions about the project and its budget. It is preferred that all stakeholders be involved in these decisions as they were during value engineering. Once construction is underway some decisions have to be made very quickly or the project will fall behind schedule. This can make the communication among stakeholders more difficult and unreliable. As a result, it is important that all parties make the extra effort to communicate important developments to everyone involved (Price, 2003).

Facility Opening. Finally, when the project is completed it is tradition to hold a dedication or grand opening ceremony to celebrate the completion of the project and introduce the facility to the campus community. This ceremony may include tours for VIPs, recognition of the project's leaders, and perhaps the unveiling of the facility's name, especially if the facility is to be named in honor of a major donor or other individual.

Conclusion

If planned and managed carefully, student affairs facilities can enhance the learning environment for students as well as the work environment for student affairs and other staff. Quality facilities can facilitate the meaningful interaction of campus community members and promote the celebration of campus life. To create such quality facilities, student affairs leaders must start with a clear understanding of the facility's mission and a careful, thorough prioritization of the facilities' goals and objectives. These priorities will guide student affairs staff throughout the planning, design, construction, and operation of facilities that will advance not only the mission of the facility but also that of the institution.

References

Akel, M. "A Greener Attitude." [http://www.universitybusiness.com/viewarticle.aspx?articleid=549]. 2006.

APPA [formerly the Association of Physical Plant Administrators]. "Facilities Performance Indicators Survey." [http://www.scup.org/knowledge/cfi/index.html]. 2007.

Association for the Advancement of Sustainability in Higher Education. [http://www.aashe.org]. 2007.

Association of College Unions International. [http://www.acui.org/tools/]. 2007.

Association of College and University Housing Officers-International. [http://www.acuho-i.org/Resources/Benchmarking/tabid/87/Default.aspx]. 2007.

Astin, A. W. *What Matters in College?* San Francisco: Jossey-Bass, 1993.

Banning, J H. "Preface." In J. H. Banning (Ed.), *Campus Ecology: A Perspective for Student Affairs.* Cincinnati: National Association of Student Personnel Administrators. [http://www.campusecologist.org/files/Monograph.pdf]. 1978

Banning, J. H. "Where Do I Sit? The Landscape of Informal Learning." *Campus Ecologist*, 13(4). [http://www.campusecologist.org/cen/newsletter.htm]. 1995.

Campus Consortium for Environmental Excellence. [www.c2e2.org]. 2007.

Hornfischer, D. "Expanding Within Your Urban Boundaries." *Business Officer*, 2007, 40(12), 28–35.

Kuh, G. D., Arnold, J. C., and Vesper, N. "The Influence of Student Effort, College Environments, and Campus Culture on Undergraduate Student Learning and Personal Development." Paper presented at the annual meeting of the Association for the Study of Higher Education in Boston, Mass., November 1991.

Kuh, G. D., Kinzie, J., Schuh, J. H., Whitt, E., and Associates. *Student Success in College.* San Francisco: Jossey-Bass, 2005.

Kuh, G. D., Schuh, J. H., Whitt, E., and Associates. *Involving Colleges.* San Francisco: Jossey-Bass, 1991.

McClellan, G. S., and Barr, M. J. "Planning, Managing, and Financing Facilities and Services." In M. J. Barr and M. K. Desler (Eds.), *The Handbook for Student Affairs Administration* (2nd ed.) San Francisco: Jossey-Bass, 2000.

Mills, D. B. "Assembling the Project Team." In J. M. Price (Ed.), *Planning and Achieving Successful Student Affairs Facilities Projects.* New Directions for Student Services, no. 101. San Francisco: Jossey-Bass, 2003.

National Intramural and Recreational Sports Association. [http://www.nirsa.org/research/Default.aspx]. 2007.

Price, J. M. "From First Design Brainstorm Session to Final Coat of Paint: Communication, an Essential Constant." In J. M. Price (Ed.), *Planning and Achieving Successful Student Affairs Facilities Projects*. New Directions for Student Services, no. 101. San Francisco: Jossey-Bass, 2003.

Sabo, S.R. "Tapping Partnership Potential." *Business Officer*, 2006, 40(5), 22–28.

Schuh, J. H., and Upcraft, M. L. *Assessment Practice in Student Affairs*. San Francisco: Jossey-Bass, 2001.

Society for College and University Planning. "Campus Facilities Inventory." [http://www.scup.org/knowledge/cfi/index.html]. 2007.

Tinto, V. *Leaving College: Rethinking the Causes and Cures of Student Attrition*. Chicago: University of Chicago Press, 1987.

U.S. Green Building Council. "Leadership in Energy and Environmental Design." [http://www.usgbc.org/DisplayPage.aspx?CategoryID=19]. 2007.

CHAPTER THIRTY

TECHNOLOGY

Innovations and Implications

Kevin Kruger

Technology is integrated into virtually every facet of the college and university experience. This chapter explores several key questions related to how technology has affected student affairs. First, how has technology affected the ways in which students interact with each other and the college setting? Next, how have online and distance education programs changed the delivery of student affairs? Third, what technologies used by colleges and universities positively affect student learning and the delivery of critical student services? Finally, what technology trends will affect student affairs during the next few years?

Any article, book chapter, or publication that addresses information technology faces the challenge of the time horizon for technology. Innovations and market forces in technology occur quickly, and as a result, discussions about how students use technology as part of their daily lives can change rapidly. E-mail is a case in point. E-mail was only recently hailed in technology circles as a *killer app*, a technology that changes the way in which tasks or work is conducted or a technology that has become so ubiquitous that it is seen as vital and critical by technology users. On college campuses, college administrators saw e-mail as a cost-efficient way to communicate with students. Within the span of a few years, however, college students' attitudes about e-mail changed from a favored technology to a requirement. "The presence of email in teens' lives has persisted, and the number that uses email continues to surpass those who use IM (instant messaging). However, when asked about which modes of communication they use *most often* when communicating with friends, online teens consistently choose IM over email in a wide array of contexts" (Lenhart, Madden, and Hitlin, 2005).

This change largely occurred between 2000 and 2005, a span of just five years. Information technology—its use and innovations—changes and evolves quickly. The challenge for this chapter, then, is to discuss current technologies and issues that will have lasting effects on the practice of student affairs and not on the latest technologies and gadgets, whose effects change very quickly with time (Kruger, 2005). The best student affairs conversations about technology ought not to be about the actual technology itself but about the process of using technology and how it does and might affect student learning and the delivery of services to students.

Students and Technology

The extent to which computers, the Internet, and all forms of technology are woven into the fabric of college student lives has been well documented by the popular media and in such national research projects such as the Pew Internet and American Life Project. It is through this type of research that we are able to obtain a full picture of the ways in which technology affects so many aspects of college student lives. This section of the chapter examines new and emerging technologies and their effect on the college student experience.

Web 2.0

Technology writers often describe the current state of Internet applications as *Web 2.0*. Web 2.0, a term first used by Tim O'Reilly (2005), describes a second generation of Web-based applications such as social networking, blogs, wikis, podcasts, video, and photo archival sites. Web 2.0 has become a common reference that describes the widespread use of Internet technologies and the dramatic increase in the number of Internet users who create, publish, and share content online (Rainie, 2007). It is Web 2.0 that defines the nature of the college student interaction with technology. Participation in Web 2.0 applications affects nearly every component of the college experience. The following highlights some of these effects.

Instant Messaging

As discussed earlier, instant messaging (IM) has become one of the most frequently used technologies by college students. The IM market is dominated by AOL, MSN, Yahoo, and ICQ (Sines, 2003). The Pew Internet and American Life study (Jones, 2002) found that 29 percent of college students use IM daily, compared to just 12 percent of the general population. Many nonscientific studies at colleges since this study was published now show IM usage as high as 90 percent (Lenhart and others, 2005).

The popularity of IM as a communication tool has created opportunities to leverage this technology for educational purposes. Many faculty use IM to conduct office hours and to communicate with students outside of class. Students who use IM with faculty "found it easier to communicate, felt a stronger sense of community, and had more venues for informal and social communication about class material, the school, and their common degree program" (Jeong, 2007, p. 30). These same positive benefits to student learning can be achieved through the use of IM by student affairs staff. Despite the educational advantages of using IM, student affairs has been slow to adopt IM in its program offerings. To this date, most campuses primarily use IM as a broadcast tool for campus emergencies. For example, Mississippi State University has implemented a program called "Ping MS State," which allows students to register with the campus emergency notification system (Mississippi State University, 2007). In the wake of such campus tragedies such as that at Virginia Tech in April 2007, emergency notification using IM has become widely used across the country.

Student affairs offices should consider developing other strategies to use IM with students. Student organization advisors, residence hall staff, peer educators, leadership educators, and student government advisors, to name a few, could use IM communication. IM could be used to open communications avenues with parents and could provide scheduled access to key administrators such as the president or vice president for student affairs.

Conducting Research

Ask a college librarian and you will find out very quickly that students use the Internet for conducting their research and rarely roam the stacks for native sources of books and journals. While the Internet provides access to millions of potential sites that house research for students, none have become as popular or more widely used than Wikipedia (Educause Learning Initiative, 2007). A *wiki* is a collaborative Web site which can be directly edited by anyone with access to it. Wikipedia is an example of a wiki that attempts to become a worldwide collaborative online encyclopedia. Wikipedia has quickly evolved from a novelty to one of the most frequently accessed Web sites in the world. "*Wikipedia* is more popular on a typical day than some of the more prominent activities tracked . . . including online purchasing, visiting dating websites, making travel reservations, using chat rooms, and participating in online auctions" (Rainie and Tancer, 2007, p. 2).

Student affairs divisions have the same opportunity to take advantage of the comfort students have with wiki technology by developing wikis that serve to connect students with the campus. Oberlin College, for example, has developed a wiki that is accessed by prospective students and also contains resources about residential life, student government, and health education as examples. Since the content is organic and will change over time, it is a cost-efficient way of conveying content and is flexible enough to add content (Oberlin College, 2007).

Social Networking

Social networking sites are the virtual equivalent to the residence hall or student union lounge. Social networking is "an online place where a user can create a profile and build a personal network that connects him or her to other users" (Lenhart and Madden, 2007). Social networking became popular in the past few years through the dramatic increase in the use of sites such as Facebook.com and MySpace.com. Over half of youth ages twelve to seventeen use an online social networking site (Lenhart and Madden, 2007). In a 2005 survey of students from Harvard, Massachusetts Institute of Technology, and the University of Oklahoma, 91 percent reported having a Facebook account. Students also report frequent usage of their Facebook profiles (Jones and Soltren, 2007).

While the advantages of social networking seem clear, many student affairs professionals also grapple with the negative consequences of social networking sites. As Facebook participation has become virtually universal among college students, colleges and universities are presented with the dilemma of responding to the photos and other content posted by their students. Photos of illegal drinking, vandalism, and person-to-person violence increasingly appear on students' social networking sites (Watson, Smith, and Driver, 2006). Another serious issue relates to the practice of students posting personal information on their profile. In a study of Facebook usage on campus, Jones and Soltren (2005) found that the vast majority of students post personally identifying information on their profiles. Through orientation and other transition-related programs, student affairs professionals need to address the dangers and risks associated with too much openly available personal information.

One of the most vexing problems facing student affairs administrators is whether to access students' profiles and whether to take judicial action against those students who post pictures of illegal activities. This creates a striking example of the conflict between individual rights, privacy, and claims of free speech and the responsibility of colleges and universities to monitor the behavior of their students. "If universities set a precedent of aggressively searching Web sites for violations, it could create new expectations that institutions will and should be doing this as part of their ordinary course of business, which could place more legal responsibility on institutions" (Dahne, 2006 p. 24). By routinely reviewing student Facebook profiles for illegal activities, the college may create an increased duty of care and may increase their potential liability (Steinbach and Deavers, 2007).

Many colleges have attempted to move from enforcement to education as Facebook incidents have increased. Increasingly, colleges include social networking policies in their orientation programs and inform students that the photos and information on their site may be used in a disciplinary process. These programs emphasize the importance of educating students about posting photos of illegal activities (underage drinking) and being careful not to defame or harass other students in their posts. Many campuses, such as the University of Missouri, have appointed Facebook task forces comprised of students, faculty, and staff to monitor Facebook incidents (Dahne, 2006).

While much of the press surrounding social networking sites often has a negative slant, there is also evidence that these sites play an important role in the social experience of college students. Students establish their own social networking sites as soon as they are admitted to a college in order to begin establishing relationships with their fellow freshmen (Lombardi, 2007). A 2007 search of sites such as Facebook revealed significant numbers of college sites devoted to the class of 2011, almost all created by students and not the colleges (Lombardi, 2007). Many campuses also use Facebook and MySpace to survey students on important issues and use the sites to track student reactions to campus events (Simmons, Boyle, Silverman, and Khoury, 2007). Facebook and MySpace communication was one of the primary ways in which students communicated during and in the aftermath of the Virginia Tech tragedy of 2007 (Singel, 2007).

Gaming

The Pew Internet and American Life study of gaming among college students found that 65 percent of college students reported being regular or occasional game players (Jones, 2003). For most students in the survey, playing games was a positive experience. Nearly two-thirds (60 percent) "agreed that gaming, either moderately or strongly, helped them spend time when friends were not available" (Jones, p. 1). One in five (20 percent) believed that gaming helped make new friends or improve relationships with existing friends.

As is the case for any technology, problems can result from investing too much time in gaming. In the same Pew Internet and American Life study, almost half (48 percent) of college students reported that gaming keeps them from studying some or a lot. One third (32 percent) of students in the Pew survey report playing games during class (Jones, 2003). An emerging trend over the past few years has been the numbers of students who participate in what are known as "massively multiplayer online role-playing games" (MMORPGs). MMORPGs are a category of online games where large numbers of players interact with one another in a virtual world. MMORPGs include hugely popular games such as World of Warcraft and Everquest. How popular are these games? In July 2006, the World of Warcraft had 6.5 million subscribers (Woodcock, 2007).

Gaming, while largely a recreational activity for college students, also has enormous potential for learning and education. Increasingly, faculty are experimenting with gaming technologies as part of the academic offering (Gee, 2003). Increasingly, educators believe "games should be part of a whole curriculum, connected to texts, Internet sites, discussions, and lectures" (Dungy, 2005, p. 28).

Virtual Worlds

A solid example of the interest expressed in gaming has been the significant increase in the number of faculty and student affairs administrators who are participating in virtual worlds. The most popular of these virtual worlds is Second Life, which as of June 2007 had more than 5 million subscribers. While technically not a "game," virtual world applications are similar to the MMORPGs discussed previously. "Virtual worlds are richly immersive and highly scalable 3D environments. People enter these worlds via an avatar which is their representation in that space, moving their avatar through the space as if they were physically walking—or in some cases, flying" (New Media Consortium, 2007, p. 18). There are increasing examples of faculty use of Second Life, as many courses now meet in a virtual world allowing interaction among students and faculty (New Media Consortium). "For example, more than 70 universities have built island campuses in *Second Life*, according to Stuart Sim, chief technology officer and chief architect of Moodlerooms, which builds structures in virtual worlds and offers course management software" (Olsen, 2007). The potential for the use of Second Life in the classroom has led to the creation of Campus: Second Life to facilitate the use of the program in college classes.

Despite its increased popularity, not all higher education observers support the use of Second Life in the classroom. Some users find the interface for Second Life complex and difficult to use, so that "fewer than one in six who try it are still online 30 days later" (Kirkpatrick, 2007). In addition, critics question the potential conflicts associated with commercial advertisers in the Second Life environment and the reliability of Second Life servers to handle the Web traffic for a growing audience (Kelton, 2007). Finally, the Educause Center for Applied Research (ECAR) has identified several key questions to be addressed before colleges adopt the widespread use of Second Life in the classroom: "Is there sufficient proof of educational value to consider, continue, or increase institutional investment in *Second Life* and how does one assess the instructional work that will go on in virtual environments, and should the same scale be used for instruction provided face-to-face?" (Kelton, p. 10). More research will need to be conducted before Second Life will be widely adopted in the classroom.

Although slow to adopt, a small group of student affairs departments have also begun to experiment with using Second Life to work with students. Eric Van Danen identified a range of potential applications for student affairs' use of Second Life. "Career centers could hold pre-counseling sessions to direct student traffic to specific counselors or other resources; academic advising could be provided to first-year students prior to arrival on campus; residence life could host virtual hall parties for new and returning students as segues to real-life, shared residential experiences; counseling services could establish support groups in non-threatening anonymous spaces for students; and student activities could post information in a virtual student center about each student organization" (Van Danen, 2007, p. 33). While not replacing face-to-face contact, applications such as Second Life will continue to provide alternative methods for interacting with students.

Beyond the Administrative Core

Information technology has altered virtually every business practice within higher education during the past decade. While higher education has never achieved the paperless office that was promised in the early years of this latest technology revolution, technology advances have transformed the majority of administrative functions. In particular, admissions, financial aid, registration and student accounts, commonly described as the *administrative core*, have undergone significant change through the adoption of new technologies (Burnett, 2002; and Shea, 2005). Replacing old, legacy-based databases with campuswide or Enterprise Resource Planning (ERP) solutions for student accounts, financial aid, and registration has become standard practice across the country. As a result, campus information technology resources have been directed towards these expensive, time-consuming enterprise-wide software installations. Peoplesoft, SCT Banner, Datatel, and other software companies have become part of the higher education lexicon, in some cases due to the positive effect on administrative functioning and in other cases due to the cost and administrative headaches associated with these complex installations (Wheeler, 2007).

While the administrative core has been the primary focus of these systems and has received the bulk of institutional resources, key student affairs functions are increasingly becoming more technologically integrated. "For example institution-wide student record applications can also track and record student involvement in various clubs and activities and may include modules for career portfolio design for individual student use. System wide applications offer space-management components, room reservation options, and other facility-related applications viable for student affairs use" (Moneta and Nisbett, 2005, p. 7). In the Learning Anytime Anywhere Partnership (LAAP) project funded by the U.S. Department of Education, Web student services were divided into five suites, including the administrative core (mentioned previously), academic services, communications, student communities, and personal services. The student services suites are discussed in more detail in Chapter Fifteen of this book. The suites outlined in the model are as relevant for student affairs professionals working with campus-based students as they are for those working with online students. It is clear that campus-based students want the same 24/7 convenience for using student affairs functions. Online student services have bridged an important gap between office hours and the hours during which students want access to information, programs, services, and support programs.

Go Ask Alice!, Columbia University's Internet-based health information service, is an excellent example of the personal services suite in the area of student health and mental health (Columbia University, 2007). The program provides more than 3,000 questions and answers to health related topics. Topics include alcohol, fitness and nutrition, emotional and general health, sexuality, sexual health, and relationships. Go Ask Alice! provides students with important health information in a safe, anonymous setting and is unencumbered by office hours.

The personal services suite has also seen an increase in educationally sound commercial solutions that many campuses have adopted. Alcohol Edu, produced by Outside the Classroom, a for-profit company, is a three-hour online course that uses lectures, surveys, and tests to educate students about alcohol and the effect of alcohol on behavior. At the time of this publication, Alcohol Edu is used at more than 500 schools nationwide and is required at more than 100.

Online orientation programs are examples of implementing the academic services suite. Online orientation programs provide opportunities for students to interact with their prospective institution without stepping on campus. Students at Saint Leo University create an online profile and receive customized information based on their status as a freshman, transfer, resident, or commuter student (Saint Leo University, 2007). The University of South Florida has created a virtual advisor that allows admitted students to ask questions before they arrive on campus (University of South Florida, 2007). In both of these cases, online orientation supplements live orientation programs offered by the campus.

"By merging both technology and the personal touches that have long been the cornerstone of orientation programs, institutions can continue to meet the needs of our diverse student populations" (Conway and Hubbard, 2005, p. 27).

The widespread use of courseware such as Blackboard and WebCt to deliver online education to both distance learners and campus-based students creates opportunities to use the same courseware for student affairs applications. This courseware can be used to build programs in any of the non-administrative core suite of programs previously identified. Any student affairs function that delivers content to students could be adapted to an online format at a relatively low cost point. The following traditional functions could be enhanced through online delivery using courseware:

- Career development workshops on resume building and interview skills,
- Resident assistant training,
- Peer educator training and health related programming delivered to students,
- Leadership programs,
- Student organization development topics such as budgeting, program planning, and meeting management, and
- Wellness and personal development topics presented by counseling center staff.

As was the case in the online orientation programs, using courseware to deliver programs traditionally done live by student affairs staff does not replace personal contact with students. It simply shifts some of that contact to the online world in which students spend so much time. Student affairs professionals that use courseware to accomplish student learning objectives should incorporate lessons from faculty who have been using online courseware for years. Faculty engaged in online teaching should be open and flexible, comfortable communicating in a written environment, and appreciate the value of online learning as equivalent to traditional teaching (Swann, 2007). Interactions with student affairs staff in an online environment will be just as important as working with students in a live environment. The quantity and quality of interactions with course leaders (presence) is critical to the overall experience of the students (Swann). Anderson (2005) suggests, "Instead of simply posting notes or a copy of a PowerPoint presentation, online instructors should incorporate frequent opportunities for both public and private interaction into the course design. We value and create opportunities to interact with students on the physical campus because we know it is an effective way to educate. Why wouldn't we do the same in the online environment?" (p. 26).

Electronic Portfolios

Electronic portfolios are one of the most promising technologies to affect the ways in which student affairs staff might interact with students. "What are electronic portfolios? They are digital collections of personal and educational information presented in a format that allows personalization and collaboration" (Kruger, 2003, p. 22). Using electronic portfolios, students can document and record campus experiences by uploading writing samples, photographs, audio and video files, and any text file. Many campuses are helping students catalog their involvements, leadership roles and service learning experiences to create a co-curricular transcript that can be sent to potential employers. The possibilities for using electronic portfolios are numerous. This author, in another article on the subject (Kruger, 2003), identified several emerging options for their use:

- Admission applications could include the high school transcript, test scores, and an electronic portfolio of files and documents demonstrating the applicant's experiences and competencies.
- University 101 courses could include the construction of a portfolio for each new student.
- Involvement in leadership and service learning experiences could be recorded. Student affairs staff would play key educational and advising roles in collaborating with students.
- The career development process could include the student's portfolio as a tool for career planning and assessment and as a companion to the transcript for employment and graduate school applications.

Campuses with senior-year experience programs could use electronic portfolios to guide students during the reflection and assessment process (Kruger, p. 23).

Florida State University has been using electronic portfolios with students since 1997. Their portfolios highlight skills identification, planning of coursework and co-curricular activities, preparation for marketing in a job or graduate/professional school search, and providing a mechanism for reflection and personal development. At George Mason University, the Office of Student Life is helping students create leadership portfolios. Students upload documents and reflection related to identities, relationships, and community engagements. Students then receive feedback on their portfolios from faculty, staff, and peers participating in the program (Inter/National Coalition For Electronic Portfolio Research, 2008).

Technology Challenges

It is clear that while information technology is transforming the academy and the student learning process, there are many negative consequences that have developed from students' use of technology. Student affairs professionals must be aware of these issues and the strategies to address them.

Online Gambling

In July 2006, the U.S. Congress passed legislation putting restrictions on online gambling. The legislation bars online gambling companies from using the Internet to transmit bets and prohibits credit card companies from processing online gambling transactions (Murray and Grimaldi, 2006). This legislation will serve to curtail, but not to eliminate, online gambling—a growing problem among college students (Brown, 2006). In the 2006 National Annenberg Risk Survey of Youth, researchers found weekly card playing increased from 12.7 percent to 16.3 percent from 2005 to 2006 among eighteen- to twenty-two-year-old males, reflecting the increased popularity of Texas Hold'em and other poker games covered on television. In a parallel manner, online gambling increased for male youth from 2.3 percent in 2005 to 5.8 percent in 2006, a statistically significant jump of more than 100 percent (Annenberg Public Policy Center, 2006. Another study from the University of Connecticut Health Center found that 20 percent of college students participated in online gambling. Of more concern was the finding that 25 percent of the online gamblers fit the clinical definition of pathological gamblers (Schwartz, 2006).

One of the challenges in addressing the Internet gambling problem is that it is often very difficult to identify students with online gambling addiction problems. The first notice of a problem may be in associative behaviors such as alcohol use and financial issues (McClellan, Caswell, and Hardy, 2006). Many campuses have developed comprehensive strategies to educate students though Web sites, advertisements, speakers' series, and programs directed toward high-risk students such as Greeks, athletes, and freshmen. For example, the University of Alabama has formed a University Gambling Action Team, a cross-functional team of student affairs staff, to address the issue of gambling on campus through programs, mentoring, and awareness advertising. Programs such as this are necessary to address this complex issue. An excellent resource for additional campus examples can be found in "The Gambling Action Team: A Cross-Divisional Approach to Gambling Education and Intervention" (King and Hardy, 2006).

Illegal File Sharing

When technology is discussed among student affairs administrators, often the conversation turns to the vexing problem of students illegally downloading music and video using the college and university broadband access. Illegal downloading has been a major issue on campuses, as it often slows down campus networks and uses large portions of available bandwidth. In addition, since the Recording Industry Association of America (RIAA) has decided to prosecute individual students who participate in illegal downloading of music, student affairs administrators have been drawn into this issue. "At the core of the controversy is whether students are violating copyright law through the use of peer-to-peer (P2P) filesharing networks. P2P filesharing is facilitated by the Internet, which allows students to utilize free software to share music or movie collections on their computers with other network users" (Petersen, 2006, p. 27). Thirty percent of young people ages eighteen to twenty-nine report sharing music files online, and 59 percent of those ages eighteen to twenty-nine say that the file-sharing networks, not the individual user, should be responsible for the illegal download (Madden and Rainie, 2005).

While many campuses have taken an active role in policing illegal downloading, many have contracted with for-profit online services to make it easier for students to legally download music. In some cases, the institution has paid a license fee that allows unlimited music downloads as part of their contract. "Institutional arrangements expose students to legal alternatives and potentially minimize the chances for any consequences resulting from violations of law or campus policy. As the range of options grow for consumers to legally access music and movies, students will increasingly arrive on campus with preferences and experience using legitimate alternatives" (Petersen, 2006, p. 29).

Implications for Student Affairs

The widespread use of technology throughout colleges and universities has also created a range of issues in traditional student affairs programs and services. Student affairs professionals, historically educated in student development or counseling programs, will need a new set of skills (Kleinglass, 2005). Student affairs professionals will need to develop skills in technical areas such as Web design and database-driven Web sites, as well as expertise in social networking, online community building, and communication (Kleemann, 2005; and Kleinglass, 2005). These skills and competencies will be critical in advancing the technology agenda for student affairs.

It is also important to note that despite the advantages of widespread use of technology by students, there are also downsides. For example, while instant messaging provides many communication opportunities for students, it can also open up opportunities for harassment and abusive behavior. The immediacy of IM can also create unrealistic service and response expectations by students during their interactions with student affairs (Educause Learning Initiative, 2005).

Finally, as the number of hours students spend on the Internet increases and as their interaction patterns continue to favor virtual communication, many educators are concerned about the loss of social and interpersonal skills. Some research suggests excessive reliance on technology may result in loneliness and difficulties interacting with others (Henderson and Zimbardo, 2001). As technology usage by students evolves, it is important for student affairs professionals to be aware of both the positive and negative effects on student development and learning.

Conclusion

In the same ways technology has changed virtually every facet of our life, it is changing the learning enterprise at colleges and universities. While bricks-and-mortar institutions will continue to exist, increasingly the student experience will be a hybrid experience. A world that meshes live, in-person experiences with rich virtual-world experiences in which students interact with faculty, staff, and their peers using a wide variety of communication and community tools will increasingly be the norm. Facebook may or may not be the primary social networking site in five years. But social networking will still be a major tool among traditionally aged college students. Second Life may become the biggest new influence on student learning, or it may go the way of satellite education. However, virtual worlds are here to stay and will become more and more sophisticated and widespread over the next five years. Students will continue to IM and text message, but in the near future these messages will include broadband video. The iPhone may not be popular in five years, but the convergence of personal digital assistants (PDA), the phone, Internet browser, and personal computer will continue to advance and become as common as the cell phone. The challenge for student affairs professionals is to stay current with new technologies. Use IM, try text messaging, and create an avatar in Second Life. Only then will you be able to understand the potential of these new and existing technologies and the ways in which we can leverage them to enhance student learning and the delivery of student services.

References

Anderson, C. "Technology Reconsidered." *Leadership Exchange*, Fall 2005.
Annenberg Public Policy Center. "National Annenberg Risk Survey of Youth." [http://www.annenbergpublicpolicycenter.org/NewsDetails.aspx?myId=32]. 2006.

Brown, S. "The Surge in Online Gambling on College Campuses." In G. McClellan, T. W. Hardy, and J. Caswell (Eds.), *Gambling on Campus*. New Directions for Student Services, no. 113. San Francisco: Jossey-Bass, 2006.

Burnett, D. J. *Innovation in Student Services: Planning Models Blending High Touch/High Tech*. Washington, D.C.: Society for College and University Planning, 2002.

Columbia University. "Go Ask Alice!" [http://www.goaskalice.columbia.edu]. 2007.

Conway, J., and Hubbard, B. "Build an Online Orientation." *Leadership Exchange*, Summer 2005.

Dahne, M. "The Fuss Over Facebook." *Leadership Exchange*, Spring 2006.

Dungy, G. J. "The Gamer Generation." *Leadership Exchange*, Summer 2005.

Educause Learning Initiative. "Seven Things You Should Know About Instant Messaging." Washington, D.C.: Educause, 2005.

Educause Learning Initiative. "Seven Things You Should Know About Wikipedia." Washington, D.C.: Educause, 2007.

Gee, J. P. *What Video Games Have to Teach Us About Learning and Literacy*. New York: Palgrave/Macmillan, 2003.

Henderson, L., and Zimbardo, P. "Comparing Social Fitness and Technology Use at the High School and College Level." Palo Alto, Calif.: Stanford University and the Shyness Institute, 2001.

Inter/National Coalition For Electronic Portfolio Research. "Third Cohort." [http://ncepr.org/cohort3.html]. 2008.

Jeong, W. "Instant Messaging in On-Site and Online Classes in Higher Education." *Educause Quarterly* 2007, 30(1).

Jones, H., and Soltren, J. H. "Facebook: Threats to Privacy." *The MIT Computer Science and Artificial Intelligence Laboratory*. [http://www.swiss.ai.mit.edu/6095/student-papers/fall05-papers/facebook.pdf]. 2007.

Jones, S. "The Internet Goes to College: How Students Are Living in the Future with Today's Technology." *Pew Internet and American Life Project*. [http://www.pewinternet.org/pdfs/Pip_College_Report.pdf]. 2002.

Jones, S. "Let the Games Begin: Gaming Technology and Entertainment Among College Students." *Pew Internet and American Life Project*. [http://www.pewinternet.org/pdfs/PIP_College_Gaming_Reporta.pdf]. 2003.

Kelton, A. J. "Second Life: Reaching into the Virtual World for Real-World Learning." *Research Bulletin Center for Applied Research*, 2007, 2007(17).

King, C., and Hardy, T. W. "The Gambling Action Team: A Cross-Divisional Approach to Gambling Education and Intervention." In G. McClellan, T. W. Hardy, and J. Caswell (Eds.), *Gambling on Campus*. New Directions for Student Services, no. 113. San Francisco: Jossey-Bass, 2006.

Kirkpatrick, D. "Second Life: It's Not a Game." *Fortune*. [http://money.cnn.com/2007/01/22/magazines/fortune/whatsnext_secondlife.fortune/index.htm]. January 23, 2007.

Kleemann, G. "Weaving Silos: A Leadership Challenge." In K. W. Kruger (Ed.), *Technology in Student Affairs*. New Directions for Student Services, no. 112. San Francisco: Jossey-Bass, 2005.

Kleinglass, N. "Who Is Driving the Changing Landscape in Student Affairs?" In K. W. Kruger (Ed.), *Technology in Student Affairs*. New Directions for Student Services, no. 112. San Francisco: Jossey-Bass, 2005.

Kruger, K. "Electronic Portfolios: The Next Big Thing?" *Leadership Exchange*, Spring 2003.

Kruger, K. "Improving the Learning Experience." *Leadership Exchange*, Winter 2005.

Lenhart, A., and Madden, M. "Social Networking Websites and Teens: An Overview." *Pew Internet and American Life Project*, January 7, 2007.

Lenhart, A, Madden, M., and Hitlin, P. "Teens and Technology: Youth Are Leading the Transition to a Fully Wired and Mobile Nation." *Pew Internet and American Life Project*, July 27, 2005.

Lombardi, K. S. "Make New Friends Online, and You Won't Start College Friendless." *New York Times*, March 21, 2007.

Madden, M., and Rainie, L. "Music and Video Downloading Moves Beyond P2P." *Pew Internet and American Life Project*, March 2005.

McClellan, G. Caswell, J., and Hardy, T. W. "Learning and Living with the Genie." In G. McClellan, T. W. Hardy, and J. Caswell (Eds.), *Gambling on Campus*. New Directions for Student Services, no. 113. San Francisco: Jossey-Bass, 2006.

Mississippi State University. "Emergency Notification Through Instant Messaging." *Ping*. [http://www.its.msstate.edu/Information/Workshops/pdfs/ping/janfeb07.pdf]. 2007.

Moneta, L., and Nisbett, C. "Technology and Student Affairs: Redux." In K. W. Kruger (Ed.), *Technology in Student Affairs*. New Directions for Student Services, no. 112. San Francisco: Jossey-Bass, 2005.

Murray, S., and Grimaldi, J. V. "House Passes Bill to Restrict Internet Poker: Legislation Would Forbid Use of Electronic Payments." *Washington Post*, July 12, 2006.

New Media Consortium. *The 2007 Horizon Report*. Washington, D.C.: EDUCAUSE, 2007.

Oberlin College Wikipedia. [http://en.wikipedia.org/wiki/Oberlin_College]. 2007.

Olsen, S. "Universities Register for Virtual Future." *CNET News.com*. [http://news.com.com/2100–1032_3–6157088.html]. February 7, 2007.

O'Reilly, T. "What Is Web 2.0: Design Patterns and Business Models for the Next Generation of Software." *O'Reilly Media*. [http://www.oreillynet.com/pub/a/oreilly/tim/news/2005/09/30/what-is-web-20.html?page=1]. September 30, 2005.

Petersen, R. "Sharing Is a Virtue: Except When It Comes to Music and Movies." *Leadership Exchange*, Fall 2006.

Rainie, L. "Web 2.0 and What It Means to Libraries." PowerPoint Presentation to the Computers in Libraries Conference. [http://www.pewinternet.org/PPF/r/94/presentation_display.asp]. April 2007.

Rainie, L., and Tancer, B. "Wikipedia Users." *Pew Internet and American Life Project*, April 4, 2007.

Saint Leo University. *Center for Online Learning*. [http://info.saintleo.edu/col/default.cfm]. 2007.

Schwartz, M. "The Hold-'Em Holdup." *New York Times*, June 11, 2006.

Shea, P.A. "Serving Students Online: Enhancing Their Learning Experience." In K. W. Kruger (Ed.), *Technology in Student Affairs*. New Directions for Student Services, no. 112. San Francisco: Jossey-Bass, 2005.

Simmons, M., Boyle, J., Silverman, S., and Khoury, G. *Best Practices for Leveraging Social Networking Communities*. New York: Extreme Entrepreneurship Education, 2007.

Sines, S. "Instant Messaging Is Changing the Way We Chat." *Columbus Dispatch*, March 17, 2003.

Singel, R. "Lessons from Virginia Tech: A Disaster Alert System That Works." *Wired*. [http://www.wired.com/culture/education/news/2007/04/vtech_disaster_alerts]. April 17, 2007.

Steinbach, S., and Deavers, L. "The Brave New World of MySpace and Facebook." *Inside Higher Education*, April 3, 2007.

Swann, K. "Pedagogy 101—Tips and Techniques." [http://nursing.buffalo.edu/documents/Pedagogy_101_Tips_and_Techniques.pdf]. 2007.

University of South Florida. "Virtual Advisor." [http://usffl.askadmissions.net/usffl/aeresults.aspx]. 2007.

Van Danen, E. "Second Life: Connect Through the Virtual World." *Leadership Exchange*, Summer 2007.

Watson, S. W., Smith, Z., and Driver, J. *Alcohol, Sex and Illegal Activities: An Analysis of Selected Facebook Central Photos in Fifty States.* ERIC Document No. ED493049. 2006.

Wheeler, B. "Open Source 2010: Reflections on 2007." *Educause Review*, January/February, 2007.

Woodcock, B. S. "An Analysis of MMOG Subscription Growth." [http://www.mmogchart.com]. 2007.

CHAPTER THIRTY-ONE

RESPONDING TO CAMPUS CRISIS

Keith M. Miser and Cynthia Cherrey

A day on a college campus usually is filled with students attending classes, researchers making discoveries in laboratories, debates, cultural and intellectual activities, rehearsals, presentations, recreational and athletic events, and celebrations such as convocations and commencements, all of which create idyllic and indelible impressions of campus life. At times, unfortunately, on nearly all campuses, tragic events also leave an indelible impression, altering the lives of some, many, or all in the campus community. Tragic deaths of students, faculty, or staff from suicide, alcohol poisoning, drug overdose, accidents, shootings or infectious diseases occur; natural disasters such as tornadoes, floods, hurricanes, and earthquakes leave their destructive marks; human-made crises such as riots, terrorism attacks, and even social protests or unrest turned violent have changed society, but often at an extreme price for many on our college campuses.

This list is not exhaustive, but many of us will see some aspect of our work in this précis. It is nearly impossible to work for any period of time in student affairs without facing and working through a campus crisis. The effective management of crisis is an essential skill for a student affairs administrator. In today's global society, it requires planning skills in collaboration with our institutional colleagues and with those outside the walls of our campuses. It requires skills in handling the immediacy of the crisis, which is made even more complex by managing the immediacy of the media in a technology, communication-driven world: "live at the scene" television and cable TV, radio, Internet, blogs, and cell phones, especially cell phones with the ability to take pictures and instantly download to the Internet. Also, it requires leadership skills to help others heal and move on. Crisis work in student affairs requires a blend of compassion, expert training, and wisdom that comes from experience.

This chapter concentrates on the complexity of crisis. First, it defines the types and levels of crisis. Second, it describes the management of crisis work: the required preparation, the work that we do during a crisis and the recovery process. Third, it outlines the leadership needed from student affairs professionals after a catastrophic event. Finally, it describes lessons learned from student affairs colleagues who have experienced institutional crises. Each crisis gives us an opportunity to reflect upon and learn from the crisis.

Crisis Defined

Bejin and Morin (1976) discuss the origins of the word *crisis*. In Greek tragedies, *krisis* meant a critical event that required a decision. This interpretation suggests a flexible process for a college or university to assume when responding to a crisis. The Chinese ideogram for crisis consists of the combined symbols representing danger and opportunity (Lagadec, 1993). Student affairs professionals can use this Chinese wisdom to see the opportunity in each crisis and the subsequent recovery process to promote healing and ways to improve the institution.

Student affairs colleagues have developed ways to define the crisis work that is done on college campuses through the listing of situations that define the crisis, situations such as death of a student, life-threatening injuries, loss of life and/or property. Some campuses have separate crisis plans defined by their specific region of the country for earthquakes, tornados, floods, or hurricanes. Others may define *crisis* simply as a situation that requires immediate action by the dean or vice president or any situation in which a parent is already involved or will be. Harper, Paterson, and Zdziarski (2006) offer a more formal definition of *crisis* as "an event, which is often sudden or unexpected, that disrupts the normal operations of the institution or its educational mission and threatens the well-being of its personnel, property, financial resource and/or reputation of the institution" (p. 5).

Types of Crises

There are many different types of crises. Researchers (Clement and Rickard, 1992; Mitroff, Pauchant, and Shrivastava, 1988; and Shrivastava, 1987) propose that there are typologies of crises. Three of the most common in higher education are human crises, facility crises, and environmental crises.

Scale of Crisis

In addition to typology, every crisis has a dimension of scale. Zdziarski, Dunkel, and Rollo (2007) define *dimension of scale* as the level of the crisis: critical incident, campus emergency, or disaster. A critical incident is usually focused in one department and/or an individual or small group of individuals. It can include, for example, a student or faculty death, a disruptive student in a class, or a bomb threat. A campus emergency affects most, if not all, facets of the university and may result in a disruption of the daily operation of the campus. Examples of a campus emergency would be civil unrest or large campus demonstrations. The largest scale of crisis (for example, a disaster or catastrophic event) are those events that have far-reaching impact beyond the borders of the college campus. Hurricane Katrina adeptly illustrates such an event.

Stakeholders

There are stakeholders who must be considered in the planning, response, and recovery with every type and level of crisis. Primary stakeholders include those on campus, such as students, staff and faculty, patients, and campus guests. Secondary stakeholders are those closely related but not on campus, such as parents, alumni, donors, media, neighbors, and admission counselors. Tertiary stakeholders such as political leaders, higher education leaders, and business leaders all need to be taken into consideration during the emergency planning, during the crisis and the aftermath.

Management of Crisis Work

Although major campus crises rarely occur, it is critical to develop an institutional plan as well as a plan within the division of student affairs to deal effectively with a crisis event. Many well-prepared campuses develop plans that anticipate likely events in their regions. A university in the southeast coastal region, for example, may have detailed plans for dealing with the potential of a deadly hurricane sweeping across campus, or a California campus may have specific plans for responding to an earthquake.

Although it seems logical to develop very detailed plans outlining options and choices for decisions to be made during a crisis, this approach is seldom practical or effective. Each major campus crisis is unique and likely occurs only once during an institution's history. Detailed and rigid plans do not place institutional and student affairs leaders in positions flexible enough to deal with a specific, unique crisis and the subsequent events as they unfold.

The key to good preparation for a crisis is to develop master plans, including a portfolio of protocols that can be used in a wide range of crisis situations. Examples include death of students, bomb threats, and a natural disaster plan of evacuation of a geographical region, such as specific plans for earthquakes, tornados, and hurricanes. Some campuses may have multiple options in the general plan, depending on the unique location of the campus. As an example, the University of Hawai`i at Hilo has a comprehensive approach and plan, with specific guidelines for responding to tsunamis, earthquakes, volcanic eruptions, and hurricanes (Ikeda, 2006).

Developing a Plan

A good crisis plan includes a framework for decision making during the actual period of a crisis. The plan should outline both philosophical and pragmatic issues and should identify individuals in positions who should participate on the decision-making team. The crisis plan should articulate the lines of organizational authority and responsibility within the institution. Such clarity will facilitate both the decision-making process and implementation of decisions.

A comprehensive communication and media plan should be in place before a natural disaster occurs. First, the plan's components should include a means to contact key personnel so leaders and other staff can be notified quickly as the crisis unfolds. Second, methods must be designed to allow communication with internal constituents, including students, staff, and faculty, from the beginning of the incident until the crisis has been resolved. Third, a framework needs to be in place to communicate effectively with external constituents, such as government officials, local citizens, parents, alumni, and other interested individuals and groups. Internal and external constituents and the media will demand information about the campus's response to the crisis. Without a comprehensive communication plan in place, chaos may result because decision makers will be drawn into designing a communications plan rather than addressing the responses to and recovery from the crisis itself.

Practice in Preparation for Crisis

After a comprehensive university plan is developed, it is important to practice and subsequently update the plan on a regular basis. By having at least an annual crisis or disaster practice, the plan can be strengthened by adding new approaches and technologies. The practice session should be taken seriously, and the entire institution must participate at least at some level. Practices can identify problems with the alert and warning systems, changes that can be made in personnel and leadership roles, as well as policy and coordination concerns. A significant key to a successful practice is a link to and involvement with local and state agencies like police, fire, and civil defense programs. Frequently, successful coordination is the most difficult to achieve with these agencies because of their lack of direct involvement with the institution. A good practice simulation can help build communication and instill a good working relationship with critical agencies. Often staff and even college and university leaders are reluctant to participate in a disaster simulation because of time. Institution leaders must assure the full participation of the campus to make sure the campus is ready for potential problems.

Policy Review

To prepare for a possible crisis, each campus must review policies and procedures that may be needed during such an event. These documents could include financial polices; expenditure and authorization procedures; purchasing, bidding, and approval policies; insurance documents; construction approval policies; environmental, health, and safety policies; and student record policies and procedures. Many of the standard processes, including any approval procedures a campus uses, may have to be altered significantly to allow the campus to respond quickly to the crisis.

The procedure for responding to a crisis can and should be planned in advance, allowing for maximum flexibility and knowing that even during an actual event these planned procedures may need to be altered. In many ways, the response to a crisis is an art more than a science in a continually unfolding and unstable postcrisis environment.

The Leadership Role of Student Affairs

When a campus crisis occurs, there usually is a short period of chaos before the process of response and rebuilding begins. The regular routine and institutional responsibilities are disbanded and the response to the crisis becomes the norm. During a crisis, the best in an institution appears when politics and the usual problems are set aside as the institution strives to mitigate the effects of the crisis (Siegel, 1994).

When a physical crisis occurs, people's safety is the first concern, followed by immediate efforts designed to implement temporary situations for facilities. Such efforts aid a return, as quickly as possible, to normality. Frequently, the initial response is directed toward the physical plan, particularly when the media focus on the intense and dramatic visual images showing the campus destruction. The trauma to and impact on people, however, may exceed the damage to buildings. It is critical for campus leaders, especially in student affairs, to focus a significant amount of effort on assisting and supporting people effectively. In the end, this response will determine whether the campus response was of high quality.

Student affairs professionals are trained to work with people, and from this foundation, they become key leaders in responding to campus crises. Needs may include counseling, loss therapy, the rescheduling of academic programs, communicating with families, supporting faculty colleagues, and working with individuals who may have lost their life's work and research. Facilities such as student unions, Greek houses, residence halls, and student health centers under student affairs management responsibilities may be demolished or damaged during a natural disaster. Student affairs leaders must be actively involved throughout the entire process of rebuilding the physical plant. If there is a loss of life or severe injuries, a significant time must be spent with family, friends, and colleagues of those individuals affected by the crisis. The campus will depend on student affairs staff to use their experience and skills to make significant contributions to the human community through the response period and the rebuilding process.

Each campus is a unique organization with a special culture, shaped by history, mission, and leadership. The important role of student affairs in a crisis will be defined both by the campus culture and the nature of the crisis. The senior student affairs leader often serves as a key figure and as a central campus leader during this period. This individual should define the specific responsibilities of student affairs programs and staff during the crisis. In any crisis the contributions of student affairs professionals are significant in determining the outcome of the response and rebuilding process, especially with regard to the well-being of the campus community.

Crisis Coordination and Administration

In the administration of a crisis, the key organizational structure that contributes to successful outcomes in the recovery effort is a campuswide coordinating committee. Depending on the nature of the campus, the extent and nature of the crisis, and the resources needed to analyze the issues and to make decisions, the institution's president should appoint a special crisis coordinating committee to accomplish this task of response and recovery.

During a crisis there may be a breakdown in the normal systems of communication and analysis on campus. Consequently, the core crisis coordinating team should be relatively small, and members need to be professionals with specific expertise. The team must analyze and make decisions with regard to the structures and processes to deal with the crisis. When issues are brought before the committee, decisions must be made quickly. After each meeting, committee members must implement the decisions made at the meeting within their own departments or organizations as well as gather more information from their units to bring back to the next meeting. This structured process guarantees smooth decision making and eliminates confusion and miscommunication. Student affairs representatives typically are key members of such a committee and indeed may chair the group. Following the 1997 flood that caused a significant crisis at Colorado State University, a crisis coordinating committee was appointed, with members including the vice president for administrative services, vice president for student affairs, director of housing, director of the student union, director of purchasing, director of facilities services, university general counsel, director of public relations, provost, director of telecommunications and information services, chief financial officer, and the student body president.

Financial Management

During a crisis involving damage to buildings, personal property, and information technology infrastructure, excellent financial management is essential. Decisions must be made about immediate expenditures to bring the campus into a position where normal functions and activities can be resumed. A long-term financial strategy also must be implemented to return the campus back to its precrisis state and do so in a financially stable way.

Insurance plays a large role in the financial recovery from a campus crisis. Student affairs professionals must be involved in the damage assessment process as well as the implementation of the recovery using insurance funds. In particular, students may suffer from great personal and financial losses, including the contents of residence hall rooms, cars, and other personal materials. These losses must be assessed immediately and verified to allow students to make insurance claims and receive funds as soon as possible for housing, food, and daily necessities. At times, state and federal insurance agencies may be involved in the recovery, creating an environment of conflicting rules, procedures, and outcomes. Student affairs professionals, because of their training, experience in human issues, and their communication skills are key in assisting colleagues and students with these issues and their successful resolution.

Legal Issues

As with any issue today, many complex legal concerns have to be addressed during a campus response to a natural disaster. Institutional lawyers must be involved with every decision, from the beginning of the crisis through the entire recovery process. Primary issues include student information privacy laws, financial aid, regulations, and insurance claims. Legal counsel must be consulted to review insurance claims and policies, state and federal regulations affecting the crisis recovery, open record laws, and possible lawsuits.

Communication and Technology

Recent years have seen a dramatic increase in new technology that can be used effectively in communicating with campus constituents in preparing for or during a crisis. E-mail communication is by far the most popular and widespread form of communication. Because it can be sent and received from desktops, laptops, or handheld devices, it is a good choice in many cases. Many institutions have listservs with e-mail addresses of all students that can be used for mass distribution of information. This medium, however, is not always the best choice. It can be ineffective if the IT infrastructure is damaged or there is an electrical power outage. In a crisis several years ago at Colorado State University, administrative offices received more than 5,000 e-mails. This ripple of e-mails and subsequent rumors they generated nationwide resulted in communication about the crisis that was not only misleading but also inaccurate, thus creating false perceptions to readers, many of whom were family members and supporters. The campus was nearly paralyzed in its effort to respond to and manage the e-mail communications. The institution used its Internet Web site to release press statements about the crisis, but this effort did not reduce significantly the e-mail challenge. Thus, the readily available and heavily used medium of e-mail can create problems, yet it also can provide solutions for student affairs professionals in their effort to communicate information accurately and in a timely manner to students and other internal constituents, as well as to external groups.

An older technology is the use of 800-numbers that families can use to call a "call center" staffed by individuals with the latest information on the crisis. Telephone companies can assist the university in establishing the numbers quickly to use for one-on-one communication.

In the past few years, cell phones have become an increasingly popular method of communication for students, faculty, and staff. The best feature of using cell phones to communicate crisis information is their practicability, although in some weather-related disasters the use of cell phones may be disrupted due to the destruction of transmitting towers. Many institutions are including cell phones in these communication plans, especially using text messaging as the medium of communication through cell phone technology. Many campuses today have implemented a text message emergency communication system. Members of the campus community can register to have their cell phone numbers included as part of this alert system (Milian, 2007).

A crisis or disaster Internet technology can also be used to help students process the impact on their lives. Colleges and universities are using chat rooms, blogs, and comments on Facebook to allow the much-needed discussion to occur with campus constituents.

Student Affairs Response to the People on Campus

Student affairs professionals are critical in establishing and maintaining a climate of support during a campus crisis, the immediate response, and recovery period. Of course, campuses that have developed a supportive environment before such a crisis occurs are able to continue and advance this ethic during a time of high stress.

Students and Their Families

Students are the key target constituency for a student affairs response. Teams should be created within the division of student affairs to assist students in any way possible by using their resources, skills, and training. Helping students process the personal meaning of the disaster and, through this process, helping them deal with all their losses are important responsibilities of student affairs staff. Many students feel disoriented and frightened. All students, particularly seniors, will struggle to learn how the crisis impacts their academic progress or their graduation. A number of students will have lost personal possessions of great value to them. Some may have lost friends or relatives to death. In all these cases, student affairs staff can be the student's vital link to the campus by providing counseling, academic advising, financial advising, grief counseling, personal support, and information about the institution's decisions and actions through the recovery process.

Student affairs staff often are the connection to students' families. If 800-number telephone lines are installed to allow parents, family members, and friends access to a single information source after a crisis, these lines can be staffed by student affairs professionals who will give accurate and updated information about the response and recovery process.

Newsletters sent to the parents and other external constituencies after the crisis are another vehicle to present an update on the recovery process. Student affairs professionals may ask for the assistance of parent organizations and others to assist with newsletters and other forms of communication during the crisis period. For families who have not received information, the unknown usually is much worse than the known, especially if a family lives a great distance from campus. If communication with students' families and friends is handled well, their support likely will expand and continue to grow long after the campus has returned to its normal routines.

Student Leaders

In a crisis situation, student affairs professionals play another critical role by immediately and actively involving student leaders in the response and recovery process. Student leaders have excellent ideas for how to communicate effectively with their fellow students. Student leaders, along with student affairs professionals or institutional officials, should sign letters, memoranda, e-mails, and press releases. Student government leaders usually are more than willing to become involved, and they are an invaluable communication link in reaching the general student population. They have good ideas on how to solve problems that will better meet the student needs. In the 1997 flood at Colorado State University, student leaders met with groups of students across campus to answer questions and to engage them in dialogue about current events and procedures. They also assisted with getting accurate information to the student newspaper, coordinated their efforts with administrators by meeting with them daily for updates, and kept their own families informed so they could help quell the fear of other parents nearby. In 2007, during fall orientation week at the University of Hawai`i at Hilo, a Category 5 hurricane approached the island, three earthquakes rocked the buildings in two days, and a tsunami alert was issued by the National Oceanic and Atmospheric Administration. The university was closed by the state, and orientation and residence hall leaders under the supervision of their respective student affairs directors made immediate plans to disseminate information to all students and parents at regular intervals and in regular places on campus, to provide any assistance needed for safe shelter, and served as a calming influence in the midst of a chaotic and frightening time. When two days passed with little or no damage, the student leaders then turned to salvaging as much as possible of the program and garnered support from the chancellor and faculty to help make the week be a success. Parents left with great admiration for those who had cared so well for their sons and daughters.

In addition to engaging student leaders in problem solving and facilitating good communication, many other campus and external constituents and governance systems should be directly involved. Faculty councils, staff councils, the alumni board, governing board, city council, and chamber of commerce may be helpful and will appreciate being asked to share their expertise and leadership. Specific student affairs staff also are central to helping with internal and external communication, including residence hall staff, Greek advisors, student union advisors, and student government advisors. These staff members will help disseminate information to student constituents and bring ideas and concerns to the central coordinating committee.

Responding to Staff

During a crisis, student affairs staff also will have personal and professional needs. Student affairs staff will work extraordinarily hard for very long hours to help students with their emotional, financial, and personal needs. At the same time, these staff members likely will have some of the same needs, fears, and concerns as students. Senior student affairs professionals and counselors are instrumental in assisting students and staff throughout the recovery process. The strategies of taking scheduled breaks, changing venues, seeking personal support, getting appropriate rest, and eating nutritious meals are critical to maintaining a staff that continues to be effective, even after the first several days. It is critical for student affairs leaders to communicate to staff members the importance of taking care of themselves during a crisis and subsequent recovery so they can be effective in supporting others around them, particularly students, during this difficult period.

After the immediate shock and disarray of the disaster and the beginning of the orderly and often mechanical response and recovery process, student affairs leaders and staff must develop strategies for healing that will return the total campus community to a normal routine. A mandatory step in a return to normalcy is for the campus community individually and collectively to find ways to grieve their losses. There must be a period of mourning, transition, and regeneration for everyone, whether they are concerned about buildings, organizational design, administrative structure, relationships, or any combination of these. Regardless of the nature of the crisis, it also is important to recognize that the campus likely will never be the same as it was before the incident happened, and student affairs staff have an integral role in ensuring a positive outcome in this process of rapid change. One essential word of caution: Leaders and staff at colleges and universities may make the serious mistake of believing that when buildings are repaired and furniture, books, and other supplies are replaced, everything is back to normal. Later they find that personal scars from the crisis have been so deep that the postcrisis organization has become dysfunctional. So, equal attention must be paid to these hidden wounds in order to promote healing and hope for the future, in spite of recent losses.

After the response and recovery period, it is entirely possible that the restored institution will be better than it was before the event occurred. Replacement of and repair to buildings may improve and update them to better meet campus needs.

Relationships among staff are strengthened through their participation in the process of crisis management and working together. New relationships and linkages developed during the crisis can improve communication and coordination throughout the institution. Through innovative and steady leadership, the institution's culture can be strengthened because it now believes it is strong and able to accomplish anything by working together. Student affairs staff and leaders are essential in helping to ensure these positive outcomes at the end of the crisis period.

Debriefing and Evaluation

Debriefing and evaluating all components of the crisis and the subsequent campus response are critical. This may be almost as important as the actual recovery process, because it provides useful insights and information into the processes and policies that might be changed for a future crisis response. It also may help bring closure for those who were intimately and directly involved with the crisis from the beginning to end. This period of debriefing and evaluation also allows campus leaders to personally and publicly thank everyone who helped with the response and contributed to the recovery.

The review process is especially significant for the student affairs staff who are the campus human response specialists. Occasionally, student affairs staff feel they could have done a much better job during a crisis. This comment is common during a situation when there is such organizational and physical disarray that staff members are not able to maintain their normal expectations in responding to needs and demands. In truth, no one can meet every immediate human and institutional need during a major crisis. It is important for student affairs leaders to continually assure staff and believe themselves that they have done an excellent job, especially in view of the complexity and the comprehensive nature of any crisis.

The final step is to transition the student affairs staff into a more routine and normal work environment and to address the myriad of projects that were postponed or delayed during the crisis. If this closure process is handled successfully, not only will much be learned in order to handle a future campus crisis, but also the campus community will feel empowered and capable of overcoming any challenge.

Transitions After a Catastrophic Event

The aftermath of a college crisis is difficult enough, but the resulting transitions from a catastrophic event to the new reality are even more challenging. The 2007 Virginia Tech shootings that resulted in thirty-three deaths on the campus and Hurricane Katrina in 2005 that closed Gulf Coast universities for extended periods would be defined as catastrophic events. Each resulted in a life-changing experience for both individuals within the university and the universities themselves.

Transitions are phases that individuals and organizations pass through as they come to terms with a given situation (Bridges, 2003). The leadership ability of student affairs is critical in helping students, parents, staff, and faculty colleagues work through the transitions. Authors (Allen, 1993; Bridges, 2003; and Mitchell, 1993) propose various phases that individuals or organizations experience. Most commonly experienced are the phases of letting go, the "tweener" stage, and new beginnings.

Letting Go

Transitions start with endings. Individuals must be given permission to let go of the past in order to prepare for the future. This is brought about in a number of ways (Cherrey, 2006).

- Describe the reality. Explain what has been lost individually and as a group.
- Acknowledge that each and every person reacts differently to loss.
- Do not be surprised at overreaction or time-delayed reactions to the event.
- Accept and encourage the rituals that individuals and groups must practice as they let go.
- Provide continual communication on the latest developments and repeat the information again and again. Individuals will be ready to accept information at different times.

Understanding the "Tweener" Stage

During the crisis the entire community comes together, the media are swarming, and your colleagues are there to support and offer assistance. Shortly after the crisis, the media may continue to give the crisis visibility, and colleagues are still there to offer support. The most challenging time is when others go back to their normal working lives while the affected institution is trying to determine what its "new normal" is all about. Some at the institution will have one foot planted firmly in the old ways of doing things, while others are searching for solid ground for the new direction. Old problems and old resentments may resurface at this time in the organization. Key indicators that individuals are feeling the pressure of this stage include a rise in anxiety and a decrease in motivation; feelings of isolation and loneliness causing some to retreat; and unsettled feelings that leave individuals in a state of flux.

Beginning Anew

Although hope is an espoused virtue that can help us maintain optimism during a crisis, it is not a strategy that gives direction and focus to an institution in its rebuilding efforts. As Charles Montagu, the Earl of Halifax, said, "Hope is generally the wrong guide, though it is very good company" (Foxcraft, 1896, p. 703). Student affairs professionals have a unique vantage point and the needed capabilities to assist higher education institutions and the members of the campus community to move through challenging times in their history. To promote healing and renewal, the following should be taken into consideration (Allen and Cherrey, 2000; and Cherrey, 2006):

- Reward experimentation and innovation, not perfection. Give permission to experiment, and encourage staff to look at issues from different perspectives.
- Take small steps and big steps simultaneously. Institutional members need to see immediate successes, and students will be looking for and demanding new types of programs and practices that reflect the changes the institution went through. Develop transitional programs that honor the past and celebratory events that reflect the future of the campus community.
- If you have the opportunity to hire new staff, do so with a focus toward the future. Select professionals who are excited about the opportunity to be a part of the change, who are creative and innovative. Look for individuals who display a strong sense of resilience, flexibility, and optimism.
- Shift from a fragmented to a networked approach to work. Counsel staff to abandon territorial approaches to problems and consider themselves as part of the bigger picture. In making this important shift, staff can be encouraged to join forces with colleagues across units. They may eventually recognize that the whole is greater than the sum of its parts, and those collaborative efforts can create synergy which can have amazing results.
- Create partners in learning. Interact with community organizations and create new partnerships in the process of renewal. Initiate conversations with stakeholders to explore what it means to be part of the renewal efforts, to identify the role of student affairs in actualizing the plan.

Student affairs professionals have a special role in times of crisis and the resulting transitions. Beyond the crisis management skills, student affairs staff bring perspective, team-building skills, and the capacity to help in the transformation of an institution that has gone through a catastrophic event and the ensuing renewal efforts.

Lessons Learned

After each and every crisis, an important aspect of crisis management is to reflect upon and assess what went well and where improvements can be made. The following are reflections and observations from colleagues on what they learned from their respective crisis experiences (Harper, and others, 2006; Sherrill and Siegel, 1989; Siegel, 1994; and Zdziarski and others, 2007). These lessons learned are from student affairs staff who experienced critical incidents on their campuses such as the death of a student; and large-scale crisis such as collapsed bonfires (Texas A&M), fires in campus residence halls and other facilities, natural disasters such as hurricanes, tornadoes, and earthquakes. The lessons learned are clustered under the areas of communication, technology, protocol and policy decisions, and leadership.

Communication

Communication is critical. The need to know what is happening and what the university is doing about the crisis is important for all stakeholders involved. Before an emergency, institutions should know their various audiences and where they are likely to go for information. During the crisis, the management and dissemination of information is paramount, and after the crisis how the university ensures that the college or university reputation is intact and that the right messages are delivered to the campus community and general public. Student affairs professionals who have experienced critical incidents, campus emergencies, and disasters echo the following consistent messages:

- Designate one spokesperson so there is one unified and consistent message. The type and level of crisis will determine if the spokesperson is the president, the public relations office, or a student affairs professional. Know the public relations staff and make sure they know the leadership team in student affairs so that the right person can be chosen to represent the university.
- Designate main ways to communicate with the campus community and make sure faculty, staff, and students know the primary source. In today's technology-driven society, there are many forms of communication that can propagate rumors and spread them quickly. Even today's radio and television news stations can add to the misinformation. Having one main source, usually the university's Web page, is the preferred communication medium.
- Web communication is critical, but it cannot take the place of human contact. Many student affairs staff stressed the importance of setting up phone

banks managed by student affairs. In doing so, make sure that the individuals on the phones are selected carefully and trained thoroughly. Others stressed the importance of town hall meetings to communicate with campus members, share information face to face, and allow for questions. Contingent on the type of crisis, others talked about the importance of the president and vice president to be seen out walking the campus.

Technology

Not a day goes by that we do not use technology. Higher education institutions rely on technology for data storage, communication processes, and network systems. Often it makes jobs easier. In times of crisis it can be of great help. Likewise, technology can also hinder operations and response if it goes down or is overloaded. Student affairs staff had these points of advice regarding technology:

- Create an emergency command center that is well equipped with the technology needed to communicate effectively and respond quickly. Test it prior to the need to employ the command center and its technology. Make sure it has diversified ways to communicate with the emergency operations team.
- Redundancy is good. Multiple ways to communicate and backup systems off site were two aspects of technology that staff reiterated from their experiences, primarily when the crisis is of a large scale. Multiple methods of communication such as the Internet, phone banks, two-way radios, battery-free radios, campus plasma screens, or prominent message boards should be incorporated into the emergency plan. Maintain off-site records management to ensure that important records are preserved in the event that the campus is non-inhabitable or destroyed. Have servers at different locations, either through relationships with sister institutions or through a business vendor. Cell phones have made communication with staff and students much easier. However, they also go down when circuits are overloaded or cell towers go down. University e-mail accounts are easy ways to communicate, but again, require staff to have alternative e-mail accounts in case the university server is inoperable. Provide off-site capabilities for payroll and business operations.
- Leverage the technology. Continually look at ways to increase communication through technology. Explore the newest business and security measures that are being promoted that use multiple forms to automatically notify campus members. Maximize the ways that students use cell phones, text messaging, MySpace, and Facebook. Check the blogs; use a blog analyst to

determine what information and misinformation is circulating about the crisis, and use the blog to distribute accurate information through the university's official Web site.

Protocol and Policy Revisions

One of the aspects of emergency planning that was noted earlier in this chapter is the importance of debriefing with campus colleagues after any campus crisis. Administrators will often convene to review their emergency plans after the latest catastrophic event that occurs on a college campus, when, in fact, this should be done on an annual basis. The following are consistent themes that emerged from student affairs staff regarding emergency planning and policy decisions that occur during a crisis that have long-term implications for the institution:

- Always take the time to debrief, review, and, if needed, revise emergency protocol plans after each critical incident.
- University emergency plans should be just that—university wide. Make sure students, staff, and faculty are involved with the planning, and that all members of the institution know their roles and responsibilities during a campus emergency or disaster.
- Establish partnerships with vendors and other institutions as a part of the emergency plan. Standing purchase orders for essentials and relationships with other student affairs colleagues to supplement staff primarily for psychological and medical assistance can save valuable time in the midst of the crisis.
- Policy decisions regarding classes: When does an institution decide to cancel classes, and when is it best to keep to the schedule? This question is answered on a case-by-case basis. It takes into consideration the type of event, magnitude of the event, loss of lives, and loss of campus property. Canceling classes can range from one day to one semester. The general sense is the sooner you can get back to the normal academic schedule, the better for the individual members and the institution. For example, California State University, Northridge (earthquake) and University of Miami (Hurricane Andrew) had to ensure that their facilities were safe prior to reopening after their respective campuses. Gulf Coast schools after Hurricane Katrina had no choice but to close for the semester. Texas A&M decided it was important to continue the academic class schedule after the bonfire accident. Other catastrophes like the Virginia Tech shootings and the Los Angeles riots occurred at the end of a semester. Classes and final exam periods were canceled, but graduation ceremonies took place as scheduled.

- Suspending of long and time honored traditions: There are times when the university needs to suspend traditions that have taken place on a campus for the community members to heal and/or for an investigation of the incident. The Texas A&M bonfire is such an example.

Leadership Lessons

In a time of crisis, strong, decisive leadership is required. The university needs to move quickly and steadfastly. The scale of the crisis and the culture of an institution will determine the designated person in charge of the response. For example, for most campus emergencies and all disaster-level crises, the president is likely the person in charge. Contingent on the type of critical incident, it may be the senior student affairs officer or for facility or environmental crisis it may be the chief operating officer or chief financial officer of the institution. Regardless, these individuals are successful only if they are surrounded by an effective group of leaders who are prepared to lead in times of crisis. Leadership lessons learned by various student affairs leaders are as follows:

- Do what is right. First and foremost put the needs of the academic community first. Make sure that basic needs are taken care of for all community members, along with communication that is candid and caring. Litigation and the concern for the financial costs should never supersede doing the right thing of helping to care for students and their families and responding to affected faculty and staff members in the community.
- Strengths and weaknesses are amplified during crisis. Know your staff. It is important to know the depth of skills and abilities of individual staff. Learn to leverage the strengths of individual staff and departments and work outside the organizational structure to reduce the weak points. After the crisis, get proactive and make the changes that were needed before the crisis occurred.
- Symbols are powerful. Symbolic leadership and symbols during a crisis are important cues that can reassure a campus community. Demonstrating compassion, communicating actions taken to maintain or restore campus safety, and promoting healing are ways administrators make their leadership visible. The act of the college president and senior student affairs officer walking the campus for all to see reassures people. During the Los Angeles riots (1992), the president of the University of Southern California stayed on campus. After Hurricane Andrew, the president and student affairs staff at the University of Miami were visible every evening at the campus cafeterias to speak to students who remained on campus. Rituals are another important

element of symbolic leadership. College campuses embody the memories, feelings, and identities of the people who attend and work there. Memorial services, vigils, convocations, or places to convene are all important for community healing and community bonding.

Conclusion

The effective management of a crisis is an essential skill for a student affairs administrator. In fact, a successfully managed crisis can result in positive visibility, increased confidence, and deepened appreciation and understanding of the role of student affairs on campus. By that same token, a poorly managed crisis can result in a very different outcome. Loss of respect, influence, and trust, individual reassignment, or even dismissal is also possible if the crisis is major and if it is poorly handled.

More important, how student affairs professionals deal with crisis will have a lasting influence on the lives of the students who are touched. No greater opportunity exists for our profession to provide support and understanding than to individuals who are affected personally by a crisis. Many will come through that experience either strengthened or diminished. The role of student affairs in the management and response both to the crisis and its aftermath can make a crucial difference. In response to the national dialogue over the role of student affairs in responding to campus crises, the National Association of Student Personnel Administrators (NASPA) invited a group of senior student affairs professionals to publish a white paper entitled, "In Search of Safer Communities: Emerging Practices for Student Affairs in Addressing Campus Violence" (Jablonski, McClellan, Zdziarski, and others, in press).

In many respects, the student affairs profession is uniquely positioned to manage these most difficult moments. We have support services in place, we work in communities with shared values, and our ongoing communication and relationships with students, faculty, and staff provide a positive context for dealing with crisis effectively.

In other respects, we are not so well positioned or prepared. We may have a general understanding of the federal and state laws, as well as case laws, that apply to higher education. However, our legal knowledge rarely extends to the world of litigation and the complexities of that process. The same gap often applies to the world of media relations. We all have a basic appreciation of the importance of public relations, and we often have regular interaction with the student press, but how many in our profession have the training to be successful in a press conference or to appreciate the subtle differences in dealing with the print versus the broadcast media or with the national "entertainment" journalists versus the national or regular news?

The process of becoming more familiar with such areas as litigation and media relations increases the likelihood that we will be better equipped to handle a crisis when it comes. Moreover, those issues provide wonderful opportunities for staff development and interaction within the student affairs division and across campus. The successful practitioner will recognize that crisis management can be as critical a task as any that we engage in and will take whatever steps are necessary to prepare for a sound performance in that role.

References

Allen, R. D. *Handbook of Post-Disaster Interventions*. Corte Madera, Calif.: Select Press, 1993.

Allen, K., and Cherrey, C. *Systemic Leadership: Enriching the Meaning of Our Work*. Lanham, MD: University Press of America, 2000.

Bejin, A., and Morin, E. "Introduction." *Communications*, 1976, 25, 1–3.

Bridges, W. *Managing Transitions: Making the Most of Change*. Cambridge, Mass.: Perseus, 2003.

Cherrey, C. "The Aftermath of Katrina: Learning Opportunities for SSAOs." *Leadership Exchange*, 2006, 4(3), 5–11.

Clement, L. M., and Rickard, S. T. "Managing Crisis." In L. M. Clement and S. T. Richard (Eds.), *Effective Leadership in Student Services: Voices from the Field*. San Francisco: Jossey-Bass, 1992.

Foxcraft, H. C. "The Works of George Savile, First Marquis of Halifax." *The English Historical Review*, 1896, 11(44), 703–730. [http://ehr.oxfordjournals.org].

Harper, K. S., Paterson, B., and Zdziarski E. II. *Crisis Management: Responding from the Heart*. Washington, D.C.: National Association of Student Personnel Administrators, 2006.

Ikeda, K. *Emergency Operations Plan for* Hawaii *Community College and the University of* Hawaii *at Hilo*. Hilo: University of Hawaii, 2006.

Jablonski, M., McClellan, G. S., Zdziarski, E., and others. *In Search of Safer Communities: Emerging Practices for Student Affairs in Addressing Campus Violence*. Washington D.C: NASPA, (in press).

Lagadec, P. *Preventing Chaos in a Crisis: Strategies for Prevention, Control, and Damage Limitation*. London: McGraw Hill, 1993.

Milian, M. "National Emergency Exchange." Diamondback. College Park: University of Maryland, May 1, 2007.

Mitchell, J. T. *Critical Incident Stress Debriefing: An Operations Manual for the Prevention of Traumatic Stress Among Emergency Services and Disaster Workers*. Ellicot City, Md.: Chevron, 1993.

Mitrof, I., Pauchant, T., and Shrivastava, P. "The Structure of Man-Made Organizational Crisis: Conceptual and Empirical Issues in the Development of a General Theory of Crisis Management." *Technological Forecasting and Social Change*, 1988, 33, 83–107.

Sherrill, J., and Siegel, D. *Responding to Violence on Campus*. San Francisco: Jossey-Bass, 1989.

Shrivastava, P. *Bhopad: Anatomy of a Crisis*. New York: Ballinger, 1987.

Siegel, D. *Campuses Respond to Violent Tragedy*. Phoenix, Ariz.: Oryx, 1994.

Zdziarski, E. II, Dunkel, N, and Rollo, J., and Associates. *Campus Crisis Management: A Comprehensive Guide to Planning, Prevention, Response, and Recovery*. San Francisco: Jossey-Bass, 2007.

Other Resources

Derrington, M. "Calming Controversy." *Executive Educator*, 1993, 15(1), 32–34.

Hoverland, H., McIntruff, C. S., and Rohm, T. *Crisis Management in Higher Education*. San Francisco: Jossey-Bass, 1986.

Maguire, M. "Here Comes Trouble: During an Emergency, A Run-of-the-Mill Crisis Plan Isn't Enough." *Currents*, 1993, 19(3), 26–30.

Mitroff, I., and Pearson, C. *Crisis Management: A Diagnostic Tool for Improving Your Organization's Crisis-Preparedness*. San Francisco: Jossey-Bass, 1993.

Pruett, H. L. and Brown, V. B. *Crisis Intervention and Prevention*. San Francisco: Jossey-Bass, 1990.

Snyder, T. "When Tragedy Strikes." *Executive Educator*, 1993, 15(7), 30–31.

Stevenson, R. (Ed.) What Will We Do: Preparing a School Community to Cope with Crises. Amityville, N.Y.: Baywood, 1994.

EPILOGUE: CONTINUING THE CONVERSATION

George S. McClellan and Jeremy Stringer

The chapters in Parts One through Six represent the collective contributions of the authors to the ongoing professional conversation in student affairs. Like all good conversationalists, the authors have listened carefully to what has been said before them as they extend and enrich the discussion. The Epilogue is to highlight a series of conversation topics synthesized from the authors' remarks in this handbook and to add our thoughts on those topics to the continuing discussion of our profession.

Change as Metatheme

Change has arguably served as the metatheme for student affairs since the 1960s, so it is not surprising that countless changes in our profession are identified throughout this handbook. They include changes in the larger milieu in which higher education is practiced, such as tightening fiscal pressures on our institutions, strong public demand for accountability on our campuses, and a heightened regulatory and litigious environment for our practice. Changes on our campuses, such as an energetic focus on student learning as the essential component of student affairs practice, dissolving barriers between student affairs and academic colleagues on many campuses, and emerging models of both organization and practice are also addressed. Finally, and most important, the conversation reflects changes in our students, including the centrality of technology in their lives, higher numbers of students with serious mental health concerns, increasingly diverse student populations, and the need to redefine traditional notions of what "student development" entails, both in theory and in practice.

Barr and Desler (2000) observed, "The future of higher education and student affairs is anything but predictable" (p. 629). While we may be able to discern the direction and implications of change only in retrospect (Levine and Cureton, 1998), it should be apparent to anyone involved in student affairs that we are and will continue to be thoroughly drenched in the white water of change (Vaill, 1996). How then are we to practice our profession in the face of uncertainty and unpredictability? We concur with the advice offered by Woodard and Komives (2003) that student affairs professionals must "generate and influence change anchored in our core values but reflective of a changing context" (p. 646). It will be up to each of us, working in conjunction with our campus communities and other stakeholders, to determine the most appropriate responses to the challenges and opportunities that changes present to us.

Timeless Values Frame Our Practice

Another thread throughout the conversation in this handbook is that the timeless values of the student affairs professional have been essential in consistently framing our practice even as we undertake it in an environment of change. Among these values, perhaps none is more important than the focus within our profession on the development of the whole student. The importance of this concept predates the recognition of student affairs as a profession, but it was expressly stated in 1937 in *The Student Personnel Point of View* National Association of Student Personnel Administrators (American Council on Education, 1937) in which it was asserted that higher education has an "obligation" to consider "the person as a whole" (p. 49). Since the publication of the original *Student Personnel Point of View*, the development of the whole person has been the profession's most significant professional linchpin.

Other enduring values of the profession include:

- An emphasis on student learning, both inside and outside of the classroom
- Student ownership of their educational experiences,
- The shared responsibility of all educators to collaborate to support student success,
- Leadership in developing diverse, multicultural, and global communities, and

- The necessity for student affairs professionals to continue to engage in assessment and research in order to better understand the students we serve and their college-related experiences.

The discussion in this handbook provides ample evidence that these values, all of which were articulated in *The Student Personnel Point of View* (American Council on Education, 1937, 1949) and other foundational documents, remain vital to contemporary professional practice in student affairs.

Alexander Astin observes, "Values are at the very basis of education. . . . Just having a curricular requirement is a value. We can't escape values; they are embedded in everything we do" (cited in Gair and Mullins, 2001, p. 23). While our lasting values provide solid bedrocks for practice, they may also cause us to miss valid antitheses or partially hidden truths about our students and their education. This Janusian dilemma should motivate us to ask what it is that we overlook, look away from, or fail to see as a result of our focus on cherished values. Our ongoing professional conversation must include an active review and interrogation of our professional values.

Ethical Principles Inform Our Actions

Just as values frame our practice, ethical principles inform our actions. Everyday ethics, as defined in Chapter Nine of this volume by Dalton and his associates, are a living element of our decision-making processes. Our shared ethical principles (Council for the Advancement of Standards in Higher Education [CAS], 2006) are critically important as we address issues of conflict, crisis, legal affairs, staff supervision, diversity, student health, confidentiality of student records, and other arenas of daily practice.

The CAS standards for graduate preparation programs in the student affairs field stipulate that "graduates must be knowledgeable about and be able to apply a code of ethics or ethical principles sanctioned by a recognized professional organization that provides ethical guidance for their work" (CAS, 2004, Part 5a). We assume that most graduate preparation programs prepare new professionals to recognize ethical dilemmas and apply accepted ethical codes to their resolution. Graduate preparation programs, however, are not the only gates through which professionals enter the profession, and we can all benefit from opportunities to reconsider and refresh our ethical frameworks. We suspect that more needs to be done to ensure that ethical principles are enduring topics of conversation within our profession.

The Importance of Context

Another consistent topic of the authors' conversation in this volume is the importance of contextual variables in defining professional practice in student affairs. Two particularly salient contextual variables are institutional mission and sociopolitical environment.

Institutional mission influences the organizational model employed, relationships both within and outside of campus, institutional governance, political practices, staffing patterns, and characteristics of the student body being served. While institutional mission is subject to change, such changes are often more symbolic or subtle than substantive. However, it is clear that the institutional mission, whatever it may be espoused to be, affects the nature of student affairs practice (Hirt, 2006).

On the other hand, sociopolitical context is more fluid and dynamic. The issues addressed in student affairs practice are a reflection of sociopolitical context. Bud Thomas (Woodard and Komives, 2003) put forward a typology of three types of issues that confront student affairs: ongoing national issues, emerging national issues, and local campus issues. The defining dimension of Thomas's typology is sociopolitical context.

The sociopolitical context in which student affairs professionals engage their practice is constructed at the local, state, national, and international levels. While commitment to diverse, multicultural, and global communities is one of our core values, engagement in these areas might look very different at an open access institution in the Southwest or in the Upper Plains than it does at an urban elite private institution in the Northeast or a rural public research institution in the Southeast, and the work might look very different at any one of those institutions at a time when program resources are more readily available than at a time when such resources are more scarce. Student affairs' role in governance is likely to be constructed differently in a state where higher education labor is unionized than it is in a state where unionization is not prevalent. Our work with student organizations is different when the national political discourse is highly charged (for example, as we near national elections or at times of war) than is the case when the national political scene is more mundane. At the international level, we are all too familiar with the ways in which international incidents can shape our work. The impact can be short term, such as the emotional response and subsequent philanthropic activity on campuses following the tsunami of 2004 in the Indian Ocean. The effects may also be long term, such as the ongoing emotional, enrollment, curricular, and programmatic effects as a result of the terrorist attacks of September 11, 2001.

Investing in Higher Expectations

In the previous edition of this handbook, Barr and Desler (2000) identified as one of its themes the need for student affairs to support institutional efforts to meet the high expectations of its various constituents. There is no doubt that the publics we serve (students, families of students, business interests, governmental entities, and others) have high expectations for those of us in higher education. Why wouldn't they or shouldn't they? Higher education in the United States has been one of the nation's great success stories and continues to be one of its greatest assets (Secretary of Education's Commission on the Future of Higher Education, 2006). Still, as the importance of a college education continues to increase at the same time that the costs of pursuing such an education escalate, it is not surprising that the high bar of expectations established as a result of our historical performance is raised even further (Immerwahr and Johnson, 2006).

There is evidence in the preceding chapters in this volume and in many corners of student affairs that our profession is taking note of these increased expectations and attempting to address them. The work of CAS in updating standards of practice for student affairs and the focus of the two major student affairs professional associations on assessment (as evidenced by their creation of assessment-related organizational infrastructure, development of stand-alone assessment workshops, and inculcation of assessment skills and strategies through workshops at national conferences) are examples of such evidence.

Still, we cannot help but wonder about the extent to which the assessment and accountability movements afoot in student affairs reflect our profession's reaction to external stimuli versus an internalized value in our field. Much of our professional discourse, perhaps too much, reflects a defensive dimension of the former rather than an affirmative expression of the latter. It is understandably difficult to make time for assessment, particularly well-done ongoing assessment that involves students and academic colleagues across our institutions, when there is so much work to be done every day on our campuses. It is also the case that assessment, especially quantitative assessment, is not something that appeals to the humanists who are attracted to the student affairs profession. We ought to move beyond our view of assessment and accountability as being simply an adaptation to external demands. Incorporating the additional perspective of assessment and accountability as a strategy for pursuing the higher expectations we hold for ourselves would be an important step forward in fulfilling our role in supporting institutional and student success. The ability to conduct high-quality assessment and interpret the results to other campus educators should be core professional competencies of student affairs educators.

Technology is another area in which higher education and student affairs is confronted by higher expectations. It is impossible to think of renovating or constructing facilities without giving thought to the possibilities that technologies present in the project, but the impact of such technologies on the original project and ongoing maintenance budgets is equally inescapable. The potential for global recruitment using Web-based communication strategies is enormous; so, too, is the new scope of competition for students as a result of the emergence of such strategies. The opportunities available for students to take courses from a variety of sources in an array of formats most suitable to their learning styles and personal circumstances offers the promise of reducing stratification as a result of structural barriers. However, those same opportunities may be priced or presented in ways that perpetuate privilege rather than challenge it.

Fiscal pressures are a challenge for student affairs practitioners as they work the heightened expectations they and others have for higher education. As noted in several chapters, constraints on fiscal resources continue to be a central concern for student affairs in a variety of ways. Among them are issues of access to and affordability of higher education for students, availability of resources for student affairs programs and services, and the costs and availability of health services and student health insurance.

It appears likely that higher education will continue to find itself competing for the fiscal resources it requires in order to provide the programs and services expected by the various constituencies it serves. While it would be understandable, and perhaps somewhat therapeutic, for student affairs to engage in bemoaning the scarcity of resources and the perceived tendency for cuts to come first and deepest to student affairs programs, to our profession's credit it appears that we have chosen instead to focus our conversation on creative and cost-effective ways to achieve our programmatic goals and on sharing information on how to identify and pursue new funding opportunities through grant writing, fund raising, or auxiliary revenue operations.

Sandeen and Barr (2006) note that student affairs has become a mature profession. This means that professionals in the field may no longer struggle for professional recognition and respect for their expertise. However, leaders in the profession may find that this recognition comes at a cost. Arthur Levine and Jeanette Cureton (1998) state that mature industries experience demands to "control growth, reduce cost, measure achievement, and require accountability" (p. 155). These challenges are echoed in the final report of the Spellings Commission (Secretary of Education's Commission on the Future of Higher Education, 2006). The public and governmental agencies not only want an increasing amount of data on the attainment of defined educational outcomes, but also increasingly want to know that measurable objectives have been achieved in a cost-effective manner. The themes of access, affordability, and accountability will continue to be present in the public discourse about higher education. Student affairs will need to be invested in meeting the challenges they pose *for* higher education in order to receive their requisite share of the public's investment *in* higher education.

Fostering Learning

Student learning is one of the foci of the discussion of higher expectations of higher education. Much of the discourse regarding student learning addresses the importance of creating collaborations between academic affairs and student affairs colleagues to foster comprehensive, engaging, integrated, seamless, and learner-centered experiences for students. The partnership between student affairs leaders and their academic colleagues in shifting the emphasis from teaching to learning was "projected and thoroughly discussed" (Manning, Kinzie, and Schuh, 2006, p. 151) in *The Student Learning Imperative* (American College Personnel Association [ACPA], 1996), *Powerful Partnerships* (American Association for Higher Education [AAHE] and others, 1998), and *Principles of Good Practice for Student Affairs* (ACPA and NASPA, 1997). Subsequent works such as *Learning Reconsidered* (Keeling, 2004) and *Learning Reconsidered 2* (Keeling, 2006) have done much to advance this conversation across the full spectrum of academe.

It is helpful and healthy for student affairs and academic affairs colleagues to engage one another in discussions related to facilitating student learning. However, it is worth noting that framing the practice of student affairs as a form of teaching is hardly new (see, for example, Lloyd-Jones and Smith, 1954).

Robert Fenske (1980), writing about the history of student affairs, suggested that in the future the field might well be subsumed back into the faculty from which it sprang. It seems unlikely that the field would disappear from the higher education landscape given the degree to which it is structurally entrenched at individual institutions, in statewide systems, and through established professional associations. It seems very possible, instead, that there will be continued discussion and action around various organizational models that place student affairs in the portfolio of provosts, or about hybrid organizational models (or professional positions) that are a blend of the traditionally distinct academic and student affairs domains (Manning, Kinzie, and Schuh, 2006).

Developing Whole Students and Whole Communities

Much like the conversation in the chapters in this volume addressing the importance of engaged, integrated, and seamless learning, there is also discussion throughout regarding strategies for pursuing the development of whole communities and whole students. As one dimension of this discussion, it is apparent from comments of our authors throughout this book that student affairs remains at the forefront of supporting students' exploration and celebration of their identities and of promoting structurally diverse, multicultural, and international campus communities. There have been substantial changes over time in the quantity, diversity, and complexity of identities of both our students and our institutions. Some of those changes, such as the increasing proportion of women and part-time students enrolled in higher education, have emerged gradually. Other changes, such as the explosive growth in the enrollment of students with disabilities or the rapid emergence of online students or for-profit institutions, have been much more sudden.

Our theories and models of practice are being challenged, interrogated, and revised (or new models developed) to better inform our work with a continuously changing body of students. Similar changes are underway with regard to programming, facilities development and management, staff supervision, and graduate preparation. All the while, we as individuals are engaged in exploring the intersections of our own identities, epistemologies, and professional endeavors.

Student affairs professionals are also engaged in supporting the development of healthy students and healthy communities. In doing so, practitioners are addressing both ongoing issues, such as the consequences of students' choices related to the use of alcohol and other drugs, and emerging issues, including the rise in the number of students experiencing mental health problems and the alarming severity of those problems.

Another dimension of the healthy student and healthy community conversation is crisis management. Concern in this area reflects the perceived threat of global pandemic, experiences with natural disasters such as Hurricanes Katrina and Rita, and incidents of campus violence such as occurred at Virginia Tech, Northern Illinois University, and the University of Memphis, among others.

The resurgence of interest in student affairs regarding student spirituality helps enrich our conversation regarding developing whole communities and whole students. The work of Alexander Astin, Helen Astin, and Jennifer Lindholm (Higher Education Research Institute, 2004) offers a valuable stepping-off point for long-overdue consideration in this area. Their national study indicated that 75 percent of third-year college students surveyed were "searching for meaning and purpose in life" and were actively discussing spirituality with friends (78 percent). Yet more than half of the respondents (56 percent) said that their faculty "never provide opportunities to discuss the meaning and purpose of life" (Higher Education Research Institute, 2004, p. 6). The same might be said of many student affairs professionals, particularly in public institutions, who, despite student yearnings for engagement about the larger questions of life, approach the topics of meaning and spirituality as if they were taboo subjects.

Just as spirituality is an important issue in the lives of our students and our campus communities, and hence in the future of student affairs, issues related to broad international social movements are also critical to our students' development. Sharon Parks (2000) has pointed out that "one way young adults find a sense of meaning and purpose" (p. 187) is to participate in social movements. We are heartened that many students get a "double win" (Waitley, 1984) by participating in such causes as the international green and peace movements: they are developing their own sense of identity while at the same time striving to make the world a better place for all of us.

Contemporary practice must also address the growing challenges to traditional notions of *whole* or *community* presented by computer-mediated communication. For example, how does computer-mediated communication affect our understanding of the development of either identity or community? More fundamentally, is our notion of a single, integrated, whole identify still appropriate given that students today increasingly take on multiple, whole, distinct, and diverse identities (Turkle, 1997)? And what do Boyer's (1990a) principles of community mean in a world where students participate in cyberworlds in such astounding numbers?

Eroding Boundaries

These questions bring us to another of the themes of conversation in the preceding chapters. Across a variety of dimensions of practice historic boundaries are eroding. They include:

- Boundaries between academic affairs and student affairs as a result of the shared emphasis on student learning, assessment, and accountability
- Boundaries of the classroom, library, and major, as practices such as service learning, digitized resources, and interdisciplinary programs become increasingly common
- Boundaries implied by traditional notions of identity. Challenges to conventional constructions of race are necessitated by the growing numbers of multiracial students, and our theory base must embrace emerging paradigms of gender and sexual orientation, as well as the collision of concepts of human identity and the cyberexperience

- Boundaries of time and personal space as a result of the increasing use of text messaging and 24/7 interaction through omnipresent technologies,
- Boundaries between educational endeavors and economic interests as higher education is increasingly explicitly seen as an instrument of economic development and technology transfer (Slaughter and Rhoades, 2004), and
- Boundaries of national systems of higher education as increasing number of students study abroad, the world economy becomes increasingly globalized, and higher education pursues internationalization.

While the full array of implications of such changes for student affairs professional practice is difficult to foresee, there can be little doubt that the implications will be profound. How then should student affairs professionals prepare themselves for the new reality of renegotiated, reduced, reconfigured, or removed boundaries?

Strengthening Networks and Relationships

Strengthening our networks and relationships, may be one answer to the aforementioned question. Relationships marked by mutual respect and trust are an essential element in developing and sustaining effective partnerships with our colleagues in academic affairs. Similarly, relationships play a significant role in our ability to work through issues, negotiate for budgetary support, and prepare for and respond effectively to incidents of campus conflict. In student affairs, our relationships with a variety of individuals both on and off campus in no small part determine the extent to which we succeed in the political dimensions of our work. Networking and nurturing professional relationships are among the benefits of participation in professional association activities. Relationships are vital in interacting with legislative partners, in friend making and fund raising, and in matters of campus governance. Most important, student affairs practitioners' networks and relationships with individual students and groups of students are vitally important in fulfilling our professional role supporting student and institutional success.

Keeping Our Profession Vital

The final discussion thread is the importance of maintaining the vitality of the student affairs profession. One observation about student affairs that is evident in the chapters in this book is that we are blessed with a rich professional history.

Our predecessors in the field have moved us over time from a set of ad hoc institutional positions and responsibilities to a recognized professional field. They framed theories of practice, articulated ethical standards and standards of practice, promulgated organizational models, and fostered graduate professional training programs. These became the essential building blocks of the contemporary practice of student affairs. Paraphrasing the words of Jim Rhatigan in Chapter One, one way we pay our debts as professionals to those who have paved the way for us in student affairs is through our efforts to do the same for those who will follow us in this grand profession.

Boyer (1990b) described the characteristics of scholarly practice as being based on theory, data driven, inclusive of peer review, tolerant of a variety of perspectives, unselfish, adaptive, cautious and critical, heedful of matters of regeneration, and autonomous. One way to assure the continued vitality of student affairs is to recommit ourselves to the scholarly practice of our profession. This includes engaging in conventional forms of scholarship as well as the scholarship of practice. Simply put, we must seek to better understand our students, our institutions, our contexts, and the complex interactions between them. We must then share those understandings through presentation and publication, subjecting our findings to the scrutiny of others while sharing our newfound knowledge.

In addition, keeping student affairs vital requires that we critically examine structural issues within our profession. How will the growth of specialization and increasing stratification of employment opportunities by specialty and institutional type impact the future of student affairs?

Similarly, we must recommit ourselves to addressing the intractable issues that confront our profession. Why is it that, despite tremendous investment of energy and resources, we have not had greater success in positively affecting choices students make regarding the use of alcohol? How can it be that we have been unable to make greater strides in increasing retention and graduation rates, particularly for students from historically underrepresented groups or families with lower socioeconomic resources?

Our efforts to maintain the vitality of the student affairs profession must also include a focus on our future colleagues. How do we attract the best and brightest people to the profession? In what ways should our professional preparation programs be structured so as to help assure the future success of graduates of those programs as well as the success of the students they serve?

Art Sandeen and Peggy Barr (2006), in their work identifying critical issues confronting student affairs, note, "It would be presumptuous of us to claim that we have the answers" (p. xii) to the complex challenges facing the student affairs profession. We follow their lead in acknowledging that, while we hope that our efforts in raising crucial questions will be helpful, we do not presume to have the answers.

Echoing the words of Jim Rhatigan in Chapter One, "There is much to celebrate in these ordinary days of our lives, part of the fellowship we share with those who came before." We are certain that assuring the vitality of the student affairs profession requires those of us fortunate enough to be invited by students to be both supporters of and witnesses to their pursuit of lifetime aspirations acknowledge and appreciate the wonderment that is our profession.

References

American College Personnel Association. *The Student Learning Imperative: Implications for Student Affairs.* Washington, D.C.: American College Personnel Association, 1996.

American College Personnel Association and National Association of Student Personnel Administrators. *Principles of Good Practice for Student Affairs.* Washington, D.C.: American College Personnel Association and National Association of Student Personnel Administrators, 1997.

American Council on Education. *The Student Personnel Point of View.* Washington, D.C.: American Council on Education, 1937.

American Council on Education. *The Student Personnel Point of View.* Washington, D.C.: American Council on Education, 1949.

American Association for Higher Education, American College Personnel Association, and National Association for Student Personnel Administrators. *Powerful Partnerships.* Washington, D.C.: American Association for Higher Education, American College Personnel Association, and National Association for Student Personnel Administrators, 1998.

Astin, A. W., Astin, H. S., Lindholm, J. A. *The Spiritual Life of College Students: A National Study of College Students' Search for Meaning and Purpose.* Los Angeles: University of California, Higher Education Research Institute, 2003.

Barr, M. J., and Desler, M. K. *"Leadership for the Future."* In M. J. Barr, M. K. Desler, and Associates (Eds.), *The Handbook of Student Affairs Administration* (2nd ed.). San Francisco: Jossey-Bass, 2000.

Boyer, E. *Campus Life: In Search of Community.* Special report of the Carnegie Foundation for Teaching. San Francisco: Jossey-Bass, 1990a.

Boyer, E. *Scholarship Reconsidered: Priorities for the Professoriate.* Princeton, N.J.: Carnegie Foundation for the Advancement of Teaching, 1990b.

Council for the Advancement of Standards in Higher Education. *CAS Statement of Shared Ethical Principles.* Washington, D.C.: Council on the Advancement of Standards, 2006.

Council for the Advancement of Standards in Higher Education. "Master's-Level Graduate Program for Student Affairs Professionals Standards and Guidelines." [http://www.myacpa.org/comm/profprep/facressub/cas.htm]. 2004.

Fenske, R. H. *"Historical Foundations."* In U. Delworth and G. R. Hanson (Eds.), *Student Services: A Handbook for the Profession.* San Francisco: Jossey-Bass, 1980.

Gair, M., and Mullins, G. "Hiding in Plain Sight." In E. Margolis (Ed.), *The Hidden Curriculum in Higher Education.* New York: Routledge, 2001.

Higher Education Research Institute, University of California, Los Angeles. *Spirituality in Higher Education: A National Study of College Students' Search for Meaning and Purpose. Summary of Selected Findings (2000–2003).* [http://www.spirituality.ucla.edu/results/Findings_Summary_Pilot.pdf]. 2004.

Hirt, J. *Where You Work Matters: Student Affairs Administration at Different Types of Institutions.* Washington, D.C.: American College Personnel Association. 2006.

Immerwahr, J., and Johnson, J. *Squeeze Play: How Parents and the Public Look at Higher Education Today.* San Jose, Calif.: National Center for Public Policy and Higher Education, 2006.

Keeling, R. *Learning Reconsidered: A Campus-Wide Focus on the Student Experience.* Washington, D.C.: National Association of Student Personnel Administrators and American College Personnel Association, 2004.

Keeling, R. (Ed.). *Learning Reconsidered 2: Implementing a Campus-Wide Focus on the Student Experience.* Various: American College Personnel Association, Association of College and University Housing Officers-International, Association of College Unions-International, National Academic Advising Association, National Association for Campus Activities, National Association of Student Personnel Administrators, National Intramural-Recreational Sports Association, 2006.

Levine, A., and Cureton, J. S. *When Hope and Fear Collide: A Portrait of Today's College Student.* San Francisco: Jossey-Bass, 1998.

Lloyd-Jones, E., and Smith, M. R. *Student Personnel Work as Deeper Teaching.* New York: Harper and Bros., 1954.

Manning, K., Kinzie, J., and Schuh, J. (Eds.). *One Size Does Not Fit All: Traditional and Innovative Models of Student Affairs Practice.* New York: Routledge, 2006.

Parks, S. D. *Big Questions, Worthy Dreams.* San Francisco: Jossey-Bass, 2000.

Sandeen, A., and Barr, M. J. *Critical Issues for Student Affairs.* San Francisco: Jossey-Bass, 2006.

Secretary of Education's Commission on the Future of Higher Education. *A Test of Leadership: Charting the Future of U.S. Higher Education.* Washington, D.C.: U.S. Department of Education, 2006.

Slaughter, S., and Rhoades, G. *Academic Capitalism and the New Economy: Markets, State, and Higher Education.* Baltimore, Md.: John Hopkins University Press, 2004.

Turkle, S. *Life on the Screen: Identity in the Age of the Internet.* New York: Simon & Schuster, 1997.

Waitley, D. *The Double Win: Success Is a Two-Way Street.* Old Tappan, N.J.: Revell, 1984.

Woodard, D. B. Jr., and Komives, S. R. *"Shaping the Future."* In S. R. Komives and D. B. Woodard Jr. (Eds.), *Student Services: A Handbook for the Profession* (4th ed.). San Francisco: Jossey-Bass, 2003.

Vaill, P. *Learning as a Way of Being: Strategies for Survival in a World of Permanent White Water.* San Francisco: Jossey-Bass, 1996.

NAME INDEX

A

Abes, E. S., 159
Ackerman, R. L., 369
Adam, B. E., 66
Adam, E., 411
Addelston, A., 246
Ahrentzen, S., 69
Akande, B., 295
Akel, M., 582
Aleman, E., 426
Alexander, F. K., 89, 90, 91
Allen, I. E., 289, 293, 294
Allen, K. E., 321, 322–323, 377, 447
Allen, M. J., 530, 533, 537
Allen, R. D., 614, 615
Allen, W. R., 26
Almeida, L., 227
Alschuler, A. S., 15
Alstete, J. W., 188, 189, 190
Altbach, P., 234
Ambler, D., 322, 326
Amelink, C., 29
Amey, M., 391
Anand, R., 362
Anderson, C., 594
Anderson, J. A., 427

Anderson, M. S., 25
Angell, J. K., 7
Antonio, A. L., 245
Appleton, J. R., 430
Archer, J., 267
Aristotle, 169
Arminio, J., 187, 190, 195, 196, 197
Arnold, J. C., 565
Aronowitz, S., 53, 56
Ashkenas, R., 326, 327
Askew, P. E., 91
Astin, A. W., 120, 157, 453, 534, 541, 558, 565, 625, 630
Astin, H. S., 630
Aulepp, L., 555
Austin, A. E., 72, 74

B

Bacharach, S. B., 426
Bailey, W. J., 269
Bain, O., 122, 131
Bair, C. R., 395
Baird, L. L., 70
Baker, B. D., 397
Balderston, F. E., 81, 90
Baldridge, J. V., 47, 48, 430, 437, 439

Ball, S. J., 425
Banahan, L., 454
Bandura, A., 377
Banning, J. H., 61, 68, 69, 150, 155, 156, 158, 199, 321, 323, 566
Banta, T. W., 526, 530, 531, 532, 533, 537
Barcelo, N., 244, 256–257
Barham, J. D., 111, 115
Barker, R., 61, 68
Barr, M. J., 15, 19, 20, 21, 81, 90, 276, 326, 421, 439, 447, 459, 481, 493, 495, 545, 546, 553, 554, 555, 580, 624, 627, 628, 633
Barr, R. B., 66
Barratt, W., 198, 390, 392
Barshaw, C. T., 207, 208
Bartell, M., 120
Bashaw, C. T., 15
Bass, B., 157
Bathurst, J. E., 3
Baum, K., 271
Baxter Magolda, M., 153, 154
Bean, J. P., 150
Bebeau, M. J., 154
Beckhard, R., 326
Beers, C., 9
Bejin, A., 603
Belch, H. A., 232, 397
Belenky, M. F., 154
Belgarde, W. L., 26
Bell, D. A., 159
Bell, J. E., 122
Bender, B. E., 90
Benitez, M., 27
Bennett, B. R., 29
Bennett, M. J., 247
Bennis, W., 477
Bensimon, E. M., 260, 409, 420, 442, 443, 540
Benton, S. A., 272, 278
Benton, S. L., 272, 278
Bergquist, W., 440, 441
Berkner, L., 94, 95
Bernstein, A. R., 229
Bertrand, R. D., 27
Betts, J. R., 188, 189
Bianchi, S. M., 83
Bilodeau, B. L., 233
Binet, A., 8
Bingham, W. V., 7
Birnbaum, R., 322, 427, 435
Bishop, A., 255
Black, H. C., 508, 509

Blackburn, J. L., 6, 8, 9
Blaesser, W. W., 12
Blakeley, B., 299
Blanchard, K., 457
Blase, J., 425, 426
Blimling, G. S., 15, 54, 105, 110, 112, 174, 212, 245, 374, 450
Bloland, P. A., 210, 211, 407
Bloom, B. S., 538
Boettcher, J., 304
Bok, D., 53, 54, 56, 229
Bolman, L. G., 157, 322, 342, 425, 427, 428, 430, 448, 451, 459, 474
Bonsall, D. L., 452
Borden, V.M.H., 289–290
Borkowski, N. A., 399
Bostock, D., 169
Bourassa, D. M., 407, 417
Bowen, W. G., 229
Boyer, E. L., 265, 406, 631, 633
Boylan, M., 171
Boyle, J., 590
Bracco, K. R., 453
Braddock, R., 226
Brawer, F. B., 25, 51, 427
Braxton, J. M., 61, 69, 150
Breneman, D. W., 23, 29
Bresciani, M. J., 526, 527, 528, 530, 531, 533, 536, 537
Bridges, W., 614
Briggs, K. C., 156
Briggs, L. R., 5
Brint, S., 51
Broido, E. M., 233, 247, 255
Bronwyn, S., 411
Brown, M. C., 26, 27
Brown, O. G., 85
Brown, R., 5
Brown, R. D., 13, 110, 148, 154, 360
Brown, S., 596
Brown, S. C., 153
Brubacher, J. S., 9, 22
Bryan, R. A., 433
Bryan, W. A., 178, 190, 191, 361
Bryant, D. R., 149
Bryson, J. M., 447, 451
Buckingham, M., 450, 457
Buford, B., 368
Bumba, R., 453
Burack, C., 405, 414, 415, 418, 454
Burgstahler, S., 303

Burke, J. C., 106, 107
Burkhardt, J., 411
Burlingame, P. J., 15
Burnett, D. J., 592
Bush, G. W., 105
Byrnes, J., 356

C

Cajete, G. A., 33, 34
Callahan, J. C., 168
Callan, P. M., 453
Campbell, K. J., 109
Cantor, J. A., 371, 372, 382
Cantwell, B., 120
Caple, R. B., 15, 212
Carducci, R., 434
Carey, K., 105
Carnevale, A. P., 244
Carnevale, D., 295
Carney, C. M., 26
Carnoy, M., 229
Carpenter, D. S., 174, 187, 191, 335, 371, 372,
    374–375, 376, 379, 393, 400
Carr, J. L., 270, 271
Carroll, M., 526–527
Carter, L., 433
Casey-Powell, D., 298, 300, 303, 304
Cass, V. C., 152, 158
Castelo-Rodriguez, C., 231
Caswell, J., 596
Cattell, R. B., 8
Ceja, M., 159
Cervero, R. M., 376
Chambers, J., 3
Chambers, T., 411
Chang, M. J., 234, 235, 236, 245, 258
Cheldelin, S. I., 467, 468, 469
Cherrey, C., 321, 322–323, 377, 447, 602, 614, 615
Chickering, A. W., 62, 64, 110, 148, 151, 152, 153,
    156, 157, 158, 367, 474
Choy, S. P., 99
Clark, B. R., 44, 50, 63
Clark, T. A., 5
Cleary, J., 523
Clement, L. M., 105, 603
Cleveland-Innes, M., 292
Coaxum, J., 26
Coffman, C., 450, 457
Cohen, A. M., 24, 25, 51, 427
Collins, D., 29, 390
Collins, J. C., 73, 195

Collis, D. J., 49
Colvin, A. J., 449
Connolly, M. R., 70
Connolly, W. E., 243
Considine, M., 44, 53, 56
Constantine, M. G., 159
Contreras-McGavin, M., 434
Conway, J., 594
Coomes, M. D., 15, 209, 211, 397, 399
Cooper, D. L., 148, 196, 397
Cooper, M., 449
Cooper, S., 267
Corak, K., 51
Corrigan, M. E., 231
Corson, J., 48, 49
Cortes, C. E., 233
Costrell, R. M., 188, 189
Coulter, S., 5
Covey, S., 457
Cowley, W. H., 3, 5, 7, 8, 10, 11, 13
Cranston, N., 433, 434
Crawford, A. E., 16
Crawley, A., 288
Creamer, D. G., 148, 197, 372,
    380, 433
Crookston, B. B., 13
Crosby, P. C., 166
Cross, K. P., 15
Cross, W. E., Jr., 152, 159
Croteau, D., 451
Crow, M. F., 6
Crowley, W. H., 212
Cullin, F. T., 271
Cummings, W. K., 122, 131
Cunningham, M., 395
Cureton, J. S., 624, 628
Curtis, D. V., 47, 48
Cuyjet, M. J., 85, 231, 545, 555

D

Daddona, M. F., 397, 399
Dahne, M., 590
Daloz, L., 450
Dalton, J. C., 166, 452, 454, 457
Dannells, M., 149, 391, 449, 450
Dare, L. A., 292, 294
D'Augelli, A. R., 158
Davidson, D. L., 28, 29, 36
Davis, C., 304
Davis, J. E., 26, 27
Davis, R., 96

Davis, T. L., 228, 242, 247
de Valero, Y. F., 389
De Wit, H., 121
Deal, T. E., 157, 322, 342, 425, 427, 428, 430, 448, 451, 459, 474
Dean, L. A., 112
Deaton, R., 106
Deavers, L., 590
Delgado, R., 159
Delworth, U., 279, 555
Dempster, N., 433
Depree, M., 455, 456
Desler, M. K., 624, 627
Deutsch, M., 459
Dewey, J., 10, 253
Dey, E. L., 228, 229, 232, 235
Di Fazio, W., 53, 56
Diamond, R. M., 66, 411
Dickeson, R. C., 501
Dietz, L. H., 450
DiGeronimo, T. F., 271
Dirkx, J. M., 376, 382
Donahoo, S., 27
Dore, T. M., 391
Downie, R., 187
Drucker, P. F., 359, 367
Drum, D. J., 555
Dubeck, L. W., 496
Duderstadt, J. J., 108
Dungy, G. J., 110, 591
Dunkel, N., 604
Dunkle, J. H., 265, 271, 278, 280
Dunn, M. S., 397
Duran, L. R., 269
Durant, R., 270

E

Eaton, J. S., 106
Eberhardt, D., 166
Eberly, C., 393
Ecker, G. P., 47, 48
Edison, M. I., 98, 245
Eells, G. T., 275
Ehrich, L. C., 433
Eisenhart, M. A., 67
Eisenhower, D. D., 12
El Nasser, H., 233
El-Khawas, E., 227, 229
Ellingboe, B. J., 121

Ellis, S., 425, 447, 453
Enchelmayer, E. J., 450
Engberg, D., 121
Engstrom, C. M., 409
Eraut, M., 160
Erikson, E., 151
Erison, E., 149
Erwin, T. D., 198, 199
Estanek, S. M., 321, 323, 430, 435
Estevão, S., 227
Ethington, C. A., 395
Etzkowitz, H., 25
Evans, N. J., 148, 150, 151, 153, 154, 155, 157, 206, 210, 211, 247
Ewell, P. T., 107, 526, 527

F

Faghihi, F., 395
Fenske, R. H., 88, 629
Fernandes, E. M., 227
Ferren, A. S., 411
Fetterman, D., 72
Fhagen-Smith, P., 152
Field, K., 188
Figler, H. E., 555
Fincher, C., 24
Finder, A., 234, 236
Fine, M., 237, 246
Finn, C. B., 451
Finney, J. E., 453
Fischer, K., 88
Fisher, B. S., 271
Fisher, R., 467, 468
Fisk, E., 51
Fletcher, J., 168
Fley, J., 5, 6, 7
Flowers, B. S., 477
Floyd, D. L., 298, 300, 303, 304
Forney, D. S., 148
Fowler, J. W., 154
Foxcraft, H. C., 615
Franke, A., 272
Freakley, M., 433
Freed, J. E., 536
Freire, P., 447
French, J.R.P., 435, 436
Fried, J., 179, 251, 409
Fry, R. A., 244
Fuller, T.M.A., 420
Fygetakis, E. C., 454

G

Gair, M., 625
Galbraith, J. R., 326, 327
Gallagher, R. P., 272, 274, 275
Gamson, Z. F., 64
Gardner, M. M., 528, 537
Garner, B. A., 508
Gates, H. L., 236
Gee, J. P., 591
Gehring, D. D., 86, 269, 524
Gendron, M., 360
Gerda, J. J., 209
Gidycz, C. A., 270
Gilley, A. M., 376
Gilley, J. W., 376
Gilligan, C., 110, 154
Gilroy, M., 15
Gipson, E., 179, 180
Glater, J. D., 234, 236
Gochenauer, P., 190, 195, 196, 197
Gold, J. A., 190, 193
Golde, C. M., 391, 392
Goldsmith, M., 326
Goleman, D., 474, 477
Gonyea, R. M., 61, 66
Gonzalez, K. P., 392, 395
Goodman, D. J., 247
Gordon, S. E., 190
Gowan, M., 336
Grace, G., 452
Green, M. F., 121
Greenleaf, R. K., 157
Gregory, S. T., 28
Grimaldi, J. V., 596
Grubb, W. N., 51
Guba, E. G., 558
Guido-DiBrito, F., 148
Guiffrida, D., 34
Gunsalus, C. K., 459
Gupton, J., 231
Gurin, G., 228
Gurin, P., 228

H

Hagadoorn, J., 406
Hagedorn, L. S., 98, 245
Haigh, M. J., 120
Hall, L. M., 232

Hamrick, F. A., 151
Hanaka, M. E., 358
Hanson, G. S., 207, 208
Hardee, M. D., 10
Hardy, C., 438
Hardy, T. W., 596
Harpel, R. L., 106
Harper, K. S., 603
Harper, S. R., 147, 148, 149, 226, 447
Harper, W. R., 7
Harris, A. R., 15
Harris, F. H., 149
Harris, R. A., 452
Harvey, W. B., 230
Haskins, C. H., 3
Haugabrook, A. K., 420
Hauptman, A. M., 90
Hawkins, B., 358
Hawkins, P., 452
Hawley, W., 440
Haworth, J. G., 395
Hayes-Harris, M., 190
Healey, P., 25
Heard, R. L., 86
Hearn, J. C., 106
Hearn, T., 437
Heifetz, R. A., 442, 473
Heinmiller, K., 391
Heitzmann, D., 276
Henderson, L., 598
Henkel, M., 453
Herdlein, R. J., 15, 425
Hesselbein, F., 326, 327
Hettler, B., 267
Hicks, L., 451
Hill, B. A., 121
Hines, E., 47, 48, 49
Hinton, K. G., 85, 394, 396
Hirsch, D. J., 405, 414, 415, 418, 454
Hirschy, A. S., 69, 150
Hirt, J. B., 19, 29, 51, 283, 318, 321, 323, 626
Hitlin, P., 586
Hocker, J. L., 464
Hoffman, C. M., 82
Holland, D. C., 67
Holland, J. L., 69, 156
Hollingsworth, K. R., 271, 272, 280
Holmes, H., 139
Holmes, L., 7
hooks, b., 243, 249
Hoover, E., 281

Hopkins, L. B., 7, 10
Hornfischer, D., 579
Hossler, D., 61
Houser, S., 229
Howard-Hamilton, M. F., 85, 148, 388, 389, 394, 396
Howe, N., 280
Hrutka, M. E., 304
Huba, M. E., 536
Hubbard, B., 594
Huebner, L. A., 69
Hughes, P., 475
Hughey, A. W., 454
Humphrey, E., 433
Humphries, F. S., 27
Hune, S., 228
Hunt, M., 8
Hunter, B., 86
Hurley, J. L., 266
Hurst, J. C., 69, 555
Hurtado, S., 120, 129, 228, 229, 231, 232, 235, 245
Hyman, R. E., 388, 394, 407, 409

I

Ikeda, K., 605
Immerwahr, J., 627
Isserstedt, W., 131
Iwai, S., 69

J

Jablonski, M. R., 454
Jackson, B., 409
Jackson, D., 450
Jackson, J.F.L., 86
Jackson, M. L., 100, 333
Jacobs, B. C., 190
Jacoby, B., 192, 412, 413
Jagger, A. M., 254
Janis, I. L., 443, 451
Janosik, S. M., 197, 372–373, 433
Jaworski, L., 477
Jenkins, J., 166–167
Jeong, W., 588
Jewell, J. O., 26
Jick, T., 326
Johnson, A., 254
Johnson, E. A., 88
Johnson, J., 627
Johnson, J. A., 397
Johnston, A., 6
Johnstone, S., 295

Jones, H., 589
Jones, S., 587, 590, 591
Jones, S. R., 159, 246
Josselson, R., 151

K

Kadison, R., 271
Kaplin, W. A., 188, 278
Karabel, J., 51
Karagianni, P., 226
Kassop, M., 293
Kater, S., 51
Kaufman, M., 243, 246
Keating, L. A., 545, 546, 553, 554
Keeling, R. P., 61, 110, 192, 276, 350, 374, 406, 409, 416, 417, 448, 455, 529, 557, 629
Kegan, R., 154, 248
Kellom, G., 233
Kelly, K. F., 29
Kelton, A. J., 591, 592
Kendall, J. R., 294
Kennedy, J. F., 12
Kennedy, R. F., 12
Kepplar, K., 454
Kerr, S., 326
Kezar, A. J., 150, 405, 409, 410, 411, 412, 413, 415, 416, 417, 418, 419, 434, 443, 444, 454
Khoury, G., 590
Kibre, P., 3
Killen, D., 466
Killoran, D., 260
Kilmann, R. H., 458, 466
Kimber, M., 433
Kimbrough, W. M., 148
King, C., 596
King, D., 260
King, M. L., Jr., 12, 229
King, P. M., 150, 153, 154, 155
Kinser, K., 28, 29, 36
Kinzie, J., 15, 60, 61, 314, 334, 409, 438, 530, 535, 548, 554, 565, 629
Kiracofe, N., 112
Kirkpatrick, D., 591
Kirwan, W. E., 109
Kitchener, K. S., 154, 174, 175, 179
Klaus, P., 271
Kleeman, G., 597
Kleinglass, N., 597
Kling, R., 455
Knefelkamp, L. L., 148, 408
Knight, J., 121

Knock, G. H., 313
Knox, A. B., 377
Kohlberg, L., 110, 154
Kolb, D., 156
Kolins, C. A., 405
Komives, S. R., 14, 15, 90, 371, 375, 390, 397, 624, 626
Korn, J. S., 129
Korn, W. S., 120, 129
Koss, M. P., 270
Kotter, J. P., 447, 448, 458, 473
Kouzes, J. M., 362, 447, 450, 456
Kretovics, M., 297
Krueger, P. M., 397
Kruger, K., 385, 407, 417, 586, 587, 595
Kuh, G. D., 4, 15, 59, 60, 61, 62, 63, 64, 65, 66, 67, 68, 70, 71, 72, 73, 74, 75, 76, 82, 84, 150, 182, 322, 359, 405, 409, 415, 418, 421, 430, 453, 530, 535, 542, 548, 565, 567
Kuk, L., 313, 315, 316, 317, 318, 325, 327
Kwandayi, H., 227

L

Labaree, D., 53
Laden, B. V., 28
Laden, R., 150
Ladson-Billings, G., 159
Lagadec, P., 603
Lake, P. F., 279
Laker, J. A., 53, 228, 242
Lampkin, P., 179
Laney, J. T., 179, 180
Langa, M. J., 149
Larimore, J., 225
Larsen, K., 295
Ledbetter, B. E., 505
Lee, B. A., 188, 278
Lee, J. J., 120
LeGore, C., 288
Lenhart, A., 586, 588, 589
Lennington, R. L., 90, 92
Leonard, E. A., 3
Leslie, L. L., 25, 44, 49, 53, 55
Leveille, D. E., 107
Levin, J. S., 41, 49, 51, 54, 56
Levine, A., 624, 628
Levine, J., 409
Lewin, T., 235
Lewis, J. A., 555
Lewis, M. D., 555
Li, X., 94, 99
Light, R. J., 449

Lincoln, Y. S., 558
Lindholm, J. A., 120, 630
Lipka, S., 274
Little, B., 453
Lloyd, M., 226
Lloyd-Jones, E., 10, 11, 629
Locke, B., 278
Lockwood, A. T., 406
Lombardi, K. S., 590
Lomotey, K., 234
London, H. B., 71
Longwell-Grice, R. M., 246
Lopez, C. A., 190
Lopez, G. R., 440
Love, P. G., 14, 15, 90, 198, 321, 323, 430, 435, 449
Lovell, C., 394
Lowe, C. M., 8
Lowe, S. C., 26, 85, 228
Lowery, J. W., 86, 87
Lowry, R. C., 89
Lucas, A. F., 467, 468, 469
Lucas, C. J., 24
Ludeman, R. B., 138
Lynch, A. Q., 157, 367
Lyons, J. W., 70

M

Mable, P., 189
Marusza, J., 246
McAlpine, L., 395
McCann, J., 409
McCarthy, M. M., 66
McCauley, C. D., 434, 437, 439
McCaulley, M. H., 156
McClellan, G. S., 26, 85, 120, 225, 227, 228, 580, 596, 623
McClendon, S. A., 69, 150
McClinton, M., 452, 457
McConnell, T. R., 51
McCormick, A. C., 109, 289
McDonald, W. M., 448, 452
McEwen, M. K., 148, 149, 150, 159, 246
McFarland, W. P., 459
McGrath, D., 51
McIntire, D. D., 335
McIntosh, P., 253, 254
McLendon, M. K., 106
McPherson, P., 109
McSwain, C., 96
Madden, M., 586, 589, 597
Maddox, D., 493, 495, 497

Maddy, W., 450
Magolda, P. M., 71
Mahoney, K. M., 120
Maier, E., 397
Maki, P. L., 399, 526, 527, 533, 536
Mallory, S. L., 105
Mandew, M., 127
Manicur, A., 209
Mann, B. A., 190, 195, 196
Mann, H., 6
Manning, K., 313, 321, 323, 324, 325, 326, 334,
    438, 535, 554, 629
March, J., 52
Marcia, J. E., 151
Marczak, J. N., 452
Marginson, S., 44, 49, 53, 56
Marin, P., 392, 395
Marques, C., 227
Marron, J. M., 195
Marshall, C., 425
Martin, J., 409
Martin, W. B., 19
Martinez, D., 231
Marvin, C. H., 5
Marx, B. S., 69
Marx, K., 444
Mason, S. O., 390, 394, 397
Massy, W. F., 90, 93, 293
Matranga, M., 150
Matthews, L. K., 7
Maxcy, B., 426
Mayhew, L. B., 482, 495
Meisinger, R. J., 496
Mentkowski, M., 536, 542
Merisotis, J. P., 111
Metcalf, J., 106
Middendorff, E., 131
Milem, J. F., 245
Milian, M., 610
Miller, C. O., 108
Miller, T. E., 48
Miller, T. K., 148, 151, 178, 187, 188, 190, 191, 297, 375
Millett, C. M., 389, 390, 392, 393, 395, 399
Mills, D. B., 355
Minassians, H. P., 106, 107
Minor, F. D., 409
Mintzberg, H., 47, 157, 361
Miser, K. M., 602
Mitakidou, S., 227
Mitchell, B., 425
Mitchell, J. T., 614
Mitrof, I., 603

Mmeje, K. C., 149
Moffatt, M., 67
Monchick, R., 269
Moneta, L., 67, 91, 211, 333, 593
Montagu, C., 615
Mooney, P., 226
Moore, E. L., 449
Moore, L. V., 207, 208, 209, 211, 473
Moore, M., 555
Moore, P. L., 430
Moore, W. S., 190
Moos, R. H., 69, 159
Morgan, G., 425, 429, 435, 436, 444
Morin, E., 603
Morrill, W. H., 555
Mortimer, K., 51
Moses, Y. T., 226
Mourão, J., 227
Mubarak, H., 231
Müßig-Trapp, P., 131
Mueller, J. A., 246, 259, 372
Mullendore, R. H., 190, 191, 361, 454
Mullins, G., 625
Mundell, B. L., 426
Mundhenk, R. T., 115
Murphy, D., 466
Murphy, P. M., 15
Murphy, S., 409
Murray, S., 596
Musil, C. M., 244
Myers, I. B., 156, 466
Myrick, R., 69

N

Nance, M., 295
Narvaez, D., 154
Neave, G., 106
Nelson, K. A., 333
Nettles, M. T., 389, 390, 392, 393, 395, 399
Neuberger, C. G., 207, 208, 209, 211
Neumann, A., 409, 420, 442, 443
Newell, L. J., 63
Newton, F. B., 272
Nidifer, J., 6, 7
Niebuhr, R., 168
Nienow, D., 463
Nisbett, C., 593
Noble, D., 56
Nora, A., 98, 245
Norton, J., 395
Nuss, E. M., 207, 208

O

O'Connor, M., 457
Oetting, E. R., 555
O'Grady, J. P., 22
Okun, M., 51
Olausen, K. R., 53
Olsen, J., 52
Olsen, S., 591
Olson, C. L., 121, 134
O'Reilly, T., 587
Orfield, G., 235
Ortiz, A. M., 85, 231
Osfield, K. J., 120, 138, 228
Outcalt, C. L., 68
Overberg, P., 233
Owen, L. A., 138

P

Pace, C. R., 70
Padilla, L. M. A., 252
Palmer, A. F., 6, 7
Palmer, P., 449, 457, 458, 477
Palomba, C. A., 526, 530, 531, 532, 533, 537
Papert, S., 533, 536
Pardee, D., 452
Parker, C. A., 148
Parker, G., 420
Parks, S. D., 154, 473, 476, 631
Parry, L., 433
Parsons, T., 8
Pascarella, E. T., 15, 59, 60, 61, 66, 70, 98, 245, 257, 449, 453, 535
Paterson, B. G., 187, 191, 603
Patterson, G., 451
Patton, B., 467
Patton, J., 409
Patton, L. D., 147, 148, 149
Pauchant, T., 603
Pauley, R., 395
Pavela, G., 281
Pawlak, K., 440, 441
Peek, L. A., 397
Peltier Campbell, K., 244
Peltier, G. L., 150
Penney, J. F., 187
Penney, S., 454
Perlmutter, D. D., 396
Perry, W. G., Jr., 154, 155
Petersen, R., 597
Peterson, B., 335

Peterson, M. W., 70, 72
Piaget, J., 154
Pike, G. R., 70
Pimental, E., 268
Pogue, K., 294
Ponder, K. M., 434, 437, 439
Poock, M. C., 391, 392, 395
Pope, R. C., 473
Pope, R. L., 246, 247, 259, 372
Porter, L., 396
Posner, B. Z., 362, 447, 450, 456
Potter, D. L., 409
Powell, T., 210, 211
Presley, C. A., 265, 268, 276
Price, J. M., 565, 583
Prince, J. S., 148
Prothrow-Stith, D., 270
Pryor, J. H., 129, 133, 231
Pusser, B., 47, 48

Q

Quaye, S. J., 226
Quintinar, I., 231

R

Ragle, J. D., 69
Raines, M. P., 81
Rainie, L., 587, 588, 597
Rait, R. S., 3
Ramirez, S., 431–433
Ramos, J. E., 227
Ramsey, J., 454
Ranero, J. J., 206
Rashdall, H., 3
Ratcliffe, S. R., 195
Raven, B., 435, 436
Readings, B., 53
Reason, R. D., 247
Reed, B., 246
Reisser, L., 62, 148, 151, 152, 153, 156, 158, 474
Rendón, M. L., 148, 160
Renn, K. A., 233
Rest, J. R., 154
Reville, S. P., 107
Reynolds, A. L., 246, 259, 372, 473
Rhatigan, J. J., 3, 16, 207, 208, 209, 633, 634
Rhoades, G., 49, 54, 55, 56, 632
Rice, C., 121, 127
Richardson, R., 51

Richardson, R. C., Jr., 453
Rickard, S. T., 603
Riley, G. L., 47, 48
Ritscher, J. A., 346
Roberts, D. C., 15
Roberts, G., 211
Robertson, J. M., 272
Robinson-Armstrong, A., 260
Robison, J., 268
Rockland-Miller, H.-S., 275
Rodgers, R. F., 148, 153
Rogers, J. L., 450
Rollo, J., 604
Rooney, P. M., 498
Roper, L. D., 149, 447, 448, 449, 457,
    458, 459
Rose, B., 454
Rudenstine, N. L., 229, 234
Rudolph, F., 22
Rudy, W. R., 9, 22
Ruekel, P., 15
Rund, J. A., 256
Rushlau, M., 397

S

Sabo, S. R., 581
Saddlemire, G. L., 397
Saenz, V. B., 129
Sample, S., 452
Sandeen, A., 14, 15, 81, 90, 215, 216, 326,
    369, 439, 473, 628, 633
Sanders, C. S., 449
Sanford, N., 154
Santos, A., 289
Santos, J. L., 129
Saunders, S. A., 196, 397
Sax, L. J., 67, 120, 129
Scaife, J., 452
Scarafiotti, C., 292–293
Scharmer, C. O., 477
Scheef, D., 363
Schein, E. H., 72, 421
Schilling, K. L., 66
Schilling, K. M., 66
Schlossberg, N. K., 157, 367
Schneiter, S., 29
Schnitzer, K., 131
Schön, D. A., 378, 469
Schonfield, N. B., 234, 236
Schramm, J., 295
Schreiber, J., 131

Schroeder, C. C., 408, 409, 410, 414, 415,
    416, 417, 418, 419
Schuh, J. H., 15, 60, 61, 67, 81, 90, 91, 107, 151,
    191, 198, 230, 314, 334, 397, 409, 412, 413,
    417, 419, 420, 438, 447, 448, 450, 526, 527,
    528, 530, 531, 532, 535, 548, 554, 559, 565, 567,
    569, 629
Schulz, S. A., 120, 137
Schuster, J., 51
Schwartz, M., 596
Schwartz, R. A., 6, 9, 449
Scott, J. H., 111, 115
Scott, W. D., 7, 8, 10
Scribner, J. D., 426
Seaman, J., 289, 293, 294
Sedlacek, W. E., 531, 535
Seidman, E., 51
Senge, P. M., 157, 327, 377, 477
Sergiovanni, T. J., 434, 435
Shea, P. A., 299, 592
Shedd, J. D., 4
Sheeley, V. E., 210
Sheeley, V. L., 15
Sherrill, J., 616
Shireman, R., 236
Shohet, R., 452
Shrivastava, P., 603
Shulenberger, D., 109
Shulman, L., 116
Shulock, N. B., 109
Siegel, D., 606, 616
Silverman, S., 590
Sim, S., 591
Simmons, M., 590
Simmons, R., 166, 171
Sines, S., 587
Singer, T. S., 454
Skewes-Cox, T. E., 68
Slaughter, S., 25, 44, 49, 53, 54, 55, 56, 632
Smith, B. L., 409
Smith, D., 51
Smith, D. G., 234, 236, 245, 407, 430
Smith, M. R., 629
Snyder, M. B., 447, 450
Snyder, T. D., 82, 84, 88, 91, 93, 94, 95
Soares, A. P., 227
Sockett, H., 450
Soleyn, E., 209
Solórzano, D. G., 159
Soltren, J. H., 589
Sparling, P. B., 268
Spear, M., 51

Spellings, M., 105, 127
Spencer, M. G., 70
Sperber, M., 54
Stanton, W. W., 411
Starratt, R. J., 434, 435
Steele, P. E., 232
Stefancic, J., 159
Steffes, J. S., 210, 211, 219
Stein, W. J., 229
Steinbach, S., 590
Steptoe, S., 189
Stier, J., 253, 261
Stimpson, M., 374–375, 376
Stocum, D. L., 498
Stone, G. L., 267
Strade, C. B., 190
Strange, C. C., 68, 69, 148, 150, 155, 156, 159,
    199, 321, 323
Strauss, W., 280
Strayhorn, T. L., 29, 112, 449
Stringer, J., 394, 425, 463, 623
Strong, E. K., Jr., 7
Sturtz, A., 290
Styles, M. H., 555
Sullivan, M., 138
Suskie, L., 526, 527, 528, 530, 533, 537
Swann, K., 594

T

Tagg, J., 66
Talbot, D., 397
Talbot, M., 6
Tan, A. G., 82
Tancer, B., 588
Tannen, D., 474
Tarkow, T. A., 409
Tarrow, S., 451
Tate, W. F., 159
Taub, D. J., 390
Taylor, B. E., 90, 93
Taylor, P. A., 226
Taylor, S. L., 469
Terenzini, P. T., 15, 59, 60, 61, 66, 70, 98,
    245, 257, 449, 453, 535
Terman, L. M., 7, 8
Terrell, M. C., 86
Terrell, P. S., 120, 138, 228
Terry, R. W., 442
Thayer, P. B., 231
Thielfoldt, D., 363
Thoma, S. J., 154

Thomas, A. G., 292
Thomas, B., 626
Thomas, K. W., 458, 464, 465, 466
Thomas, W., 192
Thorndike, E. L., 7
Tierney, W. G., 51, 53, 229
Tinto, V., 69, 157, 160, 409, 453, 558, 565
Tippeconnic Fox, M. J., 26, 85, 228, 231
Torres, V., 70, 148, 150, 228, 335
Toth, P., 395
Toutkoushian, R. K., 92
Townsend, B. K., 63, 390, 394, 397
Tressou, E., 227
Truex, D., 6
Tseng, W. C., 272
Tucker, A., 433
Turkle, S., 631
Turner, H. S., 266
Turner, M. G., 271
Tuttle, K. N., 6, 15
Twale, D., 449
Twombly, S., 397

U

Ukpokodu, O. N., 257
Ulrich, D., 326
Underhile, R., 110
Upcraft, M. L., 90, 107, 157, 158, 191, 198, 447, 526,
    527, 528, 530, 531, 532, 559, 569
Urban, W., 22, 24, 25
Ury, W., 464, 467, 468
Useem, M., 366

V

Vaill, P. B., 371, 624
Valente, A., 166
Van Danen, E., 592
Van Deusen, K., 270
Vandiver, B. J., 152
Veloso, A. S., 227
Vesper, N., 61, 70, 566
von Destinon, M., 496, 498

W

Wagoner, J., 22, 24, 25
Wagoner, R., 51
Waitley, D., 631
Walker, B., 292
Walker, D. E., 434

Wall, A. F., 110
Wallis, C., 189
Ward, J. A., 190
Ward, R. L., 271
Warren, D., 109
Watkins, J., 107
Watson, J. B., 7, 8
Watt, S. K., 159
Webb, L., 356
Weber, M., 444
Webster, A., 25
Wei, C. C., 94, 95
Weifang, M., 226
Weis, L., 246
Weitz, S., 545
Wellman, J. V., 105, 106, 107
Wells, G. V., 259
Welsh, J. F., 106
Westfall, S. B., 409, 410, 413
Wheatley, M., 448
Wheeler, B., 592
White, J., 356, 366, 368
Whitt, E. J., 4, 15, 54, 60, 61, 67, 71, 72, 73, 75, 84,
    105, 110, 112, 179, 359, 409, 412, 413, 419, 421,
    448, 450, 530, 548, 565, 567
Widick, C., 148
Wiese, M. D., 63, 394
Wilkinson, C. K., 256
Williams, C. R., 279
Williams, J. M., 61, 66, 409
Williamson, E. G., 11
Wilmot, W. W., 464
Wilson, M. E., 209

Wilson, R., 231
Wilson, V. C., 409
Winston, R. B., 148, 151, 178, 190, 335, 380
Wise, S. L., 198, 199
Wisniewski, N., 270
Wolanin, T. R., 232
Wolf-Wendel, L., 13, 397
Wolff, R. A., 111
Wolverton, B., 100
Woodard, D. B., Jr., 14, 15, 90, 120, 227, 237,
    496, 498, 624, 626
Woodcock, B. S., 591
Wright, B., 229
Wright, I., 289

Y

Yamada, M., 51
Yerkes, R. M., 7
Yinger, J., 90
Yosso, T. J., 159
Young, D. G., 197
Young, R. B., 356, 361

Z

Zapata, L. P., 292
Zdziarski, E., II, 603, 604, 616
Zelna, C. L., 527
Zemsky, R., 293
Zhou, Q., 227
Zimbardo, P., 598
Zumeta, W., 109, 110

SUBJECT INDEX

A

ABD ("all but dissertation"), 395
About Campus (magazine), 348
Academic Profile (ETS), 140
Academy for Student Affairs Professionals (ASAP), 384
Accountability
  accreditation by student affairs professional organizations and, 112–113
  accreditation process role in, 111–112
  additional resources on, 114–115
  best practices in student affairs, 113–114
  Council for the Advancement of Standards (CAS) on, 112
  definition of, 106–107, 534
  increased demands for, 105, 107–109
  institutional productivity measures use for, 90–91
  multicultural campus communities and related, 259–260
  "new accountability" shift of, 106–107
  outcomes-based assessment component of, 534
  stakeholders in institutional, 109–110
  student affairs, 110–111
  student health centers and, 277–278
  voluntary system of, 115
Accountability movement, 60

Accreditation
  accountability and role of, 111–112
  student affairs professional organizations' role in, 112–113
  timeline and eras of standards and, 190
  See also Standards
Accreditation Association for Ambulatory Health Care (AAAHC), 113, 277
ACE Center for International Initiatives, 124
ACHA-NCHA survey, 270, 273, 278
ACPA's Commission on Professional Preparation, 398
Actual notice, 516
Addreal, 269
ADHA (attention-deficit/hyperactivity disorder), 274
Advancement of Standards in Higher Education (CAS), 148
Advocacy culture, 441
Aetna Insurance Company, 275
Affirmative action, 235
African American students
  average age for doctoral, 389–390
  enrollment rates of, 84, 274
  family and income demographics of, 83
  study abroad enrollment by, 130*fig*
  territoriality of (case study), 69
  See also Ethnicity/race differences; Minority students
Albano v. Colby College, 513

Alcohol abuse
  growing concerns about student, 13–14
  physical and mental issues related to, 268–269
  See also Substance abuse
Alice Manicur Symposium (NASPA), 210
Alumni, 454
Alumni Ass'n v. Sullivan, 515
Alverno College, 113
American Association of Colleges and Universities
    (AAC&U), 64, 122
American Association of Collegiate Registrars and
    Admissions Officers (AACRAO), 200
American Association for Higher Education (AAHE),
    406, 409, 412
American Association of Hispanics in Higher
    Education (AAHHE), 214
American Association of State Colleges and
    Universities, 115, 227, 230, 233, 236
American Association of University Women (AAUW), 6
American College Association (ACHA), 268, 270, 273
American College Health Association (ACHA),
    112, 268
American College Personnel Association (ACPA)
  *Assessment Skills and Knowledge Content Standards for Stu-
    dent Affairs Practitioners and Scholars* by, 536, 539
  Commission on Professional Preparation of, 398
  documents on past presidents of, 15
  graduate program directory by, 390, 391
  internationalization in higher education promoted
    by, 125
  job placement function of, 336
  Journal of College Student Development of, 211
  online learning interest by, 296
  origins and growth of, 208, 210–211
  Powerful Partnerships: collaboration by, 406
  professional competencies development proposed
    by, 373
  Statement of Ethical Principles and Standards of, 175–176
  student learning assessment by, 527, 528
  The Student Learning Imperative by, 110, 405, 407, 409,
    528–529, 530, 542
American College Unions International (ACUI),
    176–177
American Council on Education (ACE), 11, 110, 124,
    126, 350
*An American Imperative: Higher Expectations for Higher
    Education* (Wingspread Group), 107–108, 406
American Indians. *See* Native American students
American Life Project, 587, 590
American Personnel and Guidance Association
    (APGA), 210
American Psychiatric Association, 272

American Psychological Association (APA),
    112, 113, 278
American Society of Association Executives (ASAE),
    206–207
Americans with Disabilities Act (1990), 85, 229, 267
Annenberg Public Policy Center, 596
Annual Freshman Survey (2004), 128–129
Annual Freshman Survey (2006), 129
Anomic interest groups, 437
APA Committee on Accreditation, 112
Arbitration, 469
Army Classification System, 7, 8
The Art and Practical Wisdom of Student Affairs Leadership
    (Dalton and McClinton), 457
Asian American students, 130
Asian Pacific Americans in Higher Education
    (APAHE), 214
Asperger's disorder, 274
Assessment
  campus environment, 73–76
  using CAS standards in comprehensive, 198–199
  crisis work management, 613
  of existing facility prior to replacement, 578
  facilities operational plan, 577
  program planning and role of, 559–560
  of student affairs organizations, 330–331
  student learning, 526–542
  student motivation, 199
*Assessment Reconsidered: Institutional Effectiveness for Student
    Success* (Kelling, Wall, Underhile, and Dungy), 110
*Assessment Skills and Knowledge Content Standards for Student
    Affairs Practitioners and Scholars* (ACPA), 536, 539
Associate's colleges (community colleges)
  governance of, 50t–51
  institutional mission statements of, 25–26
  student affairs organizational model in, 320–321
  student affairs professional practice shaped by
    mission of, 33
Association for the Advancement of Sustainability in
    Higher Education, 582
Association of American Colleges and Universities
    (AAC&U), 64, 350
Association of College Unions International (ACUI),
    125, 138
Association of College and University Housing Officers
    International (ACUHO-I), 125, 138, 214, 216, 384
Association of Fraternity Advisors (AFA), 214
Association on Higher Education and Disability
    (AHEAD), 200, 214
Association for Student Affairs at Catholic Colleges and
    Universities (ASACCU), 215
Association for Student Judicial Affairs (ASJA), 214

Associational interest groups, 438

Assumption of risk doctrine, 508

Astin's inputs-environment-outcomes model (IEO), 534–536, 540–541

Audit requirements, 492–493

Authority
  for facility project authorization, 579
  moral, 435
  as political concept, 434–435
  professional, 434–435
  student affairs management, 359
  See also Power

Authority-dominated cliques, 438

Auxiliary services, 488

"Awaiting" skills, 457

B

Baby Boomers
  compared to other generations, 363*t*
  generational management challenges faced by, 362–365
  job mobility issue and, 367

Baccalaureate colleges
  institutional mission statements of, 22–23
  student affairs organizational model in, 318–319

Back on TRAC program, 269

Bakke, Regents of the University of California v., 235

Barr and Keating program planning model
  overview of, 456*fig*, 545
  planning and implementing major initiatives, 546, 548–550
  planning and implementing specific activities, 552–560
  recommendations for practice, 562–563

Beach v. University of Utah, 513

Behaviorism, 8

Benjamin A. Gilman International Scholarship, 123

Best Practices for Electronically Offered Degree and Certificate Programs (WCET), 297

Bill of Rights, 515

Blackboard, 594

Board of Regents, Sharkey v., 511–512

Board of trustees, 44–47

Bollinger, Grutter v., 235

Bologna Declaration, 122

Boosting Alcohol Consciousness Concerning the Health of University Students (BACCHUS), 13

Boston University, Guckenberger vs., 506–507

Bottom-up approach to ethics, 180

Bradsaw v. Rawlings, 513

Brueckner v. Norwich University, 512

Budget cuts
  institutional strategies for, 502–503
  unit reduction strategies for, 503

Budget cycle
  adjusting current budget, closing, and analyzing results, 502
  developing unit budget requests, 500–501
  identifying revenue and expenses, 499
  institutional parameters phase of, 499
  monitoring performance phase of, 501–502
  timetables, 500

Budget models
  cost or responsibility center, 498
  incremental, 497
  redistribution, 497–498
  zero-based budgeting, 498

Budget purpose
  allocating resources as, 494–495
  exerting control as, 495
  as means of communication, 495–496
  providing incentives as, 495
  putting business strategy into operation, 493–494

Budget types
  capital budget as, 496–497
  operating budget as, 496

Budgets
  cycle of, 499–502
  dealing with cuts to the, 502–503
  facilities operational, 569–570
  facility development, 580–581, 583
  models of, 497–498
  planning for program, 556–557
  purposes of, 493–496
  state and federal capital, 489–490
  types of, 496–497

Business Officer (publication), 348

Business-Higher Education Forum, 108

C

California State University Channel Islands, 113, 114

California State University (CSU) System, 114

Campus Consortium for Environmental Excellence, 582

Campus crisis
  definition of, 603
  lessons learned from, 616–620
  management of crisis work, 604–613
  transitions after catastrophic event, 613–615
  types of, 603–604

Campus culture
  boundary spanning between different, 440–442
  as campus environment factor, 71–72

Campus culture (*Continued*)
  different types of, 441
  facilities strategic plan consideration of, 567–568
  mutual shaping of, 72
  program development example of changing
    residence hall, 550–552
  student learning collaboration attendance to,
    418–419
Campus environment
  boundary spanning of different cultures within,
    440–442
  CAS standards used to assess, 199
  examining the impact on, 59–60
  facilities operational plan and issue of, 576
  framework for assessing influence on student
    learning, 61–72
  institutional context, student success and, 60–61
  key issues in assessing influences on learning, 72–76
  mental health aspects of, 8–9
  See also Multicultural campus communities
Campus environment assessment
  campus cultures frame of, 66–68
  climate frame of, 70–71
  culture frame of, 71–72
  ecology frame of, 68–69
  effective educational practices frame of, 64–65
  institutional mission and philosophy frame for, 62–64
  interpretive frames on, 68–72
  overview of, 61–62
  substantive frames on, 62–68
Campus environment assessment issues
  assembling credible and qualified study team, 73
  commitment of key campus personnel, 73
  obtaining as much relevant information as
    possible, 74
  seeking different points of view, 74–75
  testing impressions early and often, 75
  treating every participant and information as
    important, 75
  understanding that improvements for learning take
    time, 75–76
Campus security, 575
Campus Security Act (Public Law 101-542), 86,
    522, 523
Capital budgets, 496–497
Carnegie Classification of Institutions of Higher
    Education
  associate's colleges (community colleges) under,
    25–26
  baccalaureate colleges under, 22–23
  description of, 21

for-profit or proprietary schools, 28–29
  master's colleges and universities under, 23–24
  not-for-profit institution categories under, 22
  research and doctoral granting universities under,
    24–25
Carnegie Commission on Higher Education, 49
Carnegie Foundation for the Advancement of
    Teaching, 19, 21
Carnegie Initiative on the Doctorate, 393
CAS review
  description of, 193
  steps of, 193–195
CAS Self-Assessment Guides (SAGs), 193
CAS standards
  accountability through use of, 112
  categories of, 192
  used in comprehensive assessment, 198–199
  on domains of learning outcomes, 192–193
  ethical principles summary of, 174–175
  for health care services, 278
  origins and description of, 191–192
  research on use of, 195–198
  See also Council for the Advancement of Standards in
    Higher Education (CAS)
Case-based orientation, 180
Caucasians. *See* White students
Center for Association Leadership, 206
Center for Creative Leadership, 434
Center for Transforming Student Services
    (CENTSS), 305
Centre for Higher Education Transformation (CHET)
    [South Africa], 127
Centre National des (Euvres Universitaires et Scolaires)
    [CNOUS], 131, 138
Cerro Coso Community College, 305
Change (magazine), 349
"Characteristics of Individual Excellence for
    Professional Practice in Higher Education"
    (CAS), 374
Chicago, Terminiello v., 517
Chief diversity officer, 256–257
Chinese Education and Research Network, 226
Chronicle of Higher Education, 274, 281, 294,
    335, 349
The Chronicle Review, 349
Church-supported institutions, 489
Civil Rights Act (1965), 12–13
Co-curricular education
  barriers to, 136
  student affairs role in, 132–133
  study abroad opportunities of, 133–135

Coalitions
    building, 439
    student affairs practitioner, 451
Cocaine abuse, 269
Code of Ethics (ACUI), 177
Coercive power, 435
Cognitive development theories, 153–155
Colby College, Albano v., 513
Collaboration. *See* Student learning collaboration
College of New Jersey, 412
College Portrait (Web reporting template), 115
College Student Experience Questionnaire
    (CSEQ), 70, 74
College Student Questionnaire and Institutional
    Functioning Inventory, 70
College and University Environment Scales (CUES), 70
College and University Professional Association for
    Human Resources (CUJPA-HR), 339
Collegial culture, 441
Collegiality power, 437
Colorado State University, 609, 611
Commission on Abraham Lincoln Study Abroad
    Fellowship Program (CALSAFP), 123, 125, 126, 131
Commission on the Future of Higher Education
    (DOE), 526, 529, 542
Commission on Professional Preparation (ACPA), 398
Committed to Development, 131
Common Intellectual Experience (CIE) [Ursinus
    College], 65
Communication
    "awaiting" as skill of, 457
    budget as means of, 495–496
    crisis management lessons regarding, 616–617
    crisis work management, 609–610
    instant messaging (IM), 587–588
    as political concept, 438–439
    technological tools of, 439
    university's contractual responsibility regarding
        student, 506
    See also Listening
Community
    as ethical responsibility domain, 170*fig,* 172
    student affair practitioner relationship with, 452–453
Community College Survey of Student Engagement
    (CCSSE), 64, 70, 74, 289
Community colleges (associate's colleges)
    governance of, 50*t*–51
    institutional mission statements of, 25–26
    student affairs organizational model in, 320–321
    student affairs professional practice shaped by
        mission of, 33

Conduct procedures, 183
Conference of Deans and Advisors in Men, 208
Confidentiality issues
    parental involvement as, 280–281
    student affairs and related, 182
    student health care and related, 27–279
    See also Privacy
Conflict
    collegiality as power that avoids, 437
    definition of, 464
    handling relationship, 458–459
    interest groups and, 437–438
    internal and external responses to, 469–471
    understanding our differing approaches to,
        464–466
Conflict interventions
    arbitration as, 469
    facilitation as, 466–467
    mediation as, 468–469
    negotiation as, 467–468
    Thomas-Kilmann Conflict Mode Instrument
        for, 466
Conflict management
    creating gracious space for, 474–477
    interventions for, 466–469
    moving beyond, 473–474
Conflict resolution scenario, 471–473
Conflict responses
    changing individual behavior as, 470–471
    changing systems and structures as, 471
    cultural development as, 470
    personal reflection as, 469–470
Connecticut Distance Learning Consortium, 306
Connecticut State University (CSU) System, 290
Consolidated Rail Corporation, Heller v., 508
Consumer protection initiatives, 86–87
Contextualism (or situation-oriented) ethics, 180
Continuing education, 351
Continuous quality improvement (CQI), 527
Contracted institutional services income, 489
Contracts/grants income, 487–488
Cooperative Institutional Research Program
    (CIRP), 531
Cost budget model, 498
Council for the Advancement of Standards in Higher
    Education (CAS), 13, 112, 148, 174–175, 190,
    212, 278, 297, 373*t*–374, 530
    See also CAS standards
Council for Christian Colleges and Universities
    (CCCU), 215
Council for Higher Education Accreditation, 111

Council of Higher Education Management
  Associations (CHEMA), 212
Council of Regional Accrediting Commissions
  (CRAC), 529
Council of Student Personnel Associations in Higher
  Education (COSPA), 212
Counseling centers, 266–267
Creating Change Conference, 215
Criminal acts
  illicit drug use, 268–269
  institution responsibility for student, 514
  related to social networking, 589–590
  sexual assault, 270
  See also Violence
Crisis
  definition of, 603
  lessons learned from, 616–620
  scale of, 604
  transition after catastrophic event, 613–614
  types of, 603–604
  Virginia Tech University tragedy (2007), 279, 512,
    521, 618
Crisis transition phases
  beginning a new, 615
  letting go, 614
  overview of, 613–614
  understanding "tweener" stage, 614
Crisis work management
  communication and technology components of,
    609–610
  crisis coordination and administration of,
    607–608
  crisis policy review, 606
  debriefing and evaluation of, 613
  developing a plan for, 605
  financial aspects of, 608
  issues related to, 604–605
  leadership role of student affairs in, 606–607
  legal issues of, 608–609
  lessons learned on, 616–620
  practice in preparation for crisis, 605–606
  response to people on campus, 610
  support of students and their families, 610–611
*Critical Features of Assessments for Postsecondary Student
  Learning* (ETS), 108
Critical paradigm, 443–444
Critical theory, 443–444
Cross-constituent committees, 451
CSU Channel Islands, 114
Cultural Validation Model, 160
Culture of Evidence series (ETS), 108
Culture. *See* Campus culture

Curriculum
  education standard governing, 188–189
  international education, 127–128
  professional development CAS, 373*t*–374
  promoting multicultural campus communities
    through, 257–258
  standards for higher education, 189–190

D

Day, Smith v., 513, 514
Debt management issues, 99
DEEP (Documenting Effective Education Practices)
  Project [NSSE], 323, 530, 542
Demographics
  contemporary student, 225
  diversity of student, 226–237
  online learners, 291–293
  student affairs understanding of student, 226
  of student families, 82–83
Depression, 272–273
Development
  cognitive development theories on, 153–155
  Cultural Validation Model of, 160
  psychosocial development theories on, 150–153
  theory of psychological Nigrescence on,
    152–153, 160
Developmental culture, 441
Devry University, 28
Digital Millennium Copyright Act (DMCA), 524
Discounting tuition, 95–96
Discrimination, 260
Dissertation Academy (Indiana State University), 396
Distance education. *See* Online learning
Disturbed/disturbing students, 279–280
Diversity
  current state of, 229–233
  defining, 227–228
  future trends in, 233–234
  gender, 231–232
  as global issue in higher education,
    226–227
  history of, 229
  mental health issues related to, 274
  recommendations for student affairs practice
    regarding, 236–237
  religious differences and, 231
  structural, 228
  See also Ethnicity/race differences; Minority students;
    Multicultural campus communities
Diversity Digest, 350
Diversity, Equity, and Global Initiatives, 244

DMIS (Developmental Model of Intercultural Sensitivity) model, 247
Doctor of Education (Ed.D), 393–394
Doctor of Philosophy (Ph.D), 393–394
Doctoral education
    career paths after, 396–399
    implications for best practice in, 399–400
    journey of, 394–396
    Ph.D vs. Ed.D degrees of, 393–394
    reasons to pursue, 389–390
    selecting area of program emphasis, 394
    selecting institution for, 390–393
Doctrine of contributory negligence, 508
Documenting Effective Education Practices (DEEP) Project [NSSE], 323, 530, 542
Dram Shop statutes, 514–515
Drug-Free Schools and Communities Act Amendments (1989), 86
Due process, 516
Duke University, 133
DukeEngage program (Duke University), 133
Duty to control, 509–510
Duty to protect, 510–512

E

E-learning. *See* Online learning
Eating disorders, 273
Ecology frame, 68–69
Educational Testing Services (ETS), 108, 140
Educause Center for Applied Research (ECAR), 591–592
Educause Learning Initiative, 598
Eduventures survey (2007), 292
Eisman v. State, 514
Electronic portfolios, 595
Ely v. Murphy, 514
Endowment income, 486–487
Enlightenment, 24
Enterprise Resource Planning (ERP), 592
Environmental theories, 155–157
Ethical conflicts
    deciding and acting in situations of, 183–184*t*
    examples of common, 181–183
Ethical responsibility domains
    community as, 170*fig*, 172
    individual conscience as, 170*fig*, 172–173
    institution as, 170*fig*, 171
    overview of five, 169–170*fig*
    student affairs profession as, 170*fig*, 171–172
    students as, 170*fig*–171

Ethical standards
    ACPA, 175–176
    ACUI, 176–177
    CAS, 174–175
    NODA, 177–178
    See also Standards
Ethics
    as art of making wise and responsible decisions, 168–169
    bottom-up approach to, 180
    common issues in student affairs work, 181–183
    contextualism (or situation-oriented) approach to, 180
    definition of, 167–168, 433
    increasing concerns regarding, 166–167
    using moral compass in everyday, 184–185
    multi-lens perspective on managing and modeling everyday, 179–180
    practical reasons for paying attention to, 169
    student affairs management, 361–363
    student affairs political, 433–434
    in the student affairs profession, 173–179
    student health care centers and related, 278–282
    See also Legal issues
Ethnicity/race differences
    Cultural Validation Model on, 160
    multiracial student identity related to, 233–234
    of student demographics, 225
    study abroad vs. higher education enrollment, 130*fig*
    theory of psychological Nigrescence on development and, 152–153, 160
    See also African American students; Diversity; Hispanic/Latino students; Minority students; Native American students
European Council of Student Affairs (ECStA), 125
European Union (EU), 122
Evaluation. *See* Assessment
An Evidence-Centered Approach to Accountability for Student Learning Outcomes (ETS), 108
"Exchange perspective," 52
Expert power, 435–436

F

Facebook, 340, 589, 590, 617
Facilities development
    developing strategic plan for, 566–569
    operational plan for, 569–577
    process of, 577–583

Facilities operational plan
  components of the, 570–573
  on environment, legal issues, assessment, and
    relationships, 576–577
  establishing budget for, 569–570
  on facility partners, 573–575
Facilities strategic plan
  campus culture considered in, 567–568
  considering the user, 567
  on desired experiences and interactions, 567
  prioritizing goals, 566–567
  putting together the, 568–569
Facility development
  assessing the existing facility, 578
  issues to consider in, 577–578
  new construction, 579
  project authorization, 579
  project budget and financing, 580–581
  project construction, 582–583
  project design, 581–582
  renovation projects, 578–579
Faculty
  doctoral students aspiration to positions on, 397–398
  student affairs practitioner relationship with other,
    454–455
  study abroad opportunities for, 138–139
Fairness issue, 183
Families
  confidentiality issues related to involvement by,
    280–281
  crisis work management support of students and,
    610–611
  demographics of U.S., 82–83
  income distribution of, 83
  See also Parents
Family Educational Rights and Privacy Act (FERPA),
    86, 279, 520–522
Family Policy Compliance office (FPCO), 522
Federal financial aid, 97
Federal higher education initiatives
  access for those with disabilities, 85–86
  consumer protection, 86–87
  issues related to state finance, 87–89
  public-private dilemma issue related to, 91–92
  regulatory compliance, 86
  on state finance of higher education, 89–91
  See also State finance of higher education
Federal/state statutes and regulations
  Americans with Disabilities Act (1990), 85, 229, 267
  Civil Rights Act (1965), 12–13
  Digital Millennium Copyright Act (DMCA), 524
  discrimination, 518–520

Drug-Free Schools and Communities Act
    Amendments (1989), 86
Family Educational Rights and Privacy Act, 86
Family Educational Rights and Privacy Act (FERPA),
    86, 279, 520–522
Health Insurance Portability and Accountability Act
    (HIPPA), 279, 520–521
Higher Education Acts (1965, amended in 1972), 13
Higher Education Re-authorization Act (2002), 529
Higher Education Reauthorization Act (1992,
    amended 1998), 28
liability for Internet use, 524
Morrill Acts (1862 and 1890), 24
No Child Left Behind Act (2002), 105
Section 504 (Rehabilitation Act of 1972, amended
    1992), 85, 229
Servicemen's Readjustment Act (1944) [G.I. Bill],
    9, 12, 229
Student Right-to-Know and Campus Security Act
    (Public Law 101-542) [Jeanne Clery Act], 86,
    522, 523
Title III (Higher Education Reauthorization Act), 28
Title V (Higher Education Reauthorization Act), 28
Title VI (Higher Education Act) [HEA], 123
  See also Legal issues
15th Social Survey, 131
Fighting words speech, 517
Financial aid trends
  brief history of, 94
  federal aid, 97
  institutional aid, 97
  loan programs, 94–95
  tuition discounting, 95–96
First Amendment, 516–517
Fiscal management. *See* Student affairs fiscal
    management
Florida State University, 595
For-profit (or propriety) schools
  description of, 28–29
  student affairs professional practice shaped by
    mission of, 36
Forum on Education Abroad, 192
Fourteenth Amendment, 516
Fourth Amendment, 516
Frameworks for Assessing Learning and Development Outcomes
    (CAS), 530
Free speech, 516–517
Fullbright International Exchange Program, 139
Fund for the Improvement of Post Secondary
    Education (FIPSE), 298
Fund for the Improvement of Postsecondary
    Education (FIPSE), 123

Fund raising
    as student affairs income source, 93, 487
    student affairs practitioner relationship with donors and, 454
    suggestions on institutional, 99–101
Future of Higher Education's Commission report (2006), 275

G

"The Gambling Action Team: A Cross-Divisional Approach to Gambling Education and Intervention" (King and Hardy), 596
Gaming (MMORPGs), 591
Gender enrollment rate differences, 231–232
Generation X (Gen X)
    comparing other generations to, 363*t*
    generational challenges of managing, 362–365
    job mobility of, 366, 367
Generational workplace challenges
    description of, 362–365
    generational workplace characteristics and, 363*t*
    other supervisory concerns related to, 365
George Mason University, 595
G.I. Bill (1944), 9, 12, 229
GLBT student programs
    association focus on, 214, 215
    planning, 549
Go Ask Alice! (Columbia University), 593
Goods purchasing policies, 492
Goucher College, 125
Governance. *See* Institutional governance
Gracious space
    definition of, 475
    process of creating, 475–477
    self-awareness and self-management required for creating, 474–475
    violent energy transformed by, 477
Graduate students
    doctoral education of, 388–400
    mental health issues of, 274–275
Graham v. Montana State University, 513
Grants/contracts income, 487–488
Grutter v. Bollinger, 235
Guckenberger v. Boston University, 506–507
"A Guide to Student Services" (CHET), 127

H

Harvard University, 125, 393
Health at Every Size (HAES), 268

Health Insurance Portability and Accountability Act (HIPPA) [Public Law 104-191], 279, 520–521
Health issues. *See* Student health services
Heller v. Consolidated Rail Corporation, 508
Heroin use, 269
Higher education
    the Constitution and, 515–517
    curriculum standards of, 189
    demographics and social trends of, 82–85
    diversity as global issue in, 226–227
    doctoral, 388–400
    federal initiatives regarding, 85–92
    financial factors related to, 92–101
    "fragmented system of influence" within, 439
    internationalization of U.S., 120–140
    "micropolitics" of, 426
    See also Institutions
Higher Education Act (HEA) [Title IV], 123
Higher Education Act (HEA) [Title VI], 123
Higher Education Acts (1965, amended in 1972), 13
Higher Education Center for Alcohol and Other Drug Abuse and Violence Prevention Web site, 269
Higher Education Price Index (Research Associates of Washington), 497
Higher Education Re-authorization Act (2002), 529
Higher Education Reauthorization Act (1992, amended 1998), 28
Higher Education Research Institute, 231
Higher Education Secretariat (HES), 212
Hispanic-serving institutions (HSIs)
    institutional mission statements of, 27–28
    student affairs professional practice shaped by mission of, 35
Hispanic/Latino students
    enrollment growth among, 230, 232
    enrollment rates of, 84, 274
    family and income demographics of, 83
    study abroad enrollment by, 130*fig*
    understanding diversity among, 228
    See also Ethnicity/race differences
Historically black colleges and universities (HBCUs)
    institutional mission statements of, 26–27
    "othermothering" approach of, 34
    student affairs professional practice shaped by mission of, 34–35
History Advisory Committee (NASPA), 15
Howard University, 214
Human aggregate perspective, 156–157
Human resource issues, 493
Hurricane Andrew, 618, 619
Hurricane Katrina, 604, 614, 618

I

Ida B. Wells Black Cultural Center (My University), 388
Identity. *See* Multiple identity
IEO (Astin's inputs-environment-outcomes model),
    534–536, 540–541
Illegal file sharing, 597
Illinois Virtual Campus, 306
Illinois Wesleyan University, 371
Illinois Wesleyan University, Rabel v., 510
In loco parentis theory, 512–513
"In Search of Safer Communities: Emerging Practices
    for Student Affairs in Addressing Campus
    Violence" (NASPA white paper), 620
Income distribution, 83
Incremental budgets, 497
Indiana State University, 396
Individual conscience ethical domain, 170*fig*, 172–173
Industrial Revolution, 10
Informal organization power, 436
Information technology
    administrative core of campus, 592–594
    crisis management lessons regarding, 617–618
    crisis work management and use of, 609–610
    electronic portfolios, 595
    of health care services, 282
    See also Technology
Inside Higher Ed (online magazine), 349
Instant messaging (IM), 587–588
Institute of International Education (IIE), 124, 128,
    129, 131, 1323
Institution mission
    as campus environment assessment frame, 62–64
    linking student affairs to, 483
    purpose of, 19–20
    student affairs professional practice shaped by, 29–36
    See also Vision sharing
Institution mission statements
    associate's colleges, 25–26
    baccalaureate colleges, 22–23
    Hispanic-serving institutions, 27–28
    historically black colleges and universities, 26–27
    master's colleges and universities, 23–24
    proprietary colleges and universities, 28–29
    purpose of, 19–20
    research and doctoral granting universities, 24–25
    student affairs leadership understanding of, 20
    tribally controlled colleges, 26
Institution policies
    alcohol, 181–182
    crisis management lessons and revisions of, 618–619
    goods and services purchasing, 492

Institutional classification systems
    Carnegie Classification model of, 21
    description of, 20–21
Institutional effectiveness (IE), 527
Institutional financial health
    factors influencing, 92–99
    fund raising and, 99–101
    pressures on private institutions, 88
    See also State finance of higher education; Student af-
        fairs fiscal management
Institutional financial health factors
    college attendance and low income as, 96–97
    financial aid trends, 94–96
    revenues as, 92–93, 99–101
    student costs as, 93–94
    student debt management as, 99
    work as financing option, 97–98
Institutional fund raising
    as important revenue source, 93
    suggestions on, 99–101
Institutional governance
    challenges to the traditional perspective of, 49
    connection for student affairs, 53–55
    as institutional identity, 52–53
    institutional type as perspective of, 49–51
    lack of engagement in, 52–53
    multiple ways of viewing, 47
    narratives of, 42–47
    student affair practitioner relationship with, 453
    student affairs practitioners' response to, 55–56
    traditional perspective of, 48–49
Institutional governance narratives
    board of trustees, 44–47
    university senate, 42–44
Institutional philosophy, 63–64
Institutions
    accountability of, 90–91, 105–116
    alcohol policies and practices of, 181–182
    church-supported, 489
    contractual responsibilities to students by, 506–507
    as ethical responsibility domain, 170*fig*, 171
    financial aid directly from, 97
    mission of, 19–20, 20–36, 62–64
    noncontractual obligations to students, 507–515
    as political system, 426–430
    productivity measures as accountability from, 90–91
    public-private dilemma facing, 91–92
    purchasing policies of, 492
    responsibility for criminal acts of students by, 514
    See also Higher education
Interactionist Paradigm, 155
Interest groups, 437–438

International Academic Programs (IAP), 128

International Association of Counseling Services (IACS), 112, 278

International Center for Student Success and Institutional Accountability (ICSSIA), 114

International education
academic study abroad programs, 128–131
co-curricular, 132–135
curricular offerings of, 127–128, 136
opportunities for research and, 139
student affairs graduate preparation programs in, 137–138
student affairs professionals and opportunities in, 137
students studying around the world, 131–132
See also Study abroad programs

International education promotion
by collaborative leadership, 126–127
by college and university leadership, 125–126
by national leadership, 123
by organization leadership, 124–125
by student affairs professional associations, 125
by world leadership, 122

International Exchange Program (NASPA), 138

International Higher Education Clearinghouse, 226

International Student Enrollment Survey, 132

Internationalization in higher education
benefits of, 121–122
definition of, 121
factors leading the way toward, 122–127
history of U.S., 121

Internet
conducting research using the, 588–589
crisis management communication using the, 609–610
instant messaging (IM) using the, 587–588
MMORPGs gaming on the, 590–591
online gambling on the, 596
social networking using the, 339–340, 589–590
virtual worlds using the, 591–592
Web 2.0 technologies of the, 587

Inventory for Student Engagement and Success (Kuh and others), 73

Irish Universities Quality Board (IUQB), 126–127

J

James C. Grimm National Housing Training Institute (NHTI), 384

Jarzynka v. St. Thomas University of Law, 507, 516

Jeanne Clery Act, 86, 522, 523

The Jed Foundation, 273

Jesuit Association of Student Personnel Administrators (JASPA), 215

Johnson & Johnson, 295

Johnson v. State of Washington, 513

Joint Commission for the Accreditation of Healthcare Organizations, 277

Journal of College Student Development (JCSD), 211, 349

K

K-12 education standards, 188–189

Kentucky Virtual Campus, 306

"Knowledge of politics," 425

Knowledge (subjective), 155

L

Lamphere v. State of New York, 509

Language differences
enrollment rates related to, 84–85
multicultural campus communities and, 250–252

Latino students. *See* Hispanic/Latino students

Leadership
crisis management lessons learned about, 619–620
crisis management role of student, 611–612
of student affairs organizations, 330
student affairs professional development promoted by, 346
student learning collaboration, 416–418

Leadership in Energy and Environmental Design (LEED) rating system, 582

Leadership Exchange (NASPA), 349

Leadership Jazz (Depress), 455

Learning Anytime Anywhere Partnership (LAAP), 593

Learning disabilities counseling services, 273–274

Learning in public, 476–477

Learning Reconsidered: A Campus-Wide Focus on the Student Experience (Keeling), 110, 350, 374, 406, 407, 455, 529–530, 542

Learning Reconsidered 2: A Practical Guide to Implementing a Campus-Wide Focus on the Student Experience (Keeling), 110, 192, 350–351, 448, 455

Learning. *See* Student learning

Legal cases cited
Albano v. Colby College, 513
Alumni Ass'n v. Sullivan, 515
Beach v. University of Utah, 513
Bradsaw v. Rawlings, 513
Brueckner v. Norwich University, 512
Eisman v. State, 514
Ely v. Murphy, 514
Graham v. Montana State University, 513

Legal cases cited (*Continued*)
  Grutter v. Bollinger, 235
  Guckenberger v. Boston University, 506–507
  Heller v. Consolidated Rail Corporation, 508
  Jarzynka v. St. Thomas University of Law, 507, 516
  Johnson v. State of Washington, 513
  Lamphere v. State of New York, 509
  L.W. v. Western Golf Association, 511
  McGuiggan v. New England Tel and Tel Co., 514–515
  Miller v. State, 511
  Mullins v. Pine Manor College, 510
  Pitre v. Louisiana Tech University, 511
  Rabel v. Illinois Wesleyan University, 510
  Regents of the University of California v. Bakke, 235
  *Rosenberger v. Rectors and Visitors of the University of
    Virginia,* 517
  Scaduto v. State of New York, 509
  Sharkey v. Board of Regents, 511–512
  Shin v. Massachusetts Institute of Technology (MIT), 507, 510
  Smith v. Day, 513, 514
  Terminiello v. Chicago, 517
  University of Denver v. Whitlock, 508–509
  See also U.S. Supreme Court
Legal issues
  crisis work management, 608–609
  facilities operational plan and, 576
  federal and state statutes and regulations, 518–524
  higher education and the Constitution, 515–517
  university's contractual responsibilities to students,
    506–507
  university's noncontractual obligations to students,
    507–515
  See also Ethics; Federal/state statutes and regulations
Lewin's Interactionist Paradigm, 155
LGBT Center Director case study, 158–159
Liability for Internet use, 524
Liberal arts colleges
  institutional mission statements of, 22–23
  student affairs professional practice shaped by
    mission of, 29–30
Life Map (Valencia Community College), 302–303
Listening
  "awaiting" skill of, 457
  conflict management through, 459
  See also Communication
Loan programs, 94–95
Los Angeles riots, 618, 619
Louisiana Tech University, Pitre v., 511
Low-income students
  financial aid programs for, 94–97
  poverty and enrollment rates of, 83–84
  study abroad programs for, 123

Loyola Marymount University, 260
L.W. v. Western Golf Association, 511

M

McGuiggan v. New England Tel and Tel Co., 514–515
Maintenance (facilities), 572–573
Management. *See* Student affairs management
Managerial culture, 441
Mandatory student fees, 485
Massachusetts Institute of Technology (MIT), Shin v., 507, 510
Master's colleges and universities
  institutional mission statements of, 23–24
  student affairs organizational model in, 319–320
  student affairs professional practice shaped by
    mission of, 31–32
Mediation, 468–469
  See also Negotiation
"Medical model," 9
Medical withdrawal issues, 281–282
Meetings
  functions of effective, 343
  strategies for facilitating, 344
Men
  gender enrollment rate differences of, 231–232
  sexism impact on, 249–250
Mental health
  behaviorism on, 8
  as campus crisis, 271–272
  college environment impact on, 8–9
  disturbed and disturbing students, 279–280
  diversity issues related to, 274
  eating disorders, 273
  growing concerns about alcohol abuse and,
    13–14
  learning disabilities, ADHA, and Asperger's disorder,
    273–274
  "medical model" focus on adjustment and, 9
  post–World War II issues for, 12
  special issues of graduate, professional, and
    nontraditional-age students, 274–275
  stress and anxiety, 273
  suicide and depression, 272–273
Mentor-mentee relationship, 450
Michigan State University, 126, 127
"Micropolitics of education," 426
The Mid-Level Manager in Student Affairs (Ackerman), 369
Middle States Commission on Higher Education, 528
Millennial generation, 363*t*, 364–365, 367
Miller v. State, 511
A Mind That Found Itself (Beers), 9
Minnesota State Colleges and Universities, 306

Minority students
    Asian American, 130
    creating multicultural campus communities of,
        243–254
    effective recruitment and retention of, 258–259
    history and current enrollment of, 229–233
    Native American, 26, 83, 228, 230
    oppression and discrimination against, 260
    professional association's focused on, 214
    See also African American students; Diversity;
        Ethnicity/race differences
Mission. *See* Institution mission
MMORPGs (massively multiplayer online role-playing
    games), 591
Montana State University, Graham v., 513
Montgomery College, 302
Moral authority, 435
Morrill Acts (1862 and 1890), 24
Motivation assessment, 199
Mullins v. Pine Manor College, 510
Multicultural campus communities
    assessment strategies for accountability of, 259–260
    epistemological privilege issue of, 254–255
    identity as critical individual-institutional nexus of,
        243–245
    increasing dialogue to achieve, 249–250
    language issues of, 250–252
    pedagogical issues at the individual level, 245–249
    promoting structural transformation into, 256–260
    responsibility to facilitate, 255–256
    student affairs and identity politics role in, 252–254
    See also Campus environment; Diversity
Multicultural Organizational Development
    (MCOD), 259
Multiple Dimensions of Identity (MDI) Model, 246
Multiracial student identity, 233–234
Murphy, Ely v., 514
Myers-Briggs Type Indicator (MBTI), 156
MySpace, 340, 617

N

NASPA Forum (monthly online newspaper), 350
NASPA Journal, 349
A Nation at Risk (NCEE), 107
National Academic Advising Association (NACADA),
    2, 214, 298
National Annenberg Risk Survey of Youth, 596
National Association of Academic Advisors
    (NACADA), 200
National Association for Campus Activities
    (NACA), 214

National Association of College and University Business
    Officers (NACUBO), 212, 348
National Association of College and University Food
    Services (NACUFS), 200
National Association of Colleges and Employers
    (NACE), 192, 200
National Association of Deans and Advisors of Men
    (NADAM), 208
National Association of Deans of Women (NADW),
    207–208
National Association of Diversity Officers in Higher
    Education (NADOHE), 214–215
National Association of Foreign Student Advisors
    (NAFSA), 122, 130
National Association of Independent Colleges and
    University, 114–115
National Association of State Universities and
    Land-Grant Colleges, 115, 227, 230, 236
National Association of Student Affairs Professionals
    (NASAP), 214, 438
National Association of Student Personnel
    Administrators (NASPA)
    accountability resources available through, 114
    Alice Manicur Symposium of, 210
    on campus environment importance, 60
    distance learning task force of, 296
    diversity as defined by, 227
    on doctoral student careers, 398
    documents on past leaders of, 15
    History Advisory Committee of, 15
    on importance of national standard for certified
        counselors, 188
    "In Search of Safer Communities:" white paper
        of, 620
    International exchange Program of, 138
    internationalization of higher education promoted
        by, 125
    job placement functions of, 336
    origins and growth of, 208–210
    Powerful Partnerships: collaboration by, 406
    professional competencies proposed by, 372–373
    programs of, 209–210
    standards of ethical behavior by, 176
    student learning assessment by, 527–528
    student learning focus by, 405
    student personnel philosophy by, 10–11
    The Student Personnel Point of View by, 3, 9, 10–11, 14
    Undergraduate Fellows Program (NUFP) of, 209–210
National Association of Women Deans and Counselors
    (NAWDC), 208
National Association of Women in Education
    (NAWE), 208

National Board of Certified Counselors (NBCC), 188, 303

National Center on Addiction and Substance Abuse (Columbia University), 269

National Center for Educational Statistics, 29, 230, 233, 389

National Center for Health Statistics, 272

National Center for Injury Prevention and Control, 272

National College Health Assessment (NCHA) survey, 268, 270, 273

The National College Health Risk Behavior Survey (NCHRBS), 269–270

National Commission on the Cost of Higher Education, 81, 105

National Commission on Excellence in Education, 107

National Commission on the Future of Higher Education, 108

National Conference on Race and Ethnicity in American Higher Education (NCORE), 215

National Consortium of Directors of LGBT Resources in Higher Education, 214

National Drug Court Institute, 269

National Gay and Lesbian Task Force, 215

National Intramural Recreation Sports Association (NIRSA), 200

National Orientation Directors Association (NODA), 177–178, 214

National Research Council, 528, 536

National Survey of Counseling Center Directors, 272, 278

National Survey of Student Engagement (NSSE), 55, 64, 70, 74, 289, 291, 530, 542

Native American students
    enrollment rates of, 230
    family and income demographics of, 83
    tribally controlled colleges for, 26
    understanding importance of tribal affiliation for, 228
    See also Ethnicity/race differences

Needs assessment, 532

Negligence, 508–509

Negotiation
    as conflict intervention, 467
    techniques for, 467–468
    See also Mediation

Nembutal, 269

NetResults (bi-weekly magazine), 350

Network: Addressing Collegiate Alcohol and Other Drug Issues, 200

Network Standards, 192

"New accountability," 106–107

New England Resource Center for Higher Education (NERCHE), 414

New England Tel and Tel Co., McGuiggan v., 514–515

New facility construction, 579

New Media Consortium, 591

New York Times Careers in Education, 335

Nigrescence theory, 152–153, 160

No Child Left Behind Act (2002), 105

Nonalcoholic activity night case study, 560–562

Noncontractual legal obligations
    Dram Shop statutes and social host liability, 514–515
    duty as landlord as, 511–512
    in loco parentis theory and, 512–513
    negligence and, 508–509
    respondeat superior, 512
    responsibility for criminal acts of students, 514
    special relationship and, 509–510

Nontraditional-age student mental health, 274–275

North Carolina State (NCS), 292, 294

North Carolina State University (NCSU), 113–114, 292

Norwich University, Brueckner v., 512

O

Oberlin College, 589

Obesity, 268

Office of Civil Rights Letter, 281

On Campus with Women (quarterly online magazine), 350

Online gambling, 596

Online learners
    demographics related to, 291–293
    examining experience of, 293–294
    student affairs' responsibility for, 295–297

Online learning
    credibility of online degrees and, 294–295
    explosive growth of, 288–289
    impact on enrollment trends, 289–291
    strengths of, 294*t*
    student affairs role in, 297–298

Online student services
    best practices in, 298
    Floyd and Casey-Powell model on, 300–304
    illustrated diagram of, 299*fig*
    scope of, 298

Online student services model
    learner intake phase of, 300
    learner intervention phase of, 300–301
    learner support phase of, 301–302
    learner transition phase of, 302–303
    measurement phase of, 303–304

Open Doors report (2006), 131

Opendoors 2006 Fast Facts (IIE), 124, 131

Operating budgets, 496

Oppression experience, 260

Oregon University system, 88
Organizations
    political frame of, 428
    power within informal, 436
    systematic approach to, 328–331
    theory and research related to design of,
        321–326
    See also Student affairs organizations
"Othermothering" approach, 34
Outcomes-based assessment, 532–534
OxyContin, 269

P

P2P (peer-to-peer) filesharing, 597
Paradigms
    critical and postmodern, 443–444
    definition of, 443
Parents
    confidentiality issues related to involvement by,
        280–281
    households headed by single, 82–84
    student affairs practitioner relationship with, 454
    See also Families
Partisan-dominated cliques, 437–438
Penn State World Campus, 302
Percocet, 269
Performance appraisal, 360
Pew Internet, 587, 590
Physical activity, 268
Pine Manor College, Mullins v., 510
Pitre v. Louisiana Tech University, 511
Planning. *See* Strategic planning
Policies. *See* Institution policies
Political concepts
    authority as, 434–435
    boundary spanning as, 440–442
    coalition building as, 439
    communication as, 438–439
    critical and postmodern paradigms, 443–444
    interest groups and conflict as, 437–438
    participation s, 440
    power as, 435–437
    team orientation as, 442–443
    See also Student affairs politics
Postmodern paradigm, 444
Postsecondary Assessment and Learning Outcomes (ETS), 108
Power
    control of technology as, 436
    oppression experience and, 260
    political concept and types of, 435–437
    See also Authority; Privilege

Powerful Partnerships: A Shared Responsibility for Learning
    (AAHE), 406, 407, 409, 412, 413
Powerful partnerships, 450
Preassessment, 531
PREPARE model, 377–382
Privacy
    HIPPA on issues of student, 279, 520–521
    of student records, 522
    See also Confidentiality issues
Private institutions
    audit requirements of, 492–493
    financial pressures on, 88
    human resource issues of, 493
    public-private dilemma facing, 91–92
    purchasing policies of, 492
    state finance issues of, 87–92
Privilege
    common form of blindness to, 254
    epistemological, 254–255
    student affairs ethics related to favoritism and,
        182–183
    white, 253–254
    See also Power
Professional associations
    benefits of membership in, 216–217
    confederations of, 212
    efforts to consolidate, 211–212
    functions of, 206–207
    history of, 207–212
    internationalization of higher education promoted
        by, 125
    involvement and leadership opportunities in,
        217–219
    professional development sponsorship by, 347–348
    sample listing of, 213*t*
    specialty associations among, 212–216
    structure of, 216
    See also Student affairs profession
Professional authority, 434–435
Professional development
    association sponsorship of, 347–348
    CAS curriculum for, 373*t*–374
    commitment to, 351–352
    continuing education of staff as, 351
    continuum of, 375
    cycle of, 376
    definition of, 374–377
    examples by primary sources of delivery, 382*t*–383*t*
    exemplary practices of, 383–385
    guiding philosophy of, 345
    identifying what individuals want and need, 347
    importance of, 344

Professional development (*Continued*)
    leadership promotion of, 346
    lifelong professional learning and, 372
    management responsibilities for staff, 361
    mutual interests and mutual needs of, 345–346
    nature of, 375*t*
    PREPARE model of, 377–382
    professional competencies and, 372–374
    publications as form of, 348–351
    sample activities of the prepare model, 381*t*
    of student affairs managers, 367
    See also Student affairs professionals
Professional standards. *See* Standards
Professional student mental health, 274–275
Program planning case examples
    changing residence hall culture, 550–552
    providing a nonalcoholic activity night, 560–562
Program planning/implementation model
    overview of planning and implementing, 456*fig*, 545
    planning and implementing major initiatives, 546,
        548–550
    planning and implementing specific activities,
        552–560
    recommendations for practice, 562–563
Programs
    Barr and Keating model of development, 545–563
    definition of, 545
Proprietary (or for-profit) schools
    institutional mission statements of, 28–29
    student affairs professional practice shaped by mis-
        sion of, 36
Psychology
    behaviorism, 8
    testing performed under, 8
Psychosocial development theories, 150–153
Public Accountability for Student Learning in Higher Education
    (Business-Higher Education Forum), 108
Public institutions
    audit requirements of, 492–493
    human resource issues of, 493
    purchasing policies of, 492
    state finance issues of, 87–92
Public Law 101-226 (Drug-Free Schools and
    Communities Act Amendments), 86
Public Law 101-542 (Student Right-to-Know and
    Campus Security Act), 86
Public Law 104-191 (Health Insurance Portability and
    Accountability Act) [HIPP], 279, 520–521
Publications
    journals listed, 348–351
    professional development through, 348–351
    university's contractual responsibility regarding, 506

R

Rabel v. Illinois Wesleyan University, 510
Rawlings, Bradsaw v., 513
ReadyMinds, 303
Reasonable searches and seizures, 517
Recognition/awards, 341–342
Recording Industry Association of America
    (RIAA), 597
Recruitment practices, 334–337
Rectors and Visitors of the University of Virginia,
    Rosenberger v., 517
Redistribution budgets, 497–498
Referent power, 436
Regents of the University of California v. Bakke, 235
Regulatory compliance initiatives, 86
Rehabilitation Act (1972, amended 1992), 85, 229
Relationships
    conflict in, 458–459
    formation of, 455–458
    importance of, 448
    with individuals and constituencies, 452–455
    types of, 448–451
Religious diversity, 231
Religiously affiliated colleges
    church support of, 489
    institutional mission statements of, 23
    student affairs professional practice shaped by mis-
        sion of, 30–31
Renovation projects, 578–579
Reputations, 458
Research
    on use of CAS standards, 195–198
    international education and opportunities for, 139
    on online students, 291–293
    organizational design, 3231–3326
    professional development based on, 378
    technological facilitation of, 588–589
Research Associates of Washington, 497
Research and doctoral granting universities
    governance of, 50*t*
    institutional mission statements of, 24–25
    student affairs professional practice shaped by mis-
        sion of, 32–33
Residence hall culture case study, 550–552
Resources
    budget used to allocate, 494–495
    power of access/control over, 436
    program planning regarding available, 558–559
Respondeat Superior, 512
Responsibility-centered budget model, 498
Retention of staff, 352–353

Revenues
    fund raising to increase, 93, 99–101
    sources of institution, 92–93
    sources of student affairs, 483–491
    tuition as, 93, 95–96, 484–485
Ritalin, 269
*Rosenberger v. Rectors and Visitors of the University of
    Virginia*, 517

S

Saint Leo University, 593
St. Thomas University of Law, Jarzynka v., 507, 516
San Diego Community College, 302
San Francisco State University, 125
Sandia National Laboratories, 107
Sandia Report (Sandia National Laboratories), 107
Scaduto v. State of New York, 509
Scarce resources
    budget used to allocate, 494–495
    power of access/control over, 436
Seconal, 269
Second Life, 591–592
Section 504 (Rehabilitation Act of 1972, amended
    1992), 85, 229
Selection/hiring practices, 337–340
Senior Student Affairs Officers (SSAOs)
    generational challenge of managing for, 362–365
    management duties of, 356–359
    management mobility of, 366–368
    management roles of, 359–362
    managing up (and down) the organization, 365–366
    political map for a, 431–432*fig*
    See also Student affairs professionals
Senior Student Affairs Officers (SSAOs) study
    on organizational change and redesign, 317–318
    on organizational structures, 316–317
Servicemen's Readjustment Act (1944) [G.I. Bill], 9,
    12, 229
Services purchasing policies, 492
Seven Principles of Good Practice in Undergraduate Education
    (Chickering and Gamson), 64
Seventh International Conference on Diversity in
    Organisations, Communities, and Nations, 226
Sexism, 249–250
Sexual assault, 270
Sexual behavior health risks, 269–270
Sharkey v. Board of Regents, 511–512
Shin v. Massachusetts Institute of Technology (MIT), 507, 510
Single-parent households, 82–84
Situation-oriented (or contextualism) ethics, 180
16th Social Survey, 131

Sloan Consortium, 293–294
Sloan survey (2005), 294
Smith v. Day, 513, 514
Social host liability, 514–515
Social networking
    lessons learned about, 617–618
    sites for, 339–340
    technology enabled, 589–590
Society for Human Resource Management, 295
South African Centre for Higher Education
    Transformation (CHET), 127
Southern Association of Colleges and Schools
    (SACs), 528
Special program income, 488–489
Special relationships
    description and legal obligations related to, 509–510
    respondeat superior as, 512
Special student fees, 485–486
Specialty professional associations, 212–216
Spellings Commission (2006), 87, 114
Staff
    awards/recognition of, 341–342
    crisis management support of, 612–613
    retention of, 352–353
    study abroad opportunities for, 138–139
Stakeholders
    campus crisis and role of, 604
    facilities and other departmental, 575
    institutional accountability, 109–110
Standards
    CAS, 112, 191–193, 195–199, 278
    definition and implications of, 187–188
    different types of educational, 188–189
    for higher education curriculum, 189–190
    timeline and eras of accreditation and, 190
    See also Accreditation; Ethical standards; Student
        affairs standards
Standards of Good Practice for Education Abroad (Forum on
    Education Abroad), 192
Stanford-Binet testing, 8
State, Eisman v., 514
State finance of higher education
    institutional productivity accountability and, 90–91
    issues related to state finance, 87–89
    public-private dilemma issue of, 91–92
    review of expenditures process of, 89–90
    See also College students; Federal higher education
        initiatives; Institutional financial health
State, Miller v., 511
State of New York, Lamphere v., 509
State of New York, Scaduto v., 509
State statutes. *See* Federal/state statutes and regulations

State of Washington, Johnson v., 513
Statement of Ethical Principles and Standards (ACPA),
    175–176
Statement of Professional Ethics (NODA), 177
Strategic planning
    aligning theory in student learning assessment, 540
    Barr and Keating model of program, 545–563
    facilities development and, 565–584
    as student affairs management responsibility,
        360–361
    student learning collaboration, 419–420
    See also Program planning case examples
Structural diversity, 228
Student affairs administration
    accountability and best practices by, 110–111,
        113–114
    beginnings of, 3–4
    crisis work management by, 604–613
    deans of men in, 5–6
    deans of students in, 9
    deans of women in, 6–7
    doctoral students aspiring to positions in, 398–399
    effective management of human capital in, 333–353
    institutional governance connection for, 53–55
    modern era (1960s–1990s) of, 11–14
    personnel workers in, 7–9
    political environment of the, 425–445
    program planning role of, 560
    student personnel point of view on, 10–11
    theory-to-practice in, 147–161
Student affairs fiscal management
    budget cycle of, 499–502
    budget models used in, 497–498
    crisis work, 608
    dealing with budget cuts, 502–503
    general student affairs fiscal environment, 482–483
    public vs. private issues related to, 491–493
    purposes of a budget for, 493–496
    sources of funds used in, 483–491
    types of budgets used in, 496–497
    See also Institutional financial health
Student affairs fiscal sources
    auxiliary services as, 488
    church-support as, 489
    contracted institutional services, 489
    endowment income as, 486–487
    fund raising as, 93, 487
    grants and contracts, 487–488
    implications of, 490–491
    mandatory student fees as, 485
    special programs as, 488–489
    special student fees as, 485–486

state appropriated funds as, 483–484
    state and federal capital budgets as, 489–490
    tuition as, 93, 484–485
Student affairs management
    description of, 356
    generational challenge of, 362–365
    influencing the organizational culture through,
        258–259
    of information and money, 358
    job mobility issues for, 366–368
    managing up (and down) the organization, 365–366
    role issues for, 359–362
Student affairs management roles
    authority issues of, 359
    ethics and credibility issues of, 361–362
    performance appraisal, 360
    planning duties, 360–361
    staff development, 361
    supervision of staff, 360
Student affairs meetings
    as powerful management tool, 343
    strategies for facilitating, 344
Student affairs organization models
    affinity of service model of, 322
    common types of, 318–321
    direct supervisory model of, 322
    innovative, 325*t*
    revenue source model of, 322
    staff associate model of, 322
    traditional, 324*t*
Student affairs organizations
    design issues of, 314–318
    managing up (and down) the, 365–366
    new approaches to design and structure of, 326–328
    sample structure of, 257*fig*
    systematic approach to structural design of, 328–331
    theory and research related to organizational design
        of, 321–326
    variety of different, 313–314
    See also Organizations
Student affairs politics
    emergent political concepts and values of, 440–444
    ethical considerations of, 433–434
    important of context in, 430
    political map of, 431–433
    See also Political concepts
Student affairs practice
    cross-case example of applying theory to, 157–160
    ethical conflict decision-making in, 183–184*t*
    holistic welfare of students as moral focus of,
        178–179
    impact of technology on, 328

implications of student technology challenges for, 597–598

"knowledge of politics" skills, 425

legal issues related to, 505–525

maintaining and modeling ethics in, 166–185

using moral compass in everyday ethics, 184–185

moral landscape and common ethical issues faced in, 180–183

multi-lens perspective on managing/modeling ethics in, 179–180

other bodies of theory relevant to, 157

overview of theories that inform, 150–157

recommendations regarding diversity for, 236–237

Student affairs profession

ACPA's *Statement of Ethical Principles and Standards* on, 175–176

ACUI's ethical standards for, 176–177

as ethical responsibility domain, 170*fig*, 171–172

holistic welfare of students as moral focus of, 178–179

NASPA's standards of ethical behavior for, 176

practicing ethics in the, 173–179

Statement of Professional Ethics (NODA) for, 177–178

See also Professional associations

Student affairs professionals

common relationships of, 182, 449–450

ethical deliberation and actions by, 183–184*t*

as ethical responsibility domain, 170*fig*, 171–172

fairness of, 183

graduate preparation programs for, 137–138

holistic welfare of students as moral focus of, 178–179

how mission informs practice of, 29–36

individual and institutional perspectives on mobility of, 36–38

international opportunities for, 137

maintaining and modeling ethics by, 166–185

making exceptions, privilege, and favoritism of students, 182–183

managing human capital of, 333–353

using moral compass in everyday ethics, 184–185

multi-lens perspective on managing/modeling ethics by, 179–180

need to understand student demographics, 226

recruitment of, 334–337

resistance to theories by, 155–157

response to institutional governance by, 55–56

retention of, 352–353

selection of, 337–340

staff awards and recognition given to, 341–342

student conduct procedures/punishment role of, 183

supervision of, 340–341

time management support given to, 342–343

See also Professional development; Senior Student Affairs Officers (SSAOs)

Student affairs relationships

with colleagues and constituencies, 450–451

personal relationships with students, 182

practitioner-student, 449–450

Student affairs standards

applications of, 190–191

CAS standards of, 13, 112, 148, 174–175, 190–199, 278

case illustrations of, 200–202

See also Standards

Student affairs theories

applying to practice, 157–160

cognitive development theories, 153–155

environmental theories, 155–157

explaining resistance to, 148–150

identifying theoretical basis for program, 557–558

organizational design, 321–326

other bodies of theory relevant to, 157

psychosocial development theories, 150–153

student learning assessment and use of, 539–540

Student conduct procedures, 183

Student demographics

contemporary, 225

diversity of, 226–237

of families, 82–83

need to understand, 226

online learners, 291–293

Student Development in College: Theory, Research, and Practice (Evans, Forney, and Guide-DiBrito), 148

"Student development" movement (1960s), 13

Student enrollment

anticipated freshman study abroad, 129*fig*

comparing by ethnicity higher education enrollment to, 130*fig*

current demographics of, 84–85, 229–233

language differences and, 84–85

online learning impact on, 289–291

"student swirl" of, 289–290

Student fees

mandatory, 485

special, 485–486

Student health services

ethics/legal issues of, 278–279

historical context of, 266–267

information technology used by, 282

major administrative issues of, 275–282

for mental health issues, 8–9, 12–14, 271–275

for physical health issues, 267–271

Student health services administration
  accessibility issue of, 275–276
  accountability issue of, 277–278
  affordability issue of, 276–277
Student identity
  DMIS model on, 247
  individual-institutional nexus and, 243–245
  Multiple Dimensions of Identity (MDI) Model on, 246
  multiracial, 233–234
  student affairs and politics of, 252–254
Student learning
  campus culture impact on, 71–72
  campus cultures impact on, 66–68
  campus ecology impact on, 68–71
  "juried reviews" assessment of, 526–527
  key issues in assessing environmental influences on, 72–76
  national conversation on, 405–406
  situational constructionist, 533
  technology impact on, 415
Student learning assessment
  different approaches to, 530–536
  evaluating contributions to, 528–530
  historical overview of, 527–528
  implementing, 536–542
  "juried reviews," 526–527
Student learning assessment approaches
  Astin's inputs-environment-outcomes model (IEO), 534–536, 540–541
  outcomes-based assessment, 532–534
  preassessment, utilization data, and needs assessment, 531–532
Student learning collaboration
  associations involved in, 405–407
  attention to culture, people, and planning in, 418–420
  deepening of the, 411–414
  fortuitous timing of, 411
  history of, 407–408
  leadership for success of, 416–418
  overcoming barriers to, 408–411
  process of building, 414–415
  sustaining partnerships for, 420–421
The Student Learning Imperative (ACPA), 110, 405, 407, 409, 528–529, 530, 542
Student motivation assessment, 199
Student Personal Point of View (ACE), 110
The Student Personnel Point of View (NASPA), 3, 9, 10–11, 14

Student Right-to-Know and Campus Security Act (Public Law 101-542), 86, 522, 523
Student satisfaction instruments, 531–532
"Student swirl," 289–290
Students
  assessing motivation of, 199
  cost of attendance for, 93–94
  crisis management and support of, 610–611
  debt management by, 99
  as ethical responsibility domain, 170*fig*–171
  low-income, 83–84, 94–97, 123
  making exceptions, privilege, and favoritism of, 182–183
  medical withdrawal by, 281–282
  personal relationships between student affairs professionals and, 182
  poverty and income distribution of, 83–84
  relationships between student affairs practitioner and, 449–450, 453
  responsibility for criminal acts of, 514
  school enrollment rates of, 84–85
  student affair's moral focus on holistic welfare of, 178–179
  territoriality of, 69
  university's contractual responsibilities to, 506–507
  university's noncontractual obligations to, 507–515
  See also Financing higher education
Students with disabilities
  federal higher education initiatives improving access for, 85–86
  increased enrollment rates of, 232
Study abroad programs
  academic benefits of, 128–131
  anticipated freshman participation rate, 129*fig*
  co-curricular international education of, 132–136
  comparing by ethnicity higher education enrollment to, 130*fig*
  financial support by country, 124*fig*
  for low-income students, 123
  staff and faculty opportunities for, 138–139
  student affairs role in promoting, 136–137
  See also International education
Subjective knowledge, 155
Substance abuse, 268–269
  See also Alcohol abuse
Suicide issue, 272–273
Suicide Prevention Resource Center, 272
Sullivan, Alumni Ass'n v., 515
Summary of the Doctoral Education Literature (Carnegie Initiative on the Doctorate), 393

Supervision
  creating a meaningful relationship for, 340–341
  as student affairs management role, 360
  working relationship component of, 452
Systematic Leadership (Allen and Cherrey), 322

T

Teachers College, 393
Technology
  communication tools through, 439
  crisis management lessons regarding, 617–618
  crisis work management, 609–610
  impact on student affairs practice by, 328
  power as control of, 436
  student learning impact by, 415
  student use of, 587–592
  Web 2.0, 587
  See also Information technology
Technology challenges
  illegal file sharing as, 597
  implications for student affairs of, 597–598
  MMORPGs gaming, 590–591
  online gambling as, 596
Technology usage
  conducting research, 588–589
  instant messaging (IM), 587–588
  social networking, 339–340, 589–590, 617–618
  virtual worlds, 591–592
  Web 2.0, 587
Terminiello v. Chicago, 517
Territoriality, 69
Texas A&M University, 384
Theories
  cognitive development, 153–155
  Cultural Validation Model, 160
  environmental, 155–157
  explaining resistance to, 148–150
  identifying theoretical basis for program, 557–558
  organizational design, 321–326
  psychological Nigrescence, 152–153, 160
  psychosocial development, 150–153
  student learning assessment and use of, 539–540
  typology, 156–157
Theory of psychological Nigrescence, 152–153, 160
Thomas-Kilmann Conflict Mode Instrument, 466
Time management support, 342–343
Title III (Higher Education Reauthorization Act), 28
Title V (Higher Education Reauthorization Act), 28
Title VI (Higher Education Act) [HEA], 123

Tomorrow's Higher Education: A Return to the Academy (Brown), 110
TQM (total quality management), 527
Tribally controlled colleges
  institutional mission statements of, 26
  student affairs professional practice shaped by mission of, 33–34
TRIO programs, 123, 315
Tuition
  discounting, 95–96
  as source of student affairs funds, 93, 484–485
Typology theories, 156–157

U

U. S. Constitution, 515–517
Undergraduate Fellows Program (NUFP) [NASPA], 209–210
United Educators, 281
United States
  changing demographics in the, 232–233
  family demographics in the, 82–83
University of Alabama, 596
University of Arizona Center for the Study of Higher Education, 136–137
University of California-Berkeley, 256
University of California-Los Angeles, 126
University of Chicago, 7, 303
University and College Accountability Network (U-CAN), 114–115
University of Connecticut Health Center, 596
University of Denver v. Whitlock, 508–509
University of Florida, 128, 133
University of Florida Center for European Studies, 128
University of Florida International Center, 128
University Gambling Action Team (University of Alabama), 596
University of Georgia, 126
University of Hawaii, 611
University of Kentucky, 133
University of Maine System, 301–302
University of Maryland University College (UMUC), 303–304
University of Miami, 619
University of Minnesota, 125, 127, 256
University of North Carolina at Chapel Hill, 126
University of North Carolina-Wilmington, 384
University of Phoenix, 28
University Residence Environments Scale (URES), 70
"The university in ruins," 53
University senate governance, 42–44

University of South Carolina, 384
University of South Florida, 593
University of Southern California, 619
University of Texas Telecampus, 306
University of Utah, Beach v., 513
University of Virginia, 126, 256
University of Wisconsin, 126
University of Wisconsin-Madison, 128
Ursinus College, 65
U.S. Army Classification System, 7, 8
U.S. Census Bureau, 28, 82, 83, 87, 230, 233
U.S. Department of Education (DOE)
    Commission on the Future of Higher Education of,
        526, 529, 542
    on consumer protection of students, 86, 87
    on family ability to finance college attendance, 83
    on federal loan programs, 94
    Future of Higher Education's Commission report
        (2006) by, 275
    on Hispanic-serving institutions (HSIs), 27
    international education promotion from, 123
    Learning Anytime Anywhere Partnership (LAAP)
        funded by, 593
    on privacy of student records, 522
    on rising costs of higher education, 198
    on school enrollment demographics, 84, 85
    on student affair responsibility for online
        learners, 295
    on work as financing program, 97–98
U.S. Department of Education Office of Civil Rights
    (OCR), 281
U.S. Department of State, 123
U.S. Green Building Council, 582
U.S. Supreme Court, 235
    See also Legal cases cited
Utilization data, 532

V

Valencia Community College, 303
Valium, 269
Values
    building relationship through shared, 457–458
    emergent student affairs political, 440–444
    student learning collaboration attendance to,
        418–419
Vice President for Student Affairs case study, 159–160
Vicodin, 269
Violence
    disturbed/disturbing students and, 279–280
    gracious space transformation of, 474–477
    as health problem, 270–271

"In Search of Safer Communities:" (NASPA white
    paper) on, 620
Virginia Tech tragedy (2007), 279, 512, 521, 618
    See also Criminal acts
Virginia Tech Review Panel Report (2007), 280
Virginia Tech University tragedy (2007), 279, 512,
    521, 618
Virtual culture, 441
Virtual worlds, 591–592
Vision sharing, 457–458
    See also Institution mission
Voluntary System of Accountability, 115

W

Wake Forest University, 437
Washington State University's (WSU), 302
Washington State University's (WSU) Office of
    Distance Degree Programs (DDP), 293–294
Web 2.0 technology, 587
Web sites
    ACPA's graduate program directory, 391
    American Society of Association Executives (ASAE),
        206–207
    "Characteristics of Individual Excellence for
        Professional Practice in Higher Education"
        (CAS), 374
    College Portrait (Web reporting template), 115
    Higher Education Center for Alcohol and Other
        Drug Abuse and Violence Prevention, 269
    The Jed Foundation, 273
    University of Arizona Center for the Study of Higher
        Education, 137
    University of Chicago, 303
    University of Maine System, 301–302
    U.S. Census Bureau, 230
WebCt, 594
Weight management (Health at Every Size,
    HAES), 268
Welcoming the stranger concept, 476
Western Association of Schools and Colleges
    (WASC), 528
Western Cooperative for Electronic
    Telecommunications (WCET), 298, 393
Western Golf Association, L. W. v., 511
Western Interstate Commission for Higher Education
    (WICHE), 61, 68, 555
White privilege, 253–254
White students
    enrollment rates of, 84
    racial privilege of, 253–254
    study abroad enrollment by, 130*fig*

Whitlock, University of Denver v., 508–509
Wingspread Group on Higher Education, 107–108, 406
Women
  gender enrollment rate differences of, 231–232
  sexism impact on, 249–250
Work as financing program, 97–98
World Health Organization (WHO), 268

X

Xanax, 269

Z

Zero-based budgeting, 498